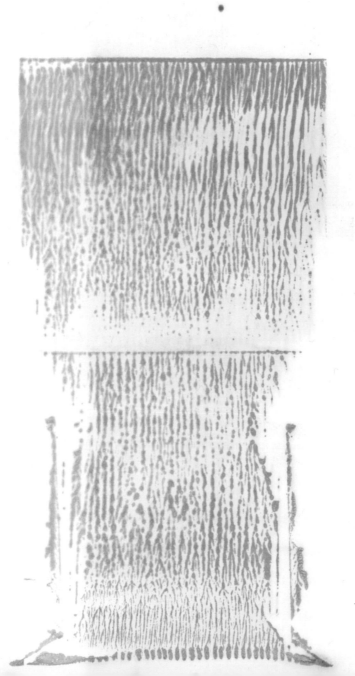

THE POLITICS OF PROVINCIALISM:
The Democratic Party in Transition, 1918–1932
(1968)

A GIANT'S STRENGTH:
America in the 1960s,
with Robert D. Marcus and Thomas R. West
(1971)

AMERICA:
A Portrait in History
(two volumes),
with Robert Marcus and Emily Rosenberg
(1974)

A HISTORY OF RECENT AMERICA,
with Paul K. Conkin
(1974)

HERBERT HOOVER

DAVID BURNER

HERBERT HOOVER

~~~~~~~~~~~~~~~~~~~~~~~~~~~~~~~~~~~~

A PUBLIC LIFE

ALFRED · A · KNOPF

NEW YORK

19 🐕 79

Library of Congress Cataloging in Publication Data
Burner, David. (Date)
Herbert Hoover, a public life.

Includes bibliographical references and index.
1. Hoover, Herbert Clark, Pres. U.S., 1874–1964.
2. Presidents—United States—Biography.
I. Title.
E802.B87 1978 973.91′6′0924 [B] 78–54912
ISBN 0–394–46134–7

To my mother
and the
memory of my father

CONTENTS

*16 pages of illustrations
will be found following page 242.*

PREFACE

"T HE BENEFICENCE OF THE CREATOR towards Man on Earth, and the Possibilities of Humanity are one and the same," lectured Leland Stanford on October 1, 1891, to the opening class at the university that carried his name. Seventeen-year-old Herbert Hoover was in the audience of students. It was a good time to study geology, the field that Hoover would settle on at Stanford. "Nature," which to an earlier generation of American intellectuals had meant the transcendent nature behind the physical, had now become the nature of the tangible universe, the soil and metals and rock strata, the bursting life that evolutionists held to be working itself into ever-subtler forms. It was also a time that favored robust work and health, and filled popular novels with clean-minded outdoorsmen. Geology had taken a major part in making the discoveries that informed the late nineteenth-century imagination of nature, and its muscularity, its direct involvement in the material world made it the right science for the time. Young Hoover was an enthusiast at it. "I have a fine man to work for and a favorite business to work in, and . . . a grand country to work over," he wrote in July 1894 from the High Sierra, where he was on a summer job under the noted Dr. Waldemar Lindgren and the United States Geological Survey. And on another expedition directed by Dr. Lindgren, in the summer of 1895 after Hoover's graduation from Stanford, he wrote: "Tomorrow we are going to make descent of the American River Canyon, a thing people here say is impossible. But," he boasted, "they are not geologists." With geology came engineering, the profession for which Hoover is better known; then big business and finance.

Herbert Hoover had grown up within a sect that makes its own affirmation of a rational, usable world. We cannot be sure that he consistently thought of himself as a Friend, yet all kinds of similarities between the Quaker mentality and Hoover's suggest themselves: a blunt plainness; a belief that people will work well together and that in rational discussion minds can be persuaded to meet; a dedication to peace; and in these things a shrewd involvement in worldly matters and a conviction that good common reason and strategy accord well with the conscience and its affairs. The universe as the engineer perceives it has the orderliness of number and physical law; the universe of the Quaker has the order and harmonies of spirit. Quakers practice cooperativeness; Hoover, who wanted a cooperative social system, spent much of his private career amidst technical and financial institutions that required the intricate combining of separate labors and intentions.

The distinguishing features of Hoover's youth were the deaths of his parents, his own brush with death (which, since it was reported, must also have been known to him), the repeated exposure to fatal illness in West Branch, and his shuttlings among relatives. Such a continual experience of abandonment and separation could easily have led to serious depression, as it did, say, for Jane Addams; but it did not do so for Hoover, although he did suffer depressive episodes. And yet the early years—arguing from silence—were so affecting that he could not cope with the experience directly. He was simply not comfortable with his own history, mixing up many dates and not caring about even his own exact birthdate. It may be more than incidentally significant that one of young Hoover's favorite books was *David Copperfield,* the hero of which is driven at hard labor by the cruel Mr. Murdstone.

What Hoover arrived at was an optimistic progressivism. If he had to be alone, so be it. He made not only a virtue out of it, but an ideology—heroic individualism, the self-reliant man expressing himself in technological mastery and personal accomplishment. He habitually looked outward. A special reflection of his early life came much later in humanitarian endeavors: helpless, bereaved, abandoned people could count on his aid; he would do for others what had not been done for him. But he distanced himself from the implication by self-control and by treating the tasks as technical administrative problems. Hoover's later dislike of passivity and of large inheritances also reflected the experience of being left on his own. He had no use for introspection or contemplative indwelling, and his culture supported and rewarded his assertiveness. When the world's mining opportunities diminished and corporate techniques increasingly dominated, Hoover would hold his world together through personal technical excellence, a sense of control, moral obligation, and humanitarian works.

Only the Great Depression shattered this formula and left him bereft in the decade of the 1930's.

This study of Hoover has as its guiding consideration the ways in which his life and thought bore upon the twentieth-century orderings of civilization, the newer collectivities within business, the economy, and public opinion that now supplement or replace the older groupings by neighborhood, shop, local government. Hoover's understanding of the collective social life, and of the place the individual has within it, received much of its strength and its limitation from the milieu, and the successes, of his own career. Skill and ability, guided by conscience and turned ambitiously and briskly upon a large social or economic problem—that was the idea of individualism and character that Hoover offered. Some sensible project, articulating the separate efforts of willing individuals knowledgeable in the technical requirements of their tasks, would provide the model for his notion of the collective existence. Hoover did not greatly perceive—or, at any rate, put to political use—the more delicate and psychological connections that make up a public, as opposed to the connections established by will and reason, conscience and mutual interest. What Hoover gave to his fellow citizens and to the world in the furtherance of their collective existence, what he failed to give, and how he came to all this are the themes of my story.

This book, intended for the general reader as well as the scholar, is a biography of the acting, writing, public Herbert Hoover. A public career, of course, has its sources in the rich and dark ground of a private interior life; but in Hoover that life is remarkably inaccessible, hidden behind an abrupt and laconic manner and a visible existence of incessantly purposeful activity. Nor does Hoover give us the high drama of a Theodore Roosevelt, Woodrow Wilson, or Franklin D. Roosevelt. As Arthur Schlesinger, Jr., one of his least generous critics, put it, Hoover had a way of transmuting all drama into business. But there is plenty of excitement in the outward circumstances of Hoover's life: a Quaker orphan, a member of the "pioneer" class at Stanford University, a self-made millionaire working on the frontiers of five continents, the supplier of relief to Belgium and later to much of Europe and the Soviet Union, the nation's President during the early years of its greatest depression, and then in the 1930's an adversary worthy of FDR.

In going through a mass of manuscripts I have found a good deal of fresh information, some of it giving a new cast to Hoover's character and activities, that I have put before the reader. Yet my interests, along with the availabilities of materials, have set limits on the study. Hoover's technical, business, charitable, and governmental activities up through his term in the White House offer a unity: they trace a widening of the field

of action, a discovery of social and economic order, a developing progressivism. And while other historians have probed more deeply into
Hoover's diplomacy or into his economics and the technical questions
they raise in economic theory, I have concentrated on different shapes
and implications of Hoover's career, including his commitments to the
professional side of engineering, the analogies between the technological
and the Quaker perceptions of existence, and the relationships between his
engineering career and his political progressivism. Since these themes have
their more appropriate subject in the years when Hoover was an engineer
and businessman and then a progressive statesman, I have ended my
detailed account with his exit from the presidency. After the bitter .defeat
in 1932—after the public figure once so popular and admired, so famed
for his works of humanitarian relief, had become defined as a heartless
reactionary—Hoover became obsessed with a hatred of the New Deal
that soured his thought and rhetoric. When Roosevelt's death released him,
Hoover mellowed and became a venerable statesman, an institution. In
one final chapter I have looked beyond his presidential days, but the
inaccessibility of hundreds of documents on the 1930's and after in the
Herbert Hoover Presidential Library also dictates that close study of
the post-presidency be the subject of future scholarship. Dr. George Nash,
working under a long-term grant from the JM Foundation, is currently
preparing a multivolume biography of Hoover. The present volume may
seem to some readers too abundant with detail and to others not detailed
enough; the finished work represents the best strategy I could attain from
among competing objectives.

DAVID BURNER
February 26, 1978

HERBERT HOOVER

I

~~~~~~~~~~~~~~~~~~~~~~~~~~~~~~~~~~~~

THE WEST

JESSE HOOVER was thin to the point of gauntness—"always in a hurry," as his niece Harriette remembered him. After attending the West Branch, Iowa, Select School, run by the internationally known Quaker educators Joel and Hannah Bean, Jesse operated a thresher on his father Eli's farm. Then in 1864, at the age of eighteen, he went into business. It suited him. The West Branch newspaper for the late 1870's is full of catchy advertisements for his blacksmith shop and farm implements store. "Ho, for Kansas!" reads one, "But if you do not go there go to J. C. Hoover and buy your Farming Implements including Three leading Sulky Plows, New Departure Tongueless Cultivator, Orchard City Wagon, Buck Eye Reaper, Rubber Bucket Pumps . . . and Lightning Rods." "Do not go to Iowa City to buy Sewing Machines," instructed another, "when you can get any kind you want of J. C. HOOVER and save FIVE DOLLARS." The friendly advertisements grew larger, holding pace with a prospering business.[1]

Jesse was one of those small-town inventors who are part of the American story, an appropriate father to two engineer sons. He manufactured a novel rubber bucket pump devised by his own father, Eli. a cow stepped on a wooden platform that sank under her weight and poured water into a trough. And with a friend, Jesse applied for a patent on a cattle stile and hog guard; cattle could "pass from pasture to hog's water trough and return, but hogs can't get out." Jesse also introduced single-strand barbed wire into the area, covering it with tar to inhibit rust. His sons "Bert" (Herbert) and "Tad" (Theodore) also showed mechanical ability.

One of their gadgets tied a calf to a mowing machine as a substitute for their own labors.[2]

Jesse's great-great-great-grandfather, Andrew Hoover (born Andreas Huber), arrived in Philadelphia in 1738 from the Palatinate. The son of a wine merchant, Andrew grew up in a large Lutheran family of Swiss ancestry. He farmed for many years in Pennsylvania and Maryland, and moved in 1762–3 to North Carolina, establishing a profitable grist mill on the Uwharrie River. This was still wild country, but Andrew showed fear of neither "man nor beast nor terror of the night." During the Revolution he contributed £100 to the patriot cause and acquired some Tory lands. His granary was one of the more important in the South. His son John became a Quaker; needing land sufficient for a large family, he moved west in 1802 to Ohio. On September 2, 1846, John's great-grandson Jesse was born in the town of Stillwater. Some Hoovers who emigrated to the Middle West, and some born there, became successful judges and legislators, and many joined societies for pacifism, antislavery, or Indian welfare. From Ohio, Herbert Hoover's father, Jesse, moved with his father, Eli, in 1854 by riverboat and covered wagon to a farm just outside West Branch, a town in eastern Iowa founded by Quakers. *The Friend* remarked in 1854: "The immigration into Iowa . . . is astonishing. For miles and miles, day after day, the prairies of Illinois are lined with cattle and wagons, pushing on towards this prosperous state."[3]

In 1870 Jesse Hoover married Hulda Minthorn in Quaker meeting at Graham, Iowa, now the hamlet of Oasis, just northwest of West Branch; they obtained their civil marriage license at Iowa City, where Hulda had attended the university. Her American ancestry also dates from the eighteenth century. In 1725 two parents from England perished on shipboard to America, leaving four small boys, among them William Minthorn, who lived to be ninety. His own son William was baptized a Congregationalist and, according to family tradition, attended a "literary college" in New England but was expelled for marrying; this was done as a "test case," which supposedly signaled a disposition for reform. William and his son John in about 1802 took their family from the Connecticut Valley to Toronto, Canada, where John (who also lived to be ninety) married Lucinda Sherwood. On May 4, 1848, in North Norwich, Ontario, his bookish son Theodore, who founded two small libraries during his lifetime, and Mary Wasley Minthorn added a daughter, Hulda Randall, to a large Quaker family. Eleven years later they settled in Iowa on the Lone Tree farm—"a true and faithful beacon to those lost in snow"—a mile south of Yankee Corners and about 2 miles east of West Branch. Theodore Minthorn soon died, leaving his wife to raise the children, who became teachers and Quaker ministers.[4]

The girlhood of the sickly Hulda Minthorn, Herbert's mother, reveals a temperament suited for Quaker piety. At fourteen she wrote from Iowa to a friend in Canada:

> Remember me when death shall close
> My eyelids in their last repose
> Remember me when the wind shall wave
> The grass upon your schoolmate's grave

Two years later Hulda was troubled at a time of several deaths: "Cold blows the eastern breeze, upon this my home and ever anon it tells of a spirit fled and gone to that home of rest prepared for those that fear the Lord." One summer she worked as a shepherdess, writing in a letter to her home of "the greatness and solitude of the prairie." And here is a poem Hulda composed at the age of seventeen:

> The evening winds are sying
>   Sying o'er the plain
> Moonbeams now are stirring
>   Like a silver rain
> Stars are brightly shining
>   In the azure sky
>   I am fondly dreaming
> Thou art nigh

The sentiment merged well with Quaker piety. At her father's funeral in 1866, when she was seventeen, Hulda broke into song, knelt at the casket, and publicly consecrated her life to God. Thereafter she spoke frequently at First and Fourth Day meeting. Educated at public school near Yankee Corners, then for two years at the well-regarded Bean Academy at the Evergreens (just east of West Branch), and in 1865–7 at the University of Iowa preparatory division, the ambitious and popular Hulda was fit for the twin Quaker occupations of teacher and minister. While teaching at the North Star School near Muscatine, Iowa, during the late 1860's, she began the day with a Bible reading, taught the three R's "to the tune of hymns," and made daily prayers for each student. "Before the end of the year all eighteen scholars were converted," a pupil recalled.[8]

The records of the Friends Church in West Branch show the birthdate of Herbert Clark Hoover as August 11, 1874. A biographical account prepared by Hoover himself in about 1915 reads: "I was born at West Branch, Iowa, on August 11th, 1874. . . ." Yet all of his biographers and Hoover's own *Memoirs* agree on August 10. Like his only brother, Theodore, Herbert was born around midnight. Since Herbert's great-uncle, John Y. Hoover, was minister of the church and in attendance at the birth, the entry in the register and Herbert's own early account should be accepted. As an adult, Herbert remembered some confusion about the date and so would yield to the convenience of celebrants as between the tenth and the eleventh.[6]

Hulda's sister Agnes remembered Herbert's birth. On the afternoon of August 10 the two sisters had been sewing clothes for an anticipated "Laura." When dawn came the following day, Jesse Hoover tapped on a bedroom window of the house across the street: "Well, Agnes, we have another General Grant at our house." "Herbert was a sweet baby that first day," Agnes recollected, "round and plump and looked about very cordial at everybody." At about the age of two the newcomer's life was endangered; Bertie, as he was called, strangled with the croup so badly that his father summoned both village doctors. "We all thought he was dead," wrote Aunt Agnes. The eyes of the tiny figure were pressed closed with pennies and a sheet was drawn over the body. But after resuscitation by his uncle, Dr. John Minthorn, who burst in upon the family on his return from a country medical visit, Herbert stirred into life. For days Jesse and Hulda took turns sitting with the baby, closely watching his temperature.[7]

The small cottage by the Wapsinonoc Creek, in which Bert—as Herbert would be called by close friends all his life—Tad (Theodore, 1871–1955), and their young sister May (Mary, 1876–1953) spent their early years, offered delight to small visitors. Phlox and wild sweet William and columbine grew around the house. Cousin Harriette Miles would run up the walk between rows of portulaca to hear Aunt Hulda read verse, a rare treat in Quaker West Branch. Fruit trees on the front lawn, particularly a bright red Siberian crab apple, fascinated Tad Hoover as a small boy. All the children joined in making maple sugar eggs in wintertime. An eggshell was blown clean, placed in packed snow, filled with melted maple sugar, and allowed to harden. "Bert and I were clumsy and broke so many eggs," Harriette recalled, and she emphatically pronounced the Hoover household a "merry place." She pictured Tad and Bert chopping through the ground with an increasingly dulled ax, having heard that China lay on the other side of the globe.[8]

West Branch, where Herbert Hoover spent his first eleven years, provided an ample setting to acquaint a young boy with the joys and hazards of life. Groves of wildwood invited hiking and exploring; local streams could be dammed into pools large enough for swimming; and fields of purple clover hid treasures, among them wild strawberries ripe for eating. Along the Burlington railroad track, gems of agate and fossil coral awaited discovery in the ballast of glacial gravel. In cold weather Cook's Hill allowed plenty of incline for fast sledding. Such were the good and comforting things Herbert Hoover recalled about his childhood. The formidable Iowa seasons could also bring destruction. Hard work and Quaker enterprise sometimes made slight headway against natural disaster and disease. The sun could scorch the crops; restless prairie storms might tear at a spring planting or level a flimsy dwelling; and unrelenting winter favored typhus, diphtheria, and pneumonia.[9]

Memories and records give us glimpses of Hoover as a child. His aunt Mattie Pemberton remembered him as a "mischievous, laughing boy"; a first-grade teacher, Mollie Brown, recalled an average student, good at arithmetic. He had been enrolled in 1879; a later school document puts "Birdie Hoover" in a third-grade class of twenty. A classmate's autograph book carries the message: "To Addie: Let your days be full of peas / Slip along as slick as greese. Bert Hoover." Hoover's own recorded memories fix on boyish incidents and impressions. He recollected that Jesse sometimes took the boys along on trips to the country, letting them dangle their feet from the back of the buggy. As a small child he repeatedly got stuck crossing the unpaved roads one rainy summer; "Papa's little stick-in-the mud," his father called him each time he lifted the boy to freedom. Once in his father's blacksmith shop a barefooted Bert encountered a burning ember that left a lifelong scar. Later in the same shop curiosity impelled the six-year-old boy to toss a lighted stick into a large cauldron of hot tar, which billowed huge clouds of black smoke across the whole town. Forbidden by his Quaker parents to carry a gun, Bert and young Indians from a local government training school (begun by Benjamin Miles in 1882) shot pigeons or prairie chickens with bow and arrows. Hoover's brother Tad recalled a night when a tornado hit West Branch. No sooner were the children rushed into the small cellar than a tremendous noise shook the house. Afterward maple leaves thickly curtained the windows and rain beat down all night in every direction. The next day revealed tangles of fallen trees and branches, but no loss of life in the little town. Hoover remembered a friendly dentist, William Walker, and his fascinating collections of old coins, fossils, minerals, and meteorite fragments.[10]

West Branch enjoyed a prosperity doubtless indistinguishable from that of many other Midwestern towns, but especially fitting to the earthly industry and solidity of the Hoovers' pietistic sect. Though it had suffered the economic stagnation that followed the Civil War, by Hoover's youth the town, founded in 1850, was humming. In 1870 it attracted a railroad. "The West Branch [grist] Mill," the *Local Record* reported in 1879, "is so full of business, that it is now running day and night." In 1880 the town sent to Chicago the biggest load of hogs it had ever delivered there, and Messrs. Albin and Eli Hoover promised to "set up the oysters" to any man in Cedar County who could better that feat. A dairy industry specializing in cheese was also important. The fertile soil supported a variety of fruit crops as well as grain and corn. By the census of 1880 West Branch had a population of 502, compared with 365 in the year of Hoover's birth. Only one person was listed as divorced. Settlers had come from the South, the Middle West, Canada, and as far away as Norway.[11]

West Branch practiced a strict Quaker morality. Typically for its time and region, it had a children's prohibitionist organization, the Band of Hope, which Bertie joined at the age of ten. (There must have been the need, for despite the dry law passed there in 1857 Tarrant's Seltzer Aperient, declared the local paper, felt "like a ball of fire rolling up and down the chest.") Years later, Hoover could remember only a single drunk, who was also one of only a dozen or so Democrats. Yet the town was less provincial than its size suggests: Quakerism fostered an interest in the goods of intelligence and culture, and in the problems of the world outside. From its inception West Branch had provided itself with decent public and private schools. As other American Quaker communities had aided in the founding of Haverford, Earlham, and Swarthmore, West Branch had a part in the starting of William Penn College in Oskaloosa, later attended by Theodore Hoover, and of Whittier College in Salem, Iowa. The newspaper dealt more with national and international than with local events. Humanitarianism completed the West Branch Quaker morality. Before the Civil War the town had been a stop on the Underground Railroad. John Brown had received lodging and encouragement there, making many visits, at least once staying for a night at a Quaker inn immediately outside town, and spending a winter at nearby Springdale. West Branch, among only nine precincts in Iowa, favored black suffrage in 1857; in another referendum in 1868, the town went the same way by a landslide. Long after the war, the West Branch *Local Record* carried news of Friends who were seeking to furnish Southern blacks with information on areas "likely to afford them opportunity for industry and the acquisition of homes."[12]

The Quakers have stood in the special situation of being both members of a pietistic community and actors within the larger world; and this location, along with the doctrine of the Inner Light, defines the Quaker perception of the world. That a communal tradition has retained its force among the Friends may be both cause and effect of their seeing the larger world as a place for intense cultivation, a place not only needing to be redeemed but capable of it. The idea of the Inner Light also suggests an invisible decency and reasonableness and harmony within the world always ready for articulation. Among the Friends there is a distinctive blend of piety and practical worldliness and also a compounding of moral urgency with a certain optimism that the world can be enticed to put its practical arrangements into good moral order.

West Branch made a good symbolic beginning for Herbert Hoover. Transform the industry into great engineering enterprises and the reformist Quaker humanitarianism into vast works of relief and a vision of a prosperous social order founded in self-reliance and willing cooperation, and the special elements in his career can be recognized.

Hoover's family figured prominently in the town's public devotional life—a style Herbert was not to follow in his own religious observance. Jesse, it is true, was reserved in religious expression, did not take to evangelism, and was thought somewhat worldly by the local minister, who observed that he "greatly neglected his calling to God." (A friend related that Jesse had enjoyed teasing his wife with statements "palpably absurd.") His business did so well that the family moved in 1878 to a comfortable four-room house. He sold the cottage and adjacent blacksmith shop to devote more time to his store. He was also chosen town assessor and councilman. Herbert's mother and a number of relatives on both sides of the family were more public in their faith. As an adult, Hoover could remember his great aunt Hannah denouncing songs in Sunday School— where Hulda Hoover taught—for making a "the-a-ter" of the church. (The meetinghouse of Hoover's boyhood actually did become a moviehouse briefly during the 1920's.) One of Hulda's sisters and a brother became ministers. Hoover's paternal great-grandmother Rebecca was an elder who frequently spoke in church. A purist, she opposed such changes as the hygienic screening of windows to keep out flies. By a son's account, she "retained the sweetness of her young womanhood" throughout her life, and was "one of the fairest and most lovely women in the wild wood." She died in 1895 at the age of ninety-four, living to see "three hundred issue of her own body." The influence this "Aunt Becky" possessed as a matriarch of the Hoover families was at its height during Herbert's youth. His much-traveled great-uncle John Y. Hoover, minister to the local meetinghouse throughout most of the 1870's and 1880's—the local paper called his prayer meetings "a brook by the wayside"—was a study in himself.[18]

A garrulous man, John Hoover had a tall and angular figure made the more striking by a highly burnished artificial eye he had proudly brought back from a visit to Oskaloosa, earning the comment from the local paper that he was "very much improved in appearance." His grandnephew Theodore remembered John as "a minister of power," who terrified parishioners with the obsessive thought that he would see Judgment Day before he died. His memoir, *Jesus Only,* recaptures the evangelical tide that influenced American Quakerism and engulfed other Protestant sects during these decades. Like the faith of Hoover's mother, expressed in temperance and charitable activities, the religion of John Hoover and his wife, also a recorded minister, showed forth in good works and reform. In the years after the Civil War the couple aided poor whites in the Carolina back country. During Herbert's youth they took a "minute" or paid leave of some months to visit "prisons, penitentiaries, poor-houses, and houses of reform" in Iowa and Kansas.[14]

AN EVANGELIST named David Updegraff, a pale man with shiny black hair and sunken eyes, came to West Branch in 1879 preaching "conversion, justification, and sanctification." "Friends willing," he stayed for two weeks of revival meetings. Theodore Hoover wrote of Updegraff as "emotional and selfish . . . a strong individualist" of a kind that could wreck a "socialistic community," and who wrought in West Branch a "midsummer madness." As a result of Updegraff's visit, the town's Quakers divided into a conservative group of older and wealthier people and the "fast" Friends of evangelical bent. Hulda went with the younger group, though she was said to be "greatly grieved" over the rift, which in many instances split children from parents. The less evangelistic Joel and Hannah Bean, who believed santification to be a lifelong process rather than an instantaneous event, lost their parishioners' support and left their Select School in May 1882, migrating to California. After the division, Hulda's niece has noted, West Branch became an unhappy place; the church quarrel, she said, scattered the original settlers all over the American West, leaving few behind in the town. Actually, populations were shifting rapidly throughout the Middle West. The 1885 census recorded a 10 percent loss in West Branch in the previous half decade.[15]

On December 13, 1880, Jesse Hoover died of heart trouble at the age of thirty-four. Six years old, Herbert would soon have only a dim memory of what the local paper termed his father's "pleasant, sunshiny disposition." Hulda Hoover—alone of the Minthorns—remained in West Branch, gradually paying all of Jesse's debts, working for extra money as a seamstress to keep current a $1000 insurance policy, and caring for her three children. So frugal was Hulda that she delayed mailing a letter for want of a postage stamp. Hoover wrote years later of having learned "at the earliest and most impressionable age . . . the meaning of poverty from actual experience." Periodically troubled by a stomach disorder, Hulda allowed Jesse's brother Benajah or uncle Will Miles to look after the children for a time so she could extend her godly pursuits. She did so in ways commensurate with her education: as a clerk of the meeting, a teacher of Sunday

School, and a member of the committee of correspondence charged with conveying news of the Iowa Friends to England, Ireland, and other parts of the world. After a temperance meeting, she attended one on woman suffrage and remarked: "This is the next question . . . and I need only to say—let a woman be left a widow and have anything to do with business and she will emphatically be on the side of equal suffrage." Like Joel Bean, who until his departure served as clerk of Iowa Yearly Meeting, Hulda composed songs and poems that she read in Sunday School. After the death of her husband she shocked the meeting by ordering a high headstone for his grave, which had to be pounded deeper into the ground to accord with Quaker simplicity. Her interests then became even more explicitly pious. She had long spoken out in meeting, and in 1883 the Springdale Preparative Meeting acknowledged her "gift in the ministry," placing her in that office by the Quaker method of common consent. While Uncle Will Miles boarded Bert, she went late that year as a delegate to Kansas and Iowa Yearly Meetings. And like a Methodist circuit rider, she traveled to speak at revivals throughout Iowa. Increasingly serious in demeanor, she carried the message of forgiveness. "It was as I remember it," her sister Agnes wrote, "*her* message. . . . Her vision of the scriptures was clear and convincing, her testimony of Redeeming Love always seemed to be so real." A return trip home by foot from a revival meeting in Springdale quickened a chest cold into pneumonia complicated with typhoid fever. On February 24, 1884, she died—in the winter like Jesse, and only one year older, at thirty-five. Eulogies told of the important place she had held in West Branch Quakerism. Hulda had given the young Herbert two placards that he kept on the wall of his room in subsequent years. They read: "Leave me not, neither forsake me, O God of my salvation (Psalms 27:9)" and "I will never leave thee nor forsake thee (Hebrews 13:5)."[16]

Hulda Hoover left more than $2000—in those days a goodly sum—for the education of her children. Her mother had chosen as their guardian Lawric Tatum, in 1844 the first Quaker settler of Cedar County, who had run a local depot of the Underground Railroad before the war and engaged in Indian welfare and prohibitionist work in later years. The children were separated after two months together at Grandmother Minthorn's in Kingsley, Iowa. May would eventually go to Oregon with her grandmother; Tad went to Hubbard, Iowa, and later to Newberg, Oregon, with Uncle John Minthorn; Herbert stayed for a little more than a year at the farm of his uncle Allen Hoover and Aunt Millie, a mile outside of town, and then was also sent to Oregon. Years later Bert recalled enjoying his stay at the farm with his cousin Walter; the two boys were close friends and Herbert named his own second son Allan, after his uncle. As was customary, Uncle Allen received money for Herbert's board from the small inheritance. The oldest Hoover child, Tad, who might feel most keenly the loss of both parents, wrote a child's poem:

> *Orphans*
> We were orphans three
> Bert and I and little Marie.
> Bert was eight, a chunk of a boy,
> Brimful of tricks that boys enjoy.
> Marie was six and all the day
> She would sing in her bright, cute way
> A brown-haired, sweet little girl,
> With none in life to say her nay.[17]

As an adult Hoover could barely remember either of his parents. Writing from Belgium in 1915, he mistakenly told a friend: "When I was 7 years old I was removed by relations on mother's side to Oregon." Actually, he had been eleven. He once attributed his success to having been left with older people at an early age. He wrote a bit resentfully of being handed from one family of relatives to another, and in his autobiography errs about when he left West Branch for Oregon as well as about the date of his mother's death. As his parents died and the rest of the family separated, he must have felt his life going out of control. Much of his career would be occupied with getting power and control for himself, and with creating order and stability around him.[18]

ON THE EVENING of November 10, 1885, eleven-year-old Bert Hoover, in company with a Quaker family named Hammell, left by Union Pacific immigrant train for Oregon to live with the Minthorns, whose own son had died the previous year at the age of seven. Bert had two dimes in his pocket. Lawrie Tatum and the West Branch Hoovers had decided he would get better advanced schooling in Oregon. The home of John and Laura Minthorn, wrote Agnes Minthorn, "was the most cultured . . . of any in either the Hoover or Minthorn families at that time. . . . They were conscientious people always interested in education . . . [and] the church, and desirous of casting about young people the best influences."[19]

It was not Herbert's first time out of West Branch. After his father died, the children had spent summers away from home. At his uncle Pennington Minthorn's prairie farm in western Iowa, Bert lived in a pioneer's sod house and sometimes rode the lead horse in the breaking of new ground. From March until late October 1881 he stayed with Laban Miles, a kindly uncle who was superintendent on the Osage Indian reservation in

Oklahoma Territory. Here Bert spent hours reading, having access to more books than were permitted to him in West Branch. Other Iowa trips were to Uncle Davis and Grandfather Eli in Hubbard, Merlin Marshall's farm in Plymouth County, and the nearby home of Benjamin Miles, Laban's father. There were also months at Kingsley, Iowa, after Hulda's death. But now Herbert was traveling to a new kind of country and life, as he would rootlessly shift his locale ever afterward. He discovered with disappointment on his way that, as he wrote his first-grade teacher, the Rockies were made of dirt.[20]

John Minthorn sustained in his own life that compound of devotion, learning, morality at work in the world, and shrewdness about his own affairs that marked the culture of West Branch. Minthorn had run a team wagon in the Underground Railroad and, though a Quaker, had served in the Civil War. Turn thy cheek one time only, this cagey pacifist advised his nephew. Educated principally at the University of Iowa, he was a physician in West Branch for a brief period—where by account he had saved Bert's life—then took his family to the Tennessee mountains to educate poor whites. In 1882 Minthorn returned to Iowa, before going to the Pacific slope early in 1883 as one of President Arthur's Indian agents. He lectured on peace and arbitration during these years; he also set up his medical practice, joined in a "general improvement" company, and in 1885 aided in starting a Quaker school in Newberg, Oregon, a Friends' colony of some five hundred people in the Willamette Valley about 40 miles southwest of Portland. The area was growing with immigrants seeking land. Minthorn's restless energy addressed itself to the business possibilities of the situation as he had earlier put himself to more specifically Quaker works.

In 1888 he moved 20 miles south to the larger town of Salem to sell undeveloped land suitable for prune orchards. The mail circulars of his Oregon Land Company—an early instruction to Hoover on the use of publicity—claimed of life there: "NO HYDROPHOBIA, NO TARANTULAS, NO CENTIPEDES." Whether the sternness in Uncle John's temperament was of a religious character or whether he simply liked to get things done, Hoover remembered him as a taskmaster who demanded a great deal of himself and others. Another description has Uncle John as "moody" and "absorbed in his work." Even in his land office days he remained a good professional doctor, possessing a model of a skeleton, discoursing in physiology, and keeping up on medical developments. John's lack of warmth must have kept Herbert a lonely boy, a loneliness accentuated by the austerity of the Quakers.[21]

Hoover later recalled "gleaming [Oregon's] wheat fields, abundant fruit, its luxuriant vegetation, and the fish in the mountain streams." The Rogue

River was his first serious fishing spot; during a visit in the 1920's he was disgusted to find it had become a polluted stream. He had been, he said then, "so happy and so poor" in those earlier times. For two summers he worked eleven-hour days on onion farms between Newberg and Portland. In Newberg he helped his uncle and Benjamin Miles clear stumps from the forested land, chopped wood, and took care of the family's horses. Dr. Minthorn gave Herbert room and board earned by incessant hard work. Another nephew recalled that Uncle John's "strength of body and character made him the greatest disciplinarian I ever saw"; his punishment for recalcitrant Indian children, according to government records, was "moving rocks." "I do not think he was very happy," Minthorn recalled of the young Hoover in 1920. "Our home was not like the one he left with his own parents in it (indulgent) and with very little of responsibility and almost no work." One of Bert's chores was to clear a fir forest on Minthorn's lands; he dreamed of "battalions of tall trees advancing in the moonlight." The boy was said to have looked serious beyond his years as he performed heavy chores. Like his brother Tad, who came to Newberg two years later, Bert clashed with his demanding uncle. Bert's brief residence then with Benjamin Miles, Laban's father, was an even worse experience, which according to his college classmate Vernon Kellogg gave Hoover a strong dislike of strict religious forms. Some years after, Hoover spoke bitterly of having been exploited by Uncle John. Still later his views softened. Both Herbert's and Theodore's memoirs portray Dr. Minthorn as essentially admirable, if harsh, and Bert contributed toward the education of Minthorn's two daughters.[22]

In Newberg, a smaller town than West Branch, Herbert lived in his uncle's house and later with Tad at the Friends Pacific Academy (now George Fox College). Uncle John described the academy as "about the same as a good High School." The first catalogue of the school, for 1885–6, shows a picture of Bert, the smallest boy with the biggest smile. Mrs. Minthorn, who taught the elementary grades, thought he had the sunniest disposition of the three orphans. Always the youngest in his class, Bert lacked an outstanding record except in mathematics; but in 1887 he did give a commencement speech on "Keeping Your Word," and another talk, "Rome Was Not Built in a Day." In the late spring of 1888, after less than three years in attendance, he went to help Uncle John and Ben Cook open their real estate office in Salem. "I was moved to Salem," he put it years later, and the focus of the Quakerism he knew shifted from service to material success.[23]

The Oregon Land Company's most expensive parcels lay in Silver Falls City, undeveloped at the time. As a $30-a-month "assistant book-keeper," Hoover learned something of bookkeeping, typing, and office routine. One co-worker remembered that Bert knew the status of all deals, the contents of all letters, and the whereabouts of all documents. It was a large operation: buying and selling land and houses, setting out and cultivating orchards, owning and operating a hotel, a saw and a flour mill, and a street railway. "In all of this," his uncle recalled, "Bert was a factor and could at any time give information about any detail. He supplied some ideas that were of great value in the business operations. He had special charge of the advertising department which included a contract with Lord and Thomas of Chicago . . . for ads in 1000 papers." To the company "he gave all his time from early morning until late at night." Bert arranged the company meetings and so dealt with incorporators of the firm, including the speaker of the lower house of the legislature and the superintendent of public instruction. "Bert enjoyed business," his uncle recalled. Some of the customers were interested in the land's mineral content, and there was talk of drifts and leads and prospects. Later the Oregon Land Company went broke, a victim of the national depression of the early 1890's. The company—like Bert's own mother—paid all existing debts. Hoover himself lost a pittance he had invested in a tiny cottage and some promising acreage. The company's failure may have driven him all the harder toward success. At night Bert studied mathematics at Ben Cook's local business and polytechnic college in Salem, paying the $60 tuition from his inheritance.[24]

He was not all business, however, as a note to "Friend Daisy" Trueblood indicates: "(and I hope you are more than my friend, although I do not dare to head it that way yet). You do not know the extent to which I am enthralled, and I am sure that no girl should be allowed such mastery over any person's heart. . . . I do not think you care. Do you? . . . Bert." In an article years later, Hoover described Miss Jane Grey, a spinster who at about this time introduced him to the literature of Dickens and Scott. *David Copperfield* lived on in the orphan boy's memory as the most important book he had ever read. He also visited the home of his Sunday School teacher, Mrs. Evangeline Martin, who lent him books and kindled his ambition for achievement. One Band of Hope debate had Hoover successfully affirming that war destroyed more men than liquor. Later, as Food Administrator, Hoover would oppose the spirit of fanatical prohibitionism. An acquaintance remembered Hoover's outburst during a debate over moving the county seat: "You are a democrat like your father and you democrats don't want to change anything but we republicans believe in changes." Uncle John recalled that the young Hoover "made a public confession of some kind once in the Highland Meeting, when a series of meetings was being held." A founding member of Salem Monthly Meeting in 1891, Herbert contributed $2 toward a new

meetinghouse and remained on its rolls until his presidency. He was remembered by a contemporary who kept up with him over the years as "a
very quiet, introspective nontalkative lad who played a little chess and
a little checkers." In Salem, Hoover slept in his uncle's house. Nearby in a
small cottage May came to live with her maternal grandmother, beginning
in December 1888; with Tad also nearby at Pacific Academy, Salem re-
united the children.[25]

Dr. Minthorn wanted Herbert enrolled in a Quaker college and arranged for scholarships, according to Hoover, at both Earlham and Haverford. Tad Hoover was attending William Penn College in Iowa. While
visiting Salem, an Eastern Quaker mining engineer urged Hoover to attend college at the new tuition-free university in California started by one
of its senators, Leland Stanford, as a memorial to his only son, who had
died at fifteen. Dr. Joseph Swain, a mathematics teacher who came to
Portland recruiting and giving examinations for the university, was also
a noted Quaker, which may have won over the Minthorns. That Hoover
had not completed high school proved no barrier, for his desire to go to
college coincided with Stanford's need for students. The university's
founder observed: "A general Education is the Birthright of every man
and woman in America." (Years later, after World War I, Hoover as a
Stanford trustee would bow to financial necessity and argue successfully
for instituting tuition.) After flunking all of Swain's entrance exams except
the one in mathematics, Hoover in June 1891 left Oregon for a summer of pre-college tutoring at Palo Alto; then only sixteen, he was among
the youngest of the five hundred or so students who trickled onto campus
later that summer. On the final entrance examinations, Hoover showed
ability in mathematics but received a "condition" in English, which would
be removed, after the stylistic tutelage of Professor Swain, just before
graduation.[26]

Hoover entered Stanford with the university's "pioneer" class, as it
was known thereafter. "I happened to be the first boy," Hoover later
wrote, "to sleep in the Men's Dormitory [Encina Hall] before the university was formally opened—and so may be said to be its first student."
For the first time he would be absent for long periods from older relatives
and in charge of his own affairs. The university itself accentuated this
independence. Its scientific and engineering departments, with their inno-
vatively open curricula offering many electives and encouraging fieldwork,
aimed to attract energetic young men and women looking for big practical
careers, and to set them on their own purposeful way even before the end
of their schooling. As a nine-year-old child Hoover had experienced the
shattering of a well-ordered world. But at seventeen he had come to believe, with sharp Uncle John's example before him, that real security lay

in the freedom and opportunity to gain control over self and environment. His choice of Stanford itself reflected that belief. His progress through his four years there would be that of a restless, idealistic opportunist.

Hoover did, to be sure, get an excellent grounding in geology. His transcript—the school gave no grades, only pluses or minuses—shows that he took the majority of credits in that subject. He also had courses in history, philosophy, and French. His only "no credit" was in German. But while Hoover could be studious, long, pounding, obedient study was not what he was after. His classmate Vernon Kellogg remarked on Hoover's "disconcerting habit" of not completing courses. He would start on one "and then, if he found it unpromising as a contribution to the special education in which he was interested, he would simply drop out of the class without consultation or permission." At one point Hoover asked his geology teacher John C. Branner—who once complained that Hoover was immersing himself in campus activities to the detriment of his studies—if he could ignore a university rule that required the presence of students during the entire senior year. Yet Hoover advised his friend Ray Wilbur: "Do your work so your professors will notice it."[27]

Much of Hoover's life and education at Stanford had to do with business. When classes began in October, he possessed in trust $822, of which Lawrie Tatum sent about half for freshman expenses. He set up a laundry business, which he soon engaged others to run, and later sold at a profit. Some classmates remember him working as a waiter and handyman at Encina Hall. He moved to a cheaper place in town the next year. Just before his sophomore term he told a friend: "Am going into baggage business at the beginning of school. . . . Am working awful hard. Have considerable business worked up 300000000000 schemes for making more."* Various jobs on campus and summer employment in the Arkansas and United States Geological Survey helped Hoover earn his way through four years of college without having to borrow. The Salem experience had evidently paid off.[28]

In January 1894 Hoover was elected treasurer of the junior class, and that spring a special runoff election made him treasurer of the Associated Students; the post, he later wrote, "implied General Manager, of the associated student enterprises." Inheriting a substantial student body debt, he cleared it away before graduating; he also introduced a voucher system that largely removed the possibility of fraud from the management of student accounts; and he was the first treasurer to open the accounts to public scrutiny. Though an unpaid position—"I am in favor of the Treas. recieving a salary myself," he then remarked—the post led to other

---

* Hoover's own spelling and punctuation are retained throughout this book.

Hoover in later years, led the largely successful anti-fraternity fight, Zion and Hicks serving consecutively as president of the student body. Hoover himself campaigned among some sixty of the poorest boys who lived in shacks in a rustic setting near the edge of campus. (This would be his only political precinct work.) His dislike of fraternities for their snobbishness persisted in later life, and he would not allow his sons—who attended public schools—to join any at Stanford. Hoover resembled Emerson in his distaste for conformism and popular mediocrity, and his insistence on individualist striving.[34]

This continued animosity toward the fraternity system distinguishes Hoover from some of the wealthy with whom many people came to associate him during the Depression years. So does Hoover's commentary while at Stanford on the American Railway Union's strike against the Pullman Company in 1894; he objected to President Cleveland's ending it by court injunction and observed it would "come out worse next time," implying a need for collective bargaining. (Or for that matter, his lashing out, during a cabinet meeting in 1922, at Attorney General Harry Daugherty's similar use of an injunction.) The anti-fraternity position foreshadows the kind of society Hoover would be working toward in his public career, a society organized, in effect, upon the dual principles of expertness and voluntary cooperation. A taste for small voluntary communities of interest and effort could include a liking for élitist or aristocratic groups, and for associations intended to perpetuate some particular cultural and social order. But Hoover's rejection of the fraternities suggests the extent of his indifference to other, comparable fundamental orderings of society that conservatives normally favor—beyond, of course, such venerable things as the Constitution, which received his predictable loyalty. Conscience, self-interest, technical skill, a right perception of some specific problem to be solved—these, in his eyes, were to be the sources of an individualistic American communalism.[35]

Stanford suited Hoover and did a great deal for him, both professionally and personally, in a way that no Eastern school of equal caliber could have done. Hoover would do a great deal for Stanford; no other President except Woodrow Wilson so closely identified himself with his alma mater in later life. During his business career Hoover bought for the library many hundreds of books, especially on Australia and the Far East. In a letter of 1908 to Theodore H. Adams, who then taught history at Stanford, he announced he would give complete sets of several publications of scientific societies "in relation to Asiatic matters, particularly early Jesuit publications"; and he wrote Adams in 1912 that he was sending some shelves of books on China. A trustee from 1912 onward in part through the efforts of his classmate and early political ally Lester Hinsdill, Hoover would donate $100,000 toward a Student Union, badly needed by the non-fraternity students. He also helped to found the School of Business and the Food Research Institute, both of which opened after World War I. He wanted more "pre-eminent" professors and higher salaries for faculty; initially he hoped to do away with the tenure system, not for "any sudden scattering of staff" but to oust the lazy or incompetent: "I do not know of any other profession, or calling, in this whole wide world where laziness and incapacity are wrapped up in the sacred garment of perpetual tenure." Some Stanford professors, however, managed to convince him that tenure was a substitute for greater economic compensation. His most impressive achievement was to salvage quantities of fugitive literature from Europe in the same era and house it on the campus at the Hoover War Library, later renamed the Hoover Institution on War, Revolution, and Peace.[36]

At Stanford, Hoover met his future wife, Lou Henry, daughter of a transplanted Iowa banker, a widower then living in the old mission town of Monterey.* Lou, whose father often took her fishing or hunting on afternoons after work, loved outdoor life and decided to major in geology —the only girl to do so in Hoover's time at Stanford. She was an accomplished horsewoman and athlete, a tall slim tomboy. Like Hoover, she was inclined to bluntness in expression, but she would one day possess the supple graces he lacked. When asked who would marry a woman geologist, she replied: "I want a man who loves the mountains, the rocks, and the ocean like my father does." Hoover fitted the description, and of course was attracted by her scientific bent. "We have a young lady taking Geology as a specialty now a very nice young lady too," he confided in a letter of November 1894.[37]

Lou served as president of the Stanford Geology Club as Bert had before her. Together with later business associates like John Means and D. P. Mitchell, the young man and his future wife heard such papers as "A Trip to the Diamond Mines in Brazil," "Quicksilver Mines at New Alameden," and "The Metallurgy of Gold and Silver." Bert delivered one paper on the geology of Pyramid Peak, Colorado, and of Lake Tahoe, and another on that of Western Australia. These studies of geology may have awakened Hoover's interest in history, which deepened in later years.[38]

In May 1895 Hoover graduated at the age of twenty with an A.B. in geology. Summers with the United States Geological Survey had complemented his studies, furnishing college credits, a $60 monthly salary, and a desire to be a mining engineer. The first summer, four to five months in 1892, netted fifteen college credits for "modeling and mapping"; he labored in the Arkansas Ozarks, where he witnessed degrading poverty.

* Born in Waterloo, Iowa, she grew up in a genteel reformist tradition not unlike Hoover's.

The next summer he worked in the High Sierra under the noted geologist Dr. Waldemar Lindgren. He was a more confident young man now, correcting a "we" by "or rather Lindgren" in a letter mentioning an expeditionary finding. In July 1894 he wrote a woman classmate: "I have a fine man to work for and a favorite business to work in, and . . . a grand country to work over. Our territory is just S.W. of Lake Tahoe . . . mostly about 7000 feet up. Big canyons and lots of game. Shall be out for 3 months." To his mentor John Branner, Hoover boasted: "Have just returned from the roughest country that God or man ever saw—the Buffalo country if put in one corner of the Rubicon River headwaters would not have been considered worthy of notice by a USGS topographer." When the survey maps of the area came out, Hoover shared Dr. Lindgren's credit line—his first scholarly recognition. The work of Lindgren and Hoover was all the more remarkable since it came scarcely after the region had been opened up by explorers and naturalists such as John Muir.[39]

"Now we are in a new act," Hoover wrote to a Stanford friend while studying gold deposits with Lindgren the summer following graduation.

The scenery is changed and the surroundings appropriate. From quiet Palo Alto with its live oak spotted meadows and its best of people to the jagged grandeur of the High Sierra with its dregs of humanity. But this is life, the other was happiness. Slept at Donner Lake one night. Tomorrow we are going to make descent of the American River Canyon, a thing people here say is impossible. But they are not geologists.

To his sister May, Hoover wrote of his "old friend" Lake Tahoe; the writing is in a primitivist romantic vein, suggesting the wonder-filled naturalist's concern for conservation:

No prosaic description can portray the grandeur of forty miles of rugged mountains rising beyond a placid lake in which each shadowy precipice and each purple gorge is reflected with a vividness that rivals the original . . . gaunt peaks of singular strength and nobility, vast proportions combined with simplicity and grace, stand out like buttresses and turrets from a great wall, their sides splashed with snow, their passes and lateral ridges covered with a wealth of vegetation which gives the whole an air of solidity and yet affords a restful contrast from their rugged summits. . . . Southeast of Lake Tahoe there is a sharp ridge of jagged granite peaks, each rising to over 11000 their bare sides cut by deep gorges into pinnicled precipices and saw toothed crags until in the distance the whole seems a cathedral more abundantly spired than Milan. . . . There had been a storm gathering from the West and the heavy clouds of mist mingled with snow rolled up against their battlements spreading their fleeces over turret and crest sending long streamers of mist down the gorges like the limbs of some giant dragon. As the clouds blew against this great barrier the eastward currents turned upward by the mountain side tore the vapory mass into great whorls, wrapping them about the peaks and pinnacles scattering the fleecy shreds among the rock faces . . . gradually the desert dried currents from the east gained mastery and from each icy peak like a streamer from the masthead waved a snowy banner a half mile in length widening toward its outward end and fading away in bits of detached clouds until it was gone entirely.[40]

The permanent survey position at $1200 that Hoover had anticipated did not come through, and after snowfall ended the summer job he could find no work in this time of economic depression other than pushing an ore car. Branner had encouraged his students to take up mine labor for a time. Hoover worked for some months at the deepest level of the Reward Gold Mine in Grass Valley near Nevada City, California—the storied locale of Bret Harte and Mark Twain—at a rate of $1.50 to $2.50 a day, on a ten-hour night shift and a seven-day week. After the Reward slowed its pace, Hoover lost his job and spent weeks searching before finding work on a $2.50 per day graveyard shift with Cornishmen at the nearby Mayflower Mine. "Professor" Tommy Nunnis later claimed he "learned Bert Hoover everything he knew about mining." For a time Hoover lay ill with a chest cough, which a neighbor aggressively treated with mustard plasters. By Christmas 1895 he had saved $100 and went back to Berkeley to join Tad, May, and his visiting cousin, Harriette Miles. In the summer of 1896 he registered to vote in Oakland, where he was then sharing a house with Tad.[41]

Originally Hoover had hoped to spend a year studying mining geology on the graduate level at Columbia or Johns Hopkins; his scholarly interests were well developed, and he would soon be writing professional articles. But with the economy somewhat improved, in February 1896 he sought out Louis Janin, employed by the Rothschild interests as one of the foremost legal experts on Western mining, to whom Lindgren had once introduced him. As Hoover remembers the encounter, Janin politely declined the request for mining employment, remarking that he had use only for an office typist, whereupon Hoover said he could type and would like the job. Janin was probably impressed by Hoover's references and certainly by his practical experience with Lindgren in Grass Valley, then involved in legal controversy. The older man took Hoover on at $75 a month and must have been pleased with his work for the attorney Curtis Lindley. "I was already entirely familiar with the geology of these mines, and contributed something to the winning of this case," Hoover remarked. Soon after Janin appointed his employee assistant manager of the Steeple Rock mine at Carlisle, New Mexico, which the engineering firm was examining for a London exploration group. Later Hoover and another man went to investigate a proposed hydraulic installation for gravel mines in northwestern Colorado. By the summer of 1896 Hoover had returned to work in Janin's San Francisco office at the respectable salary of $200 a month. That spring the Geological Survey position had come through, but Janin as well as Theodore urged him not to take it. Branner agreed: the U.S.G.S. gave no "dependable" employment. "You ought not to give up scientific geology entirely, but should publish occasionally whatever you can. You will be a member of the American Institute of Mining Engineers and you can bring out with them occasional papers on economic or scientific geology." Hoover's first publication, which appeared a year later, discussed Colorado placer mines.[42]

That October a cable arrived from the London mining consultants Bewick, Moreing and Company, asking for two young men skilled in American gold-mining practice, particularly smelting, to work in Australia at $450 a month. Bewick, Moreing had a promising interest in Western Australia, the world's fastest growing mining area, and desperately needed skilled men. Hoover had already done some small jobs for British firms. Janin, who hoped himself to work in London at a later time, urged Hoover to accept. It proved to be yet another kindness among the many the young man received from older men and women in the West.[43]

II

THE FRONTIERS
1897–1901

A T THE TURN of the century, a distinctive composite frontier
stretched across the world, taking in great chunks of Asia, Australia, Africa, and the American continent. Its flat wastes and mountains,
its sparse deserts and thinly populated provinces, invited not permanent
settlers but people of energy and technical skill who could dig out ores,
build bridges and railroads, organize archaic economies and politics, and
then move on to yet another region that awaited the quickening touch of
modern technology and administration. This frontier exists today in other
places and will take new forms as long as technical advances or political
disruption open territories to swift development. But a few decades ago it
was vast and disordered, with new technologies and their experts bursting
in upon lands still unused and peoples knowing nothing of machinery and
science. Young Herbert Hoover, venturesome and eager to put his engineering skills to work, was well fitted to join the international community
of technicians, capitalists, and administrators who drifted across its surface.[1]

Workers of many nationalities were trooping to Western Australia to
mine its gold, discovered at Hall's Creek in the Kimberley district in 1882,
then at Coolgardie in 1892, and at an even richer site in Kalgoorlie in
1893. As part of the British Empire, the colony looked to London; and in
the depression of the nineties London capital, deprived of attractive investments elsewhere, was ample. Gold was particularly desirable because of its
fixed price in a deflationary period.

The London mining engineers Bewick, Moreing and Company had
achieved prominence in Western Australia through investing in and managing a successful mine at Kalgoorlie. A reputation for broad knowledge and

good judgment of mines, at a time when other concerns occupied more narrowly with investment were afflicted with scandals, also helped the firm to win a strong following on the London stock exchange. As the number of mines under its direction multiplied, Bewick, Moreing searched with mounting difficulty for capable engineers willing to live in a vast desert where summer temperatures sometimes stayed near 100° even at night. Mining was not a gentleman's profession in Britain. The British Geological Society avoided the study of mining because it smacked of commerce, and technical schools lagged behind their counterparts from the United States in technical methods and knowledge. The American West, with a history of precious metals, respected mining talent, and some of its young universities such as Stanford valued practical knowledge. American engineers, moreover, had done well in the gold mines of South Africa. Herbert Hoover's combination of geological training and practical experience was highly suitable for gold mining.

On about March 25, 1897, after drinking a farewell cup of coffee with friends at a San Francisco café, Hoover left for London. He stopped cross-country on the twenty-eighth at West Branch, where the local paper said he would work for the "Rothschilds." Three days later he boarded the White Star liner *Britannic* in New York; the ship's passenger list recorded: "H. C. Hoover, Age 36, Mining Engineer." Hoover had meanwhile grown a mustache to look older than his twenty-two years. In England a long weekend at Charles Algernon Moreing's country estate went well. A large man with a booming voice, Moreing liked the young American and took pleasure in showing him some landmarks of English history. Hoover left by the Australian-China mail train for Brindisi; there he sailed by way of the Suez Canal and Indian Ocean, arriving at Albany, in Western Australia, on May 13. Detained in King George's Harbour a few days by an outbreak of smallpox on board, Hoover took the opportunity to learn more about Australian telluride gold from its discoverer, Modest Morylansk, a Polish mining man also under quarantine. Hoover first traveled to one of Australia's loveliest cities, the seaport capital of Perth on the Swan River; from there a day's railroad journey took him across undulating plains some 350 miles inland to Coolgardie.[2]

Coolgardie—a place of "sin, sand, sorrow, sickness, and sore eyes," according to a popular description—suffered, as Hoover wrote to an Oregon friend, from "red dust, black flies, and white heat." So distant were the amenities of civilization that he once spent a nickel apiece for fresh strawberries shipped in from the coast. Local whirlwinds called "willie willies" could carry away a flimsy house in a cloud of dust. Through the surrounding bush country—Hoover called it "a sort of aggrandized Sagebrush" in one of his letters home—naked aborigines wandered, living off ants, snakes, grubs, birds' eggs, and the town's garbage. "It may interest you to know something of the native customs," he wrote to his family, in a letter that demonstrated how quickly he could pick up local stereotypes. "Most of them are disgusting and brutal, to a degree; others show strange foresight," four or five of their drugs having been adopted as standard medicines. Hoover went on to give a crude description based on prejudiced local conceptions:

The tribes are always small, seldom over 200 and can never . . . associate with another tribe, except in war or to steal a wife. If a member of one tribe be caught by members of another, even when peacefully hunting, he is killed instantly. Infanticide is universal . . . when a man dies, his father falls on his body and is beaten by other niggers. . . . Curiously, they have no religion. They have a devil-devil who is not a spirit but a real live nigger, who acts as executioner for the tribe and is therefore the medicine man's partner. His services can be secured on payment and he can be legitimately killed on sight, so he wears on his feet feathers pointing both ways, to prevent his being tracked. . . .

The aborigines have no hell, Hoover observed. "The sky is inhabited by a great man, woman, and child, which they can see in the stars. . . ." On dying they rise heavenward and then fall into the sea to live happily forever.[3]

Of Coolgardie Hoover wrote home: it "is three yards inside the borders of civilization. Perth is about a mile, and of course San Francisco is the center. . . . Stanford is the best place in the world." An octagonal building on Hunt Street housed Bewick, Morcing's headquarters, where the quiet and ambitious Hoover served "fourth in command" under an irascible Welshman, Ernest Williams. In 1898 the firm moved its headquarters some 20 miles, to the richer fields of Kalgoorlie. But Kalgoorlie was no better. "It is a terrible place," Hoover wrote home. "You cannot imagine the dust, it is so deep in the streets." The wind drove it, irritating his already reddened eyes.[4]

The young engineer's duties included the sampling, surveying, and evaluating of mines offered his firm for purchase; he noted that the current depression provided opportunities for "advantageous deals" with prospectors. The mines were various: a few deep like those in South Africa, a larger number like the placer mines Hoover had worked in Colorado. Given the enormous variations, good judgment was a priceless commodity to a firm like Hoover's. Hoover traveled by camel—an even "less successful creation than the horse," he observed—to one mine after another, with improbable names like IOU, Siberia, and far-away Never Never. Suffering frequently from indigestion and from physical debility brought on by overwork, he would sometimes travel lying on a mattress in the back of an open wagon. "It is uncomfortable," he noted, "to go a week without washing." Homesick, he wished for "fresh news from U.S.A., the dearest place on earth." He purchased for himself a one-fifth interest in one small mine that caught his eye. Generally his early judgments of mining properties proved accurate in the years ahead, though he erred in believing that Kalgoorlie possessed native gold sulfide. Hoover's careful technical reports signed "HH" are still on file at the Western Australia Department of Mines in Perth. He had great opportunities in Australia and apparently missed few of them.[5]

A set of three enthusiastic reports dated late in 1897 went beyond mere accuracy and his usual care. In company code—Hoover's codename was "textbook"—he wholeheartedly recommended a remote mine some 130 miles north of the rich and familiar Kalgoorlie lodes. Geoffrey Blainey, literary master among Australian historians and author of that country's mining history, *The Rush That Never Ended,* credits Hoover's co-worker Edward Hooper with first recommending the fabulously wealthy Sons of Gwalia mine. Other Australian writers, some of their accounts bursting with nationalism, have echoed Blainey. But in a letter to a mining acquaintance Hooper himself withdrew his earlier claim, which Blainey had relied on:

Owing to further examination of my records . . . you were practically correct in attributing to H. C. Hoover the responsibility for the original purchase of the Sons of Gwalia. . . . I instructed Hoover to sample the mine and make a report to me thereon. On receipt of this report, I cabled to London recommending . . . purchase.

Hoover claimed to have stumbled on the mine late that summer while riding on camel from Menzies to Lawlers, and to have cabled Moreing directly about it; this is not quite correct, for in August the firm asked that either he or Hooper inspect it, and Hoover did so. His cable of September 11 to London read: "I consider it a most valuable property . . . very great possibilities." Largely on Hoover's highly detailed examinations Moreing, working through the London and Western Australia Exploration Company, purchased the mine for more than $1 million and registered it in London in January 1898. The prospectus for the new property quotes Hoover's telegrams. In 1903 Moreing described the Sons of Gwalia as the "mine out of which we made the most profit of any business we did." Not until the 1960's did this most famous of Western Australian mines enter receivership.[6]

Now second in line after Williams and with a salary of $12,500, Hoover became chief engineer over eight Kalgoorlie mines. He immersed himself in technical mining problems. He had worked at gold smelting under Janin at Carlisle, New Mexico, and for just such an arid land as Australia he had written an article that discussed separating gold with insufficient water supply; Skinner's *Mining Manual* for 1897 defined Hoover's purpose in going to Australia as the installing of a new process for gold smelting. In any event, he urged his firm to adopt the filter press for recovering water for further use in metallurgical processes. Three months after his arrival in Australia the press was being used effectively at Hannan's Brownhill, where Hoover was then in charge, and more presses were ordered. On July 16, 1897, he wrote home: "We are building two very large, dry crushing cyanide mills. . . ." His *Memoirs,* though, may give him too much credit for introducing the device. While Hannan's Brownhill was first to put in the press, Lake View Consols had ordered one earlier in the year; and in letters sent a few years later to the editor of the *Engineering and Mining Journal,* wherein he claimed to have had a leading role in his company's adaptation of the device, Hoover termed it the "Diehl process" after the Bewick, Moreing metallurgist Ludwig Diehl.[7]

Hoover dreamed of gathering the mines of Kalgoorlie into one efficient amalgamated unit. In his fantasies about making Kalgoorlie the Johannesburg of Australia—so an acquaintance reports—"he was himself always controlling engineer, organiser, and administrator." He soon got his chance to assume that composite position, though not at Kalgoorlie. Moreing appointed him manager of Sons of Gwalia, and late in April 1898 Hoover moved to nearby Mount Leonora, a semi-arid place studded with straw-colored spinifex and mulga. There he could experiment as he chose, largely free of anyone else's domination, introducing mining techniques and specialists from his native country. He drew up plans for a large metallurgical plant installed by a successor. He picked out able men and promoted them; the New Zealander John Agnew moved from underground laborer to underground manager in a few weeks. Now Hoover controlled a mining adventure entire.[8]

That, in Western Australia, meant dealing with scarcities of water, timber, fuel, and other materials, with a high cost of living, with the soaring labor costs distinctive of Australia. So Hoover, who as President would pursue a strong conservationist policy, had to think about conservation. He wrote later that the best policy was to mine quickly, get a profit, and then reinvest in better equipment. Hoover's successor complained about mine machinery "in such bad repair almost run to a finish"; Hoover had here chosen swift profits over the preservation of shoddy equipment. With labor, that other costly element in Western Australian production, Hoover practiced still harsher economies.[9]

Companies were hiring immigrants, and Hoover, who supervised some one hundred workers at Leonora, eagerly experimented. On May 12, 1898, he wrote to Pietro Ceruti, a recruiter or contractor, asking for "three good

Italian miners" and remarking that a satisfactory result would "open the way to the employment of many more. . . . They will receive the usual wages." The request initiated a heavy use at Leonora of Italian miners, twenty of them hired in preference to available Australians. More tractable than native labor, the contract workers came cheaper, too. Hoover also wanted to economize with employees he already had. At East Murchison he had reduced wages during a railroad strike that temporarily increased the labor supply; and a report of November 10, 1897, on East Murchison United that Hoover revised and approved carries a recommendation to raise from forty-four to forty-eight the weekly hours for some employees. A report from preponderantly unionized Leonora announces: "We have changed the working hours of the men in the mines from 44 hours to 48 hours per week, and after some trouble things have quieted down and work is proceeding smoothly." On May 23, 1898, Hoover wrote to London from Leonora:[10]

During the week I have had two strikes. In the first instance I asked the men to change shifts at point of employment instead of on the surface—each man by this means cut twenty minutes per diem from his time underground. The men met and determined to strike and I therefore promptly posted a notice that we would not grant the usual hour off on the Saturday shift, but the men would have to work the full forty-eight hours [raised by Hoover a few weeks previously from forty-four], and intimated we were prepared for any strike by importing Italians. The men sent a delegation then asking for a Meeting, at which I agreed to compromise allowing them the Saturday hour as before, if they would change at point of employment.

Again the Truckers in the lower level struck for a rise in pay owing to the wet ground. We discharged the entire crew at that level, and replaced them with men at the old rate.

Again it had been formerly the custom to pay double pay for Sunday Work, which we stopped, and six men working on Sunday refused to proceed. We discharged them and replaced them with new men.

I have a bunch of Italians coming up this week and will put them in the mine on contract work. If they are satisfactory I will secure enough of them to hold the property in case of a general strike, and with your permission will reduce wages. We now pay 5/—per day more than any other mine on the field. . . .

This episode Lou Henry Hoover years later called self-serving. We could take into account current conditions at Australian mines, where scarcity of labor made wages and hours of work among the best in the world. Usually single men, and therefore relatively free to strike, unionized miners were aided by a sympathetic government. They sometimes forced the closing of marginal ventures, including some under the control of Bewick, Moreing. By American or British standards, most of Hoover's workers received ex-

cellent treatment, and conditions were good even by the Australian measure; Hoover may have believed he was holding out against prohibitive
costs. An article in the *Engineering and Mining Journal* of December 17,
1898, has Hoover taking a tough managerial line, but being responsive to
some measures of social progressivism. "Although it is a country of un-
paralleled democracy," Hoover wrote, "it sometimes seems to the manager
that the sole object of Government is to hamper him in relation to his
laborers. It is not the high wages, however, of which Western Australian
managers complain most, but the inefficiency of the men . . . they accomplish about two thirds the amount of work of a California miner." Italians
accomplished one-half more work, Hoover observed, "but they possess
certain disqualifications," among them presumably a disinclination to
learn English. Hoover did credit the government with building railroads
and telegraphs, and with refraining from direct taxation. Further improvements in working costs, he believed, should come from lowering tax rates
on mine ownership, shortening the time that the holder to a title of a site
must work it, and removing restrictions on Asian labor.[11]

As severe as he was capable of being about labor matters, Hoover could
also write home from Cue (in Western Australia) with evident feeling
about his having to fire an employee:

I had to discharge an old accountant, a man 72 years old, and entirely incapable
of doing this work. But when I told him we would need a younger more energetic man, he broke down and cried, and told me of his wife to whom he sent
his entire salary. I have learned he even does his own washing to send her every
cent. I am dreadfully put out about it. I have been to see three of our boys.
We have made a purse of $300 for him and we think we can get him another
place in Perth. . . . If this were my own business, I would be too tender-
hearted to let him go, but I have to get things into shape for the company.[12]

In 1898 Charles Moreing was in China to see after European mining
investments. Perhaps the young engineer who had done much to lift Moreing's fortunes in Australia could do the same in China, where the government threatened to hamper his operations. Besides, an American would
be attractive to Chinese government officials beset with pressures from
European interests. And Hoover could bring to the delicacies of the Chinese situation his skills in bargaining. He had engaged in public relations
work, the Coolgardie *Miner* remarked, as a highly active member of the
important Coolgardie Chamber of Commerce. Though the Chamber records are lost, an Australian contemporary recalled that Hoover was "a
very live member . . . more work [was] done and more promptly done
than at any other [chamber] in the state." Moreing, who liked a man conscious of the need for public relations, said that these chambers should
represent "the capitalist, professional man, and the miner"; they should, in

effect, serve as organs of collective bargaining—and chambers of mines in fact served as arbiters on occasion, which kept pay relatively high and hours of work generally restricted to forty-odd per week. Here, perhaps, was a source of Hoover's concept of community organization along functional lines.[13]

Edward Hooper later claimed that Hoover's talent for hard bargaining, which would suit the Chinese, had led him to recommend the American for service in China. But the main reason Moreing thought of sending him was to keep peace in Australia, where Hoover and his boss Ernest Williams were feuding openly. While chief field engineer for Bewick, Moreing, Hoover had persuaded four American mine managers to conspire with him against Williams, who thereupon vainly attempted to fire his rival. These American cohorts in Australia affectionately called Hoover "chief," an appellation that stuck throughout his life. Moreing cabled from Peking, offering Hoover $7500 plus 10 percent of the company's profits for serving in two jobs: as the Chinese government's resident chief engineer of the Bureau of Mines for the northern Chihli and Jehol provinces, and as Bewick, Moreing representative in China. The dual position suggests a conflict of interest but was in conformity with Chinese practices of the time.[14]

The move to China with a better salary impelled Hoover to consider his personal life with a new earnestness. Late in 1898 Hoover cabled Lou Henry, "Will you marry me?" Once the telegram had been removed from the men's bulletin board at Stanford, where she was working for John Branner, and given to its proper recipient, she quickly accepted Hoover's proposal. It is possible that some objection had been raised to an earlier betrothal. Hoover in 1919 told the young man Claire Torrey, whose fiancée had not shown up for the wedding, "I had a similar experience when I was young." Hoover ransacked the shops in Perth for books on China, and on December 11, 1898, left Perth on the S.S. *India* for London. After consultation on Moreing's affairs in China, he traveled to California to be married. On his way to Monterey he stopped at San Francisco, smoked a 50-cent cigar in the Palace Hotel, and talked with a former classmate, who remarked on Hoover's growth in self-confidence. He seemed to be on top of life.

Lou Henry had resolved to become a Quaker, but since no Friends meeting existed around Monterey, the local Roman Catholic priest, a family acquaintance operating in his civil capacity under a special dispensation, on February 10, 1899, married the couple, each wearing unconventional brown traveling suits. Nominally Episcopalian, the Henrys were said to incline toward freethinking and so accepted the ceremony by the charming Monseigneur Raymond Mestres, who had helped Lou Henry control unruly students in a school where she had taught after her Stanford graduation.

Hoover gave his Stanford diploma to a friend for safekeeping, only to have it turn up in someone else's attic when Hoover was eighty years old. Ten days later the newlyweds boarded a steamer bound for the Orient. On shipboard they would consult several dozen more books on China. Hoover wrote that he was "in for two years siege in Northern Manchuria on the Siberian border. . . . I don't relish it a bit, but it can't be any worse than Western Australia."[15]

Australia had trained Hoover in technology and in management. China would work both an enlargement and a transformation of his Australian experience. He became for the first time manager over varied resources, confronted with major problems in economics and at one point with the task of keeping refugees alive.

The young engineer would have to come to working terms with the Chinese, but he shared the American perception that identified efficiency with Western ways and a look of briskness. The busy and preoccupied Hoover was not to acquire whatever feeling for Chinese culture a knowledge of the language would have brought. His *Memoirs* candidly note that, while Lou Henry Hoover made great progress in Chinese lessons, he never learned more than a hundred words in his nearly three years in the country. "HH" 's newspaper sketch, made during the Boxer Rebellion in 1900 (see insert of illustrations), shows two effete Chinese, one of them a rebel and the other an opium-smoking soldier, lounging on some railroad tracks, in classic ethnic stereotyping. Hoover came as a technician, with large responsibilties, to a land unschooled in Western technological methods and pace. He compassionately observed shocking poverty, convinced that a different set of national habits would rout it. He was right; but it was a form of communism that changed Chinese customs a half-century later, not American know-how or values.[16]

Hoover found China frustrating. In an article of 1899 he put the effectiveness of Chinese laborers at about one-fifth that of Westerners, but concluded that since the Chinese were paid only 1/25th as much, and "their tendencies to dishonesty are probably no greater than those of other human beings under the same condition," the cheap labor was an asset. Three years later he expressed a more pessimistic opinion:

The simply appalling and universal dishonesty of the [Chinese] working classes, the racial slowness, and the low average of intelligence, gives them an efficiency far below the workmen of England and America. Neither is the Chinese working man in China to be judged by his countrymen in America, who, coming from natural selection from the best working class, are freed from a maze of custom and superstition, and imbued by the spirit of another country. . . . For crude labor, such as surface excavation, he has no equal, but as we proceed up the scale of skill he falls further behind. . . . The disregard for human life permits cheap mining by economy in timber, and the aggrieved relatives are amply compensated by the regular payment of $30 per man lost.

Upper-class Chinese also exasperated Hoover. "Their smallest weakness," he remarked of native administrators of his company, "is unfamiliarity with the business." His wife wrote to Professor Branner: "The managers and most of the officials (all Chinese) have never been down [into the mines]!" Hoover estimated that "under Chinese administration . . . every deficiency of the workman is multiplied many times by the innate lack of administrative ability in his superiors and their more consummate dishonesty. . . ." Politics, he learned in China, does not mix with administrative efficiency. He theorized that the Chinese had no sense of personal responsibility but did have a group life that entailed common obligations. A portion of the *Memoirs* written before the United States entry into World War I also speaks sensitively of the Chinese character. Hoover distinguished between American graft and the less offensive Chinese "squeeze," which prevailed only in situations not covered by contracts or clear understandings. "There were bad persons," he wrote of the Chinese, "just as there are in all races. What the relative proportion of good and bad there are depends a great deal on how much they have to eat. I doubt if Americans would average as well . . . if they had so little."[17]

How much of the West Hoover himself aimed at bringing to the Celestial Mines of China—especially in the way of skill and pace and attitude, to be urged on Chinese workers and administrators or stimulated by the very presence of Western industry—we may only speculate about. His task in any event was to import the West for the good of the nation that had appointed him its resident chief engineer and the good of the Western financiers for whom he worked. In a sense, therefore, the same qualities of Chinese life that he thought hindered his work also gave it its definition and purpose. One of Hoover's first recommendations on arrival at Tientsin in northern China, where he would reside for much of his stay in the country, looked to improving the lot of Chinese laborers and perhaps also to awakening new attitudes among them toward work. He proposed an end to the system of secure long-term contracts—a slave system, he called it—and its replacement by a system rewarding individual merit. His larger problem was to create conditions favorable to the entrance of Western capital and technology.[18]

In the 1890's the Chinese government considered a vigorous new policy of developing Chinese mines. In his *Memoirs* Hoover credited a German civil servant of the Celestial Throne, Gustav Detring, with the introduction of these ideas, which became part of the "Young Emperor" Kuang-hsü's "reform and progress" program. But Detring's plan, whatever it may have offered to the Chinese economy, included forcing the weakened government to give substantial territorial concessions to foreign countries. It was an era of plunder, when Europeans stole from the Celestial Kingdom everything from temple bells to whole provinces. At the very time Hoover went to China, a nationalist reaction to these losses threatened to endanger both foreign interests and even native development of natural resources. After a surge of reform culminated in the execution of the reformers, a series of new "Regulations" adopted by imperial edict in June 1899 required in substance that no more than one mine, rather than a large area of mines, be granted to foreigners; that the government receive 25 percent of the profits; and that administration of the companies be entirely Chinese, although foreigners could own half the plant and assist in technical capacities. Under these conditions no applications were being made.[19]

Speaking of the restraints on foreign operation of mines, Hoover wrote Moreing in January 1900 that "the game is not worth the candle" without control. Moreing had already secured $1 million for the Chinese Engineering and Mining Company's deepwater port at Ch'in-wang-tao. Why should Europeans want to invest more in any business plagued with incompetent administration? Hoover himself proposed a comprehensive mining law allowing equal rights to foreigners under strict government supervision, with royalties to the Chinese and safe title for the foreign investor. The time for formal enactment was inopportune, but Hoover with nine subordinate engineers nevertheless pursued development of the Chinese Engineering and Mining Company, protecting already committed European investments.[20]

In 1899 he had sent for members of the Sons of Gwalia staff, John Agnew and D. P. Mitchell, along with two geologists from America and a British harbor engineer whom he set to work in subzero weather on the port, which connected the interior coal mines with the outside world. The Chinese government's Director of Mines, Chang Yen-mao, urged Hoover to find gold. He, his assistant, and sometimes Lou—herself a licensed mining engineer—traveled over much of Shantung and Shansi provinces and even into Manchuria. G. B. Wilson, one of the American geologists, tried hard to make some of the existing mines profitable. But he wrote Hoover on his attempts to reduce wages: "I received the astonishing information that a Chinaman's salary cannot be reduced. If so he must resign or 'lose face.'" In a later communication he recommended a "benevolent institution in Tientsin, where we may relegate the useless members and 'friends' of the staff here to life long ease and plenty." The only Oriental manager familiar with the mine got up daily at noon and smoked opium until weak and pale. Hoover suggested that Detring set up a small company for selling the mines explosives, insurance, machinery, shipping, and so forth, the company to be subscribed to by Hoover, Detring, Chang, Hoover's secretary, and an Oregon friend. Hoover meanwhile spent much of his time seeking and developing the enormous coal deposits that constituted China's true mineral wealth. In 1899 he placed a £8,125,000 value on coal in sight at Chihli Province's Chinese Engineering and Mining Company. Hundreds of millions of tons lay behind this; in addition, the company ran cement and brick factories, a busy port, and steamship lines that plied an extensive coastwise trade. At the end of his first year in China, Hoover was fretting because the government would act on none of his suggestions and he lacked the power to implement them.[21]

Before very much could be accomplished, the young emperor had been imprisoned by his aunt, the Empress Dowager, and the extreme nativist insurrection known as the Boxer Rebellion broke out. Believing they possessed supernatural powers that protected them from harm, swarms of Boxers (short for "righteous harmonious fists") set out in 1900 to extirpate every foreign thing in China—railways, telegraphs, houses, and people—and any Chinese associated with foreigners or Christianity. They aimed to "drive them into the sea." Anthropologists have described their frenzied effort as a "revitalization movement," seeking to restore old values threatened by a sudden influx of new ones.[22]

Hoover was surveying the vast anthracite coal deposits in the northwestern hilly interior that June when he heard of sporadic violence near Shanghai. He quickly returned to Peking and took his wife, who was ill, to Tientsin, which he initially saw as a refuge. A settlement of hundreds of foreign families, the area included, besides good medical facilities, a small Western college where Hoover had delivered a series of lectures on mining. According to an interview with Hoover late in 1900, the Allied fleets' capture of Taku on June 16 had "united all factions of the natives in opposition to us." The naval men responsible must have been "insane," Hoover observed, because they had left Allied settlements largely unprotected. However, some fifteen hundred soldiers of several foreign countries, whose armament included two cannon and a dozen machine guns, promised safety from tens of thousands of poorly armed peasant Chinese. An additional contingent of seven hundred Russian soldiers arrived and made the district still more secure. But then the foreign-trained Chinese thought to be protecting the area fell under Boxer influence; from a section known as the Old City they sent a hail of shells and bullets that continued intermittently for some thirty days. Some three hundred people were killed; only the presence of the Russian troops saved the settlement. Years later Mrs. Hoover recalled reading her own three-column obituary, which had been published in California. Atrocities took place on both sides; in fighting between

Boxers and Chinese soldiers, casualties were horribly mutilated.* Hoover estimated that about 2000 corpses floated down the river that bounded the settlement.[23]

The Hoovers put themselves into the thick of the city's defense. Lou looked after a dairy and commissariat and worked much of the day in one or another of the hospitals. She carried a Mauser automatic 38-caliber pistol and was considered a good shot, she remembered in a letter. She was captain of the guard around the house where the Hoovers were staying, and "took my turn in these night watches. . . . I could do it as well as the men." But "Bert and I left the killing to the soldiers." She was certain, she remarked, that Herbert had "never had a gun in his hand to aim at the enemy," but whether this reflected his Quaker principles she does not say. She declared that she had had a fine time during the Boxer Rebellion, and would not have missed it for anything. Hoover helped direct the building of barricades composed of sacks of rice, sugar, and grain along the exposed sides of the town. He also joined in fighting fires. Getting around by bicycle, for nearly three weeks he directed the carrying of food and water to some six hundred anti-Boxer Chinese who had taken refuge in settlement compounds. One of his Stanford classmates at Tientsin recalled shortly afterward that Hoover was "everywhere and everything to everybody." He appeared oblivious to the constant shower of stray bullets. The episode resembled in microcosm what he would do on a great scale for much of the European world during the era of World War I. On July 13 Hoover sent a one-word cable—"Safe"—from Shanghai to Lou's father in Monterey.[24]

Among the Chinese Hoover looked after at Tientsin were Chang Yen-mao, whose venality had increasingly troubled Hoover, and T'ang Shao-yi, Director of Railways and later Premier of China. Amidst suspicions that some shooting was coming from the Chinese under Hoover's care, or that they kept in touch with the enemy by carrier pigeon, a British captain took Chang, T'ang, and others into custody, executed some of their underlings, and began to try them all under summary proceedings. Hoover and others —John Agnew, Jack Means, William Newberry, Edward Bangs, Dr. Tenny —prevailed on the chief officer in the town, a Russian colonel, to order their release. In the opinion of T'ang, who years later publicly thanked Hoover for his help in 1900, Hoover's intervention probably saved their lives. After T'ang's wife and baby had been killed by a stray shell, Hoover and Agnew carried the other T'ang children to safety at Hoover's house. Eighteen years later one of T'ang's daughters, then the wife of the Chinese

* Joaquin Miller, the California lyric poet who swallowed fish whole during his reading tours, came out of retirement from distilling 110-proof whiskey to cover the Rebellion for the Hearst Press. Sporting a long white beard and accompanied by a pregnant woman not his wife, the Sweet Singer of the Sierra called at Tientsin on Hoover, who intentionally directed him away from the conflict.

ambassador to the United States, surprised Hoover at a social gathering in Washington by remarking that he had rescued her when she was a young child.[25]

During the Boxer Rebellion, Chinese Engineering and Mining properties had been taken over variously by Russians, British, Americans, Japanese, and Germans. Fearing that such seizures meant an end to free commercial access to China, the American Secretary of State, John Hay, in July sent these powers his second "Open Door" note, urging them to guarantee its administrative and territorial integrity. Hoover's classmate wrote from Tientsin to Dr. Branner in Stanford that partitioning was "very probable." Early in August 1900 Chang and Gustav Detring, in an effort to keep the financially ruined mine properties intact, had Hoover accept as trustee a deed dated July 25 on behalf of a contemplated new British corporation for, in Hoover's well-chosen phrase, the "benefit of all concerned." Detring, with power of attorney from Chang, signed the document for the Chinese government. The new company would provide both protection and capital. Gleeful at this turn of events and confident of the property's enormous potential under efficient foreign management, Hoover left for England on August 14 with his wife on a German mail boat. "Trust peace is being fixed up," he wrote Detring from the *Weimar,* complaining "table atrocious, service worse." The Hoovers arrived in England by way of Suez—the Trans-Siberian Railway was not quite finished—on October 8.[26]

Until this point Hoover had been simply a well-paid employee; now he became more. Moreing, who held £100,000 of bonds in the Chinese company, was naturally grateful. After some delay Hoover assigned his power of attorney to Moreing, who used it in December to establish a British-based Chinese Engineering and Mining Company. Hoover got a partnership in Bewick, Moreing the following year, earning then $12,500 annually and 20 percent of its profits; already a director of the new Chinese company, Hoover also received some quarter of a million dollars of the company's stock.[27]

In early January 1901 Hoover returned to China with Lou and assumed the position of acting general manager. He brought with him a letter from Moreing to Detring asking for some changes in the agreement. After an arduous battle of persuasion, Hoover prevailed on Chang and Detring to sign a revised deed bearing the original July 1900 date, ostensibly as protection against Russian claims to some of the properties. No longer simply a trustee, Hoover was given wide latitude in transferring the assets of the old company. Moreing's aim was to obtain clear title—a deed of sale, not a trust—to reassure Belgian investors, and to gain promotional profits. Chang signed with his official seal, an act doubly assuring the legality of the transfer, and greatly expanded the area granted to include not just the mines previously worked but the entire Kaiping Basin. The transaction placed both Chang and Detring in uncomfortable positions: each making more than $250,000 on the arrangements, they needed now to show they had not betrayed China. And so in exchange for the transfer agreement, all the parties signed a memorandum dated February 19, 1901, guaranteeing Chang a large degree of supervisory rights and assigning to a Chinese board a vote equal to that of the foreign owners.[28]

Two days after the signing, the Brussels Banque d'Outre Mer cabled $500,000 to the company's account. Belgian interests, led by Émile Francqui, wanted full control; and in 1901 Hoover worked in China with a Belgian mine manager, Chevalier de Wouters d'Oplinter. After several months Hoover and Francqui were at angry odds. On October 1 the Hoovers left for California, taking with them the beginnings of an outstanding collection of exquisite Ming and K'ang Hse blue porcelains. Francqui would later tell Hoover's friend Edward Eyre Hunt, "Hoover's quiet withdrawal cost . . . the Company about five million dollars."[29]

Hoover's retirement from the field must have made it easier to disregard his memorandum with Chang. The new firm now quickly denied having empowered him to sign it. It "is only step by step that we have succeeded in becoming the master," noted de Wouters. The memorandum "does not bind us to anything." Detring, who after Hoover's departure began protesting the Western coup within the company, claimed in 1902 that Francqui was exercising "supreme power for the [Western] board." Francqui told de Wouters to do whatever was necessary for progress, regardless of the Chinese board. That body, now powerless, was useful for not much more than temporarily saving Chang embarrassment. And what was Hoover doing as the Chinese were being denied a voice in the management of the company's resources?[30]

In a letter sent early in 1902 to the English-language *North China Herald,* a communication intended for the foreign settlements and for educated Chinese, Hoover claimed to have abided by the division of power. And though Detring accused both Hoover and de Wouters of ignoring the memorandum, he did concede that Hoover had initially tried to keep to that agreement. Three years later he would denounce "arbitrary . . . repudiation" by the board of directors "of an agreement [that] had been something more than plain." But as early as March 9, 1901, Hoover in a letter to Moreing had been arranging "complete control" for de Wouters, free of "any interference from the Chinese board," which he labeled a Daly opera.* In a note of July 7, de Wouters told the London office: "Mr.

* Augustin Daly (1838–98) wrote for a comic theater he owned on Broadway in New York City.

Hoover and myself are doing what we want informing the China board only of those things which it may know without danger and going squarely to the front without it when necessary." T. R. Wynne, a later general manager, testified in 1905 that Hoover had advised him in August 1902 to ignore the memo; Hoover explained himself to the court as having meant only "that it was necessary that the detailed administration of the mines should be in the hands of the manager, subject to the board." Hoover, in any case, remained on the board—because, in Mrs. Hoover's account, he could thereby be a more effective critic—and did not relinquish his profitable seat until 1912, four years after Moreing's resignation.[31]

Perhaps any complaints Hoover later made about violations of the memorandum agreement represent his translation into moral terms of some relatively self-interested power contest between the Belgians and himself: the press of 1902 is full of reports of what one editorial called "internecine conflict" between Belgian and English directors of the company. But it is likely that even though he wanted the technical operation of the company in hands he considered competent, he had a notion of an ultimate Chinese voice and veto in defense of their national welfare and found the Belgians to have encroached on that minimal indispensable right; perhaps even de Wouters had some similar ambivalence. Impatient, confident to the point of arrogance, craving efficiency and results, Hoover used shortcuts against the slow, genteel Chinese establishment. He also wished to do well by China—had, indeed, a feeling of personal engagement in that nation's progress—and would not want the Chinese insulted and exploited by Western interests. If Hoover himself could have dominated a company divested of all but a ceremonial vestige of Chinese control, he might have been pleased, not only because he liked having his unencumbered way at work but because he would have trusted himself, correctly or not, to act fairly. But sharing with other foreigners in the control of Chinese resources —that was something else.[32]

The British Foreign Office wished the firm to be solidly British. In answer to a request by Hoover, British troops in February 1901 occupied territories relinquished by Russians and later helped to restore the port of Ch'in-wang-tao to company control. But one foreign service officer called the company's new board "morally . . . wrong," and Arthur Townley, the British chargé d'affaires, complained later that an "Anglo-Belgian gang" had "fleeced" the Chinese and that Moreing and others had "made a pretty pile at [their] expense." But Townley also observed of the defenders of the Chinese interest: "What makes such as Detring . . . and Chang Yen Mow wild is that they thought themselves rather smarter than most people, and yet got themselves had by a Yankee man of straw [Hoover] acting for Moreing." Detring, according to Townley's colleague, Sir F. Bertie, was "notorious . . . a fearsome scalawag adventurer." But he wrote of the whole affair, "this is a wasp's nest into which we had better not poke our fingers."[33]

Through Chang, as an architect of the company's reconstitution, the Chinese government acted in 1903 to regain control. For his part in the reorganization Chang had lost favor with a court and country wounded in pride. In 1905 he appeared in London in full Mandarin dress to represent the cause of the Chinese government in a well-publicized civil suit for control of the company and to protest what amounted to a diffusion, if not a watering, of the stock. Hoover's testimony helped Chang win a temporary victory that was struck down on technical grounds on appeal to a higher court. Yet the trial gave Hoover for a time a somewhat unfavorable reputation in the City, the financial center of London. In 1920 he tried unsuccessfully to get an exonerating statement from Judge Joyce or from a surviving attorney for the plaintiff; later he obtained, and evidently destroyed, the only remaining full copy of the court minutes. From 1905 the terms of the memorandum, according to Hoover, were adhered to "after a fashion."[34]

Whatever the legal and moral issues might be, the company and its Chinese investors thrived. Before and during the Boxer troubles the company had possessed insufficient funds; property was damaged in the violence and production interrupted. Hoover pointed out that at the time of the memorandum transaction the old company, bearing "monumental debts," had faced ruin or a Russian takeover. After Hoover returned as general manager in 1901, he almost immediately turned a losing business into a prospering one. The management worked to eliminate ubiquitous graft, firing hundreds of Chinese functionaries. The new company attracted more investment capital; and it instituted a host of modern technical procedures, some of them over Chinese objections. In addition, funds went to support local hospitals and a mining college. The company became the largest single commercial undertaking in China. The Chinese government developed adjacent coalfields, and in 1912 the competing fields combined on terms favorable to the Europeans.[35]

In the course of making creditable achievement, the company also provided indelicately large profits for some of its officers and investors. Moreing, who arranged for financing by selling the deed to the sinister-sounding Oriental Syndicate, made at least half a million dollars. To counter the danger from the Russian presence in North China—Kaiping lay in the Russian sphere of influence—the concern persuaded Belgian financiers influential with the Russians to take over half of a large bond issue, offering the Belgians' company shares as an inducement. The king of Belgium himself invested substantially. Hoover's justification for the generous terms given privately to new investors was that the company remained a risky enterprise undertaken in a period of tight money. The old company had many debts that the new firm paid off; and all of the property, as Hoover remarked, was "in the vortex of war," with claims on it by five countries at the time of the agreements. The Syndicate formed the new British Chinese Engineering and Mining Company with 1 million £1 shares, yet the securities were never offered to the public.[36]

All that occurred in China had to do with great economic forces, new techniques for financing companies, a swifter international flow of capital, a worldwide organization of mineral resources, the beginnings of the multinational corporation, and beneath it all, of course, the continuing revolution that was technology. We cannot assume that Hoover gave to these forces any essential shape or direction they would not otherwise have taken, but his work in China was vividly expressive of them. From the Chinese mines he returned in 1902 to Australia and involved himself once more in a large economic activity—the production of zinc in answer to the world's demand for high-grade steel. Hoover's Zinc Corporation was to become one of the twentieth century's giant industries. The flotation process he perfected for the production of zinc was a technical accomplishment on a scale with the cyanide metallurgy he had helped to introduce at Kalgoorlie. The only prime areas of the world's mineral development where Hoover failed to have an important part were Iran and South Africa.

In the summer of 1904 he did pay a mysterious visit to South Africa. One journal reported that he had taken the trip "mainly to recruit his health"; another called it a "professional visit" for studying "mining methods." The journey came exactly at the time when the gold-mining industry was awaiting results of importing the first coolie labor to the Rand, and at least one contemporary source indicates Hoover was looking into this innovation. Shiploads of Chinese, under irrevocable contract for specific periods, had embarked from docks and facilities owned by Chinese Engineering and Mining. They would provide cheap, non-union labor in territory where some mines would cease to be profitable otherwise. The Archbishop of Canterbury called the practice a "regrettable necessity." In a July speech to the Transvaal Chamber of Commerce Hoover dismissed the use of Chinese labor as unprofitable, and there is no evidence that he took any role in the experiment. We may of course suspect that he was called in as a consultant on the labor matter. The Chinese Engineering and Mining Company reported in September on two shipments of coolies to the Transvaal from the North China company port of Ch'in-wang-tao. "The directors anticipate these shipments will continue," reported the *Mining Journal* of September 17.[37]

While traveling through China, Hoover had visited ancient gold mines

—some dating back forty centuries. The sophistication of these works astonished him. It was there that the native scholars he had employed to read ancient manuscripts told him of a great silver mine in Burma, on a road between Mandalay and Peking. This Bawdwin mine would later be the chief source of Hoover's fortune. In China, however, everything had been mined down to water level except coal, the solitary remaining wealth of the country's mines. Lacking minerals to be retrieved, and resistant in Hoover's view to Western technical and administrative methods, China at the end offered him only limited opportunity for the kind of work he wanted to do.[38]

A scholar, a diplomat, or a missionary who has lived in the Orient might be expected to acquire from the experience some sensibility toward another culture, some perception of what subtle needs and motives fill the lives of people in a remote land. What the East taught Hoover, however, was almost the opposite. He learned to think of Western technology and the rationalized method of work it presupposes as offering a means of reordering whole societies. The East influenced the kind of progressive Hoover became, a kind historians have recently found to be common in the early twentieth century—the reformer who looked not to a simple and purified democracy but to modern administration and experts. Hoover's ideas of reform would have their strength in a social vision founded on the virtues of hard intelligent work, sensible cooperation, commonsensical decency, and good neighborliness. His practical and humanitarian Quaker past was falling into place along with his professional character—the expert engineer, the capitalist bargainer, the public relations man, the manager, the indefatigable American promoter who believed in progress. These were some of the qualities a good politician can use. But they would fail to take into account the more intangible components of a full community.

III

THE FRONTIERS
1902–1913

BETWEEN 1902 and 1907 Hoover circled the globe five times, often accompanied by his wife and Herbert, Jr., born in London in 1903. The baby began journeys around the world in a basket at the age of five weeks. He had circumnavigated the world twice by the age of two, his father expressing alarm at his geometrically proportional rate of growth. Both parents contracted malaria but shook it off swiftly. Travel took up several months of each year; "Mr. Hoover was always in a hurry," remarked a Stanford classmate who visited him in London. He traveled widely in order to oversee other people's work and evaluate business arrangements offered his company. His London partnership in Bewick, Moreing required a combination of engineering skill, financial judgment, and dealings with people—fellow mining company directors, employees, stockholders, the press, and ultimately the general public. A former associate deprived of his job by Hoover insisted that "a score of men in West Australia knew every phase of the technique of mining far better than Hoover did," and that Hoover got praise for many engineering innovations more properly credited to Dr. Ludwig Diehl, the noted metallurgist employed by Bewick, Moreing. Yet no other major mining figure acted at once as financier and promoter as well as geologist, engineer, and metallurgist. Hoover also enjoyed a rising fame within his profession. Only twenty-nine in 1903, he had acquired an international prominence. Everyone spoke of "young Hoover." He was already the "great engineer."*

* The American Institute of Mining Engineers later named Hoover "Engineer of the Century." In 1943 he advised his friend Ralph Arnold: "I was not a founder or promoter of . . . companies. I was always an engineer. . . . You will find that point of view holds public esteem."

In 1901 the Hoovers rented a flat at 39 Hyde Park Gate, Kensington, and in December 1907, just after the birth of their second son, Allan, they moved to the nearby Red House in London's Campden Hill, a modest old eight-room home they filled with books. They welcomed friends, especially Americans, with a hospitality deriving from years abroad in lands with few of their countrymen. Summer days were spent in the large rose garden behind the Red House or at a country home in Stratford-on-Avon; Hoover accepted the post of honorary treasurer in the Shakespearean International Alliance of the actor Sir Frank Benson. These were happy years. There were trips to the country, Sunday afternoons spent adjusting rudders and sails on the Round Pond in Kensington Gardens, and evenings spent with friends over good food and wines. The Hoovers met Joseph Conrad and other well-known people in the arts, including H. G. Wells, of whom Hoover later disapproved for having fathered a child out of wedlock. A young Stanford instructor remembered Hoover full of emotion viewing Tintern Abbey's ruins, and again at the restored Parliament house of miners in the Forest of Dean, where legend ascribed the first democratic assembly of Englishmen. He knew all there was to be known about the history of the places visited.[1]

Some Englishmen found the Hoovers ungraceful socially; Herbert suggested artificial fogs for London drawing rooms since the British had better manners when a fog hit town. He frequently derided Britain's firm class distinctions and called its society parasitical. It surely conceded little status to an engineer; that calling was far more prestigious in America. Hoover told the story of a British lady on shipboard who on learning his profession exclaimed, "I thought you were a gentleman!" The low productivity of British labor also troubled Hoover. He later told Lloyd George he had equipped an English coal mine with machinery that could be worked to death, but the miners refused to use it and he lost most of his investment. The British, Hoover said, preferred to work the workers to death. In London the Hoovers did not attend Quaker meeting. The couple lavished far more attention upon their children than British custom mandated; for a time Mrs. Hoover, not wishing to leave them with servants, would not accept invitations to lunch. She was supportive of the British woman's suffrage movement but remained in the background. "I never can feel I can play the 'Progress of Women,' against the 'Abstract Right for Humanity,'" she explained to a friend. Hoover once had to pay bail for a Stanford classmate, Anne Martin, who was arrested for beating up a policeman, but he did not think Americans should become deeply involved in British reform movements.[2]

The Hoovers never considered England their permanent home. In 1902, together with Lou's father, they built a small house in Monterey, California, and five years later the couple had a six-room cottage constructed in Palo Alto, which they did regard as home. Hoover also rented office space in San Francisco. Later political charges that he preferred life abroad and had applied for British citizenship were unfounded. His name did appear on a British voting list, but one composed of all residents, subjects or no. Of the sixteen years he lived in England overall, there were only four in which he failed to make a trip to the United States, and beginning in 1909 he spent an average of three to four months each year at home. Called "Hail Columbia Hoover" (in conformity to his initials) because of his decided preference for American mining experts and techniques in Australia, he came to rely on Americans primarily. He made good choices. W. A. Prichard and W. J. Loring, who worked on ore flotation processes, were trained technicians and practical miners who gave new life to many pinched-out mines. His associates of these years remember his almost chauvinistic love of America and his desire to return there to live and work. The presidency of Stanford especially appealed to him; not long after, both this position and the deanship of Columbia's engineering school could have been his. He also dreamed of operating a chain of newspapers like Hearst's and talked of reforming American cities, starting with New York. And as early as 1909 he was planning "a book of business or social philosophy"—a project that came to fruition with *American Individualism,* published in 1922.[3]

WHITTAKER WRIGHT, London's most glamorous mining promoter, for some years had been indulging in remarkably conspicuous consumption. The catalogue for his bankruptcy sale of a 2,800-acre estate in Surrey described 22-carat gilding in the ballroom—he was a goldfieldsman for sure; a "lovely chain of lakes" with a glass-roofed cocktail lounge underneath one of them; "temples of classic design"; and a "fine carriage drive terminating in a Balustraded Court." Wright also enjoyed a steam yacht, quite a novelty for those times and an object of particular disapproval to Hoover, who preferred that capital be used for reproductive purposes. In 1901 the speculative venture that supported this elaborate establishment suddenly collapsed. Accused of fraud, Wright committed suicide in the dock during his trial, pulling a pistol from his frockcoat and shooting himself through the head. Lake View, his richest Kalgoorlie mine, came under Bewick, Moreing's control in 1902, thanks to a shipboard friendship between Hoover and the mine's chairman, the suave, well-educated London stockbroker Francis A. Govett.

Govett brought to mining "a sincerity of purpose and an honesty of performance that was a distinct gain to the mining industry of Western Australia," London's *Mining Magazine* remarked of him a decade later. In London he was regarded as eccentric, especially in board meetings, where he sprayed his throat with an atomizer and talked of "my" mines and "my" board. Hoover and Govett invested Lake View's wealth in the profitable Broken Hill South Blocks mine and in a series of efforts to extract zinc and lead from millions of tons of tailings at Broken Hill, New South Wales, some 450 miles north of Melbourne.[4]

Hoover brilliantly realized that new metallurgical methods could unlock the wealth of Broken Hill, which he called the dreariest place on earth. Any mass of mineralized materials, he correctly perceived, was exploitable if close to transport. The Zinc Corporation, registered in Melbourne during September 1905, is a record of his own fallibility as well as his genius.

An informal meeting of the Zinc Corporation in London in August 1907 revealed costly false starts. Speaking for the firm, Govett mysteriously alluded to its having lacked a "free hand" until March of that year. But in any event it had not stepped in to prevent two expensive failures, the Potter and Mineral Separation Company's processes for separating the zinc from the tailings, both undertaken by Augustin Queneau, a young and enthusiastic American appointed by Hoover.[5]

Govett and Hoover made bold financial decisions and lent the firm large sums of their own money; and using the Elmore vacuum process—installed by D. P. Mitchell, another of Hoover's choices—it earned some modest profits. Mitchell praised Hoover for erecting both a large plant and a small experimental one simultaneously so that the flaws in the smaller one could correct the other. Had not zinc prices fallen sharply in 1908, the Elmore process would have been very successful.[6]

Higher profits came in the years from 1910 to 1912 when Tad Hoover, who had completed his engineering degree at Stanford with financial help from his brother, conducted numerous experiments in Australia. The two held the patents on a separation process that had been tried earlier without success. Dominating the Zinc Corporation board, the Hoover brothers installed the new process. Moreing thought Theodore's $10,000 fee exorbitant and called him an "ill-mannered, ill-tempered cur." Although one of the company's directors agreed that Theodore was "something of a liability," his later publications on the project received praise throughout the mining press. Certainly the Zinc Corporation first demonstrated the large commercial value of the flotation process for extracting lead and silver from tailings. Many of its methods were imported into American mines. Difficulties in the World War—much zinc concentrate was treated in Germany and Belgium—were temporary. After many mergers the corporation became Conzinc Riotinto, one of the world's largest mining companies.[7]

As early as April 1898 Hoover had written home to a friend that "no country in the world has witnessed such rank swindling and charlatan engineering as Australia." The inauguration of the Commonwealth in 1901 helped to diminish financial chicanery in both Melbourne and London. Hoover himself did much to rationalize the business of West Australian gold mining—an easier task in the more mature Commonwealth years than in the boom times of the 1890's. His *Principles of Mining* (1909) observes that the "engineer's interest is to protect the investor, so that the industry which concerns his life work may be in honourable repute and that cooperation may be readily forthcoming for its expansion." In 1902 he became general manager for Australia. On his trip there that year the innovative manager bought the first automobile to be used on the Northern goldfields; and in subsequent years he continued to make working visits. In this fieldwork he fired dozens of inefficient employees (including several he had worked with before 1900) and set up large profitable purchasing units for his company's mines, using his firm's power and prestige to eliminate costly middlemen. This important policy reduced working expenses without lowering wages on the mines under Hoover's supervision—particularly Lake View, Great Fingall, West Fingall, Cosmopolitan, Boulder Main Reef, Hannan's Star, the Oroya Links, the Great Fitzroy, the Sons of Gwalia, and the Lancefield (perhaps the company's largest failure).[8]

The young engineer was instrumental in the formation of several enlightened policies enacted in about 1904: reporting mine developments in Western Australia at the same time as their publication in London, giving the press access to the mines, requiring managers to file with the Department of Mines copies of the assay plans, publishing monthly the estimated yield of ore exposed, publishing the working costs of mines while the company was paying the highest wages on the goldfields. The most distinctive improvements, of course, were in technology. With the help of a pipeline which Hoover had recommended that the government should build over the desert to bring water from the coast, his techniques of management enabled the state's mines to be worked to a greater depth than they might have been. Although the gold yield per ton declined after 1903, tonnage increased sufficiently to offset the loss, at least until 1909. Thereafter conditions worsened, and by 1912 the Australian mining industry was in deep depression. From time to time during Hoover's years, members of Western Australia's Parliament worried about monopoly and blacklisting, but in 1906 that state's *Mining Journal* said of Bewick, Moreing that it had done more for the country than any other firm.[9]

An incident early in Hoover's partnership had done much to earn for him and his firm a reputation for honesty. Anthony S. Rowe, a recent partner in Bewick, Moreing, had been speculating in mining shares with company funds. To cover his losses of some half a million dollars, he had forged shares, embezzled from the firm and its clients, and at the end of 1902 fled to Canada. Later it was discovered that Rowe had served a prison term for embezzlement, which Edward Hooper, who resigned when Rowe came in, said was known to Moreing at that time. Hoover responded quickly to the situation, telegraphing Moreing—who was hunting tigers and climbing mountains in Manchuria at the time—that the company and probably the partners themselves were liable for debts that would require payments stretching over some years. "If we go bankrupt," Hoover advised with the backing of another partner, T. W. Wellsted, "we shall be held for full amounts in our personal capacity and shall be ruined for all future and firm destroyed." Having just handed 50,000 shares of Chinese Mining and Engineering stock to Detring, Moreing was loath to take on the burden; he returned to London, Hoover said, "in a towering rage" that the company had assumed full liability— Hoover and Wellsted thought restitution imperative to their own business survival. Moreing exacted a long-term contract providing that he would retain his firm's management if it came to the aid of the Great Fingall, whose stocks Rowe had forged. Hoover himself lost about $127,000 and Moreing had to carry him for some time; but the company regained public confidence, a reputation that would be only somewhat tarnished in the Chang affair. A stockbroker named Edgar Storey sued Hoover, alleging joint responsibility for a bad account belonging to Rowe, but Hoover eventually won the case. In December 1905, when the last funds had been earned back by the company, Hoover opened an excellent claret in Kalgoorlie to celebrate. He helped to support Rowe's family while he was in prison and later sent small sums to Rowe himself.[10]

After a discussion in December 1903 between Hoover and Ralf Nichols, a manager of the Great Boulder Perseverance Mine, Hoover's firm purchased at least 40,000 shares of Great Boulder at £1 7s. 9d. and assumed management of the mine. The consequences put a palpable blot on the company's record. Prichard and Loring, who took over the management, soon found the mine to be worth some 30 percent less than the former owners had estimated. The news came as a "thunderclap," Hoover said. It was probably because of this discovery that for a time the field people sent their assay reports to Great Boulder in London by way of the Bewick, Moreing office rather than directly, as the contract with the mine ownership had stipulated. Moreing, acting for his company, then sold its shares in the mine for some 13s.7d., at a loss of more than £27,000. A Western Australia government investigation of the mine, published in 1905, indicated relative good faith in the whole affair on the part of the firm. Hoover claimed to have lost $85,000 on the transaction.[11]

Coming not long after the Rowe affair, the financial loss was a blow to Bewick, Moreing. But its reputation survived, and Geoffrey Blainey concludes that the firm's ethics "were superior to those of the mining companies and the share market of the day, and [Hoover's] conduct . . . was more commendable than that of a man who earned an unblemished record in an industry which had no scope for fraud."[12]

The company's treatment of its workers during Hoover's partnership, though unacceptable by later standards, was notably humane for its time. When profits declined in 1905, Hoover's close associate Francis Govett insisted on maintaining wages against a proposal by other firms to reduce them. Hoover wrote: "My firm, since I joined it four years ago . . . had never been an advocate for cheap labour or reduced wages." Both men believed that well-paid workers were more efficient and more willing to endure hardships. Some productive employees could earn up to 50 percent more than the normal wages. To prevent unemployment, the firm sometimes moved its men to productive mines. But when the State Arbitration Board, after considering an appeal from workers at the East Murchison, actually lowered wages, they threatened to strike, and Hoover forced them to return, warning of orders from London to close the mine. After the arbitration ruled in favor of Sons of Gwalia workmen, Bewick, Moreing evidently retaliated by increasing the number of Italian laborers, who were considered more tractable.[13]

Since Hoover's management of Sons of Gwalia in 1898, Bewick, Moreing had increasingly used Italian labor, which some Australians considered non-white. In response to a government inquiry of 1904 into immigration that directly blamed the influx for arresting the gains of native Australian labor, the company introduced a reform that was moral only by the nativist standards of the day. The firm decided that after May 1904 it would hire no one who lacked a thorough understanding of English and would fire workers already employed who were deficient in the language. The company wanted to prevent accidents where cautionary signs and verbal warnings could not be understood; but pressure from unionized Australian labor had most to do with the decision, for the Italians often worked for contractors at reduced wages. Yet mines under Bewick, Moreing's direction continued to use some Italian labor, even after a 1906 law required a knowledge of English. Safety measures were sporadically enforced, and the practice went on, even after some foreign laborers were badly mangled and died as a result.[14]

Bewick, Moreing reflected virtues appropriate to the civilization that Hoover as technocrat-statesman would later speak for. This is not the virtue, such as it may be, of "individualism"—a phenomenon Hoover incorporated only imperfectly into his good society—but a certain compounding of productivity, rectitude, and humaneness, with rationalism as element and agent. Such an attribution is generous to Bewick, Moreing, a relentlessly profit-making enterprise, ruthless when it chose to be. But the days of Hoover's partnership did give him the chance to bring about and experience an ordered world in which careful fact-gathering and publication amounted to an ethic, while efficiency and technological expertness made possible a certain generosity toward the workers.

Western Australia's mining law provided that title could be held only for a mine being worked almost without pause, and this kept prospectors from searching for new reefs to replace exhausted sites. Hoover had complained of this restriction as early as 1897; and later he claimed that its zealous enforcement had made for a decline of some 90 percent in prospecting and the absence during the new century of any major finds. What hurt the industry most, however, was that money for investment in machinery had dried up with the collapse of the gold boom of the 1890's, the widespread fraud in promotion of West Australian mines, and the reappearance of other kinds of attractive investments. Forced to look elsewhere, Hoover continued to locate promising new mines, traveling in these years to New Zealand, Tasmania, Burma, India, Egypt, Italy, Canada, and the United States.[15]

As early as 1900 Hoover had heard about the rich Bawdwin silver mine in Burma, which had been worked by Chinese for centuries until about 1850. In 1904, a casual shipboard acquaintance on a steamer en route from Penang to Colombo again piqued his curiosity. After two appraisers had sent back enthusiastic reports on the mine, Hoover in 1905 visited the area, sealed off from civilization by deep gorges and mountain ranges. After some political preliminaries—he saw the Dalai Lama, then just a boy on a bicycle riding round and round in a small courtyard—he found a metallurgical bonanza that would become one of the most profitable mines in the world. Hoover first inspected slag heaps left on the surface from earlier Chinese excavations for silver; most of the minerals—the mounds contained some 50 percent lead and 16 percent zinc—were surely recoverable from 100,000 tons of slag. Then in an old tunnel he found silver and zinc deposits of a richness that astonished him. Only a Bengal tiger's large fresh footprints sent him hastily back to the surface.[16]

At Hoover's insistence Bewick, Moreing secured an interest and took on the initial job of opening the mines, while Hoover eventually acquired an 18 percent investment for himself. Labor was seasonal, chiefly Chinese and Muslim, none of it "forced," as certain opponents of Hoover later claimed. Hoover became a director of Burma Mines (later the Burma Corporation) in 1906, managing director in 1908, and chairman of the board in 1914. After several years of travail with labor, transport, and fuel, more years than Hoover had supposed would be needed, the Bawd-win mine struck the rich ore bodies he had insisted were there. With a 50-mile railroad, an excavation 800 feet long and 350 feet deep, and a drainage ditch under the old workings, the mine started earning money in 1913 and became enormously profitable.[17]

Hoover was now finding Charles Moreing a reactionary; he would soon denounce his kind in lectures at Columbia University. Moreing, moreover, played the stock market constantly, charging losses against the firm (according to a later manager of Sons of Gwalia) and placing the profits, if any, into his private account. He probably got Hoover into a "number of scrapes," this source observed. Moreing was famous for devising secret mining codes. Hoover himself wrote that after he became a partner, "I soon learned that these profits were made by jobbing in the stock market as a result of the tremendous position which the firm had in the control of the management of 7 or 8 mines; and Moreing was also receiving commissions on supplies furnished these mines, and so forth. . . . I cleaned out the speculation, commissions, etc. . . ." Hoover and Moreing disagreed fundamentally about whether their firm should simply manage mines or, as Hoover preferred, purchase and operate them. Moreing was no doubt troubled by the slowness with which the Zinc Corporation was developing, as well as by the unsuccessful workings of deep lead companies in Victoria then under the supervision of Dr. Waldemar Lindgren, whom Bewick, Moreing had hired late in 1903. Lindgren, then head of the United States Geological Survey, Western Division, had been touted in the press as the "world's greatest authority on deep lead mining and geology." There is another possible reason why Hoover in 1908 left Bewick, Moreing, selling his interest to W. J. Loring for $169,000. A recurring report has it that he was suffering a breakdown at about this time and decided to retire from the mining business. Hoover explained to Moreing that his retirement, on account of "consumption of the brain," was "in consequence of ill health, a result of continuous overwork." After dissolving his partnership, however, he became at once extremely active and by 1910 had increased his earnings. Bewick, Moreing's business at the time of his departure was triple what it had been when he joined the firm in 1897; but he found Moreing "a wholly impossible partner."[18]

Less than two years after Hoover had quit the firm, his former associates Moreing, Loring, and Wellsted brought suit against him for engaging, contrary to their agreement, in mining activities based in England that competed with the old firm, and for hiring away its ablest employees. The main point at issue concerned the exploitation of oil in the Western Hemisphere—especially in Peru, Mexico, California—and in Russia and Galicia, and whether it constituted a mining operation. While the terms of the separation refer specifically to ores and minerals, the Lincoln's Inn judge then thought otherwise, and Hoover paid a $125,000 out-of-court settlement in 1911. Though viewing Hoover as superior in character to his associates, Moreing believed that the American and Francis Govett were plotting against him. Loring felt aggrieved as well, claiming he had purchased Hoover's partner share on the understanding that Hoover would not act as a competitor to Bewick, Moreing. "The contract was never drawn which I cannot break," Loring reported that Hoover had boasted to him. For his part, Hoover remarked that Loring was "steeped in Melbourne views of business honesty" and that his new "partners will lead him into trouble in time." In 1916 Moreing sued Hoover again, this time to gain a more equitable division of the losses from Rowe's defalcation. Since Moreing had borne a disproportionate burden of those losses in 1902 and Hoover had become wealthy in the meantime, Hoover agreed to pay him £4650, even though it had been Moreing who had chosen Rowe.[19]

Hoover's later business and engineering career, from the end of the Moreing partnership in 1908 until his wartime direction of Belgian relief, became more varied and concentrated less on mining operations. Working from a new office at 1 London Wall and from others in Paris, Petrograd, San Francisco, and New York City, Hoover listed his occupation in a professional registry as "mining engineer," but alone of the 246 engineers he added: "No professional work entertained," perhaps because of his agreement not to compete. A financier of new projects, he claimed access to "unlimited capital" and sometimes straightened out tangled corporate finances. Hoover worked best as a reorganizer, a keen definer of values of merging units, and for this he commanded large fees. Like most mining engineers and metallurgists near a stock exchange, Hoover took an interest in speculation incidental to mining. He gave financial support for the start of his friend T. A. Rickard's *Mining Magazine,* which would soon become the outstanding such publication in Europe. An anonymous article on mining shares in 1909, the first year of publication, is accompanied by Rickard's testimony to the "good faith and unusual knowledge" of the author. The essay's bias against South African shares and its placing some of Hoover's properties on the "best" buy list suggest the identity of the author. The few shares the article put on the "excellent" list increased in value in the months ahead. Elsewhere in the mining press Hoover is identified as a speculator, and the Bewick, Moreing files contain ample evidence of that firm's buying and selling of speculative shares.[20]

No one could make $10 million honestly, Hoover told Anne Martin, the Stanford classmate who was visiting the Hoovers in London around 1910—but $5 million, yes. Had he made five yet? "Not quite," he replied. About this time Loring estimated Hoover's fortune at $3 million, and this is what Mrs. Hoover told her guest—who disliked the Hoovers in spite of their hospitality to her, apparently because she had invested unwisely in a firm associated with Hoover. Hoover's wealth was far more than the $1 million he speaks of in his *Memoirs;* by 1918 he was worth about $4 million. Once he remarked that if a man "has not made a million dollars by the time he is forty he is not worth much."[21]

Hoover made a good part of his fortune in Burma. Between 1915 and 1918 he sold most of his interest to Herbert F. Goedalla for about $2.5 million, after which time it declined in value. The name E. Heberlein among the Burma Corporation's directors in 1913 indicates the financial presence of Metall Gesellschaft of Frankfurt. Aron Hirsch und Sohn of Halberstadt was also associated with the Bawdwin mine. In return for a $1 million credit line—they owned some 215,000 shares—the Germans took a profitable role in smelting the ore, a process carried on first in Mandalay, then at NamTu in Burma, and finally in Belgium and Germany. This and other connections may have elicited sympathies that would explain why Germany took to Hoover as Belgian relief commissioner in 1914. Yet Hoover tried for a British government loan to establish smelters in Britain, and he sent his brother to the United States on a similar mission. "Impelled as we are largely by patriotic motives," Hoover wrote to a British firm in September 1914, "it is our desire to get the Zinc Smelting Industry established in England instead of, as hitherto, in Germany."[22]

He continued to scour the world for profitable mines. Working with a technical group that included his brother, his "chief of staff" John Agnew, Amor F. Keuhn (who would become Keene during the war), and many others, Hoover and Francis Govett invested even more widely the assets of West Australia's Lake View and Oroya Exploration. The exploration company, which controlled the rich Lake View Consols and Oroya-Brownhill, was offered some 680 mines, examined 130, and put its funds into about 20: Kyshtim and Orsk in Siberia; Leonesa in Nicaragua—a revolution, then floods, temporarily ruined the Leonesa; the unsuccessful Great Fitzroy copper mine of Queensland; Granville and Boyle's Concession in the Yukon; and a few other Australian ventures. Despite the war, Lake

View Exploration in 1915 paid a 10 percent dividend. Many of Hoover's mines were washouts, but a small number of rich ones easily carried the rest. He himself bought into a few of the richest at an early date. Beyond the Lake View agglomerate he associated with a constellation of famous mine promoters, often as a technical advisor. Among their interests were Nigerian tin, Transvaal coal, turquoise mines of the Pharaohs, and Canadian gold.[23]

Oil drew Hoover to the American continents: Langunitos in Peru, Continental Oil and General Petroleum in Mexico and the western United States, and Natomas Consolidated, located chiefly in California. Elected a director of General Petroleum in 1912, he lent it considerable financial help—a fifth of a million—and recommended it extend its pipelines, which became profitable during the war. He sold Langunitos to Jersey Standard; Walter Teagle remembered Hoover as "a queer looking fellow" in a seersucker suit and white tennis shoes—"it's a wonder they aren't all in jail," cracked Teagle's accountant about Hoover's highhanded business methods. At the closing of the deal Hoover appeared in rolled-up shirt sleeves, to everyone's consternation, and was entirely genial once he learned the buyers had a certified check. Toward the end of his business career, Hoover cast ever farther abroad. The Bishopsgate syndicate searched for Rumanian oil. Through a series of "inter" companies—Inter-Russian, Inter-Yukon, Inter-Mexican, Inter-California—Hoover was trying, so it seemed, to grasp whatever else might be hidden beneath the earth's surface.[24]

Getting in on a venture at its inception was Hoover's formula; flotation profits by his own admission became in aggregate an important source of his personal fortune. One such endeavor proved the formula fallible. The Granville mine, which he joined in 1911, was a slightly irrational undertaking on Canada's Upper Klondike River. One idea, reminiscent of *Gulliver's Travels* and discredited upon implementation, got Hoover's approval: instead of injecting steam into frozen ground, the company would remove the topsoil of an area and let the sun thaw the frozen surfaces. Two high steel towers costing some half a million dollars supported huge carriers that gathered the muck and deposited it in piles, which became too large to allow any progress in the workings. The project gave entertainment to the local Canadians, who gathered each day to watch and make comments. After a temporary row with a fellow director—sourdough promoter Joseph Boyle, who later became the lover of the queen of Bohemia—Hoover gave up on this Yukon adventure in 1913.[25]

On the other side of the world, Hoover worked in Russia, where the extent of his activities has become a matter of dispute. The Australian historian Geoffrey Blainey believes Hoover played only a minor part there and never visited the country. But the *Memoirs* describe a large involvement, and as early as 1917 in testimony before a Senate committee Hoover listed Russia first among the many countries where he had worked as an engineer. Company records perished in the Revolution except for some technical correspondence now in the state archives in Leningrad, and the principals are all gone. Hoover, who briefly visited the Urals and Siberia as early as 1908, would have been looking in such places then, since by terms of his separation from Moreing he could not develop new mines within the British Empire. He first became rather heavily involved with Lindon Bates in the Maikop oilfields on the east coast of the Black Sea, but they never produced successfully. He probably visited Maikop in 1909. In 1910 Hoover became chairman of the newly created Inter-Russian Syndicate, with a capitalization of 2 million rubles. In the same year he rearranged the Kyshtim Corporation's finances and imported Butte, Montana, engineers who were to design a new copper-smelting plant in the Urals, which he visited and wrote about firsthand the next fall. In the prewar years Hoover returned to Russia several times (totaling seventy-two weeks by his own account), once bringing back a baby bear for Theodore's family. *Mining Magazine* early in 1914 singled out Hoover and the Scotsman Leslie Urquhart, the best-known foreign mining man in Russia, as being commonly associated with the Russo-Asiatic Corporation "on account of their prominence in Russian enterprises." Russo-Asiatic, the magazine elsewhere observed, "is controlled by Messrs. Leslie Urquhart and H. C. Hoover with whom are associated two banks at Saint Petersburg." Urquhart, however, wrote in 1932 that Hoover's role had been negligible, although he remembered the prominence of American engineers in his enterprises. Some two decades later Urquhart's widow protested Hoover's published description of his Russian work.[26]

The memories of various mining men support Hoover's claims about the scope of his activities. Amor Keene noted in 1932 that Urquhart, manager of the Baku oilfields during the Russo-Japanese war, later got control of Kyshtim and tried to run it as a gold mine but could not make it pay. American engineers told him that he could make money by mining for copper, and Hoover's circle became involved at least as early as 1909. "In 1911," Keene wrote, "Urquhart could not sell his bonds for 50¢ on the dollar in London markets [this is roughly correct]. Hoover pulled Kyshtim out of the hole and made huge profits." Hoover lent Urquhart $175,000 in 1911 and Chester Beatty lent the same sum. *Mining Magazine* for August 1911 confirmed that Kyshtim was losing money and that £50,000 in debentures had recently been issued; and Skinner's *Mining Manual* of 1913 calculated that over two years £400,000 of new capital had gone into a copper-smelting project. *Mining Magazine* similarly noted that "a large interest [in Kyshtim] is held by Hoover and Beatty, who recently assisted the company financially to enable the erection of a smelter." According to a friend's account, Hoover forcibly moved the entire working force of several thousand families to better housing near the site of the ore; and instead of modernizing the old plant he simply constructed an enormous new smelter, ore crushers, and even mine shafts. Kyshtim and other Russian mines became highly profitable after the intervention of Hoover and Beatty.[27]

An invitation in 1912 from the Czar's family to Hoover and Urquhart to survey East Siberian mining properties got Hoover more deeply involved in Russia. He used as a guide the 1891 eyewitness exposé, *Siberia and the Exile System,* written by George Kennan, Sr. Kennan, who had spoken at Stanford in Hoover's student days, recommended improved living conditions for workers and better health care as a means to greater productivity. At Irtysh in Siberia, Amor Keuhn reported to Hoover on a solid, continuous 150-foot ore body of copper, lead, zinc, silver, and gold. The Irtysh Corporation, floated in December 1914, had on its board three mining engineers, including Hoover and his friend D. P. Mitchell; and Hoover took up thousands of shares in the company. Mrs. Urquhart insisted that Hoover exaggerated when he claimed his group had contributed $20 million. The figure may be high, but the company was an offshoot of the 1912 exploration firm Russo-Asiatic (itself an extension of the old Anglo-Siberian, owned by Hoover and Urquhart), which turned over to Irtysh the Riddersk and Kirgiz mines in the beautiful Altai region of Siberia. *Mining Magazine* called Irtysh a British-American-Russian enterprise. Even Urquhart's Tanalyk copper and gold mines in the Urals had 50,000 shares under option to the Inter-Russian Syndicate that belonged to Hoover and Beatty.[28]

Until the revolutionary régime confiscated them, Hoover's Russian interests promised millions; stories relate that he dynamited the mine openings when he left, hoping the Soviet presence would be brief. At Kyshtim, as a listener remembered a frustrated Hoover telling it, harmless lunatics took "control of orderly situations . . . gradually transforming the order into chaos and themselves into maniacs, with the accompaniment of assemblies and discussions and legislation and committees and principles. . . ." Had the mines been restored after the war, it would have been not Hoover, whose interests were then nil, but the British and French bondholders who would have profited. During Russian relief activities in the early 1920's he learned that the great mines he had helped activate then lay dormant.[20]

One of Hoover's favorite endeavors during these last active business days was to take poorly run or corrupt mining boards and completely reorganize them. After the drain of excessive promotion profits, the Santa Gertrudis silver mine in Mexico suffered a financial collapse. The situation threatened Hoover's General Petroleum holdings, and in the spring of 1914 he came in to overhaul the mine along with Messina copper. As he wrote to Ray Wilbur: "I have been obliged to take an interest in the matter because of the interest which many of my associates hold in these concerns. I am becoming chairman of two of the largest ones, at least for the moment." Hoover commented on "a certain amount of self-satisfaction to be called upon to take over what is undoubtedly the most important and strenuous situation existing in the mining world." Although his Belgian relief work interrupted his efforts at this time, Hoover stayed with the company until it again became solvent in about 1916. He also reordered the finances of important families, such as those of Sloss and Lilienthal in California.[30]

A good part of Hoover's work in the years after 1908, then, was of the same kind as his most distinctive labor in the partnership at Bewick, Moreing—a technical work, addressed to tightening the structure and workings of an enterprise. Yet that late portion of Hoover's business career seems almost unfocused in its incessant searching out of fields for investment.

For all his commitment to professionalism, his extraordinary powers of concentration, and his famous ability to recall facts and figures during conversation, Hoover could have a cavalier way with detail. Remembering the Hoover of 1901, his close associate W. A. Prichard remarked two decades later: "I do not believe that he cared for details." The first volume of Hoover's *Memoirs* (1951), fascinating, warm, and witty, is wholly unreliable. Written for his two sons partly in odd hours while he was traveling for Belgian relief in 1915 and 1916, it includes hundreds of incorrect dates and misspelled names.* He was confident of his own initial judgments and often gave trusted subordinates freedom to carry on their work while he investigated new projects. Hoover suffocated problems with solutions—if one did not work, another would. And in these years he learned that abundant publicity about a problem and its solution would bring change if circumstances were or could be made receptive. His business career also accustomed him to dealing with large sums of money and investing in projects that stood only a reasonable chance of success. Hoover's request in 1928 to spend half a billion dollars for agricultural cooperatives would seem as natural to a successful big businessman as it was abhorrent to congressional conservatives. During the 1930's he was

---

* Hoover's *Memoirs* have him born on the wrong day, his mother dying in the wrong year, his leaving Iowa in the wrong year, and his leaving the United States for Australia in the wrong year—the errors are legion.

perpetually disgusted with fellow Stanford trustees who would not risk investing any substantial part of the university endowment in common stocks.[31]

Even as his engineering experiences trained him in the handling of impersonal fact, and his speculative adventures taught him something of judging character and situations, his temperament and success induced in him a certain stubbornness, reflected in a capacity for self-delusion that appears in his *Memoirs*. Perhaps, as Blainey suggests, because his mind unconsciously reshaped events over an intervening half-century, he sometimes claims there a greater share of accomplishment than was the case. Hoover enjoyed the role of Sherlock Holmes. He would playfully predict the contents of sealed envelopes containing mine reports. He even assumed the persona of Holmes in a jocular letter to the editor of *Mining Magazine*. Sure of his own ability—though not to the extent of refusing to admit he could ever be wrong—he assumed a concordance between his thinking and an independent rationality. He rarely accepted stylistic criticisms, and his prose suffered. He had, after all, risen from orphan to internationally prominent multimillionaire. Like F. Scott Fitzgerald's Jay Gatsby, Hoover willed things into existence, from a Stanford grandstand to a vast fortune.[32]

Occasionally Hoover worked too hard. His letters contain many references to exhaustion, both physical and mental. He placed himself under strains that would have broken ordinary men. But faced with the prospect of taking a vacation, he almost always drew back in panic or rushed through a sightseeing itinerary in breathtaking time. On his first "vacation" in five years en route to Johannesburg in 1904, he wrote to his brother: "The rapid expansion of our business during the past two years, the Rowe frauds, the misrepresentation of Ralf Nichols have all been too much for my nerves. I found myself slipping memory and unable at concentration of thought—and . . . able to sleep but 3 to 5 hours." On picnics he spent his time—and persuaded friends to join in—damming streams, building complicated sluices and elevated canals. Vernon Kellogg would sit back smoking a pipe and perhaps supplying some small stones, while Hoover stood to his knees in mud carrying vast rocks against his suitcoat until he looked as if he had rolled in dirt. Any job he undertook quickly expanded in dozens of directions; Hoover needed a wide world to work in. Even after his presidential term he soon became bored in Palo Alto and moved to New York to be at the center of things, though keeping up the fiction of living in rural California. Hoover hated to eat alone; at the Red House in London and at the White House during the presidency, he would surround himself with dinner guests virtually every evening. He spoke little himself, except discursively among intimate friends, and was once observed to eat a five-course dinner in eleven minutes flat. If not for his faith in the eventful triumph of rationality, he would have found existence—the existence that he met with inexhaustible and nearly frenetic energy—a baffling or horrifying experience.[33]

Until 1914, engineering had been the fastest-growing American profession, and the one that offered perhaps the most opportunity for upward movement and accomplishment. "Within my lifetime," Hoover wrote in his *Memoirs,* "it had been transformed from a trade into a profession." Not quite two years before World War I broke out and Hoover entered Belgian relief work, he gave an interview to the *New York Sun.* The mining industry, he said, had small opportunity for growth; further discoveries of large mining districts appeared unlikely, and with techniques now able to recover 90 rather than 60 percent of ore, little space remained for technical progress. Elsewhere, he wrote that at some point in 1913 the world's existing mines would attain their maximum profitability, with a decline thereafter being almost certain. Hoover may have been wondering about his future in mining. But there was another career for him. In achieving wealth, a Quaker takes on a trust to bring a portion of the world to order; the engineer in Hoover must have compounded that imperative. His farflung businesses had given him a sense of international politics and his working experience had made him aware of vast economic potential wasted in inefficiency and ignorance. And he had achieved such success and was of so restless a talent as to be in pursuit of alternative activity. As early as July 1907 Hoover had told President David Starr Jordan of Stanford, at an accidental meeting in a Melbourne railroad station, that he had all the money he wanted and wished to try something else. He spoke then of translating Agricola, a sixteenth-century student of mining, and of working on ancient record stones from a mine in Mount Sinai. "There were rents that needed mending in American politics," Jordan remembered of his conversation with Hoover. "There were lines of administration into which he might fit." "The ending of my professional work," Hoover observed when he entered public service, "coincided with the ending of the Golden Age of American engineers in foreign countries."[34]

Hoover had an early try at the management of public sentiment with his efforts to secure British participation in the Panama-Pacific Exposition of 1915, a trade conference designed to publicize the rich resources and markets of the American West Coast, particularly in the San Francisco area, now recovered from earthquake and fire. The delicacy of English politics dictated tact and strategy.

In 1912 he consulted first with Arthur Balfour, the former Conservative Prime Minister, whom he enticed with the notion that "the only certain and enduring alliance would be between peoples of the same race." Sir Edward

Grey, the incumbent Liberal foreign secretary, gave his personal support as well. Hoover also implored *The Times* to publish a supplement on the exposition. And he convinced the American Committee for the Celebration of the Hundred Years of Peace Among the English Speaking Peoples that no less a personage than King George V should come through the Panama Canal to San Francisco on a planned trip to Vancouver. "My own attitude," Hoover wrote the California committee chairman, "has been largely that of a missionary . . . in the hope of stimulating them to action."[35]

Congress ruined Hoover's smooth machinery in August 1912 by exempting American ships from Panama Canal tolls. Refraining from participation at San Francisco was one obvious means by which the British could object to the discriminatory toll arrangement. Observing that the "Panama position hangs as a . . . cloud over everything here," Hoover then adopted a many-sided publicity program and *The Times* came out with his supplement in June 1913. That August the Prime Minister announced his intention of declining President Taft's invitation to participate at San Francisco. Hoover pushed on. Writing a letter to the editor of *The Times,* he combined sentimental remarks on the Canal as the "great engineering triumph of the races" with the hard argument that, thanks to the Panama route and the area's lack of coal and iron, "the Pacific slope will become largely a province of Europe from a manufacturer's and a shipping point of view." Then Hoover persuaded the San Francisco backers to hire a British journalist, William Goode, as secretary of a purely British committee to be formed to advance the exposition. Insistent on controlling the whole campaign, Hoover not only guided Goode's hand but also eliminated another exposition representative in London whose work threatened his own. Fifty leading commercial men made up Goode's committee, which adopted a memorandum prepared by Hoover and Goode arguing for participation. In addition, the two men elicited editorial support from papers throughout the United Kingdom. Sir Arthur Conan Doyle presented to the Prime Minister a petition of British authors asking for participation. Still, there was no change in policy.[36]

Late in 1913 a weary Hoover tried what he called "a rather dangerous ballon d'essai." He had discovered an additional reason for the British government's stubbornness: a secret agreement with Germany to boycott the exposition jointly in protest against the canal tolls. Acting entirely on his own, Hoover warned Foreign Secretary Grey of possible consequences should Americans learn of the agreement. And then he broke the story to the press through second parties—a display of "fighting blood," he called it. *The Times* revealed that Hoover had called the refusal of Great Britain "a political act unfriendly to the United States." He also went

further than the San Francisco committee wished when he visited government figures in Paris and Berlin and wrote to an influential mining friend
in St. Petersburg about Russian policy toward the meeting. To Baron V.
Meller-Zakometsky, an associate from his days with Kyshtim, Hoover
had also expressed a year earlier the wish that "the unfortunate people in
Russia," the Jews, be treated reasonably.[37]

Goode took another step in April 1914 by obtaining signatures on a
letter asking for participation from a majority of Parliament through the
medium of an ad hoc committee of members. The Liberal government—
harassed by events in Ireland and at home—still refused to take part.
Finally Hoover suggested special exhibits sent with government approval
as an ultimate compromise; these were shown in San Francisco. He could
take satisfaction in having noticeably coaxed public opinion toward his
position. According to his *Memoirs*, he continued to work to secure participation of other European governments until his efforts were interrupted
by war. He was, as Craig Lloyd demonstrates, a man "behind the scenes."
Yet Hoover knew how best to get his own way. It is difficult to improve
upon Lloyd's summary of this unplanned rehearsal for his subsequent
activities in Belgian relief:

. . . we catch a glimpse of his self-confident assertiveness, his pleasure and
excitement in taking part in a large "public" venture, his knowledge of the international political economy, and his hitherto unsuspected stature among powerful segments of English society as well as at the American embassy in London.
Here clearly was a man of large affairs.[38]

IV

THE ENGINEER AS CRITIC

LATE IN 1911, Hoover wrote to an actress friend in California a description for a play to be based on the firing of a giant smelter:

These are big machines. a front elevation would fill the whole back of the stage. . . . The equipment of these great copper mines has been in progress for two or more years. The ore has hitherto to all other comers resisted treatment. These men have tackled it on novel and bold lines involving new departures in furnace construction. . . . Their professional future and the financial success of the enterprise depends on this furnace. . . . I've whiled away many idle hours constructing a drama to represent to the world a new intellectual type from a literary or stage view—the modern intellectual engineer.[1]

Hoover was a reader of Thorstein Veblen. Phrases and classifications from the work of the great sociologist—an admirer of the modern engineer—appear in Hoover's writing. We cannot know just how, and with what critical attention, he responded to Veblen's thought. But one thing that might have piqued, disturbed, or delighted him is a distinction Veblen made in *The Instinct of Workmanship,* which appeared in 1914 and was elaborated in his later studies.[2]

Veblen's technicians, schooled in the impersonal precisions of a mechanical matter-of-fact world, fulfill themselves in exacting workmanship; and their task compels them to seek a smoothly performing economy. Modern techniques bring together and perfect the differing goods that Veblen implicitly associated with the "instinct of workmanship": the moral imperatives and the artistic relish that compound in the doing of a precise, difficult job, and the morality that addresses itself to the public well-being. Business as Veblen described it is of a nearly opposite charac-

ter, training its practitioners to shrewdness rather than to technical exacti-
tude, and interesting them not in economy and efficient technology but in
the disruptions that make for profits. Veblen did find the element of accounting in business to require the same discipline to fact that science
and the machine impose, and he respected the role of management as essential to modern industrial society; but he wanted that role to be assumed
by technical experts, in whose keeping he would place machine civilization.

Hoover was in many respects a figure out of the future Veblen imagined. During the twenties he would be considered a representative of
"technocracy," as the idea and the new order espoused by the Veblenians
came to be called. His rise to the directorship of mining companies was a
Veblenian event, for previously these positions had usually gone to retired
military gentlemen picked for the dignity they would lend to the office
rather than for their technical or even financial knowledge. The world
he mentally inhabited was a little like a factory. When interviewed, Hoover
would answer a question curtly and then, until there was another, stop
like a machine that has run down. He could irritate with his air of omniscience about financial and other matters, and with such observations as
that engineers could build waterfalls superior to those in nature. But
Hoover was also very much Veblen's calculating and persuasive businessman; and his engineering could involve the guesswork and the wasteful
exhaustion of machinery that we would expect of the business mentality
as Veblen analyzed it.

Hoover did a good deal of writing—much of it concerned with specific,
limited problems of finance or management—that touched on the character of those who are in charge of modern industry. There he displayed
something like the appetite of a Veblenian technician for finding solutions
to concrete difficulties. But many of the problems that drew him were
financial, and he wrote as though he looked on the business sector as
simply another functioning part of modern industry, its mechanics to be
understood in just about the way that a question in engineering was to be
grasped. It is important for an evaluation of Hoover's public and presidential career, in its characteristic procedures and perhaps its limits of
perception, to realize how thoroughly he had conditioned himself, in his
earlier days, to perceive human society from the standpoint of an entrepreneurial engineer.

An article published in the *Engineering and Mining Journal* of 1903
represents Hoover well. It proposes a uniform systematic bookkeeping,
and calls for the recording of the working cost for each lode of gold as a
means of preventing fraud. Costs, Hoover suggested, should be recorded
for each department according to some common unit. The article suggests
that such methods would transform gold mining from a speculative venture

into an industrial enterprise. An industrial enterprise—that is the note; and the implicit assumption that exactness, honesty, and productivity make up a single compound.[3]

The piece is typical of Hoover's work also in addressing the problem of arriving at exact financial evaluations. In an article of 1904 he attacked the careless techniques of mine valuation that merely added 40 or 50 percent to the value of the mineral in sight, urging instead a subtle taking into account of adjoining mines, bores, and continuities. This ordering of mine finance, he argued, would benefit the investor without sacrificing "the very necessary position of the vendor or promoter." At the same time he wished "to adjust the engineer's viewpoint to the ultimate purpose of the valuation of mines for sales purposes." In another essay he set a reasonable return on mining investment at 6 percent, a figure considerably below what most stockholders thought fair in a risky enterprise.[4]

An extensive proposal for reforming mining speculation, advanced by Hoover in *Mining Magazine* for October 1912, began by listing eight factors for arriving at the assured profit on a mine; prospective value, on the other hand, was to be established by individual opinion based upon psychology and geology. Patterning his design on the "great railway systems," Hoover observed that assured profit should be represented by debenture capital, redeemable out of such profit, and that all of the share capital should be assigned to prospective value. It would be wholly speculative, pure risk; having offered to the public the whole of the debentures, promoters were justified in retaining much of it for themselves. Observing that the general public suffered its largest investment loss in new issues, Hoover continued: "If the promoter or vendor under-estimates the capital necessary to bring the mine to production, he will have to pay the penalty in the loss of his entire share-interest through foreclosure of the debentures, or, alternatively, to supply the money to prevent such an event."[5]

In the same article Hoover also envisioned a time when investment trusts would hold the less speculative securities in mining enterprises; this too would rationalize the industry, placing more completely in the hands of engineers the decision as to where capital was deserved and needed. In any case speculative investment by the general public should be discouraged. "From an economic point of view . . ." Hoover wrote, "capital in the hands of the Insiders [promoters, vendors, brokers, and so forth] is often invested to more reproductive purpose than if it had remained in the hands of the idiots who parted with it." In some cases, he conceded— one example being Nigerian tin—a speculative fever might help to secure adequate capital for exploiting a mineral deposit worthy of development. But in boom times, "a multitude of worthless ventures are started; these represent a great economic loss." Society's interest lay in having promoters who did not become "drones on the community, or establish families of drones, or squander [their money] on riotous living. . . . The most hopeful view is that they will reinvest their takings in reproductive work and continue to devote their experience and abilities to the augmentation of the national wealth."

Any notion of a definable fair profit, or fair wage, is shaky. It requires measuring in some financial way the moral value of such things as an expenditure of effort, or an exercise of skill, or an act of risk. Hoover's attempt to establish a fair profit on investment says something about his perception of the industrial system as a whole. He stood in the broad tradition, inclusive of Marxism and capitalism, that tries to understand every element within a legitimate economy to be an element of production, measurable and justifiable by its degree of productivity or by the achieving human activity it embodies; and as for investment, at any rate, he would not consign that measurement to the play of the market. He wanted a moral economy, which he thought to be the same as the most efficient economy, and he was prepared to use planning and control, at least from within business, to get it.

An example of Hoover's ability to change his thinking during this period is his attitude toward Western Australia's arbitration law. Hoover rejoiced in March 1906 that Western Australia had recently "freed itself from a Labor government." Now the arbitration law might be revoked, along with mining title legislation under which a leasehold was granted subject to the constant employment of one worker for every 6 acres. The "fear of inability to hold ground," he believed, had driven the prospector largely from the field and throttled the growth of the industry. The new government, however, did not act as expected, and after experiencing an arbitration court ruling at Broken Hill in New South Wales favorable to the company, Hoover changed his views. In 1909 he wrote: "Some years of experience with compulsory arbitration in Australia and New Zealand are convincing that although the law there has many defects, still it is a step in the right direction, and the result has been of almost unmixed good to both sides. One of its minor, yet really great, benefits," he added, "has been a considerable extinction of the parasite who lives by creating violence." Years later, however, he was skeptical of a postwar law in Kansas imposing binding arbitration on labor disputants. He noted that while the Australian and New Zealand systems worked well in prosperity, hard times eventually brought as many strikes as ever. Difficulties inherent in trying to establish a fair profit and a fair wage would work against the Kansas law. But Hoover, always willing to experiment on the state level, said that the scheme was "worth trying on American soil."[6]

By 1909, Hoover had adopted a matured and fully humane view of the labor issue. In his *Principles of Mining,* published that year and based on previous articles and on talks given at the Columbia School of Mines and at Stanford, he scolded reactionary capitalists. Noting, as would Veblen, that engineers in executive positions should guide employers in their relationship with labor, he defined engineering as a blending of technical skill and administrative ability. Unions he described as "normal and proper antidotes for unlimited capitalistic organization." After their initial stage of demagoguery and violence, unions sought harmony. They "are entitled to greater recognition. The time when the employer could ride roughshod over his labor is disappearing with the doctrine of 'laissez faire' on which it was founded. The sooner the fact is recognized, the better for the employer." Strikes hurt business, Hoover realized, and good relations between union and employer reduced their number and duration. Part of the blame for reactionary ideas lay with the academic economists; and Hoover proposed his own unorthodox wage theory: When the professors "abandon the theory that wages are the result of supply and demand, and recognize that in these days of international flow of labor commodities and capital, the real controlling factor is wages and efficiency, then . . . an educational campaign may become possible." Hoover believed that "in the design and selection of mining machines, the safety of human life, the preservation of the health of workmen under conditions of limited space and ventilation, together with reliability and convenience in installing and working large mechanical tools, all dominate mechanical efficiency." He recommended that management pay high wages to able workers and take "a friendly interest in the welfare of the men," offering them "justifiable hopes of promotion." Always a lover of efficiency, he endorsed piecework and cash bonuses.[7]

Principles of Mining became a standard textbook for a generation of engineers and helped give shape to a faction of progressive engineers who after the war briefly led the Federated Engineering Societies and elected Hoover its head. One review commented on the book's "clear, straightforward style, avoiding the use of technical terms and miners' jargon"; another complained about involved and cumbersome sentences, careless punctuation, and abruptness. W. R. Ingalls, editor of the *Engineering and Mining Journal,* which published the book, wrote of the manuscript Hoover submitted: "It was atrociously bad—bad in handwriting, in spelling, in grammar and syntax, and in composition." Hoover grinned when informed that Ingalls had edited it extensively; the author did not look at the proofs. During World War I Hoover told a startled and unappreciative Stanford professor that writers were worth a dime a dozen. W. J. Loring claimed that many passages appearing in the text had been lifted almost verbatim, and without credit, from technical papers he himself had written. In 1905 Hoover had written to D. E. Bigelow saying he had depended on Bigelow for some papers on dry crushing of Kalgoorlie ores in South Kalgoorlie and for another on condensation; and a letter of June 1909 to John Agnew acknowledges "a good deal of assistance to yourself." The evidence is too slim to charge Hoover with anything like plagiarism; he may simply have relied on the work of others in the same manner that many scholars do.[8]

Hoover had become devoted to the idea of the mining professional and relished the dignity of professionalism. He joined nearly a dozen mining organizations before the war. In an early essay he had proposed forbidding mine managers and engineers to hold any financial interest in the firms that employed them; and at Bewick, Moreing he once advised a mine manager against such investment. A comment of Hoover's in a 1909 issue of the *Mining Journal* recommends making choices that bring an advance in professional status at the expense of personal financial gain. People with formal training, he remarked to his teacher John Branner in a letter the same year, have more "professional feeling" than do those up from the ranks; and he urged a broad academic training for mining engineers. It had to be so, for it must embrace mechanical, electrical, and civil engineering, as well as mineralogy and chemistry. As Brooks Adams writes in his *New Empire:* "mineralogy and geography elucidate history, for the one helps to explain the forces which have moved the seat of empire, the other obstacles which have fixed its course by determining the path of least resistance." According to friends, Hoover did show a remarkable ability for grasping how topography influenced the course of European wars, and he was intimate with worldwide geography even before he worked in war relief. In 1904, *Science* had published Hoover's argument that this training, coming after thorough work in the humanities, should emphasize "the purely theoretical ground work of the engineering profession," especially scientific studies. The schools should not try to reproduce practical working conditions; they ought to encourage students to take jobs during the summers. Bewick, Moreing itself offered young mining school graduates a two-year apprenticeship—a training in all departments of their main interest. Here, said Hoover, the young "can get an adequate balance of what constitutes commercial vs. theoretical conditions." In the university education of mining engineers, America was doing a better job than other countries in combining administration and purely technical skills.[9]

For all in Hoover that was abrupt, impatient, even tending to recklessness, he was a moralist. He had, first of all, the ascetic morality of the technician, the care for the exact disposal of impersonal things and abstract figures. Pretty much at his core, it took him into the larger sphere of organization and public responsibility where he had his later career. He never lost his technician's character: it simply discovered implicit within itself a purpose, a method, and an ideology—this last never fully formed —essentially humane. The distinction Richard Hofstadter makes between the "hard" side of farming, its self-interested and businesslike quality, and its "soft" side, its myth of the virtuous yeoman, suggests a way of thinking about Hoover the technologist. The "hard" side of Hoover the technician was simply his urge to efficiency; the "soft" technician thought, skeptically or naïvely, that people could be trusted with the techniques of industrial organization, which would quite naturally adapt themselves to decent ends.

Some of Hoover's earliest articles concern the history of mining, and in 1912 after five years of work that absorbed evenings and other free time, he and his wife published an edited English translation of *De Re Metallica,* a classic Latin work of 1556 by Georg Bauer (1494–1555). A doctor and burgomaster from the great mining region of Joachimsthal in Bohemia, Bauer, writing under the pen name of Agricola, had worked in a difficult medium, a language offering limited resources for the age and techniques of sixteenth-century mining. But after moving to Chemnitz, the center of the Germany mining industry, in 1531, he produced a work that became the major mining textbook for two centuries, with copies sometimes chained to the church altar and translated by the priest between religious services. Lou had owned two copies in her Stanford days, one of them published at Basel in 1561. An English version of 1670 also existed, itself rendered from a Spanish translation by Barba. But other attempts at translation never came to fruition, for Agricola—subsequently known as the father of mineralogy—had invented new Latin words to describe phenomena unknown in ancient Rome. Hoover and his wife had the distinct advantage of combining linguistic ability with mineralogical knowledge.[10]

The purpose of Hoover's work was to "strengthen the traditions of one of the most important and least recognized of the world's professions." In this joint project, its authors shared knowledge about geology, mining, metallurgy, and Latin. Together they visited many of the areas in Saxony that Bauer had written about; most records of the era had been lost, and they had laboratory experiments conducted in the chemical processes he had described. Lou Hoover, assisted by three Latin scholars, did much of the translating, while Herbert contributed the introduction and lengthy footnotes, occasionally garnished with touches of wry humor. Theodore and his wife, Mildred Brooke, also helped. All of their mining knowledge was essential for the translation. The Hoovers paid over $20,000 for outside experimental help and ordered translations of other mining books that might clarify their understanding of Agricola. The handsome 637-

page translation appeared in 1912, bound in vellum with facsimile engravings of the original woodcuts, many of them depicting objects Hoover had been able to identify; the paper, type, and illustrations imitated the original. Although Agricola describes without protest the harsh conditions of mining labor, he also argues for institutions and policies that we would associate with an enlightened modern system: the eight-hour day, various forms of insurance and charity, guilds for the interchange of knowledge—and Hoover's notes allied him with that responsible tradition. The Hoovers dedicated *De Re Metallica* to Stanford's John Branner, who had inspired Hoover's longing to be a scholar as well as a mining engineer.[11]

The appearance of this scholarly book was a reason for Hoover's appointment in 1912 to be a trustee of Stanford. Of the three thousand copies printed, more than half were given free to mining engineers and students—a generous gesture, but also a self-publicizing one. Hoover undertook other scholarly projects. He issued privately a lengthy bibliography of mining works published up to 1700. And Lou and he also made a draft of a translation of Agricola's *De Natura Fossiliarum;* years later he would try to persuade a Latin scholar to translate Agricola's "Bermannus" and "Probier Büchlein," so as "to bring into English all of the literature of the profession down to and including 'De Re Metallica.' " Lou herself undertook scholarly projects; one of her articles was a study of an important botanist. Another, "John Milne, Seismologist," reflected what was for a Californian a natural interest. She later organized the Engineering Woman's Club in New York City. Together the Hoovers gathered hundreds of old scientific books, including some incunabula. This striking and well-chosen collection is now housed at Harvey Mudd Library at Claremont, California.[12]

Hoover's practical experience as an entrepreneur undoubtedly quickened the growth within him of a feeling for the efficient ordering of people and things. Once he began to control chunks of the private economy and to make public statements about business and technology, he appeared to be seeking the ways in which large economic situations could be organized into the workable conjunctions of resources, technology, common sense, and ethics. The principle of rational and beneficent order that Hoover would come to detect as latent within economic activity is not like the coldly impersonal order the classical economists had perceived; it is looser, more kindly, and more dependent on human articulation. The progressivism he espoused had a good deal in common with that of his hero, Theodore Roosevelt, and of other people in this time when professionals and reformers, as recent studies have shown, were fascinated with the methods of technology and the prospects for planning.

Hoover's austere twentieth-century ethos was not inappropriate for a

West Branch Iowan whose parents' sect recommends work in the world, approves of careful business practice, has been known for success at it within the bounds of proper stewardship, and seeks the harmonies within the world, the reasonable resolution of conflicting needs and claims. Whatever Hoover may have retained of Quakerism, his writings on business and, later, on society and politics would contain little that suggests either a skepticism about the world's inclination to moralize itself or a sense of the mystery surrounding mundane life and work. He was envisioning a community of professionals and consumers—their welfare to be achieved by a right allocation and use of resources, their proper morality that of devoted and serviceable workmanship, their social bonds an amalgam of self-interest and altruistic working cooperation. Yet Hoover had little taste for the "mechanical" perfection that some technocrats projected as the ideal future. In a comment made in 1933 on futurist speculation of this kind, Hoover allowed that he did not want to live to see its arrival. He feared a robot society similar to those later depicted by such anti-utopians as George Orwell and Aldous Huxley.[13]

V

BELGIUM

BEFORE WORLD WAR I, Hoover recollected in his *Memoirs,* "Men were able to move practically without any restriction across frontiers. . . . Russia and Turkey alone required passports." Then, suddenly, "the diplomatic lightning began flashing from capital to capital, the world was in a storm," and a long era of peaceable progress had ended. Hoover wondered how the war would affect America. And "what would happen to our [mining] business and all the people we employed? I found myself cabling over the world to slacken production since we could not sell the products." From London he wrote to a friend: "There seems to be little hope of making a living here during the war."[1]

In bright sunshine on the morning of August 4, 1914, German soldiers, expecting that Great Britain would delay before entering the war, marched into Belgium on the way to Paris. Tiny Belgium chose to fight back, gaining precious time for French and British troops to form solid lines along the Marne River. Throughout the war Belgium would be acclaimed for the heroism of that choice. The Germans shot Belgian resisters, burned the ancient library at Louvain, and nearly destroyed the city. A relief worker tells of visiting a nearby orphanage where the children, all under four, were playing in pens: "One of the tiniest, with blue eyes and curls, ran over to me laughing and calling, 'Madame, mon père est mort.'" Throughout a country smaller than the state of Maryland, and at that time the most densely populated white nation in the world, bayonets marked crossroads and food became scarce. Since the Hague Convention said nothing about the duty of an occupying army to feed civilians—on the contrary, it allowed armies to subsist on the products of civilian life—the Germans refused to supply food. Belgians, however, customarily imported most of their food. By the end of August they were appealing for help. The plight of the beleaguered country drew a tide of sympathy.[2]

Hoover's great projects of food relief for Belgium and Europe would be in a way a more purely Veblenian task than his earlier career had afforded him. If the new work did not set him to being an engineer, neither did it call on him to act in the capacity of a businessman except insofar as it required such strategies as making a smart purchase of food on the commodities market. What he brought to the work was technical and managerial skill, but more particularly that relentless energy and forcefulness that had both sustained and at times, perhaps, overwhelmed his technical expertness during his business years. Hoover's personality suited the job at hand; a righteous cause often demanding urgent action needed his direct, insistent ways. "This man," stated his German passport, issued late in 1914, "is not to be stopped anywhere under any circumstances." And he proceeded as though he took the mandate literally.[3]

Hoover began the work of managing Belgian war relief almost by accident. When the war came, he happened to be in London preparing for one of his increasingly frequent trips to California, where he was arranging to purchase the Sacramento *Union* with his friend Ben Allen of the Associated Press. Opportunity came as it had in China when he lived there during the Boxer uprising. On August 3, 1914, the United States Embassy staff, besieged by stranded American travelers, asked him to help relieve their "acute temporary destitution." Hoover happened then to be head of a small committee charged with aiding Americans, particularly seamen, to reach their native shores. As the best-known American engineer in London, he easily persuaded several others to subscribe loans and to raise other funds for cashing checks and converting American currency refused by nervous London bankers. Three days later in a ballroom of the Savoy Hotel, Hoover and some friends set up the American Citizens' Relief Committee, a sort of Travelers' Aid, to serve the tens of thousands of Americans hurrying in from Europe. The 500 volunteers accommodated some 120,000 Americans. Mrs. Hoover headed a women's division. These groups gave time and money generously and with a communal spirit that encouraged Hoover's belief in voluntarism. The women's committee, Lou Hoover later reported, worked "without one incident of friction, without one word of misunderstanding between any of its members!" Yet Hoover forced people to divulge their own resources, sent the destitute home by steerage, and criticized a congressional appropriation that later in the month paid for "a complete shipload of [administrators] over here at high salaries [and] kept them at fabulously expensive hotels." The relief work taken over by this government group in mid-August could have been better left in the hands of local committees, he said. An overlapping, short-lived private "Tourists Committee" also dealt out money carelessly. All this argued for Hoover's conservative, competent presence.[4]

Meanwhile, in Brussels that August, an American Relief Committee had been formed by Dannie Heinemann, a businessman experienced in German affairs, to help his countrymen stranded by the war. By the end of the month, Heinemann, an engineer named Millard Shaler, the American minister, Brand Whitlock, the Belgian multimillionaire Ernest Solvay, Hoover's old nemesis from China, Émile Francqui, and others were trying to do something for needy Belgians. They organized initially a Comité Central under Solvay, which was succeeded by the Comité Nationale de Secours et d'Alimentation, a private agency under Francqui's chairmanship. The Comité Nationale took steps to secure German patronage, which would allow unhampered distribution of food, and placed orders in London. Britain, not yet having instituted its naval blockade, agreed to export food to the Belgians provided that it was distributed under the aegis of the American ambassador to Britain, Walter Hines Page, and Whitlock.

When Whitlock cabled for help to Page, he had already been impressed by the efforts of Hoover to secure British participation in the Panama-Pacific Exposition, as well as by his relief work. A deputation of Belgians, including Francqui and the Chevalier de Wouters d'Oplinter, agreed in late September that Hoover would serve effectively. (Shaler had been sent to see Hoover by another American engineer in London, Edgar Rickard.) On October 4, personnel of the American Citizens' Relief Committee became the nucleus of what was first known as the American Commission for Relief in Belgium; the word "American" was later dropped from its title. Though a private agency, the commission, or "CRB," would operate under patron ministers of neutral nations and through channels open to it could deal with the belligerent governments. It drew numerous American volunteers.[5]

For years Hoover had been remarking to visitors from Stanford that he wished to embark on some great public service for America. And now came Belgium; "the greatest job Americans have undertaken in the cause of humanity," he called it. The task was not simply to provide food, but to "prevent any useless disturbances and slaughter of the civilian population." "We are turning barren neutrality," Hoover said later, "into something positive, a thing which has never been done before." The result would be "a monument in American history" and "the greatest charity the world has ever seen." It was in fact the first recorded moment in history in which a group of humanitarians contained on such a scale the civilian suffering brought about by war. In previous wars as much as a third of belligerent populations had died of famine; the relief work done under Herbert Hoover saved hundreds of thousands of lives.[6]

The coupling of neutrality with relief, administered by impersonal expertise, calls to mind once again the curious compatibility between the cool, workmanlike world Veblen envisaged and that realm of the spirit the Quakers perceive existence to be. Both are places of peace and cooperation; and in both, economics and daily work compose much of the activity by which people discover and make the concordances among themselves that the world is capable of assuming. We shall find Hoover later working hard to replace militarism with commerce. If he had been more explicitly a Veblenian, or more articulately a Quaker, he might have put together out of his wartime experiences a philosophy of peace more valuable than the philosophy of individualism he lumbered away at.

After returning from a conversation with Page at the American Embassy in early October, Hoover checked his watch to note that the wheat exchange was open for another hour in Chicago and promptly telegraphed a large order for the commission before news of the relief activities reached there and drove up the prices. An appeal for American charitable help, the first of many, went out on October 12; although Hoover wrote it, he signed Shaler's name to it to avoid personal publicity. A shipment of food—the first of some 5 million tons that fed 7 million Belgians and 2 million French—left for Rotterdam on November 4. Stevedores fought to unload it and pack it for transshipment by barge over canals to Brussels and from there throughout Belgium. Here began a decade-long saga of food distribution throughout Europe under American auspices, with the CRB in Belgium being the first phase. While the Dutch and Spanish ambassadors to Washington were among the patrons of the commission, it drew its effectiveness from the United States—the most powerful neutral nation and the one most cultivated by belligerents. The chief administrators of the Belgian relief would be Hoover, Brand Whitlock, and Émile Francqui of the Comité Nationale.[7]

Whitlock was the American most Belgians identified with *ravitaillement,* or relief. A man very unlike Herbert Hoover, he had been a reform mayor of Toledo, Ohio, and a successful novelist. During the war he generously praised the organizing genius he recognized in Hoover: "Darkness brings out the stars." Ever the diplomat, Whitlock was perhaps coating the sensitive Hoover with praise; yet the favorable comments extend to both his journal and his letters. At the same time, Whitlock thought Hoover lacked refinement. His blue suit, Whitlock remarked, was usually unpressed and unbrushed, the shoulders covered with scuffs, his boots seldom clean, and the laces broken and tied in rough knots. On their first encounter, as Whitlock later recalled, Hoover's shirt front lacked a stud and showed a badly soiled buttonhole that looked to Whitlock as though Hoover had been fingering it.

"But you have lost your shirt stud," Whitlock remarked on the way to a formal dinner at Francqui's plush residence.

"No, I didn't lose it; I forgot to bring one. But it doesn't matter, does it?"

"No, it doesn't matter much, except . . ." Whitlock narrowly averted disgrace by borrowing one from Francqui's valet before introducing Hoover to the leading people of Belgium. Nor did Whitlock appreciate the Quaker's blunt humor. In 1919 one of the queen of Belgium's ladies-in-waiting inquired of him in San Francisco: "When are we to have the pleasure of seeing you again in Belgium, Mr. Hoover?" Reflecting on his years of travail there, Hoover answered, "Never, I hope." When he heard of the remark, Whitlock was aghast.[8]

Knowing the troubles that beset Whitlock, Hoover paid the urbane diplomat some compliments. On several occasions Whitlock managed to hold together uneasy alliances and to soften irascible tempers. Whitlock once remarked about the relief: "Human nature, which seems to have enjoyed such a striking renaissance all over the world in the last few years, expresses itself here in all kinds of pettiness, envies, denunciations, anonymous letters." Hoover depended on Whitlock to placate the touchy American poet-consul at Ghent, Henry van Dyke, and to keep him from importing food independently against British wishes. More important, Whitlock worked effectively with Hoover because their talents so often proved complementary. Enjoying the CRB's status as virtually a separate state, Hoover could go to Berlin and work in an atmosphere of high diplomacy, while Whitlock took on the important job of mollifying German bureaucrats in Belgium who bristled at Hoover's direct approach. In conferences, moreover, Whitlock's excellent command of French made him an asset to Hoover. But the sensitive Hoover must have been hurt by Whitlock's repeated pleas for tactful men who knew the language and culture of Belgium.[9]

At the same time, Hoover thought Whitlock too easily influenced by the smoothly sophisticated Francqui, whom the minister thought "the drollest, the best and the most charming of men." Hoover also believed that Francqui and the able Spanish ambassador, the marquis de Villalobar (whose association with the CRB Whitlock insisted on), dominated the American diplomat, spelling trouble for relief. Villalobar was a breathtaking figure: born with disfigured limbs and ears, and no hair at all, he artfully disguised his physical presence and became one of the most powerful diplomats in Europe. Hoover later called him a "monster." Rarely taking a moment from practical work, Hoover also perceived Whitlock as essentially a passive figure, a procrastinator and neurasthenic. "Often he retreated outside Brussels for months on end," Hoover recalled later, "to write, to paint, and out of sensitiveness to avoid meeting the hard and cruel facts of war." Hoover particularly resented Whitlock's "failure to rise to the duty of defending Edith Cavell," the English nurse executed by the Germans for spying. Hugh Gibson, also of the American Embassy at Brussels, did try to help Cavell, but after German protests was transferred to London early in 1916. Gibson considered Whitlock nearly incompetent and Hoover "a really *wonderful* man . . . a joy to work with." Thriving on work like Hoover— the two became fast friends—Gibson wanted his chancery office "as rigidly businesslike as an operating room" and refused to allow "visiting between members of his staff," an order that he extended to the minister. Whitlock, Gibson complained, left *"EVERYTHING"* to him and played golf or went on rides in the country. But as late as 1917, Whitlock told Hoover he was "distinctly of Cabinet rank." "Hoover was my friend," Whitlock later wrote, "until Gibson, like a snake, insinuated himself into Hoover's confidence by flattery and soon had him turned against me." Here, as Robert Crunden observes, there may have been a clash between the partisan progressive Republican Gibson and Whitlock, who was rather bedazzled by Wilsonian rhetoric and widely mentioned as a vice-presidential running mate for Wilson in 1916—thanks to his Belgian work. When asked later in the war whether Whitlock should be replaced, Hoover said yes; apparently it was a difficult response. Later, in 1919, he recommended to Wilson that Whitlock be appointed ambassador to Paris.[10]

Hoover worked on the highly important and delicate matters of Belgian relief with one of the few men who had resisted his wishes, Émile Francqui. Whitlock characterized the stout Francqui as without "illusions . . . born to command." Francqui, for his part, described Hoover to Whitlock as "the type of American business man, a face somewhat *fruste* [inelegant], very direct, positive, able, speaks little but everything he says counts." As Whitlock summed up the pair: "M. Francqui was a strong man who came from Belgium and spoke one language and Mr. Hoover was a strong man who came from California and spoke another." Open anger seldom if ever erupted between the men—each so used to dominating grand operations— probably because of Francqui's imperturbable blandness, which had so infuriated Hoover at an earlier time. What disturbed Hoover most was that during the war Francqui consciously used the Comité Nationale as a base for postwar political leadership; the Comité went so far as to pay former government officials part of their old salaries. Both Francqui and Whitlock seemed self-serving to Hoover, who worked without pay while his own entrepreneurial and professional career—partly because of the war, partly because of his inattention—"had simply gone to pieces."[11]

The CRB began during the fall of 1914 amidst false starts and recurrent crises as well as conflicting personalities. Hoover threw himself into the work, but stupendous difficulties lay before him and his hastily assembled staff. Communication from England to Belgium took days. All available ships were outfitted for the war; yet Hoover needed ships to carry food and crews willing to navigate around minefields and over submarines. While the Germans officially exempted CRB vessels from submarine warfare, a few well-marked ships were sunk, and in some twenty-odd crossings Hoover made he was risking his life. Once a British bomber repeatedly struck a ship he was on so that he suffered a crick in the neck for months from gauging the plane's movements. Insurance companies charged high premiums to take on such risky ventures. The economic and engineering problems were compounded by political and diplomatic ones. The most bothersome personal friction during the first months occurred between Francqui and Captain John Lucey, the American in charge at Rotterdam, which received supplies destined for Belgium. Frustrated by the lack of organization in Belgium, Lucey wrote frequently to Hoover accusing Francqui of attending to personal banking matters of the Société Générale rather than building the internal distributing organization of the Comité Nationale. Lucey, whom even Hoover called a "bull in a china shop," took umbrage when the literal translation of Francqui's letters had the Belgian "insisting" or "demanding" that certain things be done. After Francqui had ignored his complaints, Lucey wrote in November 1914 insisting "on the intelligent organization of your branch of the business. . . . [While] Mr. Hoover . . . is a very big man, and deals with business in a big way . . . your office, as far as we can see, is the only one that lacks system and organization." When imminent starvation threatened, Lucey did not hesitate to borrow food from the Germans. "You will be the death of me," Page told Hoover on hearing of the incident. Yet Hoover, like Whitlock, admired Lucey's executive ability and urged him to postpone a planned return to his oil supplies firm in the United States, asking Edward L. Doheny and others to refrain from penalizing him. Lucey stayed with the CRB for more than two years, working in Rotterdam, Brussels, London, and then New York; and after the war he played an important role in European relief. Like most of the men Hoover drew to him, Lucey later boosted Hoover for the presidency, worked in his campaign, and developed a lifelong affection and loyalty for him.[12]

By late fall Francqui was faring only a little better. He told Hoover, in a comparison both could appreciate, that communication was easier from the center of China. No telephone or telegraph was at first allowed his Comité, and he encountered "continual and unforeseen troubles, inertia of every description, a chaos of difficulties paralyzing everything." Francqui blamed the delay in part on completing arrangements so that Belgians of substance would pay enough for food to enable the CRB to supply the poor from its profits (the wealthy and the agricultural population would eventually be excluded from the relief); such monies were also used to keep up hospitals and other welfare institutions. One American CRB man, Robinson Smith, termed the early relief structure "an organization without any."[13]

Late in November Hoover made his first trip to Belgium. He likened the country to a prison. To an old friend he wrote that "a revolution" was needed there to bring efficiency to the relief work and to prevent scandal. "I first brought Whitlock to my side in 20 minutes," he boasted. (Whitlock had previously written in his journal that "if conditions would permit of an organization Hoover wants there would be no need of sending food into the country." Then, during the visit, he found Hoover "so direct, so energetic, yet so diplomatic.") Hoover continued:

I had the Belgians my way in 24 hours and in a week the Americans in control were either bashed into line or were eating out of my hand. I moved the office, consolidated the work of the two committees, insisted on nominating my own Belgians to the executive administration of the Comité Nationale. . . . I have . . . generally revamped the situation until it is under our control, and if we go wrong it is our fault.

Applying principles he had learned in private business, Hoover believed in a simple administrative structure with ultimate authority in one man, himself. He also favored decentralized operation, with reasonable latitude given to the men in the field where local problems could not be predicted.[14]

Whitlock and Francqui had been content to turn everything over to the Comité Nationale; Americans would investigate only reported cases of abuse. But Hoover brought Captain Lucey to Brussels with orders to institute tighter American supervision, which pleased the British. He soon limited the kinds of food imported to those that best fitted nutritional needs: wheat that was milled in Belgium, rice, peas, beans, bacon, lard, yeast, cocoa, condensed milk, and corn (which the Belgians at first refused to eat, believing it fit only for cattle). Whitlock thanked Hoover in mid-January 1915 for sending Lucey: "He is a remarkable man . . . pure good." Lucey, however, moved on to London, where he would not offend Francqui. His successors in 1915, A. N. Connett and Oscar Crosby, presided over a diminution of American control, partly because the Germans strictly limited United States personnel in Belgium to a few dozen at any one moment.[15]

The CRB from here on *was* Hoover. He manipulated the British, the Germans, the Americans, and even Francqui usually with ease, just as he had earlier usually brooked no interference when running great mining enterprises. This benevolent despot wrote in January 1915 to Henry James, Jr.: "Things are going fairly well with the Commission." Hoover purchased wheat abroad, transported it to Belgium, and resold it to millers there at a fixed charge—the world price plus shipping costs. Millers then sold the flour to bakers at controlled prices, and the same system prevailed for the making of bread. Domestic grain dealers could only sell to licensed middlemen at set prices. The leading citizens of the towns assisted in equitable distribution of food, a model used during Hoover's later relief work in Russia and elsewhere. The cooperative economic associations of Belgium were another paradigm to Hoover's eyes; they protected members by influencing production and distribution. Problems of supply were continuing, he said—now an avalanche of potatoes, later none at all—but distribution within Belgium was proceeding fairly smoothly. Whitlock agreed, welcoming the "hours of quiet and days of peace" that Hoover's visit had brought. Whitlock would have been amused by a swift little sharp-nosed water launch, called the *Hoover,* which scooted through the complex Rotterdam waterways intent on important business.[16]

At first, Hoover apparently believed that the CRB could be run as a charitable undertaking, with contributions from all over the world and from Belgian bank resources abroad. Beginning in November 1914, however, he pressed for government support from both sides, and obtained subsidies or loans of $5 million per month from Britain after the Germans ceased requisitioning food and imposing a war indemnity on Belgium; later, France contributed. And after its entry into the war in 1917, the United States gave large sums, amounting to more than half the total. All told, 78 percent of the CRB's funds came from government sources.[17]

Hoover needed Americans to superintend the distribution of food; the British, particularly after instituting a food blockade, demanded assurances that none of it would fall into German hands. The use of American army officers as inspectors was rejected as too dangerous. In his *Memoirs* Hoover called the idealistic young American Rhodes scholars who went to Belgium for this purpose a great asset. Privately, he soon regretted sending them, except for a few like Tracy Kittredge and Perrin C. Galpin: "My confidence in the college boy has been rudely shaken. . . . I no doubt overestimated their possibilities. I have had to remove some 10 or 12 idealists." Whitlock wanted the students shipped home; he did not wish Belgium to be "filled with a lot of impulsive, ignorant young doctors of philosophy." Gibson made a similar plea, saying that "those already sent have driven us nearly frantic." Their work was not arduous. Many lived in splendid châteaux, drove cars, and drank fine wines. Essentially their role was that of diplomats operating between the Belgians and the Germans, and they were all required to sign pledges to refrain from discussing their work with the press.

Few, unfortunately, held to the pledge. At least one young American became so unneutral as to supply British agents with information on German war movements. The Germans charged three with espionage, and Hoover had to remove several whose anti-German feelings had become too vocal. Another young man who arrived for service in January 1915 and talked of how much he was sacrificing to come was returned to the United States as unsuitable. Of the first 150 men in the CRB, according to Whitlock, 2 went to asylums and 30 suffered various sorts of nervous breakdowns. Hoover asked for and got older volunteers—mature men, fluent in French and with business experience. They were undoubtedly a fine group, fulfilling the British requirement of American supervision, serving without pay and often without expenses. These were times when idealism took the form of selfless patriotism. After the war Hoover set up a fund designed to assist any of these men should hard times come; the fund, accruing interest, was much larger by the time the Great Depression fostered increased borrowing.[18]

The Germans stationed in Belgium under the stubborn Governor General Baron von Bissing sometimes treated CRB personnel with scant respect. Von Bissing, who appeared for interviews complete with helmet and sword, was described by Gibson as the only German general who could strut sitting down. When Von Bissing temporarily denied passes to CRB men in the winter of 1915, Hoover was, according to Whitlock, "boiling with rage." An interview with the German published in the New York *Staats-Zeitung* suggested that members of the CRB were motivated by personal profit. A series of similar incidents prompted Hoover to go to Berlin. He preceded his trip with an Associated Press statement that focused American public opinion on Germany. The German high command overruled Von Bissing, at least in principle.[19]

Hoover brought back from his visit a medallion struck in celebration of the sinking of the *Lusitania*. Both he and Whitlock despised the Germans. "They are," Whitlock said, "like a tribe that has wandered down into modern times out of the middle ages." Hoover thought them evil because they denied the idea of progress, which he considered a historical inevitability. In an unsent telegram to Professor Ephraim Adams of Stanford, Hoover commented that the Germans had a "Roman empire 'Masters of the World' sentiment, a contagion of which the English had already gone through a mild case and are pleased to sit under the illusion that they are already the masters of the world." Armaments were necessary in the United States, the telegram proposed, for someday "the civilized world has got to fight these people to a finish"; concerned with the submarine's threat to both citizens and commerce, Hoover complained that "Americans in England are humiliated with interpretation put on [Wilson's] Philadelphia speech that we are too proud to fight." He knew that Colonel House's efforts to bring about political negotiations were useless, given the strong emotions generated by the war. Hoover witnessed the slaughter at the Somme through a German officer's fieldglasses. Finally accepting the inevitability of United States entry into the war in 1917, he tearfully said he did not want his sons to grow up in a world of German militarists.[20]

Despite General von Bissing's obtuseness, the Germans never posed a grave threat to the CRB. They violated the spirit of their agreement on occasion, but usually obeyed the letter of the bargain. Once Britain had imposed its naval blockade, Germany simply lacked the food to feed the Belgians; it was difficult enough to feed the German troops from the homeland. The high command knew that suffering in Belgium would bring reactions in neutral countries, and that civil unrest across the German line of supply would threaten the war effort and require a diversion of troops. Backtracking on an earlier promise, the Germans exported some meat and grain from Belgium the first year of the war. But with some troublesome exceptions, Germany ceased requisitioning local food in 1915 and cooperated with the CRB in keeping both imported food and ultimately most of Belgium's own crops relatively inviolate from German troops.[21]

Great Britain, on the other hand, grew reluctant about the work of the CRB. Lord Kitchener—hero of the Boer War and the face on the famous recruiting poster—and Winston Churchill, whom Hoover would always intensely dislike, led a military faction that regarded feeding Belgians as "a positive military disaster," since it released the Germans from that obligation. Churchill called the stubborn Hoover a "son of a bitch." But Kitchener, according to Whitlock, offered Hoover the post of Minister of Munitions in 1916 (probably it was the post of technical director of production under the minister), contingent on his becoming a British citizen. Page conveyed the offer of British citizenship. Hoover refused. While he never persuaded the militarists, he got his way by browbeating other British leaders, who appreciated what he did to curb profiteering and sympathized with his humanitarian motives. One reason the British accepted Hoover was that Walter Hines Page, an outspoken Anglophile, liked him. In addition, Francqui threatened to go over to the Germans if the Allies did not support Belgium's passive resistance; German money was refused since it demanded labor for the war in return. This made the CRB essentially an element of Allied strategy, though both belligerents tolerated it because each courted neutral support. The "undiplomatic diplomat," as Whitlock called Hoover, spoke strongly to Prime Minister Herbert Asquith about such matters as a British refusal to loan some Canadian wheat at a critical juncture. During the confrontation, Asquith, who also then believed feeding the Belgians to be against British interests, complained of Hoover's manner. Hoover by his own account replied that the repercussions of a refusal would justify any tone he wanted to use. Asquith said to him: "You told me you were no diplomat, but I think you are an excellent one, only your methods are not diplomatic."[22]

Hoover simply believed that the British food blockade of the continent made it incumbent on Great Britain to allow the CRB to do its work. The gruff humanitarian also got his way early in 1915 with an important English minister whom he asked for clearance papers. "Out of the question," said the distinguished minister. "There is no time in the first place, and if there was there are no good wagons to be spared by the railways, no dock hands, and no steamers." "I have managed to get all these," Hoover quietly replied. "Other men have gone to the Tower for less than you have done," the minister shouted at Hoover before granting his wish. "Tact," Lloyd George observed on another occasion, "is not one of his many qualities." The British leader noted in his *Memoirs* that Hoover "had a surliness of mien and a peremptoriness of speech." To the press in late January 1915, Lloyd George was more restrained: "For fifteen minutes [Hoover] spoke without a break. By the time he had finished I had come to realize the practicality of granting his request. I told him I had never understood the question before, thanked him for helping me to understand it, and saw to it that things were arranged as he wanted them." Hoover had argued that since the British had made the invasion of Belgium their *casus belli* by entering the war to protect the rights of small nations, they could ill afford to risk starvation there. That would also be a betrayal of the many Belgians who had found refuge in Great Britain late in 1914. Most of Hoover's later dealings were with Lord Eustace Percy, whom the Foreign Office put in charge of liaison with the CRB. Percy also wondered how it was that "the bluntest man in Europe is able, without apparent effort, to handle a situation involving more irreconcilable elements than any other situation in this war?" For his part, Hoover believed that one good way to accomplish things was to go directly to the ultimate authority and state frankly what was needed.[23]

In August 1915 Hoover was critical of the British blockade, claiming that it was a failure since it angered the war-drained Germans and inspired them to continue fighting. Hoover suggested that an end to submarine warfare on merchant ships might be traded off for a relaxing of the blockade. The Germans only wanted to retain Alsace, he added, and if the western line stabilized in the autumn of 1915, a truce might be possible. But he recognized that the food blockade and submarine warfare combined with aerial bombing made attitudes of mutual hatred so fixed that negotiation was unlikely.[24]

The 1915 Belgian harvest was one of Hoover's most serious problems.

The Germans had helped to plant and cultivate it and expected to take their share. The British told Hoover the CRB would have to cease operations in mid-August if the Germans proved intransigent. Whitlock deserved much credit for working out a satisfactory compromise, which included the agreement that native crops, except for oats and hay, would be reserved for the civilian population. A fair division of the helter-skelter planting was guesswork, but Hoover carried it off. Another storm would blow up over the next year's French harvest, which German planting in the occupied areas had helped to expand. Hoover went to Berlin that summer (1915) as a guest of the German general staff, and after an emotional meeting with General von Sauberzweig, whose son had just been blinded on the eastern front, he obtained a promise that satisfied the British. Von Sauberzweig had given the orders to execute Edith Cavell as an enemy spy. Widely criticized for this action, he evidently wished to make amends by ensuring the continuation of relief.[25]

Another crisis came in January 1916, when British intelligence discovered that some 18,000 tons of CRB food had been sold to Germany on the black market by individual Belgian consumers and merchants. The shipping of CRB food to the Germans "made me so angry that I almost choked," Hoover raged. Francqui observed philosophically that leaks were as inevitable as crime itself, but Hoover found the British in no mood for philosophy; he called the exports to Germany "the worst blow against our personal integrity." Then the British discovered that some German hand grenades had been made from CRB condensed-milk cans. At once the Americans were made responsible for pounding the used cans deep into the ground with pile drivers, while packaging was gradually switched to other materials. Hoover wanted relief to cover only necessities; he could not appreciate Francqui's and Whitlock's insistence on providing such relative luxuries as beer and oil, which he thought would bring "caustic comment."[26]

Compared to Belgian relief, the assistance to 2 million people in northern France beginning in the spring of 1915 was almost easy. The French government refused to subsidize the relief publicly, but contributed indirectly through private banks. Without consulting Whitlock, Hoover sent the famous conservationist Gifford Pinchot to coordinate the beginning of French relief. Pinchot did excellent groundwork for the job. But after staying en route to Belgium with his brother-in-law, the British minister at The Hague, he took two of the minister's mailbags to the border, whereupon the Germans would not let him pass without search and barred him from further work. "Probably my fault," Hoover wired Van Dyke, "for not having attached serious importance to one's wife's relations in these extremely strenuous times." Nonetheless, the Comité for northern France worked smoothly. In contrast to the Germans in Belgium, the occupation troops in France lent active help in distributing food and enjoyed excellent relations with the able CRB director there, Hoover's friend Vernon Kellogg, a biologist on leave from Stanford. The French CRB man in Paris, Louis Chevrillon, was an old engineering acquaintance of Hoover's. By midsummer the French wanted provisioning entirely separate from that of Belgium, and this matter was arranged despite Whitlock's objections. Even in France there were problems: "Trouble No. 7921," Hoover labeled a need for clothing. And later such a food shortage developed that provisioning through neutral Switzerland was seriously entertained. Hoover came in touch with French President Raymond Poincaré and other government officials in the course of his work. No other American, with the exception of Wilson's advisor Colonel Edward House, developed such a wide acquaintanceship with the leading political figures of Europe.[27]

Meanwhile, Hoover encountered difficulties from an American source. After initial gifts amounting to $1 million, the Rockefeller Foundation sent representatives to Belgium whom Hoover cultivated closely. Then, when he had taken many steps with the expectation of further assistance, the foundation decided to cease for fear of deterring governments from supporting the relief. A furious Hoover wrote a carefully controlled letter of protest, asking for a united American will. Privately, he lamented that the foundation's public announcements, which ignored the CRB and discouraged smaller gifts, had lost Hoover's group some $2 million in charitable help.[28]

Worse was to follow. In 1915 the Rockefeller people approached the Germans to make arrangements to feed Poland, and then Germany returned to the CRB for help. Hoover—who was carefully seeking a solution to the difficult problem—was beside himself from that time on: "The responsibility of people starving in Poland was up to them [the Rockefeller contingent]." He would try again to do something if the Germans would announce that they would make no further requisitions in Belgium and that the Rockefeller mission for Poland had failed. Hoover believed this might persuade Britain to lift the blockade for ships carrying food to Poland. By late spring of 1915 he knew, as he wrote Francqui, that hundreds were dying there daily, and he believed that "because of the confidence we have gained," the CRB was the only hope. Ambassador Page noted that London "keenly" opposed Polish relief, hoping that Polish distress would place both economic and propaganda pressures on Germany. After Vernon Kellogg had reported on grim scenes in Poland, Hoover publicized various reports on conditions there, hoping that the British Foreign Office would be influenced by public opinion. In February 1916 Hoover prepared a plan to feed four million Poles; Ambassador Page officially handed it to Lord Grey. But even though President Wilson pleaded with George V, Britain refused to countenance any scheme for Poland or Serbia that did not force Germany to acknowledge control over regions of Austria-Hungary and refrain from requisitioning Polish produce for its own armies. German jingoes took an equally stubborn position. The CRB's activities, together with those of Polish relief groups in the United States, at least pressured Britain to allow the shipment of some food for children, publicized the Polish cause, and contributed to Poland's postwar territorial integrity.[29]

It is difficult to accept Hoover's hard attitude about the feeding of Serbia. He cautioned an assistant that the first appearance of trouble was premature, given the tendency for people "to hide every resource in the country." It would be the "wildest folly to jump into a situation of this kind half-cocked and without proper international understandings." Hoover was probably correct in thinking not only that private charity was wholly inadequate to the task, but also that the situation had to "become sufficiently black to induce governments to mobilize resources, the financial assistance of belligerent Governments, etc." Yet only two months later a report to the Rockefeller Foundation held that "many thousands" had perished. Hoover thought the case hopeless, owing to the intransigence of Britain. Meanwhile, war came closer to America, and the provisioning of Belgium across both German and British minefields became extremely risky.[30]

As early as the spring of 1915, Hoover was seriously wondering whether the CRB ought to continue. He was angry about the sinking in April 1915 of the British-owned relief ship *Harpalyce,* with the loss of its chief officers and many of its Chinese crew. The act, he said, "is absolutely in its complete barbarism without parallel in the last century." After the *Lusitania* went down in May, he feared that American intervention would force an end in any event. He was anxious lest a rupture between the United States and Germany have serious consequences for Belgian relief. At the same time, Hoover probably would not have wished the relief to stand in the way of United States intervention in the war. In fact, as Lord Percy feared, President Wilson sometimes used Belgium as an excuse for not being harder on Germany—for avoiding extremes. Continued conflict with Francqui and with the Spanish ambassador Villalobar also persuaded Hoover that it might be well to place control entirely in Belgian or Dutch hands. The Belgians could afford the costs and the Comité Nationale could direct the work. Like most observers, Hoover had not expected the war to last long; he had worked to get food to people quickly rather than to perfect an administrative and technical model of distribution.[31]

At the time there was some feeling within the Comité for assuming control, or at least for restricting the CRB's role to that of inspection and advice rather than executive action. Hoover's highhanded ways probably had something to do with it; so did the Comité's annoyance that Belgians gave America so much credit for the relief. Villalobar, Francqui, and another Comité official, Jean Baron Lambert, went to London in the spring of 1915 to seek greater authority for themselves. They were severely rebuffed by Sir Edward Grey, who correctly suspected that Germany itself wanted greater control of the relief and could get it through the Comité. Hoover's proposal to Ambassador Page in July that he himself quit seems to have been sincere; but he also knew that if Britain vetoed the Comité plan, his own hand would be strengthened against it. The Comité, realizing the danger of not having the major neutral power at hand in case of trouble, in fact shifted its position against independence. Hoover's power was once again dominant. But early in 1916 Belgian efforts to reduce United States participation to minuscule dimensions resumed, and Hoover again offered to quit. In October he wrote to Kellogg: "Francqui has, unfortunately for us, finally disclosed his whole intent and manner by closing up the [jointly administered] Bureau of Inspection and Control by violence, and delivering himself of the general dictum that we are a purely ornamental body . . . that he represents the Belgian Government," and that the CRB's presence only gave "a colour which may satisfy the British." Francqui, a victim of "war vanity," had descended from "pure philanthropy into the realm of ward politics."[32]

Vernon Kellogg agreed with Hoover on Francqui, saying that the Belgian had made

numerous misstatements of facts and distortion and misrepresentation of conversation. . . . He is so preoccupied with the . . . political status . . . and such a large portion of his time is taken up by his important and absorbing banking and private interests that he has not had time to acquaint himself with the extent and details of the Commission's work. . . . He has not visited our central offices except incidentally on two or three occasions, nor has he visited the provinces at all during the whole of my residence in Brussels.

Francqui did not realize, Kellogg continued in a summary of the CRB's work, that "the whole of the internal transportation in Belgium, the control of the milling, the detailed study of food conditions and the determination of rations, carefully adjusted distribution to provinces and regions, the constant investigation and impartial correction of minor abuses, and the burden of daily negotiations with the German authorities not only in Brussels, but in all the provinces, rests continually on the shoulders of the Americans!!" The situation was as Hoover had put it: the question was not between Hoover and Francqui, as Francqui insisted, but between the British government and the Belgians. Kellogg seems to have been the one person in the relief effort who was universally respected and rarely criticized.[33]

A specific cause of friction between Hoover and Francqui was the policy desired by socialist elements in the Comité of providing a dole for certain of the unemployed. Hoover would have nothing to do with filtering even Belgian funds for this purpose from England by way of the CRB. The dole was intended to promote strikes against the Germans and, Hoover argued, would jeopardize the whole relief operation; the dole, moreover, was "socially wrongly founded, giving money as a right to the unemployed." Charity "was out of place in every civilized community," though "the bare fact of the world's negligence" made it necessary. Yet the "fond de chomage" by mid-1915 kept some 750,000 Belgians from having to work for Germany, which eventually put an end to the program. Despising idleness, Hoover himself expanded on a Dutch plan for a Neutral Industrial Commission for Belgium that would put the unemployed to work in their own prewar industries and exchange contraband manufactures for food. One reason for the plan was that vast numbers of working-class people were increasingly unable to pay for their food. Hoover pushed hard for the idea, but Germany would not allow it to be undertaken by the CRB, and Britain would not permit it otherwise.[34]

Finally determined to "transfer the whole fight to London" and "lay a train of powder to blow up Francqui," Hoover late in 1916 persuaded the British to draft with his assistance a contract on how the relief must work. It stipulated that the CRB have full independent control in Belgium straight to the consumer; the CRB, with the assistance of the Comité, would also see that Germany honored its guarantees. Francqui thereupon accused Hoover of using a sledgehammer to kill gnats; Hoover replied he would use a pile driver to kill a malarial mosquito. After his humiliating defeat Francqui threatened to quit, but Hoover dissuaded him and he signed the agreement giving Hoover control. Lord Percy chastised Hoover for oversensitivity about Francqui. American dignity would be preserved, he said, but the CRB's status must become increasingly anomalous: "We must negotiate, compromise . . . and put up with seeming ingratitude." Whitlock observed, however, that Hoover had tried many times to compromise, while Francqui had been unyielding and spoke of the "American invasion." Percy further warned: if by "any action of yours, you at this eleventh hour . . . act a part in preventing the destruction which threatens to follow upon the growth of German despair, you will lessen . . . the dignity of America."[35]

The relief efforts of other groups in the United States also were a constant bother to Hoover, largely because their activities—often with higher overheads, more inefficient plans of distribution, and a penchant for self-publicity—became associated in the minds of Belgians and Germans alike with the operations of the CRB. The naïve and big-hearted William C.

Edgar, editor of the *Northwestern Miller* in Minneapolis, had published a glossy booklet picturing himself, his relief ship, its contents, and happy Belgian babies. Hoover planned to "hypnotise" Edgar in Europe and send him home "with a lot of thanks documents from the Belgians." Another problem concerned destructive competition between Catholic and Protestant relief groups. One New York group, unlike that city's CRB office, made wide use of decorative names—a practice Hoover had scorned for company prospectuses and mining director boards. He telegraphed Henry van Dyke at The Hague: "A New York Committee headed by some glory hunting Belgian pinheads and professional charity workers is refusing cooperation with us claim in press they will feed Belgium through you . . . this is subversive to the whole organization." A particular problem was the anti-Germanism of the rival relief group in New York. It was all Hoover could do to convince touchy German officials that the group was separate from his.[36]

Then the CRB's New York office itself went wrong. Its head and Hoover's partner in Maikop oil, Lindon Bates, had been a victim of unsubstantiated gossip about waste and extravagance in 1915. In Hoover's opinion, Bates had become completely unhinged after the loss of his son on the *Titanic*. In a communication to the State Department that October, Bates charged Hoover with violating the century-old Logan Act that forbade any American to deal directly with belligerents. In a sense, the charge was valid; the CRB flew its own flag and made contracts with belligerents somewhat comparable to treaties. An official of the British Foreign Office termed it "a piratical state organized for benevolence." It "evoked powers and immunities, was neutral—but . . . waged frequent controversy with both belligerents." Bates's allegation was in part a reaction to Hoover's insistence on absolutely dominating the office and to some typically blunt criticisms of New York publicity organs; the women's "Little Princess Movement" disgusted him. Such advertising, he said, gave the CRB a "Barnum and Bailey aspect." He called the charity appeals exaggerated and saccharine. Perhaps he was thinking of notices like this, which came from the New York office: "For the lack of sufficient nourishment, the little ones in Belgium are now in a pitiable condition. Underfeeding has sapped their strength, and they are rapidly becoming a prey to tuberculosis . . . and many are dying from weakness." Finally, Mrs. Bates seemed to him "hysterical" and vocally anti-German.[37]

Hoover returned to the United States in October 1915 to confer with the State Department and President Wilson about Bates's charges, which Senator Henry Cabot Lodge was investigating. Page had telegraphed Secretary of State William Jennings Bryan:

The CRB is Hoover and absolutely depends on Hoover who has personally made agreements with the Governments concerned and has carried these delicate negotiations through only because of his high character and standing and unusual ability. If he is driven to resign the Commission will instantly fall to pieces. The governmental sources of money will dry up and the work will have to be abandoned.

Hoover meanwhile had met with a powerful group of newspaper editors and publishers in New York. Though he still wanted no official connection with the relief, the President decided to throw the full prestige of the government behind Hoover. He asked some prominent New York businessmen to serve on a reorganized New York committee under the engineer W. L. Honnold, with whom Hoover had stayed in South Africa. The committee included Henry L. Stimson, Oscar Straus, Elbert H. Gary, and Frank Vanderlip. Hoover then sought out and calmed Lodge and enlisted Theodore Roosevelt's aid in the same cause. Possibly because Hoover had turned up seeming irregularities about Bates's American business career, Bates finally withdrew his charges and took a nominal role in the organization, making no further trouble.[38]

Hoover moved through the events of these years with a self-protective sensitivity to publicity and criticism. His numerous and lengthy memoranda about what he said and did might have been indicative, as Colonel Edward M. House remarked, of a seeking for a place in history. Or they could have reflected a concern that he might be implicated in any misadventure or scandal. His distressing experience in the Rowe affair and in the Chang Yen-mao trial had made him chronically wary. He remarked to Bates on the near-infamy of "being set up in the world as a previous associate of C. A. Moreing." One of Hoover's first acts had been to secure the services of a firm of prominent London auditors to oversee the vast charitable monies that moved through his personal bank account. Otherwise, as the London CRB transportation man John Beaver White remarked, someday "some swine will rise up and say we either made a profit out of this business or that we stole the money"—as in fact several people eventually did.[39]

In the face of attack Hoover could act hotly, swiftly, and with effect. In September 1914 a testy professor of history, C. C. van Tyne of the University of Michigan, called Hoover's London relief committee (which had evidently lost Van Tyne's baggage) "an elaborate system of graft . . . an incompetent, dishonest organization." Hoover brought the matter straight to the attention of Michigan's president, and the professor apologized. Early in 1915, when unfounded charges of extravagant salaries and foolish purchasing policies circulated among prominent Belgians concerning the CRB's New York office, Hoover exploded, went to the exiled Belgian cabinet, and threatened to go to the king if necessary. The allegations were quickly disproved.[40]

Hoover sought plenty of good publicity for the CRB, particularly the American role. He was chagrined that Australians and many others were contributing much more than Americans and smarted at "widespread denouncement of our countrymen as being fishers for profit in this pool of blood." To counter the argument that his country was making a profit from the world's calamity under the guise of charity, he arranged for a number of journalists, including his old college friend Will Irwin, to tour Belgium. Irwin, William Goode of the Panama-Pacific Exposition affair, and Ben Allen, head of the Associated Press's London Bureau, all became members of the CRB for a time; and they contributed their skills to enhancing the public standing and clout of the organization. Hoover's concern for the favorable publicizing of the American effort flowed not only from his nationalism but also from a keen awareness of what publicity could do. It was, he said, necessary to use as a negotiating instrument "the club of public opinion." Above all he wished to cultivate Americans, calculating that if the United States perceived the CRB as a symbol of itself in Europe, the commission's survival was assured. As Whitlock put it, the CRB's "press campaign in America . . . created a public opinion in the world that Germany and England always take into account, a public opinion that has not only saved Belgium from famine and worse, but from destruction and dismemberment as a nation. It pays to advertise!" While Hoover's salesmanship of the relief work was sober and careful, it could also be aggressive in his abrupt way. In 1915 he cabled the governor of Kansas that because of the state's preeminence in wheat-growing, the governor "must" contribute several shiploads of wheat. The responses to publicity revealed shrewdness, crankiness, and idealism; if one American wanted to adopt a Belgian baby, another was looking for dependable household help. Meanwhile, American merchants were making a 40 percent profit from the sale of Belgian lace, the country's largest cottage industry; anyone in the CRB who dealt in lace, so it was said, gradually went crazy and had to retire.[41]

Hoover was honestly uncomfortable with personal publicity. "The commission has not been founded," he rebuked its New York office, as he had previously chastised Ben Allen, "to advertise its chairman, members, or employees." While "stuck here [in Paris] waiting for a train," Hoover wrote in longhand to William Edgar condemning his "rotten" article in his "damned" *Bellman*. "In London these days I have given up riding on Buses because all the old ladies tap me on the back with the handles of their umbrellas and demand to know, 'Young man why are you not in kakai' (or however you spell it). Next it will be 'oh you are the Relief man aren't you?' " Extremely shy—he failed to show up for an early speech—he loathed publicity. When Whitlock in February 1915 gingerly proposed an award for the departing Captain Lucey, Hoover objected: "It is undemocratic, and from my point of view, at least, is not the kind of reward which I am searching for in this world." In June of that year he pleaded with Francqui not to make a review of charitable aid public lest it be "made a basis for any expressions of gratitude with which we are already overwhelmed." "I do not really care," he later wrote Francqui, "whether Belgian relief is ever heard of once we can get the job done." And he infuriated Whitlock by not showing up in 1919 to receive an important medal in Brussels. Hoover had what looks like a simple Quaker distaste for such things. In Quakerism good works became tainted if promulgated; all his life Hoover made a secret of his hundreds of benefactions. Page wrote in a letter of January 12, 1915, to President Wilson: "Life is worth more, too, for knowing Hoover. But for him Belgium would now be starving. . . . He is a simple, modest, energetic man who began his career in California and will end it in Heaven; and he doesn't want anybody's thanks."[42]

At the same time, Hoover could not bear to be misread. It was as though two forces warred within him: the need of an orphan to show the world he had made good, which can be interpreted as a fear of failure, and the Quaker aversion to public tribute. He accepted only two decorations right after the war: the French Legion of Honor (which he said he would have refused, given the opportunity) and that of Honorary Citizen and Friend of the Belgian Nation, along with a Belgian passport stamped "Perpetual." The British, however, denied him the Order of Merit.

By January 1917 all signs pointed toward an early end to the American work in Belgium. German submarines sank CRB ships, and on February 3, Wilson broke off relations with Germany. When Von Bissing's civil aide, Baron von der Lancken, curtailed the freedom of CRB representatives early in 1917, Hoover once again threatened to withdraw his men immediately and completely. Again, his opponent admitted defeat. After Von der Lancken made it plain he did not wish to be held responsible for the departure of the Americans, Francqui—returning from a long session with the Germans—laughed, and even Villalobar remarked: "Hoover is the best diplomat of all of us."[43]

On a trip to the United States in late January, Hoover asked President Wilson for an outright government subsidy for the CRB, which was soon forthcoming. Hoover's California friend, Secretary of the Interior Franklin K. Lane, offered to make him the department's first assistant secretary. Whitlock wrote to Secretary of War Newton Baker that he hoped Hoover would not take the Interior job, "for I don't know how we could carry on

the relief work without him. The position has so many delicate points
. . . this is not the time for any bull to come into this china shop." Interestingly, Whitlock goes on: "I think he is precisely the man that the
liberal movement in America, as you and I understand it, needs . . . his
hardness is all on the surface. He is a gentleman of rather wide culture
. . . of a most democratic nature and with great human sympathies; his
work in the Commission of course is one of the modern wonders of the
world." Lane introduced Hoover to the economist Adolf Miller. Whitlock
wanted him to meet the single-tax proponent Louis Post. In New York,
Hoover dined with Herbert Croly, editor of *The New Republic*. His list of
important acquaintances was growing. Hugh Gibson described a trip to see
Teddy Roosevelt at Oyster Bay: "We were ushered into the Trophy Room
and in a minute or two the Colonel came in swinging an ax and covered
with leaves and twigs as though he had pushed his way through a mile
of jungle." In early February, Hoover said that while he hoped to avoid
war "I am no extreme pacifist." On February 17 he advised Colonel House
in a long memorandum to provide the Allies with munitions, money, and
food. Without the prestige and influence of a neutral, the United States
obviously would have to stop directing Belgian relief.[44]

Hoover wanted the Dutch to take over the relief from the Americans.
He reasoned that they held a strategic position *vis-à-vis* Germany, that
relief ships had an established routing through Rotterdam so the Dutch
already controlled supplies, and that Americans esteemed the Dutch. He
spoke also of what he called unfortunate racism in the United States toward Spaniards. He was uncomfortable with Villalobar's closeness to the
Germans and feared for the reputation of the relief. Failing Dutch control,
Hoover suggested Danish or Swiss. Page, however, informed Hoover that
it would be essential to include Spain, since that nation was now the most
influential neutral. Whitlock wanted other neutrals to join the CRB.
Hoover said he knew no neutrals he could trust, a comment that reflected
his general feelings about Europe. In mid-February Hoover, influenced
by Page, wanted Whitlock and other Americans to leave Belgium; then he
quickly reversed himself. "This Commission," he wrote, "has now become
a national trust . . . any voluntary withdrawal on our part would impress
the American people as cowardly." He also decided that Villalobar was
too influential in Belgium to be stopped. The result was the Comité His-
panico-Hollandais, headed by the king of Spain and the queen of Holland.
Still, Hoover had the final word: "All large decisions now must have Washington approval." Whitlock complained that Hoover, some 3000 miles
away, lacked touch with the most serious element of every situation—its
atmosphere. Secretary of State Robert Lansing directed Whitlock and
other Americans to leave by March 23; a few stayed on, the capable

"volunteer" Prentiss Gray remaining until June. A congressional commission continued the relief and Hoover ran the operation from Washington until just after the war. Things went much the same: Hoover called Villalobar "childish" and Francqui "insulting," but the job got done. When Belgian relief finally did end in 1919, auditors estimated the overhead costs at slightly more than one-half of 1 percent; the child mortality rate in Belgium and northern France was lower under the CRB than it had ever been before. Altogether, 2.5 million tons of food valued at $300 million had been shipped to feed more than 9 million people in Belgium and France. Belgium was Hoover's prime example of the value of intelligent economic assistance. Had similar help been given to all of Europe after the war, the chronic problems that gave way to another war might have been avoided.[45]

If ever a historical institution was the "lengthened shadow" of a great man, the CRB was Hoover's. As Tracy Kittredge, the author of a distinctly nationalistic, privately published history of the CRB, put it: "Hoover, with his odd persuasiveness, drew men to him. . . . [The CRB] was an organization based on good will, on the spirit of volunteer service, on the sense of pride in participating in an organisation so humanitarian in purpose, so extensive in its operations, so efficient in action." And as Hoover wrote home to a friend: "I am hoping that we have been able, in addition to relieving the suffering of Belgium, to advance the interests of our country abroad." The CRB, in the midst of war, was also a vestige of internationalism and the solidarity of civilization.[46]

Belgian relief, along with the great projects in Russia and elsewhere that Hoover would direct in the following years, constituted a superb accomplishment, technically, morally, and practically. It was of the essence of what Hoover was fitted to do well, as an engineer, a Quaker, an American, and provides a good situation for appraising his virtues and their limits.

A fundamental fact about the project was that because of its size and composition Hoover was able to control and manipulate its workings in the most direct way. He had, to be sure, to cope with governments he could not order about and personalities that could thwart him; and he graciously cajoled when he could, compromised when he had to, and played one force against another—his British support, for example, against the Comité's resistance. But the people he had to deal with were within the reach of his personal confrontation and argument; he pounded away at British officialdom until he got what he was after. Persuasion of a more delicate sort—the charming or inspiring of an audience, the composing of large social factions—was not part of his work, so that the strengths he displayed were not necessarily transferable to electoral politics. But how deceptively reasonable it would be to think that someone so successful in the running of large projects could easily run a still larger one: the United States of America.

Why did Hoover, after making millions, turn so abruptly away from his personal affairs to relief work? It is not difficult to speculate. In China he had helped organize relief within a city, and since then had done much writing about the social responsibilities of modern enterprise. He was no sudden convert to humanitarianism. Moreover, the urge to make money or expand a business expresses a deeper appetite for power, for putting big units together, for imposing shape on some vast material. Belgian relief could offer satisfactions of that appetite. It could also be a basis for a more extensive public career. And its peculiarly nonpartisan nature demanded an engineer's ethic of operating above the battle for the long-time good of the commonweal. But the immediate motive surely was that the condition of Belgium, and Hoover's ability to do something about it, presented a very simple and commanding moral imperative. There is not the slightest reason beyond crude cynicism to doubt that what drove Hoover in this period, making him at one moment push around a British cabinet minister and at another order a state governor to send wheat, was his knowledge that lives needed saving.

Hoover in this time made no eloquent or even groping statement on the meaning of suffering in the world, no suggestion of identifying with the poor, nothing expressive of a tortured and reflective sensibility such as we have recently come to associate with a social conscience, especially in its religious forms. He would not have known how to talk or act like that, though what he may have experienced inside is another question. Instead, he gave us the homelier side of conscience, its committing of itself to getting a needful task competently done.

VI

"FOOD WILL WIN THE WAR"

HOOVER ACTIVELY SOUGHT the post of United States Food Administrator, even though he later claimed it had been thrust upon him. He had been angling for the prospective job of managing the war effort, perhaps from abroad, at least since late in 1916. In a letter from London dated April 3, 1917, just three days before America entered World War I, he described his qualifications to Colonel Edward House, who on European trips had used Hoover as a listening post on the war. He also telegraphed his friend Hugh Gibson in Washington, saying that he was available for "appropriate service"; Gibson passed on copies of the telegram to influential Wilsonians. House replied that he, along with Samuel Gompers and a number of others impressed by the Commission for Relief in Belgium, had urged the appointment on the President. Hoover was not above issuing a press release on how food crises "may possibly result in the collapse of everything we hold dear in civilization"; he also had British war associates boost him for service in America. Public opinion itself quickly centered on the "Almoner of Starving Belgium" as the proper choice to manage food supplies at home. Hoover noted with distress demonstrations in major American cities against high food prices; later in 1917 he called the Russian Revolution a "food riot." Already knowledgeable in the conduct of the war and quite well acquainted with the Allied leaders, Hoover was the natural, almost inevitable choice for political as well as administrative reasons to be United States Food Administrator. Europeans and Americans both regarded him as one of the unique creations of the war; even those who questioned his methods could not quarrel with his success.[1]

Woodrow Wilson, who had consulted with Hoover early in 1917 on ways to avoid American entry into the war, signified through Colonel House in the midst of the campaign for Hoover that he wanted to use him in some capacity connected with food administration. The Council of National Defense—a civilian preparedness committee set up in 1916 with representatives chiefly from industry and labor—soon invited Hoover to investigate food requirements abroad and then to cross the sea to advise in Washington on matters pertaining to food supply, which was in effect an invitation to a prospective office. The British had already assumed Hoover would serve in such a position. On his arrival in New York on May 3, Hoover made it clear that neither he nor other volunteer administrators would accept a salary for any wartime services. While Secretary of Agriculture David Houston wanted food management under his own direction, and the army and navy were jealous as well, Hoover convinced Wilson that a separate agency would be more easily disbanded after the war. He stipulated that the possession of sufficient authority was a prerequisite for his service, yet he bargained and beguiled Wilson with talk of voluntarism and help from business leaders who (unlike bureaucrats) would retire at the end of the war. House warned the President that Hoover was "the kind of man that has to have complete control in order to do the thing well."[2]

On May 19, Wilson asked Congress to establish the post of Food Administrator with power to regulate the distribution and consumption of food, its export, import, price, purchase, requisition, and storage. In many respects a continuation of Hoover's work in Belgian relief, which had been widely copied by other governments, the new, more partisan job meant winning the war as well.

As a witness to the stumblings of Allied governments early in the war, Hoover knew the cost of inadequate centralization and coordination. He realized that virtually none of the historical conditions that had fashioned the existing presidential cabinet was military, and since wartime demands swelled the normal duties of cabinet officers, fresh, centralized authority capable of striking across the existing departments would be required. Unquestionably, Hoover wished to be a food dictator. There must be one, he told Secretary of the Navy Josephus Daniels on May 7.[3]

But with a difference: While Hoover wanted great power and would berate Congress for not giving him more, he had an idea of the sort he would later develop during the 1920's, of a free public cooperation enlisted by the government in pursuance of a national project. Such voluntarism was to be encouraged by publicity and slogans, and disciplined by a range of powers that might not have to come into use: their mere existence would warn off profiteers and hoarders and supposedly strip the money-making apparatus of private enterprise into an austere war machine. Voluntarism needed inspiration from an individual leader, Hoover told Wilson, not from a board. "There ain't going to be a Food Control Board," Wilson informed a jobseeker. The ambivalent Hoover, shunner and manipulator of publicity, knew that the reputation his work in Belgium had gained for him could help to win the war.

Hoover prepared for a brief war. By relying for leadership on volunteers, he could evade both Civil Service rules and political patronage—and secure as well a large degree of personal power. His volunteerism functioned in an élitist fashion, drawing personnel often from the wealthy who could, for example, afford accretions to their staff if needed to secure advantage. Such men as Hoover and Bernard Baruch were in some respects beyond the control of the President or Congress. Yet, given their idealistic motives and superior technical skills, they scarcely realized their unique positions. Hoover in his presidential inaugural would say: "One civilization after another has been wrecked upon the attempt to secure sufficient leadership from a single group or class."[4]

Speaking to the Senate Agriculture Committee four days after his return, in a session at which he dazzled his interrogators with his detailed knowledge of the worldwide flow of commodities, Hoover began by telling the curious senators that in recent years he had engaged in a rather strange occupation—"being called in to build up new concerns." This earlier work was something of a model for wartime administration. Hoover then proceeded with a recital of his varied experiences, until one senator finally interrupted: "It might be easier for the record if you would tell us what you have not been doing." "Simply those matters relating to engineering," Hoover replied with attempted modesty. "It does not traverse the whole field of human activities."[5]

The witness and the senators then waxed enthusiastic about beans. They possessed a food value, Hoover observed, "very high in protein and fat—higher than any other vegetable. One could almost maintain a population on beans alone, it is so admirable a food. It has the great advantage of endurance." When Senator Thomas Gore of Oklahoma asked about the price of beans per bushel, Hoover replied: "I have always bought them by the ton." He convincingly used beans as an illustration that each agricultural product must be treated from the beginning as an international commodity.

The way flour and other goods crisscrossed the country before reaching the consumer brought Hoover to a favorite subject, that of waste. The man who had grown up in thrifty Quaker communities lashed out at wasteful trade practices, including inefficiency of threshing machines, faulty loading for transportation, slow transportation, failure to unload goods promptly, buying in larger quantities than needed, duplication of delivery service, a lack of standard sizes for such items as loaves of bread, and customs such as the acceptance by bakers of the return of stale bread. "Every household in America consumes more food than is absolutely necessary from a dietetic point of view," Hoover observed, "and practically every household wastes something." Soon he would be preaching the doctrine of a clean plate. "In public places," he said, "[a man] eats and destroys twice as much as he does in his home [where] he has the machinery of feeding. In Belgium . . . we were the tyrants, and we abolished the hotel and restaurant," except for the traveler more than 5 miles away from home.

Price-fixing—Hoover preferred the phrase "profit-fixing"—he termed for the congressmen "the most obnoxious job in history." In place of a minimum or a maximum price, he proposed the device used in Belgium: a "fixed price, a definite price at which the stuff was purchased throughout the whole year and backed by the Government." Elsewhere he wrote of controlling prices "not by futile legal maximum or minimum prices but by injecting the government as the sole buyer and seller at one link in the distribution chain." This managed price would reflect prewar business profits. It was impossible to serve both God and Mammon, objected James Vardaman of Mississippi, and businessmen should not be allowed any profits; Hoover replied that the economic system would break down in twenty-four hours without them. He then suggested "withholding licenses" from "skunks" who did not cooperate with wartime goals. Hoover believed that the government's proposed Food Department should have cabinet status, which would encourage its being taken seriously in matters of price and licensing. The food division should perhaps have more power than other cabinet offices, since it would have to negotiate with other governments. The food agency should have control "from the soil to the stomach." And the new agency "should die with the war."[6]

"War," Hoover observed, "is a losing business, a financial loss, a loss of life and an economic degeneration. . . . It has but few compensations and of them we must make the most. Its greatest compensation lies in the possibility that we may instill into our people unselfishness. . . . We have gone for a hundred years of unbridled private initiative in this country," he lectured the senators, "and it has bred its own evils and one of these evils is the lack of responsibility in the American individual to the people as a whole, the unwillingness of personal selfishness to sacrifice to national interest." In a different context, Hoover noted, "We have in this country a class of the population given over to more or less idleness and a great deal of extravagance. There grows out of this a certain amount of class feeling in a country where there should be no class division." Wartime unity required that the wealthy reduce their scale of living.[7]

The British blockade had impressed on everyone the importance that food would have in the war. In the early months after American entry, food was critical, more urgent than getting men for the armed forces. Well before Congress acted, Hoover had organized a temporary food administration, staffing it with volunteers like the muckraker Ida Tarbell, his friend Ray Lyman Wilbur of Stanford, and the faithful engineer Edgar Rickard. They coordinated help from fraternal groups, women's organizations, and state defense councils. A massive campaign sought to enroll as members every woman in control of a household. As a result, housewives came to cut down on some of their normal use of bread and sugar; it is hard to say how much, given already declining consumption, higher prices, and heavier imports. The enlisting of American women played a large part in awakening public opinion in behalf of the war; this was probably more valuable than the conservation of some 16 million bushels of wheat. More savings could be made through the trades than through consumers, Hoover admitted. Volunteers also mailed curricula on food conservation to the nation's teachers colleges in time for use in summer sessions; "talks" were supplied to the Chautauqua circuits. In an effort to induce people to substitute potatoes for wheat, one school leaflet called for a potato campaign. It suggested an essay contest on "The Life of a Potato." Children could sing a song, "The Patriotic Potato," enact a play, *The Crowning of the Little Brown Prince,* learn about a potato's "eyes" and what *au gratin* meant, and carry home a cross-section of a potato that would make them "enthusiastic about the potato situation." "When in doubt," the Hoover poster commanded, "serve potatoes." The campaign got endorsements from the pulpit.[8]

After almost three months of debate the Lever Food Control Act finally passed the House on August 10, 1917, by a vote of 365 to 5. Hoover bitterly complained that the delay inhibited increased production by creating uncertainties for the producer. Fiorello LaGuardia called the bill a "Democratic job grab," and several senators attacked it as unfair to farmers. The law gave the President authority to control food and fuel with such agencies as he chose to create with the object of feeding Americans, their armies abroad, and their Allies. Food would be diverted from neutrals who might sell to Germany. Certain senators had deleted important provisions relating to smaller retailers, but the law prohibited manufacturers, wholesalers, and large retailers from hoarding, profiteering, and mischievous speculating. Senator William Borah of Idaho complained that there were "enough generalities in the bill to bring on the millennium."

The language was mostly broad and elastic; the legislation was based on the war power, not control over interstate trade. But specific price fixing powers were granted only for wheat, a most important war material owing to its ease of transportation and storage and the great demand for it in Europe. Congress set a minimum price of $2.00 a bushel for the 1918 crop.[9]

The Food Administration that came into being under the Lever Act to control the 1918 crop lacked a rigidly bureaucratic structure, or so Hoover liked to boast. Since "it is a purely temporary organization," he observed in his first annual report, "created to deal with . . . emerging problems . . . the scope of the Food Administration can't be accurately defined nor strictly limited." Hoover believed that the war would be relatively short; he elected simply to treat each problem as it arose, selecting for his staff the man best fitted to handle each particular difficulty and regularly checking his work. He chose people for technical skill (Alonzo Taylor), for political associations (Robert Taft—the former President's son), for influence with farmers (Gifford Pinchot), or for importance in the business community (Julius Barnes). When two workers overlapped, they met and worked out their individual jurisdictions; competent men would find new ground to map imaginative plans. Every branch in the Food Administration held running sap; when the sap stopped, the branch was pruned. When Felix Frankfurter of the War Labor Policies Board asked for an organization chart, he was told disdainfully that none existed. "The Government kept sending efficiency experts to us," said Hoover, "and the first thing they all wanted to do was to draw a 'chart of organization.' I wouldn't let them. . . . An organization isn't a chart: it's a body of men—and any new organization that can be charted is badly launched." In reality, more and more bureaucratic traits crept in and power became increasingly centralized as the war continued. Hoover himself, as in his Commerce Department years, was always reaching out beyond his bureaucratic boundaries.[10]

In accordance at least with Hoover's moral preference for decentralized organization, his new agency chose state food directors, serving mostly on a voluntary basis. Each of these directors was supposed to conduct statewide educational work with advice from Washington's educational division. Library directors were to set up community centers for detailed information on the saving of food; a merchant representative would provide for visual displays in stores; and a director of home economics (always a woman) advised on technical matters. The county level of work became most important. The head of the largest bank in the county was to call a meeting of bankers, editors, and fraternal groups, who would nominate a county food administrator; a committee with representatives from each town, appointed by the administration, would investigate complaints, distribute educational literature, and publish maximum fair prices and costs to merchants in local papers. Such boards existed in counties throughout the nation by December 1917 and in the cities later. Hoover directed local units to settle their own problems as much as possible. Milling operations also were directed by zone instead of nationally.[11]

To most Americans the Food Administration was an agency of exhortation. Using slogans like "Food Will Win the War" and employing a rich poster art, it mined the American talent for advertising. Ben Allen of the CRB headed the publicity section for much of its existence, persuading newspapers, magazines, motion pictures, and even an outdoor electrical talking billboard company to contribute free advertising space, which added up to some $19 million. Twenty-one thousand letters went to newspaper editors, asking that they urge food conservation on their readers, and the press entered a veritable partnership with Hoover. American Telephone & Telegraph assisted by having each of thousands of district managers call clergymen and request that they announce Food Conservation Days. Meatless and wheatless days (with substitutions of fish and vegetables), victory bread composed of as little as 50 percent wheat, and even a campaign to keep a family pig—"no more unsanitary than a dog," Hoover remarked, and pigs could live economically on scraps—became a part of the war effort. People "should be given to understand that as their patriotic duty they are *expected* to observe them," one directive said of the Food Administration "days." Edward Bok's *Ladies' Home Journal* stopped commissioning articles criticizing cats as foes of birds and published from six to sixteen pieces a month on food conservation. Blood sausage took on the new name of victory sausage. On January 28, 1918, the fifty-fifty rule went into effect, requiring every purchaser of wheat flour to buy at the same time a like amount of substitutes. On February 3, commercial millers were instructed to mix 5 percent of other cereals with their wheat flour, and were told that the mixture was to be 20 percent by February 24 and 25 percent by April 14. To "Hooverize" came to mean to economize with a worthy purpose; the word for a time entered the English language. One woman, reading his instructions to save bread, brought twenty-eight loaves into the Washington office and asked what she should do with them.[12]

The early Food Administration assumed that Americans were eager to do the right thing, amenable to persuasion. "Working with Hoover," one admirer wrote, "gave me an understanding of the tremendous power of voluntary cooperation that exceeds the power of law or threats of punishments." As ever, Hoover appealed alike to selfish and to altruistic motives: decency in feeding Europe, practicality in keeping the war from the Eastern seaboard. And in involving the citizen early and intimately in the war, the Food Administration became an important propaganda agent. The personnel were drawn in part from the Belgian relief, in part from other public-spirited men and women, particularly Californians, anxious to help in the war effort. A coterie of advisors met daily at 7:00 A.M. in Hoover's house for a discussion of the day's problems: Mark Requa, Julius Barnes, Theodore Whitmarsh, and others. These men determined policy and displayed devoted loyalty to the "Chief," whose physical stamina and grasp of detail astounded them all. Hoover directed the agency's publicists to give credit to junior people to the fullest extent warranted. Even Thorstein Veblen worked briefly on two agricultural studies for the Food Administration: one asked that the demands of the Industrial Workers of the World be granted as a wartime measure to conciliate the working class; the other argued that the Food Administration was a businessman's racket and that the government should displace the middlemen. Veblen also spent time on drawing for the Navy Department a device to catch submarines with lengths of stout binding wire trailed from ships.

Rather than use the contract system of purchasing supplies, the Food Administration employed a device that set an important pattern for other war agencies. Large firms and trade associations, supervised by the government, allocated the work among the relevant industries and set the prices. Their representatives, possessing skill to draft technical regulations and contracts with foreign countries, came to Washington for varying periods as consultants. Price was to be a function not of market conditions but of prewar profit added to the delivered cost of the commodity. The regulatory scheme was a foreshadowing of the cooperative trade association efforts setting business practices and standardizing parts, the pooling of statistics and scientific information that Hoover in the 1920's would be encouraging within business. During the war the government suspended antitrust laws and the distinction between the public and private sectors became increasingly blurred.

The presence in Washington of some experts from within the trades introduced the danger that decisions would be influenced by self-serving bias. Hoover, sensitive to congressional and public criticism on this point, tried to find people free of financial interests; this was especially important among the worst profiteers, the millers and packers. With partial success: accounts were consistently audited and various schemes attempted for limiting even accidental excess profits, including one that allowed the sale of grain to the government at reduced prices and another that compelled gifts to the Red Cross. Profits, however, were not well restricted in 1917, and Hoover became a firm advocate of a wartime excess-profits tax.

The Food Administration did possess licensing powers that could force companies into submission. In the hands of Roland Boyden, the independent Enforcement Division revoked dozens of licenses for varying lengths of time. By withholding supplies of ammonia for a while, Boyden forced Armour and Company to comply with his wishes. He was known as "Hoover's hangman." But such practices sometimes hurt the consumer and even interrupted the flow of war goods. Hoover stated a preference for publicity, particularly against hoarders, but also for action that would deprive the convicted profiteer of his past gains and make imprisonment mandatory for anyone willfully destroying commodities for the purpose of driving up prices.[13]

Despite Hoover's good intentions, some companies did make enormous war profits. As time went on, an increasing number of commodities came under the Food Administration's control; by March 1918, Hoover was saying that set prices should be paid for all scarce goods. A $5000 fine or two years in prison helped to enforce price schedules against large retailers. Small retail violators were publicized as unpatriotic, or their sources of supply were effectively cut off under a rule forbidding wholesalers to deal with those not conforming to regulations. The Enforcement Division issued 3769 legal decisions for fair trade, a figure that does not include tens of thousands of similar actions by state and local food administrators. Yet, by December 1917, Hoover was asking Wilson for more general price-fixing power than his executive order on adhering to pre-1914 profits. Fairness to the wheat farmer, so definitely restricted compared to the Southern cotton grower, demanded it, he said; the abuse of voluntary price agreements was setting off "great currents of injustice." The difficulty of determining prewar profits was another reason for going to fixed prices. Hoover settled for whatever course brought the greatest promise of increased production. But in 1920 he wrote that one great revelation of the war was the "unnecessarily wide margin of cost that exists between producer and consumer."[14]

Most of the Allies were food-importing nations, and had traditionally drawn their cereal foods from eastern Europe and Russia. After the war began, Argentina, India, and Australia proved good sources of cereals. But Argentina's 1916 wheat failure forced an embargo from that government, while the increasing scarcity of ships made the long haul from Australia or India more and more difficult. Canada and the United States might provide 60 percent of Europe's needs in 1917, but with a poor wheat and corn harvest expected, only conservation could raise the figure to an amount sufficient to wage war unhindered. In the meantime, the instability of demand along with speculation threatened to raise cereal prices. Hoover's job was twofold: to control prices—the poor, he said, suffer most from high bread prices—and to increase production in aid of the war effort. War, he pointed out, becomes largely a matter of political administration. The Lever Act gave Hoover broad but limited powers to accomplish its complex job of establishing priorities within trades. A strategy of encouraging one food product might unintentionally discourage output of another needed item, or create dislocations of varying degrees of seriousness. Closing candy factories, for example, would throw a quarter of a million women out of work. The handling of food became therefore a matter of political tactics.

For various reasons Hoover wished to maintain a $2.20-per-bushel ceiling on wheat. With Wilson's creation of a carefully selected committee provided with specific Food Administration data, he accomplished his goal. The mechanism consisted of an eleven-member Fair Price Committee, chaired by Harry A. Garfield, head of Williams College and a close friend of Wilson. It included a majority of representatives from farm organizations, but with important minority sentiment from labor and the public wanting to check the high cost of living. The recommendation to set the price at $2.20 in the Chicago market was unanimous. According to the committee's chairman, "Hoover had absolutely no part in this matter," but this is only technically correct. The price seemed reasonable to him, and he opposed later increases. The fixed price itself stood 20 cents above the minimum price for 1918 set by the Lever Act and 60 cents above the 1916 average. The income of wheat farmers rose during the war years, and the price was sufficiently high to encourage larger crops in the future.[15]

Without the fixed price speculation would have been uncontrollable, and a rise in the cost of wheat would have brought a sympathetic increase in the prices of other cereals as well as a diminishing of the acreage reserved to them. Hoover argued that without the agreed price the buying power of the Allies could have withheld orders and forced a lower one. Perhaps they could have, but there is no evidence that they thought seriously of doing so. Before the fixed price wheat had indeed bounded upward, but the reason, Hoover said, was competitive bidding among the Allies. He held that the benefit of higher prices went chiefly to speculators who wished to protect themselves in a fluctuating market, not to the farmers who had divested themselves of most of their crop at low prices early in the year.[16]

While the government did not directly impose the fixed price, Hoover had adequate means of enforcing it. He called the millers to a conference at Buffalo and warned that the Food Administration would revoke the licenses of any of them who paid more than the minimum price. He pooled the buying of wheat for the Allies and the military. And he was Chairman of the United States Food Administration Grain Corporation, a government owned firm that President Wilson set up for bringing order into the movement of wheat. This agency displaced a large number of middlemen by limiting the storage of wheat beyond thirty days and prohibiting contracts for sale of flour (known as futures) beyond the same period. The grain chief Julius Barnes, a dealer who by 1917 was the principal grain exporter in the United States, used a government fund of $150 million, and additional borrowings, to buy and hold grain until it was needed domestically or by the Allies. Tom Hall concludes in his study of the Grain Corporation that it "managed prices by astutely and continuously manipulating the wheat market." Its unvarying "fair price" served as the form of insurance for producer, miller, and buyer that hedgings on the market normally provided. Barnes kept the mills operating, unified loading operations, and eliminated the inefficient movement of grain. As a result, twice as much flour was milled from an equal amount of wheat, and the production of grain had tripled by the end of the war. Wilson vetoed bills to raise the guaranteed price of wheat, and, owing to this and the discriminatory treatment allowing cotton prices to rise unchecked, lost the House in the 1918 elections. But after the Armistice the Grain Corporation, against Hoover's desire, allowed the wheat price to climb above $2.20.[17]

Stabilizing the wheat price was the Food Administration's most far-reaching political act; its consequences followed Hoover into the 1928 campaign, when it was charged that he had cheated the farmer by holding it down. During the war, Senators Thomas Gore and James A. Reed—who called the Food Administrator "J. Rufus Wallington Hoover"—made life difficult for him. In Senate committee testimony, Reed elicited some degree of discrepancy between the stabilized wheat price and Hoover's original promise not to permit price-fixing. ("There is no provision for price fixing, and no such thing can be carried out under the bill," Hoover had testified on June 19, 1917.) In response to Reed's charge, Hoover pointed out that the farmers had a voice in the determination. Reed, a lawyer, attempted through relentless and ill-mannered cross-examination to brand Hoover a liar. He submitted data in the *Congressional Record* about "Food Dictator" Hoover, noting for instance that sugar prices had risen after Hoover had taken over his new job. As people like Gifford Pinchot, now of the Food Administration, and Henry C. Wallace of *Wallace's Farmer* would see it, the Iowa farm boy in Hoover had been done in by the mining engineer. Despite the laws giving special interests like the meatpackers "completely into Hoover's hand," Pinchot complained, they suggested their own prices and were pressured only to make changes voluntarily, while the farmer received a fixed price by government fiat. Pinchot was more right than wrong. But as much as Hoover might be enraged by the meatpackers, the success of his work depended on their cooperation. Their monopolistic machinery of production had to be used, and Hoover found himself defending its operation. To the extent that he greatly encouraged wartime production, Hoover perhaps can be held indirectly responsible for some part of the farmers' problems in the 1920's. Possibly that is a reason he later gave them so much attention.[18]

Prohibitionists grasped the value of a patriotic campaign to eliminate the brewing of beer and distilling of liquor as a waste of needed grains. Hoover took a practical but somewhat evasive point of view on this. To the dry Josephus Daniels he said he had always favored national temperance. To Senator Morris Sheppard he wrote that if beer were prohibited, saloons would sell hard liquor from substantial stocks. As a result of Hoover's wishes, the quantity and alcoholic content of beer were limited, giving impetus to the total prohibition that followed the war.[19]

A serious Food Administration problem lay in distribution. Blizzards in January and early February 1918 crippled the nation's railways, and Great Lakes shipping had to be overseen by a mobilization committee. Hoover thought William Gibbs McAdoo a disaster as Railway Administrator, and criticized him until he obtained partial control of McAdoo's work. Daniels believed that Hoover was nine-tenths right in his dispute with McAdoo, but Hoover went too far in one of his blasts and had to apologize. Working with Harry Garfield, now Fuel Administrator, Hoover shut down industry for five days to stop the flow of manufactured goods so that coal could reach waiting ships. "There was nothing to do," wrote Wilson, "but retire to the cyclone cellar," so strong was the outburst of public criticism that followed.[20]

The Food Administration faced no more pitfall-laden situation than in its efforts to stimulate pork prices. Owing to the high price of feed corn, hog stocks had declined in 1917; and yet fats remained a vital need in overseas food. To determine how best to encourage production, Hoover in September 1917 called a meeting of the United States Livestock Committee, which endorsed a principle advanced by Henry C. Wallace, later Secretary of Agriculture in President Harding's cabinet, that the price of hogs would be the sum of the market value of corn fed to them and a reasonable profit. Gifford Pinchot presided over a meeting of Iowa hog producers which recommended a ratio, based on Chicago prices, of 14 to 1 between the price of corn and the profit on hogs. Hoover hoped to secure the voluntary consent of packers to maintain some such price, while Secretary of Agriculture David Houston—himself much disliked by farmers—preferred that Hoover simply encourage voluntary increases in production and regulate packers' profits. Nonetheless, Hoover quickly appointed a Swine Commission that was to investigate the cost of producing hogs.

The chairman, Professor John M. Evvard of Iowa State University, finished his report late in the month, recommending a ratio of 13.3 to 1. The Food Administration, employing control over the buying power of the Allies, the armed forces, the CRB, and the Red Cross, and working through a packers committee, then set stimulative minimum Chicago prices "so far as we can affect them" at $15.50 per 100 pounds. All the buyers for whom Hoover could speak would pay that price. J. P. Cotton, Hoover's Chief of Meats, promised to the extent of his agency's ability a minimum ratio for the 1918 crop of 13 to 1.[21]

In spite of the Food Administration's reasonably swift action, the volatile Pinchot and his co-worker Edward C. Lasater, a Texas stockman, resigned over the treatment they believed the producer was getting from Hoover and his first assistant, the blunt California oilman Mark Requa. Pinchot and his chief did not work comfortably together. Hoover had found Pinchot abrasive in the CRB and the Food Administration, and as director of the federal agency had tried to send him abroad. Hoping to avoid any sort of price guarantee, Hoover had been disappointed at Pinchot's reporting the failure of the campaign to get farmers to increase animal production voluntarily and thought inflationary the 14-to-1 ratio Pinchot brought back from his Iowa conference. President Wilson consoled Hoover about Pinchot's resignation, saying it "always happens" with Pinchot. For his part, Pinchot labeled Hoover "not a real Republican or a real American" and "more autocratic than Mr. Wilson."[22]

Hoover's persisting desire to have the hog farmer accept some of the risk of overproduction was probably a mistake. Wallace wrote him a long letter arguing persuasively that regardless of the individual will of producers, the play of the marketplace dictated a stable price as a spur to production. Experience proved Wallace correct. Hoover came to accept stabilization as necessary, and was thankful that he had avoided calling on Congress over the issue. He despised special pleading in wartime from packers as well as from farmers. At one point he sent Professor E. Dana Durand to tell the packers that if they precipitated a material increase in the price of hogs, he (Hoover) would ask Congress to give him charge of packing plants for the war's duration. He was angry at packers for refusing to take on the risk of stabilizing prices and for making high war profits before the Federal Trade Commission limited them to 9 percent in mid-1918. Requa and the Illinois Food Administrator, Harry A. Wheeler, had overestimated the packers' patriotism, Hoover said in 1920. "A small minority profited, but even if this minority goes unpunished in this world they can never have the pride of having given national service." Pinchot, along with the Federal Trade Commission and many others by August 1918, would have liked the government to take over the packing industry. But

Hoover perceived that the packers, unlike the railroads, were strong and efficient, and that socializing them would be injurious to the war effort. Their abuses called for "permanent legislation," not wartime experiments, he said.[23]

Until the fall of 1918 Hoover managed to hold hog prices within reasonable limits by depressing the high price of corn and by withholding European orders when hog prices rose too much. But in September, exorbitant corn prices forced what may have been a calculated interpretation of the corn/hog ratio by the Food Administration. While Wallace's livestock committee had specified the Chicago price of corn, Cotton's agency directive had not specified, and Hoover was free to predicate a lower cost of production. That this approach was weaseling (Hoover said the Evvard formula was "substantially followed") is suggested by the arbitrary exclusion of Kansas from a list of eight leading corn states, perhaps because of the high cost of corn there. Wallace denounced Hoover for backing down on his bargain; years later his son, Henry A. Wallace of the New Deal, declared that Hoover had acted with integrity. With rumors of peace the price of corn suddenly dived. Now Hoover dropped the ratio entirely, as unfair to producers, and established a price of $17.50 per 100 that was honored from November until the agency's authority expired in early March 1919.[24]

A mixture of voluntary agreements and formal and semi-formal commitments left the Food Administration at the war's end with tremendous quantities of pork in production. Success in stimulating pork production now threatened to overwhelm it. Britain in particular looked to cheaper sources in the Argentine, Australia, and elsewhere as an end to hostilities promised freedom of shipping. At the same time that Britain and its continental Allies canceled their orders, they maintained the German blockade against American imports—despite Hoover's pleas, both practical and humane—to let neutrals ship to the Central Powers. The canceled orders were an effort to prevent quick recovery in Germany. And "Relief," as the historian Gary Best observes, "was something of a misnomer in Hoover's frantic desire to unload high-priced pork and grain (except in the sense that almost all American credits advanced for food were never repaid)." Then it became clear that Britain and the other Allies lacked sufficient shipping and would have to buy from the United States in return for sufficient credits. Hoover lobbied Congress for the $100 million it appropriated for this purpose in February 1919, and Secretary of the Treasury Carter Glass acceded to a liberal interpretation of Liberty Loan provisions, granting sums that represented a disguised subsidy to American farmers. The blatant argument that the food was a military measure against the threat of Bolshevism convinced Glass, temporarily, to extend additional credits far beyond Congress's intent. Whether it was fear of Bolshevism or a desire to get safely over a mountainous economic problem that chiefly motivated Hoover is a matter less scrutable than some scholars have made it seem. As Best points out, "to sell food at artificially inflated support prices on credit terms was clearly a strange and expensive way to use it as a weapon against disorder." Hoover bluffed his way to success by ordering the Grain Corporation in December to buy another 50 million pounds of pork and lard and the CRB to take another 20 million, and more tens of millions for Germany. In the period before the Allies restored their orders and finally ended the German blockade, Hoover had worked out a skillful delaying action.[25]

For months after the outbreak of war, Hoover had tried to avoid placing sugar under government supervision, especially since much of it came from outside the United States. He sent an agent to investigate reported unrest in Cuba, and his agency employed the slogan: "If you have a sweet tooth, pull it." Before a Senate committee in January 1918 he demonstrated detailed knowledge of the movement and costs of raw, granulated, brown, and confectioners sugar; of Cuban, Puerto Rican, Louisianian, and Hawaiian. By mid-1918 the government was limiting sugar sales to 2 pounds in cities, 5 pounds in rural areas, and holding grocery retailers to a profit of only 1 cent per pound. In 1918 the Sugar Equalization Board was created for purchase of the entire Cuban crop, with the power to allocate it among the United States and its Allies. Hoover was its chairman, and it was one job where he had no difficulty acting as dictator. After the war the government, over Hoover's opposition, lifted price controls on sugar; and this, added to postwar demand, sent sugar from about 10 cents a pound to a peak of almost 20 cents after July 1919. To embarrass Hoover, Senator Henry Cabot Lodge forced him to testify on the complex sugar situation before the Committee on Manufactures chaired by his arch-critic, James Reed. The Missourian remarked that Hoover's power during the war had been one "such as no Caesar ever employed over a conquered province in the bloodiest days of Rome's bloody despotism."[26]

Not long before the ending of controls on sugar, the government had relinquished controls of hog prices; here too Hoover had resisted, and again prices rose. The supervision of the economy that war had brought about was passing. Hoover requested funds that would continue some activities of the Food Administration beyond July 1, 1919, when it was to expire; but Congress refused.

Hoover's conduct of the Food Administration would sometimes suggest that his idea of cooperation was to have everybody get together and do just as he said. If he was the ablest administrator since Caesar, Mary

Austin wrote, he acted "wholly in the Caesarian manner, with all the reins in his hands." Even Colonel House, who made a hero of the administrator-reformer, thought Hoover's desire for "complete control" his "besetting fault." Hoover continued to avoid publicity, complaining that "our people have a perfect mania for personalizing everything." The post office, however, knew instantly where to deliver a letter addressed to "The Miracle Man, Washington, D.C." At least in wartime Hoover acted under compulsion to be a sort of dictator.[27]

Reflecting on the war experience in 1924, Hoover told a congressional committee that in wartime, "men must make instant decisions and take instant responsibilities." So for future wars he would have Congress authorize single administrators over munitions, food, fuel, shipping, railways, and overseas trade. Authority must go to the President to fix prices, wages, transportation charges, and embargoes, and to suspend habeas corpus. In war, Hoover observed, "the great bulk of our ordinary safeguards of life must be forgotten. Perhaps the reason democracy won through the last war was its willingness to yield to dictatorship; and the unwillingness of some of our continual allies to yield to dictatorship for periods of . . . one to two years after they had entered the war was one of the causes of its prolongation and enormous losses."[28]

From one point of view, Hoover's work in the Food Administration and in Belgium relief was no more than an extension of the kind of engineering project, turned to economic and social engineering, that had occupied his earlier days. But these wartime activities take on a more complicated meaning in the light of the social philosophy Hoover would one day be shaping. For each of them in its way seems to violate some part of that philosophy: the Food Administration, by mixing compulsion with voluntary effort; European relief, by its implicit acknowledgment that the economy cannot generate out of its own abundance and its more local voluntary agencies the cure for its ills. We may, of course, simply acknowledge that war creates its own special emergencies requiring extraordinary measures, and let it go at that. But it may be more interesting to consider Hoover's wartime activities as against several models of social philosophy to which he may have subscribed.

Hoover had grown up amidst scenes of missionary effort and organized Quaker charity. The Friends have a sense of the world as community—not the complex, hierarchical community subscribed to by, say, Roman Catholic social philosophers, but one more simple and spontaneous in its orderings and its charitable impulses. If any of his Quaker boyhood remained with him, Hoover could have taken to relief as the most simple and obvious moral response to a calamity; and he could have understood the moralistic and hortatory features of the Food Administration as representing the way society ought to think about itself in times of emergency—although war was not precisely the sort of emergency Quakerism was intended to address.

What then of the individualism of Hoover's later social philosophy; how comfortably would it sit with the collectivizing of the massive Food Administration, and, in another sense, that of highly ordered Belgian relief? The individuality Hoover would describe in *American Individualism* (1922) is not a matter of small-scale hardbitten entrepreneurship and property-holding. It is not, to be frank, very clearly described at all. But it seems to have to do with freeing the imaginations of individuals and enlisting their incentives in all sorts of general public projects. Take out the references to capitalism, and give the rhetoric a different ideological ring, and "American Individualism" will sound like the calls to self-help in the service of the nation that we hear in present-day China. And so the sense conveyed by the directives of the Food Administration that the impulse and specific planning for food conservation are to come from specific groups is quite harmonious with the philosophy of American Individualism. And this individualism is not so far from Quakerism.

The unifying element is the engineering. What Hoover would implicitly mean in 1922 by the American individualist was Herbert Hoover; and as acts of initiative, of moralism, and of engineering genius, the Food Administration and Belgian relief were quite consonant with the individualism that Hoover would later more generally be enunciating. The concept of an engineered society that he half articulated—society putting to work its resources of technological knowledge and social sophistication—conveys the impression of individual energies mobilized and efforts gently ordered: a society not unlike that of the Quakers or that of American Individualism. Hoover's voluntarism was, of course, an élitist concept—a combination of the nineteenth-century gentry's noblesse oblige and a romantic view of the twentieth-century professional. Voluntarism brought such representatives of the status quo as Bernard Baruch into government; in turn, business in wartime should accept a lot of guidance. Volunteers lacking financial interest in the products but conversant with business ways were the right people to handle the problem; and those of the World War I generation were assuredly more idealistic and sensitive than more recent crisis managers.

Hoover had been the instigator of Wilson's war cabinet and a member since its first meeting on March 20, 1918. Coming together weekly to coordinate matters related to the war and the economy, and quickly becoming more important than the regular cabinet, this group included Baruch, Edward Hurley of the Shipping Board, Vance McCormick of the War Trade Board, Fuel Administrator Harry Garfield (his office a spinoff from the

Food Administration), and members of the regular cabinet whose work bore importantly on the war. Service on it, like his responsibilities in the Food Administration, kept Hoover attentive to international conditions, and served as a bridge to postwar global problems. In mid-July 1918 he journeyed abroad, taking on the chairmanship of an Allied Food Council that was to anticipate postwar problems of food, clothing, and medical supplies.

VII

~~~~~~

HUNGER

O N NOVEMBER 7, 1918, Woodrow Wilson named Hoover to transform the Food Administration into an agency for the relief and reconstruction of Europe. Once again Hoover had solicited the job. Near the
war's end, he had told Wilson that a capable man should go to Europe for
about a year to take charge of economic rehabilitation.* "I have learned
to value your judgment," the President had said. When Hoover sailed for
Europe on the 17th, he was acting not only as Food Administrator but
also as chairman of the United States Grain Corporation, which served
as the relief's fiscal agent; head of the Sugar Equalization Board; alternating
chairman of the Inter-Allied Food Council; a member of the War Trade
Council; and Commissioner for Relief in Belgium. He would soon become
director general of the American Relief Administration—a technical device
designed to satisfy Congress, which appropriated $100 million for it on
February 24—economic director of the Supreme Economic Council, chairman of the European Coal Council, and head of the European Children's
Fund. While not a formal member of the Peace Commission, he said he
dealt "with the gaunt realities that prowled outside," and frequently advised Wilson and others on a full range of matters economic and political.
Hoover was assigned rooms with the peace delegation at the Hotel Crillon.[1]

Hoover himself termed the undertaking a second American intervention.
Now the object was the economic rehabilitation of a ravaged and disordered continent, to "save life and prevent anarchy" while the peace was
being negotiated. The means amounted to joining the economic strength of

* Hoover hoped for a quick end to the war, having no patience with those who wanted
"a triumphal march down the Unter den Linden."

the United States to what remained of Europe's. This Wilsonian dream required, as Hoover later put it, the imposition in certain regions of "absolute dictatorship over economic forces," and the virtual control of the world's food supply enabled him to do this. The economic organization of Europe proceeded under Hoover's direction while the talk at Versailles dragged on. By this second intervention, the United States, Hoover said, "saved civilization." He was so proud of this work—saving 100 million lives, he calculated—that he came back to the period in two books, *An American Epic* and *The Ordeal of Woodrow Wilson*.[2]

Hoover brought with him to Europe, as the historian Michael Hogan points out, certain convictions: that in an interdependent world, economic power must come under some guidance; that an absence of economic cooperation leads to war; and that excessive intervention by government in the economy also dangerously politicizes international affairs. And he was convinced that American capitalism—the same system that had carried him to great personal wealth—would be a great liberating element, raising standards of living throughout the world. His aim was not to assure large export markets; he wished to limit United States exports to 10 percent of the gross national product. The chances of war, he felt, would be reduced by selling and buying on roughly equal terms.[3]

Running his own organizations on precedent, he urged Wilson to forget about turning the League of Nations Covenant into a "constitution for the human race" and to make it simply an international forum. Perhaps even more than Wilson, Hoover looked to the League as a means of remedying wrongs in the Versailles Treaty. He also advised Wilson and Colonel House not to underestimate the opposition of Allied reactionaries to their kind of peace; he warned the President about "second story men." By June Hoover had criticized Wilson severely on the Versailles Treaty, and was dropped from the staff of presidential advisors. The reparations it exacted would lead Germany to either reaction or Bolshevism, he warned; and in Germany's behalf he observed that there was no recognition of the sea rights of neutrals in wartime. Hoover, like House, had urged Wilson not to come to Europe at all.

The Allies were unwilling to endorse an independent American relief agency, fearing it would weaken their position in negotiating the peace and securing trade advantages. But Hoover, who could not bear to work with the "pinheads of bureaucratic Europe," opposed European control. He wanted the United States, as the provider of food and credits, to hold full sway over postwar rehabilitation (and thereby political control): "We can use our resources," he wrote to a receptive President, "to . . . maintain justice all around." A board composed of only one nationality would impede efficiency; one of four different nationalities, with all the centrifugal forces involved, could mean only disaster. And since the United States was contributing 95 percent of the food for relief, it was Americans who should supervise and determine its distribution. It was absurd to let the purchasers, who were buying mostly on credits, have a dominant role in price and distribution. Hoover also believed, like the American general Tasker Bliss, that food distribution should be designed to strengthen Wilson's hand "in securing from the European Allies agreement to the things we want to obtain at the Peace Conference."[4]

After some two weeks of fruitless discussion in London, Hoover accused the Allies of using "the pressure of starving millions in Europe and the American desire for their relief in the general trading which they propose to open with the President." He went on to Paris and simply informed the Allies that because of the emergency he was beginning relief operations. In late December 1918 ships were entering the Mediterranean en route to Trieste. At Allied insistence there came into being the Supreme Council of Supply and Relief that would show a united front to the defeated enemy; but Hoover managed to retain control by ignoring it. He soon ceased attending its meetings. American taxpayers, he explained, would support the relief only if it were known as an American project. Despite an obvious need for Allied cooperation, Hoover termed the council "a futile chatterbox." It was supplemented and then replaced in February—when the imminent removal of the blockade required more centralized power—by the Supreme Economic Council. Lord Robert Cecil understood very well that Hoover, because he thought Cecil cooperative, wanted him as Britain's representative on the council. As director general of the food section, Hoover managed to dominate the new council by choosing its staff and by sheer force of knowledge about the economic affairs of Europe. When he found himself restrained as Director General of Relief, he could act as Food Administrator and report directly to the Big Four.[5]

Hoover pieced together the economic reconstruction of Europe with typical cold aggressiveness. He helped to secure government credits for the Allies, and infuriated Treasury Secretary Glass, who complained more than once of Hoover's "unbridled extravagance." His mind always ran toward administrative simplification, and he opposed government censorship. For much of southern and eastern Europe Hoover coordinated the distribution of food and the means of financing its purchase, restored to useful service river craft and rolling stock, took charge—or attempted to— of ports and canals and traffic on the Rhine, the Elbe, the Vistula, the Danube, rebuilt telegraphic and postal communication, renewed coal production for homes and industry, eradicated much contagious disease including typhus, and arranged barter where food could be moved in no other way. He coordinated Congress, the Treasury, the Shipping Board (where he could), the armed forces, and his own food agencies. Anyone who wished to communicate among European countries had to do so through Hoover. The first American Relief Administration (ARA) mission was established at Warsaw on January 4, 1919. During the following week, missions were set up throughout northern, central, and southern Europe and the Near East, extending from Helsingfors and Copenhagen in the north to Trieste and Salonika in the south, and to Tiflis in the east. Hoover also issued a special appeal for American funds to keep European universities functioning.[6]

Hoover's subordinates often matched him in their capacity to display initiative. To most of them he explained that "there are four Associated Governments [in Paris], that each one of them has seven different Departments who are interested in every commercial transaction between enemy and Allied territory . . . it is far better that you should give directions and make arrangements locally yourselves than to refer up here or to the various governments for detailed approvals, as you can be sure that the people will be dead before the approvals can revolve amongst these 28 departments." The most Hooverian operator, perhaps, was Colonel William B. Causey, a roughneck Westerner who took orders from no one except his boss. When a line of soldiers with bayonets halted a train at the Yugoslav border, Causey got out, parted the bayonets with his hands, and beckoned the locomotive on. "They didn't know what to do with that kind of man in eastern Europe," James Shotwell admiringly observed. By taking direct action, Causey solved many problems utterly unsolvable by the parties themselves, quickly obtaining much of Germany's rolling stock and promises from reluctant leaders to return locomotives and cars crossing borders. Colonel W. G. Atwood summed up the staff's attitude on the meddlesome Allies in a note to Causey: "We have, however, in the past broken most of the laws that existed." Another ARA man stepped in and arranged a truce between two warring eastern European tribes. Still another, A. Conger Goodyear, needed authority in Upper Silesia. Hoover replied that there was none available and "proposed that I manufacture my own," as Goodyear remembered it. So he composed two telegrams for Hoover to sign, telling Berlin and Warsaw he would soon be in Upper Silesia as representative of the Inter-Allied Commission (which no longer existed) and requesting the opposing military forces to withdraw behind lines which he determined. Hoover signed the telegrams, grinned, and said: "It's all right if you can get away with it," which Goodyear said he did. Later, when Goodyear experienced more trouble, Hoover supplied him with a letter to the prime minister of each country he dealt with, alternatively threatening a cessation or promising an increase in food delivery, depending on the country's cooperation over coal supplies. Goodyear's work resulted in the establishment of the remarkable European Coal Commission, an organization that might have brought about a European economic community had it not broken up after the Americans left.[7]

Hoover showed up at his Paris office each morning, pockets stuffed with all sorts of memoranda written on dinner menus and newspaper margins— assorted scraps of paper containing ideas that sometimes became life-saving operations. When the Supreme Economic Council opened a debate on ways and means to send ships down the Danube, Hoover announced he had been running craft there for two weeks. He arranged the exchange of two Austrian locomotives for two million eggs from Galicia. He accepted IOU's made out to him personally. The revered diplomat Henry White praised Hoover for running communications, shipping, railroads, for showing outstanding administrative ability, and for choosing able subordinates. Colonel House, himself an expert diplomat, also commented favorably on Hoover's work, as did Lloyd George, Norman Davis, Vance McCormick, and more; all of these, however, qualified their praise in one manner or another.[8]

Hoover's work was complicated by a problem that originated in his wartime role of Food Administrator. Having guaranteed pork prices and being charged with enforcing the congressional price of wheat, he now had the task in Europe of disposing of huge agricultural surpluses resulting from plans to support a war lasting into 1919. On December 31, 1918, after the United States Treasury refused a major loan, Great Britain, desiring to recapture its foreign trade, canceled its food orders, threatening to buy more cheaply from distant sources such as Australia and the Argentine. The other major Allies followed, and Hoover approached apoplexy. But the continued scarcity of ships necessitated purchase from Hoover in any case, and his promises to farmers were soon fulfilled. Edward Hurley of the Shipping Board wanted to use most American ships to encourage domestic manufacturers to compete in world markets. By late March 1919, once the blockade of Germany was lifted, Hoover got all the shipping he needed, driving Hurley to a nervous breakdown in the process.[9]

His activities complemented those of the peace negotiators. He was obligated particularly to protect the newborn democracies being carved at Versailles out of the carcasses of the Austro-Hungarian and Russian empires. Without food in these countries there would be anarchy and revolution, which in turn would prevent the distribution of food. Hoover's policy, therefore, was generally to support existing governments.

It has been charged that he withheld food to discourage the advance of Bolshevism in eastern and central Europe. Fear of that movement pervaded Versailles; it was the first significant, tangible challenge to international capitalism. When the peace conference opened, Bolsheviks were extending their power into eastern Europe and Germany. And the Allies, including the United States, were confronting Bolshevism in Siberia and Archangel in 1918 and early 1919. Thorstein Veblen called containment of Bolshevism "the parchment on which [the Treaty of Versailles] was written." No doubt, Hoover was hostile to Bolshevism; so was Woodrow Wilson, and every major statesman at Versailles. "As a tyranny," Hoover wrote to Wilson, "they have resorted to terror, bloodshed, murder to a degree long since abandoned even amongst reactionary tyrannies." It is naïve to express surprise that anything besides humanitarian motives should have entered Hoover's mind in 1919; Hoover never thought that way, and most assuredly not about a continent he knew to be seething with economic and political rivalries. But if he were placed in a spectrum of anti-Bolshevism, he, like General Bliss, would fall near the center, with David Hunter Miller representing the most inflexible position and William Bullitt the least. But even Bullitt had written, before the Armistice, a State Department memo on the use of food in stabilizing European economies against Bolshevism. Congress and, particularly, Treasury Secretary Glass were receptive to anti-Bolshevik sentiment, and the Americans in Paris played it up to obtain government grants and credits, most notably the $100 million loan for relief in January 1919. Hoover did use food to establish order and allow peacemaking on a Western style to proceed; he was under great pressure to use food as a political weapon, given the Big Four's lack of any other anti-Bolshevik strategy. But his most blatant employment for political purposes of his control of food distribution was in fact for the displacement of a reactionary Habsburg monarch, Archduke Joseph of Hungary.[10]

Hoover's dealings with Bolshevism in 1919 were complex. At least up until 1917, no régime in Europe had been so abhorrent to him as that of Imperial Russia. The Revolution, Hoover said, was "spiritual," and in December 1917 he told Josephus Daniels that he expected to see Russian laborers acquire more widespread ownership of property. In a speech after the war, he suggested that revolutions might be necessary in parts of Europe for the attainment of justice. Revolution was coming of the war: the "inequalities and injustices of centuries" became unendurable with its added burdens. The weakened governments freed the masses to respond to "great theories spun by dreamers to remedy . . . pressing human ills." In a letter of March 28, 1919, suggesting a scheme for feeding Russia, Hoover told Wilson that military intervention in Russia would do "infinite harm," since emotion will "ferment and spread under repression." The letter counseled patience in dealing with Bolshevism. "The American people," he observed, "cannot say that we are going to insist that any given population must work out its internal social problems according to our particular conception of democracy." Hoover believed, in fact, that Bolshevism had not the soundness to survive and would soon collapse.[11]

Yet he wanted the West to turn revolutionary Russia from interference abroad. The postwar problem in Europe, as he discerned it, was to maneuver between "warding bolshevism off on one side and reaction on the other in order that the new born democracies could have an opportunity of growth." His proposal to Wilson—which was similar to an idea Wilson himself had held a year before, and to plans of Vance McCormick, Colonel House, and William Bullitt—was for a "second Belgian Relief Commission for Russia" that would supply food in exchange for an end to all hostilities with other nations and all subsidies of unrest in eastern Europe. The plan did not "involve any recognition or relationship by the Allies of the Bolshevik murderers now in control any more than England recognized Germany in its dealing with the Belgian relief." Nor did it require any withdrawal of foreign troops from Russian territories. "From a political point of view," Hoover said, "the urgent necessity of setting up supplies need not be placed on a higher plane [than] to stem the tide of Bolshevism."[12]

Having obtained Wilson's approval, he went on to present his plan to the Allies. He gave his motives as "solely humanitarian and entirely non political." They were something more than that. Wanting to contain a Bolshevism that would spread disorder in the countries he wished to feed, Hoover desired also to restrain the Allies from invasion—a military enterprise that would require aid from the United States, since Great Britain was the only European country not effectively bankrupt. Churchill and other leaders did want to invade. Hoover's plan got an enthusiastic reception. The hitch was that the White Russians under Admiral Kolchak were winning some victories. Foreign Minister S. M. J. Pinchon of France complained that it would be "a moral and material reinforcement of the iniquitous Bolshevik government"; similar charges were to be made against Hoover's feeding scheme of 1921 to 1923. His response was that the plan would give surrounding states a respite from aggression and would illuminate the weaknesses of Bolshevism.[13]

In April 1919 the Council of Four endorsed the plan for a neutral Commission of Relief, putting it under the explorer and diplomat Fridtjof Nansen of Norway. Even then Hoover had difficulty in getting his offer delivered. Georges Clemenceau promised Hoover that the message would be beamed to the Soviet Union from the Eiffel Tower radio station; it never was. Finally, after considerable delay, Dutch diplomats got it through. In May, Grigorii Chicherin, the Commissar of Foreign Affairs, declared that the Soviet Union would not accept political demands parading as humanitarianism. Chicherin asked Nansen to meet with him directly so that they might work out an acceptable relief plan. Nansen eventually provided modest quantities of food and clothing through an international commission supported by various groups, but the general poverty of Europe after the war precluded any substantial degree of help. Under State Department orders, Hoover fed White Russian civilians in Riga (Latvia) after the Bolsheviks withdrew in May 1919. But he "did not like the looks of the expedition against Petrograd" conducted by the Whites, he would later claim.[14] And in February 1920, Secretary of State Robert Lansing would record his disagreement with Hoover's desire to raise the trade blockade against the Soviets, which would help feed both them and many central Europeans.

Socialism, Hoover believed, worked in wartime because of "the great patriotic impulse of war," along with the contributions of expert managers. But he had little confidence in the system and expected the fall of Bolshevik Russia imminently. Once war ended, he explained, "the normal day-to-day primary impulse of the human animal took over"—that is, self-interest for himself or his family and home—with a certain degree of altruism, varying with his racial instinct and his degree of intelligence. Socialism, in short, wrecked itself on the rock of production. Without rewards for individual initiative, production would inevitably slacken. Socialism merely replaced a monied with a bureaucratic aristocracy that ignored comparative abilities. Hoover's analysis neglected the difficulties of postwar scarcity of raw materials, the changing to peacetime production, and the political rearrangements of Versailles. His benign vision of capitalism emphasized that its basis was not "taking advantage of other persons"; rather, it aimed through specialization to increase "the total and variety of production and secure its diffusion into consumption." Thus, "we often lay too much emphasis upon its competitive features, too little upon the fact that it is in essence a great cooperative effort."[15]

The establishment on March 21, 1919, of Béla Kun's Bolshevik government in Hungary, which much alarmed the statesmen at Versailles, threatened Hoover's goals of restoring trade among nations, efficiently ordering transportation over national boundaries, and producing coal for the transport and supply industry. The internal dynamics of Bolshevik economic theory plainly militated against the repair and reconstruction of democratic systems. Kun was a student of Lenin sent back to his native Hungary and supplied with Russian gold. Like Ho Chi Minh in Vietnam some years later, he effected a compound of nationalism and communism, and quickly became the object of Allied intrigues to depose him. Marshal Foch wanted war; Hoover opposed it, saying, "We should probably be involved in years of police duty," and would be "a party to reestablishing the reactionary classes, which would give our soldiers Bolshevik ideas." Most of Kun's difficulties came from within, stemming from clashes among leftists and from his own dogmatism. Recently historians have come down hard on Hoover for not feeding Hungary during the period of Kun's ascendancy. But toward Kun's régime, as toward that of the Russian Bolsheviks, Hoover's policy was in fact surprisingly temperate.[16]

Well before Kun, the American Relief Administration had estimated Hungary's food needs as far less pressing than those of neighboring countries such as Austria. So no ARA feeding of Hungary had occurred before Kun came to power, and the country had actually exported some food. Hoover told a congressional committee sitting in Paris that with food in Serbia 60 miles south and in Rumania 80 miles east, the United States should not send shipments from 4,000 miles distant.[17]

After Kun took over on March 21, Hoover continued to allow Hungary to purchase food outside its borders and permitted more than one trainload to reach Budapest. He told Wilson on that date that he preferred any combination of democratic and Soviet government to Allied occupation. The "provisioning of Hungary should go on," he said a week later, "so long as no excesses are committed by the Government. . . . If the feeding of Hungary were put on this basis and dissociated from all political interest except the one requirement, it would do more than anything else to hold this situation in check." General Tasker Bliss agreed with Hoover. Some members of Hoover's ARA staff such as Claire Torrey also opposed military intervention in Hungary, although most, like Joseph C. Grew and Captain T. T. C. Gregory, advocated it.[18]

Hoover's principal aim was to distribute the coming harvests across Hungary's strategic railway system and down the Danube. In an April 3 telegram to Gregory, Hoover advised not only sending all food shipments to Hungary that had been paid for, but also maintaining "a thin stream of food which we will for the present charge to the President's fund, subject to ultimate arrangement for payment." By mid-April, it increasingly troubled Hoover that Hungary should be treated similarly to other countries, since this might encourage Bolshevism elsewhere. Soon he secured Wilson's consent to a plan—never implemented—to send food into Hungary only in exchange for that country's cooperation in supplying other lands. Inter-Allied commissions working in the area could establish economic relations with the Hungarians. This "side entrance" might open the river and railroad lines. Hoover admitted that this action could strengthen Kun, against whom the Allies had now instituted a food blockade; he then suggested that Kun might remain in power so long as he could attribute all hardships to the blockade. Hoover suggested another scheme to Secretary of State Lansing:

supply food and police the country with neutral troops, though he admitted that this would probably be unacceptable to Kun.[19]

By early June, Hoover's opinion of Kun had fallen precipitously. The Hungarian leader had used Russian funds to proselytize for industrial centers outside the country, which might add to the disorder and the decline in production that were Hoover's main problems. The régime had carried out hundreds of political executions; Kun had purchased munitions and artillery from Italy; his armies threatened to link up with Russia's Red Army through Galicia; he had doubled his troops beyond Armistice terms; above all, the Hungarian revolutionaries had turned to violence and threatened to overflow their borders, and this posed an "economic danger to the rest of Europe." Now Hoover endorsed Gregory's thinking and began toying with the notion of allowing eager French divisions into southeast Europe to effect Kun's overthrow. So, "much as I dislike to suggest it, I can see but one solution and that is for the French troops which are now in Jugoslavia to advance on Budapest without delay. Otherwise, it appears to us, that both the Czecho-Slovakian and German-Austrian Governments will surely fall." The Hungarian régime had become a "tyranny of the minority."

But Hoover quickly reversed himself on military intervention and became its staunchest opponent before the heads of delegations in Paris. In a memo of July 17 to General Bliss he again presented opening the Danube and vital railway lines as an alternative to overturning Kun's government by force, which he termed "military interference in the internal affairs of Europe." Military interference, he now realized, would destroy Wilson's grand vision and his own program for a liberal, economically restored Europe.[20]

In an article written some time later (which evoked Hoover's dissent) Gregory remarked that "way down in my heart [I was] also fighting Bolshevism," and of that war observed that "bread is mightier than the sword." Gregory tried in mid-July to convince Hoover to support a *coup d'état* being planned by a defecting General (or Lieutenant) Boehm. Hoover would at first have nothing to do with private parties; but he became interested when Boehm promised to establish a leftist social-democratic government and pledged to open food distribution routes, and he passed the proposal on to the Big Four, who, however, lacked troops to use against the Hungarians. Georges Clemenceau asked Providence to provide a solution. Hungary, meanwhile, had invaded Czechoslovakia, and Rumania had attacked Hungary with great success, ravaging the land. When Hungary withdrew from Czechoslovakia according to an agreement with Rumania, the latter refused to pull back in turn. The heads of delegations promised an end to the Supreme Council's food blockade if a new government should come to power in Hungary. Kun then fled to Russia in a largely peaceful overturn by the trade unions, whose government Hoover termed "relatively radical." Without sufficient military strength, the major powers had employed Hoover's control of food to stop the advance of Bolshevism in central Europe.[21] But Hoover, to his credit, had resisted some of the arguments made familiar in a later generation under the rubrics of containment, the domino theory, and the role of world policeman.

Hoover became angry at the plundering Rumanian army, which, he said, even stole food from a children's hospital and was thus responsible for the death of eight youngsters there. A coup in August by the Habsburg Archduke Joseph, supported by certain British and French elements, took place while Rumanians trained machine guns on the building where the Hungarian ministry sat. Hoover believed the Hungarians would prefer Kun to Joseph. The Bolsheviks, he said, could now justly claim that the Allies were reestablishing "reactionary government in its worst form."[22]

Hoover telegraphed Frank Polk, acting for Wilson after the President's departure for home: "Do not believe that we can permit Hapsburg government to continue but not prepared to say now what steps we should take." Polk, fearful of the Bolsheviks coming back, complained to his diary: "I told him we were trying to get the Archduke out slowly, but Hoover said he was for prompt action." Polk was willing to allow the archduke to run in an election. On the same day, Hoover practically gave orders to Polk:

[Archduke Joseph's] recognition and encouragement by British General Gordon is the worst thing. . . . Did the British authorize this? If not, replace Gordon by Admiral Troubridge who has some sense. If . . . Commission would demand Archduke's retirement and the formation of a ministry representing labor and socialist middle classes and peasants it could be done easily.

And he told the Council of Five: "I consider that the American Army fought in vain if the Hapsburgs are permitted to retain power." Finally, he sent an interview to the United Press saying that he would resign and have nothing to do with the American Peace Conference unless the Hapsburgs were cleaned out. *The Nation* editorialized: "Bravo, Mr. Hoover! It is beyond the endurance of any red-blooded American to see his Government tolerate the restoration of the Hapsburgs, as the United States entered the war to banish from the world that for which the Hapsburgs and the Hohenzollerns stood."[23]

Hoover got his way. It was, as the *Literary Digest* remarked, an "almost singlehanded performance." With the permission of the Big Four, he sent by way of his Food Administration wires a telegram to Gregory to present to the archduke, saying that the powers refused to recognize him. Gregory replied with a secret message in American slang: "Archie on the carpet at 7 P.M. Went through the hoop at 7:05 P.M."[24]

Austria was another country whose cities particularly were in desperate need of relief. Vienna, Hoover explained to the Paris congressional committee, was "a population based upon an empire, with the empire cut off . . . the financial and economic center of a very large area, and contained a largely centralized government, with a great mass of civil employees. . . . We have here a large idle population of some 2,000,000." Austria would one day become part of Germany again, he argued. The Austrians in their desperation for food proffered their national gallery of art in exchange. Hoover refused the offer and drew food from Serbia and Hungary in the early winter of 1919. Since the terms of an amendment introduced by Henry Cabot Lodge prohibited direct loans to former enemies, $45 million of United States funds had to be filtered in through the Allies. During the Kun régime Hoover, with Wilson's permission, got broadsides distributed on May Day through Vienna: they proclaimed, "Any disturbance of public order will render food shipments impossible and will bring Vienna face to face with absolute famine." He later claimed that this tactic had kept a centrist government in power. "Food is not politics," Hoover observed in 1920; but inevitably it was.[25]

Italy, one of many countries to use food as a political weapon, obstructed the sending of supplies to Austria and the rest of central Europe from the crowded port of Trieste and across a single railway. The Italians promised in January to dispatch 30,000 tons, but sent only 4000. They were attempting to force the English government to furnish them with ships, coal, and money. In February 1919 Hoover urged Wilson to withhold credits to Italy until the food got moving. "The uses to which the blockade on foodstuffs is being put," Hoover said, "are absolutely immoral." And "the stoppage of American foodstuffs to starving people cannot be used as a political weapon." Prodding from the Italian prime minister Vittorio Orlando finally sent food moving eastward in March, when the Allies agreed to mediate disputes between Italy and Yugoslavia. When Yugoslavs would not pass on food to Serbian regions, Hoover refused food to Yugoslavia.

His ultimate aim was to stimulate the independent initiative of peoples rather than to "nurse them through all sorts of difficulties." American resources could not be stretched that far; the congressional appropriation of $100 million became part charity, part revolving fund. But the Treasury itself was already having to advance credits in excess of $1 billion. Hoover especially resented aid given to warring nations; for, as he put it, every dollar of food gave them a dollar of military equipment. Thus, each country

took over the transportation and distribution of its own food through existing political structures. This would enable the ARA to concentrate on
stimulating their commercial life and solving their international monetary
and supply problems.[26]

Hoover was moved by the plight of Russian prisoners-of-war in Germany. At Christmas 1918 he wrote to the State Department: "The most
terrible suffering in Europe today is that of the Russian prisoners in Germany and Austria and enroute home. They are dying wholesale." The
Quaker War Secretary, Newton Baker, flatly turned down Hoover's plea
for helping the prisoners. When France also refused to help, Hoover arranged to borrow food from United States army stocks and charged it to
France. In the months that followed, Hoover was persistent about the care
of these prisoners, although many continued to die. Here, as with many of
Hoover's plans, there was also a tactical consideration: he feared that the
Russians, as they were released and wandered starving eastward across
Poland, would be drafted into the Bolshevik army. Partly through his ef-
forts, the situation was finally relieved during the spring.[27]

When an invitation came from the postwar German government to negotiate with Dr. Reith and Baron von der Lancken, who had earlier hindered Belgian relief efforts, Hoover rebuffed them in December 1918 with
the widely quoted "You may tell the pair to go to hell with my compliments." This remark, which was published in George Sylvester Viereck's
American Monthly and elsewhere, was used against Hoover with German
voters in the 1928 presidential campaign. Yet Hoover worked for a speedy
fulfillment of the Allies' Armistice agreement to end the blockade against
Germany. The Allies threatened to boycott his surpluses if Germany were
restored to economic health too soon. According to Jane Addams, who
went to Europe to promote the feeding of Germany, Hoover's offices in
Paris were about the only place she could obtain a hearing. She was
pleased that Hoover persuaded United States Navy ships to feed Finland
in spite of the blockade.[28]

Lifting the blockade speedily was partly a matter of self-interest, since
large food surpluses were awaiting shipment in British warehouses. As
Hoover's friend Norman Davis put it on January 3, 1919: "[it was] difficult sometimes to draw the line between the requirements for relief and the
requirements for an outlet for the surplus." Hoover also portrayed a united
Germany as a bulwark against Bolshevism. He warned repeatedly and no
doubt sincerely against the Spartacists, who in January were gaining
strength in German cities. He was also aware that Germany had gold with
which to buy surplus American food. Hoover accused the blockade of forcing a worldwide speculation in commodities that was driving up the cost
of living in the United States and elsewhere, as well as risking an agricul-

tural collapse once the blockade should end and Germany prove unable to absorb the foodstuffs that had been gambled on. Sporadically, the Allies declared the blockade ended. They did so in late December 1918, then in March 1919 with the Brussels agreement, whereupon Hoover quickly shipped in food before it was paid for. He boasted to Wilson of getting food in two weeks early by "anticipating." Closed again in late June, Germany was not permanently opened to freighter commerce until July, after it had accepted the peace terms.[29]

At first, Hoover did not believe that American charity for Germans was necessary—beyond the countless sausages, butter, and lard that poured in from the Milwaukee and Yorktown post offices after the blockade had ended. He thought that German efficiency would bring quick recovery, and he did not anticipate the "hideous piece of bad faith" by which the Allies would not compensate Germany for their use of its fleet after the war. By the fall of 1919, however, moved by the desperate plight of German children, he had changed his mind.[30]

Hoover relied largely on the American Friends Service Committee (AFSC) as the vehicle for dispensing relief to Germany. With 250 years of American ancestry and an enviable reputation for probity, the AFSC was above reproach. Hoover generally minimized his relationship to German relief, fearing that it might do injury to his other appeals, but in November 1919 he did accept co-chairmanship of the Quaker program. "The United States," he said, "is not at war with German infants." The money, it was believed, would come chiefly from German-Americans, with the ARA seeing to purchase and transportation. Rapport failed to develop, however, between Hoover and the ultrasensitive German community in the United States. He was still touchy toward Germans; and the attitude of Viereck's *American Monthly* that Germany, vanquished but brave, deserved the "best treatment possible" grated on him. Viereck, for his part, labeled Hoover a "philanthropic prig." Jane Addams reported that Chicago Germans were angry at having to work through someone so prominently identified with the war, but that the use of Hoover's name quieted criticism from non-Germans. He allowed the AFSC to serve as a buffer between the ARA and the German-Americans. His chief interest, in any case, was not in soothing them but in making relief of Germany palatable to the American public at large. To *McClure's Magazine,* tales of German misery constituted a "smokescreen behind which the former empire . . . is busily evading its responsibilities"; and the newly formed American Legion disrupted a Los Angeles concert and other activities designed to raise funds for German relief. German contributions proved comparatively small alongside those that Americans of Polish, Yugoslav, or Hungarian extraction sent to their ancestral homelands. Hoover quietly transferred $5 million of ARA funds to German relief. And Germany came under the ARA charity program launched in December 1919, which realized $29 million; this fund was administered under the European Relief Council for the feeding and medical care of European children. Hoover also argued vigorously against the displacement of ethnic Germans into neighboring countries, declaring that this would provide fuel for future wars. He opposed as well leaving Germany with any substantial army, encouraging the survival of the military caste system.[31]

Poland, the neediest of the European countries Hoover served, captured the American imagination. Here the plight of children was most pathetic. For Poland the great pianist Ignacy Paderewski had played and lectured throughout the world for years. And Poland was soon fighting the Bolsheviks.

Hoover and his associates had a large presence in postwar Poland. They first concentrated on removing German opposition to shipping food down the Vistula; substantial shipments began in mid-February. But Germans in Silesia interfered with the distribution of food and coal, as did the continued existence of the blockade against Germany. In January 1920, with the help of the new American envoy, the equally indefatigable Hugh Gibson, Hoover forced the Socialist Józef Piłsudski to appoint Paderewski as premier in the government; the United States then became the first nation to recognize the new Polish state. Piłsudski and Paderewski he regarded as "two out of the six or seven great idealists of the world." Hoover demanded and got an independent American commission, which at his suggestion included Henry Morgenthau, to investigate the slaughter in Poland in April 1919 of some 280 Jews, in an incident connected with hostility to Bolshevism. While the anti-Semitic implications of the incident may have been somewhat exaggerated, the spotlight Hoover placed on it may have mitigated the very serious problem of Polish anti-Semitism. (Gibson himself was a vicious anti-Semite, though apparently somehow unaware of the fact.) When Hoover drove his private car to Poland by way of Austria in August 1919, a crowd of five thousand schoolchildren marched by, repeatedly singing "The Star-Spangled Banner." Some caught an astonished rabbit in the roadside grass and brought it to him; Hoover wept at their exuberance. At about this time, he had insisted that fund-raisers "rigidly suppress the use of my name" in the work of the American Child Health Association then being started at home.[32]*

---

* When Lenin and Trotsky invited neighboring peoples to join the Soviet Union in international communism, the Red Russian army advanced westward early in 1919. Hoover's child relief work, which continued into 1920, no doubt aided in Piłsudski's ultimate victory over the communists.

The technical advisors who served in Poland, starting in 1919, were part of a new and private American Relief Administration that came into existence on July 1 of that year, after congressional authorization for the old agency ran out. Hoover employed his dominating position over the exchange of money to coerce Poland, Austria, Czechoslovakia, and Yugoslavia into accepting technical assistance. It was part of his overall plan to foster trade among nations.[33]

Except in Yugoslavia, the technical advisors strove to exercise a neutral role in building up war-torn economies. In Yugoslavia, Colonel Atwood was of assistance in lending his railroad skills, but, as Gary Best points out, he was "ever alert to possible opportunities for American capital and American sales." Atwood planned for Western Electric to rebuild the telephone and telegraph system and for United States Steel to replace railway and highway bridges. The coordinator of the technical advisors' project, James Logan in Paris, tried to restrain Atwood's unabashed economic imperialism, but complained that "it is pretty hard to drive a nail in oak." Hoover at least once looked a little like Atwood. Writing to Bernard Baruch about Rumania, he warned of an Anglo-French group seeking oil rights there. United States companies should have a share, he said, "if we are to continue to make advances to Rumania." In most of the countries involved, the ETA program bore resemblances to President Truman's Point Four program. Similarly, Colonel Causey's European Coal Commission prefigured somewhat the European Coal and Steel Community after World War II.[34]

The European Children's Fund did what UNRRA would accomplish a generation later. Cooperating with this private charity's state-by-state organization at home were the American Friends Service Committee, the Federal Council of the Churches of Christ, the Jewish Joint Distribution Committee, the Knights of Columbus, the Red Cross, the YMCA, and the YWCA. Beginning in 1920, Hoover played one nationality against another in an effort to raise $33 million. With his series of "invisible guest" dinners —an extra place set as though for a hungry child—and with the help of General Pershing and many others, he raised almost $30 million for the children of Europe. The work kept him in Pullman cars for some sixty nights. The feeding of the children thus extended into the early 1920's, particularly in Austria and in Poland, by then recovering from the war with the Bolsheviks. In an effort to bring back school life, food was distributed in schoolhouses. Hoover insisted that his work with children was largely a preventive health measure and denounced "sob stuff" like pictures of dying children. But as typhus began to move westward from Russia, the ARA distributed millions of tons of soap and underwear and disinfectant against the lice that spread it. Even with children's relief, Edgar Rickard noted that a grateful generation would later become natural economic friends with the United States.[35]

The United States delivered *in toto* about $5 billion in American food to Europe. Much of the money was in loans, since, Hoover said, lavish charity is "highly detrimental to the development of initiative and a sense of responsibility." But private and government contributions made up a substantial amount. Most went to Allies: $1306 million to the United Kingdom, $1289 to France, $800 to Italy. Belgium got $697 million and Germany $294, Poland $201, Czechoslovakia $115, Austria $145, Russia $63 (after 1920), and Rumania $53. The ARA's own deliveries were chiefly distributed to central Europe. Hoover went through his documents in the 1950's to write his history of the relief, *An American Epic:* they breathed "the awakening of the kids from lethargy to chatter" as "my tendrils of memory began to clothe [the papers] with life." The story of American relief, he wrote in his *Memoirs,* would constitute the unwritten third volume of Frank Norris's great epic of wheat—not in Norris's "despairing tones of tragedy" but in those of triumph. Had Norris lived, "he would have found this—'The Song of the Wheat'—a theme in the world's regeneration."[36]

Hoover in 1919 offered his long-term solution for European reconstruction. Attacking massively "demoralized productivity" and advocating "a better division of the profits," he rejected revolutionary experimentation because there was no margin for it. Europe also had to avoid militarism, inflation, and discriminatory national policies. If it did, American capital could be used for economic rehabilitation. Hoover attempted to form an International Economic Council pending the establishment of the League of Nations. After losing out to the Treasury Department and to British intransigence in his recommendations, he turned to launching the Foreign Trade Financing Corporation under the Edge Act. The scheme to make safe private bank loans of $100 million would avoid statism yet offer centralization. It would be American capitalism's answer to Bolshevism. Wall Street, however, would not cooperate, and Hoover instead worked toward the same ends through the Harding administration while he was Secretary of Commerce. No wonder that he later found the seeds of world depression in the turmoil of the Versailles peace.[37]

THE GREAT Soviet famine of 1921 to 1923 had its origins in three years of struggle against Germany followed by three years of civil war. The disruptive economic policies of the Bolsheviks produced additional disorder; Allied intervention and a severe drought in 1921 made the situation acute.

Without international aid "the government will perish," Lenin wrote that March. Almost a year before, Hoover had issued a press release that showed a close knowledge of the Russians' desperate situation:

Today three-fourths of their railways and rolling stock are out of operation. The whole population is without the normal comforts of life; the cities are plunged into the most grievous famine of centuries. People are dying at the rate of hundreds of thousands monthly from disease the result of underfeeding. . . . The function of the town and city to provide manufactured goods and other comforts in return for the produce of the land has entirely disappeared.

Such, Hoover went on to say, are the results of socialism or of any system in which there is lack of equality of opportunity or freedom to compete.[38]

On July 13, 1921, the Soviet writer Maxim Gorky issued a plea to the world for food and medicine. Hoover, now Secretary of Commerce under Harding, promptly responded as head of the American Relief Administration with demands, as a condition of food aid, for the immediate release of seven American political prisoners and the freedom to move about in Russia for his ARA representatives. The Soviets replied that they wished to meet for an accord. There followed a "dialogue by proxy" in which at each stage Walter Lyman Brown, ARA director for Europe, acted under specific directions from Hoover, and Maxim Litvinov spoke for Lenin. The agreement, signed on August 20 after ten days of strong debate, outlined conditions for Russian relief similar to those under which the ARA had operated in Europe: freedom for Hoover's people in the selection of personnel, areas, and method of operation. Hoover agreed, however, that the Soviets could check on political and commercial activities by ARA employees, both American and Russian. Earlier he had cabled Brown about the importance of keeping out of Russian politics: "our mission is solely to save lives." When a woman complained in a public meeting that August about relief aiding Bolshevism, Hoover leapt to his feet and angrily banged on the table: "Twenty million people are starving. Whatever their politics, they shall be fed!"[39]

The Bolshevik régime had cause to be suspicious of Hoover's motives and those of the ARA. The Commerce Secretary's sentiments toward the régime were well known. And the influence of the ARA, most particularly in Hungary and Vienna, had aided democratic capitalism. Hoover's European Children's Fund had distributed food, clothing, and gasoline to the Menshevik resistance in the offensive against Petrograd during the summer and fall of 1919; and in the summer of 1920 it had fed Polish children while Russia and Poland fought. But the ARA in January 1921 did give funds to the Quakers for their relief activities in Russia. As Secretary of Commerce, Hoover stated his strong opposition to recognizing the new

Soviet state and expressed doubt that it had worthwhile goods to trade. The Bolsheviks were not ignorant of Hoover's personal business enterprises when he had invested before the war with Leslie Urquhart in Kyshtim and elsewhere. But once the ARA men in the Soviet states demonstrated their efficiency in food distribution, suspicions receded.[40]

As head of the Russian relief operation, Colonel William N. Haskell, a West Point graduate with a distinguished war record and earlier ARA experience in Rumania and Armenia, had established a reputation for getting things done without involvement in politics. Perhaps because he was a military man used to accepting orders, Haskell throughout the twenty months of relief in Russia continued to work under the close direction of Hoover and Brown. Although Haskell and the men in the field frequently made important decisions, Hoover received reports regularly from special investigators: Frank Golder, Lincoln Hutchinson, Harold Fisher, and many others. He also met frequently with representatives returning to the United States who brought news about conditions and ARA activities. While Haskell took care of the day-to-day dealings with the Soviets and ARA representatives, matters of principle or major problems that threatened the flow of food and its proper distribution usually went to Brown and Hoover.[41]

The initial ARA food ship, the S.S. *Phoenix,* docked at Petrograd on September 1, 1921; it brought 700 tons of balanced rations to a city whose death rate had risen sharply. The first feeding kitchen opened on September 7. The big problem was sending food to the Russian interior. Connections between port and rail lines were often nonexistent. Food reached Moscow from the Baltic via Petrograd in one to four weeks, although passenger trains made the trip in fourteen hours; one train, carrying forty-three cars of food, took one month to get from Odessa to Simbirsk, 1500 miles away. Rivers and roads were often impassable in the winter and sudden spring thaws flooded roads and waterways alike. When requests for aid came to Moscow headquarters, an ARA special investigator went to the area to meet with local officials for determining anticipated crops, numbers of children to feed, available hospitals or shelters for children, total population—all the statistical data necessary before the food distribution could go on. Usually the basic findings were wired to Moscow and within days an ARA representative was present to secure an abandoned restaurant or open a closed school for a feeding station, and to hire local workers who would supervise, distribute, cook, and manage the kitchen. Many died from starvation before ARA assistance could come, but it saved millions.[42]

Among the motives that have been ascribed to Hoover for offering relief to Russia was that of helping American farmers to get rid of their surplus corn. And this strategist, who in a philosophical way liked to perceive concurrences of morality and self-interest and in practice knew something about managing people, did indeed use the fact of the surplus to obtain congressional approval of funds for the ARA. But it is not easy to say whether his own thoughts were on unloading the surplus, or on manipulating Congress for the sake of the hungry, or both. He also used the shipping lobby to promote Russian relief. We have seen his attempt, in 1919, to trade relief for a modification of Bolshevik foreign policy. But the simplest explanation for Hoover's response to the famine is that he had been, for several years, an administrator of world relief; his conscience, compassion, workmanship, and pride were now fully committed to this task.

Golder and Hutchinson give an idea of the conditions the ARA encountered. In Simbirsk, six hundred sickly children in a receiving home lay three and four together to a cot with one blanket. In Odessa, one entire floor in a children's home had been ripped out for fuel, which was so scarce that many who did not starve froze to death. Bread was commonly a mixture of 20 pounds of crushed dry clay with 10 pounds of flour. Typhus was only one disease to reach epidemic proportions. In the Ukraine the chief hospital in Elisabetgrad was poorly equipped and badly managed, "inexpressibly dirty and foul-smelling," itself a breeding house of disease. On a trip to the Urals and Caspian, the American organizer at Orenburg confronted thousands of Polish war refugees huddled in boxcars in the railway yards, waiting to be repatriated; hundreds died before the train pulled out. Filth of all kinds lay embedded 6 inches deep in Orenburg's streets, breeding rampant disease. Human beings ate dogs and cats. There were numerous cases reported of murder for cannibalism, the meat of the victims being used in sausages.[43]

At home, Hoover drafted two memoranda for President Harding to approve, one of them assigning the United States Grain Corporation to act as purchasing agent for the ARA and transferring to the ARA some $12 million in funds left over from the war years; the other, an order making the ARA the sole agency for accepting and distributing food to Russia from America. The Soviets deposited a total of $10 million in gold in the United States for the purchase of grain; the Ukrainian government deposited an additional $2 million. Hoover realized that funds were needed immediately. There was no time for public solicitation, especially when America itself was in the midst of a depression and an appeal through the European Relief Council for some $30 million for European relief had just been completed. He had Harding recommend that federal funds be appropriated for Russian relief, and Congress approved $20 million. One month later the President signed an additional bill authorizing $4 million in army medical surplus for use in Russia. Working through the ARA were the American Red Cross, the Jewish Joint Distribution Committee, the Federal

Council of Churches, and the Young Men's Christian Association. These and other organizations raised several million dollars in public appeals.[44]

Hoover had faced difficulties at home with the American Friends Service Committee. In January 1921 he had given $100,000 of ARA funds to the AFSC for food and medical supplies to be distributed in Moscow. Hoping to get supplies to political prisoners through the Quakers, he urged them to seek the release of American prisoners in exchange for relief. They refused, preferring not to mix politics with their work. When the ARA was offering to work in Russia, the Soviets wanted to continue the arrangements made with the Quakers in the distribution of food; yet Hoover's effort, far wider in scope, had its own system long practiced in Europe. He asked the Quakers, already active for over a year in Russia, to work through the ARA. But they feared that the scheme would compromise their ability to secure funds and to work directly with Soviet officials; and English Friends with whom the American Quakers worked believed that alliance with the ARA, given its quasi-political reputation, would do damage to the "moral and spiritual values" of Quaker work. The two groups compromised by restricting Quaker relief to specific areas.[45]

A greater complication arose when Hoover discovered that certain Friends were supporting the Russian Red Cross, an arm of the Soviet government that had attacked Hoover and the ARA as politically motivated. After an exchange with Rufus Jones, chairman of the AFSC, Hoover apparently realized that the Quakers had no intention of backing such propaganda against himself or the ARA. "If there is anything in which I have implicit confidence," he wrote Jones, "it is the right-mindedness of the people with whom I have been born and raised." Still, he carried resentment. Various liberal papers and magazines criticized Hoover and questioned his motives while praising the work of the Friends. One such was *The New Republic,* which, in a series of articles, claimed that Hoover had used food as a weapon to weaken Communist control in Hungary during 1919, and lauded by way of contrast the methods and motives of the Quakers.[46]

Hoover had some trouble when, at a time private agencies were still campaigning for funds, he announced that poor transportation in Russia precluded the consignment of additional food. Some suspected him of cutting down on the food distribution purposely in an attempt to weaken the Soviet government. But Walter Lippmann in the New York *World* answered that attack in some detail. The real problem, as Lippmann pointed out, was that thousands of tons of food awaited train transport inland from the already crowded docks.[47]

Radical relief agencies gave Hoover additional problems. Walter Liggett, the American publicist for the Soviet-supported American Committee for

Russian Famine Relief, wrote a series of letters to President Harding, requesting a personal interview so that he might explain his agency's purpose and connections. Liggett, whose committee had enlisted support from several prominent politicians and religious leaders, accused Hoover of working to discredit the organization. The FBI soon uncovered a large discrepancy between the funds collected and the actual relief sent; much of the money was used for Soviet propaganda in the United States. Liggett charged that Hoover was using relief for political ends, but Hoover could well have made the same accusation against Liggett.[48]

The Soviet government, in desperate need of machinery and other goods, calculated that it could export grain from its 1922 harvest in exchange for manufactured goods if the ARA continued to serve the famine areas. Hoover objected to supporting the Soviet state in this fashion, and at least partly for that reason he declared that he hoped to stop aid to Russia after the harvest. Liberals and humanitarians attacked his decision. Walter Duranty of the *New York Times* predicted a new famine and stated that 7 to 8 million people were still in want. Hoover realized that if the ARA pulled out completely, children would starve. Mainly because the Russian government had cut back its own efforts and thereby increased the need, he decided that relief could extend through the following spring. In the meantime, private agencies were calling for another fund appeal. Hoover indicated that he would not object to a public drive for funds if the Soviet government would not export the grain it had planned to trade for manufactures. He threatened to release correspondence revealing the character of the Russian plan. There was no appeal.[49]

Hoover never formally advocated recognition of the Soviet Union, but most Russian commercial leaders were anxious to set up trade and even political relations. Toward the end of their stay in Russia, ARA men like Haskell, Golder, and James Goodrich all came to believe that diplomatic and economic relations with Russia were desirable and that trade agreements should be tried experimentally. In the spring of 1923, disagreement developed on this matter between Hoover and his directors. On his own initiative Haskell called for foreign financial aid and economic assistance to Russia outside of the ARA; Goodrich advocated formal recognition; Golder wanted a commission from Russia to survey possible trade areas in the United States. In an open letter to C. V. Hibbard of the YWCA, Hoover gave a detailed response to all these suggestions. Russia, he argued, had nothing of value to trade or export, and its manufacturing was almost at a standstill at the same time that the drought had brought almost total crop failure. Hoover had his way against recognition and trade. President Harding issued a statement to this effect, dated July 31, 1923, which Hoover had helped to prepare.[50]

The feeding of Russian children, according to a detailed report Hoover submitted to Harding, worked through nearly 18,000 stations set up by ARA personnel who never exceeded 381 Americans, most of them volunteers. The Soviet Union paid for all expenses within the country, such as internal transportation, storage, and salaries of Russian workers. The ARA only distributed food that could be eaten at the feeding station and only to those who showed undernourishment. The majority of those fed were children and the sick. In twenty-four provinces the ARA took care of 10.5 million people; five thousand institutions were supplied with medicines as well. Eventually over $60 million sent more than 700,000 tons of commodities to Russia.[51]

What seems most impressive about the ARA operation is that the organization managed to keep close and strict management. Almost daily reports came in, giving details of food supplies, anticipated food needs, numbers sick, numbers being fed. Most of the ARA men lived in boxcars while on tour, and two died of typhus. How did these people come to volunteer? Half had served under Hoover in earlier relief work, the other half had received military training. Hoover carefully chose as administrators experienced and knowledgeable men such as Golder and Hutchinson who had lived in Russia and studied the nation's history, and others like Haskell with a reputation for efficiency and results. James Goodrich tells of traveling through the Berkshire Mountains with his wife after his gubernatorial term in Indiana and receiving from Hoover a call to Washington:

I went to see him and he told me to go to Russia.
"I don't know anything about Russia," I told him.
"That's why I want you to go," he replied.
I felt that appealed to me a hundred per cent, and asked if he had any instructions. No, he had none; he depended upon others to use their heads. So I went to Russia.

Hoover never went to Russia during the relief. The administrators, including Haskell, came to New York to consult with him.[52]

On July 18, 1923, at a banquet given for Haskell and the ARA directors, a scroll was presented which read, in part:

. . . in the name of the millions of people who have been saved, as well as in the name of the whole working people of Soviet Russia and of the Confederated Republics and before the whole world, to this organization, to its leader MR. HERBERT HOOVER, to its representative in Russia, Colonel HASKELL, and to all the workers of the organization to express the most deeply felt sentiments of gratitude, and to state, that all the people inhabiting the UNION OF SOCIALIST SOVIET REPUBLICS never will forget the aid rendered to them by the AMERICAN PEOPLE, through the agency of the AMERICAN RELIEF ADMINISTRATION, holding it to be a pledge of the future friendship of the two nations.

The scroll was signed by Lev Kamenev, acting president of the Council of the People's Commissars; N. Goburov, chief of the Administrative Department; and L. Foticf, secretary of the Council. A further effect of the ARA's work was one that neither Hoover nor the Bolshevik régime would have wished to acknowledge: the organization, George Kennan has said, "importantly aided" the revolutionary government, "not just in its economic undertakings, but in its political prestige and capacity for survival."[53]

VIII

PROGRESSIVISM AND THE PRESIDENTIAL CAMPAIGN OF

1920

Hoover, said John Maynard Keynes—who proved a severe critic of both Woodrow Wilson and Lloyd George—was the only man who emerged from the ordeal of Paris with an enhanced reputation. . . . This complex personality, with his habitual air of weary Titan (or as others might put it, of exhausted prize fighter), his eyes steadily fixed on the true and essential facts of the European situation, imported into the Councils of Paris, when he took part in them, precisely that atmosphere of reality, knowledge, magnanimity and disinterestedness which, if they had been found in other quarters also, would have given us the Good Peace.[1]

Hoover arrived in New York on September 13, 1919, telling reporters he never cared to see Europe again. (Like Jefferson and Franklin, as he saw more of other countries, he became still fonder of his own.) Wilson fell ill a fortnight later. And since many of the President's renowned wartime administrators, such as William Gibbs McAdoo, had returned to private business, Hoover almost alone remained as a prominent spokesman for the grand and optimistic vision that had commanded the national rhetoric during the war. He was "the biggest figure injected into Washington by the war," wrote Louis Brandeis.

To many Americans during these postwar months, Hoover became a vehicle for the idealism the conflict itself had been too brief to spend. For he represented a contrast to Wilson that pleased anti-Wilsonians: this hard-headed moralist was a perfect antidote to the abstract moral rhetorician that Wilson was now perceived as. After his outstanding accomplishments at home and abroad, Hoover's reputation for being the "Great Engineer"—the practical idealist—took firm hold in the public mind.[2]

Hoping for a rest from public service and for time to get reacquainted with his family, Hoover went home to Palo Alto. For nearly six years he had been away and had been apart from his wife and children for most of that time. He announced he would not answer the phone, speak publicly, or read letters longer than one page. Mrs. Hoover, celebrating the release from public life, directed the building of a modern house in the Hopi style. But Hoover, still deeply involved in the rehabilitation of Europe, undertook the job of vice-chairman (and often acting chairman) for Wilson's Second Industrial Conference, which began in December. The American Institute of Mining Engineers had already named him its president. In 1920 he presided at a number of dinners for the "invisible guest" represented by the empty seat and candle at the banquet table— the dinners that raised almost $30 million for the European Children's Fund he headed. And it was at this time of enormous prestige that Hoover proceeded to make some of his most extensive social commentary.[3]

"A society's inspiration," he wrote in 1919, "is individual initiative. Its stimulus is competition. Its safeguard is education. Its greatest mentor is free speech and voluntary organization for public good. Its expression in legislation is the common sense and common will of the majority. It is the essence of this democracy that progress of the mass must arise from progress of the individual." The teaser is that "voluntary organization for public good" dropped so assuredly in with the rest. "I believe we in America are developing a new economic thought, a new basis of community action . . . cooperation," he wrote elsewhere.* It was American individualism that had awakened this communal spirit, which was revealing itself in a striking increase in cooperative bodies—the American Federation of Labor, the Chambers of Commerce, farmers' organizations, professional groups of engineers, lawyers, doctors. These agencies possessed institutional lives quite apart from that of Congress but were still subject to regulation by government. And the American people themselves, Hoover believed, rejected social Darwinism in favor of cooperation. One important point here is that idealism can originate in self-interest: community awareness grows from communal organization. Hoover was the engineer improvising, always improving and progressing. As technology makes for better living conditions, so can society improve itself.[4]

The problem is not that Hoover was mistaken in believing individualism

* This is a recurrent theme in American history. Alexis de Tocqueville 150 years ago described the spontaneous working of a creative public spirit as a unique feature of the American system; he was referring to the many outlets for personal caring and concern. John Gardner of Common Cause wrote in 1978: "If, in a local community, a citizen becomes aware of a human need which is not being met, he thereupon discusses the situation with his neighbors. Suddenly a committee comes into existence. The committee thereupon begins to operate on behalf of the need and a new community function is established."

to be conformable to cooperation. Even if the concept of individualism is left with its narrower connotations of competitive self-serving, it could be partially accommodated to the kinds of organizations Hoover referred to, insofar as these represent the self-interest of their members and have also a stake in good relations with the rest of the country. That this tactical associationalism may be part of what Hoover was getting at is suggested by his argument that a cooperative program for rationalizing the schedules for producing bituminous coal could free more than 100,000 people for work elsewhere. It is implied as well in his proposing for cotton, which was then sclling below par, that planters and bankers get together with the government in providing European countries with credits necessary for buying the cotton they so badly needed. But Hoover knew in any case that human nature is a mixture of self-interest and altruism—the dominant impulses being selfish, he said; and some of the properties he discerned in people—a desire for self-expression, a wish to be adulated, a pride in service—are motives simultaneously of self-interest and of involvement in community, a fact that Hoover likely also recognized.

Hoover's progressive American individualism, he said, meant the guarantee to all of equality of opportunity—the "fair chance" of Abraham Lincoln—so that the individual's place in the world would be determined by intelligence, character, ability, and hard work at the emery wheel of competition. To keep the system open, to discourage the formation of classes, and to protect the infirm, Americans also practiced "neighborly obligation and a higher sense of justice . . . self-sacrifice and . . . public conscience." Private enterprise worked as a vital, innovating force; but government had to eliminate greed and assure social justice. Public opinion —what is fashionable—corrects wrongs as do legislative provisions. In America each person strives within a competitive society; the crowd does not build. Only a few meritorious individuals reach the pinnacle where those of highest capability make the most important decisions. But each person can achieve happiness through personal accomplishment accompanied by a sense of service. Ruthless individualism untempered by a sense of community is destructive and must be eliminated by education or restrained by law; equality of opportunity is the "negation of class." Reaction deceives the people through subtle obstructionism and progressive platitudes. Hoover called for "pioneers" to invade "continents of human welfare of which we have penetrated only the coastal plane."[5]

So Hoover gives us little to dispute. And that is the real problem. Ideas flow together: we see no particular motives in their stubborn separateness, or in their difficult conjunctions; nor are we invited to think about the political and cultural strategies for selecting among them or harmonizing them. Hoover's ideas reflect well the particular experience of individualism that was most available to him—his own confident, repeatedly successful, inexhaustible energy, which grasped for wealth, poured itself into a problem in technology or administration, wrote tracts on individualism, and rescued the starving. He evidently felt no reason to distinguish the acquisitiveness from the desire for admiration, the public morality of service from the private morality of excellence in workmanship, to look at each in its distinctness and to puzzle at how they went together. What we have, particularly in *American Individualism*—a compilation of statements, most of them from the immediate postwar period, that Hoover published in 1922—is a prose that blurs edges and unites opposites by proclamation. And his commitment to the engineering ethos would further complicate matters.

Although, as Hoover said, there had figured in his own life a "vast preponderance of the commercial over the technical," he was powerful within his profession. He had joined the American Institute of Mining Engineers in the 1890's and over the years had repeatedly published in its journal. He later made substantial financial contributions to the institute. While in London he had organized American engineers, and he drew heavily on this group in the war relief; all but one of the several American relief directors in Belgium were engineers. In 1919 the American Institute of Mining and Metallurgical Engineers elected Hoover its president. In November of that year he became head of the new Federated American Engineering Societies (FAES), "created," he observed, "for the sole purpose of public service." Conservative engineers liked Hoover's rhetoric about individualism and the evils of socialism; progressives saw in him an aggressive planner. For the solving of industrial problems he turned to his professional constituency. He spoke of the "objective" scientific engineers, free of bias, who stood "midway between capital and labor." With their "training in quantitative thought" and their "intimate experience in industrial life," they could assist in building "a bridge of cooperation." During Hoover's presidency he refused to allow the FAES to join the United States Chamber of Commerce. Engineers could subtly calculate the proper length of the working day, considering not only strain but the need for "recreation, family life, and leisure for citizenship." Coordinated engineering projects must now replace haphazard development with its great speculative profits. Professionals could organize water and rail transport, provide future resources of fuel, conserve coal, oil, and timber, plan for irrigation and the reclaiming of land, and develop and distribute electrical power. Hoover proposed that the government investigate the possibilities of establishing "a great electrical trunk line throughout the great power consuming districts of the northeast," the line to draw power generated at coal mines and water sources. A few years later he urged a "superpower project" to join the nation's power systems into one giant network. The engineer, according to Hoover, "dissolves monopolies [through advancing technology] and redistributes the wealth [by mass production]." The engineering function, as Edwin Layton has observed, worked as a "sort of social catalyst"; "We had better reduce the volume of science" in the curriculum, Hoover said, "to make room for some stimulation of their public relationships." He urged the engineer to "come out of your shell," take classes in public speaking, and speak out on public questions.[6]

Hoover could have drawn from his own experience had he chosen explicitly to connect his idea of individualism and voluntary organization to his idea of engineering. He knew how large an opportunity the field afforded for craftsmanship, for private, imaginative speculation, even for frontier adventuring; and he had worked in projects requiring free cooperation among specialists. To perceive the whole modern technological complex as a vast workplace gathering independent artisans would offer a useful antidote to laments about collective enslavement to the machine. If individualism and voluntarism are still possibilities, they must be reconciled to twentieth-century technology in its other character: centralizing, disciplining workers into industrial armies, not obeying the whims of its attendants but imposing the inexorable commands of mathematics, the sciences, the principles of matter. Modern technological or administrative systems *may* seek and educate ability; provide a liberating abundance; recognize how greatly individuality depends on cooperation and fellowship; and make of twentieth-century technical imperatives a schooling and a discipline. But these possibilities Hoover does not discuss, or at least not with care.

So the grand sentiments of his prose give us no convincing inquiry into just what individualism is, morally and psychologically, or how it can be congenial to cooperation, or how the precise orderings that engineering effects can co-exist with either. But his pronouncements, in posing these quarreling goals, expressed a robust, balanced progressivism that over the years would make a partially successful attempt to articulate itself in specific programs.

The United States just after the war entered a time of confrontation and social violence. During the winter of 1919, Seattle suffered a general strike; a bomb scare occurred about May Day—thirty-seven prominent citizens were sent incendiary missives by mail; race riots in Chicago and elsewhere killed dozens of people; in September the Boston police struck; and major strikes occurred that fall in the coal and steel industries. In 1919, 3374 strikes took out four million workers. Angry Americans blamed the Bolsheviks for the unrest. Elsewhere in the world there was real revolution. Over the years, businesses associated with Hoover's own career had come under attack from revolutionists. It was the importation of Chinese labor into South Africa that gave Gandhi his first radical leanings. Sun Yat-sen often cited the Chinese Engineering and Mining Company as an example of European aggrandizement; and Stalin spoke of the massacre of 213 workers by owner-hired mercenaries at Russia's Lena goldfields as the single biggest incitement to revolt.

For all he knew, Hoover said, the European revolutions were essential historical events. As for the troubles at home, he preferred a piecemeal approach to change. He objected to "the transgressions against real civil liberties by the use of war powers in peace such as injunctions against strikers, nontrial by jury of Reds, action of Albany legislature [in refusing to seat duly elected socialists], etc." Europe had proved repression inherently self-defeating, leading to resistance and instability. Likewise in America, the source of postwar violence lay in prewar inequities. Hoover did suggest that port authorities should check on incoming Bolshevist agents. But, rejecting the notion that Bolshevism lay behind domestic unrest, he set about to aid in finding conciliatory solutions.[7]

President Wilson had called representatives of labor, capital, and the "public" to meet in Washington during October, but the steel strike prevented any agreement then on the questions of unionism and collective bargaining. The Second Industrial Conference met on December 1, 1919. By President Wilson's instructions it was to accomplish "a genuine democratization of industry, based upon the full recognition of those who work." The principles to be followed were those that the League of Nations Covenant had laid down, which demanded good wages, equal pay for men and women doing the same work, limitations on child labor, freedom to associate, and a forty-eight-hour week. Hoover provided quarters in the Food Administration building; and for about a third of the time, in the absence of Secretary of Labor William B. Wilson, he led the meetings. Among the other members were the Sears philanthropist Julius Rosenwald; Henry M. Robinson, previously of the Shipping Board; Owen D. Young of General Electric; and former Attorney General George Wickersham (who opposed trade unions), all of whom Hoover would later call into public service. Hoover, an observer remarked, was perhaps the "foremost" figure in the meetings. One participant described Hoover and Young as being "for pretty sweeping reforms." Hoover's most insistent advocacy was of a Federal Employment Service, a Department of Public Works, and a Home Loan Bank. And he viewed the root problem under discussion as the inequitable distribution of income between capital and labor.[8]

The meetings continued until March 6, 1920, when in a report written largely by Hoover to the ailing President—who took no subsequent action —the conference endorsed the forty-eight-hour week, a minimum wage, equal pay for men and women, prevention of child labor, improvement in housing, and "promotion of the insurance principle, and for converting Liberty Loan savings into some form of annuities." It concentrated on establishing procedures for the settlement of industrial disputes. It proposed shop committees within factories that would speak for employees and meet regularly with management; these were to be sharply distinguished from company unions. The report also called for a nine-member national tribunal representing capital, labor, and the public. But the core of its program was a regional machinery of arbitration. Twelve regional boards of adjustment, composed of employers and workers, would meet with aggrieved parties. If one of the two sides to a conflict agreed to accept the unanimous opinion of an appeals board, that party could have a seat on an investigatory board that would possess broad powers of subpoena; if both agreed, the initial board would become a collective bargaining agency. Such procedures promoted the recognition of labor unions. Legally binding arbitration would take place only when both sides requested it. In the absence of an agreement on the part of both contestants to abide by a board's solutions, the system would rely on the publicizing of findings that would be founded in expert testimony. Publicity, said Hoover, meant the "enfranchisement of public opinion as a force for settlement." Compulsory arbitration, then under experiment in Kansas, would not work since it ultimately resulted in a minimum wage for all industries, and workers would usually be paid the minimum. "If a court may control wages," Hoover further observed, "it will in effect control industry and in the end [by destroying competition] stifle it."[9]

Hoover was attached to the principle of collective bargaining, which suggests other forms of peaceful talk and agreement that this heir to Quakerism espoused: the national conference, an instrument that he would make much use of both as Secretary of Commerce and as President; and a League of Nations that (in an alternative version he proposed) would consist of one representative of each member country and would meet daily, sitting under obligation to discuss every issue before the body until it should reach an accord. He had a humanitarian concern over the physical deprivations of labor: he proposed government credits for homes, complained of "industries in which we find inhuman hours and conditions of labor and living," and called for some mode of profit-sharing and for "provision against unemployment and the terror of illness." He urged job insurance of some variety as both a safeguard against suffering and a bulwark of social stability. But he made a special point about giving labor a place of larger dignity and more positive will in the industrial system, and it is probable that he valued collective bargaining for this as well as for its more utilitarian advantages.[10]

Acknowledging that shop committees were no substitute for unions, Hoover nonetheless liked these local collective bargaining units for being on a scale that allowed immediate participation and held promise of making capital and labor a community. Perhaps he was attracted more to the democratizing of corporations—or at least to a system in which workers would support and help to implement managerial reforms—than to the establishment of countervailing power in unions. One of Hoover's best-known speeches, delivered before a frosty Boston Chamber of Commerce audience in March 1920 and containing a much-quoted warning that "there is no surer road to radicalism than by repression," made some of those pleas for an easing of material hardship, but put much of its thematic emphasis on the question of the place and stature of labor. Industrial unrest, Hoover argued, expressed a desire not only for better wages and hours but for "a larger and more organic influence in the processes of industrial life"—"the contribution of the worker's intelligence to management," he wrote in italics elsewhere. He stressed the need for "actual organization" in big industries that would "reproduce the mutuality of interest and sympathy" between employer and worker "that existed in the smaller units of years ago." He urged that workers have "unrestricted opportunity to discuss and make recommendations on the conduct of the business." Here we have Hoover's concern with tangible community—something he knew to be impossible with the concentration of power in government or business. In "The Paramount Business of Every American Today"—a title that says as much about his style as about the stature he had attained in the public view—he wrote:

We are wasting our time if we think of the human relationships in industry only as matters of wages or hours or unwillingness to work as compared with a former willingness to work. In that view we are treating labor as a "commodity" —the employees of the country are looking for a position of right instead of a position of consideration; that is, they want their rights instead of benevolence. Exactly what these rights are . . . is our largest national problem.

Hoover visualized a future in which "those who work with their hands will obtain a larger proportion of this world's goods and those who work with their brains will obtain less."[11]

One interesting by-product of Hoover's FAES work was a closer relationship with the AFL's Samuel Gompers. The two met to discuss the plan of a young engineer, Robert B. Wolf, to bring order to industrial relations. By publicizing facts relating to all industries, Wolf believed, engineers could correlate the production processes. Hoover extended the discussion, proposing that savings from more efficient work might go to unemployment and sickness insurance. The program harmonized with the study of waste in industry initiated by the FAES. Unions, under Hoover's plan, would have to increase productivity and allow shop committees in exchange for management's recognition of labor and acceptance of collective bargaining. While the industrial conference met, Hoover spoke to groups of businessmen, urging closer liaison with the AFL; "the idea got a very cold reception," one industrialist recalled in his memoirs. The association with Gompers continued when Hoover became Secretary of Commerce.[12]

Hoover persuaded the American Engineering Council, set up in January 1921 by the Federated American Engineering Societies, to undertake a study of waste in industry, a "survey," he called it, that "will attempt to visualize the nation as a single industrial organism." Edward Hunt, director of the project, was identified with the scientific management theories of Frederick Winslow Taylor, and the study was termed "a clear presentation of the Taylor program." Hunt praised Hoover for bringing Taylor's principles to the national level. Hoover himself characterized a shift in scientific management from its prewar concern with the minutiae of shop and office routine to "broad questions of policy-making." The fifteen engineers who conducted the study aimed, in Hoover's estimation, to improve living standards for poorer workers by increasing production; here were echoes of Walter Weyl or Simon Nelson Patten. It concluded that management was responsible for over half the waste, while labor accounted for less than a quarter. Employers denounced both this study and another Hoover had inspired that condemned the twelve-hour day for steelworkers as inefficient. The American Institute of Mining Engineers withdrew from FAES in 1922 over the report attacking the steel industry. The trade journal *Industrial Management* complained that the waste study contributed to "the spirit of class antagonism." The popularity of engineering progressivism had already declined rapidly late in 1920 when the FAES voted down organizational reforms; the engineers later attempted to dissociate themselves from the study. Hoover remarked: "Maybe we will have to wait for the death of some of the older members."[13]

Nowhere does Hoover appear more subversive of upper-class interest in this period than in his ideas on taxation. Believing the distribution of wealth to be more unequal than was necessary for stimulating enterprise, he argued that the income tax began too far down on the scale of income and amounted to a tax on necessities. He would tax high incomes more heavily: the rich must come to see the bearing of a heavier burden as a social duty. He also advocated a steep graduation in inheritance taxes, contending that the tools of production should go to the person or agency most fitted for their use, not to a relative or friend. "The ruthlessness of individualism" had caused unjust amassings a wealth. He urged a swift redistributing of "the larger industrial accumulations . . . that our rapid development has made possible." Besides taxes, a "larger representation of all elements of the community in the control of the agencies" of economic domination could redistribute the nation's wealth.[14]

In this postwar time the nationalist Hoover was vigorous in his loyalty to Wilsonian internationalism. The "justification of any rich man," he observed at a New York State Chamber of Commerce meeting, "is his trusteeship to the community for his wealth"; "the justification of America . . . is her trusteeship to the world-community for the property which she holds." Noting a growing European bitterness toward the United States, he lectured: "The money which has come to us . . . is money in trust, and unless America recognizes this trust, she will pay dearly and bitterly for its possession The requital of the obligation which comes with riches . . . should not be alone her duty, but should be her crown." The war had put the ideal of service to international works and Hoover hoped that this expanded awareness would persist into the postwar period.[15]

He must have seen in the activity of the League a microcosm of the work he had been a part of as a member of the fourteen-man Supreme Economic Council. There for some seven months he had labored by persuasion with representatives of major countries toward peace, stability, and the solution of enormous logistical problems. He became a forceful member of the League to Enforce Peace, a pressure group for ratification of the Versailles Treaty, and on October 28 argued unsuccessfully in its executive committee against reservations. Slowly alienated by President Wilson's intransigence in the face of powerful political opposition, Hoover by the end of 1919 had abandoned his earlier stand, and observed that the "whole process of peace has been necessarily one of compromise." Yet he was one of the last pro-League Republicans to accept reservations, and did so only out of political necessity.[16]

Hoover's argument when he did come around to rejecting Article X of the Covenant, which committed member nations to some sort of united response to aggression, was of a piece with his larger reasoning for the League itself. The article could involve the United States in armaments and bloody international adventure. Nations "become aggressive largely through the permanent military class that grows out of the maintenance of large armies and navies—a reduction of armament would directly lessen the influence of these groups who are themselves the cultivators of war." Without disarmament Americans would have to "tax ourselves a couple of billions a year and enter a race of preparedness."[17]

Economic strategies dictated entry into the League. Though he later supported membership in the Reparations Commission, Hoover opposed

American engagement in commissions set up under the Treaty of Versailles, since they worked for European self-interest. But he warned that with the United States outside the League, it could become "a political league against us, for we are the creditors of the world today." Peace was good business, Hoover demonstrated in urging ratification of the Versailles peace—which also meant acceptance of the League. Without peace, the United States could not supply monetary credits to Europe. Without credits, Europe could not purchase raw materials for industrial production, and without credits or production, Europe could not buy United States agricultural surplus. While consumers deserved relief from high prices, too hasty a slackening would hurt the American farmer.[18]

Hoover believed the League to be a means of protecting and encouraging the spread of democratic institutions patterned on those of the United States. He shared in the large notions Americans had of their country's benevolent importance. Had America not entered the war, he maintained, German-dominated autocracies would have swept over Europe. As a result of United States intervention, the soundness of its democracy had influenced countries like Finland, Estonia, Lithuania, Czechoslovakia, and Bulgaria in the building of their new governments. Hoover counted the governments of England and Italy among those liberalized through the American example. He did in fact have some experience in bringing the American example to another people. The pianist-politician Ignacy Paderewski—whose 1894 visit at Stanford had been arranged by Hoover as a young geology student—imported a few American political institutions into Poland, with some guidance from Hoover. And from January 1919 until that year's harvest, the Poles were supported by American food. Hoover spoke of America's obligation to Thaddeus Kosciusko and his corps of engineers, who had helped in the American Revolution. "Are we really to say that our job is complete after we have inspired all of these things?" Hoover asked. "Are we to withhold the influence of America for stability in the world and the influence of America for the upbuilding of humanity? These are the things which will prevent war." "The American people, who have been advocates of human liberty and of democracy during this whole one hundred and fifty years," he wrote later, "cannot stand here, having stimulated all these efforts in all parts of the world amongst down-trodden people and then desert them after we have launched them forth on the road to freedom."[19]

At the request of former President Taft, who later called it "a great speech," Hoover summarized his views on the League of Nations at Stanford on October 2, 1919. He acknowledged the Covenant's imperfections, pointing out that there had been "five hundred conflicting minds in Paris," representing twenty-three nationalities. "Greater things were accomplished by this conference than by any other in history," he said, and he cited particularly the destruction of autocracies that wage war "for the profit of their class." Opposition to the League in Paris "arose entirely from the representations of the old militaristic regimes and from the reactionaries of the world in general." As for the danger to America's own independence, Hoover interpreted the League Covenant's controversial Article X as requiring the assent of Congress for the use of U.S. military forces. The League's "most potent weapon" was not arms but "the determination of the rights and wrongs of international quarrels; and the enlightenment of the world upon them, and by consequence the moral isolation of the aggressor. . . . Every line of [the League Covenant] is the complete negation of militarism." Only "the egotism of insanity" would suppose that the United States could prosper while Europe suffered because of the breakdown of the treaty. Not to join was to ignore the investment Americans had made in "the lives of our sons and an enormous portion of our wealth." Hoover concluded:[20]

I am one of those who hold that this war would never have happened if the nations of Europe had accepted the invitation of Sir Edward Grey to a conference of civilians in July, 1914. I believe that if the intelligence of the world can be aggregated around a table, the pressures from these responsible men for a solution which will prevent the enormous loss of life and the fabulous amount of human misery created by war will be such that no body of decent men in these times can resist it. We have now seen the most terrible five years of history because the reactionaries of Europe refused to come into a room to discuss the welfare of humanity. From this mighty political, social and economic upheaval there has resulted a host of outstanding problems which can breed war at any minute. The liberal world is asking us to come into a council to find solution for these things. That world is not asking for soldiers; it is asking for our economic and moral weight, our idealism, and our disinterested sense of justice. Are we not to take the responsibility that rests on the souls of those men in Europe who refused this invitation in 1914?

The following month, before the first Senate vote on the League, Hoover addressed Wilson and Democratic leaders on the desirability of accepting reasonable reservations. "I am impressed," he wrote, "with the desperate necessity of early ratification." Above all, delay slowed European economic recuperation and endangered the lives of the hungry peoples he was struggling to feed. He worried that Americans were confusing the League and the treaty. If the treaty should get to be an issue in the presidential election, he argued, "it will become confused with our own domestic issues, our own racial prejudices, the constant blame of every difficulty in Europe."

HOOVER DID NOT energetically promote his presidential candidacy in 1920, and did not have any substantial expectation of winning the office. Like other successful people he had a large ego, and despite his shyness there is no reason to suppose he would not have been receptive to the presidency in 1920 had it been offered him. But his engagements in politics were by way of pursuing impersonal goals, particularly the League's ratification.

At first it was unclear, even perhaps to Hoover himself, which party he would be most likely to identify with. He had grown up a Republican; he spent his first years in a town where Republicans outnumbered Democrats by fifty to one, and in both his Oregon and Stanford days he declared himself one. By his own account to a congressional committee he had never voted in a presidential election, but had from 1909 to September 1917 belonged to the Republican Club of New York, an organization supporting his hero, Theodore Roosevelt. "I can never forget the enthusiasm with which I supported TR," he remarked in 1920 in conversation with Carter Glass. "As you know, I was one of his great backers." Hoover contributed $1000 to the Bull Moose candidate in 1912. *Who's Who* listed Hoover's party affiliation as Republican. But a letter of November 5, 1918, that stated, "We must have united support to the President," had earned Hoover the condemnation of the Republican National Committee, which regarded it as an oblique call for a Democratic Congress. Hoover had seen Wilson on the very day the President wrote his letter asking for a Democratic Congress. As a member of Wilson's circle, he was popularly supposed to be a Democrat or at least an independent, and he had attended Democratic party luncheons during the war. At a January 1920 meeting that his friend Owen D. Young of General Electric arranged between him and Homer S. Cummings, the chairman of the Democratic National Committee, the two agreed that he was close to being a Jeffersonian Democrat. This was a fairly shaky designation for a modern engineer, an administrator of vast programs, and a representative of some of the most centralizing tendencies of twentieth-century life, notwithstanding his espousal of individualism and free community.[21]

That Hoover would meet with the Democratic chairman at all was an indication of interest; and he readily agreed to a testing of how receptive Democrats might be to his running for President. Colonel House had several meetings with Hoover, who apparently exhibited considerable interest in his own candidacy. Wilson's secretary, Joseph Tumulty, also seemed responsive to the idea. Democrat Bernard Baruch, though always somewhat peevish about Hoover and inclined to think his reputation over-blown, urged him to refrain from committing himself as a Republican: "I felt," wrote Baruch, "he had a utility to my party." But Baruch complained that Hoover had "delusions of grandeur—he really believes all the wonderful things he has written about himself. . . . As a mining engineer he never had a success in his life." Hoover professed "a disdain for political organizations, as now constituted," Baruch reported. "He railed a bit at the essential similarity between Republicans and Democrats today, at the political bankruptcy of both platforms." William Gibbs McAdoo thought Hoover was using the Democrats to get the Republican nomination.[22]

A number of Democrats looked on Hoover with favor. Franklin D. Roosevelt wrote to Hugh Gibson: "He is certainly a wonder, and I wish we could make him President. There couldn't be a better one." Hoover's friend, Secretary of the Interior Franklin Lane, claimed he would be able to win fifty delegates in 1920 and so get an edge on the nomination for 1924. The first major endorsement of Hoover came in late January 1920 from a Democratic organ, the New York *World,* which expressed a willing-ness to support him regardless of party. The publisher, Ralph Pulitzer, and the editor, Frank I. Cobb, had discussed Hoover's possible candidacy at a lunch the previous month with Hoover, Colonel House, Cyrus Curtis (publisher of the *Saturday Evening Post*), the financier Cleveland H. Dodge, and Sir Edward Grey, then British ambassador to the United States, with House acting as host. (Grey's presence at the luncheon alarmed Anglophobes like Missouri's Senator James A. Reed, who termed Hoover "that recent acquisition to our population.") Perhaps Hoover could have drawn well on Democratic ethnic voters for his relief work. Reports in the *New York Times,* the Detroit *News,* and the Philadelphia *Public Ledger* had it that Wilson himself wanted Hoover. In one of his blunter moments, however, Hoover later described Wilson as having been a great man until he became insane and wanted to rule the world with Hoover to help him; and Wilson spoke with similar sharpness of Hoover: "I have the feeling that he would rather see a good cause fail than succeed if he were not the head of it"; Hoover, he declared, was "one of the most selfish people I have ever known." Whatever went wrong between the two men—Hoover came to favor the League with the Lodge amendments and he had earlier disagreed temporarily on American membership on League commissions—he could, as Arthur Link has written, probably have had the Democratic nomination. As it was, the Republicans perceived him as a Trojan horse.[23]

On February 8 Hoover had told the *New York Times:* "I must vote for the party that stands for the League." Even in late March he was an-

nouncing that he would favor the party that had the better platform—
meaning especially the better platform on the League. Julius Barnes (himself a Republican) at Hoover's private instruction had already announced
in mid-January that Hoover was a "progressive Republican," as he was
well known to be in his Belgian relief days; this aborted the Democratic
interest in his candidacy. The public declaration of Republicanism came on
March 30. Its tone implied a slight aloofness from the political process,
a civic volunteering for office on condition; and this was no pose, but rather
an instance of the public role and manner that had by now become a facet
of Hoover's self-understanding:

If the Republican party, with the independent element of which I am naturally
affiliated, adopts a forward-looking, liberal, constructive platform on the Treaty
and on our economic issues, and if the party proposes measures for sound business administration of the country, and is neither reactionary nor radical in its
approach to our great domestic questions, and is backed by men who undoubtedly assure the consummation of these policies and measures, I will give
it my entire support. While I do not, and will not myself, seek the nomination,
if it is felt that the issues necessitate it and it is demanded of me, I can not
refuse service.

"In effect," observed one newspaper, "Mr. Hoover tells the Republican
party he would like to belong to [it] if [it] will be the kind of a party to
which he would like to belong. And that, if he belongs to it, he would have
no objection to leading it." Above all, there was the issue of the League.
Whatever may have been Hoover's other reasons for going Republican, his
solicitude for the League would have been a good strategic one. Like other
political observers, including Wilson's canny son-in-law, William Gibbs
McAdoo, Hoover saw that 1920 was not likely to be a Democratic year.
He later told Edgar Eugene Robinson: "I knew no Democrat could win in
1920 and I did not see myself as a sacrifice." It was therefore the Republican party that held the fortunes of the League, he could have calculated,
and the party must be brought to support it. Doggedly identifying himself
with the world organization as it became politically unpopular, Hoover in
the time of his candidacy and the time of Harding's presidential campaign
would strive to move the party toward its support.[24]

Republicans, he had contended even before his March 30 commitment,
must be for the League with reservations, for such a body had been not
only Wilson's idea but Theodore Roosevelt's, expressed in his address
accepting the Nobel Prize. "I . . . hope," Hoover wrote, "that the more
than a thousand clubs that have sprung up in this country advocating my
name at the Chicago Convention will . . . use their utmost influence that
the Republican platform shall endorse the prompt ratification of the Treaty
and approve the reservations." Hoover explicitly asked his supporters in

Oregon to give their backing to the League first and to him second. In California, where he and Ben Allen had purchased the Sacramento *Union,* he let his candidacy be entered so that Republicans there could "express themselves in favor of the League of Nations with proper reservations." The "issue was whether we should join the moral forces of the world [or] by pretense of an insularity we do not possess, sit by in face of growing armies, navies, national antagonisms, reaction or, in reverse, the spread of Bolshevism, through much of the world." Certainly the League was no political asset: "in choosing the League of Nations as the chief issue," the El Paso *Times* remarked, "the former food Administrator has placed his bet on a dead card."[25]

Hoover's party declaration of March 30 was for the purpose of permitting him to file in the Republican presidential primary in California against that state's isolationist Senator Hiram Johnson, whose opposition to the League, Hoover said in May, was as "destructive" as President Wilson's demand for unqualified approval. California friends had been urging him to run. For southern Californians in particular, he was attractive as a migrant from the Midwest. He chose a clear-cut fight on the issue of the League. Senator Johnson's supporters responded with posters reading "Vote for 'Erbert 'Oover." Enthusiastic amateurs like Ralph Arnold, building on remnants of the Food Administration precinct units and supplied with ample campaign funds, could not overcome the solid labor, farmer, and machine support that gave Johnson a vote of 370,000 to Hoover's 210,000 in the April primary. Yet it was a sufficient showing to dampen the Johnson campaign, and Hoover had accomplished what may have been his real goal: to spoil Johnson's campaign for the presidency. (He did this again in 1924 by helping to carry the Republican primary for Coolidge against Johnson.) Even before March 30, Hoover had already won three of the four Republican district races in New Hampshire, and the allegiance of most of the unpledged delegates. In Michigan during early April, where differing supporters had entered him in both party primaries, he came in first (over McAdoo) in a light vote on the Democratic side, and fourth on the Republican. On the whole, he performed well in the primaries, yet won few delegates.[26]

Hoover had become the prime candidate of independent progressives. Within the citizenry at large he was most popular among independents and women. The roster of those who advanced his candidacy in 1919 and 1920 is thick with the names of reformers: William Allen White (who with Franklin K. Lane had written numerous letters boosting Hoover), Franklin Roosevelt, Herbert Croly, Jane Addams, Louis D. Brandeis, Walter Lippmann, Edward Bok, Oscar Straus, Edward A. Ross, Ida Tarbell, Ray Stannard Baker, Frederick Lewis Allen, Heywood Broun, and

Frank W. Taussig. Much of the progressive press supported his candidacy, including the anti-Treaty *New Republic* (closely associated with Colonel House and always prone—as one of its historians, Charles Forcey, has observed—to invent heroes) and the Scripps newspaper chain; the *Saturday Evening Post,* associated Curtis publications, and the *Ladies' Home Journal* also boosted Hoover. Engineering societies, scientific management groups, and particularly university communities joined in. The Harvard University faculty voted in a poll for Hoover by a 2-to-1 margin. Hoover's supporters had as their common theme their candidate's independence and ability; and as their goal, to "Hooverize" politics, making it less partisan and more idealistic.[27]

Hoover himself, busy with the Children's Relief Fund and the Second Industrial Conference, refused to campaign. He was "deeply and sincerely bored by the whole affair," wrote Hugh Gibson. When the rumor floated that he might employ in his own behalf a part-ownership in the Washington *Herald* acquired in December 1919 with Julius Barnes and the Wilsonian Charles R. Crane, Hoover exploded: "If I hear anybody say that, I'll kill him." He considered the venture "an attempt at public service," since there was much deficiency in covering Washington news. A Hoover Publicity League kept its candidate before the nation. This organization was run by the exceptionally competent Edward Eyre Hunt, a co-founder with Walter Lippmann of the Harvard Socialist Club and director of the Madison Square Garden pageant depicting the IWW strike in Paterson, New Jersey. "Seven out of ten men who work with Hoover," wrote Mary Austin, "become his permanent press agents." Edgar Rickard, Julius Barnes, Robert Taft, William B. Poland, John Lucey, George Barr Baker, Thomas W. Lamont, and hundreds of devoted followers publicized Hoover, who wrote numerous articles during this period on the League, labor, and education.[28]

The *Literary Digest* straw poll taken just before the Republican Convention in June gave Hoover an impressive 260,000 votes, including 94,000 among Democrats, compared with 263,000 for Johnson and 277,000 for General Leonard Wood. In total primary votes Hoover had come fourth. If the three Republican front runners—Frank Lowden, Wood, and Johnson—deadlocked at Chicago, perhaps Hoover would still win. But while the galleries were with him, the party leaders assuredly were not. On the critical tenth ballot Hoover won only 10½ votes, while Senator Warren G. Harding of Ohio took the nomination. Some months before, Hoover had predicted the result to his son Herbert, Jr., now at Stanford. His candidacy would be a good deal like Herbert's flivver: starting it would take a lot of people, it would make a lot of noise, and they would all have to walk back home in the end. Irvin Cobb, the journalist, wrote from the convention that if he wanted to commit the perfect crime he would leave the corpse at Hoover headquarters, where it would never be discovered. Hoover loyally and cordially congratulated Harding—since Harding would win, he explained to his secretary Lewis Strauss, he must "be 'regular' and give the Old Guard as much trouble as possible from the inside."[29]

On a variety of issues Hoover supported the Republicans against the Democratic candidates, James Cox and Franklin D. Roosevelt. He was pleased at Harding's interest in reorganization of the government. Early that year Hoover had spoken to a group of engineers on the need to reshape each of the great departments of government more nearly to a single purpose. He attacked the Wilson administration: "Its actions on social questions have been . . . in the main reactionary." In a campaign speech he lamented:

It was the business of the Democratic party to have assembled the best brains in the United States before each of these problems, to have prevented the advancing cost of living, to have found solutions for the difficulties of our agricultural industry, to have inaugurated constructive methods of resettlement of the land, the development of our industrial employment relationship, the protection of child life, the solution of our deficient housing, reorganization of the business administration of the Federal Government, and a host of other domestic questions. . . . The failure in these domestic necessities has already imposed a terrible cost in our daily lives and will yet impose vast unemployment. . . . The responsibilities of government should now, therefore, be transferred [to the Republican party].

He blamed the Democrats for the Senate's failure to accept the treaty of peace with the League Covenant embedded within it; theirs was a "failure in statesmanship" for ignoring "one half the people of the United States" and making a partisan peace. The party had shown itself unwilling "to make those compromises necessary to secure the League of Nations and the peace of the world." Hoover recommended to New York State voters that they defeat Governor Alfred E. Smith in his bid for reelection because he would have no influence in a national Republican government charged with "new and definite" policies of reconstruction as well as efficient business administration. Elsewhere he selectively supported progressives like Wisconsin's Senator Irvine Lenroot but opposed California's James Phelan—who had rather ineptly defended Hoover against Senator Reed. Rising prices, which he termed "the visualization of insufficient production," Hoover blamed on Wilson's inactivity. In August Hoover suggested deleting Article X of the League Covenant, since moral, not military, strength was at its core, particularly "wide publicity and the force of the public opinion of the world." He also recommended possible later withdrawal from the body should Europe not disarm, and endorsed economic boycott over force of arms.[30]

During the campaign he pressed Harding firmly on a league, demanding on August 3 that the candidate repudiate Senator Johnson's isolationist interpretation of his acceptance speech. On August 12 George Wickersham urged Hoover to "join with say fifty Republicans" warning the candidate to reject isolationist pressures. Hoover wired back: "Exceedingly anxious that such a protest shall be made vigorously." Wickersham termed Hoover's response "the first encouragement I have had to go on with the idea." Hoover and Wickersham were prominent in organizing a protest. In correspondence over the wording of a document that finally emerged under the aegis of a committee of thirty-one prominent Republicans, Hoover urged incorporation of the point that "any other action by the Republican party" than joining a league would "be a betrayal of its own support." Under pressure, Harding announced on August 28 that he favored with "all my heart" an association or league of "free nations." The statement was in conformity with the Elihu Root straddle in the party's platform.[31]

In a public letter to Mrs. Robert Burdette, director of food conservation for California, Hoover said that if the party "fails to provide peace on terms" of a league, "it deserves no more consideration four years hence than the present party deserves today." When the candidate requested help among "your [California] friends . . . upon whom party ties rest lightly," Hoover assured him that help would come if Harding acknowledged the existence of a moral obligation to join a league. In an Indianapolis speech on October 9, Hoover pushed strongly for a league: "The carrying out of that promise is the test of the entire sincerity, integrity, and statesmanship of the Republican Party." On October 11 he sent another wire to Harding and the next day he received an endorsement of the substance of the letter to Mrs. Burdette. This statement, which he released on the twenty-seventh with the candidate's permission, proved far stronger than the declaration extracted by the famous appeal of the committee of thirty-one Republicans. It was a signal personal triumph for Hoover.[32]

After the election President-elect Harding appeared unable to decide about a league. As late as mid-December Hoover returned from Marion, Ohio, with the impression that the present treaty would be modified and then adopted. Later that month, however, after meetings with Massachusetts Senator Henry Cabot Lodge, Jr., the President-elect turned strongly against any league. In January 1921 league supporters formed the American Association for a League of Nations. After Elihu Root had declined its presidency, the association offered it to Hoover, who also turned it down. Hoover's recommendation, George Wickersham, accepted.

Hoover had to refuse, for he had already been privately offered the post of Secretary of Commerce.

After the election Hoover had tried to leave public life, which he found exhausting and financially draining. On the day following the election, however, Harding raised the possibility of having him in the cabinet; the President-elect said he wanted the "best minds" there. A letter in the Hoover Papers, dated December 22, is an apparent refusal of a post, or at least an expression of fearfulness that the old guard would find him unacceptable. He had already embarked with Julius Barnes in founding the Intercontinental Development Company (a failure from its inception), and he considered the offer an attempt to "use" him. He also "did not think the position of Secretary of Commerce a wide enough field to appeal to him." Charles Evans Hughes finally persuaded Hoover to accept the job; he preferred it to Interior, which was also tendered him. Many old guard Republicans, men like Senators Reed Smoot and Charles Curtis, opposed his entry into the administration. So did isolationist progressives like Senators Johnson, Norris, and Borah. When the nation's wheat growers adopted resolutions against his appointment, Hoover replied: "I indeed will be glad if your opposition shall succeed." Harding blunted opposition among conservatives by agreeing to appoint the multimillionaire industrialist Andrew Mellon, of Pennsylvania, as Secretary of the Treasury. Hoover's telegram of acceptance, sent on February 23, set an ambitious program: government reorganization would have to bring all relevant bureaus into his department; a "vigorous policy of leadership" on his part would persuade industries to cooperate in standardizing products and reducing waste (this would not include alteration of the Sherman Act—companies holding too great a percentage of any market, Hoover believed, should be prosecuted); and joint work with the Labor Department would reduce friction in the "employee relationship." Hoover was about to set out upon another major project; his Democratic friend Franklin K. Lane shrewdly guessed that "unless he gets to be the leading adviser he'll have to get out."[33]

In these postwar years Hoover showed he could respond constructively to a range of problems. As his confidante Mary Austin put it: "Things came up in his mind and turned over, showing white bellies like fish in a net . . . he had the conception of great ideas." In this period he continued to fit rather closely the description of progressives advanced by the historian Robert Wiebe: those who believed that expert skills could be brought to bear in a continuing administrative way on society. Like Veblen's engineers, the new professionals such as Hoover might be capable of mastering the century's technical and economic forces. These were among the most intellectually fertile years of Hoover's life. Here are found the origins of most of what he later attempted in employment stabilization, housing and mortgage finance, statistical work, reform of the coal industry, and European reconstruction. But such ideas would reach maturer definition in the Commerce and presidential years.[34]

IX

COMMERCE

A BUSINESS PERIODICAL singled out some words and phrases as being characteristic of Hoover's language: reason, knowledge, patience, good will, quiet negotiation, restraint of passion, moderation, and calm, prudent common counsel, what are the facts? These words and phrases even in their austerity sound more Quakerly than technocratic, and tell of Hoover's involvement in the larger, less exactly manageable affairs of statesmanship. But the expectation remains that the world is resolvable into harmonies, which reason and skill can find. Such were the assumptions on which Hoover's Commerce Department implicitly proceeded. We may see his labor for a more free-flowing international trade as a proposal that commerce go forth to seek the underlying unities, which can replace the relationships of force and war; even Hoover's efforts to bring about standardization of parts and measurements suggest this sense of the harmonies in things. However arbitrary he had been in business and in public administration, and however impatiently he may have wielded power, he had at least a theoretical liking for projects with a wide participation. The Commerce Department had little desire for supervisory control; it wanted to be a center for communication among manufacturing and distributing bodies. The lessons of war, its achievements in self-regulation such as Baruch's War Industries Board as well as the Food Administration, served as inspiration to the elite corps of Commerce administrators. For if businessmen could be public-spirited enough to curb their appetites during the tempting inflation of wartime, they could do it as well in peace. And Hoover's unique brand of cooperative capitalism was a lesser danger than the marketplace kind, with its momentum away from freedom towards fascism, socialism, or centralized corporate state capitalism.[1]

One of Hoover's objectives for the Commerce Department therefore was a collectivizing of free individual initiative, a light but efficient ordering of the nation's private and local energies to national purposes. A notion of that delicate synthesis was not uncommon during the decade. It is implicit in the romance of the stock market, where small investors thought themselves individualists for throwing in their lot with some huge enterprise, and, beyond that, with the projected growth of an entire economy. It appears in Henry Ford's insistence that a technologically advanced factory puts large demands on the intelligence and steadiness of the workers—in effect, that individuals can prove and fulfill themselves within a tightly ordered collectivity. In a large way the idea or image of huge sophisticated collective efforts is almost inseparable from a modern technology, and almost unthinkable without it. But Hoover's particular rendering emphasized the polar elements: centralization and individualism.

Another objective in the Commerce years was the mobilizing and application of expertise. In some senses this reliance on the expert accorded with Hoover's taste for cooperation. His conferences were to an extent the gathering of experts, and his trust in the existence of an objectively perceivable right way of doing things suggested the possibilities of progress without government coercion. But expertise and the technologies that accompany it may require centralized projects of the sort that Hoover would design for the use of Western waterpower.

Aside from the farm cooperatives, which would be mainly a preoccupation of Hoover's presidency, the device that most neatly represented his thought was the national conference or commission. This was a way of accomplishing change particularly suitable at a time of conservative government. The national conference called by the federal government was not an innovation. In various forms the idea went back to the Civil War and progressivism had adopted it: President Theodore Roosevelt, for example, had held a conference on child welfare in 1909, and President Wilson had appointed numerous commissions. But Hoover's Commerce Department and then his presidential administration used them with unprecedented regularity. And with a twist: these were gatherings not merely of concerned citizens but of functional leaders speaking for the interests of their constituencies. His Commerce assistant Edward Eyre Hunt called the method provided by fact-finding conferences "one of the most important by which public and private policy is determined."

The purpose of a conference was to gather exact information on a large economic or social subject, formulate ideas for legislative or administrative or private civil action, and disseminate ideas and facts by publicity.

Publicity accorded well with the timbre of Hoover's morality, which liked the call to duty muted by the appeal to fact. Specialists planned and executed the studies, but a group of prominent laymen usually presented the findings to the President. The principle of voluntary cooperation was embedded both in the proceedings of the conference itself, which were those of inquiry and talk, and in its way of organizing national resources, through persuasion rather than directive. This approach resembled that of a Quaker meeting, with its abhorrence of coercion which sets people against one another. For government to coerce was to violate the respect and freedom that are required if the Spirit within is to develop. There was, however, a degree of manipulation. Hoover used conferences to insinuate his thinking into public practice; he employed quantitative data to impress and convince; and some of his choices for participants were people he believed would come to the same conclusions he had reached. Hoover "left nothing to chance" in planning conferences, observed one of his press secretaries, Theodore Joslin. His grandest conception was to invite an economic advisory commission to Washington in 1921; but he had to back down when he discovered too great a variety and multiplicity in American commerce to allow such a thing.[2]

Between 1921 and 1928 Hoover and his associates succeeded in transforming the Commerce Department from a miscellaneous collection of small technical bureaus into an organization of 1600 employees mainly concerned with promoting, guiding, and protecting American economic development. While the department never fulfilled its more grandiose ambitions—a highly rationalized American economy and the virtual elimination of poverty—it added a variety of new agencies and programs, reorganized and expanded its existing bureaus, pushed its influence into nearly all of federal economic policy, and proceeded to link public with private action through a series of important cooperative conferences. The department seemed a dynamo under Hoover. One small-town California editor insisted in the mid-1920's that he had received a piece of Hoover's Commerce Department publicity every day for several years; they were like flakes of snow in a heavy storm. Commerce became the epitome of "progressive government," its activities combining scientific management, organized cooperation, and private initiative into a new and superior political economy. The department took on a vigorous esprit de corps. Plans were made for a huge new building to house the expanding organization; it was completed during Hoover's presidency.[3]

The three organizing bureaus of the Commerce Department were Standards, Census, and Foreign and Domestic Commerce. By tradition, the Bureau of Standards tested materials purchased by the government. Under Hoover it increasingly offered to assist business in the solving of complex

scientific problems; by the mid-twenties it was known as the largest research laboratory in the world. It also set many additional safety standards,
notably for automobile brakes, rail joints, building cement, and elevators.
Hoover pleaded with Congress for more salary for government inspectors,
who might otherwise become prey to corruption. The Bureau of the Census
grew into a foremost statistical office, furnishing more and more useful
information to business; its valued statistical monthly, *Survey of Current
Business,* began publication under Hoover in July 1921, listing current
industrial production and inventories. A Goodyear executive called the
Survey "the most important step in our industrial life since the inauguration
of the Federal Reserve System." *Commerce Reports* became a valued
compendium of trade data. The widely heralded Division of Simplified
Commercial Practice, a subdivision of the Bureau of Standards, followed
from the recommendation that Hoover had prompted the Federated American Engineering Societies to make on the "Elimination of Waste in Industry." The concern grew out of similar aims during the war. Before accurate
statistics could be collected, products had to be manufactured in standard
shapes and sizes. By persuading manufacturers to reduce variations in
everything from baby bottle nipples to screws, the Division cut waste and
prices to consumers even as it increased profits. The government exerted
some influence here by stipulating, at Hoover's urging, standard specifications for its own purchases. To critics of standardization Hoover replied
that the "man who has a standard automobile, a standard telephone, a
standard bathtub, a standard electric light, a standard radio, and one and
one-half hours less average daily labor is more of a man and has a fuller life
and more individuality than he has without them."[4]

The new functions joined old ones. The Lighthouse Bureau floated its
buoys and whirled its lights, adding radio beacons as an aid to coastal navi-
gation. The Bureau of Fisheries applied selective breeding to improve the
quality and quantity of fish across the nation, and to conserve the fish supply. Hoover vetoed a proposed patronage appointment to head the bureau
and chose Henry O'Malley, a twenty-five-year veteran of the service who immediately attempted to restore closed fisheries, undertake needed research,
and, as Hoover particularly wished, encourage and regulate commercial
fishing. "As you are aware," Hoover wrote in 1924 to a Calvin Coolidge
exhausted by his many proposals, "we have for the last four years been
pounding away at the necessity of fisheries conservation." The job of
looking after seal herds off the Pribilof Islands brought the Coast Guard,
at Hoover's insistence, to patrol international waters to prevent wanton
slaughter of the animals by Japanese hunters. Atlantic coast interstate conferences were stymied by conflicting interstate regulations, and the fishing
industry lobbyists themselves were so highly individualistic that they

could agree on few proposals. But despite scarce funds and the opposition of the Hearst papers, there were substantial improvements in restocking streams and lakes throughout the nation and in reversing the gradual disappearance of many species such as Hudson River shad and Alaskan salmon. The department accomplished these improvements by favoring established firms over new ones and restricting seasons and areas of catching. Hoover got private fishing clubs to accept newly born government fish on condition that half of them at maturity be placed in public waters; and he doubled appropriations for stocking fresh water with fish.[5]

Radio and the airways famously came under Hoover's jurisdiction. In 1922 he held the first of four annual conferences at which industry and government discussed regulation of radio. The number of receiving sets had risen twelvefold during the previous twelve months, and attendance at the conferences rose from fifteen in the first year to more than four hundred in the fourth year. Hoover early saw the possibilities of national radio networks and worked with Owen D. Young and others to speed their completion. His department cooperated by setting up a commercial wireless news service. Hoover did not want the new instrument of communication in the hands of the government. He advocated giving the industry a chance to regulate itself; and despite what he spoke of as the medium's great capacity for slander, he opposed government censorship. He hoped that the stations would not permit ceaseless advertising "chatter." The Radio Act of 1927 established ultimate public ownership and limited regulation of the airwaves. A federal commission could assign frequencies, limit hours of operation, and specify standards of equipment. The radio station of the great California evangelist Aimee Semple McPherson wandered all over the dial. When Hoover's inspector sealed her station, she telegraphed him: "Please order your minions of Satan to leave my station alone. You cannot expect the Almighty to abide by your wavelength nonsense. When I offer my prayers to Him I must fit into His wave reception. Open this station at once." McPherson also proceeded to elope on a motorcycle with Hoover's inspector. A wavelength for amateurs, according to a sixteen-year-old boy, was regulated this way in one city: "If anybody . . . does not stick to the rules, we will beat him up."[6]

As early as 1922 Hoover called a conference on the development of aviation to promote industrial codes and regulation, but Congress was in an economizing mood and did not provide an increase in air mail subsidies until the Air Mail Act of 1925. In 1926 Hoover proposed a Transcontinental Airway, from New York to Chicago to California, and a Southwestern Airway from Chicago to Texas. Plans for passenger and mail service went on in cooperation with the army and navy. Europe was far ahead of the United States in passenger routes; not until 1927 was there a scheduled airline between New York and Boston. Here, as in shipping, private enterprise had to be coaxed into such undertakings by lucrative mail contracts. Hoover believed that the federal government had to regulate and encourage airways as it had shipping.

The Air Commerce Act of 1926 set up an Aeronautics Branch within the Commerce Department. The new body had the task of tripling the number of lighted runways in three years and providing more sophisticated weather and navigational equipment, all in the cause of promoting commercial aviation. Rules were instituted on everything from certification of flying schools to quality of parachutes, engines, and propellers. Charles Lindbergh's tour of the United States in 1927 following his transatlantic flight popularized both passenger travel and air mail. In 1930 Congress passed an important amendment that Hoover's Postmaster General Walter Brown wrote into the Air Commerce Act. The McNary-Watres Act gave Brown power to extend and consolidate existing air routes in the public interest—virtually dictatorial powers. The idea here, typical of Hoover, was to develop the industry to the point at which it was competitive and self-sustaining. In the meantime, larger companies transporting passengers were favored, and many smaller ones disappeared. Under this program the air industry developed quickly, so that by the mid-thirties passenger flying was common and reasonably safe.[7]

The biggest problem Hoover faced upon becoming Commerce Secretary was the severe unemployment—up to 5 million—generated by the depression of 1920–2. He rejected the conservative formula of reducing wages and prices until supply and demand set the system right again. Instead, he urged business to avoid wage cuts and recommended that government finance public works projects, particularly road building. The vehicle for his plans was the misnamed "President's" Conference on Unemployment of 1921, the first experiment in American history to respond to hard times with plans for economic stabilization.

Hoover wrote to President Harding on August 12, 1921, proposing a conference of national leaders that would arouse "public sentiment" against unemployment, encourage cooperative action, suggest emergency measures, and put forward means of preventing future depressions. The membership would include prominent business and labor leaders, and also a number of academic economists. Having received the President's approval, Hoover chose three central figures: Professor Edwin Gay of Harvard; Otto Mallery, originator of an experimental public works project in Pennsylvania; and Edward Eyre Hunt, who became secretary of the conference. These and other experts served on an Economic Advisory Committee that met in early September; ten of its nineteen members had belonged to the progressive prewar American Association for Labor Legislation. Its recommendations emphasized local action as having the most immediate beneficial effects, particularly community employment bureaus and voluntary relief agencies. Support was to come from local governments as well as from organizations and individuals. The committee urged solvent businesses to make improvements and repairs that would quicken employment. The federal government should speed up public works, particularly road building, expand the United States Employment Service, and, if necessary, issue bonds to be lent to states for further public works. Hoover added some of his favorite reforms, such as limitation of world armament, which would allow for a reduction in taxes, and the entry of the United States into the Reparations Commission.[8]

In the way of permanent reform, the same committee suggested that the government refine the collection of statistics and proposed a federal agency responsible for planning public works in advance for ready use in hard times. Public works not needed immediately, Edward Hunt argued, should be put off to moments of economic crisis, when they could act as a "balance wheel." In 1923, after the depression had ended, Hoover, in keeping with this recommendation, asked Harding to delay public works to avoid inflation, since the building industry was fully employed. Hoover also promoted the work of the American Construction Council under the chairmanship of Franklin Roosevelt, with the purpose of maintaining full employment in the building trades.[9]

A standing committee of fourteen had the task of carrying out the conference recommendations. Colonel Arthur Woods, who had helped ex-servicemen to find jobs after the war, was to coordinate the work of national, state, and city governments. Focusing on municipalities, Woods mailed the conference report to more than three hundred mayors. Hoover also sent out hundreds of letters demanding action, including an exhortation to state governors. By December, 209 mayor's committees on unemployment had been formed; many of them set up employment bureaus. As reports of ingenious local job-making schemes and public works programs flowed in, Woods conscientiously spread them abroad. The use of churches and women's groups, the optimistic pep talks, the endless publicity, the Protestant tone of self-denial, the theme of voluntary cooperation—all suggested Hoover's own wartime relief work.[10]

But the bureaucratically top-heavy largest cities failed to respond to these techniques, and later in 1922 local and private resources began to dry up. The national industries that Hoover appealed to as a second line of defense were largely unproductive. He warmly endorsed a $400,000 congressional appropriation to the U.S. Employment Service that failed to pass. But a generous Federal Road Act, with Washington paying half the cost of new highways, easily went through in the fall of 1921. Woods's efforts partially restrained the traditional practice of government and business retrenchment during depression. For if waste, as Hoover's earlier study indicated, could be traced largely to management, then recovery ought to come about without liquidating labor.

In 1922, employment started to revive. The conference had some moderate effect on alleviating unemployment, although no evidence supports Hoover's claim that 1 to 1.5 million people had found employment as a result. The reluctance of Congress and many members of the administration to cooperate, and perhaps Hoover's own unwillingness to involve the federal government more extensively, prevented it from becoming an important test of what such action might achieve. When Senator William Kenyon introduced a bill proposing a reserve fund of federal public works, a swarm of objections arose. Conservatives found any number of reasons to oppose it. And the progressive Senator George Norris of Nebraska remarked: "We had better let God run [the economy] as in the past, and not take the power away from Him and give it to Hoover." Through the twenties Hoover continued to support the idea, with Otto Mallery as agent in its behalf. He had Governor Owen Brewster of Maine, after the election of 1928, offer a $3 billion reserve fund program to the National Conference of State Governors. The President-elect called it a "construction reserve fund to do for labor and industry what the Federal Reserve has for finance." But at a time when the federal budget was so small, the helpfulness of such a program was in any event dubious. Hoover could obtain only paltry funding for the collection of economic statistics.[11]

In an able study of this conference, Carolyn Grin argues that its educational effects were its real contribution, particularly some permanent research committees headed overall by Hoover. In 1923 the Committee on Unemployment and Business Cycles, under Owen D. Young's chairmanship, published *Business Cycles and Unemployment*, blaming slumps on speculation, waste, extravagance, and poor credit facilities. Professor Wesley Clair Mitchell directed the National Bureau of Economic Research publication of twenty-one supporting economic studies, including one on unemployment insurance. Other research projects were carried out cooperatively by the Bureau, the Russell Sage Foundation, Frederic Feiker of the National Conference of Business Editors, and the Commerce Department; the most important, the valuable two-volume *Recent Economic Changes in the United States*, appeared in 1928. The experts were learning about the mystifying economic life of America. Part of the answer to the costs and problems left by war, Hoover believed, was an increase in productivity, and these studies all looked to that goal.[12]

An economist has found in Hoover's work "the roots of government responsibility for the overall performance of the economy" through what

Hoover himself called "the better control of economic forces." Hoover's guidance for corporate planners and the semi-official business cycle study itself "provided a model for future joint public-private economic policy formulation." The postwar period, with its new technologies requiring more fixed capital investment and more highly trained personnel, had introduced more costly dangers into the business cycle. Hoover spoke of a need for "national planning of industry and commerce" to achieve broad economic goals such as preventing unemployment. By this he simply meant that corporate planning should take place with "a larger perspective than the individual business." As for the unemployment conference itself, the long-range goal was *"prevention* rather than *cure,"* as Hoover put it. It was the work of war agencies that had made the unemployment conference possible in America. The minor recession of 1927 brought a flurry of activity with a Committee on the Present Economic Cycle set up in the Commerce Department, and Hoover asked New York foundations to finance a second business cycle study—the genesis of *Recent Economic Changes.*[13]

Among Hoover's research projects, the National Academy of Sciences was one of the most imaginative. The aim was for industries to support university projects of pure scientific research that would later have practical application. Hoover proposed a board of trustees consisting of such figures as Elihu Root and Andrew Mellon, asked for Coolidge's blessing, and gave him a letter to sign. The result was a National Research Fund with Hoover as chairman and Charles Evans Hughes, Owen D. Young, John W. Davis, Julius Rosenwald, and the banker Felix Warburg as trustees. The National Electric Light Association pledged $3 million, AT&T $2 million, and Rosenwald $1 million. But the pledges were matching grants never fully paid. Hoover was properly cynical: "Don't fool yourself that they care a damn for pure science. What they want is to get into their reports, which will soon be examined by the Federal Trade Commission, that they are giving money for pure science research." The project died during the Depression.[14]

FARMING, the most complicated and baffling economic problem of the decade, was itself a business, or a multitude of small businesses, amounting to half the country's commerce, and did not escape the Secretary's attention. Hoover shared the American convention that admired agriculture as natural and character-building, set apart, as he said, from "the insidious forces of moral degeneration which are such corroding influences in the life of our great cities." Many kinds of farming did well enough, dairy products and fruit in particular; but trouble pursued the wheat growers. The war had exacerbated their worst problem, that of overproduction.

From the outset Hoover believed that a partial solution lay in "the larger development of the cooperative principles"; he supported the Capper-Volstead Act of 1922 exempting farm cooperatives from antitrust prosecution. The agricultural cooperative could secure advantages in distribution and the elimination of waste that individual competitors could not. Waste would be reduced by bypassing excess middlemen, by the diversification of crops, the improvement of waterway transportation, the gathering of more reliable census reports (such as the agricultural census undertaken by the Commerce Department in 1925), the standardization of seeds, loans for exports from the War Finance Corporation, the minimizing of spoiled produce with more shipping facilities and better storage at terminals, and the curtailment of speculation. The Secretary cautioned that no single solution would be wholly satisfactory: "I am all for cooperative marketing. It will help. But it can not solve all the problems. We must get a bigger vision and build an economic system governing all industry, including agriculture, that will not permit [economic] slumps." Hoover said repeatedly—in 1926, for example, after a two-day tour of the proposed Columbia River Basin irrigation project—that growth in population would improve the market for food: "In . . . five or ten years we are going to be a food importing country . . . and when the day comes the return to agriculture in proportion to the effort given is going to be larger than that in industry." In the meantime, however, flagrant overproduction would yield only "prices low enough to make production unprofitable for some part of the acreage in use."[15]

In 1921 Hoover wired Harding that the nominee for Secretary of Agriculture, Henry C. Wallace, was "admirably fitted for his work." The two cabinet officers maintained superficially cordial relations, and supported the newly formed Senate farm bloc and American Farm Bureau Federation in efforts to obtain congressional passage of important credit legislation, as well as laws regulating grain trading and stockyards. The Farm Bureau leader O. E. Bradfute later said that Hoover may have been an essential ingredient in the passage of these bills. Hoover, however, favored credit machinery in a revolving fund that would become self-sufficient after an initial governmental investment. Specifically, he advocated limitations on the size of trades. Private credits must be extended to such underconsuming areas as eastern Europe and Germany, which could then purchase American food. When Hoover came to oppose the plan of Senator George Norris for a government agency to finance exports, an angry Norris lashed out at him as an "Englishman devoted first to . . . the British Empire." Hoover helped to draft the important Agricultural Credits Act that permitted the War Finance Corporation to extend credit to cooperatives, country banks, and foreign buyers.[16]

Part of the difference between Hoover and Secretary Wallace was a matter of style. Hoover had optimistic faith in the preponderance of decent, well-intentioned men in such private institutions as the Chicago Board of Trade: "I have great respect for human invention and its ability, on one hand, to solve almost anything after a little experience with it, and, on the other, to evade most regulation." One reason for the passing of old-fashioned commodity cornering, Hoover said, was that "the growth of business morality has put a large taboo on that kind of operation." Self-regulation, as against government rules, placed "the institution itself on a constructive basis." At one point, however, he wished to do away with these middlemen completely in order to stop speculative activity as distinguished from necessary hedging in futures. Wallace himself wanted co-operatives to come about not through active promotion on the part of the federal government but through the farmer's "wholehearted voluntary support." Wallace's adherents, however, employed a populist rhetoric that gave them a monopoly on the reputation for agricultural reform. Issues of jurisdiction divided the two secretaries.[17]

In 1922 Wallace created a data-collecting Bureau of Agricultural Economics. From Dr. Henry C. Taylor's leadership of this agency came the statistical arguments for the McNary-Haugen law, which won Wallace's support in 1923. The new plan provided for a federal export corporation to buy the farm surplus for resale at the world price abroad; a tax on producers would make up the difference between the domestic price arbitrarily set by the government and the world price. Wallace, Hoover remarked in his *Memoirs,* "was in truth a fascist, but did not know it, when he proposed his price- and distribution-fixing legislation in the McNary-Haugen bill." Hoover's plans for correcting the duplication of work that prevailed between Agriculture and Commerce were another cause of dispute. Believing that the function of the Department of Agriculture should end when produce left the farm, he thought that the Bureau of Markets should be transferred to Commerce where it would encourage cooperative marketing; and he wanted to bring into his department the collection of statistics on foreign agricultural production. (He did succeed in acquiring the Geological Survey and the Bureau of Mines from the Interior Department.) Commerce took the lead in controlling a 1924 hoof-and-mouth epidemic in California, on the grounds that it interfered with interstate commerce and was alarming bankers. Hoover was tempted to sue George Peek, a major architect of McNary-Haugen, for circulating an Agriculture dossier prepared under Taylor on "Encroachments of the Department of Commerce upon the Department of Agriculture"; the dossier complained of Hoover's inconsistent statements and implied duplicity. Later in the decade he did manage to get Taylor fired.[18]

Coolidge liked neither Wallace nor his programs. When the Secretary died in 1924, Hoover refused an insistent presidential offer in January 1925 to replace him, and he was said to favor Eugene Funk, a farmer-businessman he had worked with during the war. The eventual appointee, William Jardine, president of Kansas State Agricultural College, shared Coolidge's disinclination for an activist policy. Nevertheless, soon after Wallace's death Hoover advanced numerous cooperative projects with the Department of Agriculture. And the administration, in its opposition to McNary-Haugen, relied on a long memorandum of objections drafted in the Commerce Department.[19]

The document observed that McNary-Haugen would "continuously stimulate American production and . . . pile up increasing surpluses"—as in wartime. Hoover himself styled the plan a "profiteering" scheme "that guarantees the profits of every packer, flour miller and grain handler in the United States." One scholar, Gary Koerselman, has observed that it would have indeed profited "key bankers, middlemen and processors" by a bounty ultimately paid by farmers and consumers in higher prices and taxes. This argument is probably exaggerated: most packers were against the law. Yet Hoover had opposed similar interference by foreign governments in international commercial affairs in the cases of rubber, coffee, and potash. He also feared retaliation from abroad in the form of high tariffs or embargoes. The scheme would interfere with the repayment of international debts, according to the Commerce critique. Domestic food prices would go up as speculation in land increased, and wage earners in turn would demand inflationary wage hikes. The plan would benefit most large farms and lead to oligopoly in farming; other failing industries would demand similar treatment and Congress would be under constant pressure from lobbyists.[20]

On March 29, 1924, Hoover handed Representative Arthur B. Williams of Minnesota a draft of a cooperative marketing plan. It was based, he said, on ideas shaped during the Food Administration (such as the daily disseminating of marketing data), on recent Commerce Department investigation, and on ten months of consultation with Gray Silver of the American Farm Bureau Federation. Hoover's plan also owed part of its inspiration to cooperative societies in Belgium. The resulting revision of Williams' bill by Hoover had strong federal regulatory features under a board that would encourage diversification of crops. The tariff would protect only those farmers agreeing temporarily to reduce acreage. The Capper-Williams Bill—a forerunner of the Agricultural Marketing Act of 1929—did not, however, pass Congress. Cooperatives opposed it as "bureaucratic," and in fact, despite its intentions, it would have hindered large coops and producers. Although it became the administration's alternative plan to McNary-Haugen, Coolidge himself was uncomfortable with the scheme. A President's Agricultural Conference held in Washington in 1924–25 recommended a version of it; the President himself virtually ignored the conference. Even Secretary Jardine called the federal cooperative "paternalistic"; a congressman termed it "the politician's alibi, the farmer's lullaby." Hoover's plan also came under attack from the largest producers, who would have been greatly affected, and from the Chicago Board of Trade.[21]

Hoover worked through the Commerce Department to encourage domestic consumption, support an increase in the tariff on foreign agricultural goods, expand exports of food, and get financing for them. He urged a lowering of transportation rates on farm products, the building of better inland waterways that would cheapen transport, and a decrease in personal property taxes (because the farmer "is bearing an undue burden in proportion to his income at the present time"). He also proposed that businessmen should make sure local banks and realtors were not exploiting farmers. He thought there might be merit in a plan to charge depressed commodities lower railroad rates. In 1926 he tried to get bankers to finance the surplus cotton crop on condition that farmers restrict the acreage of cotton during the next year. He also supported the Norbeck-Burtness Bill making $50 million available for crop diversification. Finally, he wanted farmers to move to smaller towns, for "the very best result of all the forces in American life . . . are in towns from one thousand up to one hundred and fifty thousand"—hardly the West Branch he was supposed to idolize. Hoover wrote to Coolidge's secretary in 1925 criticizing Congress for not acting on the Agricultural Conference's proposals; without their implementation there would be "socialism," he said, meaning price-fixing. His persistent fear was of continuing overproduction.[22]

The idea that various units of the economy could regulate themselves under some degree of supervision, an idea so clearly represented in Secretary Hoover's farm program, had currency among spokesmen for business. It was related to the concept of business as a profession, which was reflected in the founding of business schools at Harvard and Stanford in the 1920's—and in the existence of more than two thousand trade associations. Associationalism, aiming to rationalize industry, drew inspiration from the War Industries Board and the progressive engineers who were set upon a Tayloristic quest of efficiency. Ellis Hawley has labeled the movement "associational progressivism." This was a "corporatist" ideology, a concept of society as organized into functionally independent economic units—voluntarily decentralized while self-governing and self-regulating. These units, each with its own agency of representation in a community, would work harmoniously out of a shared sense of social responsibility and devotion to efficiency. The ideal was not alone the absence of government but the presence of community. Hoover himself wrote of "a new era in the organization of industry and commerce in which, if properly directed, lie forces pregnant with infinite possibilities of moral progress." Businessmen would spend varying periods working in the Commerce Department, lending their special skills and expertise.[23]

Hoover encouraged a reasonable degree of cooperation among companies involved in marketing the same or similar commodities. He wanted broad representation, and urged, for example, that a proposed National Coffee Roaster Association include members from labor and consumer groups. Frederick Feiker of McGraw-Hill aided the department in supervising and promoting cooperation throughout industries. Commerce, Feiker believed, was becoming a profession with "a new sense of service"; this would be America's greatest contribution to the world. Much of his activity in Washington was aimed at rationalizing production, particularly —for the practical, undogmatic Hoover—in industries that were not doing well. The department assisted in the standardization and simplification of parts; and its *Survey of Current Business* ingeniously provided a public forum for the interchange, within an industry, of statistics bearing on cost accounting and economic trends. Hoover hoped that open and full publicity of statistics would permit cooperation short of monopoly, and he opposed collusion and price-fixing, although some of his advisors, such as W. E. Lamb and F. T. Miller, wanted the Justice Department to condone such practices. The trade associations gave a strong clientèle backing for the expansion of his department's activities.[24]

Attorney General Harry Daugherty, touchy about arrangements that looked monopolistic, moved against certain associations under the antitrust laws. The Lockwood Committee of the New York State Assembly had also viewed them as leading to administered shortages and monopolistic prices. Their views were bolstered by the Supreme Court's Hardwood decision of December 1921, which limited the scope of open price associations. Two months later Daugherty temporarily compromised by sanctioning the circulation of statistics through the Department of Commerce. The compromise sparked a coordinated effort within Commerce to help work out the complexities of standardizing products and processes. No particular company's scheme received Hoover's endorsement, and Daugherty briefly reinstated Justice's campaign against certain manufacturers' practices. Even after Daugherty's resignation, Hoover proceeded cautiously in most cases. With the Chamber of Commerce headed by Julius Barnes as an ally, he pressed the receptive and morally impeccable new Attorney General, Harlan Fiske Stone, for a ruling permitting the department's current policy. William E. Humphrey, a 1925 appointee to the Federal Trade Commission, also worked for greater freedom for the trade associations. The Supreme Court in June 1925, with Stone writing the decision, obliged by ruling in cement and maple flooring cases to permit industry-wide statistical exchanges.[25]

Hoover in effect came to embrace a nice distinction advocating a partial protection from antitrust in certain businesses—notably coal and oil—that had failed to prosper under a competitive system. He reluctantly requested such exemptions directly of Coolidge in 1924; he also suggested that cure for the troubles of the bituminous coal industry would be "a period of continuous operation under free competition and full movement of coal." Hoover supported the Federal Oil Conservation Board's proposal of 1926 —he was a dominating member—for unit operation of oil pools; the means would be an interstate compact allowing uniform state conservation laws. Specifically, he recommended in 1926 "an amendment to the Sherman Act permitting oil companies to curtail their drilling activities in small localized fields, which may threaten to upset the condition of the entire country." Conservation itself, which the control of overproduction would promote, was a secondary but important end. For most industries Hoover, while perhaps favoring some relaxation of the antitrust rule, would stay short of permitting cartelization; he did not advocate cartels even at the bottom of the depression, when some associations seemed to want them while others desired a revival of competitive individualism. Many historians have seen Hoover's activities in behalf of trade associations as a forerunner of the New Deal's National Recovery Administration; but he never countenanced monopolistic practices and as President had the Justice Department prosecute many monopolies, including that of his old friend Owen D. Young of General Electric. He also refused to pressure construction firms to join the American Construction Council as requested by its head, Franklin Roosevelt.[26]

Perceiving labor both as a separate unit within a cooperative society and as belonging to its various industrial components, Hoover regretted the loss of personal relationships attendant on the growth of large industrial plants, for it meant a diminution of mutual respect and responsibility between workers and owners, the crystallization of each party into an interest group. He wished to raise the bargaining power of labor to an equality with that of capital in order to restore to the individual worker something of the old independence. All major industries, he told Samuel Gompers, should be unionized. Strikes were sometimes necessary and reasonable weapons, but they caused waste in productivity. The answer, in Hoover's words, was "a definite and continuous organized relation . . . between the employer and the employee." Discussion would bring out the harmony of interest between the two sides and minimize the unavoidable conflicts, which was the proper intent of collective bargaining. The force of public opinion would impel parties to take advantage of regional government machinery. In 1924 Gompers, Owen D. Young, Julius Barnes, and other representatives of labor and capital came together at a dinner at Hoover's Washington house on "S" Street. The aim was to agree on certain principles of industrial relations, such as collective bargaining, that would put an end to strikes. But Hoover refrained from aggressively promoting union- ism: his high regard for progressive managers like Alexander Legge, John D. Rockefeller, Jr., MacKenzie King, and Charles Hicks, who were sponsoring various forms of employee representation under company aus- pices, kept him neutral as among differing modes of bargaining. He did denounce the use of shop committees as devices for the control of labor.[27]

Hoover played a big part in the campaign to end the twelve-hour day in steel, which half the employees worked (a quarter worked seven days a week). Nothing so affronted his belief in the perfectibility of the existing economic system as this primitive exploitation of men in steel. No indus- trial worker so manipulated, he believed, could play his assigned role of contented and loyal member of what some called the "new economic system." For two years Hoover used relentless persuasion, if not intimida- tion, to cajole the steel leaders into moving to the eight-hour day. He en- listed in his cause prominent engineers and university faculty, and of course the press. President Harding, at Hoover's suggestion, invited recal- citrant steel executives to dinner at the White House. Afterward, Hoover lectured the press on the industry's deplorable lack of social consciousness, and he redoubled his efforts to swing public opinion against steel. Pro- fessor Samuel Lindsay of Columbia also contributed a great deal, particu- larly through foundations, to overcome the powerful opposition, and the Federal Council of Churches was highly active. When the steel leaders continued to resist, Attorney General Daugherty advised Harding to take some public act that would win wide popularity and embarrass the industry. Sensing demagoguery, Hoover headed this off by sending Julius Barnes of the United States Chamber of Commerce to lunch with Judge Gary of United States Steel, who agreed to respond favorably to a presidential letter prom- ising the reform as soon as possible. The *coup de grâce* was a letter the implacable Hoover drafted for Harding's signature; it cleverly forced Judge Gary either to admit that the twelve-hour day was at least theoreti- cally undesirable or to isolate himself formally from the twentieth century. Gary replied that the industry would institute the eight-hour day when the move was "practicable." Hoover had the ailing Harding, then on his fatal Western trip, reply with vociferous congratulations. Complete victory came in 1923; and it had the effect of promoting the eight-hour day in other industries. Hoover boasted that the task had been accomplished "without the aid of a single law," by voluntary effort and publicity. His approach with the steel owners had been high-minded yet practical, and essentially

paternalistic. The steel industry, however, moved toward greater employment of the unorganized poor, and for another fifteen years managed to
live without unions. The eight-hour day was therefore a major but only a
partial victory for the steel workers.[28]

Hoover regarded bituminous coal, one of the depressed industries of
the twenties, as "the worst functioning" of all. Working conditions were
unsafe and the work itself irregular; savage competition made things hard
for management as well. Hoover believed that the owners would be delighted to sell out to the government at any time. In coal, as in farming,
World War I had overstimulated production and postwar demand had not
kept up. Rationalization of the industry, Hoover thought, could come with
voluntary consent, persuasion, a natural growth of larger units, and better
government statistics. But the industry's importance to consumers and the
war's role in causing suffering among the miners would justify some federal
intervention. Hoover's first attempt, through the Frelinghuysen Bill of
1921, to secure legislation for the collecting of statistical data was defeated
by suspicious Southern lobbyists who viewed it as a precedent for unioni-
zation.[29]

In the spring of 1922 a half-million members of the United Mine
Workers struck the bituminous industry, causing a coal scarcity, speculation, violence, virtual bankruptcy for some owners, and hunger among
workers and their families. For a time Hoover, contemplating the shortage
of coal, encouraged the employment of unorganized labor. His practicality
in this case so diluted his fairness as to bring him near to sanctioning the
violent anti-unionism of the Appalachian fields. At the same time he
recommended the use of a federal mediation commission with public representatives. The killing of dozens of men in Williamson County, Illinois,
brought stronger pressure from the administration toward settlement.
Hoover arranged a White House conference at which Harding proposed a
return to the higher prevailing wages of 1920; the opposition of the Mellon
coal interests assured this plan's rejection. With Harding's backing, Hoover
also tried to push through a settlement reverting to higher wages and
voluntary price controls. Neither plan succeeded. Hoover, now angry at
the selfish "swine" who plundered the consumer, eventually persuaded
Harding to force a rational system under which the Interstate Commerce
Commission would give priority to the movement of non-profiteering coal
under war powers. In late August a wage agreement engineered in part
by Secretary of Labor James Davis, who held formal responsibility for
handling the problem, ended the strike on terms favorable to the union's
position. Even after this, a law was passed and signed that established for
one year an office of Federal Fuel Distributor, whose task was holding
down prices.[30]

Since the settlement solved none of the industry's problems—if anything, it increased them—Hoover worked for district-wide associations in the bituminous industry that went almost to the point of federal dictation. A system of unemployment insurance under which operators who continued to produce on a regular basis were to make smaller payments would squeeze out part-time operators. A similar regional arrangement required part-time producers to shut down except in time of peak demand; the more efficient operators would compensate them. The plan also sought to accomplish savings through cooperative selling and an end to competitive transportation waste. This ingenious scheme garnered little support and many criticisms—some of them valid, as Hoover himself came to admit.[31]

In the face of a 1923 strike of some 150,000 Pennsylvania anthracite workers, Hoover supported the use of the 1922 United States Coal Commission, which had as its chairman the mining man John Hays Hammond and as its secretary Edward Eyre Hunt. The investigators rejected most of Hoover's earlier suggestions and produced a lengthy, confusing report that did no one any good. Governor Gifford Pinchot of Pennsylvania soon settled that strike, but at the cost of much higher coal prices, which sharply diminished anthracite's share of the market and contributed to future troubles.[32]

President Coolidge and Secretary of the Treasury Andrew Mellon opposed any significant degree of governmental interference in coal or any other industry. Hoover's tactic, therefore, was simply to encourage cooperation and reform from within. In February 1924 the bituminous mine owners, still under Hoover's threat of federal legislation, signed the Jacksonville agreement, extending the wage level of 1922 until 1927. The Commerce Secretary worked with John L. Lewis on this pact, which maintained the important bargaining regions. As late as 1926 the United Mine Workers *Journal* called Hoover "brilliant" and "a gifted economist." Lewis shared his thinking on the workability of capitalism, wanting only a larger slice of the profits for labor. Later Hoover disclaimed responsibility for enforcing the Jacksonville understanding, for doing so, he claimed, would violate the neutrality appropriate to the Secretary of Commerce. By the end of the decade the agreement had collapsed and the union grew weaker. Similar events occurred in the anthracite fields. Hoover observed in 1926: "It has been a deplorable business from every angle . . . especially depressing as indicating that we have not yet reached a stage of civilization where we can settle such primary things." Again he encouraged larger coal companies to force out the wasteful marginal ones. But by then Hoover had virtually given up; what he sought was impossible. The difficulties in the coal industry would be reflected in the checkered existence of the New Deal's Bituminous Coal Commission.[33]

The 400,000-member railway brotherhoods struck shortly after the bituminous miners in the spring of 1922. Strengthened by the war, these shopcraft unions operating as a national federation were challenging consecutive wage reductions by the Railway Labor Board and changes in working rules. The union grievance was chiefly with discriminatory implementation of the board's decisions. Attorney General Daugherty, siding with management, moved toward the use of an injunction, while Hoover worked to influence the more reasonable capitalists toward an equitable settlement. The railroad leaders crudely rebuffed his attempt and sought to deny strikers their seniority rights; Hoover later remarked that "their social instincts belonged to an early Egyptian period" and that they drove him to Bolshevism. Years afterwards he observed that while the Western railway men had social consciences, the Easterners "had their offices in New York. . . . [Many] still dodder around their clubs, quavering that 'labor must be disciplined.' " Hoover also became angry at the unions, as Harding was, for refusing to negotiate on seniority issues. The President fell under the influence of Daugherty, who in September asked Judge James Wilkerson of Chicago to issue an injunction, which was largely ineffective. Hoover declared himself "outraged by its obvious transgression of the most rudimentary rights of man," and, with Secretary of State Charles Evans Hughes, denounced Daugherty in a cabinet meeting. Returning prosperity ultimately aided most workers to reach a status quo agreement with management; others faced the restoration of the open shop.[34]

Hoover blamed the "reprehensible" railway construction of the previous generation of promoters as being responsible for the "witches' cauldron out of which we have been unable to secure any sanity." An amalgamation of weak and strong systems would make possible the replenishing of equipment for national needs. As long as rates were regulated, competition was largely diminished anyway. Farmers deserved lower rates than manufacturers. The railroads should receive aid in the form of purchases of their securities by the War Finance Corporation.

Reaction against the Daugherty injunction helped bring about the Railway Labor Act of 1926, one of the most important federal labor statutes. A number of times Hoover had criticized the Railroad Labor Board of 1920 for not enforcing its decisions against carriers. He lent his support late in 1925 to a plan accepted by both sides that he claimed was close to a solution he had proposed two or three years before. This act of 1926 set up a United States Board of Mediation in place of the previous board.

While its decisions were not binding, the board guaranteed unions collective bargaining and added a presidential fact-finding group that would operate during a cooling-off period prior to a strike. At the same time the board recognized company unions. The new law—an ancestor of the New Deal's Wagner Act—was a compromise favorable to labor (if to anyone). Hoover, along with the union lawyers Donald Richberg and David E. Lilienthal, deserved credit for its enactment.[35]

HOOVER WAS CONSCIOUS of the nation's undeveloped water resources as a source of great wealth. He visualized a coordinated national transportation system of inland waterways, including the Great Lakes; a St. Lawrence Seaway that would revitalize the Midwest's economy; flood control of the Mississippi and its tributaries; a mammoth Columbia River Basin reclamation project; and above all, the Colorado River project with its multiple aims. In the mid-twenties he widely distributed copies of his talks on the social consciousness of utilities, which he claimed profited only 6 to 8 percent on their investment, and on the superiority of state to federal regulation. This was part of an acknowledged administration campaign against public ownership of utilities. But he perceived the need for "giant power" and knew that this meant at least a uniformity of state regulation. Hoover called the Colorado his "favorite horsepower . . . pregnant with much larger possibilities than any other"—an oblique allusion to the favorite of his adversary Senator Norris, Muscle Shoals on the Tennessee River.[36]

The Colorado River, architect of the Grand Canyon, posed a continuing threat of treacherous floods in much of California's Imperial Valley, which could be drowned out by the breaking of the river into the Salton Sea. At the turn of the century Theodore Roosevelt had recognized the Colorado's potential for benefiting the Southwest through irrigation. He recommended federal funds for flood relief, but Congress refused. By 1919 the seven states of the Colorado Basin had agreed that federal aid and direction could ensure an equitable development of the Colorado's power as well as flood control and irrigation through an "All-American" canal route that avoided Mexican territory.

Congress in 1921 approved an interstate compact to be negotiated under the direction of the President's personal representative. Harding chose Hoover, who eagerly asked that he be appointed chairman of the Colorado River Commission and made a personal inspection of the area. At Bishop's Lodge, north of Santa Fe, Hoover and the Colorado attorney Delph Carpenter negotiated with seven states for a compact: "To get to the place you are obliged to wriggle in an automobile over a convolution of roads that dizzily sweep up and down like a switch-back roller coaster and hang precariously to the steep sides of the desolate landscape," wrote Hoover. When more delegates than he wanted registered at the lodge, he forced the manager to evict them under threat of moving the conference elsewhere. Wearing his famous frown, he warned recalcitrant Californians: "I'm going to disband this conference . . . and [say] that you are the people who killed Cock Robin." To Hoover's disappointment, all but two of the Californians then left the conference. Hoover avoided further trouble by what he called his "Wild Indian" article: "nothing in this compact shall be construed as affecting the rights of Indian tribes." Norris Hundley, a careful scholar of the negotiations, credits Hoover with "artfully and patiently" using his position of chairman: asking "probing questions" and suggesting essential compromises, including a proviso on the quantity of water delivered to each basin. Hoover wrote William Allen White that he had accomplished this "treaty between more fractious elements than any . . . I saw in Paris" only by "keeping them in a sanitarium for eighteen days. And I now have," he continued, "the pleasant job of ratification with seven Legislatures and Congress. . . . Some fellow is going to find an Article Ten in it if he can." As Hoover told Harding, "this is the first occasion when more than two states have under the direct provisions of the Constitution accomplished through this method the solution of interstate difficulties outside the Courts."[37]

In June 1922 Hoover testified in Congress on "the pressing emergency of the situation and the necessity for early action"—the "construction of a large storage dam." He added later: "These canyons on the Colorado are the most ideal spots in the world for dams of large storage and power possibilities." At one point he spoke of building a smaller dam that would avoid certain political problems, but was offended when critics accused him of backing down from earlier promises. Hoover consistently urged that Congress proceed, but Arizona's failure to ratify in 1923 brought stalemate; he suspected power company lobbies. He then visited each of the other six legislatures to obtain an amendment allowing the compact to hold for ratifying states even if one state should fail to join. Next, California added a stipulation requiring Congress to finance a dam on the river. This meant four more years of delay while Hoover sought the approval of the other states again. Had he submitted to his own state's pressure and included the dam project in the Santa Fe compact, it would never have been approved.[38]

The Boulder Canyon Project Act, written by Representative Phil Swing of California, passed in December 1928. Despite the dramatic example of the Mississippi flood, the bill had died in filibuster in May. But Hoover's election forced its passage. The disclosure of huge sums spent on lobbying by the power companies added to the margin of support. Appeasement of conservatives dictated that the bill, drafted in its Senate version partly by Hoover, should list power as a minor purpose of the project and leave the matter of extent of federal control largely up to the Secretary of the Interior. The act would pay for irrigation, flood control, and aqueducts to Los Angeles. But power was the real object. Senator Reed Smoot of Utah saw through the rhetoric about flood control and irrigation, protesting angrily to Coolidge that "its primary . . . object is the production of electric power." The project, said Smoot, was "ten times worse than Muscle Shoals and it violates fundamental and precious principles of our form of Government." The governor of Arizona attacked "nationalizing" the river. Hoover boasted that for three years he alone had prevented the Federal Power Commission from granting licenses for private development of the Colorado. And he emphasized: "All this [power] will belong to the people, developed by them, owned by them and for their benefit."[39]

While public power groups fought among themselves, advocates of private power, with notable exceptions such as Owen D. Young, did what they could to stall the building of Boulder Dam. But the facility was so closely identified with Hoover's leadership that utilities were cautious in opposition. Congressman Swing and Elwood Mead, Commissioner of the Bureau of Reclamation, sparked the early construction of the dam. It would be twice as high as any yet built. At Black Canyon tunnels diverted the river and left a dry stretch of bed on which to build. The Depression hastened work by Six Companies, Inc. Dozens of men died in accidents at the dangerous, sun-baked site, and discriminatory housing for Negro laborers set off protests. But the dam got built; and the project rivaled in magnitude the entire Tennessee Valley development.* [40]

Hoover's plan of comprehensive inland waterways would aid the farmer by cutting in half, on the average, the shipping distance between producer and consumer. He projected 9000 miles of river highways—northward from New Orleans to Chicago and Duluth, westward from Pittsburgh to Kansas City—and thousands of miles more in tributary routes. The development money would come jointly from federal and state government, with federal administration. In 1926 Hoover wrote to Senator Arthur Capper: "I am leaving . . . for the Far West where I am continuing to preach about waterways . . . that is the one practical thing we can get over at the next session of Congress even on an enlarged scale over anything we have hitherto contemplated." During the trip President Coolidge sent Hoover

---

* Las Vegas owes much of its early start to these workings; thousands of laboring men on sprees gave that town its first lurch toward its present neon sprawl.

a sharp telegram questioning the projects because they would need vast federal appropriations. But for the engineer who had visions of building an empire of dams and waterways, the Rivers and Harbors Bill of 1926, which established the Mississippi system, was only a start. The grandest idea was the St. Lawrence Seaway.[41]

The dream of joining the Great Lakes to the Atlantic by a canal that would take oceangoing vessels dates back to the nineteenth century. During the war Hoover saw the desirability of the Canadian route, but he rarely if ever invoked national security as an argument for it. The inadequacy of railroad rolling stock at harvest time was sufficient need for an alternate transportation route. But the success of the Panama Canal, which injured Midwestern agriculture and industry, delayed consideration until Congress in 1919 authorized the International Joint Commission to make a report. Finding the commission's 1922 estimate agreeable in cost, the United States then approached Canada about a mutual undertaking, and received a favorable answer. In 1920 New York's two legislative houses had gone on record in opposition: there was fear of a diversion of trade from the state's waterways and cities, despite the cheap power that would result. Some chauvinists claimed that Canada would be the chief beneficiary of its southern neighbor's investment in the Seaway. But the Midwest, economically lagging and troubled by rising railway rates, was enthusiastic for the project. In 1924 Coolidge appointed Hoover head of an *ad hoc* St. Lawrence Commission to investigate the scheme, including its technical feasibility. Eighteen states joined in an association for promoting it. In 1926 Hoover's commission issued a favorable report, which told New Yorkers that the population growth effected by the Seaway would offset any economic loss. By now the plan was looking to the use of the channeled waters for electrical power.[42]

The Secretary of Commerce wrote to a friend that the project "meant more to me than almost anything else in this world." He released an array of engineering and economic statistics to counter a proposal to dredge the Erie Canal and Hudson River for a separate route. And, of course, he put publicity to work for the Seaway. He urged the editor of the *New York Evening Post* not to exacerbate Midwestern hostility to New York by opposition to the Seaway; other letters went off to the *Des Moines Register,* the *Chicago Daily News* ("the most important public improvement since the construction of the Panama Canal"), and wherever else they might be of assistance. Hoover also toured the river and presided over a joint engineering commission in 1926 studying how to save the "face" of Niagara Falls.

Hoover's efforts in behalf of the St. Lawrence Seaway were vigorous, though scattershot in approach. Had he later employed his office of the presidency with all its power of persuasion as well as he used his Commerce job with all its channels of investigation, the Seaway could have been completed long before the 1950's. His trust that the Senate would approve such a rational project was confounded by the small political hindrances that brought a 1-vote defeat of the treaty in 1934.[43]

Hoover also partially failed in his efforts to deal with oil pollution in his capacity as Commerce Secretary. Already in the 1920's oil was polluting American waterways and its three great coasts—chiefly from industrial-grade tankers that carried water in their holds for ballast and discharged it near ports of destination. Gobs of asphaltum covered oyster beds in areas like Chesapeake Bay; in numerous estuaries and bays a skim of oil on the surface prevented fish from spawning; coagulated oil refuse washed up onto Atlantic and Gulf shore bathing beaches; waterfowl sickened; and fires broke out in harbors, among them Baltimore and New Orleans. The situation was within the province of Commerce, and Hoover took an important part in an early, unsuccessful environmental movement.

After a conference of fishing associations at the Commerce Department in June 1921 had recommended legislation, Hoover repeatedly testified vigorously before House committees in behalf of "very drastic regulation." When a congressman asked whether the industries could invent devices for recovering the oil before the discharge of the bilge water, Hoover replied: "the probabilities are that invention would follow rapidly on legislation in restraint. There is comparatively little effort going on in the shipping trades to find mechanical devices, because there is no particular pressure on them to do so." The bill that the committee worked on provided also for a general inquiry into industrial pollution. Some partially spoiled areas, Hoover believed, were reclaimable, while cleaning up others, such as New York Harbor, would involve the dislocation of too much industry for reclamation to be worth the cost. His proposal was to sort all American streams and rivers into three categories: clean, partially polluted, and beyond recovery.[44]

Only weak legislation passed in 1924. Testimony given by the Bureau of Fisheries against industrial plants was completely ignored. Hoover spoke of "my pollution bill" and called himself "the arch antipollutionist in the country." Once the bill had taken final shape, he complained to the head of the Isaak Walton League that the oil industry had "reached" key Republican legislators: "Official Washington has no knowledge that the American people give a damn about pollution, and until they do care and let the State governments and the Federal Government know that they do care there will be no great advances as to pollution"; nor, he said, did the press seem to care. Hoover's idea of centralizing all federal waterways activity in a Bureau of Merchant Marine Affairs got little support in the administration. At a small conference on international control "of which I am somewhat the father," Hoover offered his department as an international clearinghouse for publicizing information on world pollution; many countries signed an agreement stipulating zones free of dumping, but Germany and Italy refused.[45]

THE OBJECTIVES of the Commerce Department in this age of proliferating research and statistics dictated that its work in the gathering of information useful to business would grow. It was an activity that went well with Hoover's public character of spokesman for benevolent expertise. During his tenure Commerce greatly expanded its capacity to provide business with information and advice. A division of domestic commerce, established in 1923 under Frank M. Surface, made regional surveys. An area would be examined for its density and clustering of population, its income, occupations, schooling, "habits and traditions," and buying power—the prospects it offered for being a market. An *Atlas of Wholesale Grocery Territories,* for example, simplified trade terms and practices. Studies of the costs required for the enlargement of sales territories were of much use to business. Like other Commerce units, this one dealt with a growing stream of daily inquiries: "How do you treat sick bull frogs?" But by far the greater part of the effort of Commerce was in the investigation of business opportunities outside the United States. The Secretary had as one of his main goals the expansion of the country's world trade.

Hoover took the Department's tiny Bureau of Foreign and Domestic Commerce—which had little to do with domestic affairs—quintupled its budget and personnel, increased its offices abroad from twenty-three to fifty-eight while the domestic offices went from seven to twenty-nine, and put it under the able direction of Julius Klein, a Harvard professor of Latin American history and economics. It, too, would function as a "balance wheel" to stabilize the domestic economy: credits, better marketing information, and elimination of waste would all come under the bureau's program. It would become the hub of the department's activities, contributing data of immediate use to business. By 1924 Commerce had outposts in Estonia, Latvia, Batavia, Tientsin, and Soerabaja, among other distant places. Hoover at once saw a need to specialize not in countries but in commodities. He secured Frederick Feiker's assistance in creating fifteen divisions by industrial categories, and brought industry experts to Washington, where they labored with the 2500-member bureau at determining promotional policies best suited for each product. Automobile companies, for example, were urged to set up more service centers abroad. The common task was to advise on foreign competition; on the availability of financing, shipping, and raw materials; and on foreign laws, particularly import regulations. A Department of Regional Information headed by Louis Demaratzky contributed regularly to *Foreign Affairs,* compiling helpful studies on cartels and trends in international economics. Much of the bureau's work came through publications such as *What the World Wants, Monthly Summary of Foreign Commerce, Exporters' Index, Food-stuffs Around the World, Foreign Notes on Meats, Fats, Oils and Live Stock.* These new publications joined the essential annual, *Commerce Reports* (1923–   ), in aiding the international businessman. Special department reports included "Sisal Situation in Yucatan" and "Black Sea Trade Routes." Hoover urged a larger United States Merchant Marine that could increase American presence on routes of international trade; many of these routes, he claimed, simply extended inland waterways. The bureau located new markets and increased United States business by hundreds of millions of dollars a year. In 1922, for instance, it helped find a market for California's enormous rice surplus.[46]

Hoover wanted commercial, not military, expansion for the United States. Especially notable was his dislike of interference in Latin America. It was characteristic of him, as of so many Wilsonians, that he expected the American role abroad to bring a higher standard of living to the rest of the world. In the process, it was believed, the United States would eclipse Great Britain in world economic leadership.

The work of Hoover's refurbished bureau came into conflict with that of Foreign Service commercial attachés already stationed at the various embassies. The embassies had none of Commerce's commodity specialists, no close relations with American business firms, and no periodicals publicizing business opportunities abroad. Hoover's undiplomatic handling of economic matters with political implications brought him criticism. Denmark protested formally to the United States over a headline, "Danish Economic Conditions Unfavorable," in a 1923 issue of *Commerce Reports.* A book published in 1925 by Consul General Tracy Lee criticized this kind of tactlessness; Hoover persuaded Secretary of State Charles Evans Hughes to indicate that the book was unofficial. There was temporary discomfort between the two men, but Hughes was secure enough to admit frankly to a subordinate that businessmen wanted a system of economic attachés under Hoover's control. Acrimonious memos were exchanged between the two departments after Frank Kellogg succeeded Hughes in 1925; but Kellogg then advised embassies to cooperate with Hoover. By mid-decade Hoover's operations in the field of trade had outgrown and subsumed those of State. American businessmen and union publicists came to look on Commerce as the expert on foreign economies.[47]

Hoover was discriminating about where American capital should be invested abroad. He desired investments that would strengthen foreign economies, as well as loans that would increase the ability of economically healthy foreign nations to buy American goods and to repay debts to the United States. The Commerce Department exerted pressure toward making loans contingent on the purchase of American products. A stronger world economy would mean a stronger American economy: again we see the implicit assumption that self-interest and altruism can go together. "Enlightened self-interest," many Wilsonians called it.

But Hoover did not like it when cheap labor abroad, shipping costs, and discriminatory foreign tariffs led American companies to set up branches overseas; he discouraged loans to countries that had reached no agreement to pay their war debts; he was hostile to the financing of armaments; and he wanted to keep American money out of risky investments, the more so because troubled investments invited American intervention. Knowledgeable concern with world finance made Commerce personnel more cautious than State's on foreign loans, especially to Germany and France. A Senate investigation of 1932 into losses on loans proved the record of Commerce officials to have been foresighted. Hoover's attitude may have had one of its sources in a nationalistic concern for economic self-sufficiency: he did not want American manufacturers to become dependent on foreign markets, and he feared that excessive agricultural exports could disturb the balance of trade. National self-sufficiency was another Wilsonian theme.[48]

Through non-coercive methods—press releases, public speeches, and day-to-day departmental activities—he strove to influence the placing of loans. A White House conference in 1921, inspired by Hoover, articulated the principle that investors inform the State Department of proposed loans, which the Treasury and Commerce departments would then judge for their desirability. His plan was one source of bitter antagonism from New York bankers; Benjamin Strong, governor of the New York Federal Reserve, filed a vigorous protest with the Secretary of State. Figures as diverse as Senator Carter Glass of Virginia, the corporate attorney John Foster Dulles, and *The Nation*'s editor Lewis Gannett all protested against the Hoover program as interference with the traditional free flow of capital. Speculative investments abroad would have been even greater had the Commerce Department not been so vigilant. As Hoover remarked in response to an attack from FDR in 1932, no defaults had occurred "where my proposed safeguards have been followed." But he lacked the power to pass on many of the riskiest loans. Commenting on the entire loan surveillance program, Hoover in his *Memoirs* blamed Harding and particularly Coolidge and Mellon for "a retreat from our original standards."[49]

Beginning in 1921, Hoover warned against efforts on the part of foreign governments and businesses to raise profits on raw materials by constraints on their exports. In the United States, as he pointed out in a congressional hearing, such a thing would be unconstitutional under the antitrust laws. He singled out rubber and coffee as "combinations in restraint of trade" that cost Americans—consumers and industry—$300 million annually. British restrictions on exports of rubber from Ceylon and Malaya did drive up prices, and Congress in 1923 funded a survey of crude rubber and field expeditions in search of alternative areas for growing rubber. Hoover also recommended the use of substitutes, the limitation of American loans for these monopolies, and retaliatory action in the form of government subsidies or of buying pools authorized by Congress that would keep American buyers from bidding against one another. To fight alleged coffee and potash monopolies, Hoover attempted with some success to discourage loans to Brazil, France, and Germany. His attack on the potash cartel hindered one of the few instances of cooperation between France and Germany. By 1928 both countries had agreed not to engage in activities in the potash industry that the American antitrust laws would forbid for American enterprise. In the meantime Congress had made an appropriation that enabled Scott Turner, the director of the Bureau of Mines, to locate potash in American lands. "How far did you want me to take this search?" Turner asked Hoover. "Just to the point where [private] industry will take it on," was the reply. Turner spent only a little money finding potash deposits so rich that New Mexico quickly became an exporter to foreign countries.[50]

A later congressional investigation indicated that Hoover had exaggerated the extent of some of the monopolies. The *New York Times* criticized his aggressiveness toward the economic policies of foreign governments and noted that he had advocated restricting wheat production though many of the world's people were starving; and *The Nation* defended the British plan for saving rubber growers from ruin in face of the American tariff. Owen D. Young, as one of Hoover's progressive associates, questioned the Secretary's emphasis on the danger of monopolies in raw materials. "I am sincerely troubled," wrote Young in 1926, "by our national program, which is demanding amounts from our debtors up to the breaking point, and at the same time excluding their goods from our American markets, except those few raw materials which we must have. I think our position would be much stronger in criticizing their artificial restraints if we did not indulge in them ourselves, and at the same time demand extraordinary payments." Young was on the commissions to renegotiate war debts, and he had obviously attained a different perspective from Hoover's. Certainly the high American duties, as surely as the international monopolies Hoover deplored, artificially restrained trade and were a protection of the American standard of living. There was a chauvinistic tone to some of Hoover's pronouncements, and he took personal credit for driving down prices. In his mind, we should suspect, the interest of a benevolent United States was hardly distinguishable from the interest of mankind, and a benign vision of a peaceful world of enlightened productivity and trade could co-exist with his nationalist concerns. And he really did perceive in foreign monopolies the possibility of disastrous trade wars and the crumbling of international stability.[51]

Winston Churchill, Hoover's old nemesis, was behind the compulsory government restraint of British rubber production. The act drawn up by Churchill's financial advisor, James Stevenson, probably did force prices up by some 20 percent, but the United States's demand for automobile tires also contributed to the rise. There was danger that American threats to control cotton and wheat exports—or to finance separate United States rubber plantations in the Far East—would damage Anglo-American relations. While a temporary buying pool among rubber-processing companies in 1927 and 1928 aided the United States, the Stevenson plan lapsed in 1928 and then the Newton bill legalizing the American rubber pool failed to pass Congress. But given the high grain prices of the World War era, the Hoover campaign left a bitter residue, which this British quatrain catches:

> Because of rising costs of rubber
> Dear Hoover, is it wise to blubber?
> You took your whack in recent years—
> When war was on. Oh, dry those tears.[52]

Hoover's position on war debts had its public and private face, and shifted in the course of the decade. As a member of the American World War Foreign Debt Commission, he initially shocked his colleagues by joining the British in calling for the cancellation of international debts incurred by governments before the Armistice and suggesting that some of the remaining payments should go to bring foreign students to the United States. "Some sacrifices on our part," he wrote Harding, "might bring definite economic compensations [in the form of greater European stability] as well as a better world." At the 1922 Washington Conference Hoover inserted a clause implicitly relating reparations and war debts. But after the Foreign Debt Commission had given prolonged thought to political realities and congressional stubbornness, Hoover came down with "a slight case of ptomaine poisoning" when he was about to deliver a cancellationist speech. At Toledo, in October 1922, he recommended repayment of the entire $11 billion, and, probably for political reasons, refused publicly to admit a relationship between debts and the reparations he deplored. The United States, he declared, had lost economic ground on account of the war, notably by inflation and overexpansion of industry. He argued that the loan payments amounted to only about 5 percent of European buying power, that the United States paid more interest on the bonds that financed the loans than it received in interest, and that debtors spent five times as much in America on arms alone. He did suggest that interest payments should be reduced, and he had recommended a compromise on interest and the period of repayment in return for progress toward disarmament. In a letter to President Harding he went further than this by offering $500 million in loans in return for balanced budgets and armaments restrictions. The United States Grain Administration could act as the agency for this work. American public opinion was of like mind that the debts ought to be paid. The liberal *New Republic*'s TRB, in a comment worthy of Babbitt, complained of "all the skepticism I have felt from the first as to the getting of real money from these people."[53]

Hoover was somewhat severe—more so than Andrew Mellon—on the French position, which offered less than half the cost in interest carried by the American taxpayer. He would, however, accept the somewhat nebulous criterion of ability to pay, a "safeguard" clause which was more generous to France than to Britain. Coolidge wanted to break off negotiations with France. But Europe had "hates enough," Hoover responded; "we must show the consideration of a great nation seeking to do the generous and just thing." He offered a plan that would be reviewed in a few years when the economy of France was stronger or at least clearer. This move the French rejected. Whatever agreement the French made, Hoover observed in 1925, they would break when they found it convenient to do so. He told his fellow commission member Senator Reed Smoot that while the United States might need some time to make a debt concession for the purpose of getting disarmament in Europe, "we had better have something in storage to concede." A reduction in armaments might enable America to reduce its military costs and therefore forgive more of the debt.[54]

Each country was dealt with differently. The settlement with Great Britain was perhaps generous to the United States. For years France refused to settle at all; in 1929, ratification of an agreement with interest payments averaging only 1.6 percent narrowly passed the Chamber of Deputies. The Commerce Department adjudged France able to pay if it pursued conservative fiscal policies. Germany received many loans from American investors in spite of Hoover's repeated warnings, which were much resented by United States bankers who profited from promoting the flow of capital. Germany owed Hoover some thanks for recommending Charles Dawes—along with Owen D. Young and Henry Robinson—as advisor for the Dawes Reparation Commission, which scaled down the

German payments. "The Dawes Commission," Hoover later said, "succeeded beyond our hopes." The only cabinet member to endorse the plan in public, Hoover believed that a strong Germany would be an important buffer against the Soviet Union. In part because of his prodding, a treaty of commerce with Germany was ratified in 1925. When the Dawes plan proved inadequate, a committee chaired by Young in 1929 again revised the debt repayment schedules, joining debts and reparations. This plan lasted only until 1931, when under pressure of the Depression Hoover declared a one-year moratorium on foreign debts to the United States.[55]

DURING THE COMMERCE YEARS the Hoovers lived in a colonial house at 2300 "S" Street, its balcony overlooking the District; an acre of garden flowers bloomed for much of the year. "S" Street was similar to the Red House in London. In both, and later in the White House, guests came to dinner almost nightly. Sunday night gatherings during the Commerce years were regularly attended by the Mark Sullivans and Justice and Mrs. Stone— the Hoovers' special friends. Lou Henry Hoover retained her public anonymity throughout these years with one exception: as honorary president of the Girl Scouts, she raised over $2 million, which helped to increase its membership from 100,000 to 1 million girls. Allan Hoover entered Stanford in 1925 after attending public schools. Herbert, Jr., already a Stanford graduate, married and began work as an electronics engineer. The family occasionally took "working vacations" during the twenties, usually to Palo Alto or the Florida Keys. Sometimes—rather infrequently, in fact—Hoover fished. One of the automobile's greatest benefits, he said, was extending the fisherman's preserves. Fishermen are optimistic, he claimed; otherwise they would not be fishermen. His remark "all men are equal before fishes" was a profession of democracy; the blessings of fishing, he said, included a "mockery of profits and conceits, a quieting of hate and a hushing to ambition, a rejoicing and gladness that you do not have to decide a blanked thing until next week."

The presidency would allow him no such respites.

X

THE 1928 CAMPAIGN

CALVIN COOLIDGE, that most unspectacular and undramatic of men, nevertheless managed from time to time to rivet the attention of the nation. At about noon on the showery day of August 2, 1927, newspaper reporters in attendance on Coolidge filed into the mathematics classroom of the Rapid City High School, near South Dakota's Black Hills where he was vacationing. Coolidge was already in the room, and when the door closed, he curtly told the newsmen: "The line forms on the left." As they passed by, the slight man from Vermont handed each a slip of paper that read: "I do not choose to run for President in nineteen twenty-eight." Asked for further comment he replied, "None," and went off to lunch. The statement meant precisely what a New Englander would suppose: Coolidge did not want to run again. There was little speculation about it in the Vermont papers. Mrs. Coolidge, having made a quilt with "Calvin Coolidge, 1923–1929" embroidered on it, had already told reporters that she knew what she was about. The death of Coolidge's son at fourteen, of blood poisoning, had taken away much of the joy of being President, and the strains of the office placed a heavy burden on a man with chronic indigestion who needed to sleep a dozen hours a day. Had he run again, he would also have had to face the American aversion to a third term in office. Too prudent to risk overstaying his welcome, Coolidge in 1929 went back to live in an ordinary white house in Northampton, Massachusetts, and died there less than four years later. In the 1930's Hoover denied to a magazine editor that Coolidge had hoped for renomination: "I know it from direct, positive, intimate and complete discussion."*[1]

* Hoover offered another interpretation: when Coolidge experimented in fishing with flies, "he gave the Secret Service guards great excitement in dodging his backcast and rescuing flies from trees. There were many photographs. Soon after that [since there were 25 million fishermen] he decided he did not choose to run again."

In 1924 Calvin Coolidge had wanted Senator William E. Borah for his vice-presidential running mate. It was a sensible choice. Borah and George Norris were the two most prominent Republican progressives in the Senate; Borah's opposition to the McNary-Haugen Bill made him an acceptable agrarian candidate who could take some of the edge off rural discontent. But when Borah would have none of it, some Republican leaders, especially William Butler, wanted Hoover to be the vice-presidential nominee. Senator Reed Smoot pointed out that Hoover would appeal to many different groups, notably women and businessmen. Governor Frank Lowden, another agrarian progressive who opposed McNary-Haugen, briefly backed Hoover, and Coolidge himself was reported to be receptive. Yet there were reasons not to nominate the Commerce Secretary: friction with Secretary of Agriculture Wallace and lingering doubts about his conduct of the Food Administration had made him unpopular with many farmers, and party stalwarts remembered his semi-endorsement of Wilson's call for a Democratic Senate in 1918. On the third ballot Hoover earned 334½ votes, chiefly in the South and Far West, against 682 for Charles Dawes, a colorful banker and lawyer chosen in spite of his criticisms of organized labor. Hoover campaigned for Coolidge in California as he had for congressional Republicans in 1922; but he thoroughly disliked the political hustings.[2]

Hoover himself was far removed from the Teapot Dome scandal. For whatever reasons, no letters are to be found in the Hoover Papers touching on the affair of the oil lands leased by government officials to business acquaintances without competitive bidding. There is a calendar record of a forty-five-minute meeting on May 16, 1923, with "a Mr. Sinclair." And Hoover received some complaints from businessmen who had gotten no opportunity to bid on oil leases at Teapot Dome and Elk Hills. His relations with Secretary of the Interior Albert Fall, to whom he forwarded these for reply, were good, and it took him some time to accept the fact of Fall's involvement in the scandal. On Fall's resignation, Hoover said that Interior had never had "so constructive and legal a headship." President Harding was talking in January 1923 of appointing Fall to the Supreme Court. Hoover was antagonistic to Attorney General Daugherty, and worked to have him ousted. The Hoovers were friendly with Secretary of the Navy Denby and his wife; and when the scandal broke out after Harding's death, they made a point of being decent to Denby, who had given bureaucratic sanction to the leases but was innocent of wrongdoing. It is doubtful that either Denby or Hoover had any early knowledge of the more private dealings: those involved would have had no reason to reveal their purposes. Yet it is interesting that during the spring of 1923 Hoover sent his assistant, Lawrence Richey, to London to collect denials of his alleged wrongdoing in China. This at least raises the possibility that Hoover was considering the prospects for his own presidential candidacy in 1924. Hoover certainly had been close to Harding, in any event. In February 1923 he had worked with Senators Lenroot and Pepper, and Assistant Secretary of the Navy Theodore Roosevelt, Jr., on a progressive program they hoped the President would endorse on a speaking tour that summer. (This was not unlike a similar plan Hoover had backed with William Allen White early in 1921.) Hoover accompanied the President on the tour which culminated in his death in San Francisco that August. And in 1931, when he dedicated the huge, hollow Harding Memorial in Marion, Ohio, President Hoover would denounce old cabinet colleagues—particularly Daugherty, who was sitting in the audience. It was a way of doing homage to Harding, whose capacity for hard work had won Hoover's respect. Hoover also was responsible for getting the journalist Samuel Blythe to write a flattering article on Harding.*[3]

By the mid-twenties Hoover had emerged as the best-known party figure in Washington except for Coolidge; politically both men were prospering. *The New Republic*'s TRB put it this way in September 1925:

Speaking of Hoover, it is certainly not generally recognized in the country at large (and even here in Washington by only a limited number) how extraordinarily extensive is his impress upon the government outside of his own Department. There is reason to doubt whether in the whole history of the American government a Cabinet officer has engaged in such wide diversity of activities or covered quite so much ground.

The plain fact is that no vital problem, whether in the foreign or the domestic field, arises in this administration in the handling of which Mr. Hoover does not have a real—and very often a leading—part. There is more Hoover in the administration than anyone else. Except in the newspapers and the political field there is more Hoover in the administration than there is Coolidge. . . .

This is not because Hoover pushes himself forward and asks for them. A more modest, retiring man it would be hard to find—certainly here in Washington. He is doing the things he is because of the sheer knowledge and ability of the man and his extraordinary experience which has covered many fields and many parts of the world.[4]

Hoover was a distinctly progressive figure and certainly less parochial than many of the much-touted Senate progressives. "I am convinced," he wrote to Professor Samuel Lindsay of Columbia, "that for social reasons we need an entirely revised inheritance tax. . . . I would like to see a

* In 1934 Hoover summed up his view of the scandals. "There was much wrong-doing and much hysteria . . . these men were stock promoters, they were not so much interested in what oil they got or what bargains they made with the Government. . . . The moral damage was immense. Harding had no part in it, and most officials, such as Denby, Bain, and others served their Government well in driving good bargains, and had no corrupt relations. As to Fall, Doheny, Sinclair, etc., that is another matter."

steeply graduated tax on legacies and gifts . . . for the deliberate purpose of disintegrating large fortunes." Hoover regretted that he could not support Secretary Mellon's tax program without such a stipulation. "If . . . it is desirable," he continued in the election year 1924, "that I should come up and express my frank views on this whole question, I am not afraid to do so." He had already lectured President Harding on the need to tax "earned" income less and the stocks and bonds of the "well to do" more. The impatient Hoover sometimes irritated Calvin Coolidge, who relied even more heavily on him than had Harding. Proposals in a slew of letters from the Commerce Secretary to Coolidge early in 1924 would go far beyond what the President wanted. Hoover remembered Coolidge in his *Memoirs* as "a real conservative, probably the equal of Benjamin Harrison." "He fished with worms," fly angler Hoover observed disdainfully. Coolidge did not like to spend money on such projects as waterpower and no doubt was bothered by the extra work and controversy generated by Commerce. But he must have regarded Hoover's nomination in 1928 as inevitable.[5]

In the spring of 1927 the Commerce Secretary dominated the headlines in a drama restating all the best that he represented of the engineer, the humanitarian, and the administrator. The great Mississippi flood ruined the South, someone commented, and elected Hoover. After an enormous snow that winter and then rain for two weeks along the entire watershed from Minnesota southward, water spread like an inland sea over an area 1000 miles long and up to 40 miles wide. Seven hundred thousand homes were inundated, along with virtually all the crops; thousands of livestock died and some 600,000 people were made destitute. The country was unprepared. But the obvious parallels to wartime led six governors of the region to request help from Hoover. Coolidge appointed a special Mississippi Flood Committee with Hoover as chairman; this established a precedent of federal responsibility for floods. Hoover exercised plenary authority as in wartime. The phases of relief were rescue work, refugee camps, and then rehabilitation— all directed by telegraph or radio from Hoover's headquarters in Memphis high on the Chickasaw Bluffs and from his private railway car, which kept circling the flood area from Cairo to New Orleans. For three months Hoover, who called the flood "the greatest peace-time calamity in the history of the country," stayed in the news: on national radio hook-up and in thousands of photographs, one of them catching him in Opelousas, Louisiana, beaming over newborn triplets named Highwater, Flood, and Inundation.[6]

There first appeared a fleet of six hundred vessels, sixty government airplanes, hundreds of Red Cross nurses, thousands of National Guardsmen, then more thousands of volunteers, including some from Hoover's previous relief organizations. The work was supported by a Red Cross relief fund of $16 million, supplemented by emergency state credit corporation funds of $12 million, Federal Intermediate Credit Corporation funds of $10 million, and $10 million from the Flood Credits Corporation—a private business group with further financing. As in the use of war relief, administrative overhead accounted for less than 1 percent. "For Hoover," the historian Bruce Lohof wrote in a study of the flood, "bureaucracy was a source of nourishment for grass-roots activity." Hoover's centralized organization aimed to coordinate and rationalize individual efforts. Some 325,000 people moved into 150 refugee camps in a kind of instant urbanizing of a rural people. The camps went up under local direction, and Hoover praised this American ingenuity and leadership. He also persuaded the Rockefeller Foundation to finance one hundred county health units; these worked so successfully that when he became President, he tried to get them set up in every county. "Mr. Hoover's masterly handling of the situation," a British observer wrote, "has aroused universal admiration. An administrative task of this nature is exactly what his particular talents are best adapted to tackle and he has shown that he has lost none of his old organizing ability."[7]

Hoover helped design the Mississippi Flood Control Bill of 1928, which would make the federal government responsible for rebuilding levees and for preventing and controlling floods on the river. He had wanted a special session of Congress to meet November 1, 1927, but Coolidge would have none of that. Hoover the engineer recommended higher and wider levees, their extension to tributary streams, a spillway to protect New Orleans, and the possible building of flood and storage basins. He estimated the cost at $15 to $20 million for each of twenty years, a sum in addition to $18 million to prevent recurrence in 1928 and to improve navigation. The Senate adopted the Jadwin Flood-Control Plan, named after the Army Engineers chief, partly because its projected safety-valve spillways and secondary levees were cheaper than other schemes.

In the midst of the relief effort of 1927 Hoover asked the Red Cross to increase the number of Negroes on its relief staff, and over the objections of Southern white politicians recommended that an official Negro advisory commission oversee the work. One of its members, Dr. Sidney Redmont, was a forthright critic of peonage in the South. Walter White of the NAACP charged that Negroes in the refugee camps, penned in like prisoners, had been held until claimed by the owner of the plantation they had left. White wanted an inquiry into unequal treatment of Negroes on the part of the Red Cross, and Hoover in May appointed Dr. Robert Moton, president of Tuskegee Institute, to investigate and visit the camps. Hoover blamed the trouble on the "economic system which exists in the South," and observed that only three people, none of them black, had died in the camps. But when Moton presented a report highly critical of the camps, Hoover appointed Negro assistants in each county to search out and report to the Red Cross "each case of failure and neglect," which the Red Cross would investigate "at once."

In September Moton asked Hoover for a second review. Upon receiving this report Hoover, according to Moton's later account, again acted promptly, dismissing one particularly objectionable relief worker. Hoover, however, chastised Moton for not giving generous credit to the work of the Red Cross. Both men wanted nurses and social workers in the camps who would give some education to the poor blacks. Moton wrote of Hoover in April 1928: "he has taken immediate and radical steps not only to correct whatever abuses occur, but to prevent any recurrence. I am satisfied that the colored people of America have nowhere a more intelligent, just and sympathetic friend." Moton's committee absolved Hoover of any personal blame and reported that he had tried to remedy wrongs; but the more militant NAACP found him slow to take action or to express indignation publicly.[8]

The Mississippi disaster sharpened Hoover's consciousness of the plight of black and poor white tenants and sharecroppers. On some lands, in fact, the flood by bankrupting the planters had broken the system and opened up the possibility of change. Hoover early got the idea of giving the rural poor, particularly blacks, funds left over from relief to buy the land they worked. As his friend Edgar Rickard wrote in his diary, Hoover was working on an "enormous land scheme which will place the negro in possession of a small plot and give him chance to make good." When the Red Cross summarily refused to aid the plan, he approached Julius Rosenwald with a proposal for a large-scale project; but the Chicago philanthropist thought a small experiment wiser. Hoover wanted a "land resettlement corporation," with $1 or $2 million in capital, able to buy big amounts of the best land in the delta. His plan would allow the poor "to take nominal title . . . and to acquire a real title by installment paying, largely in the form of crops. . . ." The initial management of the scheme would have to be strict, involving even a company store. But by means of getting good land cheaply and "selecting thrifty and industrious Negroes graduates of such institutions as Tuskegee and the state agricultural colleges—a good class of Negro farm owners might be developed." Unless we are to suppose that Hoover thought the Deep South to be thick with graduates of these places, we may presume that he would have argued only for a leavening of the scheme through the inclusion of the educated. In any case, the emphasis on technical excellence among the participants is quite Hoover-like. The plan was as ambitious and imaginative as it was paternalistic. In 1929 Hoover invited Tuskegee's Dr. Moton and a group of philanthropists to a White House luncheon and discussion of the idea. The scheme, however, became another casualty of the Depression. The Mississippi work did nonetheless show dividends in sharply reducing hookworm, pellagra, and malaria in the poorest areas of the South through improved methods of sanitation and hygiene.[9]

In other ways, Hoover in his Commerce years did well on Negro affairs. He encouraged the National Urban League, particularly its program of jobs and training for migrants from the South. The Interracial Commission received his support. He worked especially hard for the National Negro Businessman's League, appointing an advisor on black economic development to the Commerce Department. He secured financing for an experimental black economic community in Mound Bayou, Mississippi, and attempted to get further financing later through the Reconstruction Finance Corporation. Hoover's desegregation of the Commerce Department toward the end of his tenure there became the subject of caustic comment during the election year of 1928. Senator Coleman Blease of South Carolina reprinted disapprovingly in the *Congressional Record* a Washington *Post* story:

Hoover Changes Racial Policy in Census Office—
Colored Clerks in All Departments:

Colored clerks in the Census Bureau yesterday sought to learn why they have been brought up from the basements and other segregated sections where they have worked for years and placed in all departments of the bureau on equal terms with other workers. It was learned that the order to abolish segregation and racial discrimination in the department came at the order of Herbert Hoover, Secretary of Commerce.

The story went on to say that the change had come about after an investigation pursuant to a complaint from the NAACP. A constituent of Blease charged that Hoover had obtained black Southern delegates by giving them Red Cross hams during the Mississippi flood. She went on to refer to black women who used government "white" toilets as "Hoover chocolates." While Republicans in the 1928 campaign pledged to enact a federal anti-lynching law, the Democratic platform and Al Smith himself virtually ignored blacks.[10]

Hoover, his associates, and most of his generation, including a sizable part of the academic world, accepted racist notions with an offhanded ease. Ray Lyman Wilbur thought it was all right to mix the blood of American Indians with that of whites since they were of "good stock." Hoover and his wife came to a similar opinion of the potentialities of American Negroes, believing that they needed only education. (Lou Henry Hoover once observed that she could lick the Depression if she had the help of a few good Negroes.) He was glad that the Klan had turned away after 1924 from persecuting Negroes, Catholics, and Jews; but expressed pleasure at its anti-communism. In his *Principles of Mining* (1909), which refers to both Negroes and Asians as the "lower races," Hoover had claimed that the Asiatic and white races do not mix well; all the good in both races was lost in the offspring, he explained, giving Natal, South Africa, as an example. And in a letter written in 1924 to Coolidge he said that "there are biological and cultural grounds why there should be no mixture of Oriental and Caucasian blood." He urged avoiding offense to the Japanese, but observed that complete exclusion might end agitation about the issue. Since this is what Congress desired, Hoover had dropped his preference for a small quota.[11]

On the general subject of immigration, he agreed with the broad spectrum of Americans who wanted rather sharp restrictions imposed. And on the subject of hyphenated loyalties, he could be querulously nationalistic. A speech of 1920 to a Polish audience in Buffalo catches him at an unpleasant moment: "Your first and primary duty is to the country of your adoption. . . . Many foolish ideas are being circulated amongst the foreign-born populations of the United States. . . . If reforms are needed in the United States, they will be carried out by those whose parents have grown up amidst our institutions and those who have become, in sentiment and spirit, a part of our people." But in a letter to Coolidge he opposed the way the new law distributed quotas among nationalities, complaining of its favoritism toward Great Britain and Ireland and calling for a "humanizing" of the law so that it would be more difficult to break up families. His remarks had little bearing on the reduction in quotas of southern and eastern Europeans. Hoover belittled the whole business of keeping the population to some aboriginal purity: it was "impossible," he noted, "to determine what the national origins of the Americans of 1789 had been." Yet he settled for the year 1890—a year, championed by some Nordic racists, that the new law employed.[12]

THE 1928 Republican campaign was to a considerable extent orchestrated by an expert at public relations—Herbert Hoover. His reputation was a "work of art," Walter Lippmann later wrote. Yet he wished above all to shield himself from political bargaining.[13]

Early boosting of Hoover was alternately premeditated and spontaneous. Since mid-1926 the newsman George Akerson had been publicizing Hoover quietly but effectively, making political allies and placing favorable articles in national magazines. To Hoover's way of thinking, Akerson had simply replaced a previous department secretary a year before and was doing his job of carrying on correspondence with those who approached his chief. The candidate heatedly denied before a Senate committee in May 1928 that he had made, or would in the future make, any promises of political rewards to his supporters. The very idea of his candidacy, he declared, somewhat disingenuously, lay "perhaps not so much in my own mind as in the minds of others." Much of Hoover's support arose unaided from former workers in relief agencies—Perrin Galpin, Edgar Rickard, Thomas T. C. Gregory—women, former Bull-Moosers like Walter F. Brown, and various admirers. Considerable help came from many progressive Scripps-Howard papers, which had endorsed La Follette in 1924. To acquire delegates, Hoover's publicity directors—Henry Allen and Alfred Kirchhofer—made good use of his relations with nationals he had helped during his relief days: Poles, Czechs, Yugoslavs, Russians, and particularly Germans. Emotional movies of Hoover doing relief work aided in recruiting these groups, and photographs and films of Hoover and Mississippi flood work helped greatly with Negro voters. Congressman James W. Good of Iowa (later Hoover's Western campaign manager) and Colonel Horace Mann (helpful in the South) organized the pre-convention campaign. Congressman Franklin Fort of New Jersey would become a major figure in post-convention activities. Meanwhile Hoover himself continued to work hard at Commerce, and partly in calculated response to criticism from Wall Street dramatized his closeness to Coolidge and the Republican party. He asked Coolidge's permission to run in the Ohio primary against Senator Frank Willis, whom they both disliked. "Why not?" said the sometimes laconic Coolidge. But Coolidge himself did not endorse any candidate for nomination.[14]

Hoover lost three primaries to favorite sons—Indiana to Senator James Watson, who received substantial Klan support, Ohio to Willis, West Virginia to Senator Guy Goff—but won in California, Oregon, New Jersey, Massachusetts, Michigan, and Maryland, and clearly was the front runner. Generally, he ran best in urban areas and worst among farmers. Much of the Senate, partial to one of its own in the White House, opposed both him and Governor Frank O. Lowden of Illinois. Republican congressmen clearly favored Hoover as a political asset to the entire party ticket. He had testified impressively over the previous decade before many House committees. A major coup, an endorsement from the prohibitionist progressive Senator Borah, came about after Hoover, in reply to a public letter from Borah, said that he did not favor repeal of prohibition. Hoover was quoted during the twenties as calling it a moral failure and an economic success; he evidently wished to give it a more serious try. Senator Carter Glass offered $1000 to anyone who found anything Hoover had said in favor of prohibition. Borah and Hoover were also of the same mind on the unwisdom of intervention in Latin America and on the need for restricting American loans abroad. Borah's speeches in Hoover's behalf helped to minimize factionalism within the party, taking the edge off farm protest against a candidate who had opposed McNary-Haugen.[15]*

Pennsylvania's Andrew Mellon had given Hoover a highly qualified endorsement: Hoover, said the greatest Treasury Secretary since Alexander Hamilton, "seems to come closest to the standard that we have set for the Presidency." But Mellon also told reporters that Coolidge might run, that Hughes would be an excellent candidate, and that Pennsylvania's seventy-nine delegates would go to the convention uninstructed. One newspaper said Mellon damned Hoover with faint praise. Just before the convention, William Vare, the Philadelphia boss, announced publicly for Hoover. Without Pennsylvania, a movement to stop Hoover could not succeed. Then Mellon came out unhesitatingly for the candidate, as did William Butler, the chairman of the Republican National Committee. Neither Charles Dawes, whom campaign chairman Hubert Work feared most, nor Governor Lowden had received enough support to prevent Hoover's nomination. Hoover was known to want a dampening of stock market speculation; and a few days before the nomination, as it became increasingly apparent that he would be chosen, stocks fell. The publisher Moses Straus wrote to Chief Justice Taft: "Financial men say that they have a grievance against Hoover, dating back to the food administration days." The Republican congressman Charles D. Hilles had tried hard to cultivate a Draft Coolidge movement, which was an expression of Wall Street's distrust of Hoover.[16]

The convention, an expeditious four-day affair that opened in militantly dry Kansas City on June 12, heard a stolid keynote address by Senator Simeon Fess of Ohio. A reporter wrote that it inspired the delegates as much as the appearance of a large iceberg cheers the captain of a North Atlantic steamer. But Senator George Moses of New Hampshire stirred his audience in the speech he delivered as permanent chairman of the convention: "Bring on the Tammany Tiger and we will bury him. We welcome him with hospitable hands to a bloody grave." Moses became Hoover's campaign manager for the East. The social worker Lillian Wald complained that Hoover was using men he had said four years before "made him vomit." After a parade in opposition to the leading candidate, the adversary of McNary-Haugen, about five hundred farmers loitered outside, and some tried with hoes, rakes, and shovels to storm the doors. One hundred thousand agrarian protesters had been promised. On July 1 the Agriculture Department would announce that farm-purchasing power had

---

* During Hoover's administration Hoover and Borah were to disagree repeatedly: on hearing that Borah had gone horseback riding, Hoover opined that it was hard to imagine Borah and his horse both going in the same direction.

reached its highest point since 1920. The agricultural issue has perhaps been overrated in the campaign. Only wheat growers were doing somewhat badly in 1928.[17]

Hoover won 837 out of 1089 votes on the first ballot; Lowden came in second with 74, and Senator Charles Curtis of Kansas got 64. The nominee won heavily among delegates from every section but the Midwest. Coolidge's message was untypically ebullient: "I wish you all the success that your heart could desire." Possibly his reason for withholding support from Hoover, whom he later spoke of as the "wonder boy," was that he wanted to wait and make sure the candidate would support the President's record. During the campaign Coolidge would send brief messages of support. Worried about the farm vote, Hoover had seriously considered asking Senator George Norris to run with him, but he settled on the regular Curtis, a dry who had voted for the last McNary-Haugen Bill but not to override the Coolidge veto. The flamboyant "Egg Charlie"—a former jockey (at the age of eight) whose characteristic rhetorical device was to inveigh against the price of eggs—was the choice of both Senators Borah and Smoot for the vice-presidential candidacy, and perhaps the preference among the delegates. After saying he would "never" accept the second place, the son of the prairies accepted it. But he caught a severe cold while lecturing to Indians (he was one-fourth an American Indian himself) about the tariff, and for much of the campaign was unable to speak outside. Recovering his voice, he was to enliven the debate (he was derisively termed "half windmill and half wild Indian") when he called a Kansas heckler "too damn dumb" to understand Hoover's agricultural policies; the Democrats thereupon tried, with understandable failure, to organize leagues of "dumb farmers."[18]

Walter Lippmann noted that "the two platforms contain no difference which would be called an issue." The more specific Republican platform talked of eight years of Republican government that included four measures for reducing taxes, removing from the tax rolls "millions of those least able to pay." Despite the tariff, the document said, imports had grown more sharply during those years than exports. The labor plank, drafted in part by Donald Richberg, later a New Dealer, suggested the need for a law curbing injunctions. On conservation, the platform called for "avoidance of waste so that future generations may share in this natural wealth." It recommended a federal anti-lynching law. And it recited accomplishments attributed to the Department of Commerce. The document was a typical Republican statement with a dash of reform. The Democratic platform was not dissimilar in temper: it denounced "bureaucracy," demanded "a revival of the spirit of local self-government," and advocated a tariff with stiff rates.[19]

The Democratic candidate, Governor Alfred E. Smith of New York, was burdened by his Roman Catholicism; by his hostility to prohibition, a measure that after years of lawbreaking and controversy could still enlist some moral and reasoned argument; and by an identification—a parochial self-identification, in fact—with the streets and Tammany Hall politics of New York City that antagonized the parochialisms of the countryside. It might be more proper to say that Smith took his politically disadvantageous public character from these elements in compound: for his religion heightened the sense of him as the city Irishman—he was Irish on the maternal side—alien to the ways of the hinterland; his New York ethnicity gave his faith an air of foreignness that other Catholics in public life, such as Senator Thomas Walsh of Montana, avoided; and it was not merely as an opponent of prohibition but as a product of the corrupt and rum-ridden city that he appeared in the eyes of prohibitionists. Above all else, there was prosperity in these Republican years, and Hoover must have seemed the very figure of that affluence. In this favorable political moment Hoover, comformably to his own temperament, muted controversy and, although he resigned from his Commerce post on June 14, he relied on the platform and seven major speeches. The content of his addresses was prosaic but reassuring, some of it a succession of statistical abstracts, although he would become more animated when he talked about the application of expertise to mankind's needs. His most provocative comment in his statement of June 14 to the convention was: "Shall prosperity in this nation be more thoroughly distributed?"[20]

Accepting the nomination at Stanford on August 11, his fifty-fourth birthday, Herbert Hoover delivered his famous declaration: "We in America today are nearer to the final triumph over poverty than ever before in the history of any land. The poorhouse is vanishing from among us. . . . We shall soon with the help of God be in sight of the day when poverty will be banished from this nation." This part of the speech referred to progress through technology. "Intellectual, moral, and spiritual progress are not the products of poverty," he had observed earlier. "Upon the structure of material progress as a base we are erecting a structure of idealism that would be impossible without the material foundation." Hoover called his own youth one of "poverty." He went on at Stanford to call for a shorter work day and an augmentation in the laborer's purchasing power; he championed collective bargaining and an end to the abuse of the injunction; he advocated an increase in public works, an enlargement of educational opportunity publicly financed, and the spending of "hundreds of millions of dollars" for farm relief. In response to progressive critics, he cited an 80 percent reduction under Harding and Coolidge in tax revenues from incomes under $10,000. The speech recalled how much of the architecture of modern society had been built by Republicans, who had instituted laws on civil rights, civil service, antitrust, consumer protection, and conservation. Perhaps only a Quaker could observe, as Hoover did, that "every drop [of water] which runs to the sea without yielding its full economic service is a waste."[21]

At Stanford, Hoover stated that "farming is and must continue to be an individualistic business of small units and independent ownership." At West Branch he warned against a sentimental longing for a more purely agrarian past, a time of "lower standards of living, greater toil, less opportunity for leisure and recreation, less of the comforts of home, less of the joy of living." Still Hoover spoke wistfully of his youth—"the glories of snowy winter, the wonder at the growing crops, the joining of the neighbors to harvest. . . . It is the entry to life which I could wish for every American boy or girl." He also remembered his Aunt Hannah's bitter denunciation of modern ways and recreation, "even to the godlessness of sliding downhill." In Newark he again referred to the abolition of poverty. At one point in a speech at Elizabethton, Tennessee, he remarked that when the government already owned power-generating plants it could operate them in pursuit of some major purpose, and he inspired national headlines when he told a Scripps-Howard reporter: "You may say that means Muscle Shoals." "Hoover Wants Government to Operate Muscle Shoals," trumpeted a front-page story in the Washington *News*. But Hoover, whatever he was thinking of at the moment, never supported the massive federal project at Muscle Shoals that Senator George Norris, the great advocate of public power, sought.[22]

In Boston Hoover argued for the morality of collecting the war debt and retaining the tariff. In New York City toward the end of his campaign, without mentioning the Democratic candidate by name, he delivered a demagogic and politically effective denunciation of the governor's "state socialism"—Smith believed that New York State should build plants for leasing to private companies. The phrase does not appear in the published version of Hoover's campaign talks. Julia Lathrop, a well-known social worker, immediately refused to speak further in Hoover's behalf. Hoover returned in the same speech to his earlier concern that "the points of contact between the government and the people are constantly multiplying." He had witnessed, he said, "not only at home but abroad the many failures of government in business. I have seen its tyrannies, its injustices, its destructions of self-government. . . . I have witnessed the lack of advance, the lowered standards of living, the depressed spirits of people working under such a system." At a final campaign speech in St. Louis on November 2, he talked of a full network of interstate highways financed by the federal government; a system of waterways and adequate flood control for the Mississippi; a St. Lawrence Seaway; apportioning immigration by the census of 1890 in place of the "national origins" of 1789; a higher tariff on agricultural goods; and a Federal Farm Board, to be established in a special session of Congress that Hoover would call for the purpose. The board would have a revolving fund of $500 million for the purchase of domestic surpluses. It went unsaid that if after the sale of a surplus abroad there was an unsold surplus at home, the government would bear the loss. The promise of a Farm Board, according to *Wallace's Farmer,* was "the turning point in the farm vote."[23]

Hoover got into the spirit of a campaigner when he accepted a 110-pound watermelon that, he was told, needed to be on ice for thirty hours. He turned down offers of a free dromedary, a balloon ride over Kansas, and a goat that ate Campbell's soup for dinner every day, can and all. Little in the way of debatable issues separated the two candidates. Prohibition, a strong and elusive issue still, did not enter articulately into the presidential argument. When Hoover in his letter to Borah referred to prohibition as an "experiment noble in motive," he effected a neat and undoubtedly sincere straddle: there were a good many Americans with reasonable doubts that the experiment should be abandoned. In the course of the campaign the *New York Herald-Tribune,* the Philadelphia *Public Ledger,* and the Chicago *Tribune* all told their readers that the best way to modify the Volstead Act was to elect Hoover. Democrats put their hopes on holding much of the Solid South, winning the great Eastern states, and carrying some farm areas; Illinois with its urban center and its wheat-growing counties was particularly tempting. The Democrats also expected to implicate Hoover in the farmers' troubles. His policy in the Food Administration of encouraging farmers to produce heavily could bear some of the blame for postwar surpluses.

As Secretary of Commerce, Hoover had intervened in farm problems without bringing about substantial improvement. But Smith, identifying perhaps with his accustomed urban constituency, refused to endorse the McNary-Haugen device of the equalization fee, which Professor E. R. A. Seligman of Columbia had analyzed for him and reported on unfavorably; and this, along with Hoover's presentation of the scheme of a Farm Board, pinched the ideological distance between the two tickets on the farm question. In his *Memoirs* Hoover described the development of waterpower as an issue "on which there was no great difference between Governor Smith and myself"—this from the man who had attacked Smith's "state socialism." He would in some instances allow public development of power and the municipal purchase of power. Although Senator Norris bolted the Republican party to support Smith, he was bothered at his candidate's hesitancy about public electrical power, and Norris noted that among Hoover's intimates there existed some sentiment for public ownership.

Despite Smith's excellent record on labor, few union endorsements came his way. John J. Raskob, whom he named as national chairman, had been a tough member of the employers' group at the Industrial Conference of 1919 and had sat on the board of unorganized General Motors. Hoover's position on labor was good for a Republican. He was, moreover, expected to win, and after its disastrous support of Robert La Follette in 1924 the AFL was in no mood for endorsement of another likely loser. Hoover claimed that the Unemployment Conference of 1922 had given jobs to 5 million people. When his Committee on Economic Trends reported that the nation's per capita productivity had increased by 35 percent in eight years, Hoover commented: "I do not claim the credit for this, but certainly the [Commerce] department helped."[24]

In this contest without issues, Smith multiplied his special political difficulties. He sent the Houston Convention a strong telegram against prohibition that contradicted the platform. (Raskob was a prominent Catholic opponent of prohibition.) The sentiments of Senator Carter Glass, writing in irritation at the choice of Raskob, came close to a popular apprehension about New York City: the Tammany crowd seemed to have "not only . . . distaste, but an actual contempt for the South." Most of Smith's executive committee was from his city. In a Fourth of July speech in New York, he went out of his way to defend Tammany Hall. In all his gubernatorial races Smith had never carried one distinctly agricultural county in upstate New York. He had opposed such general progressive reforms as woman suffrage. He reacted negatively to honest fears about his Catholicism, failing to respond candidly to rational if unfounded worries, undeserving of the term "bigotry," that the temporal Church would demand a part of a Catholic president's loyalty and that its faithful were not schooled in American ideas of civil liberties. He flaunted his New York characteristics, emphasizing his accent and tastes when they came into question; and while this could be an assertion of place and culture in the face of prejudice, it was neither good politics nor in every instance necessary. Asked, in a meeting with reporters, about "the needs of the states west of the Mississippi," Smith replied half-jokingly: "What are the states west of the Mississippi?"[25]

Ultimately, as already noted, Smith had no issues against Hoover. Both favored nonintervention in Latin America, high tariffs, and governmental reorganization. They even had many personal congruencies: rising from poverty and proving themselves leaders, they adhered to a rigid work ethic, efficiency and honesty in government, the institution of the family, and a diffuse belief in progress. Although both men inspired confidence, only Governor Smith inspired affection. But with little of substance to separate them, Smith's personal attributes became the major issue of the campaign.[26]

"I come of Quaker stock. My ancestors were persecuted for their beliefs. . . . By blood and conviction," Hoover said during the campaign, "I stand for religious tolerance both in act and spirit." "I abhor bigotry," he would say again in 1960, when another Catholic ran for the office. "I denounced it half a dozen times in 1928 and thousands of other times." Hoover stipulated in 1928 that his associates were to wage only a positive campaign and to omit mention of religion, prohibition, or the social bearing of the Irish and Catholic Mrs. Smith. He himself never mentioned Tammany Hall. But the new Republican national chairman, Hubert Work —a psychiatric doctor who had served as postmaster general and Secretary of the Interior—chose as a campaign speaker Assistant Attorney General Mabel Walker Willebrandt, who appeared to have a less civilized understanding of things. Mrs. Willebrandt—who later converted to Roman Catholicism—assailed Smith on religious and prohibitionist grounds before an Ohio audience of 4000 Protestant ministers. "To your pulpits!" was the culminating slogan of her fiery talk. The origins of the speech are obscure: Mrs. Willebrandt attributed it to Hubert Work, and to a speech writer at party headquarters who worked on her materials. Hoover, according to Senator George Moses, thought "we should let her alone rather generously." At the same meeting Senator Simeon Fess characterized the political campaign as having "on one side all of the loose element of morals and on the other the very highest and best morals." Chase Osborne, the progressive ex-governor of Michigan, was not far behind Mabel Willebrandt in his campaign oratory against the Church; when Osborne wrote that Smith was cheap, ignorant, and vulgar, he was reflecting a widespread view among genteel Americans. The Eastern campaign head, Senator Moses, was caught offering "red hot stuff" (anti-Catholic materials) for publication in North Carolina papers, and in a private letter to a campaign worker in Kentucky he advised an anti-Catholic strategy. An Alabama national committeeman, Oliver D. Street, mailed 200,000 anti-Catholic circulars throughout the South. In September Hoover repeated that "religious questions have no part in this Campaign," and he sent a personal message to Smith expressing regret that some would use the issue against him. When a national committeewoman from Virginia sent out a letter on Republican stationery saying that Hoover depended on America's women to prevent a "Romanized and rum-ridden" republic, the candidate publicly repudiated her. Work suggested that the signature on the letter had been forged, whereupon Hoover again denounced its contents to the press:

"Whether this letter is authentic or a forgery . . . I resent and repudiate it. I can't fully express my indignation. . . . I have repeatedly stated that neither I nor the Republican party want support on that basis." In 1929 Work would be succeeded as national chairman by Claudius Huston. Hoover would conspicuously fail to give posts in his administration to Work and to Southerners C. Bascom Slemp, Coolidge's White House secretary, and Horace Mann. "I reprimanded many of those who agitated this question," he said in his *Memoirs*.[27]

There was not much, really, for the Republicans to complain of from the Democratic side, but now and again some tactic rankled as might be expected of any campaign. Chief Justice Taft observed that Smith's campaign trip through Massachusetts "was almost a religious ceremony," and he noted the priests and nuns who, having renounced the world, were staging a temporary return to work and vote for Smith. In a letter to Bernard Baruch just before the election, Hoover showed his hypersensitivity to situations of abrasive conflict: "I am afraid the religious issue . . . is not all one-sided. We have suppressed most voluminous reports from all over the country of virulent activities on the Catholic side. I have insisted that such reports be suppressed. . . ." Hoover also thought, with reason, that it was dirty politics for Eleanor Roosevelt to write on stationery of the Democratic National Committee that she had been served wine in the Hoover household in the 1920's, and for Clarence Darrow to tell the press similarly that he had taken a drink with Hoover during prohibition. At the time of the Mississippi relief, Hoover had shaken hands with a mulatto lady prominent in Washington's black society and asked her whether she remembered their last dance in Washington; a story was then spread that he had danced with a black girl in Mississippi.[28]

In August Hoover visited his birthplace in West Branch, Iowa, population 745. He came into town as though he had always lived there, setting out to find the old swimming hole he had used as a boy. Then this epitome of the American dream of success visited his first-grade teacher, Mollie Carran, who remarked: "I never thought Herbert was bright, but he was a good boy always, studious and obedient." The survival of the tiny cabin of his birth stood him well in the iconography of American presidential boyhoods. Rain washed the landscape, intensifying its brilliance and settling the dust. It was a John Steuart Curry painting, the myth—or reality —of the garden. All this Hoover could add to his imposing modernity, his brilliance at engineering and his administrative skill. So much had happened in recent years: cars, radio, appliances, electricity, Zeppelins, moving pictures; even television had been invented, with Hoover's as the first image to be carried in a public display. In Hoover, as in the aviator Charles Lindbergh who endorsed him, was seen a new age in old garments, an acceptable metaphor for change. Kent Schofield suggests Hoover's commanding stature came of this combination in him of harbinger of the new technology and embodiment of a rural time of self-sufficient individuals, an evocation of nostalgia and confidence.[29]

Then, too, engineering seemed intrinsically to carry a certain largeness and virtue. Hoover's training appeared to give him special powers to do anything; according to a dithyramb by a delegate who had nominated him: "He sweeps the horizon of every subject. Nothing escapes his view. . . ." The *New York Times* grandly observed that Hoover's decisions were based on a memory encompassing "all experience." He was "destiny driven," according to the Brotherhood of Electrical Workers *Journal*. A popular belief that he was above politics added to his immense prestige, and a good technocrat would have liked to argue that to be an engineer is to be above politics. Another source listed his virtues simply: achievement, ability, experience, knowledge, integrity.[30]

Hoover had more particularly the image of an activist. Indeed, some Democrats charged him with an excess of activity. Franklin D. Roosevelt complained in a letter to the shoe manufacturer Ward Melville that "Mr. Hoover has always shown a most disquieting desire to investigate everything and to appoint commissions and send out statistical inquiries on every conceivable subject under Heaven. He has also shown in his own Department a most alarming desire to issue regulations and to tell business men generally how to conduct their affairs." Jane Addams listed her reasons for favoring Hoover: his stand for collective bargaining, his ingenious plan of farm cooperatives, his "war" against poverty, his relief work, his promise to enforce prohibition without federal gunmen. Miss Addams had voted for the socialist Debs in 1920, the Progressive La Follette in 1924, and Hoover in 1928 and 1932. Of sixty-six replies by other social workers to a circular letter sent out by Lillian Wald, forty-five preferred Hoover to Smith. We may reasonably suppose that it was the Republican candidate who stood most visibly as the representative of energetic government.[31]

Prosperity and peace assured that a Republican would win in 1928 against any Democratic candidate. Hoover received 21,392,000 popular and 444 electoral votes, Smith 15,016,000 and 87. Hoover cracked the Solid South, taking Virginia, North Carolina, Florida, and Texas, and won the border states as well. His work in the Mississippi flood presumably got him many votes in the South; the filtering of Northern Republicans into the industrial regions of the Appalachians seems to have had something to do with the vote there; and Smith's attitude toward prohibition undoubtedly helped Hoover in the Southern and border states (both ministers and moonshiners wanted him). But the principal reason for the shift in Southern voting was religious. Outside New York City Hoover did well with blacks. (At the Democratic Convention in Houston, Jim Crow chicken-wire fences had separated Negroes from whites.) In Chicago, the Germans went heavily for Hoover, while Smith carried the Irish. Hoover did not do well in areas of militant agricultural politics. Smith won Massachusetts and Rhode Island and came close in Connecticut and New York. The vote signified Smith's popularity in the big Eastern cities and among Catholics and opponents of prohibition, and foreshadowed his party's coming dominance of the large urban centers that would be a major future influence. The Republicans increased their majority in the House by 30 seats, attaining a margin there of 100, and gained by 7 seats in the Senate for a margin of 17. Again, a shift in the South aided the Republicans. The size of the Republican majority in both chambers was abnormal, and under any circumstances due for a shrinkage in 1930. The popular vote in 1928 was enormous. Some 70 percent of the eligible voters cast ballots in the presidential contest, an increase by almost half over the percentage of 1920. The vote was swollen in much of the South by a female electorate that had previously been slow to take advantage of the Nineteenth Amendment. Senator Lee Overman of North Carolina attributed the Republican sweep in his state to the women, "a new and disturbing element."[32]

From November 19 to January 6, the President-elect went on a journey that took him away from officeseekers and to eleven Latin American countries. Hoover, who had publicly disagreed with Coolidge over the latter's use of marines in Nicaragua, wished to demonstrate his sense of the "good neighbor," a phrase he employed repeatedly. His desire for an improvement in trade relations exemplified his compounding of idealism, practicality, and national self-interest. On the trip he thought about appointments. Afterward there was the conferring with Coolidge, congressmen, and others with advice to offer, and prospective appointees.

From the Coolidge years Hoover kept only Andrew Mellon in Treasury and James J. Davis in Labor, a post John L. Lewis wanted. Mellon was so venerated in the business world that his departure would have raised problems. Yet Hoover later spoke of Mellon as a hopeless reactionary. James Davis, his biographer correctly notes, had compiled a record of "moderation and practical humanitarianism." He fervently espoused collective bargaining. A dedicated member of the Loyal Order of Moose, he took up government time in behalf of his fellow fraternity brothers; he left office to run successfully for the Senate from Pennsylvania in 1930. After he died in 1930, an eternal flame burned for some time in the James J. Davis Memorial Alcove in the Museum of Moose History at the now-defunct Moose College. The successful labor arbitrator William Doak of the railroad brotherhoods (whom Hoover would have appointed in the first place but for AFL objections) replaced Davis.[33]

Some of Hoover's selections had participated in his campaign. Walter F. Brown was appointed Postmaster General—a department where Hoover had many suggestions; James W. Good, the Iowan notable in regulation of public utilities, became Secretary of War. Upon Good's death in 1929, the Oklahoman Patrick Hurley came to occupy the office. Lawrence Richey, George Akerson, and the writer French Strother went from campaign work to the White House staff.

Charles Evans Hughes, Harlan Fiske Stone, and (probably for financial reasons) Hugh Gibson all turned down the post of Secretary of State. So, possibly, did Senator Borah; the job—or one as Attorney General—one journalist had it, was "grudgingly tendered and gleefully declined." Colonel Henry L. Stimson, governor of the Philippines, received the appointment. As President Theodore Roosevelt's friend and federal attorney for New York, Stimson had assiduously prosecuted trusts; under Taft he was Secretary of War; he became a colonel in World War I; in 1927 he distinguished himself as a mediator in Nicaragua; and he gave up a substantial law practice to go to the Philippines. More willing than Hoover to use instruments of American power but reasonably compatible with his President, Stimson was known for his wealth, elitism, conscience, experience, capable administration, fluency in French and Spanish, and internationalist views.[34]

For the post of Attorney General, friends of the Catholic anti-prohibitionist William ("Wild Bill") Donovan, an Assistant Attorney General under Coolidge, pushed him hard—too hard, perhaps. In Hoover's judgment Donovan was lax in enforcing antitrust laws, and he evidently pursued political motives in prosecuting Senator Burton K. Wheeler for alleged influence peddling with the Interior Department in 1925. Donovan turned down an offer to replace Stimson as governor of the Philippines. Hoover's choice for Attorney General, and Chief Justice Taft's, was Coolidge's Solicitor General, the hardworking Democrat William D. Mitchell. Experience, administrative ability, a sense of duty—the virtues were Mitchell's as they were Stimson's.[35]

Charles Francis Adams, Jr., a naval officer himself, brought hauteur to the Navy Department. One of Adams's first acts was to send some sailors to the White House to wash off a blackened pate Coolidge had charcoaled on the picture of Adams's grandfather, John Quincy Adams, to prevent its shining in his eyes. Hoover later wished he had made Adams Secretary of State. Robert P. Lamont, an engineer and prominent businessman, was Commerce Secretary until 1932—but Hoover later said that he had "no initiative and no imagination." The automobile executive Roy Chapin succeeded him in 1932. Chapin—who "put the sex in Essex"—was a welcome symbol of a still vigorous American industry; he would build a new model car at the very bottom of the Depression. Hoover let go Coolidge's Secretary of Agriculture, William Jardine, who said in 1929 that relief for farmers would come in "the real old-fashioned, practical way—the only way they have ever gotten relief and that has not been through man-made laws in the Nation's Capitol." When his frozen grapefruit juice scheme failed, Jardine was appointed minister to Egypt by Hoover. After Senator Charles McNary and others had declined it, the agricultural post went to Arthur M. Hyde. As governor of Missouri, Hyde—a supporter of Frank Lowden at the convention—had given his state an efficient, businesslike administration. Later in the 1930's Hyde took advantage of what he had learned in the department to make a half-million dollars in grain speculation. Dr. Ray Lyman Wilbur, like Hoover a Californian born in Iowa, was Stanford's president. Wilbur became Secretary of the Interior, where he worked in close rapport with the President. Hoover listed Lowden, Dwight Morrow, Henry Robinson, and Julius Rosenwald as some who turned down cabinet offers.[36]

"The cabinet," the respected Judge Learned Hand wrote to Taft, "seems to me on the average very good. . . . The Attorney General was certainly a splendid appointment. . . . Stimson and Adams are also of the highest class, and I should suppose Wilbur was, too. One cannot say so much for some of the rest." Among the nine cabinet appointees, none was a Catholic or Jew or Southerner. Most were millionaires. If Hoover projected a reformist administration, why did he not put together a more militantly progressive cabinet? His preference, apparently, was for people of a sort he called administrators—a type suggestive of Veblen's impersonal technologists. Some of the new cabinet members, notably Wilbur, Mitchell, and Adams, seemed remarkably capable of taking the public point of view. Certainly their temperament coincided with that of Hoover. The President, we might suppose, also had a political purpose behind his appointments: the Republican old guard and a sizable segment of the business world distrusted him; a cabinet generously peopled with the wealthy could do him no harm with conservatives generally. The wealthy, too, were generally immune from scandal, and the Harding years were still of recent memory. Hoover believed, moreover, that within the business conditions then prevailing the most effective way to get reform was to institute reasonable measures acceptable to the dominant element in the Republican party, and by extension to the nation at large. Various undersecretaries and secondary appointments were generally to the liking of progressives.[37]

On January 22, 1929, Hoover left for a Florida vacation at the home of J. C. Penney. Before an open fire at the island house on Biscayne Bay, a pensive Hoover remarked to the editor of the *Christian Science Monitor:* "I have no dread of the ordinary work of the presidency. What I do fear is the result of the exaggerated idea the people have conceived of me. They have a conviction that I am a sort of superman, that no problem is beyond my capacity. . . . If some unprecedented calamity should come upon the nation . . . I would be sacrificed to the unreasoning disappointment of a people who expected too much."[38]

XI

THE REFORM PRESIDENCY

THE GREAT CRASH and Great Depression dominate the memory of Hoover's administration. A proper reconstruction of his presidency, however, requires that it be examined not backward from the collapse but forward, from the moment of national self-confidence when he won the election and entered the office. For he came to the White House representing the technical proficiency, turned to humane needs, that the nation could then perceive as constituting much of its better self and its future. His early tenure was a remarkable experiment in developing new approaches to old problems.

An ailing Chief Justice William Howard Taft worried that the President-elect, a "dreamer" with "some rather grandiose views," was "much under the Progressive influence" and might appoint to the Supreme Court "some rather extreme destroyers of the Constitution." The Inaugural Address, brief and packed with generalities, gave no cause for alarm. But reporters, a journalist would recall, expected Hoover to bring back the energies of progressivism after years of rule by standpat Republicanism. The newly installed President should have been no disappointment. During the first week he observed publicly that "excessive fortunes are a menace to true liberty by the accumulation and inheritance of economic power"—a statement with broader implications than Teddy Roosevelt's warning against "malefactors of great wealth." As early as 1927 he had worried to his old friend Edgar Rickard that " 'big business,' flushed with prosperity and a helpful administration has become arrogant and must be checked. He thinks they need it more than in Roosevelt's time. They have interfered with the passage of excellent measures for public security, most notably killing a bill giving the President authority to set up a Fuel Administration in case of coal strikes also lobbying in Muscle Shoals and Boulder Dam business." Hoover did not hesitate to alarm defenders of private wealth when he remarked at a press conference that he wanted to lower federal income taxes on "earned" as against "unearned" income. On March 14, 1929, he fulfilled a long-standing goal of congressional progressives when he ordered that all large government rebates of income, estate, and gift taxes be made public. When a group of business leaders asked him for a favor, he replied: "Remember, gentlemen, when I was Secretary of Commerce I was devoting myself to your interests and now that I have become the leader of the nation, I must take the point of view of all people."[1]

Other acts discouraged Republican leaders. Hoover put first-, second-, and third-class postmasters under Civil Service. Eight days after his inauguration he set limits on oil drilling on government lands—"a wise and farsighted policy," *The Nation* commented. While he would also refuse to sanction any federal agreement offering the oil companies immunity from antitrust laws, an arrangement conducive to price-fixing and the restricting of production, the action of March 12 aimed to prevent overproduction. From the beginning of his administration he publicly divulged the names of politicians who urged, or protested, judicial or certain other appointments; this had the effect, presumably, of easing the pressure from office-seekers. He promptly retired the presidential yacht and closed the White House stables.[2]

Some of the most important and least-known actions of Hoover's tenure concern civil liberties. His attitude toward individual rights had not changed since the Red Scare a decade earlier. He repudiated a campaign by the right-wing periodical *National Republic*, which claimed to have government backing for a fund to "fight the Reds." Late in 1929 he asked for the release of Communists who had peacefully picketed in front of the White House. And he ordered the Justice Department to investigate the use of third-degree police methods in the District of Columbia. A newspaper editorial and petitions alleging "political prisoners" disturbed Hoover; he requested Attorney General William D. Mitchell to provide their names and offenses. To Jane Addams' inquiry, he replied that all such prisoners had been released years before and pardons granted those who applied. Miss Addams later must have been pleased at the order to grant a passport to the executive secretary of her organization, the Women's International League for Peace and Freedom, with the word "defend" omitted from the oath of allegiance. Hoover even wanted to inquire into the case of the labor martyr Thomas J. Mooney—his new

Quaker minister in Washington, Augustus Murray of Stanford, had been active in Mooney's behalf—but was held back by Mitchell on jurisdictional grounds.[3]

The President also secured the resignation in May 1929 of Assistant Attorney General Mabel Walker Willebrandt, the flamboyant prohibition-ist and prison reformer whose methods included sending espionage agents into prisons to check on administrators, female spies into houses of prosti-tution, and—so it was reported—"a naked lady on the train to Montreal." He also prohibited her bureau from distributing in public schools pam-phlets on the horrors of drink, and asked federal prohibition officers to comply stringently with all legal restrictions on invasion and search. Many drys had asked that she be placed in charge of prohibition enforcement. The President had disapproved of her 1928 campaign speech urging Ohio ministers to oppose the wet Al Smith from their pulpits. (She told the press after her resignation that the Republican National Committee had edited the offensive talks and forced her against her wishes to make the speaking tour.) Nonetheless, Hoover managed to maintain good relations with the ardent reformer.[4]

Hoover's second Secretary of Labor, William Doak, would spend much time tracking down and deporting aliens. Many Communist aliens, their deportation to Russia blocked by that nation's refusal to receive them, were held as long as the law allowed. Lawrence Richey received a letter about foreign students already in the country who were being "bounced overnight." Drew Pearson wrote that "under Doak [alien hunting] became a gladiatorial spectacle. . . . No brutality or illegality stopped him." It would appear that Hoover did not know what was happening. Reading of aliens who had been rounded up in Buffalo and Cleveland and held incom-municado for as long as eighteen months, and then extradited to Fascist and Nazi jails, he later exclaimed in disbelief to his former Attorney General, Mitchell: "I cannot imagine our Administration violating the very spirit of the Bill of Rights." Perhaps the press of detail and crisis that Hoover had to manage during the Depression kept complaints of wrong-doing from getting to his desk. But it is puzzling that Hoover did not receive information about the aliens in Cleveland and Buffalo—or, if he did receive it, it is disturbing that he evidently failed to institute some kind of inquiry.[5]

Overall, however, the defense of civil liberties belongs among a number of facts of Hoover's presidency that tempt us to look beyond the engineer to the Quaker, or at any rate to the culture that attended Quakerism— humane, reformist, respectful of the mind's privacy. More directly sug-gestive of the Quaker heritage were Hoover's efforts on the race question, which for their time marked a distinctly new commitment on the part of the executive.

The Hoovers had refused to sign on their "S" Street residence in Washington a restrictive covenant against Negroes and Jews. It was not a small gesture at a time when the existence of such agreements was a matter of course. The Hoovers used the executive mansion for more public demonstrations of their feelings. The President met on May 14, 1929, with Dr. Robert Moton of the Tuskegee Institute—it was a deliberate emulation of Theodore Roosevelt's invitation to Booker T. Washington—and Lou entertained many blacks as White House guests. In June, probably without thinking of the matter of all, she included at a congressional tea at the White House Mrs. Oscar de Priest of Chicago, the wife of a black representative. Rude protests quickly came from Southerners who had been courted during the campaign. The final guest list that included Mrs. de Priest was small, but Mrs. William D. Mitchell and Mrs. James Good were conspicuous among three cabinet wives present. By calculation the tea became the last of several to be scheduled, and Southerners were thereby denied the chance to boycott subsequent gatherings. The incident was a strain on the administration's Southern policy. Despite the success of the election campaign in the South, Hoover had appointed no Southerner to his cabinet and relentlessly refused patronage to the corrupt Republican organizations there. Mitchell prosecuted some wayward Negro Republican officials. Recent Supreme Court decisions outlawing the "white only" primary in Texas and Virginia were irritating the race issue, as was a proposal by Republican Congressman George A. Tinkham of Massachusetts to enforce penalties against racial discrimination. So Southern bitterness was marked when the Women's International League for Peace and Freedom formally congratulated Mrs. Hoover on the tea for Mrs. de Priest, and Congressman de Priest ten days later aggressively used the incident in a public meeting to bait racists.[6]

The President put his office to work for racial justice in more tangible ways. The first sentence Hoover commuted under his presidential pardoning power was that of a Negro, convicted of murdering a white woman in a case in which there had been no eyewitness and the verdict had depended on a confession, as Hoover pointed out, "signed in the presence of police officers." He wrote in 1931 to an aide that he was thinking of addressing Congress on the subject of lynching: "With the modern expedition, through aerial and motor forces of Federal troops located at all important centers throughout the country [the Quaker was not unobservant of military tactics] it is possible to bring them almost instantly to the assistance of local authorities if a system were authorized by Congress that would make such action swift and possible." Advised that constitutional difficulties precluded the use of federal troops without a request from a state governor or legislature, the President condemned lynching publicly but sponsored no legislation against it. He raised the number of blacks in federal employment to 54,684 by the end of his term and appointed more to middle-level jobs than Harding and Coolidge together. For the black Howard University, Hoover demanded an increased budget, which enabled its School of Law to become accredited and more faculty to be hired; and appropriations for the Freedmen's Hospital almost doubled. Hoover made efforts to increase minority employment on public works, and he sponsored a federal program that aimed to diminish illiteracy among blacks. He also improved opportunities for army Negroes at Fort Benning, where, a Southern black acquaintance had complained, they were restricted to menial work. When considering the makeup of a new federal parole board, he recommended that the proportion of Negroes and women in the prison population be taken into account. And he persuaded the Julius Rosenwald fund to support a conference on the Economic Status of the Negro.[7]

Hoover's most imaginative and far-reaching scheme to help blacks would have operated outside government. During his presidency Hoover continued to try to persuade foundations to support his plan for giving tenants and sharecroppers of both races the means to buy the land they worked. He held a White House luncheon with Moton and a group of financiers for discussion of the project. The Depression prevented its implementation; but the Farm Security Administration embraced something of the idea on a larger scale. The plan suggests that particular variety of social reformism, committed to the spread of small private ownership, that would be a distinctive part of the New Deal. The special feature of Hoover's scheme at the time was that it would attempt to reach the whole system, while a proposal successfully pushed by Henry C. Taylor, an old adversary now with the Social Science Research Council, was for a small pilot project.[8]

Hoover's relations with the black community were nonetheless flawed, and there is evidence that he opposed full racial integration. The administration's purge of the Republican party in the South was no help. Press commentators were wrong in perceiving a "Southern strategy" of systematically ousting blacks from the party. The objectives were to remove corruption and, in so doing, to make the Republican party a genuine Southern alternative, for white voters would not turn to a party that tolerated notoriously corrupt Negro leaders. After the Depression ended Republican ambitions about the South, Postmaster General Walter Brown began to court some of the old "black-and-tan" leaders Hoover had attempted to eject. But the purge itself had a lily-white appearance.

Another abrasive was Hoover's alliance with such representatives of the Tuskegee philosophy as Dr. Moton, which alienated Walter White and W. E. B. DuBois of the NAACP; that conflict was so intense that any friendship on Hoover's part for either side had inevitably to invite a reaction from the other. When Congress provided by appropriation for some ocean liner trips to Europe for gold-star mothers and widows of the world war dead, Secretary of War Patrick Hurley offended Negroes by arranging, in compliance with custom, that the black women travel separately. Injustices in the military added to black resentment. Government flood relief projects on the lower Mississippi River paid black workers less than whites. Hoover issued orders to end the discrimination and to employ more Negroes both there and on the Colorado River project, but his lieutenants evidently made only token changes.[9]

Hoover was also a prison reformer. Little more than a decade before his presidency, the two federal prisons at Leavenworth and Atlanta had held scarcely two thousand convicts. But new federal crimes—traffic in drugs, Volstead Act violations, car theft—resulted in serious overcrowding. On the recommendation of Mabel Willebrandt, Hoover put Sanford Bates, formerly the innovative director of the Massachusetts prisons, at the head of a Bureau of Prisons, established in 1930. Bates found the federal penitentiaries a nightmare: a single doctor, for instance, covered each institution, unskilled inmates providing nighttime medical care. The Attorney General urged that the prison crowding be eased by establishing camps on public lands, where convicts could be set to building roads and train tracks. But national park personnel feared that their presence would alarm vacationers, and the plan was abandoned. Nonetheless, by the time a riot broke out at Leavenworth in early August 1929, Hoover and Bates had already begun to prepare a $5 billion program of federal penal reform. Frank Tannenbaum, the proponent of prison reform, expressed confidence in Bates and called the plan "a courageous first step."[10]

Eight reform bills drafted by the Bureau of Prisons passed the Seventy-first Congress. A new penitentiary, graced by an architecturally notable library and chapel, soon rose on a 1000-acre stretch of the Susquehanna Valley near Lewisburg, Pennsylvania. Prisoners farmed outside the walls and there were light and air within. In a new El Paso reformatory, prisoners worked on the irrigation and reclamation of dry lands; in Chillicothe, they learned industrial skills (prison officials boasted of a five-day week and a seven-hour day). A federal school for prison guards was founded, and all prison employees came under the Civil Service. Elementary education programs were made available, and the Public Health Service staffed the major centers adequately. Some 10 percent of prisoners were moved to government reservations and did outdoor work under light security. Supervised by a new full-time board, prisoners on parole multiplied during the Quaker President's administration. By 1932 some thirty thousand prisoners were out on parole, compared with nineteen thousand early in 1928, and three times as many of those convicted were being placed on probation.[11]

The overcrowding in prisons reflected in part the crime that was spawned by prohibition. The oath of office and Lou Hoover's teetotalism committed the President to the enforcement of the dry law. His reference to prohibition as "a great social and economic experiment noble in motive and far-reaching in purpose"—"noble experiment" is a misquotation—did not constitute an endorsement. "My own impression," wrote Walter Lippmann, is that Hoover "regards both wets and drys as substantially insanc." The drys liked neither his reference to prohibition as an experiment nor his appointment to the cabinet of Robert Lamont, who had been on the board of the Association Against the Prohibition Amendment, and of Charles Francis Adams, Jr., another prominent wet. Hoover himself had drunk alcohol, at least from his mining years onward. As early as 1897 he crustily rejected a case of vinegary wine sent out to Leonora, Western Australia. "We are in receipt," he wrote Messrs. Milne and Company in Perth, "of the liquor and cigars sent forward by you. . . . [The claret] is so far from being 'first class' as to be undrinkable." In London Hoover acquired a distinguished wine cellar. In California he purchased part of Senator Stanford's wine cellar, which in 1919 Lou gave away without his permission. During the war he customarily drank a cocktail and then wine with his dinner. He also on occasion took champagne and gambled at the Deauville Casino; on the way out of the Deauville dining room one evening he took the baton from the orchestra leader and briefly conducted. A lady from those days wrote in her diary on July 20, 1919: "to Inn of William the Conqueror. Fine lunch—good wine—all pleasantly tight—sing old songs. Hoover life of the party . . . wears boat cloak—looks like benevolent priest . . . Bertie says green [crème de menthe] is artificially colored. Bertie keeps us up." Hoover told Josephus Daniels that he was a lifelong advocate of temperance, but as Food Administrator he opposed introducing prohibition into wartime law; it added to existing problems, he said. In 1918 he remarked that he could not see how 2.75 percent beer could make anyone drunk; and at Paris the next year he spoke in opposition to sumptuary legislation. Two fairly reliable authorities have it that during the 1920's, en route home from the Commerce Department, he would stop at six o'clock for two legal cocktails at the Belgian Embassy. Certainly most of his 1928 campaign staff, especially George Akerson, drank heavily. There are even reports of Hoover serving cocktails at the White House, but this is dubious, since his wife let it be known that she would leave social gatherings where drinks were served. From the 1930's onward he drank martinis ritualistically ("stirring them to the right"), insisting on a larger glass late in life when his doctor limited him to one. The cocktail hour was his favorite time; "the pause," he called it, "between the errors and trials of the day and the hopes of the night."[12]

"I resolved in the campaign," Hoover wrote in his *Memoirs,* "not to commit myself to prohibition as a fixture of American life but first to see if the law could be enforced." "If a law is wrong," he told an Associated Press reporter, "its rigid enforcement is the surest guarantee of its repeal." Very early in his presidency Hoover announced that his enforcement policy would contain no "dramatic displays or violent attacks in order to make headlines." Attorney General Mitchell also opposed such methods as wiretapping and illegal searches and seizures, and the generally aggressive character of earlier enforcement. He ordered his staff to refrain from violating the law they enforced. Perhaps the sinking of the *I'm Alone,* a Canadian-registered rumrunner, on March 22, 1929, by the Coast Guard using undue force in international waters had given Hoover pause.[13]

On May 29 Hoover appointed a distinguished National Commission on Law Observance and Enforcement under former Attorney General George Wickersham. The President estimated that prohibition should only take a third of its time, since only a third of federal prisoners were dry-law violators. Hoover was certainly concerned with law enforcement generally. The publisher of the Chicago *Daily News* called on him and said that Chicago was in the hands of gangsters. Between thwunks of early morning exercise with a heavy medicine ball,* Hoover directed Attorney General Mitchell to "get" Al Capone, sparing no expense but using no publicity. Hoover saw economic benefits in prohibition, and had documented them in press releases as Secretary of Commerce. He also valued the attempt at reform, since, he said, it showed that property rights did not dominate American ideals. He considered prohibition a democratic experiment against powerful financial interests and an important expression of the feminist movement. But the drys took the Wickersham Commission as a clue that revision was coming; only one known prohibitionist had been appointed to it. Reporters "learned" that Hoover "was not really a dry at heart," and that the law could be changed "a year or so after his reelection." During his presidency Hoover came to believe that prohibition could not be given an "honest trial"; it was simply unworkable. As early as December 1930, according to Henry Stimson, the President endorsed Congressman Franklin Fort's plan for a constitutional amendment to be

---

* Hoover's only exercise in Washington took the form of passing an 8-pound medicine ball over a 10-foot net on a court laid out as for tennis and scored the same way; he was joined in this undertaking for half an hour each morning by Justice Stone, Secretary Wilbur, and several other close friends.

submitted to the people through constitutional conventions. And in that same month the President told Edgar Rickard that the youth of the country would eventually force repeal. Earlier that year he had secured transfer of the Prohibition Bureau from the Treasury to the Justice Department, and it came under the purifying influence of Civil Service. This shift improved enforcement on certain levels. Years later Attorney General Mitchell sadly observed that prohibition had prevented his doing a good job of improving the Justice Department. Prohibition was, as Walter Lippmann observed, "the north pole in the realm of unreason."[14]

Overshadowing these efforts was the Wickersham Commission's final report, submitted in January 1931. Although seven of the eleven commissioners favored revision, the report advised that the country attempt more rigid enforcement before changing the law. Both wets and drys had wanted a more clear-cut decision; one paper called the report a "Wickershambles." Hoover, in transmitting the report to Congress, refrained from recommending future revision, noting that his duty was "to enforce the law," and expressing satisfaction that progress had been made in enforcement since 1927. A careful reading of Hoover's statement, however, will show that it did not argue for prohibition on principle, and he may have been quite ambivalent on the issue. "Editing and rewriting Hoover on Wickersham" messed up the statement, said Edgar Rickard; "in the original draft Hoover had left no doubt that he was still open-minded about repeal."* But if Hoover's remarks cannot be counted as strongly supportive of the amendment—he emphasized that localities and states had the main responsibility for enforcement, and implied that its success depended on their zeal—they came short of the attack on it he might have made. He in effect ignored the mountain of evidence the Wickersham Report produced discrediting the law; and the public was turning against it. "As things are at present," noted the Wickersham Report, "there is virtual local option."[15]

MUCH OF Hoover's domestic reform had its medium in the Interior Department, the traditional home or "frontier" department. There he worked through Ray Lyman Wilbur, his trusted old friend from Encina Hall at Stanford. "Public health, education and other forms of social welfare are to be given great emphasis by the new Secretary of the Interior," de-

---

* Henry Stimson gives a similar account in his diary (January 12, 1931): Hoover complained to his Secretary of State that the summaries were illogical in relation to the findings: "The findings are wet and the recommendations are dry." Hoover wished to express a lingering hope for the eventual success of prohibition but, as Stimson put it, "he has an open mind about the very powerful findings of the shortcomings of prohibition; and . . . he is quite as ready as anybody else to work out a solution."

clared the *Kiplinger Washington Letter* on March 11, 1929. One of Wilbur's first acts was to substitute for the department's existing coat of arms, an eagle with outstretched wings, a picture of an American bison. The programs of the department represent Hoover's brand of social activism, with its balance of governmental initiatives and federal restraint, its preference for voluntarism stimulated by publicity from Washington and organized on a vast scale.

The conference idea, which Hoover had extensively employed in Commerce, also gave its character as a reform instrument to his presidential politics. One critic protested that "tentacles of the commission octopus will be seen swarming out from the White House to the Capitol, the liberties of the people will be in danger, the Constitution will be on its deathbed, our republican institutions will be seen falling before an oligarchy of scientists, professors, specialists, and technologists." By mid-1932 some thirty conferences and commissions had made recommendations, only seven of which had been funded by the government. Out of these came a coordinating of veterans' affairs under one bureau; and also recommendations for the locating and constructing of a double-decker bridge across San Francisco Bay, for the eradication of illiteracy in the United States, for the development of water resources for southern California, for the "Haitianization" of the government of Haiti and the gradual withdrawal of the Marines, for "saving" the California redwoods and expanding recreation facilities, for relieving the 1930 drought conditions through seed loans, establishment of agricultural credit banks, and postponing of reclamation payments, for timber use and conservation, for street and highway safety, and for restoration of wage cuts for certain employees of Southern railways—an indication that government mediation under Hoover fully considered the employee—as well as various remedies for the Depression. But these were not Hoover's most important commissions.[16]

On the second day of his presidency, Hoover responded to Senator James Couzens' concern for crippled children: "I would like to discuss the children question with you . . . as I have a notion that we might develop something of rather broad character." The President, whose past career had embraced extensive work in behalf of children, called for a White House conference on child health and protection. Financed by a half-million-dollar grant from the American Relief Administration, the repository of surplus contributions for Belgian relief, the conference in the fall of 1930 gathered more than 2500 delegates, some of them federal, state, and municipal authorities, others representing the great voluntary organizations.[17]

The group worked out a report on child welfare that was more exhaustive than any before or since. Published in thirty-five volumes, it would serve for many years as the handbook and bible of social workers, and in its wake came state and municipal conferences, legislative action, and a heightened public awareness. Among its recommendations were the licensing of obstetric hospitals and nursing homes, the extension of the school year and the age of compulsory education, and the grant of funds to states for various welfare purposes. But Hoover explained to Theodore Roosevelt, Jr., that the "national mood" did not permit much follow-up on matters of public health.[18]

"I would be obliged," Hoover wrote his budget director on October 16, 1929, "if you would treat with as liberal a hand as possible the applications of . . . the Children's and Women's Bureaus. I have great sympathy with the tasks they are undertaking." For some time he had urged temporary federal aid for state and county services to root out communicable diseases and improve the health of children. Although he thought its head, Grace Abbot, to be self-righteous and inflexible, Hoover increased appropriations for the Children's Bureau—the first federal social welfare agency—by 10 percent for 1930. The Democratic Congress refused an additional 10 percent increase the following year; but until 1932 Hoover regularly enlarged the appropriation for the bureau. Some reformers objected to his efforts, endorsed by the Child Welfare Conference, to shift to the Public Health Service the functions the bureau was carrying for maternity, infancy, and child hygiene. He and Wilbur believed that the PHS, which they wanted moved to the Interior Department, could provide expert professional guidance in these fields, leaving the "welfare" work within the existing agency. But the idea endangered the life of the bureau, as did Senator Edward Costigan's bill for hundreds of millions in relief to be dispensed through it. Hoover was either unwilling or unable to persuade Congress to strengthen the bureau. In 1931 he did urge passage of the Rural Health Bill, offering federal subsidies to states and counties for the establishment of public health units—each to be composed of a doctor, a sanitary engineer, and a nurse—that would provide maternity and child services. The bill, growing out of Hoover's American Child Health Association and Mississippi flood work, would have strengthened the most important features of the Sheppard-Towner Act. In a time, however, of weakened economy and of decline in women's political influence, and in face of potent resistance from the American Medical Association and Father John Ryan's National Catholic Welfare Council, the bill languished under a filibuster by Oklahoma's Senator Elbert Thomas and sharp opposition from Senators Borah and David I. Walsh.[19]

The Inter-American Commission of Women, meeting in February 1930, approved a treaty providing that "there shall be no distinction based on sex in . . . law and practice relating to nationality." The aim was to give men and women equal protection against deportation. At the ensuing Hague Conference the United States refused to sign a convention codifying international law, for it lacked this proviso, which the United States was the only nation out of forty to favor. Section 213 of the Economy Act of 1932 required reductions in the number of employees at the expense of those whose spouses worked for the government; Hoover protested this provision but signed the act. Late in 1932 he issued an order against sexual discrimination in hiring for new jobs.[20]

A major ARA-financed conference addressed to housing conditions and practices, which Hoover had called for as early as 1920, went into planning in mid-1929.[21] Again, fact-finding committees—at this conference, twenty-five—would apply microscopes to their subjects and produce a multivolume report. The meeting of 3,700 registrants began late in 1931, with an address by Hoover stressing the need for new first and second mortgage money. For the national level the conference emphasized voluntary action on the part of banks and other lending agencies, and the introduction to its report observed that "the effects of an undertaking of this sort are largely intangible." But it recommended help to small homeowners making mortgage payments; in 1932 Congress passed Hoover's Home Loan Bank system. Where voluntarism, or the states, would not put adequate controls on economic waste or social injustice—here as in child labor and elsewhere —Hoover generally favored federal legislation. The report also suggested non-profit, limited-dividend companies that would provide credit for low-cost housing, cooperative apartments for congested areas, and modern conveniences in rural homes. Careful attention to the layout of lots and streets would assure both beauty and utility. For jurisdictions below the federal, the report proposed building codes for the reduction of safety hazards, licensing of real estate brokers, regulation ensuring the abatement of smoke, control of billboards, and restrictions on the advertising of homes. To the President's gratification, hundreds of state and local laws on housing and zoning were soon passed. Hoover described the eradication of slums as the next pressing order of business, and in 1932 the Reconstruction Finance Corporation lent funds for this purpose. Each city or community, he believed, should have a master plan since slums arose because of lack of planning.[22]

A National Advisory Committee on Education, appointed by Secretary Wilbur in May 1929, was another of Hoover's priority items. It included a dozen Roman Catholics and three Negroes out of fifty-two members. Hoover and Wilbur asked the conferees to arrive at a definition of the national government's proper role in education; the committee came up with a controversial report and a solid book of facts. Noting that the federal government was already engaged extensively in education, it called for a more centralized control and an end to wasteful duplication of effort. While rejecting federal dictation of the curriculum, the educators endorsed using the federal tax system to give financial aid to the states for schooling. The most controversial recommendation, passed by a heavy majority and opposed by Wilbur (who simply elevated the existing bureau to "office" status), was "that a Department of Education with a Secretary of Education at its head be established in the Federal Government." Departmental status would permit the agency to present its programs forcibly to Congress. Wilbur himself in 1930 suggested a new name for his department: Conservation, Education, and Health. Hoover, who warmly commended the committee, had himself wanted a separate cabinet-level Department of Health, Education, and Welfare. Congress ignored the recommendation to create a new cabinet department, but in 1930 it did set up another agency, the National Institute of Health, that had Hoover's early and warm support. A related project under Hoover's initiative was an Advisory Commission on Illiteracy, funded by Julius Rosenwald and John D. Rockefeller, Jr.; working through active branches in forty-four states, the commission relied on churches and fraternal and patriotic organizations, as well as state and local government, for help in eradicating adult illiteracy.[23]

The President had strong reason for addressing himself to the problems of American Indians. Indian children had been his early playmates, and two uncles had served as Indian agents: Dr. Minthorn and Laban Miles, whom Hoover had visited on the Oklahoma Osage reservation as a boy and received as a guest at the White House in 1929. Knowing the Quaker tradition of fair treatment for Indians, Hoover dismissed the insensitive Charles H. Burke and selected a Quaker, Charles J. Rhoads, as Indian Commissioner. Rhoads, a former president and then treasurer of the Indian Rights Association, and the new Assistant Commissioner, J. Henry Scattergood—also a Quaker—were Philadelphia bankers noted for their leadership in charitable work; both gave up high salaries to come to Washington, where they discovered what Rhoads called "a wilderness of past misadventures." One major thrust of the new administration was against government welfare programs that had merely "coddled" the Indians. The Indian Bureau also reflected Hoover's and Wilbur's propensity for enlisting academics in government service: W. Carson Ryan of Swarthmore and Earl A. Bates of Cornell assisted in Indian educational work. Wilbur himself belonged to the fairly militant Indian Defense Association.[24]

John Collier, head of the Defense Association and later Indian Commissioner under the New Deal, called Rhoads's appointment "well nigh incredibly fortunate." Collier represented a philosophy somewhat at variance with that of Hoover's bureau. All concurred, as the government in general had agreed since the late nineteenth century, that the Indians must cease to be wards of Washington and become independent; and all favored the continuation, in some form, of Indian culture. The difference, which never quite crystallized into debate, was over how much of the Indian communal structure and traditional customs must be deliberately perpetuated. Or, to put the case more metaphysically, how densely and absorbingly "Indian" the experience of the American Indian ought to be.[25]

The government's Advisory Committee on Education came down on the side of preserving the separateness of the Indian experience. Hoover had obtained financing for the Brookings Institution's prestigious Meriam Report of 1928 from the Rockefeller Foundation, and his appointee W. Carson Ryan had helped to write it. Although this masterful piece of reform propaganda would leave unhindered those who wished to live apart in the old culture, it opposed the "glass case policy" of separatism. Under Collier's tenure the bureau would work rather in a preservationist direction, trying to stimulate Indian crafts and otherwise intensifying communal life on the Indian lands. Favoring collective tribal ownership of Indian lands, Collier pushed Senator McNary's bill for turning the Klamath tribe into a legal corporation, which Collier said "marked a great historical change in Indian policy."[26]

The purpose of the measure, however, was not so much to determine the eventual shape of the Indian community as to provide the Klamath Indians with some independent economic base; and Rhoads, who leaned to individual ownership, endorsed the bill. It was a step toward the corporate bodies established in the Wheeler-Howard Act of 1934. Wilbur was another advocate of individual property, for which he was willing to use the tribes as intermediate agencies. In a letter to Coolidge's Secretary of the Interior, Hubert Work—responding to an article in which Work had described Indians as "primitive, nomadic people without . . . social or political entity"—Wilbur contended that Indians should be given title to their lands so that they would be economically self-sufficient. That, of course, might not mean a great modification of the older communal or cultural ways, but one of Rhoads's first efforts did point to that end: he worked toward the goal of bringing Indian children into the state educational systems; boarding school enrollments declined steadily under his tenure. The bureau also encouraged the acquisition of modern vocational skills such as that of automobile mechanic, as well as the continuation of the traditional arts and crafts. A few formulas suggest the integrationist persuasion that influenced Indian affairs during Hoover's presidency. Wilbur had written to the *Forum* in 1924: "The Indian cannot be saved on the asylum basis." He said in 1930 that he wanted to "blend" the Indians "as a self-supporting people into the nation as a whole." But he made it clear that he meant integration, not assimilation. Hoover was still more direct in summing up the department's work in 1933, saying he wanted "the ultimate breaking up of the reservation system and its artificial islands in our civilization."[27]

When Hoover's Washington did speak of preserving Indian culture, it was in no special contradiction to the objective of putting property in the hands of individuals and families, or conforming the education of Indians to that of other Americans, or making for an easier access to the cities. Partly it was a matter of not assaulting ways and sensibilities. As Rhoads observed: "all successful work . . . has aimed not to 'fill' the youth of another race with 'the white man's enthusiasm for accomplishment,' but to try to discover and build upon ambition as *he* knows it, that is, to use *his* not an alien motivation." In part, also, Washington was bringing something like a conservationist feeling to the issue, wishing merely to preserve one more element of the national inheritance. Hoover's desire for a permanent record of Indian sign languages suggests the work the government would do, notably under the New Deal, to preserve other fragments of American culture in slave reminiscences or the voices of folk singers. In 1907 he had encouraged his sister-in-law to complete a dictionary of the Paiute language. Wilbur wrote in 1932 that his department was implementing a program for saving "much of what otherwise would have been lost." Then, too, administration leaders would probably have agreed with the mild if often imprecisely thought-out belief, especially prevalent in our own time, that the possession of some kind of ethnic "heritage" is a desirable component of personal individuation. But the real point is that the government wished to increase the knowledge and the practical options available to the Indians, and was not electing in a firm theoretical way for any one of these.[28]

Perhaps the most definable accomplishment for Indians during the Hoover administration was in budgeting. Although appropriations had increased throughout the decade, the Interior Department report of 1927 entitled one section "The Poverty of the Indian Service." Strong criticisms that the Senate Committee on Indian Affairs in 1928 and 1929 made of the inadequate funding helped form a sentiment for change. Then, between 1929 and 1932, expenditures almost doubled, from $16 to $25 million. This increase escaped the fierce economizing that followed the crash, for Hoover knew Indian conditions to be deplorable. Secretary Wilbur insisted on the appropriations with exactly the rationale he must have known Hoover would like: "We have two honest capable men [Rhoads and Scattergood] ready to do their best. We need to put the Indians in a creditable position before passing on to them responsibility for themselves . . . we need to spend more now in order to spend less later." Wilbur added a revealing remark about how he expected to show results within eight years; that was the span of time Hoover had originally planned on being President. The money, appropriated over strong objections from the Director of the Budget, went for better schools, hospitals, and health care for Indian children. Adult Indians continued ill nourished and vulnerable to disease, but between 1929 and 1932 the percentage with trachoma declined by 50 percent and the capacity of sanitoriums increased by 15 percent. Direct federal aid went to Indians once the Depression had set in.[29]

Collier later observed that the real shift toward recognition of Indian rights had occurred under Hoover. He had praised Hoover for signing a bill authorizing payment to the Utes for forest lands appropriated under Theodore Roosevelt. Collier also aided in drafting early letters from Rhoads to Congress, and he approved the dividing of the bureau in 1931 into five sections—health, education, agriculture, forestry, and irrigation— each with a technician at its head in close touch with the reservation superintendents. On occasion, nonetheless, Collier criticized the administration severely. It was, he claimed, the first to be aware of Indian needs but did little to effect its goals. He was particularly anxious that the Flathead Indian power sites, the third largest in the nation, not be developed by the Montana Power Company. The opposition that he and others raised to Montana Power had perhaps more to do with their advocacy of strong governmental regulation in power development than with the issue of Indian rights. Collier urged approval by the Federal Power Commission (FPC) of an application by Walter H. Wheeler, a Minneapolis engineer. But Wheeler, who promised cheap power, would not reveal his own financial backing, and offered only vague hope of drawing fertilizer industries— an industry in flux over manufacturing methods—to the area of his plant. Assistant Commissioner Scattergood recommended award of the permit to Montana Power, but with more FPC regulation and a far larger rental to the Indians than either Montana Power or Wheeler had offered. The Montana company got the lease; but upon the insistence of the bureau commissioners, Wilbur, and the FPC itself, and in face of great political pressure to capitulate to the power company, the Indians received the higher revenues. Although the objection to Montana Power had been in the cause of a more rigorous federal policy, the lease was a great advance since, as *The New Republic* remarked, it provided a "firm footing for federal regulation of generating costs, for their accurate determination, and for the sale of the resulting power, at a reasonable and known price, to the distributing company."[30]

The effort to preserve Indian culture accorded with the President's wider work in conservation. Donald Swain, author of a study of federal conservation policies in the period, calls Hoover "a key conservation figure" and "the first conservationist President since Theodore Roosevelt."

Hoover's work, according to Swain, laid much ground for the better-publicized resource management of the New Deal.[31]

Hoover appointed Horace Albright, a well-known conservationist, to be Commissioner of the National Park Service, and supported him with numerous executive orders. Emphasizing public access to park lands, the two men pushed through Congress the Shenandoah, Mammoth Cave, Isle Royale, Great Smoky Mountains, and Morristown national parks. The Park Service budget grew 46 percent in Hoover's first three years, and funds for public works were directed toward the national forests. Wilbur and Hoover began a program of moving forest land into the national preserve—some 2 million acres in four years—and increased the area of national parks and monuments by 40 percent. They also urged acquisition of private holdings in the national parks. In 1931 Hoover directed the Department of Agriculture to cease leasing national forest lands. Large timber interests welcomed Hoover's order, since it would reduce production. The President and his Secretary, both of them outdoorsmen, were responsive to pleas to save endangered species or places of national beauty; Wilbur particularly labored to protect Southwestern desert lands as game preserves. An executive order of 1929 imposed sharp limits on the taking of migratory birds; duck-shooting seasons were shortened; and the two Californians set aside redwood groves and coastal lands in the Northwest; Wilbur founded the "Save the Redwoods League."[32]

The Secretary perceived waterpower and irrigation projects to be threats to national parks. At the urging of Commissioner Albright, he worked to prevent the building by Insull power interests of a dam above the beautiful Cumberland Falls in Kentucky. A member of the Federal Power Commission, Wilbur regretted the limits of the agency's powers to forestall such power projects and helped persuade the President to ask Congress repeatedly for expanded regulation "urgently needed in public protection." Hoover wanted an overhauling of the Federal Power Commission, to interlock it "with the regulating commissions of the states as a kind of extension of their powers." He also recommended that full-time commissioners should replace the established membership of the FPC, which then consisted of the secretaries of Agriculture, Interior, and War. The new commissioners he appointed were, according to the progressive historian Charles Beard, "grey" men not from the utilities interests. The chairman, Frank McNinch, was an old-time North Carolina Bryan Democrat turned Hoover Republican, prominent in his state's "anti-Smith" organization of 1928; he had inveighed in earlier speeches against "financial groups squatting on power sites." The commission had power only to act in the absence of state control, and this restricted its jurisdiction to a small minority of power projects. Yet Hoover directed Secretary of War

Good to investigate whether in assuming authority to supervise the smallest tributaries to interstate waters and to deny the right of way through public lands to power sites the FPC was violating the Constitution. He also intervened to secure a Justice Department ruling on Appalachian Power's application that proved favorable to the utility. And the commission fired two employees who had worked flagrantly against the utilities. Still, the weight of the administration was behind the commission's fight to regulate the company. And the Geological Survey tightened its control over mineral and water resources in the public domain.[33]

The Commission on the Conservation and Administration of the Public Domain was created in April 1929. Named the Garfield Commission after its chairman, James R. Garfield, Theodore Roosevelt's Secretary of the Interior, it was to determine land and conservation policies for the Far West. The commission brought back exactly what Hoover had hoped it would: recommendations for increasing reserves of oil and mineral lands, national parks and forests, and wildlife refuges. It also suggested that the surface rights to lands useful only for grazing should be returned to the states for more effective conservation of the soil and water that overgrazing threatened. Any revenues from the lands would be spent on education or conservation. Wilbur and the President had already brought up the idea; Hoover liked the notion of shrinking the federal secretariat, and thought that the states might be able to exercise a tighter control over the use of the lands. For a quarter century the Interior Department had unsuccessfully recommended stiff laws. The states, on the other hand, had land agencies already in operation, regulating and profiting from the lands in their possession. When some conservationists objected, Hoover affirmed that the idea was "tentative"; and the administration asked Congress to restrict grazing. Conservationists were correct to warn of danger: private interests were strong in state legislatures, and it would have been dangerous to allow individual states to own watershed areas important to their neighbors. In late August 1929 the governors of public-land states met in Salt Lake City to consider the proposal; seven of the ten states signified interest in it. Congress, however, largely ignored the mission's ideas, as it so often ignored the work of assemblies called by the administration.[34]

Since the early twenties Hoover had worked for the expansion of water-power facilities. The Colorado River Compact and the resulting Boulder Canyon Project Act of 1928 established a multipurpose project for water development financed by the government. Instead of selling "falling water," the government was to build the powerhouse and allow Californian municipalities to install the necessary machinery and buy most of the power. This was acceptable to the House appropriating subcommittee only because the Los Angeles Bureau of Power and Light operated much like a private power company. Nevertheless, *The New Republic* editorialized: "Secretary Wilbur's plans for the distribution of Boulder Dam power are so much better than his earlier announcements that the advocates of public ownership may well congratulate him." Wilbur himself later explained: "I belong to that strange group of Americans who have never developed a religion about the production and distribution of power—I favored that method of development and use that supplied the most for the least money right at the spot where the lights were turned on." Construction began in the fall of 1930. Ninety-one percent of the waterpower went to publicly owned corporations. Hoover, who had said in 1926 that "the Colorado River system should be embraced in a national program of major water improvement," in 1931 and 1932 quietly promoted legislation that would have given the government responsibility for flood control of the Palo Verde Valley, which diverted water from the Colorado. He made plans for building Grand Coulee Dam on the Columbia in his second presidential term.[35]

Hoover concerned himself with the building up of inland waterways. Both as Commerce Secretary and President he put particular effort into getting a St. Lawrence Seaway, which he considered chiefly a transportation project. In a major speech of 1929 on inland waterways he asked for $525 million for five years of work on the St. Lawrence, the Mississippi, and connecting waterways; the money would come from savings on naval construction—"nothing could be a finer or more vivid conversion of swords into plowshares." He also revitalized the International Joint Commission with new appointments, attempting to make it an instrument for forwarding the Seaway. But Canada still stalled. That nation was having internal political problems, and the port of Montreal feared losing commerce. Then, in the summer of 1932, Governor Franklin Delano Roosevelt of New York sent Hoover a letter of objection that further hampered the project. The Seaway—which was conceived as part of a network including a waterway from the Great Lakes to the Gulf and an Ohio River canal—would be competitive to the "all-American" Erie Canal route through New York State. After a disappointing meeting in Washington with Conservative Prime Minister R. B. Bennett, Hoover by pounding away negotiated a treaty with Canada in the summer of 1932, by which after disposing of electrical power the project would cost each country only $10 million annually for ten years. During the 1932 campaign, however, FDR dismissed the project as "too expensive," and by one vote the Senate failed to ratify in 1934.[36]

During World War I the national government had built a power plant at Muscle Shoals, on the rapids of the Tennessee River in Alabama, for the purpose of producing nitrates for gunpowder. The plan introduced by

Senator George Norris would have authorized the government to increase the power at Muscle Shoals, retaining ownership of the operation, producing fertilizers, and otherwise developing the region. By the time of Hoover's presidency Muscle Shoals had become so highly politicized that its second approval in Congress in 1931 did not necessarily mean that most national legislators favored federal operation. The Norris version passed, said Congressman James B. Aswell, "because of the politics involved . . . and because of an impatient desire to be rid of the question." Hoover objected that it had become a "political symbol. . . . To be against Senator Norris' bill appears to be . . . in league with the power companies." Like McNary-Haugen, it appealed to many constituencies: farmers desiring inexpensive fertilizer from nitrates, business looking for cheap power, liberals wanting a more public economy and cheaper power for consumers. As a major advocate of developing waterpower, Hoover was not the likeliest of opponents. Norris himself said that the Colorado River project—with its highest dam in the country within transmission distance of major cities, its flood control and irrigation projects represented by the all-American canal—eclipsed what he proposed for the Tennessee. The tone of Hoover's repeated technical requests to the secretaries of War and Agriculture, the governor of Alabama, and others, suggests that he wished to know whether the Norris proposal was feasible. On February 28, 1931, Hoover said: "this happens to be an engineering project and so far as its business merits and demerits are concerned is subject to the cold examination of engineering facts." The first part of his veto message concentrated on the project's financial shortcomings: "this legislation will show a loss," he said. Muscle Shoals was the only major water project he did not champion. But in recoil against what he believed to be its socialist character, he labeled it "degeneration"; and he turned Norris—who called the veto wicked, cruel, unjust, unfair, and unmerciful—into one of his bitterest enemies. The manner of the veto prefigured the image of grumbling reactionary, obsessed about socialism, that would affix itself to Hoover for many years after his defeat for reelection.[37]

The Muscle Shoals Commission, an alternative scheme originating at the suggestion of the President, was composed of representatives from Tennessee and Alabama, along with War Department technical advisors and the president of the American Farm Bureau Federation. The commission's purpose was "to consider the development of the resources of the Tennessee Valley in the interest of agriculture and industry." Public hearings in the states affected were to obtain proposals on the operation of the properties. The commission unanimously concluded that it was "economically feasible and desirable to . . . operate the Muscle Shoals properties for . . . quantity production . . . of commercial fertilizer . . . [and] chemicals."

Its plan was to lease the properties for these purposes, subject to "equitable distribution and reasonable profit limitations." But the crux of the scheme was an ingenious use of lease monies for the immediate development of the river "in behalf of" the Tennessee Valley. "Under the direction of a Board to be named by organized agriculture," this Hoover-inspired Tennessee Valley Authority would begin immediate construction of Cove Creek Dam with government funds, for the purpose of controlling floods. States, counties, and municipalities, along with chemical operations, would have first choice on power resources. Some of the profit would go to research, but most of it would enter a revolving fund for improving manufacture, storage, and distribution of fertilizer by a farmers' cooperative. Region appears to have been a stronger determinant of the vote than general principle. In the House of Representatives the "Hoover" Bill received 74 percent of its votes from the New England and Middle Atlantic states and only 11 percent from the South and the border states. Some urban Democrats of a generally progressive character voted for it. This was not the New Deal's TVA, but it was a progressive and in some ways strikingly bold plan for development of the area—a plan that might have had more national influence than TVA. It did not balance politically against the veto of Muscle Shoals and the pointless belligerence with which the conservationist Hoover had seemed to choose the course of reaction in his largest presidential controversy over conservation.[38]

Upon coming to office, Hoover had noted that the United States, with 20 percent of the world's oil, was responsible for 65 percent of its consumption. Vast pools of natural gas in Texas and California were being wastefully "blown off" into the atmosphere. "There is a limit to oil supplies," the President wrote later, and "the time will come when . . . the Nation will need this oil much more than it is needed now." A sequel to Hoover's generally well-received order to restrict use of government oil lands resulted in a deadlocked conference of Western governors who met at Colorado Springs late in 1929 to discuss means of conserving oil. Much of the time was taken up by protests against the edict. Senator Borah criticized the meeting for discouraging difference of opinion; but its chairman, Mark Requa, received considerable praise. At least the need for state agreements was publicized. After a taste of federal planning imposed under the New Deal, the same industry leaders who had rejected the interstate compact proposal advanced by Hoover would embrace just such a plan. The government and the Federal Oil Conservation Board, composed of leaders in government and industry, did make some progress against waste and overproduction of oil, though the uncooperative attitude of Texas was a major obstacle. Moderately effective were the President's ban, the enforcement of "unit operation" on land, most of it federal, in California's model

Kettleman Hills, and pressure on the states from Hoover and the Oil Conservation Board, of which he was a member, to control production. One reason for progress in conservation was the industry's awareness that curtailing overproduction would raise prices.[39]

An obvious alternate policy to curb the disordered competition that produced overproduction and inefficiency, one of modifying antitrust policy and encouraging consolidation, was generally not to Hoover's liking. Early in his presidency he would frequently urge Attorney General Mitchell or Assistant Attorney General John Lord O'Brian that one of them look into alleged violations of antitrust law. And he asked O'Brian to investigate a 1929 meeting of oil producers in Texas.[40]

During the Depression, Hoover came under great pressure to endorse efforts at price cooperation, particularly in oil. He asked Congress to undertake a revision of antitrust laws, but only insofar as they discouraged conservation. Even here O'Brian and Mitchell publicly argued that any relaxation of competition must be accompanied by effective regulation in the public interest. In the fall of 1930, according to Stimson, Hoover moved toward weakening antitrust enforcement because of the "great national emergency." After limited state action to curb oil production by the end of 1931, prices rose in 1932, enhancing the industry's health and its ability to sustain conservation endeavors. Hoover had been prepared to endorse a national agreement to restrict production had the states not begun to act. Success in the form of a durable interstate compact came only later in the 1930's, after the Supreme Court declared the NRA unconstitutional. The administration was interested in similarly steadying other industries. "Particular attention," Hoover said in December 1931, "should be given to the industries founded upon natural resources, especially where destructive competition produces great waste of these resources"; he specifically mentioned coal and lumber as well as oil. The Timber Conservation Board in October 1932 recommended that the government give "permission, under competent Federal supervision, of reasonable agreements to adjust production to consumption; avoid waste; conserve natural resources and provide continuity and security of employment." And the government sharply restricted lumbering on federal land.[41]

Still, Hoover in the politics of the Depression could not appear to be too friendly with "big business." Competition, he sincerely observed, was "not only a protection to the consumer" but "the incentive to progress," although wasteful production, impoverishing "both operator and worker," deserved investigation. The Justice Department actually proceeded in the Depression's worst days with antitrust action against RCA, General Electric, and Westinghouse as well as Appalachian coal producers. When some of his closest business friends protested that such suits threatened confidence, Hoover suggested legislation to exempt certain forms of communication like the transatlantic telephone. Frederick Feiker's appointment in July 1931 to head the Bureau of Foreign and Domestic Commerce raised speculation that Feiker would push the kind of associationalism promoted earlier. He did little of the sort. With the assistance of Hoover and the Commerce Department, cotton textile groups managed to curtail some overproduction by abolishing night work on the part of women and children. The following September Hoover attacked the plan of the Democratic industrialist Gerard Swope for strengthening business. "Aside from wiping out the Sherman and Clayton Acts," Hoover grandly wrote to Solicitor General Thomas Thacher, "this plan is thoroughly unconstitutional." It would lead to "gigantic trusts such as we have never dreamed of in this history of the world," and was an attempt to "smuggle fascism into America through a back door." And the President in 1932 resisted the campaign of the Chamber of Commerce's new president, H. I. Harriman, to get revision of antitrust laws. More indictments for violating antitrust laws came under Hoover than in any previous presidential term; forced to choose between stabilization and liberty, he embraced liberty as the more fragile and deserving of protection. In the 1932 campaign Franklin Roosevelt, not Hoover, leaned the farther toward changing the laws.[42]

An American Bar Association study of appointments to the federal judiciary shows that of all presidents since Grover Cleveland, only William Howard Taft appointed fewer members of his own party than did Hoover. Using schooling, judicial experience, and ABA rating, the study judged the Hoover choices to be of higher quality than those of Harding, Coolidge, or FDR, and found that fewer of them were from big business. While imperfect (he pushed his own secretary for a federal judgeship in February 1933), Hoover's devotion to appointment on merit is impressive. He had gone on record as wishing to treat judicial choices "above politics," and he meant it; Mitchell consulted with senators but reaffirmed that politics would not dictate inferior choices. Only one or two such compromises were made among dozens of appointments.[43]

A common standard for evaluating any President's progressivism lies in the character of his additions to the Supreme Court. Hoover had an unusual number, three appointments during his single term. The men he chose —he told Mitchell, "I should like very much to appoint a woman to a distinguished position if I could find a distinguished woman to appoint"— were all of high caliber: the former Associate Justice Charles Evans Hughes as Chief Justice, and Owen Roberts and Benjamin Cardozo as Associates.

The President's nomination of Charles Evans Hughes in 1930 to return to the Supreme Court called up substantial opposition. Hughes's recent law service to some of the country's largest corporations worked against him, as did his resignation from the Court to run for President in 1916. In his first tenure he had been a judicial moderate on the constitutionality of progressive federal and state legislation; and as governor of New York he had impressed Hoover with a memorable early defense of five socialists expelled from the state assembly during the Red Scare. But progressives perceived him as a conservative and were also voting against the conservatism of the Court itself. Carter Glass had a different reason for opposing Hughes: his opinions, as Glass understood them, had weakened states' rights. Hughes won confirmation by a 52-to-26 vote.[44]

Hoover was less fortunate, however, with his next nominee. John J. Parker of North Carolina was recommended by six presidents of the American Bar Association and by the bar associations of half the states. There was a political aspect to the choice of Parker: a Southerner had been the previous incumbent, and Hoover, having no representative of the South in his cabinet, wished to consolidate his election gains there. Parker's work for underdog clients and his strong anti-fraternity position may also have attracted Hoover. The President and Mitchell, along with the liberal Justice Stone, who recommended Parker, either overlooked or disregarded his decision in a district court to uphold an injunction enforcing a yellow-dog labor contract requiring a written promise not to strike. A Supreme Court precedent had apparently left Parker, as he claimed, with "no latitude or discretion," and that Court refused to grant an appeal against Parker's decision. He had also upheld, however—and without a word of sympathy for the underdog—the right of mine companies to evict miners from company towns when they struck. Also ignored in the nomination was Parker's remark in 1920, aimed to mute the racial issue that had erupted in North Carolina's Democratic primary, that the Negro was not ready to participate actively in the state's politics. In mitigation of this, Parker in 1930 offered the weak pronouncement that he had "no prejudice whatever toward the colored people." Carter Glass worried that if Parker were defeated for his racial comment, no Southerner could win the Senate's vote. A strong coalition of labor and Negro organizations, aided by Southern Democrats troubled about Republican implications of the nominee and the lack of a preeminent judicial record, led to Parker's defeat by 41 to 39. He served subsequently as a circuit judge. For that work the *New York Times* termed him "one of the most distinguished jurists on the federal bench," and in 1946 the ABA *Journal* called the Senate's refusal to confirm him the "most regrettable combination of error and injustice that has ever developed as to a nomination to the great court." Parker's substitute, Owen Roberts, whom the Senate approved unanimously one minute after receiving the nomination, had a less progressive record than Parker. But Roberts had gained favor, especially with the press, for his prosecution of the oil scandals, and for reputedly saying that "prohibition has no place in the Constitution."[45]

The anti-Parker drive was an event in the emergence within national politics of a tough urban and labor Democracy, given a further militancy by growing unemployment. The episode foreshadowed the great urban-based coalition of liberals, unionists, and minorities that would constitute much of the strength of Franklin Roosevelt's party.

Benjamin Cardozo, nominated in 1932, enjoyed vast respect; and Hoover had been impressed by Cardozo's integrity in a personal meeting at which the President had unsuccessfully asked the jurist to serve on the law enforcement commission. Cardozo, a Democrat, would be the second Jew and the third resident of New York City to sit on the Court. He was the choice of the Holmes-Brandeis-Stone party, as well as Stimson; in his earlier writings he had aligned himself with Holmes's constitutional philosophy and, like Brandeis, believed that legislatures had broad powers to experiment with social problems. Yet his was a judicial, not primarily a political or economic, philosophy. Cardozo's appointment shone as a sublime moment for good government, one liberal scholar commented enthusiastically. The journalist William Allen White wrote to Senator George Norris: "I have not had a good drink since I left Kansas City to come to Emporia nearly 40 years ago. . . . Hunt up . . . a good long brown drink of nose-choking, hair-raising, gullet-gugging, hard corn liquor and then and there . . . take one happy untrammeled drink for me in celebration of Justice Cardozo." Hoover himself later wrote to Chief Justice Stone: "As you know, I have never been one who felt it was the business of the Court to fasten the past onto the present in such a fashion as to block all progress." During the 1930's Cardozo and Hughes usually teamed in opposition to the "four horsemen" who so ardently resisted the New Deal, while Roberts became the swing man on the Court, which finally moved toward acceptance of FDR's programs.[46]

THE AGRICULTURAL MARKETING ACT in its implementing tells a story of the transition of Hoover's government from prosperity to depression. It was drafted in part by the President's old friend Representative Franklin Fort of New Jersey and owed much to Hoover's private prodding and plans he had outlined during the Commerce years. Passing the House by a margin of 10 to 1, the legislation promised "to promote the effective merchandising of agricultural commodities in interstate and foreign commerce, so that the industry of agriculture will be placed on an economic equality with other industries." The bill gave an eight-member Federal Farm Board wide powers to lessen speculation, control surpluses, and prevent undue fluctuations in price. The aim closely resembled that of the McNary-Haugen Bill; George Peek said that if the equalization fee had been included, "we would have pretty much the whole McNary-Haugen." Both McNary and Haugen were conspicuously present if unenthusiastic when Hoover signed the bill on June 15, 1929, each receiving one of the signing pens. But instead of providing for an equalization fee and dumping of the surplus abroad, the new act set up a half-billion-dollar revolving fund with which to encourage farmers' cooperatives and, if necessary, to buy and sell agricultural products in the interest of raising prices. In some ways the new act seemed more far-reaching than the export-debenture plan that the Senate had narrowly approved and Hoover had rejected as a subsidy of greatest aid to grain dealers and speculators. "Washington," wrote a farm journalist, "is startled with the broad powers proposed to be granted to the new farm board. In many respects it is the most far-reaching bill presented to Congress since the Federal Reserve Act . . . or the Interstate Commerce Law. . . ." Though Hoover cautiously termed the Farm Board an "experiment" and a "beginning," and he worried greatly about the government entering the commodity market and sustaining high losses, it would react to the Depression more quickly than any other government agency. It could loan to favored organizations of farmers and buy farm surpluses. Yet the Agricultural Marketing Act purposely lacked the more coercive means at the heart of the McNary-Haugen or export-debenture bills. Hoover praised the new act as "democratic." Though for chairman of the Farm Board he chose the blunt Alexander Legge, once known to him as vice-chairman of the War Industries Board and now head of International Harvester, his other appointees came from prominent farm groups.[47]

Hoover's program was widely regarded at the time as both community-oriented and politically progressive; in some respects it anticipated the New Deal plans of price supports for agriculture, and constituted one of the most extensive programs for the reorganizing of the economy the federal government had ever undertaken. Its governmental support and coordination of private cooperative activity was just the sort of thing Hoover would have relished for much of American life. And it would permit farming, he declared in 1930, to "continue as an individualistic business of small units and independent ownership."[48]

The President was particularly eager to promote the cooperatives, which he thought would reduce acreage. In the meantime, their rational marketing would stabilize prices; and their ownership of the means of distribution— purchasing, storing, processing, and marketing—would avoid speculators and unnecessary middlemen. The extent and incessant nature of the board's efforts to increase cooperative activity can be overlooked because of the dramatic quality of its stabilization policies. "Every penny of waste between farmer and consumer that we can eliminate," Hoover said to Congress, "will be a gain to the farmer and the consumer." In a memorandum to Legge and board member Carl Williams of the cotton cooperatives—both stayed at the White House on the weekend before the board's first convening on July 15—he urged applying the revolving fund to the building of marketing institutions owned and controlled by farmers. Later he suggested calling leaders of wheat cooperatives to a Chicago meeting and proposing to them what he termed a "Producers' Own Wheat Marketing Company." This was at the core of it: Hoover had roundly criticized the Non-Partisan League of North Dakota for getting that state to build warehouses and establish clearinghouses for marketing; but he approved of employing for the identical marketing process agencies dependent on governmental funding, so long as they were private. The board would lend money to this farmers' organization for use in leasing or building facilities for efficient marketing. Sam McKelvie of Nebraska, the wheat farmers' representative on the board, explicitly described its policy as being designed to substitute for the private owner of a grain elevator a public warehouseman.[49]

In its first months the board set itself to stimulate the growth of farm cooperatives. It gave generous loans, allowing advances to members of up to 90 percent of a crop's current market value pending final sale. At once more farmers joined to obtain the advances, receivable upon delivery of their crops. And as other farmers signed up, the cooperatives slowly began to exert greater control over commodities after they had left the farm.

A week before the stock market crash, the board took its first major action toward stabilizing prices. It promised enough loan money to cotton cooperatives to "cover" cotton at 16 cents a pound. Political pressure from Southern areas newly won by the Republicans in 1929 pushed the board to this considerable risk. But the gamble showed the board's flexibility, and when more awesome conditions presented themselves, it would act quickly and forcefully. On October 28, as the stock market seemed to be reviving from the mild setback of "Black Thursday" five days earlier, the board began a similar experiment with wheat. By carrying 100 percent of the prevailing price, the board steadied wheat prices to prevent, as Sam McKelvie put it, "a decline in harmony with what took place in the stock market." We "turned the Board into a depression remedy," Hoover said in his *Memoirs*.[50]

In the face of the market crash the board had upheld the prices of the nation's two largest crops. Soon through various aid programs it would stabilize corn, grapes (it saved from bankruptcy the Sun Maid raisin cooperative, run by Hoover's old friend Ralph Merritt), citrus fruits (as one of its first actions it advanced money for control of an invasion in Florida of the Mediterranean fruit fly), dairy products, livestock, wool, and many less important commodities. A Perishable Agricultural Commodities Act of 1930 supplemented its work in that form of produce. Of the major crops, only tobacco proved resistant to better organization; manufacturers, dealers, and warehouse interests successfully opposed it there.[51]

By the time the Depression began in earnest, the board had a past to live with. If it retrenched, the loans it had just made to cooperatives would be lost to bankruptcies. Even before spring winds blew over the rising green of Kansas winter wheat, a new Farmers National Grain Corporation, chartered early in 1930 in Delaware by grain producers, was dealing frantically in futures. The first purchase by this corporation of 7.5 million bushels of May futures came in February, and prompted the *Outlook* to observe that the board had taken a "high dive into socialism." A former friend of the President protested: "Communism, pure and simple," and Bernard Baruch was calling the act the "most socialistic legislation this country has ever seen." Hoover himself had doubts, fearing it would serve as "a lesson for all time in Government interference." By April, with the government assuring a market for the crop, the price of wheat remained steady—just over 90 cents. The Cotton Stabilization Corporation, organized in May by cotton producers to purchase the July crop, similarly rescued the cotton cooperatives.[52]

The board was now under attack from elements of the business community. The United States Chamber of Commerce, led by Hoover's grain-trader friend Julius Barnes, was particularly vocal. Responding to an attack from the Chamber, Legge charged its members with indifference toward farmers and of holding economic theories belonging to the "horse and buggy" era. "The local elevator, the terminal elevator, the miller and the banker who financed it are happy with a perfectly hedged market operation wherein they take no chance," he said. Although he was an important businessman, Legge's sympathy lay with the farmers, and some of them were registering delight at his assaults on the Chamber of Commerce. The Chamber, said Legge, wanted "the Farm Board to hang its clothes on a hickory limb but not go near the water." The agrarian reformer Chester Davis wrote to his friend George Peek that Legge was prejudiced against the grain traders, whose speculative activities did not really harm the farmers. Hoover and Legge believed they knew better. According to J. W. Duvel of the Grain Futures Administration, ruthless speculators had deprived wheat farmers of more than 10 percent of their return in recent years.[53]

Hoover publicly supported the board's actions. Barnes claimed that the President privately opposed using the government for buying and selling commodities and fixing prices, and Hoover did write Legge in 1930 that only the current emergency warranted the use of the stabilization powers.

The Grain Corporation, as Hoover's Senate friend Henry Allen explained, was not government, even though its funds were public. It was a neat distinction, yet somewhat disingenuous. For the eight-man appointed board, not any group of farmers or their representatives, told the Grain Stabilization Corporation what to do. Circumstances, moreover, had changed sharply since the legislation had been drafted. The Farm Board was now acting as the Hoover administration's first relief agency. There is no evidence that Hoover fought this all-but-inevitable transformation of the board. So furious was the President at Barnes's Chamber of Commerce for criticizing the board on May 1 that he called to cancel a previously scheduled talk there the next day, only to be dissuaded from such a show of temper. When Legge later failed to mention stabilization in a radio speech, Hoover complained, saying that the policy had "stemmed the tide of the panic in agricultural products."[54]

Throughout the twenties, Hoover had criticized the absence in the Mc-Nary-Haugen Bill of any method for preventing surplus production. Secretary of Agriculture Hyde made the restraining of overproduction his department's policy. He wanted the government to lease land, initially accepting the lowest rentals offered by farmers, and to retire marginal land, converting it to pasture or forest. The plan "has the merit," Hoover wrote, "of direct action in reducing supply to demand and thus unquestionably increasing prices." The cost would be borne as McNary-Haugen had provided, by a manufacturer's excise tax on products affected. Legge began publicly urging the voluntary reduction of acreage. A rise in prices of farm produce, he observed on NBC's "Farm and Home Hour," could come only through a lowering of production or an increase in sales; and worsening world economic conditions militated against the latter. On another occasion he pointed out that the biggest cotton crop of the last years had been worth only two-thirds as much as the smallest. The stabilization activities had certainly encouraged production. When prices declined, the farmers reasoned, a larger crop might compensate for the loss; and why should anyone restrict a crop without assurance that neighbors would do the same? Critics of restriction also argued that it would make the people the more vulnerable to sudden wartime need or a shortage brought on by bad weather. The board, however, embarked on reduction, beginning its program with Kansas, the largest wheat-producing state. Some of its loans were made on the understanding that acreage be restricted or fertilizer applied sparingly. In mid-1931 the board proposed suspending for a generation all public activities tending to increase crop acreage, including the Homestead Act and reclamation projects, and buying marginal crop areas on a grand scale for forest and recreational use. Yet funds were simply no longer available for such costly programs. And the cooperatives themselves, which might have persuaded stubborn farmers to curtail production, were losing ground in face of bad times.[55]

Stabilization worked to the extent that it temporarily held prices well above the market minimum. That, the board decided, was sufficient reason in the midst of great suffering by farmers to resume buying futures. The decision also reflected hopes that the market would improve, along with renewed fears that cooperatives would suffer bankruptcy. James Stone, who would take over as chairman upon Legge's planned resignation in March 1931, later told a Senate committee that the frequency of bank failures had led the board in early November to think its effort at stabilization might save the credit structure of the whole country. In November 1930 the manager of the Grain Corporation made dramatic appearances on the floor of the Chicago Board of Trade to purchase wheat. Hoover's enemy George Peek praised Legge's honesty and ability and commended the board for its work of organizing the farmers. "It makes me smile," said Peek, "when I think of the criticism directed against the McNary-Haugen bill—government in business, price-fixing, uneconomic, etc. . . . [The] Farm Board is in business, is in effect fixing prices, and the government is assuming all the risk." By February 1931 American wheat prices held at about 80 cents, while the world price sank to 55 cents. Meanwhile, the tariffs for the first time kept large quantities of Canadian wheat off the market. That had been an aim of McNary-Haugen: to make the tariff effective by support of the home price. Then the board announced—before that year's crop was planted—that it would cease acquiring wheat as of mid-1931; for it owned 257 million bushels (one-fourth of the world's supply), an amount, vastly larger than ever anticipated, that if sold would further depress prices. Only grape prices continued to be stabilized successfully; there the large consumption of homemade wines made the difference.[56]

Hoover disarmed some progressive critics in April 1931 by appointing as a board member the president of the Farm Bureau, Sam H. Thompson, a prominent supporter of both the McNary-Haugen plan and federal development of Muscle Shoals. But the last two years of the board's existence —until the New Deal placed farm relief under the Department of Agriculture and the Farm Credit Administration—were largely anticlimactic. The board continued to expand credit available to farmers—by $100 million from mid-1931 to February 1932. As late as 1932 the Farm Board, the Grange, and the Farmers' Union in a joint statement commended the Hoover legislation as a good start. The Farm Board, however, observed that "inequality has grown up in the country [between business and agriculture through] the ease of organization and of Government privilege to the one, and lack of organization and want of government sanction on the other." But the *New York Times* and the *New York Herald-Tribune* called for the board's abolition. The main dispenser of agricultural relief, the Reconstruction Finance Corporation, bypassed it completely. And the President himself operated more and more on his own to help farmers. He secured promises from tobacco companies, for instance, to buy more of the crop, and also spoke firmly against grain traders for selling wheat short and depressing prices. Hoover's friend Senator Henry Allen remarked to a Kansas editor in 1930: "The realization is growing clearer . . . that the grain trade is going to suffer if the marketing act succeeds."[57]

Hoover's well-received denunciation of short selling on July 10, 1931, was aimed largely at the Chicago Board of Trade, which was excluding the Farm Board's Grain Corporation. Clarence Huff, the president of the Grain Corporation, thereupon asked Agriculture Secretary Hyde to suspend the Board of Trade as provided under the Grain Futures Act of 1922. Legge's view of the Board of Trade was that its members "have set up a little government of their own" with trials barring attorneys or appeals; he wished to replace it with something better. Stone was tougher still: the board members, he said, "look upon themselves as middlemen, entitled by custom to take a heavy toll from American wheat producers for so-called services, which consist chiefly of pocketing for themselves the largest possible share of the consumer's dollar." Despite the danger of interrupted financing of the spring crop, Hyde in 1932 for the first time used the Grain Futures Act to bring the status of the Board of Trade as a contract market under official review. "U.S. SLAMS BOARD OF TRADE," read the Chicago *Tribune*'s headline when Hyde's special commission suspended the board's activities, a suspension delayed by appeal. Attorney General Mitchell, shunning a compromise, promised "to make the best possible presentation of the case against the Board of Trade." Just before the election, Hoover in the hope of raising grain prices receded from his position with an order lifting regulations on reporting trades in exchange for a promise of no "harmful short selling." But the basic hostility of the administration toward the board had not changed; that was indicated in its post-election proposals to tighten regulation of short selling and other speculative dealings.[58]

The Farm Board's main dilemma now lay in the enormous quantities of grain and cotton it held in storage. Dumping the surplus on the market would depress prices even more—its very existence may have had a dampening effect; on the other hand, high costs prohibited long-term storage. One answer seemed obvious to Hoover: distribute the surplus to the needy. In 1932, after his request to Congress, 55 million bushels of wheat (out of 85 million authorized) and 350 million bales of cotton were delivered as gifts to the American Red Cross—some $70 million worth of produce. At Hoover's prompting, 15 million bushels of wheat went to China in exchange for Chinese government bonds, and the President offered "to ac-

Hulda Hoover, ca. 1870

Jesse Hoover, ca. 1879

Herbert Hoover, ca. 1875

Mary ("May"), Herbert ("Bert"),
and Theodore ("Tad") Hoover, ca. 1881

Laura M. and Henry John Minthorn

Charles D. Henry and his daughter Lou
fishing, ca. 1895

A Hoover family
picnic, ca. 1878

Survey squad, Stanford University, 1893
Clockwise from upper left: Arthur Diggles,
R. E. McDonnell, James White,
and Herbert Hoover

Lou Henry Hoover (*right*)
and Jean Henry Large (*left*) in
traditional Japanese dress, 1901

Panorama of Sons of Gwalia mining town, ca. 1900

Hoover at 40

Lou Henry Hoover with Allan (*left*)
and Herbert, Jr. in London, ca. 1908

U.S. Food Administration
poster, ca. 1918

The California relief ship
Camino, 1915

President Woodrow Wilson and his War Council
(*clockwise from upper left*): Herbert Hoover, Edward M. Hurley,
Vance McCormick, James Garfield, Bernard Baruch,
Josephus Daniels, Wilson, William G. McAdoo, and Benedict Crowell

The Hardings (*center*), the Hoovers (*at right*), and General John J. Pershing in Griffiths Stadium, Washington, on Opening Day of the baseball season, April 15, 1922

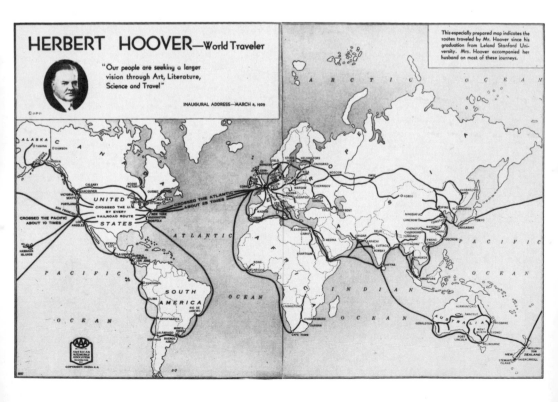

Fishing, 1928

Candidate Herbert Hoover
and fellow Republicans
at Sequoia National Park
in August 1928

Commerce Secretary Hoover
participating in the first
intercity television broadcast,
on April 7, 1927. Walter S.
Gifford, president of A.T.&T.,
spoke with Hoover before an
audience of fifty spectators.

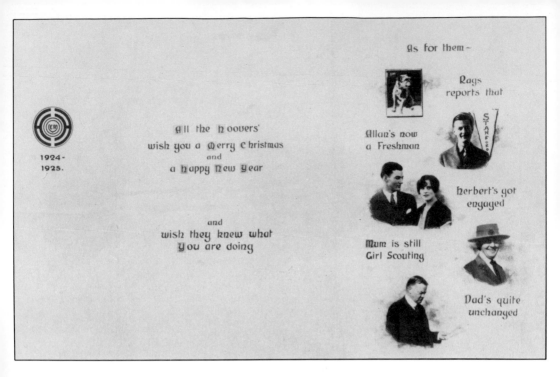

1924-
1925.

All the Hoovers'
wish you a Merry Christmas
and
a Happy New Year

and
wish they knew what
you are doing

As for them ~

Rags
reports that

Allan's now
a Freshman

Herbert's got
engaged

Mum is still
Girl Scouting

Dad's quite
unchanged

The Hoover residence at 2300 "S" Street N.W., Washington, D.C.

THE CART SEEMS TO BE RUNNING AWAY WITH THE HORSE!

THE BOXERS ON THE LINE.

"H. H." quotes from a recent telegram: "The Chinese soldiers are unable to keep the Boxers off the railway line." Could it, he asks, be anything like the above?

North China Herald
June 13, 1900

The President and First Lady
with (*from left to right*) Herbert Jr.
and his wife, Margaret, and Allan

The angle and lighting and the President's
expression, combined with the cigar
and the champagne, convey the classic image
of Hoover the hardened reactionary which is
still so popular.

Hoover in 1930

On board the U.S.S. *Arizona*
bound towards Puerto Rico
in March 1931

Clockwise from upper left: Secretary of Commerce Robert P. Lamont, Secretary of the Interior Ray Lyman Wilbur, Attorney General William D. Mitchell, Postmaster General Walter F. Brown, Secretary of the Navy Charles F. Adams, Secretary of Agriculture Arthur M. Hyde, Secretary of Labor James J. Davis, Secretary of War Patrick J. Hurley, Secretary of State Henry L. Stimson, President Hoover, Vice-President Charles Curtis, Secretary of the Treasury Andrew W. Mellon

Calvin Coolidge and Herbert Hoover in 1929

From left to right: Premier Laval of France, Hoover, Undersecretary of the Treasury Ogden Mills, and Secretary of State Henry L. Stimson, meeting on November 8, 1931 to discuss war debts and related matters

Soldiers' huts in flames after the rout
of the Bonus Army in 1932

The Hoovers departing for Des Moines
for the President's first campaign speech
after he accepted renomination in 1932

Hoover with President-elect
Franklin D. Roosevelt, en route to the
inauguration ceremony on March 4, 1933

Feeding hungry children in Poland, 1946

The Hoover Institution
at Stanford University

After fishing, 1953

commodate the Chinese Government with any amount of wheat" for refugees from the Yangtze River flood. The United States sent 7.5 million more to Germany for bonds and traded surpluses of wheat for Brazilian surpluses of coffee. Only with a caution dictated by protests from the grain trade did the government put wheat on the international market.[59]

In August 1931 the board surprised Southern governors with a telegram that urged the plowing under of every third row of standing cotton. Hoover initially favored the scheme (and wanted to kill off little pigs as well). The *New York Times* called it "one of the maddest things that ever came from an official body," and the farmers ignored it. Yet the destruction of crops—subsidized directly by Washington and, in most cases, accepted by vote of the farmers concerned—became an essential part of the Agricultural Adjustment Act of 1933. In the early 1920's both farm price supports and acreage restriction had been regarded as foolhardy; the Democratic platform of 1932 condemned the Farm Board for extravagance, government speculation, and "the unsound policy of restricting agricultural production." But the New Deal Commodity Credit Corporation would employ the policy the Farm Board had exercised of buying agricultural products at prices higher than those prevailing on the market. Hoover's board, in fact, went beyond the New Deal in its inroads on the middlemen, who absorbed some 70 percent of the costs between producer and consumer. Board personnel, such as Mordecai Ezekiel and Stanley Reed, went on to become prominent in the New Deal, and one of them, John D. Black of Harvard, helped draft the AAA.[60]

Certainly the board failed to halt the disastrous downward spiral of prices: wheat dropped from $1.02 a bushel in July 1929 to 37 cents in June 1932; cotton from 17 cents to 5 cents a pound; corn from 91 cents to 31 cents a bushel. Possessing neither compulsory restraints on production, or even supply, nor a working system for the rational distribution of produce, it was unequipped for a deep depression. But it saved farmers many times its own net loss of some quarter billion dollars, and Senator McNary said he did not see how under the circumstances the equalization fee would have worked at all. The number and size of farm cooperatives increased somewhat; without the board they would surely have declined. In the eight months from July 1930 the Farmers' National Grain Corporation made a profit of over $650 million and returned the farmer additional funds as a large and strong competitor on the world market, although foreign competitors gained while the corporation held on to its stocks. The strengthening of the cooperative movement was a mark of the Hoover administration, as the growth of large-scale farming and ultimately business was a function of the Depression and of the subsidies dispensed by the New Deal and subsequent administrations. Had the economy not fallen and the cooperative movement grown to embrace most farmers, perhaps they would have voluntarily restricted their planting without being paid directly. This was the solution Hoover wanted. In any case, the New Dealer Mordecai Ezekiel later summed up the Farm Board as "a tremendous departure," the "first real program of actual government intervention." Or, as FDR's advisor Rexford Tugwell observed in 1974: "We didn't admit it at the time, but practically the whole New Deal was extrapolated from programs that Hoover started."[61]

XII

~~~~~~

THE DEPRESSION

THROUGHOUT THE MIDDLE and late twenties, stock market speculation and banking practices had worried Hoover as Secretary of Commerce. In November 1925 he furnished Senator Irvine Lenroot with information the senator used in a letter to the Federal Reserve Board protesting against the speculation. On January 1, 1926, Hoover publicly warned against speculation in stocks, and he did so again on March 21 and August 17. In the mid-year report that he made as Secretary of Commerce, he explicitly criticized the Federal Reserve Board. Time and again, beginning in October 1925, he urged his "S" Street neighbor, Adolph Miller of the Reserve Board, to restrict credit sufficiently to deter speculation. Years later Miller credited the talks with "definite changes" in the board's policies. Hoover repeatedly asked President Coolidge to seek additional control over private banking and financial practices, especially insider trading and the dangerous use of common stock as security for customers' deposits.[1]

The drift of governmental policies was unfavorable to restriction. Andrew Mellon's tax reduction program increased funds available for speculation, and the lowering of rates on capital gains brought investors out of tax-free municipal bonds into stocks. One way the FRB might at other times have reduced speculation was through the sale of government securities, which would compel banks to draw money away from reckless investment. But the shrinking of the national debt limited this possibility. In general, the board pursued confused objectives and showed faulty logic in the use of excess reserves.[2]

The Federal Reserve could have raised the rediscount rate, the interest charge at which it lent money to other banks. In doing so, however, it would have withheld funds from the legitimate needs of farmers and business. The board might have increased the rates anyway had it not been for Montagu Norman, governor of the Bank of England, and his influence on Benjamin Strong of the New York Federal Reserve Bank. Norman urged the support of sterling at its prewar parity and of other European currencies. A drop in the credit rate and a reduction in the opportunity for the purchase of government bonds in the United States, he pointed out, could achieve the purpose by pushing Yankee investment capital overseas, where returns were higher. Most American bankers worried that if Britain devalued its currency, United States trade would suffer and its already heavy investments in the British Empire would be repaid in cheaper pounds. So New York bankers in particular, more interested in the effects of monetary matters on world trade, largely ignored the domestic consequences of "easy money."[3]

In 1925 Hoover predicted that such reserve policies would bring "inevitable collapse" in the United States, since a slowing down of domestic investment would not maintain enough new jobs to provide necessary expansion. David Crissinger, appointed head of the Federal Reserve Board by President Harding after service with the Marion [Ohio] Steamshovel Company, ignored Hoover, whose efforts to influence the board through warnings to the Senate Banking and Currency Committee also came to no avail. During July 1927, while Hoover was occupied by Mississippi Valley relief, the board to combat a recession began open market operations aimed at inflating credit, and in August it dropped the rediscount rate to a minuscule 3½ percent. Hoover was appalled. Even when the rate was cautiously raised to 5 percent, speculation picked up in earnest late in 1927 and early in 1928. The Federal Reserve also purchased large orders of banker acceptances on the mistaken notion that the funds so released would not go through the hands of avaricious bankers into the stock market. Hoover continued to worry about the "crazy and dangerous" stock market and was horrified by Strong's successful effort to subordinate the domestic economy to the needs of international finance. Coolidge and Mellon thought Hoover an alarmist; before leaving the White House the President said of the common stocks then rising in vaulting leaps that they were "cheap at current prices."[4]

Two days after he took office, President Hoover conferred with Federal Reserve officials about restraining stock speculation. He wrote a statement for a reluctant Andrew Mellon to make public on March 13, 1929, saying that bonds were undervalued. On March 16 Roy Young, a member of the Federal Reserve Board, appealed to the country's bankers for aid in restricting credit. These acts drove up interest rates slightly, but call money rates—monthly charges for borrowing money from stockbrokers to buy securities—were several times the regular market rates for interest. As call money approached 20 percent during the summer of 1929, the Federal Reserve System lost control of the situation: if it raised general interest rates to that level, normal business would sag and the delicately balanced European currencies would fall off the gold standard. Yet doing nothing only encouraged bankers to make quick profits on Wall Street, which deprived industry, agriculture, and retail stores alike of enough credit to carry on their businesses. New York financiers seemed oblivious to all this. Toward the end of March 1929, Charles E. Mitchell of the National City Bank of New York defied Hoover and Young by offering ready loans for stock speculation. Senator Carter Glass, as chairman of the Senate Banking Committee, denounced Mitchell. In April Hoover had requested editors and publishers of major newspapers to campaign against speculation. Few cooperated.

In the same month he instructed his own financial agent, his friend Edgar Rickard, to liquidate certain of his personal holdings "as possible hard times coming." By May, when car sales dipped and building slackened, he was switching to "gilt-edged bonds." Hoover also sent his friend Henry M. Robinson, vice-president of a major Los Angeles bank, to New York to warn in the President's name both speculators and bankers who loaned to them. He summoned to Washington Richard Whitney, president of the New York Stock Exchange, and asked him to encourage internal regulation. Whitney, who later went to jail for stock fraud, promised much but delivered little. The Federal Reserve Board then ordered an outright cessation of loans to banks that lent largely on stocks. In June Hoover began a drive against "bucket shops" that sold stocks they did not own. He considered for a time establishing an economic council that would coordinate government policies, with Eugene Meyer of the recently defunct War Finance Corporation as its head. Hoover also came to fear that a sharp upward movement in the Federal Reserve rediscount rate might bring collapse, and he resisted for a time the New York district board's recommendation for a rise. The rate went up from 5 to 6 percent in August, and Hoover urged Governor Roosevelt to propose legislation for regulating Wall Street, pointing out that an earlier governor, Charles Evans Hughes, had regulated New York's insurance industry. Thomas Lamont of J. P. Morgan and Company wrote Hoover on October 19 that there was no danger; and an emissary from Lamont heatedly objected to the President about his pressures against speculation. The day before the market break of October 23 Hoover complained to a visitor about the "size and extent of stock market operations." Forever afterward he was fond of saying: "The only trouble with capitalism is capitalists. They're too damned greedy."[5]

When the crash came, Hoover acted quickly. In late October, probably just after the more convulsive decline on the twenty-ninth, he sent Henry Robinson to see Julius Barnes of the United States Chamber of Commerce. According to Barnes, he and Paul Shoup called a meeting of industrial leaders, including Lamont, Owen Young, Bernard Baruch, and several others. After two days they drew up a protective agreement, putting together about $300 million for the purchase of stocks against demoralization. The money was never spent, for prices temporarily recovered to reasonable levels, in response partly to the news of this pool as it spread through Wall Street.[6]

Hoover, like many economists and businessmen ranging from John Maynard Keynes to Andrew Mellon, anticipated a healthy deflation that would soon be followed by another business revival. He used the word "depression" because it sounded less frightening than "panic" or "crisis," terms employed in earlier instances. So earnestly did Hoover believe in the importance of confidence that he later attended a World Series game in Philadelphia simply to make an example of his own serenity. The United States in 1929 lacked any valid historical model as a guide for predicting what would happen. The experience of previous depressions indicated a relatively short duration. Democrats in particular believed that Woodrow Wilson's Federal Reserve Act, and its well-advertised provision of an "elastic" currency, precluded anything like a major economic decline. The board did lower its discount rate and made large open-market purchases. But as W. W. Kiplinger observed: "The amazing lesson from this depression is that no one knows much about the real causes and effects of ANYTHING."[7]

The stock market, after a net loss of 30 percent in industrials, staged a substantial recovery during the first winter of the Depression; in May 1930 the *New York Times* average of industrial stocks stood about where it had a year before. Little in the economic statistics of late 1929 and the first half of 1930 suggested anything more than a normal, though slow, year. The October crash was widely regarded as freakish.*

Few Americans realized that stock market prices do not necessarily reflect the strength or weakness of the economy. Although experts had long worried about the precariousness of the banking system, they did not understand the deeper significance of the economic changes of the 1920's. Worker productivity had increased, but too much of the resulting profits went into the hands of employers, weakening consumer demand.

* Jude Wanninski of the *Wall Street Journal* has discerned a relationship between falling stock prices and news about the proposed Smoot-Hawley Tariff. But it is dubious that "the most important information coming to the market is political news," and the investing class generally believed that tariff increases would make investments safer and more profitable, and that few agricultural prices would rise.

Heavy installment buying had made consumers wary of taking on more debt or buying more goods. Overexpansion by American farmers to meet the artificial needs of wartime meant overproduction during the 1920's; overproduction in turn meant declining prices; and declining prices meant less spending for manufactured goods. Bumper crops throughout the British Empire and in Russia in 1930 aggravated this downward trend. All in all, the decline in consumption was the most insidious force intensifying the Depression. Official unemployment figures in the United States rose from some 2.7 million in 1929 to about 4 million by mid-1930.[8]

Still, Americans ignored these disquieting trends and focused instead upon comforting parallels in the past. The rise in unemployment, for example, was less steep than in the first year of the depression in 1920–2. Even for the second year of Hoover's presidency, when conditions worsened, the obvious paradigm was the postwar depression: severe but short. On October 2, 1930, Hoover said that the country was still better off than in the comparable phase of the earlier depression. By 1931, when calamitous events overseas had wrecked international finance and huge unemployment in the United States finally forced everyone, including Hoover, to realize how bad things really were, the contours of a solution still remained unclear. Economic experts had no fresh ideas to deal with an unprecedented situation. They merely trusted that once prices sank low enough, once unemployment rose high enough, then businessmen would reopen their plants. Meanwhile, the government should not intervene in the normal restorative process. Deficit spending, for example, would compete with entrepreneurs for available capital. Politicians, too, seemed complacent. Of forty governors who replied to a questionnaire sent out by Senator Hiram Bingham, thirty-nine claimed that their states could handle their own relief; only one reported that some people were probably starving in his state—Pennsylvania's maverick Republican, Gifford Pinchot. Most of the country's mayors told the *New York Times* in September 1931 that they were determined to get by without federal relief. By this time manufacturing volume was down by half; in 1932 the steel plants operated at 11 percent of capacity.[9]

Hoover's later writings reflect a sense of bewilderment, for all their self-serving dogmatism. He discounted the construction boom of the twenties, observing that much of it had been a matter of catching up with work suspended by wartime, and noting lulls in 1926 and in 1928–9, when the backlog of work had been largely accomplished. The very efficiency of industry in the decade contributed to overproduction, argued Hoover, who pointed to a finding by his Presidential Committee on Economic Changes that some three-fourths of profits had been going to higher industrial wages and one-fourth to business, eluding farmers and white-collar workers. Hoover put the heaviest blame on a banking system totally unequipped to deal with any jolt to the economy, and complained that Congress in 1929 had ignored his pleas for banking reform. Far from accepting his previous association with the "New Era," Hoover came to employ the term with sarcasm and contempt and sustained the role he had taken in his earlier writings, as the expert critic of business practices.[10]

Ironically, United States economic ties made it much more a member of an Atlantic community than League membership alone would have; since at least World War I American financial stakes had mandated international responsibilities. In fact, prosperity was real enough, and even international finance was not "unsound." It was, however, vulnerable to the United States' domestic policies, which helped explode the effects of the stock market crash. As Hoover correctly stated, this was an unnoticed cost of the war and one that had to be paid. He himself had correctly diagnosed world economic problems in 1919. Greater American generosity in the twenties (which Hoover generally desired), and more belt-tightening in Europe, could have paid the bill by 1930. But debt consolidation would have meant sacrifice of profits (from German investment, for example) along with a better insurance of a long-term profitable market in Europe. Tariffs were also marginally significant, but Democrats overemphasized them—and then in 1933 devalued the dollar, a much more stringent grab for national advantage. All this Hoover knew and preached unremittingly.[11]

Hoover later admitted that he had erred in the spring of 1930 when he declared: "I am convinced we have passed the worst and with continued effort we shall rapidly recover." He was not alone in this miscalculation: the American Economic Association in December 1929 had predicted recovery by June 1930; it made a similar forecast the following year. Hoover's remark suggests the misplaced optimism that Franklin Roosevelt later succumbed to on occasion, and resembled earlier assurances in similar circumstances given by Presidents Cleveland, Harding, Wilson, and Theodore Roosevelt. But he was widely misquoted as announcing that prosperity was "just around the corner," a statement actually made by Vice-President Charles Curtis. Hoover's retrospective analysis reasoned that recovery began early in 1931. Bank failures then declined, and many economic indicators moved upward. At the time he had claimed that at least America was self-sufficient and would not be adversely affected by the world's troubles; but his later writings leaned in the other direction, putting the blame on overproduction and malpractices in Europe—and behind that, the war itself. As Hoover told it, the breakdown of central European banks that spring spread malign influences into the United States, turning back the domestic recovery. The moratorium on foreign debts that summer, his version contended, prevented a panic and the recovery began again, but only briefly. When the Bank of England faltered and then collapsed despite fresh, heavy private loans from the United States and France, the American economy sailed downward until Hoover, according to his *Memoirs,* regained a tenuous hold on economic stability in the fall of 1931. The European influences proved overwhelming, however, and in December Hoover had to bring all the resources of the federal government to bear, beginning with his call for a Reconstruction Finance Corporation. June 1932 was the Depression's low point, according to Hoover's account. It requires an act of faith to assume the economy would then have righted itself. Yet, from the perspective of the mid-New Deal, Walter Lippmann would contend: "Hoover, Secretary [of the Treasury] Mills and [Reconstruction Finance Corporation] Governor Meyer had hold of the essence of the matter in the spring of 1932 when they forced a reflation policy on the federal reserve system. Believe it or not, they arrested the depression."[12]

By Hoover's reckoning, the crisis of September 1932 to March 1933 was a result of political uncertainty over the transition to Franklin Roosevelt. FDR's maneuvers against the Depression in subsequent years were largely unsuccessful, claim the *Memoirs,* and only World War II brought the country back to prosperity. Hoover sensed the delicacy of the global and national structure of finance, knew that overextension and a lack of liquidity among bankers and businessmen was a dangerous thing in good times and their morale a precarious thing always, and wanted the government to act in restraint of recklessness and in support of reasonable confidence. His analysis concentrated on the inner motions of finance and its subtle connection with the national mood. It was a predictable attitude for a chief executive presiding over the beginning of a depression, especially when the stock market was crumbling. The solution as he perceived it lay in reassuring businessmen that the decline was only temporary, that paper devaluation would be the best answer. Sustaining business investment would halt the economic decline, bolster consumer spending, and prevent disastrous drops in industrial production.

But when all that proved insufficient, when the expected recovery did not materialize, Hoover was forced to focus his attention on the banking system. Still assuming that the economy was basically sound, that businessmen were eager to expand production and needed only to acquire the necessary working capital, he concluded that irrational fears among bankers and financial leaders were eroding the supply of credit. Once again his attitudes were predictable. Most economists of the 1920's and 1930's believed that demand for credit was inextricably linked to its supply. In this instance, frightened bankers had to overcome their fears and expand credit, after which businessmen would increase production and boost employment. Hoover's commitment in 1932 to the Reconstruction Finance Corporation and the Federal Home Loan Bank system reflected his assumptions.

During his presidency Hoover failed to see that the Depression was not merely a correctable slowing of bank credit to businessmen but the state of a whole society, its causes dispersed through the entire economic system. Only the cumulative experience of the Depression itself, and the rising defense budget, would yield the economic tools Hoover's successors have employed: a public economy extensive enough to support indefinitely—with jobs and contracts, with relief money and with pensions—that fluctuating part of the population that the private economy cannot sustain.

Hoover's early response to the crisis was at least swift. The cure for such economic storms, he observed, was "action." In a space of five days, beginning on November 19, 1929, he met with leaders from business and finance, railroads, public utilities, the construction industry, agriculture, and labor, and with the Federal Reserve. In this Conference for Continued Industrial Progress, as it was termed, he outlined four essential understandings: no strikes; no reduction in wages until the cost of living fell, so that consumption would be sustained—and workers would not have to strike later to regain lost ground; a sharing of work where it was feasible; and employers to look after relief of their employees when they could. This voluntary arrangement, lent prestige by such leaders of industry as Henry Ford, Walter Teagle, Owen D. Young, Alfred P. Sloan, Jr., and Pierre duPont, sustained wages quite well. William Green of the AFL was delighted, although he said in 1930 that Hoover had done nothing for labor. Until April 1931 the arrangement was policed by Julius Barnes, through a four-hundred-member National Business Survey Conference. Big Steel held wages at their then-current levels until October 1931, and as late as 1932 Hoover forced a reversal of reductions in railroad pay. The utilities, however, refused the President's requests that they assure continuity of employment. For these efforts Walter Lippmann condemned the President for interfering with natural economic laws. A libertarian economist writing in 1963, Murray Rothbard, said much the same thing, suggesting that Andrew Mellon's cure of liquidation and deflation was the right one. As a result to some extent of Hoover's so-called "no business" meetings, real wages—for those still employed full time—may even have increased under his presidency, and purchasing power for those fortunate enough to hold jobs remained high.

In another display of leadership, Hoover asked Congress for greater public works appropriations; he also asked state governors to expedite such projects, including county and local work then in the planning stage. The shrinking of tax revenues soon diminished the impact of local efforts, however. Hoover encouraged utilities and other corporations to increase needed expansion projects, and he urged that household repairs and maintenance be undertaken during the winter months. Spending for public works had declined in every previous depression; this time it tripled within two years to some $700 million. Hoover believed that this was as much as the capacities of engineering technology and legal processes could then absorb. But more could certainly have been spent on highways. The important point is that the federal government focused on reviving finance, assuming that industrial recovery would follow, rather than dealing directly with unemployment, unprofitably low prices, and, in the case of agriculture, overproduction. This sequence, recommended by experts and businessmen, hampered and limited the administration from the outset. Consensus and ideology set the contours for Hoover's activity, as it did for Franklin Roosevelt's: it took the New Deal until 1939 to raise public works spending to $5 billion from almost $1 billion in 1930. Within this sphere, Hoover moved quickly, even innovatively; but he refused to step outside it.[13]

Perhaps this explains why none of these energetic efforts awakened any significant public imagination or commitment. As chief executive at the beginning of the Depression, Hoover could hardly present himself as the answer to it. Blame must also go to his own near-inability to present himself at all. A Quaker visitor at the White House asked the President what tenet of Quakerism was most important to him. "Individual faithfulness," responded Hoover. But a President plodding faithfully along his own private, uncommunicative course could not expect the public voluntarily to give him its trustful support. Yet it was inauthentic for a Quaker to pose. The President, who knew the importance of confidence, could not bring himself to manufacture it.[14]

Hoover had planned for a different relationship with the public. At his first White House press conference in 1929, he had greeted reporters with "smiling cheerfulness" and promised them a more "intimate" relationship. In a departure from custom, he announced that he could sometimes be quoted directly and that conferences would occur more often. On April 22 of that year he said: "Absolute freedom of the press to discuss public questions is a foundation stone of American liberty." He asked a committee of correspondents to help establish the new guidelines. His press assistant met with reporters twice daily. There was a continuation of the generally successful relations with the press that he had enjoyed as Commerce Secretary when the Washington *Evening Star* observed: "Hoover certainly has got the whole town by the neck from a news standpoint—no one can get near enough to see the dust." At the time "it became the custom of correspondents," wrote the journalist Paul Y. Anderson, "to gather several afternoons each week in Hoover's office. There he talked freely not only about his own department, but about the departments of his Cabinet colleagues and about the affairs of the presidency. . . . He was the best 'grapevine' in Washington . . . he knew more about . . . the government and the . . . country and the world than any man in the administration." But his presidential fortunes with the press would be of quite another sort.[15]

Although Hoover misled with promises he never delivered, part of the trouble lay with the reporters themselves. Most had favored Al Smith during the campaign. *The New Republic,* an opposition journal that commended Hoover for speaking at his press conferences with "freedom, force, and intelligence," complained of partisan writers who had never forgiven him for defeating their candidate and the anti-prohibition ticket and who now magnified every gaffe in the new administration and rudely pried into personal matters. News stories treated the President tactlessly. Small things were leaked: that Mrs. Hoover took sound tests to improve her voice; that a dog from the presidential kennels bit a Marine. A story about the presidential car's speed en route to Hoover's Virginia camp on the Rapidan River annoyed him greatly. An uninvited correspondent and his wife wrecked their car and suffered serious injury behind Hoover's "flying cavalcade." (Driving his sixteen-cylinder Cadillac across the country in 1933, Hoover was stopped for speeding; when his son Allan took over and reached eighty-five miles an hour, his father asked, "What's holding you back?" And Lou Hoover "terrified" cabinet members' wives with her driving.) Mrs. Hoover's habit of giving various signs to servants also became a source of fun. She had signs for secretaries, waiters, and ushers, that included dropping her handkerchief or pocketbook, revolving her eyeglasses about her fingers, or discarding something in her hand to the side or a little to the rear.* In August 1930 the Baltimore *Sun* published a palpably untrue story, circulated by an airline company; it charged Herbert Hoover, Jr., employed as a radio engineer, with influencing a government air mail contract. The President replied angrily, "I have not in my experience in Washington seen anything so rotten in an attitude of the press towards the President of the United States." This caused the story to reach many other papers across the country.[16]

The *New York World* then irresponsibly purchased for $12,000 a fabricated story from a disgruntled employee alleging corruption in Secretary of the Interior Wilbur's handling of worthless oil shale lands. The Demo-

---

* During the presidency only Lou Hoover outdid her husband in vulnerability to public criticism. "She was oversensitive," the hypersensitive Hoover explained. He consoled her with the remark that her more orthodox religion included a "hot hell" for retribution to wrongdoers. She spent her energy restoring White House rooms and took special pride in refurbishing Lincoln's study with authentic pieces—rescuing it from the boy's bedroom it had become under Theodore Roosevelt.

cratic *World* dubbed it a "second Teapot Dome" scandal and ran the stories right up to the 1930 elections, despite Wilbur's well-documented denial. Goadings on the part of correspondents had something to do with the Senate's revolt against Hoover's unsuccessful nominee for the Supreme Court, John J. Parker; they also helped to organize the opposition to making Charles Evans Hughes Chief Justice. They "buttonholed Senators and dug up precedents," the journalist Henry Pringle observed. Charles Michaelson, publicist of the Democratic National Committee, had anti-Hoover material placed in the *Congressional Record* so it could be circulated to newspapers without fear of libel; he was careful to write of the "Hoover" tariff or the "Hoover" panic. Hoover's natural sensitivity added to his troubles. He was utterly unable to emulate Coolidge's attitude: "If you don't like it, don't read it."[17]

Hoover in his turn was touchy toward the press. Even in his business he had cultivated privacy, carefully selecting what he wished the public to see and projecting a figure of cold competence and rectitude rather than a full, quirky, and accessible human being. On a post-election good-will trip to South America, his shipboard press secretary George Baker insisted on approving copy before correspondents could file it from the ship's radio. Once the Depression had set in, Hoover wanted reporters to temper their role of social critic with conformance to what he considered the national interest. Although he continued to meet the press twice weekly, he increasingly confided in a few friendly newsmen like Mark Sullivan and William Hard. His distrust sometimes became irrational. When a story particularly irritated him, he would wire Roy Howard at Scripps-Howard or some other publisher. Bewildered at exactly what was troubling the man in the White House, the newspaper owners would send personal apologies, by which time the matter had blown over.[18]

By nature desirous of dwelling and moving about within his own private space, Hoover in fact came to the presidency with little conditioning to criticism from the press. His activities during the war and the twenties had gotten a remarkably favorable reception, and in time he had acquired the presence of a statesman standing outside common politics. The dislike of rough criticism conforms to the kind of reformer he was. He lacked the messianic zeal of Wilson, the blustering righteousness of Theodore Roosevelt. It was the engineer in him, perhaps, that trusted so much to autonomous intelligence, applied to understandable materials, discovering solutions that other intellects would impersonally accept. Hoover knew controversy, of course. And he had been good at appeals to the public, and at managing people. But the appeals had been simple calls to patriotism or compassion, and the management had worked on simple, accessible motives like self-interest and pride. To cope with a quarreling, picking, boisterous press, to cultivate its friendliest elements and try some stroking of the others, to be noble, joking, raffish as the occasion demanded, and in the face of attack to be silent without bitterness or to find release in a joyous rage—these capacities were not Hoover's. Even Calvin Coolidge had had sense enough to give reporters free lunches from food sent to the White House.

George Akerson, who acted as Hoover's press secretary from 1926, was a large, hard-drinking Harvard man and a former Minneapolis *Tribune* reporter well liked by his colleagues. But repeated fumblings in the early presidential years, coupled with some heavy drinking in public, led to his departure for Paramount Pictures late in 1930. Others around the President alienated the press. Lawrence Richey occupied a White House room with the shades perpetually pulled down, and discouraged speculation about presidential visitors or motives.* All newsmen admitted to press conferences had to swear they were unconnected with any "brokerage tipping service." Secret Service men also lectured some reporters about the President's right to privacy and grilled them to discover a newspaper informant on the presidential staff. In 1931 Theodore Joslin, a former reporter from the conservative Boston *Transcript,* replaced Akerson after Julius Klein refused the job. Joslin was defensive, sour, and so obnoxious that even the President found him trying; a fellow reporter, borrowing from Winston Churchill, characterized him as "the first known instance of a rat joining a sinking ship." He dealt with journalists whenever possible by means of reading but not releasing printed statements. When he noted confidentially that the country was in an emergency "second only to war," the stock market took a dive. Joslin asked reporters to "consult with this office" before sending out potentially damaging economic news, but later insisted that "censorship never entered my mind." Hoover himself told a press conference that "leaks" about programs then being worked out could lead to oppositions otherwise avoidable: "I am asking you to suppress nothing. . . . I am giving you my feeling [about] what I think would be in the interest of the American people. I leave it to you and ask for no promises. . . . You are absolutely free to do whatever you please." Nonetheless, journalists took offense and put on skits about censorship at the annual Gridiron Club show. There he objected to "exhibitionists" who visited him to get the press's attention for their distorted versions of what was discussed. He also alluded to "dwellers in the twilight of near sanity . . . who collect around this neighborhood."[19]

It was perhaps the private man's shrinkage from rough political contact, the predilection for working by himself, and the habit of perceiving prob-

---

* It was Herbert Hoover who had recommended to Coolidge that J. Edgar Hoover (no relation) be appointed to head the Federal Bureau of Investigation in 1924.

lems as requiring rational, impersonal solutions that made Hoover uncomfortable with the rude, demanding Congress as well as with the press. Many of his achievements during the 1920's had come without congressional action. As Secretary of Commerce he had persuaded opposing groups, such as railway carriers and the brotherhoods, in effect to introduce their own legislation. Or he would work through his various conferences, which circumvented Congress. As representative of the White House on many matters throughout the twenties, he had made his share of congressional antagonists. And this loner who relished a cooperative society distrusted Congress for being a collection of hungry, squabbling interests. He believed that as President he could transcend the mentalities of congressional factions and interests and make decisions like an engineer. His administration's most impressive work, indeed, was not legislative but was accomplished in conferences or took the form of administrative actions by Interior Secretary Wilbur, the Farm Board, or Hoover himself. That the President, despite some successes with Congress, could not establish a really going relationship became, like his troubles with the press, a greater liability with the onset of the Depression, when public confidence depended on visibly energetic and effective presidential leadership.

The composition of Congress complicated Hoover's efforts. James Watson, the Senate majority leader, had started his career in national politics under President Benjamin Harrison; a gregarious rogue, he recalled the politics of the Gilded Age. "Is it my fault," Hoover asked a reporter in 1931, "if Jim Watson . . . prefers to play his own politics against me?" Hoover, who spoke of Watson's "spasmodic" abilities, would have preferred Pennsylvania's David Reed as floor leader. Having served since 1903 and schooled under such high tariff stalwarts as Aldrich, Penrose, and Lodge, the powerful Mormon Senator Reed Smoot of Utah excelled at pushing bills through Congress. But Smoot, overly concerned with the tariff and patronage, found Hoover far too progressive on such legislation as Boulder Dam. The hidebound George H. Moses of New Hampshire—the president *pro tempore* of the Senate who had branded Republican progressives "Sons of the wild Jackass"—frequently appalled Hoover. Moses, as Hoover's Eastern campaign manager in 1928, had once urged the use of anti-Catholic propaganda. Hoover—like Wilson, who had said that senators' heads were knots that kept their bodies from unravelling—disdained the Senate's intelligence. Senator Peter Norbeck, for instance, was "a well-intentioned well-driller from South Dakota" who had no business chairing the Banking and Currency Committee; another such denizen was "the only verified case of a negative IQ." On one occasion Hoover referred to Congress as "that beer garden up there on the hill." A special problem was the Republican insurgents. Such men as George Norris were too independent, and perhaps too inconsistent, to work well with Hoover, and they succeeded only in driving him away from progressivism. Each power in this political triangle—the independent Hoover, the old guard, the progressives—frequently wielded a veto on legislation.[20]

The President did feel easier with some leaders. Ohio's Simeon Fess, party whip and, beginning in 1930, the chairman of the Republican National Committee, was a solid party man he usually trusted. Fess's colleague from Ohio, Theodore Burton, was perhaps Hoover's closest friend in the Senate, but died early in the administration. Henry Allen of Kansas, an able senator whom Hoover had liked ever since they had worked together in European relief, lost his seat in 1930; and Dwight Morrow of New Jersey died suddenly in October 1931, after serving less than a year in the Senate. Only Arthur Vandenberg of Michigan, somewhat to the left of the old guard, seemed to have much influence on Hoover after Allen departed. Vandenberg briefly led about two dozen or so "Young Turks," also called "Hoover's Boy Scouts"—middle-view Republicans who sought to align all party members for the President's programs. In the House Hoover lost an able lieutenant when Speaker Nicholas Longworth died in April 1931. Longworth's successors, John Q. Tilson of Connecticut and Bertrand Snell from upstate New York, had more trouble leading than the former Speaker. Hoover preferred Tilson, who was relieved of his job by disgruntled party members in the new Congress.[21]

The President could exert slight leadership over the Seventy-first Congress, which met intermittently from March 1929 to March 1931. When it was slow to act on his many suggestions for reform, he was painly irritated but lacked able followers to push his programs. Even when he did find a warm supporter such as Vandenberg, he alternated between reticence and a stubborn refusal to compromise. The President is not merely to advise Congress, Hoover wrote in his *Memoirs,* he "is expected to blast reforms out of it." Like Dwight Eisenhower, Hoover had little taste for forcing congressional action, but on occasion he insisted on results. He had only two major defeats in the Seventy-first Congress: the rejection of Supreme Court nominee Parker, and the overriding of a vetoed veterans' bonus bill. But once adjournment came, nothing could persuade him to call another session, although Vandenberg urged one for liberalizing the lending policies of the Federal Reserve. When Hoover announced a moratorium on debt payments by Europe in July 1931, he obtained unofficial congressional approval by phone and telegram. "It is my belief, and the belief of my advisers," he wrote to one congressman, "that an extra session at the present time would create ten times the unemployment that can be cured by any possible legislation acted." If confidence was the way to prosperity, he thought, the bickering and posturing of Congress could what relief provided by government would do to the nation, he seemed not to be speaking, as right-wingers would later do, about reliefers turned into loafers. He knew that the work ethic was far from dead; and he feared most the hordes of subsidy seekers. The initiative and resources that Hoover wanted preserved would have their proper object not merely in personal scrambling but in individual and communal acts of voluntary sharing. He did announce on February 3, 1931, italicizing the words: *"I am willing to pledge myself"* that if hunger and suffering could not otherwise be prevented, *"I will ask the aid of every resource of the Federal government."** But, as Richard Hofstadter has observed, it mattered to him not only what goals were adopted, "but exactly *how* a job was done." And he actually entertained the hope that more fortunate Americans would freely rescue their neighbors. Few sentimental liberals could have had a more naïve expectation about human conduct.[24]

The decisive Herbert Hoover of European relief must remain a puzzle for critics of the Depression President. Whatever Hoover may have thought he believed in the way of conventional economic theory, he had committed himself, throughout his pre-presidential career, by words and acts to perceiving an economy that was not the market mechanism of the laissez-faire theorists but the product of the will to order. This he affirmed when he assumed the task of quickening the Chinese economy, when he put together his own industrial and commercial empire, when he organized his great relief projects, or when as Secretary of Commerce he worked for economic rationalization. And his writings put expertise and cooperation in the central place that classical economists had assigned to competition and price. His insistence on the primacy of voluntary effort reflects more than his distaste for governmental bureaucracy; it manifests the conviction, ingrained within him by almost thirty years of practice, that people are prepared to come together as expert reason dictates. Belgian relief, for example, had been effectively run on certain tested principles: decentralized administration, the absence of a paid bureaucracy, voluntary administrative services of leading citizens. Congressional aid was needed only during and after the war for nations "so disorganized by war and anarchy that self-help was impossible." Hoover hoped to use the metaphor of war to drain internal frustrations onto a common enemy. But, he analyzed, depression is a fluctuation of the economy, while war is an act of God, a force above history; so we must muddle through the Depression. War united people; the Depression set them against one another. Yet federal relief in the Depression would injure, perhaps irreparably, local self-gov-

---

* Secretary Stimson confided to his diary the day before that Hoover planned to call a special session of Congress in the unlikely event that local and private aid for suffering proved inadequate.

only interrupt the processes of recovery already at work. But this aver
to congressional politics, this lack of feeling for the play of it, meant
Hoover had to forego the uses to which the political strategist Fran
Roosevelt could put Congress in the articulating and orchestration of
port for himself and his policies.[22]

Hoover's inability to capture the public mind had its most impor
cause and consequences in the bleak fortunes of Depression relief.
agricultural policy, formulated in the first presidential months as a c
fident expression of his cooperationist philosophy, did extend itself int
relief agency. Yet about direct relief he displayed in general a hesita
and contrariness that furnish the worst memory of him. He could beco
vehement on the subject. In December 1930 he said of proponents
costly relief measures—notable among them were Senators McKell
Brookhart, Caraway, Walsh, Shipstead, Black, and Trammel—that th
were "playing politics at the expense of human misery." The vast major
of Americans shared a consensus in their distaste for relief. Some had
mind the British dole, which, as practiced in industrial cities such as Ma
chester and Leeds, was paying sixteen-year-olds a few shillings a wee
more to married people, and had become a basic component of a cultu
of poverty. Some young men, wrote a correspondent of Senator Hen
Allen, "have never worked since the world war, and . . . the [Britis]
government is afraid to make any changes." It was widely believed that th
expenses of the dole were chiefly responsible for forcing Great Britain o
the gold standard. Franklin Roosevelt and the liberal *New York Worl*
as well as Hoover, denounced a dole. Even Senator Robert Wagner op
posed direct federal relief, preferring that funds be filtered through th
states. But the President would continue to be reluctant about extensiv
relief even in the presence of a large demand for it. It was not, as was ofte
claimed later, that he had no moral perception of suffering. His "individ
ualism" included no simple notion that if the unemployed looked har
enough they would find jobs. What was it, then, that made this humani
tarian and organizer so slow to react in the face of the most obviou
necessity?[23]

Perhaps it was that some of the best things in Hoover's past and though
stood in his way now. His relief projects had trained him to believe tha
people volunteer their money and effort, and he must have recalled the
work itself as a gratifying experience of problems skillfully and freshl
solved. If liberals complained about the vagaries of private relief, Hoove
remembered its systematic efficiency. During his presidency he gave sub
stantial personal contributions to private relief, and he was pleased at such
plans as that of Sears's employees who donated one day's pay a month
to support former employees. When he began worrying out loud about

ernment. "Where people divest themselves of local government responsibilities," Hoover wrote, "they at once lay the foundation for the destruction of their liberties." The spread of government, he added, destroys individual opportunity and initiative and thus destroys character. Character is made in the community as well as in the individual by assuming responsibilities. Bureaucratic federal aid would damage the sense of an American community—the same joy he took from bringing together a small group of Americans in a foreign land, or the Quaker communities he knew in his youth, the working democracy which craves self-government and where neighbors took care of one another. "I want to live in a community that governs itself," he wrote in 1925. It was, then, not simply or even primarily the initiative of recipients that would be injured but rather that of property owners—the very group whose initiative was most needed to overcome the Depression.[25]

For years Hoover had sought to draw attention to the need for privately financed social welfare measures or "welfare capitalism." While at Commerce he had drafted a memo on government-supported old-age pensions, which he thought should be at a subsistence level. The federal role should be principally that of collecting a percentage of a worker's wages and an equivalent contribution from the employer, who, unlike the employee, would not have the choice of declining. Farmers and small businessmen could also participate, their contributions being matched by the government. But the states should handle actual disbursement of funds, making their own contributions. Hoover had supported a state plan for California. On September 26, 1929, the President invited to the White House the executive committee of the National Association of Life [Insurance] Underwriters, requesting them to write old-age pension policies based on small yearly payments, and to persuade industrial and commercial organizations to support such plans. Once private groups had begun the process, the government might subsidize the plan or assist certain groups needing coverage. Hoover also conferred on several occasions with Wesley C. Mitchell, whose National Bureau of Economic Research Hoover wanted to make an exhaustive study of unemployment insurance in foreign countries.[26]

Senator Robert F. Wagner, representing an inchoate Northern liberalism, was committed to bringing about a limited welfare state. An adroit harmonizer of diverse views, he would become a conciliatory figure as Hoover toward the end of his presidency clashed with Congress over how best to fight the Depression. Wagner, along with a few other congressional figures, had long urged action on the general problem of unemployment relief. In 1928 he introduced a trio of bills: for gathering better statistics on unemployment, improving and integrating state employment exchanges, and planning long-range federal public works. Hoover's taste for efficiency and rationalization had earlier turned him to the idea of the government's collecting unemployment statistics: he had suggested it to the Conference on Unemployment in 1921 and in a speech during the presidential campaign. The 1930 census was the first to include questions on employment (the unemployment statistics for the early depression are unreliable). Hoover signed Wagner's bill in July 1930, after it had passed the House with only one dissent.

The administration had already instituted its own idea of employment exchanges. The United States Employment Service expanded fairly sharply in 1931 with an extra $500,000 appropriation. Secretary of Labor Doak's bill for a larger federal bureaucracy failed. When Wagner's bill for federally subsidized state agencies passed, Hoover gave it a pocket veto. The plan would not soon be effective, he claimed, for state enabling legislation was needed; it would destroy the present federal service; and it would infringe the rights of states, which were not required to expand their services. "It is not only changing horses while crossing a stream," the President wrote to Wagner; "the other horse would not arrive for many months." Hoover, and the liberal *Nation,* particularly feared that locally controlled employment services would become appendages of local political machines. He also believed that a plan as extensive as Wagner's might discourage business investment.[27]

Throughout 1930 there was no concerted effort, or frequent demand, for federal unemployment relief. Wagner's mild bill in 1930 for unemployment compensation met resistance from the American Federation of Labor and the National Association of Manufacturers. Unemployment relief was scarcely an issue in the 1930 congressional elections, although the economy contributed to a narrow loss of Republican control in the lower House. "Don't change engineers in the middle of the wreck," the journalist Elmer Davis had counseled. Almost all the Republican losses came in farming areas from Pennsylvania to Nebraska. Hoover wanted the narrowly divided Senate given to the Democrats as well, but the GOP leadership, fearful of losing committee control and patronage, would not go along with this scheme to shift some political burdens to the opposition. After the elections seven prominent Democrats—James Cox, John W. Davis, Al Smith (the last three presidential nominees of the party), John J. Raskob and Jouett Shouse of the Democratic National Committee, minority leader Senator Joseph T. Robinson, and Speaker John Nance Garner— had pledged cooperation with the President; the Democrats invariably were friendlier to Hoover's work than were the progressive Republicans. The Democratic leadership in the new Seventy-second Congress that met in December 1931 seemed satisfied with what Hoover had been doing. Senators La Follette, Jr., and Costigan introduced bills for federal unemployment relief but they died in committee or, as in February 1932, failed to pass (by 48 to 35) with as many Democrats as Republicans in opposition. A new House rule gave rebellious members an opportunity to discharge pigeonholed bills. Requiring only 145 signatures to liberate a bill from committee, the rule was used but nine times—and only one of the bills passed the House. Raskob, the former Democratic national chairman, had set the tone just before the 1930 election when he warned that "political parties in control of Congress [can] pass foolish laws that will temporarily upset economic laws. Our representatives in Congress should exercise great care to make sure that all proposed legislation square with good economics." It was a time of consensus among all branches of government. Even most Republican and Western progressives in the La Follette tradition or most Northeastern liberals agreed with Mellon's advice to balance the budget at almost any cost. True, recovery would eventually begin; but as time passed, many of them wondered whether the nation could stand the social and political consequences of waiting. The consensus would hold for the moment—but not if depression worsened and fresh leadership presented itself.[28]

During 1930 the nation suffered a disaster that may at first have seemed more spectacular than steadily rising unemployment. Drought settled over a large part of the country. In August Hoover held a conference of drought-state governors, who recommended federal loans, public works, relief through the Red Cross of which he was honorary president, and a lowering of railway rates for shipping food. A National Drought Relief Committee, with the banker Henry M. Robinson as coordinator of federal and state activities, went into action, working closely with the Red Cross. The committee spent a half-million dollars left over from Mississippi relief—a project the Red Cross had handled skillfully. Though unequipped to deal with urban distress, the Red Cross had a network of officials in the twenty-seven states most affected by the drought and pledged $5 million to do the job. Hoover believed that the Red Cross alone could tap local energies through these reference points. Had it acted swiftly and energetically, much suffering and subsequent damage to Hoover's reputation for being a great humanitarian might have been averted. But the organization moved with a strange caution. Its seventy-five-year-old chairman, John Barton Payne (Wilson's last Secretary of the Interior), sometimes proceeded as if he feared that even his efforts would be destructive of morality and local self-help.[29]

Perhaps no state was harder hit by drought than Arkansas, where folklore has it that a field of corn popped on the stalk. In early January 1931 a Red Cross agent in the town of England, Arkansas, ran out of forms. When local merchants phoned the regional office for reimbursement to feed hungry people, it hedged for lack of standard application blanks. Amidst a threat of riot, frightened merchants gave out food. Although the incident received nationwide publicity, Red Cross personnel continued to be obsessed with their suspicion of imposters, turning away supplicants who seemed too warmly dressed. The Arkansas governor declared that he saw no need for federal assistance. And only about a third of the state's newspapers considered massive Red Cross aid necessary. The lame-duck Congress that met in November 1930, and the state's two senators, thought otherwise. Hoover's opponents there had an easy target. Referring to the $20 million food relief gift to the Soviet Union Hoover had previously administered, Kentucky's Senator Alben Barkley observed that "the best way to feed the unemployed would be to move them to China and Russia.[30]

Meanwhile Payne, who had spent only $1 million on drought relief by early January 1931, told a congressional committee that the Red Cross could handle by itself the problem in the stricken states. But Hoover, while claiming in his message to Congress on December 2, 1930, that there was "minimum actual suffering," asked for emergency legislation—specifically a $25 million loan to the Department of Agriculture for the purchase of seed and animal food. The notion here that the money was a loan and not a grant was for him a necessary fiction. And a friend described him as "desperately anxious" to avoid the "dangerous precedent" of direct government support of relief, for fear it would dry up private charity. Secretary Stimson quoted him as saying, "it will be the beginning of the dole in this country and will also be the end of the wonderful activities of the Red Cross." Hoover sent his aide, General C. B. Hodges, and Colonel Arthur Woods to investigate. They reported in February: "After visiting some 16 [Arkansas] counties we could find no present suffering from hunger and cold." Senator Norris was incensed at Hoover's willingness to provide seed and animal food loans but not direct relief: "Blessed be those who starve while the asses and mules are fed, for they shall get buried at public expense." The Senate responded with a $60 million bill, but the House forced a compromise of $45 million, partly because urban congressmen like Fiorello LaGuardia would favor the funds only if their use were not geographically restricted. After Payne simply refused to accept any outright government grant, which he believed would weaken the voluntaristic character of the Red Cross, Congress passed $20 million in "agricultural rehabilitation" loans. Secretary of Agriculture Hyde, under pressure from Hoover and congressional leaders, said the additional $20 million appropriation could be spent for food. Little of it reached the poorest people, tenants and sharecroppers, and only 70 percent of the appropriations were used. Applicants for any relief had to submit to a "means" test, which some liberals called demeaning. Nevertheless, the appropriation seemed to many to end an era when private charity cared for those in need, and to begin a shift of responsibility to the state and federal governments.[31]

The President got fifty prominent Americans to aid the private campaign of the Red Cross and persuaded Will Rogers to head a speaking tour. Hoover's intention was to show that charity to neighbors on a national basis remained an American and Christian duty, not to be usurped by government. Greeting audiences with "Well, folks . . . glad you are starving, otherwise I would never have met you," Rogers collected a quarter of a million dollars. John D. Rockefeller gave another quarter of a million, and the somewhat eccentric Thomas A. Edison donated his eighty-third—and last—birthday cake, which the Red Cross auctioned off for $107. Junior personnel meanwhile were pushing the Red Cross into a more activist program. But Hoover had stayed by the "feed and seed" formula too long, and political enemies made capital of his dogmatism and what they called his lack of compassion. Hoover gave a large part of his own salary to private relief organizations. Yet, as Coolidge's private secretary observed: "Down underneath there is this feeling that . . . he is not in character . . . the man who has spent hundreds of millions [for foreign relief] without regard or concern as to its source." By mid-March $10 million had been raised. In May the President lectured at Valley Forge: it "is our American synonym for the trial of human character through privation and suffering, and it is the symbol of the triumph of the American soul. . . . If those few thousand men endured that long winter . . . what right have we to be of little faith?" William Appleman Williams answers criticism of Hoover's hesitance to act: "Hoover told us that if we (the neighbors of the stricken) cannot be roused to provide such help, and if the way the government helps them in lieu of our direct assistance is not handled *very* carefully . . . there will be hell to pay . . . bureaucratic statism that would devalue the human beings it claimed to save . . . imperialism in the name of welfare . . . violence in the name of peace. We now know these were legitimate fears. Unless you and I decide that she and he are as important as us then we all are going down the memory hole together. The time's long past for passing the buck to the government."[32]

In the fall of 1930, when the government count of the unemployed had reached some five million, or one in every nine out of work, Hoover responded by appointing Colonel Arthur Woods as chairman of the President's Emergency Committee on Employment (PECE). The word "emergency" echoed the hope that this one more bureaucratic agency could soon be disbanded. A former New York City police chief, Woods had worked on employing veterans after the war and had taken a significant part in the 1921 Conference on Unemployment, becoming chairman of the Unemployment Commission. Edward Hunt was appointed secretary of PECE, Edward Bernays became its publicist, and thirty leading citizens constituted an advisory committee. Three thousand local PECE committees sprang up across the country. Much reliance was placed on public relations as a way of stimulating charity.

With only a small staff and seven field representatives, Woods consulted state governors by telephone about relief plans for the winter. He reported a spirit of wartime dedication, but also a widespread desire to handle the situation without federal interference. Working his estimate out of his experience with the Unemployment Commission of 1921, Woods suggested an additional federal expenditure of $750 million on public improvements. In December Hoover recommended up to $150 million; Congress appropriated only $117 million. Conscientious and sensitive, Woods wanted to know the nature and extent of suffering and wished to acquaint Hoover with it. Woods's committee members found "desperate distress" in West Virginia and Kentucky—"deserving men, women, and children actually . . . suffering from hunger, exposure, and cold." When in February 1931 Payne told him the Red Cross could not help distressed soft-coal miners within drought areas—since their suffering had not resulted from the drought—Woods persuaded the President to order Payne "to have the Red Cross see to it very quietly and unobtrusively." Later Woods had to tell Hoover again "about the way relief is *not* being administered in the West Virginia coalfields." This time Hoover wrote to Payne that the "Red Cross must handle the relief in a broad way." In the fall of 1931 the President asked the American Friends Service Committee to carry out a program, financed by the American Relief Administration and the Rockefeller Foundation, for feeding children in coal-mining areas. Woods's office staff, which also included Lewis Meriam of the University of Chicago, worked on countless projects to increase employment in industry. Exhausted and disappointed, Woods left in April 1931, and the capable Fred Croxton took over. That summer, while planning how to deal with relief during the coming winter, Hoover admitted the government's lack of accurate unemployment statistics but claimed that the caseload for relief could be gauged by extrapolation from the previous season's figures. For his part, Croxton insisted that no one who applied for help would starve in the United States.[33]

In August 1931 PECE's functions and some of its personnel became part of the President's Organization on Unemployment Relief (POUR) under Walter S. Gifford, president of American Telephone & Telegraph. Hoover, by Will Rogers' account, had told Gifford that he had a remarkable job for him. "Why is it remarkable?" asked Gifford. "Because we are giving you no resources to do it with," the President responded.

Gifford, who had taken the job reluctantly, lost some of his staff in September when Hoover said that unemployment was exaggerated. The President quickly apologized. Gifford testified that while in theory he favored public relief supported by taxes, the country would have to depend on community chest drives because "we have . . . built up the system the other way." POUR, like PECE, was hampered by its Hoover-like overreliance on publicity and voluntary response. When its state representatives listed bad conditions—Pennsylvania had a twelfth of the country's population, a sixth of its unemployment, and a conservative legislature unwilling to take necessary action—the President asked whether Gifford could find some very wealthy men to provide $5 to $10 million to handle these. Gifford was unable to implement this wishful scheme. He merely reassured questioners like Bernard Baruch that money for relief was holding out well. In his tenure he did appoint a promising advisory committee composed of more than one hundred technical specialists on labor and industry, with subcommittees under Croxton, Owen D. Young, and James R. Garfield for expanding, coordinating, and improving relief efforts.[34]

In February 1931 Hoover signed the Wagner-Graham Stabilization Act and abruptly took credit for it; "an admirable measure," he called this advance planning bill, saying that he had been carrying on such activity for over a year and that Woods's committee had helped in Congress. At its heart was a Federal Stabilization Board with powers to initiate public works when economic indicators turned down; discretion to fund programs remained with the President, whose Commission on Recent Economic Changes had recommended a similar plan. Hoover correctly credited Edward Hunt and Otto Mallery with developing the idea for the Commerce Department. Walter Lippmann, who would always believe that Hoover had initiated the governmental activism associated with the New Deal, defined Wagner-Graham as a radical law. Hoover said that it was not a "cure for depression," and for months he failed to appoint a director of it. His eventual choice, D. H. Sawyer, did little. But Hoover's *Memoirs* boasted that his administration constructed more public works than the federal government had undertaken in the previous thirty years. He was indeed responsible for an expansion of downtown Washington that constituted a revival of L'Enfant's plans. The mood against federal relief continued to be dominant during 1931; even though some congressmen called for a special session to deal with the problem, the National Council of Social Workers refused to endorse the principle at their May convention. Henry Ford remarked that the young men and boys crossing the country looking for work were getting a good education. But in August Franklin D. Roosevelt told the New York State legislature that unemployment relief "must be extended by government—not as a matter of charity but as a matter of social duty."[35]

In 1932 the Surgeon General, relying on independent statistical sources, assured Hoover that infant mortality had declined rather steadily even in cities, a statistic that Hoover used in the campaign of 1932 as evidence that people were not starving under his presidency. During his years working in European relief he had always used such figures to gauge human needs. "No one is actually starving," the President asserted. Hoover's old friend Ray Lyman Wilbur sounded more compassionate in his later remark: "The present depression is like a forest fire which kills many trees and sears them all. In some the scars are so deep that no future growth can cover them." Walter Lippmann observed that Hoover's statistics "are contrary to common sense. . . . It would be hard to persuade the American people that destitution and anxiety are not detrimental to health. And what purpose is served by attempting to promote complacency when there is need of sensitiveness, and sympathy and deep concern, I do not know." Various hospital records in large cities showed numerous cases of death from starvation, and the New York City Welfare Council in 1933 counted 29 deaths from starvation and 110 from malnutrition, chiefly children. There is no way of knowing how much of this was the result of the Depression itself rather than "normal" cases of infirmity or neglect or unwillingness to apply for help or even what today would be called child abuse. In 1933 ex-President Hoover and the cartoonist Ding Darling, on a fishing trip in the West, were taken to a shack where one child was dead and seven more starving. Hoover raised $3000 for the family.[36]*

By the winter of 1931–2 Hoover had decided that more substantial federal relief assistance was essential: "We used such emergency powers to win the war," he said, "we can use them to fight the depression, the misery and suffering from which are equally great." He had reports of inadequacies in private charity. The 1932 community chest relief funds, while the largest yet to be raised, reached only $35 million. Hoover chose an existing vehicle, the Reconstruction Finance Corporation, to finance relief. The mayors of the largest cities of Michigan had already sent an urgent appeal to him for direct federal unemployment relief through the RFC. Schoolteachers in Detroit and Chicago had not been paid for months, and Detroit moved to foreclose their homes for nonpayment of taxes. Even the conservative Gifford acknowledged that RFC loans might

---

* In 1977 the *Journal of the American Medical Association* described the estimated medical effects of a sustained unemployment rise of 1.4 percent from 1970 to 1975: 36,887 deaths (including at least 920 suicides), 4227 state mental hospital first admissions, and 3340 state prison confinements; the editorial concluded: "unemployment rates . . . indicate a reality of human stress, illness, and death."

be necessary for states with impaired credit or legal restrictions on borrowing. In time, the RFC did give money for relief of several kinds. But its relief activities, hindered in part by the slowness of states to put through enabling legislation, were subordinate and subsequent to its role in saving the nation's banks.[37]

Like the nineteenth-century agrarian economy it reflected, America's banking system after World War I was democratic, dispersed, unrationalized, and hostile to concentrations of power or governmental restraints. The Federal Reserve Act of 1913, designed only to assure minimum reserves and liquidity, hardly qualified as bank regulation, although it was a national system funneling money to urban areas. Without the discipline of branch banking by large commercial banks, a weakness compounded by the clear inability of the Federal Reserve banks to control the money market, America's thousands and thousands of small lending institutions had no one to turn to but themselves. Lacking diversified opportunities, too many local banks overextended themselves or concentrated on financing crops and inventories, collateral easily susceptible to swings in the business cycle. Inexperience and naïveté also imperiled many banks. In the decade before the Depression, some 5400 bank failures had eroded public trust in banking generally. Most of the closures were in small towns. Too many institutions were wholly local, dependent on depopulated rural communities threatened with farm recession. Many had assets of less than $100,000, some even under $25,000. City banking suffered from investment in weak rural banks, and more extensively from dealing in risky forms of capital finance such as investment holding companies and private credit corporations, which in turn speculated in real estate, the stock market, or various exotic foreign bonds. A rapid deflation could and did topple such ill-managed, pyramid-like structures and seriously jeopardize the assets of well-capitalized institutions like savings banks, life insurance companies, and most corporations. In December 1930 the private Bank of the United States collapsed; 400,000 depositors lost $180 million. Ten thousand more banks would fail during the coming decade.[38]

Yet bankers themselves needed a prod. Between 1929 and 1931 they had to deal with ominous, debilitating events. More and more depositors withdrew more and more money from their accounts. The unemployed needed the money for living expenses; others, justly worried about bank solvency, wanted cash at hand in case they could not get it later. The assets of all banks were deteriorating. The value of collateral pledged for loans, mostly real estate and inventories, declined rapidly. To meet the demand for cash by their depositors, bankers sold off securities for only a fraction of their acquisition cost. (The Federal Reserve System, for example, did not support government bond prices, which would have provided many institutions with ready cash. The system did not want to risk huge potential losses.) So bankers in the Midwest and South took up the defense of liquidity: getting and keeping as much cash as possible into their vaults. The public, despite the President's denunciations of hoarding, did much the same. In protecting themselves, they prevented others from fighting depression, for businessmen and governments soon discovered that money was simply not available.[39]

The administration scarcely had time to understand, let alone deal with, these complex issues before the European financial crisis of 1931 drove Britain off the gold standard. Suddenly thousands of rich speculators overseas began converting paper dollars into gold. So Hoover—warning congressional leaders they must "legislate or go off gold"—pressed for an omnibus banking bill, necessarily a patchwork affair, that would improve discount facilities at the Federal Reserve banks by releasing gold held there as collateral for loans to commercial banks. This more liberal credit policy would allow discounting of additional commercial paper by the system, as well as its use as collateral for the circulation of Federal Reserve currency. In effect, it allowed funds to go to member banks that had acceptable commercial paper. He persuaded a reluctant Senator Glass, the prestigious author of the Federal Reserve Act, to sponsor it, along with Democratic Representative Henry Steagall of Alabama. The announcement of the Glass-Steagall Bill brought a sharp stock market rise. Hoover believed it would enable the country to remain on the gold standard despite massive foreign withdrawals of that metal. He termed it a "national defense measure." It passed early in 1932 under Democratic sponsorship as a companion to the RFC. It made him smile, Hoover said, to hear the bill called a Democratic measure after he had argued leaders into it. He also worked closely with Glass on new banking legislation that came about in 1933; and he consid-ered in 1931 "proposing to Congress that all banks engaged in interstate commerce be compelled to join the Federal Reserve," but was discouraged by his Attorney General on constitutional grounds.[40]

Closely bound to the banking system was the stock market. Since the Stock Exchange had undertaken no effective self-regulation in the wake of the crash, Hoover demanded an investigation by the Senate, particularly of "sinister bear raids." Most of this selling came from prominent Republicans. In 1932 he recommended full disclosure by prospectus of stocks offered for sale in interstate trade, with punishment for fraud; a listing of all promoters, who were to be personally liable; and a set of statutory rules governing all sales. At the President's request, Connecticut Senator Frederic C. Walcott, an old friend from Belgian relief, became instrumental in heading off Wall Street efforts to blunt the investigation.

The Senate finally obliged on March 4, 1932, and in the ensuing hearings men like Charles Schwab, John Raskob, William Kenny, and Percy Rockefeller were required to explain their short selling and other practices. The short selling in 1931 infuriated Hoover: "Men are not justified," he said, "in deliberately making a profit from the losses of other people . . . these operations destroy public confidence, and induce a slowing down of business." But his own Secretary of the Treasury, Ogden Mills, disobeyed his instructions to give Owen D. Young his blistering letter of June 3, 1932, attacking short selling as it affected the currency. As ex-President, Hoover would applaud the New Deal's Securities and Exchange Commission.[41]

The Reconstruction Finance Corporation, the President's most prominent structural answer to the fallen economy, took its model from the War Finance Corporation (WFC), set up in 1918 for making loans to wartime industries and sustaining the operation of the national financial system. That agency's combining of Yankee resourcefulness with a tangible expression of unity in crisis attracted Hoover. It was appealing to him also that the WFC had been strictly temporary; after the war it had functioned chiefly as a rural credit agency until its complete dismantling in 1929. But before embracing such an activist government scheme, Hoover experimented with a private equivalent—a cooperative agency that was supposed to be financed by leading banks at an initial $500 million and to lend out to weaker institutions.[42]

Eugene Meyer, Hoover's governor of the Federal Reserve Board and a former WFC chairman, doubted that bankers would be enthusiastic. He thought the plan would simply redistribute existing capital, while banks really needed new funds. But Hoover confidently predicted cooperation, and in any case wanted to avoid an early session of Congress. Meeting on October 4, 1931, with New York's financial leaders at Secretary Mellon's Washington home, the President asked first for a private guarantee system of deposits. Then he requested insurance companies to postpone mortgage collections for a year. They refused. Hoover warned that if an effective private combine to save the banks failed to materialize, a government credit organization with power to insure deposits would. His reluctance to grant government aid to the banks belies the charge that he was willing to help businessmen and not the poor. As always during his presidency, he projected an idea of self-sacrifice. And once again his hopes looked to people who were not in a position to meet them. The federal agency that Hoover threatened was exactly what the bankers wanted, and his talk of forming one countered his object. Their scenario was for the government to rescue the bankers; the naïve Hoover's was for the bankers to save industry, which would then save the people by creating jobs. To inspire confidence he journeyed to a baseball game in Philadelphia. Receiving news there of the death of his friend, Senator Dwight Morrow of New Jersey, he left the park to cries of "We want beer! We want beer!"

Nevertheless, nine days later a privately financed National Credit Corporation incorporated in Delaware with pledges enabling it to lend up to a billion dollars; a week after that officers had been appointed, and the President urged the generous disbursement of funds. "After a few weeks of enterprising course," Hoover's *Memoirs* recall, the "Association became ultraconservative, then fearful, and finally died." The bankers, Hoover observed, had picked "the worst hard-boiled representatives they could find" for its administration. In late October, when bank failures temporarily declined and stocks rallied, the new corporation held back, demanding unreasonable collateral. Then, within a month, the economy lurched downward again. The private agency became more munificent in its last weeks of operation, but showed a disinclination to lend to small banks and lacked the power to help railroads, now in desperate shape. Hoover told Thomas Lamont: "certainly the public will not blame the administration if, upon inability of private enterprise to save the situation, the government should do it."[43]

Discerning the weakness of the NCC and hearing that California's Bank of America was verging on collapse, the President submitted a bill to Congress on December 7 to restablish the WFC as the $2 billion Emergency Reconstruction Corporation. It was a large project, yet one that a successful businessman might naturally propose. Hoover, an individualist, skillfully worked on vast projects that held dangerous implications for individualism. This original name, later changed to Reconstruction Finance Corporation, reflected Hoover's intent that all such enterprises be transitory. "It should be placed in liquidation at the end of two years," he told Congress in December.[44]

Some of Hoover's strongest critics praised the new scheme. TRB in *The New Republic* wrote: "There has been nothing quite like it. . . . [I]n the face of a crisis, it amazes me that it should be going through Congress with so little modification and amendment." In fact, however, Speaker Garner knocked out Hoover's provisions permitting loans for slum clearance, the modernization of industrial plants, and assistance to farmers. Hoover became infuriated by the delay in Congress, particularly the adjournment for the Christmas holidays. In the House, forty-three Democrats and twelve Republicans voted nay. Hoover signed the RFC act on January 22, 1932, remarking: "it is created for the support of the smaller banks and financial institutions"; the larger banks Hoover pronounced "amply able to take care of themselves." The RFC took as its president Eugene Meyer, whom Hoover had placed on the Federal Reserve Board in

1930. Meyer served with three other Republicans and three Democrats. Charles G. "Hell 'n Maria" Dawes, the dramatic and popular former Vice-President, left his post as ambassador to Great Britain to become its chairman after Owen D. Young refused the job. Dawes, Hoover thought, might give the agency the element of drama he knew he could not supply himself.[45]

Hoover had conceived of a program wider than that defined in the original congressional bill. He wanted provision for lending to industries and public bodies as well as banks; and he proposed institutions for making loans to farmers on the collateral of their production and livestock. He was still faithful to his ideal of an economy of cooperatives: the capital on these agricultural corporations was to be gradually transferred to the farmers themselves through a small premium on loans. Eight months later the President was to get these powers. At the same time he distrusted the RFC for its capacities to expand. Many progressives shared Hoover's own far-sighted uneasiness over the new agency, which would in fact last twenty years and lend $50 billion. George Norris remarked that in his wildest dreams he had not thought to put "government into business" so extensively. Robert La Follette and Carter Glass kept Hoover from writing still broader lending powers into the original bill. Borah doubted the Senate's right to pass the RFC, and "would never have voted for it except for the condition of the country." Burton K. Wheeler opposed it as the opening to a welfare state, an institution that would start by loaning to businessmen and then lend to everyone else. *The Nation* worried about Hoover's "dictatorial powers." The *Kiplinger Washington Letter* tersely called it "an experiment in state socialism." It might better have been called state capitalism.[46]

So Hoover had a lending program that in its final form marked both the triumph and the denial of his politics: a triumph in providing means for lightly rationalizing the economy in concurrence with private initiative and in league with cooperatives; a denial in threatening to bring a bureaucracy Hoover did not desire, although both his business and his governmental career had in a sense acted to the furtherance of bureaucracy. He abhorred more than the duplication, the slowness, the wastefulness of bloated administration. Bureaucracy was the foe of private, voluntary decision. And it endangered popular rule. If the federal government should become the controlling element, or even a competing participant, in American economic life, business interests would be anxious to manipulate it by financing or bribing incumbents; and an enormous and unwieldy yet secretive and unchecked government would be vulnerable to corporate influence. An administration could resent responsibility for mistakes and employ tyrannical power. It was, then, not only the power of government over business but the syndicalist power of business in government that Hoover feared. At dinner in Washington one July evening in 1930 he predicted an end to representative government and that business in government would be responsible. If business controlled the state, we would have fascism; if labor, socialism. His aversion to national bureaucracy was not one symptom of a pro-business orientation but a concern shared by many progressives. What he desired was some system of balances: a government just large enough to regulate, harmonize, and effect arbitrations in American business, and small enough to preserve its efficiency and independence. To a great extent it was the old progressive ideal of Woodrow Wilson. Hoover would enjoy as President neither the length of tenure nor the political power nor perhaps the articulateness to shape a definable program of that kind. His actions in response to economic crisis, a curious mix of boldness and hesitation, would lack the cohesiveness of a visible philosophy, as they also lacked the style that his successor could bring to government. And this was a loss; for Hoover possessed a sophisticated sense of the problems of power, administration, and bureaucracy that deserved some explicit and coherent statement.[47]

Meyer and Hoover agreed that the country's economic troubles revolved around the insufficiency of credit for business and consumers. The agency's first goal, in any event, was to strengthen the banking system. And the RFC did buoy confidence: in two months it lent more than a quarter of a billion, and bank failures declined in February and even more in March. But a high interest rate, the shortness of loan periods (many for only six months), and stiff collateral requirements tied up funds that bankers might have used to activate the economy. Still, few businessmen and few consumers could muster enough confidence and ambition to apply for loans. Neither group sought credit on a scale adequate for invigorating the economy, and bankers used most of their borrowings from the RFC not for bold reinvestment but for extending old loans or buying government bonds. Atlee Pomerene, who in 1932 succeeded Meyer as head of the RFC, said that any liquid bank refusing to make loans was a "parasite on the country." Although on occasion the RFC could act with extraordinary speed, both government and business lacked the aggressiveness needed for long-range recovery. Senator Wagner complained: "I have been very much discouraged by [the RFC's] legalistic, narrow and mechanical construction of the law." Hoover's desire for a banking policy carrying greater powers and ᴙquiring less security proved wise. He consulted on particular loans with ⌐ directors and, unlike Secretary Mills, had wanted to allow outright ᴙse of bank stock.[48]

ᴙr was the target of congressional attacks by mid-May 1932, when it became apparent that the RFC was not permanently lifting the economy. Then the near-collapse in June of the important Central Republic Bank of Chicago brought a loan of $90 million from the agency for averting disaster to the city and the probable fall of the national banking system; the administration was put on the defensive again, for Chairman Dawes had been a principal of the Chicago bank, although he had resigned from the RFC just before the granting of the loan and the new Democratic member, Jesse Jones, took responsibility for it. Worse still, Dawes tried to pay off his creditors without making certain the bank itself would continue. More politically damaging to Hoover were complaints from progressives that the RFC, in its rush to save the banks, refused to furnish relief funds to the people of Chicago or make a loan to the city to help pay its impoverished civil servants. Hoover-the-friend-of-the-rich was fast becoming a stereotype. It did not help to hear that Wall Street bankers would loan money to the city only if it slashed its relief rolls, or that a municipal employee in Chicago lost his home because he could not pay $34 in taxes when the city owed him $850 in salary. But the banks and the country would have been in even more desperate shape had not the RFC lent almost $1 billion by late summer.[49]

By early 1932, if not before, the President realized that private charity would not be enough. Reports of his own Organization on Unemployment Relief revealed that federal funds must soon be provided for economic, humanitarian, and political reasons. "Hunger marches" on Washington, beginning in December 1931 and culminating in the famous Bonus Army the next summer, dramatized the urgent need to act. In January 1932 the Farm Board gave 40 million bushels of wheat to the unemployed with Congress's permission. The conservative Senator Simeon Fess sighed, "No one would feel justified in obstructing the use of such Government possessions to alleviate hunger, but at the same time it is a step . . . to making appropriations directly out of the Treasury for the relief of indigent people from whatever cause." Hoover himself disagreed with progressives, who introduced numerous relief bills in Congress, over the nature of further assistance. As early as December 1930 he had accused congressmen who introduced liberal relief bills of "playing politics with human misery." Yet he also differed with Eugene Meyer, who resisted expansion of the RFC into welfare and public works and opposed even the direct loans to business that Hoover wanted. Such disputes may have led Hoover in 1932 to replace Meyer with Atlee Pomerene, an Ohio Democrat fresh from a six-year investigation of the Harding scandals. Democrats now were a majority on the board. Prominent Democrats like Baruch and Senator Joseph T. Robinson were calling for the RFC to undertake a role in relief. Hoover now proposed that the RFC make loans to state and local governments for relief and for public works projects that would pay for themselves, as well as for loans to municipalities and farm marketing groups.[50]

The President put forward his own omnibus bill for relief and public works, which included provisions for loans to market the agricultural surplus and $300 million in RFC loans to states for relief. Senator Wagner then attempted to link diverse congressional views in a bill acceptable to Hoover. Early in July he vetoed the Wagner-Garner Bill for emergency relief and construction, which had received the votes of all but three Democrats in the House. He did not oppose the bill's provisions on state and local relief and unemployment, but he found unacceptable Garner's insistence on unsecured loans to "individuals, trusts, estates, partnerships, all types of corporations, associations, joint-stock companies, states, counties, and municipalities." Walter Lippmann called the Garner proposal "obviously, patently, and indisputably absurd." Hoover signed into law a revised bill offering almost the same amount but without the offending passage. The concept of loans had almost vanished: states would repay the monies over five years, beginning in 1935, by a subsequent reduction in federal aid for highway building. This law, providing local relief and extensive public works and including money for slum clearance and low-cost housing, represented a new course in American public policy. Yet Hoover had been turned down in still other requests to the Seventy-second Congress, including authority to make RFC loans for plant construction. With the bill's passage the President's Organization for Unemployment Relief disbanded, Congress having refused Hoover's request for additional funding. But Fred Croxton directed the new RFC Emergency Relief Division, helping states to improve their relief machinery.[51]

The Emergency Relief Division, authorized to lend states $300 million, required sometimes cumbersome and stringent application procedures. Democrats on the RFC board, notably Pomerene and Jesse Jones, insisted on caution of this sort. Late in July 1932 Illinois received $3 million, and by the end of September $35 million had gone to nine states, including another $6 million to hard-pressed Illinois. Governor Gifford Pinchot of Pennsylvania clashed with Hoover and the RFC, which claimed that that state had not exhausted its own resources for relief. The RFC was technically correct, but Pinchot could do little with Pennsylvania's legislature. In September he asserted publicly to Pomerene that Hoover had sympathy only for the rich. Coming from a prominent Republican in the midst of a political campaign, and not long after the rout of the Bonus Army, the charge had destructive impact. Pennsylvania had received almost $27 million by March 1933, when all relief loans totaled $210 million.[52]

Private charity, with Hoover pressing in 1932, again reached a new high point and cut down on its spending for causes other than relief. By 1935, however, private help would account for only 1.4 percent of the expenses for relief.

RFC loans for reproductive or "self-liquidating" public works also multiplied. But major projects required engineering studies and approval from various political and administrative bodies. By October 1932 the board had lowered its interest rate on loans and extended the period of repayment to twenty-five years. It also solicited small-scale works that could be carried out swiftly. Three major California projects, all long-standing favorites of Hoover, gained approval just before the fall election: the San Francisco-Oakland Bay Bridge (the bridge authority requested funds at the President's urging), the Pasadena waterworks, and the Metropolitan Aqueduct from the Colorado River to Los Angeles. Other loans financed Jones Beach on Long Island, a Mississippi River bridge at New Orleans, sewage systems, waterworks, railway bridges, and electric transmission lines from Hoover Dam to Los Angeles. Even by late November only $360,000 had actually been disbursed; four months later the figure had risen to some $20 million, but it is doubtful that much cash soon found its way to the unemployed. Yet Senator Glass condemned Hoover's "insane" projects—all pre-election expedients, including the "almost criminal expenditure of forty million dollars for various water power projects in California." This was "a campaign fund" for carrying the state, said Glass. The President himself noted that such projects were two to four times as expensive as direct family relief. He had lost much of his faith in their efficacy and stuck to his insistence that the loans be self-liquidating and for "reproductive" purposes.[53]

Another important constituent in need of additional federal aid was the farmer. Once it became apparent that private mortgage groups were ignoring his request for a program, Hoover in November 1931 wanted Congress and industry leaders to endorse a series of mortgage discount banks similar to the Federal Reserve System and capitalized at up to $600 million. The concept was too radical for the times. After considerable opposition developed, Hoover asked Congress to allow the Federal Farm Loan Board to limit foreclosures by its Federal Land Banks to those farmers who wished to abandon their land or had already done so. In December he also requested Congress to set up a more modest system of Home Loan Discount banks that would quicken employment in construction and secure renewals of mortgages, a particularly serious problem in farm areas. Representative Garner held up final action on the Federal Home Loan Bank Bill—Hoover charged it was for political reasons—until the following July; eight to twelve such banks were then authorized with $125 million in RFC funds.

Franklin Fort had this agency working by September. Believing that crop restrictions would soon be required, Hoover also moved to provide distributors with better credit for purchases from farmers. The RFC Agricultural Credit Division would help both these intermediate agents and individual farmers. But loans offered by the RFC at a high 7 percent interest brought few takers. Only $37 million—and that chiefly to farmers themselves—had been spent before Hoover left office. Yet the combination of this sum with an RFC grant of $130 million, dispensed through the Agriculture Department, for loans with projected crops as security, helped tens of thousands of farmers. Hoover signed further legislation in March 1933, which made possible much of the activity of the New Deal Farm Credit Administration.[54]

Hoover promoted the consolidation of railway interests into four independent systems that he thought would make for greater efficiency. When the intensely jealous and competitive railway leaders and the Interstate Commerce Commission agreed, Hoover in 1930 asked Congress for necessary enabling legislation. But Congress opposed the pooling of interests: some progressives hoped for bankruptcy and government ownership, and some conservatives opposed the plan as unwarranted government interference. Hoover then moved to put the ICC and the Shipping Board in strict supervision of the railroads' chief competition: trucks, buses, and the coastal shipping trade. In 1931 a Southern railway failed to abide by Hoover's appeal in May to rescind reductions in wages. It was the first time a carrier rejected arbitration findings under the Railway Labor Act. But at the end of January 1932, Hoover talked with both parties by phone to Chicago and obtained a compromise that reduced an announced 15 percent cut in pay to 10 percent. He had made the threatening comment that if private enterprise did not "save the situation, the government should do so" for the purpose of circumventing a strike. Despite a favorable picture of railway finance that the ICC commissioner presented to him, the President correctly regarded the railway situation, with its strikes, its shrinking of employment, and its shaky finances, as a major impediment to recovery. The Railway Credit Corporation received some $300 million of RFC funds, which prevented the worst that could have befallen the industry. In 1932 Hoover did not even submit to Congress a plan he drew up for radical reorganization of the lines.[55]

The momentum and institutional framework for RFC and other Hoover projects transferred to the New Deal. Once the $300 million relief money had been distributed by the spring of 1933, Congress gave the RFC $500 million for Harry Hopkins's new Federal Emergency Relief Administration; the states again took responsibility for administering the program under agencies the RFC had insisted they establish. In much the same manner the Commodity Credit Corporation (CCC) originated through RFC aid for domestic marketing of farm products. The CCC, really an arm of the RFC, replaced certain private institutions the RFC had used earlier. Many administrative personnel in all these New Deal agencies had served in the Hoover government. In proposing the RFC, the Federal Land Banks, federal Home Loan Discount banks, and various banking and Federal Reserve reforms, Hoover's administration foreshadowed in a general way its more dramatic successor. Achievements—as the historian of the RFC, James Olson, has remarked—outlast precedents in the historical memory. Hoover's programs had sometimes come about grudgingly and in the belief that they should be temporary. But they also occurred mainly because private banks, too selfish or frightened or vulnerable to rally, wanted federal intervention. In a sense they were asking for the same government assistance farmers had been receiving since 1929, and with the same goal: stabilization.[56]

The year 1932—in contrast to most of 1931—was a time of growing activism both for Hoover and for Congress. In January the President appointed Benjamin Cardozo to the Supreme Court. Despite the pleading of conservatives, he signed the Norris-LaGuardia Act outlawing "yellow dog" contracts and limiting federal injunctions except when danger or injury threatened; he even claimed credit for having earlier advanced the concepts embodied in the new law, which one historian has called "the most important social legislation between the Progressive Era and the New Deal." Many historians have said that Hoover signed the law reluctantly, but it was in keeping with the position he had taken as co-chairman of the Second Industrial Conference in 1919, and he played a part in dislodging the bill from a congressional committee that had buried it. Attorney General Mitchell added some warnings, perhaps in an effort to reassure the business community on the administration's attitude or to respond to opponents who called it unconstitutional. Hoover secured passage of a model District of Columbia code prohibiting possession or sale of unlicensed weapons; he also signed another bill, recommended by his committee on law observance, for remanding juveniles convicted of breaking federal laws to local juvenile courts. And Congress finally passed a more liberal bankruptcy act suggested by the President in 1930. The Senate and the House ignored many of Hoover's recommendations, including safeguards for bank deposits and railroad bonds, and compulsory bank membership in the Federal Reserve system. On the other hand, he would have none of a revived Council of National Defense or "emergency cabinet" proposed by a group of industrialists and the American

Legion. He appeared more optimistic early in 1932, and if the congressional leadership had gotten its way the cooperation might have lasted indefinitely. The sales tax rebellion of March 1932 destroyed it.[57]

Fiscal 1931 gave Hoover a $900 million deficit. In February 1932 he appointed a new Secretary of the Treasury, Ogden Mills—Andrew Mellon having been removed, to Hoover's relief, to the Court of St. James; Mellon had long discouraged Hoover on innovative economic steps, such as his suggestion that corporations cooperatively retire their funded debt. The third richest man in Washington had now replaced the richest. An important figure in the administration since the start of hard times, Mills had yachts, a racing stable, estates on Long Island and on the Hudson, a Newport villa, a Fifth Avenue mansion; he was brilliant, a graduate of Harvard at nineteen; a heavy drinker, he died in 1937 after imbibing a fifth of gin within an hour. The President privately believed that depression, like wartime, required some deficit spending; and neither he nor Mills thought that the budget could actually be righted in 1932. As Stimson remarked in his diary on May 26, 1931, after a cabinet meeting: Hoover "said in war times no one dreamed of balancing the budget. Fortunately we can now borrow on very good terms." Such critics as Walter Lippmann and Allan Nevins, however, vehemently denounced Hoover's unbalanced budgets. During most of 1931 the Treasury opposed the raising of taxes, preferring simply that the budget be balanced by borrowing and moderately reduced spending.[58]

Higher taxes for 1932 are now supposed to have been among Hoover's chief errors in combatting the Depression. Unintimidated by reasonable deficits, and through Mills an advocate of monetary expansion, he became a proponent of tax increase only during the month after Britain left the gold standard in September 1931, when gold flowed out of the country, bond prices declined, interest rates rose, and bank failures multiplied. Hoover had previously opposed a sales tax when prominent progressives like Norris and Borah were endorsing it and urging that public expenses be cut drastically. But Mills, who also disliked a sales tax, had little trouble convincing Hoover that the goal of a balanced budget should be kept in public view. Conservative Democrats like Bernard Baruch argued for balancing the budget, and congressional Democrats slashed away at the Hoover spending proposals. As Democrat Breckinridge Long put it: the Democrats "on the hill are trying to balance the budget, and that is not part of the Hoover program. . . . The Government cannot go on expending millions of dollars which it has not, whether it be for the unemployed, or for the sick or for anyone else." Many progressives shared William Borah's view that "increasing burdens of government" were the biggest cause contributing to the Depression. George Norris recommended that Hoover "should cut to the bone federal expenses." Certainly Hoover and Mills hoped that the educational campaign in favor of a sales tax might head off extravagant legislation. After leaving the matter to the House, where revenue bills had to originate, they supported a manufacturer's sales tax of 2¼ percent, insisting that it apply neither to food nor to inexpensive clothing. The idea received the approval of all but one member of the House Ways and Means Committee and, even more surprisingly, the Democratic leadership of both houses. Wary of having Republicans sponsor unpopular taxes in an election year, Mills claimed publicly to prefer a group of excise rates. He let Democrats like Henry T. Rainey, William Randolph Hearst, Smith, Cox, Davis, Raskob, Shouse, Baruch, and Speaker Garner himself proclaim the sagacity of the sales tax. In March, after its unexpected defeat in the House, Mills could say: "The so-called manufacturers sales tax was recommended by the Ways and Means Committee on its own initiative."[59]

At first, opposition to the tax came only from predictable sources like Fiorello LaGuardia, who described it as "grinding the face of the poor," "taking milk from babies and bread from mothers." LaGuardia advocated a reduction in government spending and called Hoover a "dictator." Then Robert L. Doughton of North Carolina, the only congressman to vote against the bill in Ways and Means, gathered fifty Democrats responsive to constituents who sent in heavy mail against the tax. Soon a coalition of progressives and Democrats began to dominate the House, passing a higher income tax and surtaxes on the highest incomes. Speaker Garner had cleverly if belatedly disengaged himself from the fracas, and in a rare moment of high drama he roused all of the House to stand in favor of a balanced budget, an act that seemed to cool the "soak the rich" ardor. But the sales tax lost 236 to 160 on April 1, and with it went much of the energy behind Garner's bid for the presidency.[60]

Doughton received many protests from cotton textile mills, among them one neatly typed on cloth; the congressman from North Carolina urged retrenchment in federal expenses. Hoover believed that no further cutting of the federal budget was possible. Many states having or considering such a levy did not want to be preempted by the federal government. Doughton had remarked to a constituent: "In all probabilities, the State of North Carolina will be compelled to adopt some kind of sales tax . . . and that is another reason I am opposed" to the federal tax. The Southern and Midwestern areas where the sales tax was spreading voted overwhelmingly against the federal impost. The failure of the proposal then might have constituted more a victory of the states over the federal government than a triumph of radicalism. Many affected businessmen, like the reactionary H. J. Heinz, urged its defeat. Hoover pleaded with a group of thirty-nine publishers to support the tax and asked the Senate to pass it, but when fifty-five members declared against it, he announced that he had never favored the sales tax and would be glad to accept excises instead.[61]

In the course of a memorandum to the conservative Democratic representative Charles R. Crisp, the President proposed that the maldistribution of wealth had been a major cause of the Depression. "In every society," he had written, "there will always be at the bottom a noxious sediment and at the top an obnoxious froth." The memorandum was an extensive statement on taxation. Hoover recommended against an increase in excise taxes on necessities, which "fall 'hidden' on the lower-income groups." Excise taxes on luxuries and non-essentials, however, should be higher. As for income taxes: "My view is that we should raise the upper brackets . . . to 45 per cent, as compared to the present 23 per cent, as an emergency matter and give a deduction for earned incomes as distinguished from incomes from rent, interest, etc." Capital gains taxes should be modified or abolished, since they favored the stock speculator. Hoover contended that a moderate estate tax was among "the most economically and socially desirable—or even necessary" of taxes. "The way to disperse . . . [great fortunes] . . . is by the division of estates among a number of beneficiaries. . . . My proposal is a graduated tax applied, not to the estate, but to the beneficiary, rising to a maximum of, say, 45 per cent, as against the present 23 per cent." Later a correspondence with a duPont would come to an abrupt end when Hoover, during the New Deal, told him that high estate taxes were essential. He also held that an undue proportion of taxes fell on farmers and homeowners. On June 6, 1932, Hoover signed a bill for increased surtaxes up to 55 percent, estate taxes to 45, higher corporate taxes of 14 percent, and a variety of excise taxes on items from jewelry to bubble gum. The Revenue Act of 1932 was the most progressive tax law of the decade; Hoover called it a natural extension of the graduated income tax, itself "one of the most just and efficient methods of taxation." The new rates were left essentially unchanged throughout the New Deal and for a generation after.[62]

It is too much to claim that the Hoover administration anticipated the New Deal and that Roosevelt just filled in the cracks. The New Deal was so broad in scope, such a panoply of measures came out of it, that the average citizen was made to feel the presence of the federal government for the first time. Hoover's response to the Depression, in contrast, was characterized—and deeply marred—by his tenacious adherence to a philosophy of voluntarism. The experiences of his administration forewarned its successors that an attempt to reduce government spending did not end

depressions and that voluntary agencies and businessmen would not sacrifice to end them either. After Hoover, no one could say that the federal
government had rushed in before private agencies had been given a chance.
The way was clear for a New Deal.[63]

XIII

WORLD DIPLOMACY

HOOVER brought to the White House a range of international experience greater perhaps than that of any previous incumbent: his mining years had acquainted him with the Far East and life in London, and five years of service in the World War I era had brought him as close as any American to European problems; and his recent trip to South America, along with prior mining experience there, had given him firsthand knowledge of that continent as well. (He had, moreover, been interested in occupying the office of Secretary of State under Coolidge.) He would repeatedly call on this experience during his presidency. From the start he determined to make his own major foreign policy decisions, but economic problems frequently distracted him from foreign affairs. His policies, also, did not often have the energy and boldness that characterized other administrations. Nonetheless, he won praise for his Wilsonian personal meetings in the United States with Ramsay MacDonald of Britain and Pierre Laval of France, for his dramatic moratorium on intergovernmental debts, and for the Stimson Doctrine in the Far East. He also built up the Foreign Service and increased the State Department budget by 40 percent. Although he endorsed the World Court and urged greater participation in the League of Nations' economic and humanitarian projects, he preferred a self-contained United States that could serve as a model for other peoples. This Pauline strategy of being in the world but not of it underwent great stress during his administration. For the involvement of the United States in foreign affairs expanded under the disintegrating pressures of worldwide depression and the ominous spread of militarism.[1]

In addition to the external problems of politics and economics, there were inherent conflicts in Hoover's ambitious attempts to apply Quaker principles in foreign affairs. Cooperative action in behalf of international neighbors and attempts to fight the Depression clashed with an isolationist notion of merely serving as a model for other countries. The appeal to international ethics did not accord nicely with the objectives of American business abroad. And Hoover pressed for disarmament just at a time when nations were beginning the scramble for rearmament. But whatever the difficulties in Hoover's foreign policy, Europeans by and large welcomed the change from Coolidge, who in a 1928 Armistice Day address had shown a contemptuous misunderstanding of Europe—an "apple of discord" thrown abroad on the tenth anniversary of the Armistice.

Hoover was especially interested in extending a friendly hand to the Latin American republics, where a certain restiveness had arisen in response to the United States' increasing economic involvement and persisting political interference. His basic orientation in this area was not entirely new, but rather an extension and elaboration of the policy that had been developing throughout the 1920's during the Harding and Coolidge administrations.

At a meeting of the Pan American Union in Havana in 1928, for example, the Latin nations called for a formal undertaking that "no state may intervene in the internal affairs of another." This implied condemnation of United States policy in the Caribbean prompted the chief American delegate, Charles Evans Hughes, to defend intervention lamely as "simply a wish for peace and order and stability." In 1926 Hoover had spoken out in the cabinet against meddling in Nicaragua and Mexico, and the following year he had attacked "dollar diplomacy," arguing that no country should advance loans to another except for "productive enterprise." He did not believe that United States citizens in Latin America should have their government's military protection, and he saw no merit in the rationale that the Caribbean must be a preserve of the United States for the protection of the Panama Canal route. The Good Neighbor policy, especially for Hoover, had its economic side in an era of rising anti-Yanqui sentiment but not a distinctly imperialistic one. Trade promoted both pacific relations and mutual prosperity. International air travel, as well as exchanges of students and teachers, would be good components of hemispheric friendship and Pan-Americanism.[2]

Soon after his election Hoover, anxious to avoid insistent office seekers and armed with trade analyses, journeyed to a number of Latin American capitals. His party included an official State Department representative assigned by President Coolidge. The seven-week trip took Hoover to Honduras, El Salvador, Nicaragua, Costa Rica, Ecuador, Peru, Chile,

Argentina, Uruguay, and Brazil. He avoided countries such as Panama, where relations were strained. In his first speech, at Amapala, Honduras, he gave a Quaker interpretation of a good neighbor: "In our daily life, good neighbors call upon each other as the evidence of solicitude for the common welfare and to learn of the circumstances and point of view of each that there may come both understanding and respect. . . . This should be equally true among nations." Hoover criticized kindhearted but intolerant people who judged every community by their own. He preferred that Latin American countries "work out their own salvation even with more or less disorder and a substitute loss in the efficiency of their government." In Nicaragua, he successfully brought together the outgoing president, reluctant to leave office, and the incoming one. The Tacna-Arica boundary dispute with Peru (the Alsace-Lorraine conflict of South America) was responsible for a cool reception for Hoover in Chile. He was to take credit for disinterestedly solving the quarrel in 1929, although Secretary of State Kellogg had laid the groundwork for this. Both incidents demonstrated talents for mediation rather than interference. In Argentina, where political leaders had often condemned North American arrogance and where British influence was strong, Hoover repudiated the notion of his own country as a "big brother" to the younger republics of the south. He told President Hipólito Irigoyen that the United States would "abstain from further intervention in the internal affairs of Latin America," and announced that all United States occupation forces would be withdrawn from Nicaragua and Haiti. The trip was not an unmitigated success: Hoover was booed in Buenos Aires and drew only scanty crowds in Chile. Some Latin Americans, observed a British consul, regarded him mainly as a commercial traveler. Another Britisher wrote to Neville Chamberlain: "it will take years of patient work, tact, sympathy, and a thorough knowledge of the people before the fear, suspicion, and dislike" would be eradicated. He "has gone to meet Latin Americans halfway, he has made a gesture of friendly sympathy, and he has gone to see conditions for himself." In his inaugural address Hoover reaffirmed this Good Neighbor policy.[3]

An almost immediate test of Hoover's intentions and a foretaste of difficulties inherent in them came in Mexico, where the constitutional government was threatened by revolt from a group backed by the country's banks—the "real conservatives," as Lewis Strauss described them. The President chose a policy of denying arms to the rebels and supplying them to the government, a policy at once neutral and interventionist. *The New Republic* approved. But "stay out of Mexican politics as much as possible," Hoover advised in a memorandum to the State Department. When trouble broke out in Cuba, he did not interfere. He did continue United States intervention in Nicaragua, at first withdrawing only a third of the Marines who had been stationed there since the Wilson administration. But near the end of his term the remainder departed on schedule, despite the victory in the Nicaraguan election of a candidate hostile to the United States. In 1930, after a series of political upheavals in Latin America, Hoover and Stimson had modified the Wilsonian policy of sitting in judgment on American régimes. If the new governments would promise to hold elections "in due course" and to honor international agreements, a spokesman explained, they would win recognition.[4]

The shift in Latin American policy was particularly marked in Haiti. Protest strikes and student demonstrations against the United States occupation culminated late in 1929 with an attack upon the Marine base at Cayes. Hoover disliked the Marine Corps (a feeling returned by its leaders), and he did not want the country to be represented abroad by them. So he asked Congress for immediate authorization to appoint a commission of inquiry into the future of United States–Haitian relations. (The Salt Lake City *Tribune* indulged in some crude ridicule: "Voodoo . . . beckons investigators . . . down to the land of mumbo-jumbo.") W. Cameron Forbes headed the group, which included newspapermen James Kerney of the Trenton *Times* and William Allen White. Overruling local military administrators, the commissioners allowed Haitians to hold a parade protesting the occupation. At their suggestion the impending presidential elections were placed in native hands, and a candidate neutral toward the United States was elected. A civilian replaced the military director on the island. Reporting in March 1930, the Forbes Commission commended sanitation and road-building projects but criticized the United States' racism and its policy of taking advance payment for debts rather than developing the economy or broadening education. The commissioners also wanted occupation to terminate in six years. Until that time, however, the United States would have to retain control over customs to ensure the repayment of foreign debts. If serious disturbances broke out, officials in Washington might reconsider withdrawal. Hoover also sent an all-black commission headed by Tuskegee's Robert Moton, who urged that Haitians forgo attempts to emulate whites, and instead make their own special contributions. *The New Republic* observed that the Forbes Commission had done "a difficult job and had done it well." Hoover, who wanted "to withdraw from Haiti bag and baggage, immediately if possible," said that the report, which he perceived as being in favor of returning the government of Haiti to its own people, would become the administration's settled policy. Late in 1931 the Haitian government took over control of most domestic matters except finances and the military. Delaying tactics on the part of the Haitian assembly in 1932 held up final withdrawal until 1934.[5]

Hoover hoped to pare back United States entanglements in the Caribbean still further. His administration repudiated the Roosevelt corollary to the Monroe Doctrine, the "Big Stick" which justified intervention in the Caribbean in the event of "chronic wrongdoing." For a research document commissioned in 1928, J. Reuben Clark, Jr., of the State Department had written a detailed covering letter rejecting the principle. Henry Stimson in 1930 declared the Clark statement settled policy and published it. When Panama had a brief revolution and when El Salvador defaulted on its bonds, there was no response from the administration. Hoover claims credit in his *Memoirs* for the repudiation, but the Stimson diary at one point notes that the President, out of fear of alienating Congress at a time of conflict over executive independence, did not wish the Clark memorandum widely publicized. And the State Department papers contain a letter to one correspondent indicating that the repudiation represented Clark's private view only. The historian Robert Ferrell shows that the hesitancy to acknowledge the Clark memorandum extended into Franklin Roosevelt's administration.[6]

This reluctance may have had something to do with a more general desire, especially on the part of Stimson, not to give up entirely the concept that the country had a large political interest in Latin America. Stimson resented European delvings into affairs south of the United States' borders, and Hoover and Assistant Secretary of State William Castle wanted to take British territories there in settlement of debt questions. The President wished to use British Honduras—where the United Fruit Company's shady dealings had drawn a denunciation from Stimson—as a pawn against Mexico. Hoover also imposed an embargo on arms shipments to Latin American revolutionaries, only to reverse his stand, and then shift back once again to his original position against all deliveries. Similarly, he seemed ready to threaten Liberia when Harvey Firestone's interests there became endangered. The Hawley-Smoot Tariff contradicted the Good Neighbor policy, and in the Virgin Islands Hoover grumbled about the "effective poorhouse" in St. Thomas and labeled the purchase a poor bargain.[7]

This hesitation emerged elsewhere, especially over the issue of Philippine independence in 1932. Not wishing "to be the only imperialist" or to encourage plans for naval expansion, Hoover had advocated freedom for the island archipelago; but Stimson, with his long experience in the Philippines, and Patrick Hurley opposed the idea on strategic grounds. Hurley worried about Japanese expansion, already manifest in Manchuria, and warned that British leaders might enlarge the Royal Navy in the event that the Philippines went unguarded. Stimson argued for a commonwealth status. Congress—as well as American business—had its own opinion: the legislators passed the Hare-Hawes-Cutting Bill, which provided for independence in ten years. Hoover vetoed the measure, citing America's "responsibility" for the islands, but Congress overrode the President. Then the Filipinos themselves rejected the idea. Many in their legislature feared that independence might rob the islanders of a lucrative, protected market for sugar in the United States. Critics of American policy thought Washington had contrived this outcome. Fully aware of Filipino concerns, Congress did not make those economic concessions necessary to ensure Philippine prosperity. Hoover himself was worried about a foreign policy that uneasily married imperialist substance to liberal pretension.[8]

The President's only large concern in relations with Canada was the furtherance of the St. Lawrence Seaway. Canadians, however, feared economic disruption from the Hawley-Smoot Tariff. Colonel Hanford Mac-Nider, a Republican businessman who had lacked any special qualifications for diplomacy, made an able representative. But a badly managed meeting took place between Hoover and Prime Minister R. B. Bennett in Washington during 1931. Hoover was annoyed that action had not been taken on the Seaway, and his insistence—together with the rudeness of the press—annoyed Bennett. Only the most persistent pressure from Hoover brought Bennett and his somewhat anti-American Conservative Party to support the Seaway in 1932.[9]

Disarmament was another of Hoover's important goals. As early as May 1921 he had written to President Harding, "There is nothing that would give such hope of recovery in life and living as to have this terrible burden and menace taken from the minds and backs of men." As Secretary of Commerce he had opposed loans for military purposes to foreign governments. During his Armistice Day speech in 1929, he emphasized a need for disarmament. "Levels of naval strength," he said, "could not be too low"—a reference to his hopes for a reduction in arms, not just a limit on future stockpiling. Hoover repeatedly proposed United States membership in the World Court and implementation of the Kellogg-Briand Peace Pact. Court membership he described as a realizable goal, as against the "chimerical" one of joining the League. In 1923, as Commerce Secretary, he had called for joining the Court. Before Stimson's arrival in Washington, Hoover had asked Elihu Root to go to Europe to see if certain modifications were acceptable so that the United States might join. Root was partially successful and Hoover awaited a politically opportune moment; but the Senate clearly opposed membership and, though the President persistently recommended passage, it never came to a vote. A believer in mediating disputes through peaceful processes, Hoover went ahead with systematic cooperation with the League of Nations in most of its non-political functions: global radio and airway codes, naval safety, the eradication of slavery, and surveillance against narcotics smuggling and counterfeiting. He thought that international cooperation—for various reasons he seldom used Wilson's words "collective security"—could prevent war and, more important, create a world economy so interdependent that the impetus toward conflict would disappear. A peaceful world would be a profitable one for Americans and for everyone else; disarmament also would free vast sums of capital for more productive investment. Governments could balance their budgets, and western European nations could more easily pay reparations and war debts.[10]

As a first step, Hoover wanted to make the London Naval Conference of 1930 a great success through cooperation with the British. This sequel to the Washington gathering in 1922, however, seemed unlikely to enlarge upon that earlier achievement, which had stabilized the arms race in the Pacific Ocean. The Japanese, particularly militaristic, were unhappy with existing arrangements, for the various treaties had virtually imposed a second-class status upon them. Hoover believed that a strong Anglo-American front might overawe the Tokyo leaders, so he sent Edward Price Bell, a reporter from the Chicago *Daily News,* to Britain on a quasi-diplomatic mission. After some preliminary talks uncovered much interest in Anglo-American cooperation, Bell suggested that Prime Minister Ramsay Mac-Donald visit the United States. Hoping that with Yankee support England might still impress the world, MacDonald asked to come; the trip, the first of a British Prime Minister to the United States, might also serve to bolster his own precarious position at home. That summer, after Congress passed an ominously heavy cruiser construction bill, MacDonald navigated the principle of naval parity through the British cabinet—a major concession for the British, virtually a surrender of their naval supremacy, and much in line with MacDonald's views. In early October 1929, he came to Washington and told the Senate that parity "was the only condition under which competitive armaments could be stopped . . . we would create a public psychology which could pursue the fruitful and successful avenues of peaceful cooperation." He then met with Hoover at the President's Rapidan River camp in the Blue Ridge Mountains of Virginia, the site—exactly 100 miles from the White House—that Hoover often used to bring others around to his own views. On a bright Sunday morning the two men strolled past crimson sumac and mountain pools splashing with trout; then they sat down on a log near a waterfall to chat and thresh out their differences. Although they accomplished little of a technical nature, their evident cordiality, along with the jubilant reception given the friendly MacDonald by Americans, went far to dissolve the Anglophobia that dated back to colonial times.* The meeting, a "diplomatic triumph," marked a high point in the political careers of both men. They spent much time discussing a plan for solving international disputes that relied mostly upon the force of public opinion. Conflicting parties, they thought, might choose arbiters who, if they reached no agreement, would publish the details of the dispute (although Hoover resisted Stimson's plan for compulsory arbitration). The Quaker President and pacifist Prime Minister expected that reason and public pressure together would move the disputants toward peaceful settlement. Such were the hopes of statesmen before the violent decades of the mid-century.[11]

Any disarmament agreement, whatever its scope, faced two major technical hurdles: no one really knew how to disarm or what to disarm. Hoover spoke, logically enough, of abolishing "offensive" weapons while permitting "defensive" armament. Military men claimed not to understand the distinction; the airplane and the tank, for example, could be used effectively for either purpose. Moreover, intensive training and technical polish might to an important degree substitute for weapons, yet morale and skill could hardly be measured at all. Sea powers wished land powers to reduce armies; land powers urged sea powers to limit navies. Imperialist countries and victors of World War I wanted everyone to arm up to a certain point; colonial peoples and defeated nations wanted everyone to disarm to their level. Pressure groups—often a predictable assortment of military men, super-patriots, and munitions manufacturers—propagandized against the whole idea. In America, Hoover's hopes for disarmament faced opposition from the Navy League. One of its publicists, William B. Shearer, had already undermined the abortive Conference at Geneva in 1927 by entertaining lavishly, spreading rumors, and, some thought, bribing congressmen. Shearer's dossier was on file with Scotland Yard, the Sûreté Général, and the Department of Justice. The French had asked for his extradition from England on charges of jewel robbery. News of Shearer's shenanigans broke during August 1929, and Hoover shrewdly asked Congress for a complete investigation when he divulged that Shearer's navy views were connected with his retainer by munitions firms as a paid agent. "It may be a useful public example," he wrote Stimson, "and

---

* A dinner held for MacDonald was the occasion, not for the first time, of an unseemly dispute over the seating of bachelor Vice-President Charles Curtis' sister, Dolly Gann—something of a continuing problem in the social life of Washington. William Allen White's Emporia *Gazette* observed that "if Washington does not do right by our Dolly, there will be a terrible ruckus in Kansas. We will be satisfied with nothing less than that she be borne into the dinner on the shoulders of Mrs. Nick Longworth, seated in the center of the table as an ornament with a candelabra in each hand and fed her soup with a long-handled spoon by the wife of the Secretary of State." Dolly made numerous campaign speeches for Hoover in 1932, insisting that the Depression was "over."

one that we will need before we are finished." Hoover realized that publicity, which quickly discredited the Big Navy lobby, could generate support for the London Conference. The Dallas *News* praised his "Roosevelt-like directness," and *The Nation* commended his "adroit attack" on the Shearer propaganda.[12]

Hoover believed that any conference had to be a show where diplomats ratified agreements already reached, not an arena where disputes were aggravated by displaying them to the world. The MacDonald meeting illustrated this strategy. The President's idea of a "yardstick of fighting strength," which probably worked to the United States' advantage, aimed at solving the dilemma of specific procedure. He thought that by taking into account the age, speed, size, and quality of armaments—not just measuring raw tonnage—it would be possible to establish the comparative quality of naval fighting strength. Several European countries expressed interest in this highly detailed and technical "yardstick" idea, but critics wondered aloud about its practicality. The press published various technical reports that hindered Hoover's efforts, and he requested prominent newsmen to put "patriotism over professionalism" and stop divulging information.[13]

The Naval Disarmament Conference met early in 1930. Stimson headed the delegation, a distinguished group which included Senators Robinson and David Reed, Ambassadors Dawes, Gibson, and Dwight Morrow, and Charles Francis Adams, Jr. For three months the Americans, fearful of Britain and overanxious to protect their naval power, burdened the meeting with maritime details and complicated proposals for safeguards. Other delegations were no better. In this atmosphere, comprehensive agreements were hard won. After respective agreements not to fortify the Philippines and to abrogate the Anglo-Japanese alliance, the United States did achieve parity with Great Britain, but Japan did not—the Asian power was authorized to build only seven destroyers for every ten allotted to America and England. The result in Japan was the eventual triumph of militarist factions. The final treaty also scrapped some armaments and pared building plans for the future. The President, for example, accepted fifteen cruisers instead of the twenty-five desired by the Navy Department. The naval armaments race in capital ships was halted until 1935. Hoover had sought a five-power treaty for naval reduction and instead obtained only a three-power treaty for limitations on the largest vessels, with Italy and France joining in on other compromises. The Paris government would not join in the proposed larger agreement without a military defense pact with the British; France was also irritated over not receiving treatment as a "first-class" power, which it was. The President did succeed in limiting the size of aircraft carriers and preventing the general abolition of the battleship, considered essential for American

would lead to a war the United States could win only in many years. Throughout the Manchurian crisis Hoover—and to a somewhat lesser degree Stimson (they were not so very different)—remained more solicitous of Japan's sensitive feelings than did leaders in Europe. The Depression so dominated the Western world that it diminished everything else by comparison; otherwise stronger action would have been taken against Japan. But as Senator Simeon Fess wrote to his son: "It is unthinkable under the present economic situation that great nations would be involved in another war."[19]

As the troubles of depression became of increasing concern to Hoover, he came to believe that many of America's problems originated abroad. For a time he and Stimson conducted what they obliquely called the "Russian investigation," on whether to increase trade with Russia. Hoover had privately advocated such an increase, as did most of his cabinet, including Secretaries Mellon and Lamont. (The President even hinted privately at recognition, but he and Stimson backed away from this anti-Japanese move in 1931. Still, such trade was higher during his administration than in Roosevelt's.) One reason, also, why Hoover had called a special session of Congress in 1929 was to dispose of the lingering, complicated question of higher tariffs. He opposed a general rise in rates, recommending instead specific readjustments for those industries in which "insurmountable competition" had caused "a substantial slackening of activity." Customs should equalize, or offset, rising costs in the United States or falling costs abroad. Only for agricultural products did he favor across-the-board increases. Both political parties had embraced higher tariffs during the 1928 campaign, and a host of special interests worked on Congress. Logrolling on Capitol Hill quickly generated huge boosts in many duties, all part of the Smoot-Hawley Bill. The famous appeal of a thousand economists protesting these unprecedented rates that appears in almost every American history textbook addressed itself both to Congress and to the President. Protectionists argued that cheap imports would threaten American industry as it struggled to keep up wages, a sound enough argument by itself. Critics, though, pointed to the danger of foreign reprisals and the injury American barriers could do to the world economy.[20]

Hoover himself staked his reputation on a strengthened tariff commission which, with executive approval, could raise or lower rates by up to 50 percent. (The idea was similar to a plank in the Roosevelt Progressive party platform of 1912.) Such a commission would enlist experts and operate scientifically, adjusting duties to changes in world prices. Dairy and wheat farmers during the 1920's had benefited from the work of a weaker version of the agency already in operation. Senator Borah objected, believing that the commission could diminish the authority of Congress.

"No provision for flexible tariff," the President told Republican leaders, "then no tariff bill." It was a dangerous tactic, since it could have scared Congress into demanding higher rates. But exactly the flexible provision he wanted was adopted in conference. "A Progressive advance," he called it, that "gives great hope of taking the tariff away from politics, lobbying, and log rolling." It would work, so he hoped, as the Interstate Commerce Commission's control of railroad rates had neutralized that issue. He would appoint Henry P. Fletcher, former ambassador to Italy, as chairman of the new commission. Edward Clark, Coolidge's secretary, said "those who know Fletcher best laugh at the idea of his doing any hard concentrated work."[21]

The Smoot-Hawley Bill embarrassed the President in some respects. Ten years before, Hoover had told the American Bankers Association that high tariffs were anachronistic. He had seriously considered running on the low-tariff Democratic ticket that year. But in 1928 at Boston he had reasoned: "The tariff can affect but a small percentage of the buying power of foreign countries. . . . It probably increases imports because by increasing our domestic prosperity it enables us to buy far more raw materials." Although he signed Smoot-Hawley in the spring of 1930, he was angered by its high schedules, which embodied a deal, adopted over his protest, between agricultural and industrial forces in the Senate. "Nothing would contribute to retard business recovery more," he wrote, "than this continued agitation." Hoover wanted Congress to turn to other legislative matters; the special session had adjourned the previous November 22. He realized that high rates, even only 35 percent of imports, could cause reprisals elsewhere—some forty-four countries had already adopted protective rates in recent years—and he termed the matter one of "extreme difficulty." Thomas Lamont of J. P. Morgan recalled: "I almost went down on my knees to beg Herbert Hoover to veto the asinine Hawley-Smoot Tariff. That Act intensified nationalism all over the world."[22]

In the election year 1932 Hoover justified his signature with labored argument. Declining much more sharply than American prices, the cost of foreign articles endangered American wage rates, he observed. Worldwide agricultural depression compelled a tariff act in which 94 percent of the increases by value occurred on agricultural goods. Hoover claimed that the provision for flexibility, invoked during the intervening months on 291 articles, had led to about twice as many decreases as increases. But Julius Barnes, who had defended the tariff at an international meeting in Amsterdam, admitted that the sparseness of the decreases was a failure for the commission. The figuring of costs on domestic production proved to be enormously complicated and often required rather arbitrary judgments. "As a practical matter," Assistant Attorney General John Lord O'Brian later wrote, "it was a complete wash-out! Nobody short of Omniscience can tell what it would cost to produce a thing here and abroad. The chief competing country was changing all the time." Hoover repeatedly stated that since trade was now "polyangular" among many nations, the tariff hurt no one very much. High tariffs would not hurt sales abroad because "foreign trade was no longer a direct barter between one single nation and another. World trade had become more a common pool, into which all nations pour goods or credit and from which they retake goods or credit." To proposals for reciprocal tariffs, Hoover objected that most nations wanted only the United States agricultural rates lowered and that favored treatment led to trade wars. In 1932 he vetoed a bill to give Congress, rather than the executive, the power to accept and enforce recommendations of the tariff commission.[23]

Before the Depression worsened, Hoover held openly to the position, which Congress and the public shared, that war debts should be paid. In 1928 he said: "the increase in our tourist expenditure alone in Europe since the war would enable them to take care of the entire amount. . . . The increase in our imported goods alone since 1922 could pay the whole amount three times over." He considered repayment a fair exchange for American deaths and high taxes during the war and for America's legacy of inflation and social problems. One recent scholar has noted that during the 1920's the United States "was far from being a merciless creditor and, on the question of war debts, was more accommodating than France." (That country—the only great power that wanted the peace settlement preserved largely intact—had no desire to release Germany from reparations, since they were a means of keeping it subjugated.) The World War Foreign Debts Commission was composed of moderates, including Hoover, who dealt realistically with the situation during the twenties. Inter-Allied debts, Hoover thought, should be collected; but a wise creditor must take into account the economic condition of its debtors. Like most Americans, though, he insisted that repayment of western Europe's war debts not be linked to the receipt of German reparations by the Allies. The Young Plan of 1929 had revised debts downward, but the Hoover administration ignored the extremely difficult problem of transferring these non-productive payments from country to country, especially in light of America's rising tariffs. Then, too, the whole postwar credit structure, both private and intergovernmental, depended upon continuing growth and prosperity.[24]

The onset of world depression necessarily altered Hoover's views. Debtors in central Europe, like those in South America and parts of Africa, could no longer sell enough manufactured goods or raw materials abroad to repay their private loans to banks in Great Britain and the United States. At the same time, investors withdrew more and more money from foreign countries, often by the simple expedient of not renewing loans as they fell due, and sought a safe haven for their funds in nations securely on the gold standard. This dual pressure soon forced central Europe toward financial collapse. By early 1931 Hoover was considering forms of debt cancellation, according to the Stimson diary. His main fear was that monies saved would go into armaments.

The year 1931, "that terrible year," as Arnold Toynbee has dubbed it, ended an era in Europe. During May the directors of the Credit-Anstalt, the largest bank in Austria, admitted that their bank could no longer repay its debts; liabilities exceeded paid-in capital by some six times. The dimensions of the failure defied all rescue efforts, even those by the Bank of England and the Austrian government itself. Fears of insolvency spread rapidly throughout central and eastern Europe; brokers everywhere pulled out their clients' investments in manufacturing firms, banks, and public works. Panic threatened Germany in particular. As debtors ever since World War I, the Germans had borrowed money at high rates for the short term to invest in long-term reconstruction. (Though sometimes characterized as "malfeasance," such risk-taking is one purpose of finance.) Now investors would not renew their loans, yet the Germans could not repay them, since depression had severely reduced profits from trade. The only alternative, it seemed, was default—a default so massive that it would tie up billions and billions of British pounds and American dollars in uncollectible loans. Even the strongest financial structures could not withstand such strains.[25]

Hoover acted. He heard from Frederick M. Sackett, the American ambassador to Germany, that the country was teetering near collapse. As early as the previous December Sackett had relayed to Hoover a German desire for an international economic conference. A group of South American republics was on the verge of agreement to default on all external obligations. New York bankers like Chase National—fearful of sacrificing private as well as governmental loans—pressed Hoover to grasp the only alternative to hundreds of bank failures at home: moratorium. While his *Memoirs* tell another story, Hoover knew that Americans held perhaps $10 billion in foreign loans, chiefly short-term. Taking some liberties with the Constitution—Congress alone controlled debt policy— in order to prevent a financial collapse in Europe that could easily confound American finance as well, Hoover on June 20, 1931, proposed a one-year moratorium on all intergovernmental payments, war debts, and reparations. Presumably this would free enough money to repay private investors. (The Europeans had asked for a two-year respite, and Hoover's plan in effect delayed payments until December 1932.) Hoover admitted privately that world depression had nullified earlier settlements, including his own insistence on separating debts and reparations. The proposal was the kind of psychological tonic the public needed. Its directness was especially praised, for the moratorium avoided the entanglements of painstaking diplomacy. Its boldness also gave hope for future leadership. The danger that Germans and Austrians would default on their private obligations disappeared for the moment. In fact, London and New York bankers organized large new loans to finance old ones as they fell due. There was considerable opposition in Congress; John Nance Garner regarded the moratorium as tantamount to cancellation, and minority leader Robinson offered his support only in return for tariff revision. But thirty-nine senators wired pledges of support to Hoover, and when Congress convened in December the legislators gave formal and overwhelming approval to his *fait accompli*. Though Hoover himself had taken weeks to come to his dramatic decision, the moratorium averted panic. The downward spiral of trade and prices had ceased.[26]

Hoover kept a journal of events from May 6 to July 22, 1931, beginning with the arrival in Washington of Ambassador Sackett, who warned that the German financial structure would soon collapse. On May 19 the President showed Stimson part of a speech he proposed to make, "indicating that our debt had been settled on the basis of capacity to pay in normal times; that the American people would not wish to extort more than the capacity of these nations to pay by virtue of the world-wide depression . . . and opposing cancellation." The passage was stricken from the speech, but the message was delivered to Germany "that the whole reparations and debt complex could well be reviewed in the light of capacity to pay under depression conditions." On June 5 he proposed the moratorium. Stimson approved, Mellon dissented; Mills worried over the lack of executive authority to act. A banker's panic resulting from the German minister's visit to London finally brought the official announcement.[27]

France blunted the force of the Hoover moratorium. Offended that they had not been consulted—senators whom Hoover had felt obliged to confer with had been first to leak the news to the press—and fearful that an Anglo-American alliance was forgiving Germany its debts, the French leaders delayed their assent to the proposal for three weeks, which weakened its effects on the international economy. The French had some reason for anger. As the principal recipient of reparations, they feared that any moratorium might break Germany's will to resume payments in the future. (Postwar governments had issued billions in reconstruction bonds secured only by future reparation receipts.) Hoover told Thomas Lamont on June 29: "We are all fed up with the French. They have placed every obstacle in the way of the agreement. [Their] conditions . . . have been multifarious and all of them objectionable." "Our French friends," Hoover remarked again, "need to get a stronger taste of Depression." But he made as many as ten phone calls a day to Paris, London, and Berlin— Congress insisted that he personally pay the bill—to meet French objections. And Secretary of the Treasury Mellon, now seventy-seven years old, displayed his stamina in day-long sessions on the Paris embassy's phone, located in the concierge's room in the basement. The French formally signed an agreement on July 6. The United States also arranged for conferences that were to formalize those financial technicalities required by moratorium and at the same time to "smooth out the differences between Germany and France which make practically impossible any solution of the present difficulties." The result was a "standstill agreement" to delay presentment of short-term bills against Germany until February 1932. The Franco-German animosity remained.[28]

Hoover's efforts on behalf of moratorium and the standstill agreement, as Senator Borah remarked, could be of lasting value only if the time were well used. Statesmen in Britain and the United States backed away from any direct government stimulants for the economy, arguing that deficit finance would only draft money from the private sector. Some economists, among them John Maynard Keynes, challenged such assumptions, but most contemporary experts agreed with them. By late 1931 Secretary Mills thought the world situation little improved; more trade barriers had been erected, and unemployment grew and grew.

Many nations edged toward experiments with the gold standard. If a country depreciated its currency (that is, reduced its value in terms of gold), foreigners could buy its manufactured goods for less. Domestic industries would revive to meet this anticipated increase in overseas demand. The nation's balance of trade would improve, and investment capital would flow into the country to take advantage of returning prosperity. Trading nations early became attracted to this solution for depression, while creditors—those countries with large overseas investments—shied away from depreciation. If Great Britain or the United States devalued the pound or dollar, their debtors could repay debts with "cheaper" currency having less purchasing power. Some nations, like England, were both lenders and traders.

The pound sterling, that synonym for financial probity, was taken off the gold standard by a Labor government cornered in a banking panic during September 1931. The Hoover moratorium and the various standstill agreements had trapped millions of pounds in central Europe; many bankers worried that Britain might be unable to repay its debts without those assets. Anxious to avoid possible default, investors did not extend

new loans; instead, they demanded full payment in pounds and then converted them into other currencies, principally the French franc or the
American dollar. Currency speculators joined the mêlée: by selling pounds
now, in anticipation of devaluation, then buying them back later after
devaluation, shrewd operators could make huge profits. The Bank of
England did not possess enough gold to repay foreign loans and freely to
convert its currency. American and French bankers lent their counterparts
in London and the British government several hundred million dollars'
worth of gold. But the drain continued, especially after newspapers head-
lined a job protest in the British fleet as a "mutiny" at Invergordon. Events
moved too rapidly for Hoover, or anyone else, to influence. The British
left the gold standard on September 21, 1931, their pound depreciating
quickly on currency markets.

This startling chain of events shocked Hoover, who was inclined to
cancel the war debts had Britain remained on the gold standard. Now British industry could compete more favorably with American industry for
world markets; depression must worsen in the United States. Bankers in
New York, particularly at the Federal Reserve Bank there, worried him
with reports of a potential "raid on the dollar." Speculators had made huge
profits from the British devaluation. Now, apparently, they were attacking
the dollar, exchanging it for other currencies or demanding gold. Hoover
strongly opposed leaving the gold standard or "fiddling with the dollar."
The country's huge overseas investments could be repaid in cheaper dollars
and, he thought, depreciation would destroy whatever remained of business
confidence. No one would lend money if there was the likelihood that
repayment in the future would be with less valuable dollars. So Hoover
began again, this time not with a well-publicized effort to halt panic in
central Europe but with a quiet, almost unnoticed effort to stave off a
raid against the dollar itself.

He turned to the French, now the great source of financial stability. The
Bank of France held huge gold reserves, and Frenchmen had borrowed
little from abroad. The franc, as a result, was the strongest currency in the
world. Because of large population losses during the war and its own
remarkable self-sufficiency, the French economy was not much damaged
by depression. A financial alliance between the French and the Americans
could stop speculative attacks against the world's currencies, reassure investors everywhere, and perhaps force England to return to the gold
standard. Leaders in France quickly responded to Hoover's discreet inquiries; indeed, Premier Pierre Laval asked to visit the United States. Publicly, the conference was to improve relations between the two countries
strained by Hoover's precipitous announcement of his moratorium earlier

in the year and by Laval's jealousy of MacDonald's visit in 1929. Privately, the French thought their financial power might buy major political concessions.

Laval outlined the French hopes in his meetings with Hoover during October 1931. He admitted that the moratorium had proved itself a practical idea. He wanted to preserve the Young Plan. But he preferred the United States to link debts and reparations. After all, the moratorium itself had done exactly that in referring to "intergovernmental debts." He also desired a collective security pact, a ten-year moratorium on changes in political boundaries in western Europe. This, he claimed, would ease tensions along the Rhine (or at least divert Germany eastward, away from French borders). Hoover told Laval that neither he nor Congress would accept a boundary moratorium. But the two agreed to remain on the gold standard; quite secret talks and complicated maneuvers went on between central bankers in New York and Paris to defend the dollar. Further decisions about war debts and reparations, they both agreed, must be made before the moratorium ran out. Laval interpreted as a bargain, or at least a gentleman's agreement, what Hoover had merely thrown out as a possibility: that the United States would cancel war debts if Europe canceled reparations. Hoover preferred mutual reductions.[29]

The United States survived the raid against its currency during the winter of 1931–2; speculators stopped selling paper dollars, and the drain of gold out of the country slackened, then reversed. European nations, after much preliminary jockeying, finally met during the summer of 1932 at Lausanne and largely canceled German reparations. They all clearly thought, or hoped, that the United States in turn would reduce their debt payments. But cancellation, unpopular in America, might further weaken Hoover's chances for reelection, so the President wrote a public letter to Senator Borah strongly disavowing any connection between war debts and reparations. Earlier he had pressured Congress unsuccessfully to extend the moratorium, or, as Stimson put it, to reach "a complete and final settlement" of the reparations and debt question. However much European leaders may have felt Hoover had reneged, they said little in public. The Democrats, that more internationalist party of Wilson, they thought, must soon recapture the presidency. So they waited.[30]

Hoover did not. Buoyed by his year of active diplomacy and his own restless need for work, the President concocted another scheme for recovery, one that might conceivably rescue his dimming electoral chances: a grand international conference to cooperate on measures to restore prosperity. Plans for a world meeting began to take shape in early spring 1932, and by midsummer Britain, France, and the United States had agreed on its preliminaries. War debts were excluded from the agenda upon

Hoover's request, but the diplomats hoped for projects to halt the upward spiral of tariffs, stabilize national currencies, organize joint marketing plans, and, perhaps, launch worldwide public works. Every nation sought its own parochial advantage, of course. Great Britain wanted to consolidate the gains made from its depreciated pound; France aimed at restoring the gold standard; and the United States and Germany, the two large countries hardest hit by depression, yearned for recovery from whatever source. Yet the complexity of the issues delayed action.[31]

What general principles were deduced by the administration from the Kellogg peace pact were in fact supplemented by earlier dogmas or undertakings: the Monroe Doctrine, the Open Door, the Nine Power treaty, the Senate's rejection of the Versailles Treaty. Old prejudices had still to be reckoned with. And as the presidential campaign took shape, more and more foreigners wondered whether Hoover could survive the challenge of Franklin D. Roosevelt and the Democratic party, both made politically strong by the nation's economic weakness.

XIV

~~~~~~

THE BONUS ARMY
AND AFTER

BY 1932 many Americans believed their country to be crumbling fast. Brigadier General George Van Horn Moseley, deputy to Chief of Staff Douglas MacArthur, and a trusted confidant of Secretary of War Hurley and other prominent military figures, wanted something done.

Disturbed by what he perceived as Hoover's pacifist tendencies and inadequate leadership, General Moseley on May 24, 1932, wrote the journalist Herbert Corey—at least one other copy went out, to Charles Dawes—about how improvident and unready for emergencies Americans were. The numbers of "drifters, dope fiends, unfortunates and degenerates of all kinds" were growing. Without naming them, Moseley cited the testimony of a prominent senator who called for a dictatorship and a New York minister who suggested "military reinforcement" for civilian rule. Moseley recommended as a model the Spanish-American war experience in the Philippines. There the military had "ample authority" and "utter simplicity in government," free of a "multiplicity of laws, intricate procedures . . . weak . . . officials . . . [who] complicated the administration of justice." The military could simply ship undesirables "beyond the seas." He urged that a similar power be invested in government to

gather up the leading malefactors [including] important public officials when circumstances required and send them, let me suggest, to one of the sparsely inhabited islands of the Hawaiian group not suitable for growing sugar. On such an island, in a fine climate, they could stew in their own filth until their cases were finally disposed of with the return of normal conditions. We would not worry about the delays in the due process of law. . . . With carefully selected military governors installed in all our states and the District of Columbia, great economies could also be effected, for graft could be eliminated. . . . The return to normal conditions . . . might be on a competitive basis. . . .

Whether Moseley's letter came to Hoover's attention is not known, but similar calls for a "man on horseback" to set the nation right were familiar enough by the summer of 1932.*[1]

Even at the Republican Convention, held in Chicago from Flag Day, June 14, to the sixteenth, there was a lack of enthusiasm for Hoover's renomination. Progressive Republicans were hostile, the old guard unhappy. Colonel Robert McCormick's Chicago *Tribune,* repelled by Hoover's internationalist tendencies, declared it mandatory that the convention "look elsewhere" for a nominee. Dissident factions had talked of Coolidge and Senator Dwight Morrow of New Jersey, but Morrow had died late in 1931 and Coolidge had little strength. An incumbent President in control of patronage held the renomination for the asking. After a debate that lasted through much of the second night, the prohibition plank straddle won by 681 to 472 votes after 40 percent had voted for unrestricted repeal. Each day of the convention began with a clergyman speaking a prayer at the top of his lungs into a battery of microphones, photographers all the while perched above him on chairs snapping their bulbs. Floodlights for moving pictures threw the scene into an even brighter glare, and dozens of typewriters clicked away, recording the words.

The keynote speech, from Senator Lester Dickinson of Iowa, was addressed to a hall one-third empty; it became much emptier as his speech progressed because loudspeakers garbled "Hell-raising Dick's" words. Though an ardent dry, he omitted all mention of prohibition. Dickinson credited Hoover for speeding up public works projects but criticized the Democrats for recommending additional such ventures. Bertrand Snell, the permanent chairman, thanked God that Hoover had avoided "the deadly pit of the dole."[2]

On the third day "that glorious Californian, Herbert Hoover," was placed in nomination by "Plain Joe" Scott of Los Angeles. Bands struck up "Over There" to recall Belgian relief, and the crowd demonstrated for more than twenty minutes. The display ended with Klieg lights, a blurred recording of Hoover's voice, slides of the President shown at both ends of the auditorium, and the thoughtless playing of "California, here I come, right back where I started from."

Dr. Joseph I. France, a former senator from Maryland, was offered as an alternative nominee; on the convention floor the microphone went dead

* On March 7, 1932, "Bloody Monday," four demonstrators had been killed by police on the outskirts of Detroit—this "Ford Hunger March" set the tone for events later that year.

and he was dragged off when he tried to withdraw in favor of Coolidge. A Hoover seconder, Roscoe Simmons of Chicago, added an unusual endorsement by Abraham Lincoln brought "fresh" from the Lincoln Memorial: "if you see him, speak to Hoover for me and say that his road is the one I traveled." Another seconder, Snell, compared Hoover to Washington because both were engineers. After renominating Hoover by 1,126½ of 1,154 votes on the first and only ballot, the delegates grudgingly chose the bone-dry, seventy-one-year-old Vice-President Curtis as his running mate. Two less colorful candidates could scarcely be imagined. No picture of Hoover graced the convention hall.[3]

The 1932 Hoover campaign staff was considerably different from that of 1928; Jeremiah Milbank, the Wall Street philanthropist, remained in his earlier position, that of Eastern campaign treasurer. Everett Sanders served as the fourth chairman of the national committee under Hoover. Silas Strawn of Chicago was campaign manager for the West and Felix Herbert of Rhode Island managed the East. Old friends George Akerson and Henry J. Allen helped with publicity. The Chicago headquarters reported raising about $2.5 million, slightly more than the Democrats.

Behind the campaign stood a Republican organization with some years of troubles. David Hinshaw's *Washington,* an official Republican newsletter, had died in three strokes. For the first issue, it was disclosed, he had hired a Democratic printer, and then he dwelt at length on Hoover's "handicaps," notably an "inability to talk in the political vernacular." For the second, Hinshaw employed a non-union printer and Hoover ordered that the 5 tons of newsprint be destroyed. The third issue could not overcome the poor publicity generated by the first two. Succeeding the unfortunate Hubert Work as national chairman in 1929, Claudius Huston—once the head of a small business college—had collected large sums of money from sources he could not always recall, disbursing funds to people he could not remember. A Presbyterian and Mason, he had served as chairman of the Republican National Committee's Ways and Means Committee. When it became public knowledge that he had welched on an $80,000 poker debt and illegally used the funds of the lobby, the Tennessee River Improvement Association, to speculate in the stock market, Huston resigned. The next chairman, Senator Simeon Fess, allowed his assistant Robert Lucas to enter another man named George Norris in the Nebraska primary in an unscrupulous effort to unseat the progressive Senator Norris. Edward Sanders, Fess's successor in 1932, presided over a party in disarray.[4]

NOT LONG after the nomination an army of World War I veterans descended on the small Southern city of Washington. At first not much attention had been paid to reports of some three hundred unemployed veterans in Union Pacific freight cars rocking and swaying from Portland, Oregon, to Pocatello, Idaho. Some accompanied by their families, they all were headed for Washington seeking congressional approval for early payment of a soldier's bonus not scheduled for distribution until 1945. But this "Bonus Army" picked up fresh recruits at almost every city in the spring of 1932 and finally became national news when the B & O Railroad tried to stop it at the "Battle of East Saint Louis." Local railroad union leaders averted bloodshed by moving truckloads of men, women, and children across Illinois to the Indiana border. Then state governors hurried the band as swiftly as possible past Indiana, Pennsylvania, and Maryland until it reached the District of Columbia, there to meet other veterans from every state in the Union, a total of more than twenty thousand people.[5]

General Moseley had prepared an order for Hoover to instruct federal troops to turn back the marchers before they entered the District. Secretary Hurley, according to Moseley, endorsed the plan, but "Mr. Hoover declined to execute it, calling it a 'temporary disease.' " Despite the entreaties of prominent Republicans, the President refused to follow the example of Grover Cleveland's administration, which thirty-eight years before had stopped the marchers of Coxey's army with federal injunctions. And once the veterans settled in abandoned buildings and on the largest site, Anacostia Flats in Maryland, Hoover quietly provided the District police commissioner, Pelham Glassford, with clothing, beds, tents, medical supplies, kitchen equipment, and army food free or at cost. Hoover wrote in early June that he expected no disturbance of the peace in Washington: "except for a few New York agitators these are perfectly peaceable people. . . ."[6]

Like Hoover, Governor Franklin D. Roosevelt of New York disapproved early payment of the bonus, and offered his state's veterans both transportation home and guaranteed employment. Congressman LaGuardia and Senator Norris pointed out that many of the veterans were not poor people and deserved no special treatment. All of the President's cabinet opposed the bonus. Hoover had effectively centralized all veterans activities in a new Veterans Administration under Frank T. Hines, and he had generously written or endorsed numerous pension and hospitalization bills for them. The President's disability bill for veterans was a model of generosity. By 1933 veterans' benefits accounted for one-fourth of the national budget. He had, however, made a dramatic trip to Detroit the previous October to give an eleven-minute speech to the American Legion Convention opposing early payment of the bonus and the Legion's idea of reinstituting a Council of National Defense with dictatorial powers. The

Bonus Bill passed the House on June 15, 1932; but two days later the Senate soundly defeated it, 62 to 18. Next, Hoover initiated federal loans for transportation home to any veteran who applied. But some ten thousand stayed on, waiting for something to happen.[7]

On July 9, some 250 Californians arrived, led by a navy veteran, Roy W. Robertson, who camped out with his men on the Capitol lawn. While in the service Robertson had broken his neck falling out of a hammock; he wore a leather brace supported by a tall steel column rising almost a foot above his shoulders, giving the eerie impression of a man with his head perpetually in a noose. For three days and four nights Robertson's men took turns slowly walking single file in a "Death March" vigil around the Capitol building. His head held high in the rigid brace, Robertson was a study in determination. While an angry mob of fellow veterans under Commander Walter W. Waters occupied the building's steps, Congress adjourned and its members escaped by subterranean passageways. Now the focus shifted to 1600 Pennsylvania Avenue. Hoover had earlier ordered guards not to arrest veterans or Communists picketing the White House, and he favored Glassford's policy of restraint. But after the siege of Congress the Secret Service urged the selective arrest of militant leaders, and Hoover went along when small groups of Communists attempted to draw the veterans into a bloody confrontation at the White House.[8]

General Douglas MacArthur stood ready for trouble with a large regular army force under the command of Moseley. MacArthur personally commanded the most impressive display of military might that Washington had seen in many years. On July 28 the administration forced the eviction of veterans from a small downtown area of government buildings scheduled for demolition. A riot ensued between a gathering of as many as five thousand veterans and fewer than eight hundred police. One veteran was dead, another lay dying. The police commissioner, the District of Columbia commissioners informed Hoover, had concurred that army troops were necessary; Glassford later denied having made any such request.[9]

MacArthur ordered his troops to assemble at the Ellipse behind the White House. Hoover specifically directed the general only to move the rioting veterans out of the business district and back to their camps. His staff aide, Major Dwight D. Eisenhower, was shocked when the Chief of Staff, resplendent in full military regalia, appeared personally to take command, although the President had ordered MacArthur to get his instructions from Glassford. Major George Patton was also on hand. Seeing "revolution in the air," MacArthur used cavalrymen with drawn sabers and infantry with tear gas, dispersing both veterans and spectators. After the downtown area was cleared, he stopped at the bridge leading to Anacostia for his men to have dinner. Ignoring the President, who issued contrary orders on at least two occasions, MacArthur and his troops then crossed over and the whole camp became ablaze with light. Setting fire to their own huts was a final symbol of the veterans' defiance. Eisenhower recalled "a pitiful scene, those ragged, discouraged people burning their own little things." Soldiers and District police fired the remaining, often unsanitary, empty huts. Fleeing the capital, the veterans became refugees from an apparently heartless government.[10]

Hoover might have chosen to speak with representatives of the veterans, making an effort to reassure them of his concern. He had been notably restrained and tolerant about Communist demonstrations outside the White House in 1929 and 1931, and in January 1932 had provided army quarters for twelve thousand unemployed workers who came to protest. He met with their leader, Father Cox, at the White House. In 1928 he had even apologized that his *American Individualism,* written just after the war, was "a little out of date as it was written when we were somewhat more exercized over socialistic and communistic movements than we need to be today." Once the bonus marchers had been driven from town, he could have refrained from noisy propaganda about their iniquities. But he did not: and in the meantime the public had the memory of burning shacks within sight of the Capitol steps. The Bonus Army would become one of the most compelling stories of the coming presidential campaign.[11]

The Bonus Army had posed a problem, not only for the government but for veterans in their crowded, unsanitary encampment, that any administration might eventually have responded to with some force. But why Hoover, who did upbraid MacArthur privately, nonetheless let him get away with insubordination we may only surmise. Part of the reason, perhaps, was a fear that firing the general might upset the country further. Personality, too, may have figured. MacArthur, as Moseley pointed out, "was a prima donna and insisted upon occupying the center of the stage; but he was the best performer, and that was the place for him." Hoover, not being one himself, could have had a certain grudging respect for a dramatic man of action. He was impressed that the army operations resulted in no casualties. Both men made much of Communist and criminal elements among the Bonus Army. MacArthur reported discovering machine guns and dynamite in the camps. These were, so it appeared, dangerous times: a plot to blow up Congress was discovered later in the month, and the President-elect narrowly escaped assassination during the interregnum. But Hoover's subsequent attitude toward the marchers appeared to be a part of a defensive, hard-tempered shift to the right as the presidential campaign progressed.[12]

The Democrats and the liberal press portrayed Hoover's cruelty and ineptness in burning out the innocent veterans. *The Nation,* in an article entitled "Tear-Gas, Bayonets, and Votes," announced: "Hoover's campaign for reelection was launched Thursday, July 28, at Pennsylvania Avenue and 3rd Street, with 4 troops of cavalry, 4 companies of infantry, a mounted machine-gun squadron, six whippet tanks, 300 city policemen and a squad of Secret Service men and Treasury Agents." The customarily conservative American Legion denounced his actions. Much newsprint was devoted to the death of Bernie Myers, age eleven weeks, of tear gas. The infant had been diagnosed as having pneumonia by a District hospital; his parents, however, had refused to leave the child under medical care. A veteran's ear was supposedly severed by a cavalry saber, but the shorn man was never photographed or located. In the minds of most analysts, whatever doubt had remained about the outcome of the presidential election was now gone: Hoover was going to lose. The Bonus Army was his final failure, his symbolic end.[13]

When Franklin Roosevelt heard about the rout of the Bonus Army, he turned to Felix Frankfurter and grinned: "Well, Felix, this will elect me." Roosevelt, named presidential candidate at the Chicago Democratic Convention a month before, had not won the nomination effortlessly. Some two hundred Eastern delegates who had favored Al Smith lost in a fight with their old enemy from the 1924 convention, William Gibbs McAdoo. When the Californian delivered his state's votes and the nomination to FDR on the fourth ballot, someone remarked that McAdoo had buried the hatchet—in Al Smith's neck. Feelings ran so deep that Smith's advisor Belle Moskowitz suggested to a Hoover aide that the President should campaign first in the East. When Smith did speak for Roosevelt in Newark, he stuck to lambasting the "bigots" who had voted against him in 1928. Nor was Roosevelt—who in his Acceptance Address asked for a 25 percent cut in federal expenditures—widely regarded as a strong candidate. The choice of the alleged radical, John Nance Garner, as running mate also raised doubts about the strength of the ticket; Garner had opposed Roosevelt for the nomination.[14]

But it gradually dawned on the public that this optimistic Roosevelt had survived the cruelest adversity in his own life—and might be able to overcome the nation's as well. His state had been in the forefront of those combatting the Depression; in August 1931 its legislature passed his Temporary Emergency Relief Act. The New Yorker began his campaign before the convention closed: with his family he flew to Chicago, battling storms along the Great Lakes in a Ford Trimotor, to accept the nomination. Reflecting on the performance and the temper of the electorate, the Brooklyn boss James McCooey said that Roosevelt could go to Europe for the campaign and still win. Instead, to demonstrate his good health and vigor, FDR set out on a nationwide railway campaign trip and spoke sixty times, not including whistlestops where he jollied the crowds with local pleasantries. As Republican Senator Hiram Johnson of California remarked of his appearances there: "his very pleasing personality was quite attractive . . . enormous crowds . . . cordially gave him pretty general approval." Johnson complained of Hoover: "The money we so lavishly appropriated through the RFC . . . has not filtered through to those who most need it. I am afraid we began fertilizing the tree at the top and forgot the roots." Roosevelt's talks, vague in substance and dynamic in tone, went well in a Depression campaign; and he spoke effectively in numerous radio broadcasts.[15]

The two candidates had some remarkable similarities. Both had been protégés of Woodrow Wilson. Both advocated rigid economy in government spending. Both were capitalists, Roosevelt probably being the wealthier of the two. Yet FDR had intangible virtues that, at least in retrospect, appear appropriate to a candidate in hard times: a confidence and ease and grace, the manners of inherited wealth, that could awaken trust and a sense of security within the electorate. Hoover, the self-made success and the technician, could not warm his audience. Ironically, though, he was capable of considerable personal warmth: Stimson remarked, after Hoover attended the funeral of William Castle's daughter, that "he is very considerate about these things and always goes out of his way to show human feeling and to make members of his administration feel that they belong to him." Roosevelt's presidential successes against the Depression would be in large part consistent with the character of his campaign: they were in essence political successes, a composing of diverse factions, in Congress and within the public, into a political community. If, of course, it had been Roosevelt who had presided over the beginnings of the Depression, and in consequence Hoover the victor in 1932, a historian could be pointing to Hoover's clipped competence as an asset, giving the electorate the promise of coldly sophisticated leadership. At a moment when the incumbent President was on his way out, any number of styles might have served his opponent; and FDR had a good one.[16]

The Depression had converted the special virtues of Hoover in the 1928 campaign into liabilities four years later. Given the needs of the Depression, war relief no longer counted in the political scales—except as a source of embarrassment to Hoover. To rise from poverty was in good times a testimony to the working order of the system. In bad times, when people do not find themselves in control of their lives, they perhaps wanted a leader from a different and secure background—a Roosevelt who could relax and add grace. Roosevelt also appeared to be the national figure who could best unite rural and urban America against the threats of depression. Perhaps hard times, which mocked everything Hoover had worked for, awakened and validated in Roosevelt the right style for the right time. Like his cousin

Theodore Roosevelt, he possessed a Burkean sense of a community's innate character—the sources of its energy, morale, equilibrium—that Hoover the progressive technocrat always had lacked. The astute politician, like a skillful clinician, senses the complex of elements needed to maintain the health of the organism. Hoover, as the historian Eric McKitrick has remarked, was prepared to let the most serious damage occur without quite realizing what the conservative's priorities were. He often faltered when he had to act in the medium of representative government.[17]

In March 1931 Hoover vetoed the Muscle Shoals Bill and hoped that his strong words would be a good early opening to the campaign. He even believed the public would enthusiastically support his stand against the Bonus Army. In St. Paul just before the election, the press reported his comment: "Thank God we still have some officials in Washington that can hold out against a mob." Charles Michaelson, for three years the Democrats' director of campaign publicity, made the most of Hoover's gaffes and his policy of silence. To Michaelson, politics was a game played for power; to the naïve Hoover it was a solemn obligation for public service. John Nance Garner said: "It was Michaelson's job to whittle Hoover down to our size." Hoover's failures became much larger assets to the Democrats than all of Roosevelt's promises.[18]

If Hoover's 1928 campaign speeches had seemed dull, his omnibus talks of 1932, crammed with statistics, were even duller and more platitudinous. The long, badly constructed sentences employed vocabulary on the order of *sisyphean, vacuous, supervened, attenuated, palpably.* Hoover delivered his talks in a flat, metallic voice. The speeches were unrelievedly conservative, a defense of the record, not a plan for reconstruction.[19]

His acceptance speech delivered in Washington on his birthday, August 11, reads like a primer in economics. There was almost no applause at the end, wrote a British journalist, "due to the dispiriting influence of Mr. Hoover's personality, his unprepossessing exterior, his sour, puckered face of a bilious baby, his dreary, nasal monotone reading interminably, and for the most part inaudibly, from a typescript without a single inflection of a voice or gesture to relieve the tedium." In Des Moines on October 4 he addressed an audience of hand-picked Republicans on farm problems while two thousand demonstrators led by Milo Reno stood outside "to let the world know that there's folks in Iowa who's sour'n hell on Hoover." Not only did he fail to give the support he had been considering for the domestic allotment plan, but he repudiated the price-stabilizing provisions of the Agricultural Marketing Act. Years later the retired President told Charles Lindbergh the Des Moines speech had been a mistake; in politics one "learned not to say things just because they are true." The only personal portion of the talk—boiled down from a weighty seventy-one pages—came at the outset: Hoover's comment on the depression under way at the time of his Iowa birth and the Iowans' self-sufficiency then. But the present, he said somberly, "could be so much worse that these days now . . . would look like veritable prosperity." In Cleveland he bored an audience with a dreary account of the tariff. One *bon mot* on the tariff lightened the mass, the remark that Roosevelt's was "the dreadful position of the chameleon on the Scotch plaid." Hoover also took a swipe at the leaderless, irresponsible Democratic House for holding up passage of the national system of Home Loan Banks and thereby causing hundreds of thousands of unnecessary foreclosures. In Detroit an angry mob met Hoover at the railroad station. Numerous accounts state that the exhausted President shivered and trembled while delivering some of these talks.[20]

Finally, in a vigorous speech at Indianapolis on October 28, Hoover took the offensive and sarcastically rebutted charges made by FDR. And he attacked an "atrocious slur": Roosevelt "implies that it is the function of the party in power to control the Supreme Court." On Halloween, in an overlong harangue at Madison Square Garden, he continued the attack, bravely repeating his promise of 1928 to banish poverty. If tariff protection were to be removed, he warned, paraphrasing William Jennings Bryan's "Cross of Gold" speech: "the grass will grow in streets of a hundred cities, a thousand towns; the weeds will overrun the fields of millions of farms . . . their churches and schoolhouses will decay."* It was a contemptible appeal to fear. (The Democrats jovially responded in 1936 by driving an enormous harvester through the streets of Philadelphia.) Secretary of Agriculture Hyde unleashed a similar diatribe: "If Roosevelt is elected the homes and lives of one hundred million American people might be in jeopardy." According to Stimson, Hoover stimulated fears of what FDR might do because it was his only way to overcome feelings of hatred for himself.[21]

Between June and October, as Hoover's candidacy faltered, considerable economic improvement was taking place. Stock prices increased by more than 50 percent; bank failures and applications for RFC loans declined. That August the Home Loan Bank System, with $125 million from the RFC, began to buy delinquent mortgages held by hard-pressed building and loan associations. But the requirement inserted by Speaker Garner in a funding bill, that all RFC loans be made public, may have been responsible for part of the drop in applications. In October repayments on previous RFC loans declined. And commercial lending by banks had not revived enough that industrial recovery could begin.[22]

---

* Bryan had warned: "destroy our farms and the grass will grow in the streets of every city in the country."

"Reemployment" schemes were advanced in 1932 by such varied business leaders as Julius Barnes, Bernard Baruch, and Owen Young. Hoover picked up parts of their programs when he employed the Banking and Industrial Committees of the twelve Federal Reserve banks to encourage the use of credit opportunities and so promote employment. "Enlightened self interest if not patriotism," said Walter Teagle, head of a Share-the-Work plan, required support of the scheme. Business periodicals backed the various reemployment plans. After the election, Hoover continued to press the program to make "purchasing power . . . confident and effective in speeding business recovery."[23]

If there was one issue that could remotely compete with that of the Depression itself, it was the emotional and symbolic one of prohibition. The campaign blurred it. Attorney General Mitchell claimed that Hoover's administration had brought better federal enforcement, but observed that many states had abandoned or repealed their own "little Volstead Acts." The Republican platform's "dry, wet, damp" plank was the same, essentially, as that proposed by Al Smith in 1928 and by the Wickersham Report: a federal ban on the saloon, along with a reservation to each state of the right to regulate the sale of liquor within its borders. At the time of the plank's adoption Roosevelt was continuing to fudge the issue, and the Democratic Convention had not met. In his 1932 Acceptance Address Hoover admitted that prohibition had failed as the solution to the liquor problem. In 1932 the Republicans, like the Democrats in 1924 and 1928, were caught between the irreconcilable drys and the implacable wets. The Democrats called for outright repeal.[24]

One measure of the President's troubles was that the state of Maine went Democratic by a close margin in its balloting of early September. Another was his loss of favor in the black community. Democrats reminded Negro voters of his "lily-white" delegates in 1928, his nomination of Judge Parker to the Supreme Court, and the army's segregation of black Gold Star mothers on their voyage to Europe to visit their sons' graves. FDR assured an integrated audience that his symbol of the forgotten man applied "absolutely and impartially" to all blacks as well as whites. For the first time the Republican party lost the support of most of the black press. Hoover would win a clear majority of the black voters; but 1932 forecast the loss to the Republican party of a once-faithful constituency.[25]

On returning to California just before the election, Hoover's train was stopped near Beloit, Wisconsin, where a man had been found pulling up spikes. The President's car was pelted with rotten eggs in Elko, Nevada. The state's governor refused to appear publicly with Hoover; a senator did so and lost by five hundred votes. When Hoover reached Stanford he was described as a "walking corpse." One telegram to him suggested: "Vote for Roosevelt and make it unanimous." Hoover's candidacy was moving not even toward a decent and respectful repudiation but toward something ugly. As Elizabeth Stevenson, the popular historian, put it: his "reputation was murdered publicly, noisily, and painfully—as a thing once loved." The primitive impulse to personify misfortune was easy to understand, but there was a darker side to the hostility toward the President.[26]

From 1930 to 1932, with the worsening of the Depression, a number of muckracking books had appeared, written by an assortment of critics ranging from honest radicals to dollar chasers, that purported to uncover wrongdoing in Hoover's business career: checks forged, workers exploited and chained to stakes in the sun, and other completely unsubstantiated charges. The books include *The Rise of Herbert Hoover* (1932) by Walter Liggett (the best of the lot), John Knox's *The Great Mistake* (1930), John Hamill's *The Strange Career of Mr. Hoover Under Two Flags* (1931; Hamill confessed under oath that this book was largely fabricated), James J. O'Brien's *Hoover's Millions and How He Made Them* (1932), and Clement Wood's *Herbert Hoover, an American Tragedy* (1932). Liggett —who was murdered while muckraking in Minneapolis during the 1930's— was writing in part from animosity developed out of his own work in Russian relief, which ran counter to Hoover's; O'Brien and Hamill worked together, financed perhaps by William Kenney, the New York Democrat; Samuel Roth, a convicted dealer in pornography, published Hamill's and Wood's books. Hamill's was sixth on Macy's non-fiction bestseller list. Some liberal journals like *The Nation* recommended books of this sort to their readers, and *The New Republic* said they must be answered. The scholar Harry Elmer Barnes was not untypical of certain liberal reviewers when he remarked that Hamill was "appalling if true and very likely true." At the height of the campaign Senator Norris's secretary repeatedly recommended that correspondents read Hamill and Knox: "Perhaps these books are in your local library." Democrats disagreed over whether to ignore such material. The Democratic Speakers' Handbook urged comment on opportune occasion about Hoover's "former partnerships which contracted cheap coolie labor in South African mines."[27]

Hoover lost the election by 22,810,000 to 15,759,000 votes, receiving about 41 percent of the popular vote.* Roosevelt carried all but six states, winning 472 electoral votes to 59 for Hoover. But some of Roosevelt's states went for him by margins of less than 3 percent: Michigan, New Jersey, Wisconsin, Kansas, New Hampshire, Maine, Wyoming, and Delaware.

---

* Apropos of the election James Thurber wrote in *The New Yorker:* "Herbert Hoover is a great engineer and he should be released from burdens he doesn't understand in order to go back to his real work. Anybody who built the Great Wall of China, to name only one of his achievements, should not be President of this country."

In Congress 60 Democrats and 35 Republicans would sit in the Senate, 310 Democrats and 117 Republicans in the House.

Time labeled Hoover "President Reject." The event deserved a more dignified observation, for Hoover, a good but not guiltless man, had struggled against impossible odds. He blamed Wall Street for supporting the opposition "financially and otherwise. They opposed us because we were urging banking, public utility, and other reforms." He also blamed Congress for "the deliberate delay to recovery for purposes of the election." He should further have blamed his own inept campaign. At one point Stimson had to send researchers to New York so he could deliver a speech on Roosevelt's gubernatorial career. In 1932, as after World War I, incumbents in many countries were losing reelection. James Scullin, prime minister of Australia, served as the closest parallel. Taking office in October 1929 after a sweeping electoral victory, he along with his party was hurled from power twenty-six months later. At the December 1932 Gridiron Club dinner, Hoover managed to accept his defeat philosophically: "as nearly as I can learn, we did not have enough votes on our side." But for more than a generation Hoover and the Depression would serve as the Democrats' equivalent of the "bloody shirt" of Reconstruction. One of the first measures introduced in the December "lame duck" session of Congress was Congressman Lewis McFadden's to impeach Hoover for declaring the moratorium; eleven House members opposed tabling the motion. One ditty summed up the widespread feeling toward Hoover:

> O 'Erbert lived over the h'ocean
> O 'Erbert lived over the sea;
> O 'Oo will go down to the h'ocean,
> And drown 'Erbert 'Oover for me?[28]

Just before and after the election, Nevada underwent a crisis that foreshadowed the events of Hoover's last months in office. Suffering from undiversified agricultural investments, the state banks had looked to the RFC for help. But the agency demanded very secure collateral for short-term loans. As a result, frequent and repeated requests were made to the RFC; upon refusal, the entire banking system shut down for some six weeks beginning October 31. Even after reopening—with the largest banking complex suspending operations—the state remained in desperate shape. The University of Nevada, for want of public funds lost in the crisis, was ready to close. It was probably the Nevada collapse as much as anything else that convinced Hoover of the need to use his option to extend the RFC's life beyond its one-year limit, and the RFC that its loans must be made more flexible. Only in Roosevelt's Hundred Days did authority come to loan to states directly.[29]

In the succeeding months, as more and more banks across the nation closed while others stayed shakily open from day to day, they became the focus of a large economic failure. From twelve to fourteen million workers, nearly one-fourth of the labor force, had no jobs. Many farmers lost their lands or could not sell their produce at a tolerable profit. Hoover blamed the troubles on the proposed New Deal. In the long interregnum he sought FDR's cooperation toward balancing the budget, reorganizing the government, and changing the rules controlling banking and bankruptcy; more broadly he wanted to work with Roosevelt to achieve a public mood of confidence. Meanwhile the country floundered under a lame-duck Congress and a President who used his veto power repeatedly.[30]

Another element complicated the situation: Hoover's own alarm at the New Deal's potential for radical mischief. He thought Roosevelt ill-qualified for the presidency and ill-informed about most pressing economic problems. New Dealers, he worried, might depreciate the dollar or experiment with deficit finance, controlled prices, or direct relief. Hoover was convinced that such measures would only aggravate depression, not cure it. So he set out during the interregnum to confine the scope of future New Deal reform by using the complexities of international finance, a field he thought he understood. Specifically, if the United States gave concessions for a promise to stay on the gold standard, the Democrats could not resort to monetary tricks without breaking treaties. A brazen, somewhat pig-headed effort—the people already had rejected his leadership—Hoover nonetheless pushed ahead. His was the patriotism of a higher order, he thought, for rescuing an unsuspecting country from an irresponsible man possessed of dangerous ideas.

From the time of his appointment to the World War Debt Commission, Hoover had been of all the members most willing to consider an easing of terms. After the election he thought of arguing for revision of debts as a method of reflating the economy, but Stimson and Mills dissuaded him. Hoover signaled a willingness to negotiate with Britain and France prior to the December payment, which allowed the work begun at Lausanne to proceed. On the issue of war debts he and the President-elect soon found themselves apart.

En route by train to Washington on the Sunday after the election, the President sent a telegram from Yuma, Arizona, to Hyde Park to inform FDR that Britain and most of America's other debtors had requested a review of war debts and a postponement of their December 15 payment. Hoover had earlier delayed these requests for fear of disturbing the presidential election. He asked FDR to a personal conference to discuss debts, disarmament, and the forthcoming World Economic Conference. The letter implied that the causes of the Depression were global, and Roosevelt correctly responded only in the most general terms to what looked like a more calculated political overture than Hoover wanted to realize.[31]

At a meeting between the two men at the White House on November 22, Hoover tried to interest Roosevelt in the idea of jointly reconstituting the World War Debt Commission and softening the terms of payment. FDR did not reject the plan outright, and Hoover was led to think he approved. Actually, compromising on the debts would have brought more risk than Roosevelt could afford of alienating Democratic congressional leaders. To the President, FDR's understanding of the problem appeared superficial. And he disliked Roosevelt's companion, Professor Raymond Moley of Columbia University, thinking him pompous and surmising that he had obtained his understanding of war debts from a recent *Saturday Evening Post* article. Hoover, however, was himself to blame for Moley's presence by having insisted that Secretary Mills be present. Hoover told Stimson they had educated "a very ignorant, and as he expressed it, a well-meaning young man." Roosevelt did reveal himself at the meeting to be amenable to the principle of joint or mutual action: he asked the President in a moment of private conversation whether Hoover would support the domestic allotment plan for farming. Hoover said he would look at Roosevelt's version of the plan; but he was doubtful. According to John Nance Garner's biography, Garner, Senator Robinson, and Hoover favored some joint legislation to be enacted during the interregnum, but Roosevelt would not allow any.[32]

A much more cordial meeting took place on January 9, 1933, between Roosevelt and Stimson, who would in 1940 join FDR's administration as Secretary of War. Roosevelt endorsed the Stimson Doctrine and Hoover's arms embargo message to Congress. Stimson in return agreed to express Roosevelt's views to foreign powers where possible. The Secretary of State obtained, he thought, Roosevelt's permission to negotiate an exchange of economic concessions: in return for canceling war debts, the United States would gain tariff concessions in Europe and Britain would return to the gold standard. Plans for just such a world economic conference were under way. Stimson remained in the background as advisor as the new administration came in, arranging another meeting between the departing President and his successor.[33]

Roosevelt stopped in Washington on his way to Warm Springs, Georgia, on January 20, 1933. It was a dramatic session; even a last-minute wire from a diplomat overseas was rushed into the meeting. Frank Freidel, Roosevelt's biographer, has pointed out that the question of war debts was connected to that of the gold standard. At this January meeting, Hoover, committed to gold, raised the strategy of using the debts as a means of getting Britain to go back on the standard. He hoped that a United States commitment to gold would confine those New Deal proposals for a government-manipulated economy. But Roosevelt understandably wished to keep himself free on the gold issue. Yet he authorized the Hoover administration to open talks with major European powers about war debts and the coming World Economic Conference. No unified program came about. The question, Hoover had declared to Stimson, was whether the United States would take a courageous part in stabilizing the world economic situation. Roosevelt appeared to want only narrowly focused discussions on debts with the British, not the "best brains of both nations" going to work for "weeks and months." Nor was Roosevelt willing to write to the French asking for the December payment of their war debts, left unpaid perhaps because of his own inadvertent statements. The fault probably lay with the President, however, for throwing Roosevelt into the public spotlight. Informal, private conversations would have been a fairer, more effective way of testing Roosevelt's sincerity and finding their grounds of mutual concern and interest. The spectacle of misunderstanding between the two men, Walter Lippmann observed, was a bad example to the world.[34]

Later in January the banking crisis quickened as major institutions throughout the country began to close. Near panic came in the final week of February, when banks lost over $73 million in deposits. The RFC could no longer cope with the cash demands, and state after state placed restrictions on withdrawals. Much of what FDR did subsequently—the bank holiday, the FDIC guarantee of $5000 of customer deposits, the Emergency Banking Act—was to implement plans Hoover and his advisors had articulated in this troubled period but lacked the political power to carry out.[35]

Some of the worst trouble came in Michigan during early February. Henry Ford at first gave the RFC assurance that he would not withdraw $12.5 million of deposits from the Guardian Detroit Union banks. In an interview with Secretary of Commerce Roy Chapin and Arthur Ballantine, however, Ford said that if he had given the impression he would freeze his deposits, he "had not fully understood" and in any case "had changed his mind." When told of the consequences to small depositors, he replied: "Let them fail! Let everybody fail!" *He* would start over. Senator James Couzens would not use his personal fortune to save the Guardian banks and hastened collapse by demanding better security for RFC loans. The progressive Couzens wanted to help citizens directly and saw no reason to save unsound banks. Hoover was disgusted: "If 800,000 small depositors in my home town could be saved by lending 3 percent of my fortune, I certainly would do it." On February 13, however, Couzens offered to back half of such a loan, but Ford refused to do likewise. As a result, the governor closed all the state's banks for eight days on February 14; this was prelude to the national banking disaster three weeks later. Guardian bank stock dropped from $350 to zero: the banks themselves deserved no more, some of them having paid dividends while heavily in debt. Father Charles Coughlin, the radical radio priest of Royal Oak, Michigan, inveighed against "banksters"; this too invited withdrawal of funds. By now Hoover realized the inadequacy of the RFC policies, and recommended the issuance of clearinghouse scrip. He begged its new Democratic chairman, Atlee Pomerene, to take some form of action in behalf of Michigan. But Pomerene would not go beyond the letter of the law and the banks closed. The Michigan bank closings, which were largely extended until March 6, contributed to nationwide panic and the banking collapse.[36]

After Roosevelt nearly fell victim to an assassin's bullet in Florida and the banking débâcle had taken place in February, Hoover once again sought a united policy. As pressure on the banks increased, he came to lay blame on Roosevelt for the heavy drain on federal gold reserves, which the President attributed to anticipation that FDR would take the country off gold. On February 18 Hoover wrote asking Roosevelt to make a public affirmation of orthodox fiscal and monetary principles and thereby quiet the fears that were leading to economic collapse. He proposed in effect a near-total abandonment of the New Deal. For days Roosevelt rested on Vincent Astor's yacht before he dignified Hoover's letter with a bland response. He also refused to risk his influence with Congress by supporting legislation to stop the dangerous bank runs. Hoover had a simple plan of closing the banks for a day and then placing the government behind the ones that were solvent. The President also asked Congress for greater RFC lending authority. Neither man stood ready to subordinate everything to the national interest. Hoover even asked Eugene Meyer of the Federal Reserve Board to resign at Roosevelt's accession to office.[37]

The causes of the country's sudden crisis, Hoover wrote privately on February 22, were "simple enough. The public is filled with fear and apprehension over the policies of the new administration." And the public was unnerved by inflation, fear of an unbalanced budget, fear of projects that would overtax the government. The people "are acting in self-protection before March 4." But there was no reason to suppose that the withdrawals and the hoarding were on account of distrust of Roosevelt rather than simply distrust of the banks and the unfortunate constitutional situation. Hoover was personalizing large problems—a practice that had often dimmed his capacity for insight. Since economic conditions improved somewhat under the New Deal, he could only argue later that they would have improved more without it. Given the impotence of voluntarism in the face of huge economic forces, the demonstrated wrongheadedness of powerful individuals like Ford and Couzens, and the failure of Congress to endow the RFC with broader powers and of Hoover to provide it with leaders of greater vision, the policies of the Republican President and the Democratic Congress seemed now as bankrupt as the banks themselves.[38]

To his credit, Hoover in these final days made every effort and several important compromises to try to obtain Roosevelt's cooperation. He finally chose a five-year, 50 to 75 percent guarantee on bank deposits, which Roosevelt and Senator Glass rejected, as the best answer to the crisis. Raymond Moley later called the principle "the greatest reform that came out of that whole period." Hoover also considered proclaiming a limited national banking holiday under authority of the Trading with the Enemy Act of 1917, even though his Attorney General doubted the constitutionality of such a step. But he came to prefer state holidays, and restrictions on gold exports or withdrawals, in the absence of firm, bipartisan planning about what should take place during a banking moratorium. Mills and Meyer favored the idea, and Meyer—whom Hoover later considered disloyal—conferred with FDR about it on March 2. Hoover asked Roosevelt to call a special session of Congress on March 5 for passage of the necessary emergency legislation or to promise to continue Hoover's own independent actions. But the incoming President, while he liked the notion of a holiday, refused to participate in any joint solution to the banking crisis. Hoover then asked state governors to announce bank holidays; Governor Pinchot had to be awakened from bed by a fire engine at 5:00 A.M. At least Hoover had tried. Now it was Roosevelt's turn to attempt to rise to greatness, and the bank closing announced his coming to power with dramatic force.

Saturday, March 4, was predominantly gray and bleak; the wind blew intermittent gusts of rain, although there was sometimes a ray of sunshine. The two men rode together to the inauguration, Hoover replying in monosyllables to FDR's clumsy attempts to make conversation. "My, Mr. President, what interesting steel structures," Roosevelt said on seeing some new buildings on the site of a skirmish with the Bonus Army veterans. Although Hoover scowled a bit during the famous Inaugural Address, he pressed forward to offer his congratulations when it was over.[39]

Mills and other officials remained in Washington for a time to take essential roles in finishing the Emergency Banking Act of 1933. It had already been largely drafted on or before March 4. Mills told Hoover that if he and his associates had not stayed in Washington several days, the job "would not have been done. We have a country, you know . . . I am working for the country," he explained to the surly Hoover. Hoover agreed that the bank reorganization would create "some temporary inflation" and "give a fillip to the situation."[40]

He left for New York by train, unprotected by the Secret Service. Since John Quincy Adams a hundred years before, no President had departed so caricatured as an enemy of the people. Indeed, he was another Adams in his dour public face, his heavily moral religion, his acquaintance with science, his interest in the physical plant of the United States, his familiarity with foreign countries, his long day spent at work in the White House, his embodiment of technology and education as components of disciplined character. He might have written Adams's famous report on weights and measures; his plans for developing waterways, building dams, and consolidating railroad and airlines systems recall Adams's internal improvements. And the forces that Adams had perceived as opposing him, personified in Andrew Jackson, were like the forces Hoover thought he saw in FDR: demagoguery, political patronage, opportunism.

EPILOGUE
THE RETIRED PRESIDENT

AT A WASHINGTON DINNER early in 1929, the President asked each attendant member of his new Research Committee on Social Trends to give a ten-minute review of what the committee and the country had to do for the alleviation of social misery; he listened patiently, summarized the ideas, asked whether his interpretation was correct, and left the room. The evening demonstrated his commitment to one of his administration's more remarkable uses of the device of the fact-finding committee. Some of the nation's most prominent social scientists served in the endeavor: Wesley Mitchell of Columbia University, Charles Merriam and William Ogburn of Chicago, Howard Odum of North Carolina, Alice Hamilton of Harvard Medical School, and Edward Eyre Hunt, the committee's executive secretary. Inspired by goals out of the progressive era and by the example of the federal agencies of the World War, the committee applied science to social problems for a national purpose the government had never before projected and on a scale never before achieved among governmental inquiries: the two-volume, 1600-page *Recent Social Trends in the United States,* published in 1933, outlined a program of social reform that looked to the abolition of poverty. Among other recommendations it urged a leveling of income, unemployment payments to be financed from workers' earnings, and price-fixing of thousands of commodities.

Many of the committee's recommendations would soon come into practice, for the idea of social management was becoming a reality. And with its fulfillment Hoover's own philosophy was both realized and contradicted. Expertise, benevolently applied, the expertise for which Hoover's own career had been an argument, was fixing itself in institutions of social control rather than in the voluntary associations for which the President had spoken. Perhaps it was destined to do so, perhaps his balance of voluntarism and technical proficiency had been inherently too fragile to sustain itself; or perhaps the weakness lay in the impatience of the American people, as Hoover once testily remarked. But if voluntarism could not exist in its purity, defenses still existed within the American social and political process against the corruption of expertise into coercion. These defenses consisted of America's normal democratic processes and the looseness and fragility of power throughout American society.

The concept of the survey had come from Hoover, who delegated working out the details to French Strother, his able assistant. The committee's work gave further definition to Hoover's ideas for a progressive presidency. The technician President would begin with a survey of the needs of unemployment, old age, population change, schooling, crime, child welfare, the family, housing, and natural resources. The reorganization of the government, with enormous power centered in the Interior Department, was another gauge of Hoover's intentions. He planned to divide Interior into a department of public works and a department of education, health, and recreation. Ultimately, the President and the social scientists overestimated the tractability of the problems to be attacked; the study, as the historian Barry Karl observes, lacked political awareness. Also Hoover wanted the results to begin reaching his desk within a year so that he could use them. When in 1930 he requested data on old-age pensions, he impatiently remarked that he now expected to be President for only one term.[1]

The Depression greatly complicated the relationship between Hoover and the committee. Mitchell objected to any diminution by the President of his right to revise the reports: individual authors refused to let Hoover use reports, such as data on the relationship between immigration and crime that Hoover wanted to turn over to the Wickersham Committee. Fundamental trouble arose over Hoover's approach during depression to the social problems the survey was studying. Most members of the committee now perceived Hoover as flatly contradicting their belief that the nation should be more actively combatting hunger. When Hunt asked that the delivery of the report be publicized, the committee feared that it would be used for political purposes during the 1932 campaign.[2]

Some participants in 1932 wanted to get the survey into the hands of the Roosevelt administration. Professor Ogburn took the lead. He offered a copy to his former Columbia colleague, Raymond Moley. Hoover, Ogburn remarked, had wished it kept out of the campaign so that the committee's efforts could "lay the basis for policy making on the broader national issues." The problem of political continuity had evidently occurred only belatedly to the survey team. While the report never had a major role in the formulation of the New Deal's emergency approach to depression, some of its formulators later joined the New Deal. And some social scientists had learned the lesson of political awareness, if not a humility about the possibilities of their profession.[3]

IN LATE MARCH 1933 Hoover went to live in Palo Alto; leaving the presidency, he said, was "emancipation from a sort of peonage." Thereafter he gave much attention to Stanford and particularly to the Hoover Institution. Having read a book during a wartime English Channel crossing about the loss of documents in the French Revolution, Hoover at the time of the Armistice had organized for Stanford a collection of European documents on the era of World War I. "My idea," he told Edgar Rickard in May 1919, "is simply [to] collect library material on war generally." He was instrumental in bringing critical Soviet, Chinese, German, and British papers of World Wars I and II to Palo Alto. Some of the CRB Educational Foundation and some ARA Children's Funds went to Stanford for the Hoover Institution, which is today one of the largest manuscript libraries in the world. In 1959 Hoover ignored the recommendations of a Stanford search committee and chose as its vigorous director W. Glenn Campbell. Other CRB monies endowed professional chairs in Belgium, built a new library at Louvain there, and financed fellowships for students and faculty. Hoover also contributed funds to Stanford's Food Research Institute, established in 1924. He looked on the leftover CRB and ARA funds as spending money for his favorite charities: the Boy and Girl Scouts, the Boys' Clubs, Mills College, the Herbert Hoover Presidential Library. Bitter litigation developed early in the 1960's over the foundation's gift of $900,000 to the presidential library.[4]

With Mark Requa, Jeremiah Milbank, Edgar Rickard, and others, Hoover again turned to mining after the presidency. But public affairs continued to occupy so much of his attention that his business ventures suffered. Only the generosity of friends and his appointment to such sinecures as the Board of New York Life Insurance Company kept him prosperous. He read thirty newspapers airmailed daily to Palo Alto. Finally, disturbed at being away from the centers of national life, he moved for most of each year, beginning in 1934, to Suite 31-A of the Waldorf-Astoria Hotel in New York City.

In the summer of 1933 Hoover thought he had too small an audience to speak out against Roosevelt, who, he complained, had the bravado of a fifteen-year-old boy. When he did, he said, the subject would be not economics but freedom and the Bill of Rights. He greeted the end of prohibition as "a successful rebellion against limiting of individual liberties."

Much of Hoover's attack on the New Deal—the essentials may be found in *The Challenge to Liberty* (1934) and in the volume *Addresses Upon the American Road* (1938) that covers the years 1933 to 1938—did concern the power it was bestowing on government. To friends he vented his dislike of the "hideous immorality and tyranny of the NRA boycott provisions," and of the agency's demagogic leader General Hugh Johnson, who had the faults of a "typical West Pointer." The codes, he said in September 1933, "are ruinous to [character-building] small business and favor big business," which was enjoying exemption from the Sherman Act. "I have for years advocated building up business codes," Hoover admitted, "but, of course, I have no patience with the attempts to control production." The NRA was "Fascistic." The New Deal was erecting a "Fascist-Nazi state." Hoover protested of the Civilian Conservation Corps: "I find that the military officers in one of these camps think they are laying plans for a new military arm of the government." During his administration he had rejected what he called a similar "camp of potential mercenaries . . . under sinister military leadership." The AAA, too, was "fascist," with an unhappy resemblance to the agricultural programs of Mussolini and Hitler. It was also a blow at poor Southern sharecroppers as well as consumers. Its personnel were "totalitarian liberals." State socialism and monopoly capitalism equally destroyed freedom: any strong bureaucratic government did. And as citizens became increasingly isolated, they grew more selfish and unable to contribute to community.[5]

Franklin Roosevelt's worst mistakes, according to Hoover, were going off gold (which, he said, delayed recovery from the Depression), recognizing the Soviet Union, and trying to "pack" the Supreme Court. Yet in 1919 Hoover had argued that psychological confidence in currency, not a gold base, was of chief importance in maintaining its value. The attempt to increase the number of justices to create a more favorable Court drew Hoover's sharpest public criticism. As early as the 1932 campaign he had twice criticized Roosevelt for suggesting that the Court should reflect the views of the administration. Only reluctantly did Hoover agree with Senator Vandenberg to remain silent for two weeks since the most telling attacks were coming from Roosevelt's own party. In resistance to the plan the ex-President soon organized non-partisan protest groups in some twenty states, and in February 1937 he spoke against it on nationwide radio. Hoover supplied various sorts of information on the Court to Democrats who censured FDR. He also later excoriated Roosevelt for prolonging the Depression until World War II. The New Deal's relief efforts, riddled with waste and political corruption, cost more and aided fewer people each year. He objected to jamming programs through Congress without debate, likening it to the practice in Huey Long's Louisiana; and he sponsored conferences such as the Grass Roots Convention of 1935 that put Republicans on record against the New Deal. Hoover fought a personal battle to keep the government devoid of dictatorship and the economic system free of socialism. He feared first the "left" and then when the middle class should realize its "ruin," he feared a retreat into some American version of Hitler or Mussolini.[6]

Harold Fisher suggested in the 1930's that Hoover's increasing intolerance of views that did not coincide with his own was a consequence of his bitterness over the way he was being maligned.* Still, Hoover's opposition to the New Deal was characterized by some discrimination and critical awareness. "My administration," he correctly wrote to Mark Sullivan in 1938, had "proposed a much more drastic reform of banking than that finally enacted by the New Dealers. We created the Power Commission in its present form and proposed extension of its authorities, which was defeated by the Democrats. We proposed a public health bill, which was passed by the lower house and defeated by a Democratic filibuster in the Senate." Hoover did not mind taking credit for New Deal laws. He told Sullivan:

. . . generally, I think it might be entertaining to the public to trace out the origins of a large number of these New Deal things which we can properly support if they are well founded as to method. For instance, old age pensions had been enacted by Republican administrations in 16 states. I had had the subject thoroughly investigated for federal action, but could not undertake such a measure in the midst of depression. The whole housing business goes back ten years before the New Deal. Its foundations were laid by Republicans, culminating in the Housing Conference in Washington and the Home Loan Banks. Much the same could be said as to the development of relief for agriculture. Whether it is wicked or not, it was my administration that established the scheme of loaning money to farmers on their crops to cushion fall of prices. Etc., etc.

On another occasion Hoover wrote: "I am glad to have long advocated experiments tried out. Some of it is good; much of it is terribly bad." Thomas Dewey once said to Hoover, "I have a suspicion that you would have signed practically all the legislation that F.D.R. signed." Hoover thought a minute and said, "I think I would have."[7]

Hoover refused to join the Liberty League, an organization of reactionaries opposed to the New Deal. "As to Liberty of the Wall Street

* Stories spread that the Roosevelt administration had arrested Hoover and Mellon en route to Europe with $200 million in gold. For his part, FDR relished the tale of a doctor who examined a ten-year-old boy named Herbert and asked if he knew Herbert Hoover. The doctor explained to the unknowing lad that Hoover had been President before Roosevelt—to which the boy replied, "And is he *still* living?" On hearing the story from Grace Tully, Roosevelt was delighted and told Miss Tully "he had rather a fellow feeling."

Model," he wrote, "I am not for it. Their public statements give entire emphasis on the property right. The right of individual property serves that purpose in giving security of mind and body and stimulus to effort, enterprise, and creativeness. But they give no consideration to the fact that property or the power over property can be used to abuse Liberty. It can be used to dominate and limit the freedom of others." The function of the state, Hoover concluded, was "the prevention of abuse of the right of property." During the 1930's he worked to dissociate himself from the Harding-Coolidge economic policies that had brought on the stock market crash. To Mrs. Sinclair Lewis he implored: *"Please* do not use me as a whipping boy for the 'New Era.' I was neither the inventor nor the promoter nor the supporter of the destructive currents of that period. I was the 'receiver' of it when it went into collapse."[8]

If Hoover was so unsympathetic toward the most reactionary of the forces arrayed against Roosevelt, and could claim such affinities between his own plans and intentions and those of the New Deal, what remains of a definable conflict between him and the Democratic administration of the 1930's? It was in part a war of his own rhetorical making. The scars and humiliations of his presidency and defeat, the characterizations of him as the embodiment of selfish and arrogant wealth, such gratuitous gestures as changing the name of Hoover Dam to Boulder Dam, were together quite enough to drive him into a lasting hostility, a relentless effort to find quarrels with his triumphant opponents. Then there was the real, if sometimes elusive, philosophical disagreement over the possibilities of free cooperation and the limits of government control. A more important difference between Hoover's administration and Roosevelt's, perhaps, is that of political temperament. It is a difference that suggests the inadequacy of defining Hoover as a conservative. A useful, though incomplete, distinction between conservatives and liberals would make philosophical conservatism the party of the civilized emotions and philosophical liberalism the party of technique and disciplined rationality. The element within community of traditional or emotional connection, of delicate and often unspoken loyalties and expectations, tends to fall within the province of conservatives; the element of scientific planning and private reasoned conscience, coolly addressing itself to the public good, has been historically an attribute of the liberals. Certainly there was more planning in the Roosevelt administration than in Hoover's. Yet Hoover's efforts against the Depression had more distinctly the flavor of a rationalist morality, the sort of rationality he preeminently possessed himself and expected of the public: here is what we should do, here is what would be too dangerous, I'm sure all of you decent and reasonable people will want to get together and do the right thing. Roosevelt, on the other hand, knew or sensed or stumbled upon the important fact that a community is a matter of fragile morale, a morale that for its sustaining may require the subtle intuitiveness of the gifted politician. A prime example is furnished by the banking crisis of 1933: while Hoover in hesitating to shut down the banks was undoubtedly thinking of public morale as well as the constitutional question, Roosevelt's dramatic bank holiday was the more bracing. And for much of the remainder of the Depression era, FDR and his programs—some of them, to be sure, forced upon him—and his addresses managed to sustain a resonance with the public, and a sense of public activity, that nourished the community in a way that the most sensitive kind of conservatism ought to approve.

Another instance would be the New Deal's approach to the problem of relief. It knew—and Hoover, given more time, could surely have come to know—that relief could be so designed as not only to fill empty pockets but also to restore dignity and self-esteem; and so it made its rescue measures into something larger and more affirmative. WPA and its sister programs turned reliefers into workers, sharing in grandly visionary projects for building the nation and regenerating its spirit. The decade of the New Deal was a welter of democratic assemblages, governmental programs at cross-purposes, and through it all an image—a bit romantic, and popular among intellectuals—of the American people as various, folkish, potent with collective energy. If this was not an image to please an aristocratic traditionalist of European background, it meant an American version of the Burkean taste for a concrete living social order. Hoover the conservative, truly conservative in his commitment to association and to a national heritage, should have been at home with it. He could at least have been able, as a voluntarist and as a masterly administrator, to do something toward instructing it away from the total bureaucratization that threatened its more democratic impulse.

Hoover, once a virtual non-partisan, was now a Republican loyalist. He managed in 1934 to replace Everett Sanders with Henry P. Fletcher as chairman of the Republican National Committee, and he promoted groups of young Republicans. But while a speaking tour in 1935 was calculated to indicate his availability for a draft for the presidential nomination, which would constitute his vindication, the party did not consider him either its leader or a candidate. Although Hoover won a thirty-minute ovation for his speech comparing the New Deal to rising European dictatorships at the 1936 Republican Convention in Cleveland, Governor Alfred E. Landon of Kansas easily won the nomination. Landon did not welcome Hoover's help in the campaign. Hoover, who would have preferred Vandenberg or Lowden, looked on Landon as a candidate of Eastern banking groups and criticized his acceptance of support from the American Liberty League, "the very emblem of big business." Landon would not invite Hoover in writing to speak during the campaign. When the Kansan telephoned his request for some speeches, Hoover agreed; the Landon staff denied that the two men had spoken until Hoover threatened to release a transcript of the talk.* Both Landon and Frank Lowden were suspicious of Hoover's insistence on various political plans, fearing "some personal purpose" behind them. But, along with Senators Glass, Byrd, and Vandenberg, they signed a conservative manifesto in 1937 that objected to increasing power in the executive branch of government; the congressional elections of 1938 suggested that many Americans agreed. Hoover stepped up his activities: he spent $100,000 on party matters during the year after Landon's defeat, spoke in sixteen states, and held almost daily conferences on Republican affairs. By 1940, when opposition to the New Deal was coming from old progressives and Republican moderates as well as from large business interests, Hoover's candidate—next to himself—was Vandenberg, but the delegates wanted Wendell Willkie. From 1944 through 1952 Hoover supported Senator Robert Taft against Thomas E. Dewey and Eisenhower. He never backed a winner of the nomination.[9]

Held at some distance by his own party, Hoover had other reasons in the 1930's for loneliness. The Democrats had labeled the nation's sickness the Hoover Depression, and many people held him responsible in some way. At Charleston, West Virginia, Hoover dedicated a memorial and received a twenty-one-gun salute; "By gum," said an old man, shading his eyes and peering to where Hoover was standing, "they missed him." Still a loner, Hoover had trouble working with other loners—the ex-Roosevelt aide Raymond Moley, for example. Then, in the late thirties, there came a shift in national attention, as well as Hoover's, from the domestic issues that had crushed him politically.[10]

On a trip to Europe in 1938 Hoover attended a reunion with the survivors of the Comité Nationale—one-third of the names called at a banquet were answered by "mort"—and then visited Adolf Hitler. He was careful not to be photographed in close proximity with Hitler. As Louis Lochner reported Hoover's impressions: "Hitler . . . was more intelligent and better informed than he had been led to believe. He had, however, diagnosed certain trigger spots in Hitler's mind as an emotional streak that goes into a mental loss of control like furious anger." Hitler was "partly insane," he told another friend. Totalitarianism was "on the march," Hoover concluded, and he saw ahead a long and troubled period. After Germany, Hoover resumed his sentimental journey to Finland, Norway, and Poland. In Poland he spoke against Hitler, and he did the same

---

* One of Landon's assistants said that he knew now how the Democrats must have felt about William Jennings Bryan following his many unsuccessful presidential campaigns.

on returning to New York. Soon afterward he condemned the Nazi treatment of Jews.[11]

Hoover was alarmed at the prospect of American intervention. On the matter of an arms embargo he recommended compromise—no shipment of offensive weaponry like bombs that inflicted death on civilians. He disapproved strongly of the Anglo-Russian alliance and, like Senator Harry Truman, preferred that Germany and the Soviet Union destroy each other in a war of attrition. He viewed FDR's "quarantine" speech of October 1937 as intemperate; he held to the Stimson Doctrine, as opposed to the use of embargoes or boycotts. His concern over intervention was here reinforced by his loathing of bureaucracy, since, as he said in a private letter to Arthur Hays Sulzberger of the *New York Times:* "One reason I have opposed wars is the necessity to adopt Fascism to win wars." Another, he might have added, was his disgust with the behavior European nations had displayed during and after World War I. If Hitler could not cross the English Channel, he could not reach Washington, D.C., any more easily than the Western powers could get to Moscow. In January 1938 Hoover enunciated a Gibraltar strategy to secure the Western Hemisphere against outside aggression. "Great wars," he told another correspondent, "breed despotisms." He wrote to William Castle complaining that the Lend-Lease Bill of 1941 aimed not merely to help Britain, but in effect gave the President the power to wage war. Such attitudes got him labeled an isolationist. Yet he refused to join the America First Movement; and a more valid interpretation of his ideas lies in relating them to his pacific, essentially internationalist feeling for a sound world order—a feeling that had suggested itself in his administration's emphasis on commerce, conferences, disarmament, and the sanctity of treaties.[12]

When Russia invaded Finland and Germany attacked Poland, Hoover raised some $6 million for Polish and Finnish relief, half of it from the Polish government. Finland had a special place in Hoover's new relief efforts since it had been invaded by the Soviets. He also established a National Committee on Food for the Small Democracies. After consulting with the German Embassy in Washington, he claimed he had an agreement with Hitler to feed children in German-occupied Poland: "I could get things from the Germans other people couldn't," he boasted, including certificates of immunity from U-boat attacks. One of the first ARA men in Russia, Dr. Herschel Walker, argued that the presence of American relief workers there had alleviated government persecution and in 1940, he argued, "the presence of Americans in any country is likely to serve as a restraining force for dominating governmental activities of the worst type." Hoover in 1941 got the signatures of thirty-seven senators on a petition supporting a relief plan, but Winston Churchill, who had replaced Chamberlain as British Prime Minister, effectively prevented substantial relief work. The provisioning of Greece through Turkey in 1942, however, demonstrated the workability of war relief, Hoover maintained.[13]

In the days before Pearl Harbor, Hoover tried to use his influence with mutual friends of FDR to moderate the anti-Japanese attitudes of Secretary of State Cordell Hull and his Far East expert, Stanley Hornbeck. But after Pearl Harbor, Hoover supported the war effort wholeheartedly. Drawing on his experiences in World War I, he testified before Congress that major administrators should oversee munitions, fuel, food and clothing, and the like. With the assistance of Hugh Gibson—whom Hull, at FDR's behest, had dismissed from his Foreign Service post—Hoover published *The Problems of Lasting Peace* (1942) and *The Basis of Lasting Peace* (1945). The first book offered fifty suggestions for the peace, not unlike Wilson's Fourteen Points but stressing the resolution of economic problems. He looked forward to a peace without revenge, with "final" disarmament of the Asian powers, immediate repatriation of prisoners, immediate removal of blockades, and the relief of famine. World War I was ever Hoover's guide. While he supported the war effort, he would not move, as Wendell Willkie did, toward a nonpartisan political stance. When Eleanor Roosevelt attempted to arrange for service at some good restaurants for well-to-do foreign blacks, Hoover criticized her for failing to seek full courtesies in the South for all black people. Many letters came to FDR recommending that Hoover be made Food Administrator. Later he attacked the Office of Price Administration for costing the government hundreds of millions of dollars, and argued that the Food Administration of the previous war had added to the government's revenue.[14]

In 1944 Lou Henry Hoover died of a heart attack at the age of sixty-eight; the widow of Benjamin Harrison attended her funeral. Hoover's own correspondence is almost devoid of glimpses of her. Geologist, scholar, activist in charities, this remarkable woman assumed the character of the wife of a public figure, invariably supporting her husband's opinions. During the presidency columnists had compared her cosmopolitan background to that of Mrs. John Quincy Adams. She had broken precedent by showing Eleanor Roosevelt around the White House in January 1933. After Lou's death Hoover surrounded himself almost exclusively with New Deal opponents and fervent anti-Communists.

The retired statesman who watched the end of World War II and the coming of the Cold War had changed little from the peaceful, non-interventionist President. But the death of Franklin Roosevelt in April 1945 released Hoover from an obsession that had soured his thought and rhetoric. The following June he gave President Truman a memorandum on quickly ending the conflict with Japan; the State Department prepared a detailed critique. Hoover opposed the dropping of the atomic bomb on Japan. "The use of the Atomic bomb . . . revolts me," he wrote to a friend in August 1945. "The only difference between this and the use of poison gas is the fear of retaliation. We alone have the bomb." But Hoover visited Truman in the White House; the cordial President knew he had nothing to fear from an old man who had never wielded political power very effectively—and there might be much to gain. In 1947, Congress unanimously reversed Secretary of the Interior Harold L. Ickes's decision to call Hoover Dam "Boulder Dam."

At Truman's request, Hoover took charge of postwar food relief and went on a 35,000-mile tour examining the worldwide food situation. The implementation of his recommendations, which were similar to those of 1919, brought the famine emergency under control by the fall of 1946, except in Germany and Austria, to which he made a second trip the following January.* His activities evoked political support for food relief and for the Marshall Plan as well. He also attended conferences in Washington with Secretary of Defense James Forrestal and Truman at which he urged a strong Germany as a bulwark against communism. In 1947 he proposed the rebuilding of German heavy industry and an end to reparations: this policy would be the means to a restored economy. German gratitude was shown when Chancellor Konrad Adenauer went directly to the Waldorf Towers on making his first visit to the United States, in 1953; Hoover returned the call in Bonn the following year.[15]

In 1950 the ex-President firmly opposed both the military intervention in Korea and the sending of four American divisions to Europe following the outbreak of hostilities. He favored the withdrawal of American forces from Europe and expulsion of the obstructive Soviet Union from the United Nations. He refused Truman's invitation late in 1950 to serve as chairman of a bipartisan committee to investigate Communists in government: "I doubt if there are any consequential card-carrying communists in the Government," he told Truman. Even so, Hoover's anti-communism became in some ways more rigid during these years. But in May 1945 he told Truman, according to his later account, that war with the Russians would mean "the extinction of Western civilization or what there was left of it. I stated that I had no patience with people who formulated policies in respect to other nations 'short of war.' They always lead to war." Our position "should be to persuade, hold up our banner of what we

---

* A half-hour before leaving his apartment for this second trip, Hoover received orders from the Pentagon sharply restricting his mission. True to his old form, Hoover telephoned Truman and refused to go without carte blanche. He got it.

thought was right and let it go at that." By the end of the Vietnam war liberals like Arthur Schlesinger, Jr., Hoover's habitual critics, were warning against excessive reliance on the military, cautioning about foreign entanglements, and saying that whatever leadership the United States exerted should be by way of example. Hoover's approach by adherence to principle recalled that of Woodrow Wilson.

The historians William Appleman Williams and Joan Wilson have shown that Hoover's militant anti-communism in the era of the Cold War obscured a commitment to peaceful coexistence. Despite his many similarities to Wilson, Hoover's Gibraltar strategy would de-Wilsonize foreign policy: rightfully a means rather than an end, it should not attempt to Americanize the rest of the world. The non-Communist countries of Europe and Asia could, with few exceptions, organize themselves against the Soviet Union. And assuredly, as he told the Republican National Convention in 1944, that nation would change only as forces acted from within.

Hoover was once again out of step with his contemporaries. *The Nation* on December 30, 1950, observed that Hoover was out of touch with reality and perhaps was "even more sinister." Adlai Stevenson said that the United States was not a modern Athens—Hoover wished to concentrate on improving the quality of life at home—but was entering a great Roman era. If Hoover's emphasis on the building of air and sea power appeared to support John Foster Dulles's concept of massive retaliation, that was an ironic coincidence. Dulles called Hoover's enclave approach an "accomplice" of Soviet communism. As always, Hoover labored in the early 1950's to separate American security from American expansionism. He continued to oppose United States military force, economic sanctions, embargoes, or boycotts to prevent or end other people's wars. Yet he would cooperate in reasonable international efforts to advance world peace and social and economic betterment.

Hoover's last great contribution to public service began in 1947, when Congress passed a law providing for a Commission on Organization of the Executive Branch of the Government. The commission was to aim at "limiting expenditures to the lowest amount consistent with . . . efficient performance . . . eliminating duplication . . . consolidating services . . . abolishing services . . . not necessary; and defining and limiting executive functions. . . ." Truman asked Hoover to serve as chairman, with no reports to be issued until after the 1948 elections. The work was the culmination of one of Hoover's ambitions. In 1921 he had secured President Harding's promise to support such an endeavor; in 1924 he had testified before a joint committee of Congress on the matter; and during his presidency he had unsuccessfully urged Congress to adopt a measure. Now, with a staff of three hundred experts and such friendly co-workers as Secretary of Defense James Forrestal and Joseph P. Kennedy, he would secure many of his goals.[16]

Yet the Hoover Commission actually strengthened the managerial powers of the presidency and diminished the role of Congress in carrying on the functions of the government. This was despite Hoover's use of expert conservative advisors, such as Julius Klein and Arthur Kemp. Half the membership was Democratic and three commissioners—James H. Rowe, Jr., James Pollock, and Dean G. Acheson—were quick to dissent from restraints on presidential strength. Hoover himself, by Peri Arnold's report, was influenced by his respect for the presidency. As Hoover put it: "The President . . . must be held responsible and accountable to the people and the Congress . . . responsibility and accountability are impossible without authority." The words evoke the Hoover of the Food Administration, the director of Belgian relief. He specifically referred to Hamilton's Federalist Paper No. 70: "An energetic and unified executive is not a threat to free and responsible government." Some 70 percent of his recommendations were adopted at an estimated savings of several billion dollars.[17]

The second Hoover Commission, appointed under the Eisenhower administration in Hoover's eightieth year, was supposed to contemplate changes in social and economic policy. Its right to issue subpoenas made many government officials bristle. In Hoover's moderate estimate, Congress accepted about a third of the commission's proposals. He blamed Eisenhower, claiming that the President had delayed transmitting some two hundred reports to Congress for almost two years until they were out of date. Eisenhower had indeed delayed, made hesitant by the right-wing character of some of the recommendations, such as that for selling the Tennessee Valley Authority. In an entry to his diary for 1953, Eisenhower recorded being "a bit nonplussed to find that the only individuals [Hoover] wanted on the Commission were those whom he knew to share his general convictions that many of our people would consider a trifle on the motheaten side." In 1961 Hoover said that Eisenhower as a President would rank with Coolidge.[18]

Herbert Hoover, Jr., served as Eisenhower's Undersecretary of State for Middle East Affairs. He had specialized in electronic exploration of oil deposits and succeeded during 1953–4 in working out an agreement between Iran, London, and Washington on nationalizing Iran's petroleum. He was Undersecretary from then until 1957, when Eisenhower passed over him to choose Christian Herter, a former Hoover associate, to succeed the ailing John Foster Dulles. Herbert Hoover, Jr., died in 1969. (Allan Hoover, an economics major at Stanford, managed his father's California farm for a time in the 1930's and then gradually turned from banking and agriculture to mining.) Hoover and his son Herbert had been among Richard Nixon's original supporters in his 1946 congressional campaign. But relations soured between the presidential candidate of 1960 and the ex-President. Hoover is quoted as regretting a forthcoming visit by Nixon to Bohemian Grove, the California retreat mainly for elderly, wealthy conservatives: "How do you think I feel? I'm among those who persuaded him to run for Congress, in the first place." His friendship with the elder Joseph Kennedy was strong, and it was Hoover who formally arranged the post-election goodwill meeting between John Kennedy and Nixon in 1960. He received an invitation to Kennedy's inauguration, and would have attended but for inclement weather. He was getting very old now. When asked what ex-Presidents did, he replied: "We spend our time taking pills and dedicating libraries."[19]

Hoover's last years were spent amidst some travail. In 1958 he managed to attend the Brussels World Fair; barely a dozen Belgium relief workers were still alive to celebrate their earlier fellowship. Suffering from stomach pain, he had his gall bladder removed in 1962. A sound doctor, he said, must be opposed to exercise and in favor of tobacco. His interest in finishing "Freedom Betrayed," an unpublished history of Communist influences on the West, kept him at work, though he was deaf and now nearly blind. Barry Goldwater secured a reluctant endorsement from Hoover in 1964, shortly before his death at the age of ninety on October 21 from cancer of the colon. Only one other President, John Adams, had lived longer. The funeral, at St. Bartholomew's Episcopal Church across the street from the Waldorf, had few military trappings; except for an honor guard, its dominant impression was that of a simple Quaker ceremony. There were no eulogies, only the simplest form of the Episcopal Service from the Order for the Burial of the Dead, the reading of the Twenty-third and the One hundred and twenty-first psalms, and music. The two presidential candidates, Lyndon Johnson and Barry Goldwater, paused from campaigning to attend. Bernard Baruch, now ninety-four, was the only prominent member of Hoover's generation to appear. The body was subsequently taken to the Rotunda of the Capitol, where it rested on the same catafalque on which Lincoln and Kennedy had lain. Ever given to private maneuver, Hoover had devised his will so that no one could estimate the size of his bequests, arranged before his death, except that they totaled over $1 million. Herbert Hoover and his wife are buried on a rise of land framed by two stands of evergreens on the edge of West Branch, Iowa. Two massive but simple ledger stones made of granite mark the graves: they lie close to the limestone library that holds the records of his life.*[20]

WAS HOOVER a strong or a weak President? The question implicitly favors the desirability of a powerful executive, and therefore goes uncomfortably with at least a part of Hoover's philosophy. To label him a strong President requires special and elusive criteria, for the forms of leadership Hoover preferred do not offer much drama, or even visibility. The commissions he appointed served as surrogates of him; they recommended but could not order; and their intended effect, to educate and suggest, was of necessity slow and diffusive. In public manner Hoover remained remote. "Writing about Herbert Hoover," said George Creel, "is like trying to describe the interior of a citadel where every drawbridge is up and every portcullis down," and for inspection you have nothing "but a stretch of blank wall."

At times a sense of humor emerged. Hoover liked to tell of traveling in a limousine in the Belgian countryside during 1919 with his wife, the king and queen of Belgium, and President and Mrs. Wilson. The car pulled over and gentlemen and ladies disappeared into the woods separately. Wilson, by Hoover's claim, turned to him and said: "Now I know the meaning of 'relief in Belgium.'" Hoover replied, "I'm sorry it took you four years to find out." In his Australian days Hoover would play practical jokes on his friends; later he enjoyed giving visitors exploding cigars. Talking with Mark Sullivan during the Depression, he pointed to a chart with a stock's value moving downward. "What if the stock drops another ten points?" worried Sullivan. "It can't," was Hoover's lugubrious answer; "there's the edge of the chart." But Hoover remained mostly undemonstrative, at moments abrupt, at others shy.[21]

Hoover's public personality matched his careers in engineering and finance. These would have taught him to respect the impersonal specifications of matter and numbers. Workmanship and honor here could be austere matters, like the austerities of Quaker morality. No continuing occasion presented itself for cultivating the rich sensibilities of a ward heeler or a Hyde Park patrician.

In his exercise of power Hoover could be short with subordinates. Shyness, a discomfort with the moodiness and the intractabilities of human beings, a desire to be alone with his work, could all have encouraged his

* The *New York Times* obituary repeated a mass of misinformation: that he spread the use of the term "rugged individualism"; that he never received an A at Stanford (and was "less than brilliant" there); that he said prosperity was just around the corner. Other errors follow those in the *Memoirs*. When Hoover left the Presidency in 1933, six Presidents' widows were still living; he outlived them all.

crispness. Also, Hoover would sometimes try to master a great chunk of a project, and to burrow himself into details better left to others. But there was an apparently opposite side to Hoover's dealings with people. Ada Lillian Bush, who had much to do with turning the Commerce Department toward educating consumers in efficient purchasing, recalled being summoned to the Secretary's office after she had proposed a project for the department. Hoover was brisk with her as she tried to explain her idea; at the end of the interview he almost curtly gave her the authority to implement it on her own. He was often quick to delegate responsibility. Doing so was efficient, and he may have been aware of its concordance with his notions of individualism and free cooperation. But it probably agreed also with his temperament, in allowing him to draw in to himself and his piece of the work at hand.[22]

The delegating of authority could be related to another trait, or pair of them, that might not be expected of the brusquely confident Hoover. It is startling to consider Walter Lippmann's observation that Hoover could be rendered hesitant at the instant when a battle could be won or lost. A push from him at a critical moment might have saved some important administration bills, such as that supporting the Children's Bureau. He approved major laws, like the Agricultural Marketing Act or the Smoot-Hawley Tariff, that violated some of his principles. And while his custom, upon confronting a big issue, of seeking widely for advice means in itself no more than that he had good sense and a measure of humility, Justice Harlan Fiske Stone did opine that Hoover was "peculiarly dependent on his friends"; and this, indeed, was a characteristic. Trust in associates led the later Hoover into one unprofitable business scheme after another. Vested interests, a friend believed, refused to admit that Shakespeare's plays had been written by someone else; Hoover was intrigued at the idea. Perhaps the indecisiveness and the reliance on others were additional components of a normally complex personality. It is not unreasonable, however, to propose that these qualities, identified with extroverts and conformists, can represent as well the uneasiness and the compensations of a lonely individualist; or that they betoken an inability to deal more intimately, openly, positively with people. We have, at any rate, a vulnerability here that is appealing in its contrast to the brisk assertive competence of the public Hoover.

It is hard to take Hoover's measure. A friend who knew him in London remarked: "Is it not the most significant thing I can say about him that, after fifteen years of friendly interchange of ideas, I find myself unable to judge him with absolute confidence, feel myself still open to the possibility of making mistakes about him?" It is tempting to conclude that Hoover was much more open-minded and receptive to criticism than is commonly supposed. He was full of uncertainties; Bernard Baruch termed Hoover the only man he knew who could change his mind on economic matters once it had been made up. Here perhaps we have the source of persisting reports: that Hoover tried to convince Coolidge to sign the McNary-Haugen Bill; that he leaned toward recognizing Soviet Russia; that he seriously considered Senators Borah in 1928 and Norris in 1932 as vice-presidential running mates. One of his most able assistants, French Strother, said Hoover distinguished between a closed Latin mind and an open Anglo-Saxon or American mind: before acting, Latins insisted on having "principles" that matched their philosophical preconceptions. As a result they lacked the will to get things done. The peculiarly American combination of logic and practicality formulated not principles but ideals—rough conceptions both of what must be done and how to do it. On the other hand, critics spoke of Hoover's apparent contempt for anything he did not understand and therefore could not sympathize with. He was inclined, some said, to give no consideration to, and ride roughshod over, imponderables.

By temperament and philosophy, Hoover was only partially capable of speaking for the principles he championed. "I have never liked the clamor of crowds," he wrote. "I intensely dislike superficial social contacts. . . . I was terrorized at the opening of every speech." We must of course go beyond the Quaker and the engineer to the poor orphan boy for an understanding of Hoover's shyness. No one who grew up in such a difficult environment could do other than compensate energetically for low self-esteem and feelings of insecurity, which had led him so often to exert control over situations and people. But his individualism was also one of hard work, integrity, and inner reserve; whatever there was in him that might have flourished in other sorts of dramatic or playful individuality remained closed up. He spoke for a communalism of decent, efficient cooperation; he could not evoke community, call it to self-awareness and confidence, as Franklin D. Roosevelt did. What he left for our admiration or example, what in fact his limits help to define, are the drier virtues of self-control, persistence, workmanship, and a conscience that put itself, relentlessly and without confessionalism, about the task of feeding countless war victims who might otherwise have starved. And there came to the surface at times an instinct to transcend the orthodoxies of American social and political life.

SOURCES
NOTES
ACKNOWLEDGMENTS
INDEX

~~~~~~

SOURCES

PRINCIPAL MANUSCRIPT COLLECTIONS RELATING TO HERBERT HOOVER
AT THE HERBERT HOOVER PRESIDENTIAL LIBRARY, WEST BRANCH, IOWA

George Akerson

American Child Health Association

Arthur Ballantine

Belgian American Educational
Foundation (closed)

William R. Castle, Jr.

Colorado River Commission

Frederick C. Croxton

Edward Dana Durand

Frederick M. Feiker

George A. Hastings

Campbell H. Hodges

Herbert Hoover, Pre-Commerce
Papers

Herbert Hoover, Commerce Papers

Herbert Hoover, Pre-Presidential
Papers

Herbert Hoover, Presidential Papers

Herbert Hoover, Post-Presidential
Papers

Herbert Hoover, Papers re Commissions on Organization of the
Executive Branch of the Government

Nathan W. MacChesney

Hanford MacNider

Bradley Nash

Gerald P. Nye

President's Emergency Committee for
Employment and President's
Organization on Unemployment
Relief (PECE and POUR)

Ethel Grace Heald Rensch

Lawrence Richey

Edgar Rickard

Edgar French Strother

William Hallam Tuck

United States Committee on the Conservation and Administration of the
Public Domain

United States President's Commission
for Study and Review of Conditions
in the Republic of Haiti

Lawrence W. Wallace

Ray Lyman Wilbur

Robert E. Wood

PRINCIPAL MANUSCRIPT COLLECTIONS RELATING TO HERBERT HOOVER
AT THE HOOVER INSTITUTION, STANFORD UNIVERSITY

American Relief Administration
George Barr Baker
Citizens Committee for the Hoover
    Commission Report
Commission for Relief in Belgium
Commission on Organization of the
    Executive Branch of Govern-
    ment
Joseph F. Davis
Food Administration
Perrin C. Galpin
Edwin F. Gay
Joseph C. Green
Herbert Hoover
Edward Eyre Hunt
Inter-Allied Food Council
Will Irwin
David Starr Jordan
Tracy B. Kittredge

Hulda Hoover McLean
John C. O'Laughlin
President's Research Committee on
    Social Trends
Henry Robinson
Gilchrist Stockton
Mark Sullivan
Supreme Economic Council, Paris
    Peace Conference
Alonzo Taylor
Payson J. Treat
United States Food Administration
White House Conference on Child
    Health
White House Conference on Home
    Ownership
Ray Lyman Wilbur
Hubert Work

PRINCIPAL MANUSCRIPT COLLECTIONS PERTAINING TO HERBERT HOOVER
AT THE LIBRARY OF CONGRESS

Henry J. Allen
Ray Stannard Baker
Tasker H. Bliss
William Borah
John Gutzon Borglum
Charles H. Brent
Albert Burleson
Vannevar Bush
Edward T. Clark
Herbert Corey
William S. Culbertson
Calvin Coolidge
James Couzens
James Davis
Norman Davis
Henry P. Fletcher
W. Cameron Forbes
John P. Frey
James B. Garfield
Emmanuel A. Goldenweiser
Charles S. Hamlin
John H. Holmes
Charles Evans Hughes

William E. Humphrey
William Jardine
Jesse Jones
Robert Lansing
Irvine Lenroot
Henry Cabot Lodge
Charles McNary
John C. Merriam
Ogden Mills
John P. Mitchell
Charles Moore
John Bassett Moore
George Van Horn Moseley
George Norris
John C. O'Laughlin
Gifford Pinchot
Key Pittman
Theodore Roosevelt, Jr.
Charles Russell
Everett Sanders
William S. Sims
Harlan Fiske Stone
George Sutherland

Robert A. Taft
William Howard Taft
Thomas Walsh
Stanley Washburn

William A. White
Brand Whitlock
Edith Galt Wilson

ADDITIONAL PRINCIPAL MANUSCRIPT COLLECTIONS
RELATING TO HERBERT HOOVER

Edith and Grace Abbot, University of Chicago
Ephraim D. Adams, Stanford University
Ralph Arnold, Huntington Library
Mary Austin, Huntington Library
Julius Barnes, St. Louis County Historical Society
Claude A. Barnett, Chicago Historical Society
Bruce Barton, Wisconsin State Historical Society
Bernard Baruch, Princeton University
Eleanor R. Belmont, Columbia University
Albert J. Beveridge, Illinois State Historical Society
Walter Brown, The Ohio State Historical Society
Theodore E. Burton, Western Reserve University
Nicholas Murray Butler, Columbia University
James Cannon, Duke University
Arthur Capper, Kansas State Library
John M. Carmody, Franklin Delano Roosevelt Presidential Library
Roy D. Chapin, University of Michigan
Joshua R. Clark, Brigham Young University
Enoch H. Crowder, University of Missouri
Chester C. Davis, University of Missouri
Norman Davis, Yale University
Charles Dawes, Northwestern University
Edwin Denby, Detroit Public Library and University of Michigan
Thomas E. Dewey, University of Rochester
Edward A. Dickson, University of California, Los Angeles
Robert L. Doughton, University of North Carolina
Pierre S. duPont, Eleutherian Mills Hagley Library
William C. Edgar, Minnesota Historical Society
Dwight D. Eisenhower, Dwight D. Eisenhower Presidential Library
Albert B. Fall, Huntington Library and University of New Mexico
Simeon D. Fess, The Ohio State Historical Society
John T Flynn, University of Oregon
W. Cameron Forbes, The Houghton Library
David R. Francis, Missouri Historical Society
Joseph S. Freylinghuysen, Rutgers University Library
Arthur Garford, The Ohio State Historical Society
Carter Glass, University of Virginia
Lynn Haines, Minnesota Historical Society
Warren G. Harding, The Ohio State Historical Society
George Harrison, Columbia University

Will Hays, Indiana State Library
Hill family, Oregon State Library
Edward M. House, Yale University
Edward N. Hurley, Notre Dame University Library
Patrick J. Hurley, University of Oklahoma
Arthur M. Hyde, University of Missouri
Hiram Johnson, University of California at Berkeley
Frank B. Kellogg, Minnesota Historical Society
Fred I. Kent, Princeton University
Arthur Krock, Princeton University
Thomas W. Lamont, Baker Library, Harvard Graduate School of Business
    Administration
Alfred M. Landon, Kansas State Historical Society
Franklin K. Lane, Jr., Bancroft Library
Fulton Lewis, Jr., Syracuse University
Walter Lippmann, Yale University
Henry Cabot Lodge, Massachusetts Historical Society
George H. Lorimer, Historical Society of Pennsylvania
Thomas B. Love, Dallas Historical Society
Frank Lowden, University of Chicago
Samuel McKelvie, Nebraska State Historical Society
Adam McMullen, Nebraska State Historical Society
Anne Martin, University of California at Berkeley
Annie Meyer, American Jewish Archives
Charles Michaelson, Franklin Delano Roosevelt Presidential Library
Ewing Y. Mitchell, University of Missouri
Wesley C. Mitchell, Columbia University
William D. Mitchell, Minnesota Historical Society
George H. Moses, New Hampshire Historical Society
Robert Moton, Tuskegee Institute
William Starr Myers, Princeton University
National Council of Civic Federations, New York Public Library
John Francis Neylan, University of California at Berkeley
Allan Nevins, Columbia University
Peter Norbeck, University of Missouri; Minnesota Historical Society; Univer-
    sity of South Dakota
Walter Hines Page, The Houghton Library
John J. Parker, University of North Carolina
Maurice Pate, Rutgers University Library
George Peck, University of Missouri
Frank Polk, Yale University
Atlee B. Pomerene, Kent State University
John J. Raskob, Eleutherian Mills Hagley Library
Charles J. Rhoads, American Philosophical Society
Donald Richberg, Chicago Historical Society
Franklin Delano Roosevelt, Franklin Delano Roosevelt Presidential Library
Nicholas Roosevelt, Syracuse University
Julius Rosenwald, University of Chicago

Chester Rowell, University of California at Berkeley
St. Lawrence Seaway Association, St. Louis County Historical Society
Charles F. Scott, Kansas State Historical Society
Jouett Shouse, University of Kentucky
Furnifold M. Simmons, Duke University
Bascom C. Slemp, University of Virginia
Alfred E. Smith, State of New York Library, Albany
Lloyd C. Stark, University of Missouri
Henry L. Stimson, Yale University
Swarthmore Peace Collection, Swarthmore College
Harry S. Truman, Harry S. Truman Presidential Library
Robert F. Wagner, Sr., Georgetown University
Frederic C. Walcott, Yale University
Lillian Wald, New York Public Library
Henry C. Wallace, University of Iowa
Frank Walsh, New York Public Library
Brand Whitlock, Columbia University and Library of Congress
William B. Wilson, Historical Society of Pennsylvania
Hubert Work, Denver Historical Society

PAPERS PERTAINING TO HERBERT HOOVER IN FOREIGN COUNTRIES

Administration Centrale du Minis-
tère des Finances, Paris
Battye Library, Perth, Western Aus-
tralia
Bodleian Library, Oxford University,
Oxford
British Museum, London
Department of Mines, State of Vic-
toria, Melbourne

Department of Mines, State of West-
ern Australia, Perth
House of Lords Archives, London
Kalgoorlie Public Library, Kalgoorlie,
Western Australia
Public Record Office, London

NOTES

A Note About the Notes

EVERY POSSIBLE ECONOMY in annotation has been made. Some compromise with exhaustive citations is necessary in a one-volume biography. The selective approach adopted here will benefit the student or scholar who may wish to find his way into Hoover literature without becoming lost in inaccessible documentary sources. Whenever possible, for example, recent scholarly articles or unpublished dissertations are cited if they contain reference to a group of manuscripts used in this study. The determined scholar should find what he wants by tracing citations to their ultimate primary sources. The Herbert Hoover Presidential Library has changed its method of citation during the past decade: the staff there should be able to interpret my "old series" footnotes, while the main body of papers referred to can be determined by dating unless more specifics are given. For Hoover's own works, see Kathleen Tracey and W. Glenn Campbell, compilers, *Herbert Hoover: A Bibliography* (Stanford, 1977). Lou Henry Hoover's papers, housed in West Branch, Iowa, are closed until 1984.

The following abbreviations are used:

HHPL Herbert Hoover Presidential Library
  HI Hoover Institution
 PRO Public Record Office
  FA Food Administration Papers, HI (cf. Food Administration Papers, Sutphin, Md.)
  NA National Archives
 CRB Commission for Relief in Belgium
 ARA American Relief Administration
USFR United States Foreign Relations (State Department published series).

CHAPTER I

1 Harriette Miles Odell's letters on West Branch to Lou Henry Hoover are in "Genealogy," HHPL; West Branch *Local Record,* 27 March 1879; 4 Dec. 1879.

2 West Branch *Local Record,* 29 Jan. 1880. The United States Patent Office awarded Eli patent No. 232499 on 17 Aug. 1876 for his cattle pump.

3 I am grateful to Hulda Hoover McLean, Rancho del Oso, Davenport, California, for help on Hoover family genealogy. See her standard *Genealogy of the Herbert Hoover Family* (Stanford, 1967) and her *Genealogy . . . Errata and Addenda* (Stanford, 1976). George Clarke, "Andrew Hoover Comes to Indiana," *Indiana Magazine of History,* XXIV (Dec. 1928); "Memoir of David Hoover," *Indiana Magazine of History,* II (March 1906), 17–27. Judge David Hoover, Herbert's great-uncle, owned slaves but freed them upon moving to Ohio; Henry Hoover, "Memoir of 1850 by a Friend," Yale University Library; *The Friend,* XXVII (1854), 319.

4 McLean, *Genealogy, passim;* Theodore Hoover to Maud A. Minthorn, 19 Feb. 1930; Herbert Hoover to George Robinson, 28 April 1921; David Hoover to Gertrude Newman, ca. 1894; all in "Genealogy," HHPL. The Hoovers and Minthorns can easily be traced in the various federal and state censuses: 1860, 653/314; 1870, 593/380; 1880, 331, NA; and in the state reports of 1865, 1875, and 1885, State Archives, Des Moines, Iowa; Guy R. Ramsey, *Postmarked Iowa* (Crete, Nebr., 1976); Box 5, George Barr Baker Papers; Ann Minthorn Heald, "A Canadian Childhood, 1842–1859," with Ethel Grace Heald Rensch, Rensch Papers.

5 Hulda Randall Minthorn to Miranda Stover, 3 Jan. 1863, and 3 Dec. 1865, "Minthorn/Stover Letter," HHPL; Memoirs of Miriam Bronson, West Branch *Times,* 5 Aug. 1948; Mr. and Mrs. Newton Branson to George Akerson, 16 Dec. 1929; Hoover Family Court Records, General Accession 195, HHPL; West Branch Preparative Meeting, West Branch Friends Church, p. 12; Virgil M. Hancher to Bernice Miller, telegram, 5 Aug. 1954; Public Statement 3532, HHPL.

6 Theodore remembered "being awakened in an August night and told I had a small brother." Theodore Hoover to Lou Henry Hoover, 8 Nov. 1937, "Genealogy," HHPL; Box 1, Ben Allen Papers; General Register of the Members of Springdale Monthly Meeting of Friends, West Branch Friends Church.

7 This paragraph is based on the later recollections of relatives: Agnes Minthorn to Harriette Miles Odell, 21 Jan. 1920, and Aunt Mattie Pemberton to Theodore Hoover, 15 Jan. 1907, "Genealogy," HHPL; Theodore Hoover, "Memoranda, being a Statement by an Engineer" (Stanford, 1939), p. 15, HI and HHPL; Mary Minthorn Strench, Oral history, HHPL.

8 Several letters of Harriette Miles Odell to Lou Henry Hoover, variously dated in the 1920's and 1930's, recollect many of these stories. They are in "Genealogy," HHPL; a few letters in the same collection from Harriette's mother, Hannah Martha "Aunt Mattie" Pemberton (1866–1946), are also helpful.

9 See Hoover's own attractive brief reminiscence, *A Boyhood in Iowa* (New

York, 1931), as well as Maude Stratton's *Herbert Hoover's Home Town* (West Branch, 1948).

10 For other details, see *The West Branch Consolidated Schools: Its Beginning, Growth, Characteristics, and Alumni Record* (West Branch, 1935); Grammar Department, A Grade (3rd year), West Branch Schools; West Branch *Local Record,* 1 Jan. 1880 and *passim;* Theodore Hoover, "Memoranda," p. 16.

11 West Branch *Local Record,* 2 Oct. 1879, 12 Feb. 1880; *Census of Iowa, 1885* (Des Moines, 1885) has some cumulative records; see also "Special Schedule of Manufacturers," 1880, Springdale Township, 42/A1156, NA.

12 West Branch *Local Record,* 31 July 1879; "John Brown in Cedar County, Iowa," n.d., Gordon Smith, compiler for Cedar County Historical Society; Louis T. Jones, *The Quakers of Iowa* (Iowa City, 1914); Jeannette Mather Lord, "John Brown—They Had a Concern," *West Virginia History,* XX (April 1959), 163–83.

13 Obituary of John C. Hoover by John Y. Hoover (newspaper clipping, n.d.), "Genealogy," HHPL; John Yount Hoover to Theodore Hoover, 1905, quoted on pp. 297–8 of McLean, *Genealogy;* Edwin C. Bearss and Wilfred M. Husted, "Buildings in the Core-Area . . ." (Washington: National Park Service, 1970), pp. 5–6.

14 *Jesus Only* (1905); Red Cedar Preparatory Meeting, p. 269, West Branch Friends Church and Friends Church, Oskaloosa, Iowa; West Branch *Local Record,* 6 March 1879.

15 A good account of Updegraff is in the unpublished manuscript by Lawrie Tatum, "History of the Springdale Settlement . . . ," 1889, William Penn College Library, Oskaloosa; see also Theodore Hoover, "Memoranda," pp. 5ff; Odell Letters, "Genealogy," HHPL; *Census of Iowa, 1885;* Mildred Crew Brook, "An Unfinished Manuscript of Reminiscences," 1940, HHPL; West Branch *Local Record,* 10 June 1880; David Leshana, *Quakers in California* (Newberg, Ore., n.d.), *passim.*

16 On Jesse's heart trouble, see his doctor John Minthorn to William F. Smith, 21 Feb. 1920, Box 13, "Genealogy," HHPL. The local paper wrote of "rheumatism of the heart": West Branch *Local Record,* 15 July 1880, 16 Dec. 1880; Hulda Hoover to her mother and sister Agnes Minthorn Miles, 22 Feb. 1883, and Hulda to Agnes Miles, 24 Oct. 1883, Hulda Hoover McLean Collection; Red Cedar Quarterly Minutes, Women, 1858–1885, and Minutes of Iowa Yearly Meeting, 1883, p. 34, Friends Church, Oskaloosa; Memoirs of Miriam Branson, West Branch *Times,* 5 Aug. 1848; West Branch *Local Record,* 2 Feb. 1884, 27 March 1884; Minutes of Red Cedar Preparatory Meeting, 23 June 1883, and West Branch Preparatory Meeting, *passim,* West Branch Friends Sunday School Secretary's Record, 1881–84, State Historical Society of Iowa, Iowa City; Agnes Minthorn to Harriette Miles Odell, 21 Jan. 1920, "Genealogy," HHPL; Hulda Hoover to Agnes Minthorn Miles, 24 Oct. 1883; Hulda Hoover to J. C. Chambers, 29–30 May 1880, and 22 Feb. 1883, McLean Papers; Hoover, *Public Papers, 1932–1933,* 15 Sept. 1932.

17 Odell reminiscences, "Genealogy," HHPL; Gen. Acc. 195, Hoover Family Court Records, 1859–1895; Herbert Hoover speech at Des Moines, 10 Aug. 1928.

[18] Anne Martin to Liggett, Liggett Papers.

[19] Agnes Minthorn to Harriette Miles Odell, 21 Jan. 1920; Hoover to Mrs. F. L. Maitland, n.d., "Genealogy," HHPL; West Branch *Local Record*, 24 March 1884.

[20] Benjamin Miles to Indian Commissioner Hiram Price, RG 75, Letters Received, Commissioner of Indian Affairs, NA; Bearss, "Buildings in the Core-Area," says the Miles visit took place in 1882; this probably follows Louise Witham, "Herbert Hoover and the Osages," *Chronicles of Oklahoma*, XXV, 2–3; Hoover to Mrs. Witham, 12 Dec. 1946, is not necessarily the best source. Rose Wilder Lane was helped by the family in writing *The Making of Herbert Hoover* (New York, 1920); her placing this long visit at age seven squares with the West Branch *Local Record* note of 24 March 1881, that Laban and Laura Miles left on that date for the Osage agency; Harriette Miles Odell to Lou Henry Hoover, 8 Oct. 1939, says Herbert went to Oklahoma the summer before his mother's death, "Genealogy," HHPL. Lou Henry remembered hearing that Bert had spent "months at a time with his uncle," and there may have been two visits. Benjamin and Elizabeth Miles left West Branch as of 22 Oct. 1881, according to Red Cedar Minutes, 1863–1895, p. 4, Oskaloosa Friends Church, Oskaloosa, Iowa. Lou Henry Hoover to Mary Austin, 14 June 1923, Austin Papers, Huntington Library.

[21] Harriette Odell told Theodore Hoover that she burned Bert's letters telling of unhappy experiences with Uncle John: 30 Jan. 1920; see also Anne Martin to Liggett, Liggett Papers; Elmer E. Washburn, "Westward Across Four Frontiers," manuscript reminiscence, copy in HHPL.

[22] John Minthorn to William F. Smith, 1917, "Genealogy," HHPL; Portland *Sunday Oregonian*, 16 July 1931; West Branch *Times*, 12 Nov. 1885; Mary Minthorn Strench, Oral history, HHPL; Vernon Kellogg, "Herbert Hoover," *Everybody's Magazine* (Feb. 1920); Joshua Minthorn to Mrs. Rensch, 1 Jan. 1929, Rensch Papers, HHPL.

[23] Theodore Hoover, "Memoranda," p. 87; Theodore arrived in Oct. 1887; Newberg, Ore. *Graphic*, 30 Aug. 1917; catalogues, 1885–88, Friends Pacific Academy, Barker Papers.

[24] Gen. Acc. 259, Elmer E. Washburn reminiscence, HHPL; Hoover to M. Rawlings, 14 Jan. 1937; "Marion County Records, 1888–1901," Oregon State Library; Hoover, *An American Epic* (New York, 1961), I, 285.

[25] Portland *Sunday Oregonian*, 1928 (accounts of Granville Everest and Walter Woodward); Minthorn to William F. Smith, 1917, Box 13, "Genealogy," HHPL; Dr. Burt B. Barker, Oral history, HHPL.

[26] Herbert Hoover, typescript of commencement speech, 7 June 1941, Haverford College Library; miscellaneous records, University Archives, Stanford.

[27] Kellogg, *Herbert Hoover* (New York, 1920), p. 50; Hoover to Branner, 2 Sept. 1894, University Archives, Stanford. The transcript of Hoover's grades is in the Registrar's office at Stanford.

[28] Hoover to Nell May Hill, 30 Aug. 1892, 9 Nov. 1894, Hill Family Papers; Hoover Family Court Records, HHPL; Agnes Minthorn to Harriette Miles Odell, 21 Jan. 1920, "Genealogy," HHPL.

29 *Daily Palo Alto*, 23 Jan. 1894; see also 1 March, 11 April, 18 April, 2 May, 4 May, 30 May 1894.

30 Hoover later wrote an affectionate article about Stanford, giving him credit for an act of kindness to a miner in the High Sierra at the end of his resources. Stanford *Sequoia*, XXI (March 1921), 181–3.

31 Hoover to Nell May Hill, 19 July 1894, 9 July 1895, Hill Papers.

32 An interview with Mrs. Branner is in the *New York Times*, 27 July 1928.

33 Edwin R. Zion interview: Traverse Clements to Walter Liggett, 15 and 29 July 1931, Liggett Papers; Hoover to Nell May Hill, 9 Nov. 1894, Hill Papers.

34 Jackson Reynolds recalled: "Hoover acquired quite a phobia about . . . fraternities and held himself aloof from them as being snobbish [and] . . . didn't permit either of his sons to join"—Oral history, Columbia University. Hinsdill later changed his name to Hinsdale. University Archives, Stanford; Hoover to Nell May Hill, 9 Nov. 1894, Hill Papers.

35 Hoover to Nell May Hill, 19 July 1894, Hill Papers.

36 Dr. Payson J. Treat to Herbert Hoover, 10 Oct. 1907, HI and Oral history, HHPL; Adams to Hoover, 2 June 1913; Hoover to Adams, 20 Dec. 1908, 22 Feb. 1912, 3 June 1913, Ephraim Adams Papers.

37 Hoover to Nell May Hill, 9 Nov. 1894, Hill Papers.

38 Hoover to Branner, 2 Sept. 1894, Branner Papers; Geology Club Minutes, University Archives, Stanford.

39 Two of Hoover's geological survey field books— showing much technical work as well as curiosity, interest in history, and familiarity with professional literature—for 1894 and 1895 are intact in the National Archives (copies at HHPL). Hoover to Nell May Hill, 19 July 1894, Hill Papers; Hoover to Branner, Branner Papers; Hoover Family Court Records, HHPL.

40 Hoover to Nell May Hill, 7 Sept. 1895, Hill Papers; Hoover to May Hoover, 4 Aug. 1895, Leavitt Papers.

41 Homer R. Spence, "Mr. Herbert Clark Hoover of Oakland, California, 1896," a manuscript dated 21 Sept. 1968, University Archives, Stanford; cf. Edgar Eugene Robinson and Paul Edward, eds., *The Memoirs of Ray Lyman Wilbur, 1875–1948* (Stanford, 1960), pp. 22–3.

42 Los Angeles *Times*, 8 Jan. 1933; Louis Janin to his brother, 8 June 1896, 8 March 1897, and 7 April 1897; Charles Janin to William Liggett, 30 July 1931, Liggett Papers; Hoover, "Geology of the Four-Mile Placer Mining District, Colorado," *Engineering and Mining Journal*, 22 May 1897, p. 510; Branner to Hoover, 27 April 1896, University Archives, Stanford.

43 According to one account, Attorney Lindley of Lindley and Eichoff first recommended Hoover to Morcing. Hoover frequented the law firm and Lindley worked with Janin on mining controversies. In 1914 Hoover wrote Lindley comparing Ambassador Page's reference to one Lindley had once written for him. William H. Metson to Walter Liggett, 8 July 1931, Liggett Papers; Theodore Hoover, "Memoranda," p. 95; Coolgardie *Miner*, 22 March 1897; Hoover to Judge Curtis Lindley, 7 Dec. 1914, CRB Papers, HI; Hoover to R. A. F. Penrose, Jr., 17 March and 12 April 1897, quoted in Helen R. Fairbanks and Charles R. Berkey, *Life and Letters of R. A. F. Pen-*

rose, Jr. (New York, 1952), pp. 156, 160, 199; Bewick, Moreing Papers, HHPL.

CHAPTER II

[1] These chapters are a first attempt to chart what have been termed Hoover's "forgotten years." Harris Warren, a pioneer scholar of Hoover, wrote: "History wants to know everything about such men, not just what they themselves choose to tell; but the career of Herbert Hoover before 1914 still is primarily an unwritten story. Some day someone is going to have to burrow into what records remain in an effort to eliminate uncertainties"—*Herbert Hoover and the Great Depression* (New York, 1959), p. ix.

[2] Louis Janin to his brother, 7 April 1897, Liggett Papers. The Liggett Papers must be used with great care; the only material of value, aside from certain published matter, consists of notes on interviews with some of Hoover's Stanford, business, and technical associates. Liggett's book, *The Rise of Herbert Hoover* (New York, 1932), is the work of a monomaniac. Liggett always draws conclusions least flattering to Hoover. And facts are frequently mishandled. Hoover, for example, could not have sailed to London in early fall 1898 to confront Moreing; he signed letters at Gwalia through that November. Rusty Sayers, "Mr. Hoover's Departure for and Arrival in Australia," and Don and Donna Reid to Robert Wood, 19 Nov. 1974, HHPL; *New York Evening Post,* 28 July 1928; Caspar W. Hodgson, Oral history, HHPL; Albany (W.A.) *Advertiser,* 15 May 1897; Coolgardie *Miner,* 22 May 1897.

[3] Hoover to Burt Barker, 25 October 1897; "Herbert Hoover's Accounts," HHPL.

[4] Margaret Atwater Flory of Geneva, New York, wrote me (2 Feb. 1969) concerning her vivid teen-age memories of Coolgardie and the Hoovers. Her father served at Gwalia, and she was put aboard ship to London in care of the Hoovers, whom she thought overly solicitous. Coolgardie *Miner,* 22 May 1897.

[5] J. Malcolm Maclaren, *Gold* (London, 1908), p. 38. Harriette Miles Odell remembered letters Hoover wrote to her in these years: "So many . . . discuss fun and jokes on Mitchel[l], Moore, Hooper, etc., and early ones were full of Miss Henry, Miss Rose, etc." Odell to Theodore Hoover, n.d. [ca. 1926]. "Genealogy," HHPL. The letters apparently were burned in a fire on Theodore's ranch in the 1930's.

[6] That Blainey is mistaken is clear from a letter to Spencer Crompton in which Hooper speaks of visiting Sons of Gwalia with Hoover for the first time in late November 1897. Acc/444A, Battye Library, Perth, Western Australia. A Bewick, Moreing Letterbook, moreover, on 29 Sept. notes that "the crosscut to the vein was put in during Mr. Hoover's return [*sic*] visit" to Sons of Gwalia. Acc/1614A, 1734A, Battye Library. Also, Hoover wrote home from Mt. Malcolm, 17 Sept. 1897, "I have finished the Sons of Gwalia and have recommended it." "Herbert Hoover's Accounts," Pre-Commerce subject file. Blainey is further incorrect in faulting Hoover for failing to note that the Welsh owners came from Coolgardie; an intermedi-

ary group was in control at the time of the Bewick, Moreing purchase. Detailed reports by Hoover on the mine are in the Bewick, Moreing file, Department of Mines, Perth, along with the critical cables 131C, 142C, 149C, 183C, 189C. Moreing is quoted in *Mining Journal,* 12 Dec. 1903, p. 669. The Hooper letters to C. M. Harris, dated 7 Nov. 1947 and 8 April 1948, are in Acc/444A, Battye Library. Blainey, "Herbert Hoover's Forgotten Years," *Business Archives and History,* III (Feb. 1963), 53–76. An error-packed article on Hoover by Ted McGowan appeared in *Australian Mining,* 16 June 1969.

[7] Walter E. Skinner, *Mining Manual and Mining Year-book;* and *Miner's Year Book* (1897); Hoover to Theodore and May, 16 July 1897, "Australia-Herbert Hoover Accounts," HHPL; J. W. McCarty, "British Investment in Western Australian Goldmining, 1894–1914," unpublished doctoral essay, Cambridge University, 1960, p. 133. Both Hooper and Loring disputed Hoover's important role in introducing the filter press. Hoover's firm brought Dr. Ludwig Diehl, one man who helped perfect the process, to Australia. A series of letters discusses the issue in *Engineering and Mining Journal,* LXXV, 24 Jan. 1901, 14 Feb. 1903, 21 March 1903, 15 Aug. 1903. Hooper credits W. Feldtman with the filter press; John Sutherland is also credited; Hoover mentions an American in his *Memoirs.* See Hoover's and Pritchard's own detailed examination of ore treatment processes, "The Treatment of Sulpho-Telluride Ores at Kalgoorlie," *Engineering and Mining Journal,* 21 March 1903, *passim,* 1 Aug. 1903, pp. 156–7; 14 Aug. 1903, p. 228; *Mining Magazine,* 13 Aug. 1903, *passim.* J. W. Kirwin, "Hoover in Western Australia," and "Mr. and Mrs. Hoover: West Australian Reminiscences," *West Australian,* 2 July 1966, Acc/PR82, Battye Library. Kalgoorlie *Miner,* 7 Aug. 1897; 26 Aug. 1897; 2 Sept. 1897; 9 Sept. 1897.

Hoover was fierce in his own boastful nationalism and confidence in the superiority of American engineers. Writing to an Oregon friend late in 1897 he said: "Yankees are not well received they only have us because they have to they don't know how to make their mines pay dividends we do"—Hoover to Burt Barker, 25 Oct. 1897. To another friend he observed: "No country in the world has witnessed such rank swindling and charlatan engineering"—Hoover to Penrose, 2 April 1898. To a member of his family Hoover wrote: "I never dreamed such a set of scoundrels could exist as some I have had to deal with. Only yesterday, a man offered me a bribe of $8,000"—6 Oct. 1897, "Herbert Hoover Accounts," Pre-Commerce subject file, HHPL. See also Hoover to Ben Cook, 30 March 1898; Mr. James to Bewick, Moreing, 19 Dec. 1898, Bewick, Moreing Letterbook, HHPL. Hoover was publishing regularly now: see "The Superficial Alteration of Western Australian Ore Deposits," *Engineering and Mining Journal,* 29 Oct. 1898, p. 520; cf. *Transactions of A.I.M.E.* (Oct. 1898), p. 758.

[8] Mr. James to Bewick, Moreing, 19 Dec. 1898, Sons of Gwalia Letterbook, HHPL; Hoover to R. A. F. Penrose, 2 April 1898, quoted in Helen R. Fairbanks and Charles R. Berkey, *Life and Letters of R. A. F. Penrose, Jr.* (New York, 1952).

[9] Bewick, Moreing Letterbook, 9 and 12 May 1898, Battye Library. *Votes and Proceedings,* Parliament of Western Australia, 1904, II, A7, 73ff.

[10] Sons of Gwalia Letterbook, 23 May 1898, HHPL.

[11] Hoover may also have been simply playing up to his superior in London, demonstrating his vigor in the control of costs. Moreing, a Conservative Member of Parliament, declared in his 1899 presidential address to the Institution of Mining and Metallurgy: "The State is benefited to the greatest degree by the maximum production at the minimum cost. . . . This covers the whole of the ground of adequate title, safety of investment, taxation, protection of human life, &c., for cost is the prime factor of production, and the advance of cost by misapplication of law cripples the ideal to be attained by the State." Moreing, in the words of one of his most prominent mine managers, was "a ruthless old villain. . . . He had absolutely no ethics." Charles Algernon "by the grace of God" Moreing, Hoover once called him. Atwater interview, Liggett Papers; *Transactions of the Institution of Mining and Metallurgy,* VIII (1899–1900), 409–19. In the first sentence Moreing may be quoting another source; the text is unclear. *Engineering and Mining Journal,* 17 Dec. 1898; Coolgardie *Miner,* 11 Nov. 1905; "Mining and Milling Gold Ores in Western Australia," *Engineering and Mining Journal,* 17 Dec. 1898, pp. 725–6.

[12] Hoover to "friends" from Cue, Western Australia, 9 Aug. 1897, "Herbert Hoover Accounts," Pre-Commerce, HHPL.

[13] On Moreing's earlier business activity in the Far East, see his "A Recent Business Tour in China," *Eclectic Magazine,* CXXXI (Nov. 1898), 632; "Great Britain's Opportunity in China," *Nineteenth Century,* XL (Feb. 1898), 328–36; "An All-British Railway to China," *Nineteenth Century,* XLVI (Sept. 1899), 484–92; Moreing, "Presidential Address," *Transactions* . . . , VIII, 411.

[14] Moreing's statement on why Hoover left China is in Bewick, Moreing *v.* Hoover, 1916 B, No. 1071, PRO; Sayers, "Mr. Hoover's Departure."

[15] Claire Torrey, Oral history, HHPL; Florence L. Henry to Mrs. Mason, 12 March 1899; *Daily Palo Alto,* 12 and 19 Sept. 1892, 13 Feb. 1893. On his travel schedule to China, see Hoover's letter of 5 Jan. 1899 to his "family," "Herbert Hoover's Accounts," Pre-Commerce, HHPL.

[16] Hoover, *Memoirs,* I, 54–65; the *North China Herald,* 13 June 1900, p. 1088.

[17] The long quotation and "under Chinese administration . . ." are both from *Mining Journal,* 30 Aug. 1902, p. 1175; "Their smallest weakness . . ." is in *Engineering and Mining Journal,* 26 May 1900, p. 619; San Francisco *Chronicle,* 29 Oct. 1901; Lou Hoover to Branner, 12 May 1900, Branner Papers, University Archives, Stanford; Hoover, *Memoirs,* I, 63.

[18] On the "present contractor slavery system," see Hoover to Chang Yen-mao, 7 Sept. 1899, Bodleian Library, Oxford University.

[19] Hoover to Chang Yen-mao, 7 Sept. 1899.

[20] Hoover to Moreing, Jan. 1900, quoted in Yang Lu, K'ai-lun-K'uang, . . . (Tientsin, 1932); Lou Hoover to Theodore Hoover, "Jan.–Feb., 1920," Reprints, HHPL.

[21] Wilson to Hoover, n.d., and 8 Oct. 1899; Hoover to Detring, 16 May and 5 Aug. 1899, Bodleian Library; Hoover, "Present Situation of the Mining Industry in China," *Engineering and Mining Journal,* 26 May 1900, pp. 619–

20; "The Kaiping Coal Mines and Coal Field," *Mining Journal, Railway and Commercial Gazette,* 30 Aug. 1902, p. 1175.

22 See, for example, Anthony F. C. Wallace, "Revitalization Movements," *American Anthropologist,* LVIII (1956), 264–81.

23 Hoover gives a graphic account of what happened in the New York *Sun,* 19 Nov. 1900. The obituary story is in Bess Furman, *Washington Byline* (New York, 1949). When Furman asked Mrs. Hoover in 1928 if it were true that she spoke eight languages including fluent Chinese, Lou wondered why the number was not set at twenty-three. Hoover to Chang Yen-mao, 7 Sept. and 8 Oct. 1899; G. B. Means to Hoover, 8 Oct. 1899 and n.d. [1899]; Hoover to Detring, 5 Aug. 1899, Bodleian Library; San Francisco *Chronicle,* 29 Oct. 1901; John Agnew's estimate is a total of 1500 troops, "A Narrative . . ." Auckland *Weekly News,* 24 Aug. 1900; N. F. Drake says 2000 in a letter to Dr. John Branner, 13 June 1900; see also Drake to Branner, 31 Dec. 1899, University Archives, Stanford.

24 Hoover to Charles D. Henry, telegram, 13 July 1900, Wilbur Manuscripts, Stanford; Lou Henry Hoover to Mary Austin, n.d. (1914?), Austin Papers, Huntington Library; Hodges diary, II, 161. More information may be found in the Edward Drew diary—the Hoovers stayed at the Drew house—or the William Schockley letterbooks, if and when these sources are released to scholars. Norman McGee, who died a few months later from disease contracted in Tientsin, is quoted by Archie Rice; mention of the cable is in the Ray Lyman Wilbur Papers, 13 July 1900; both sources are in the University Archives, Stanford, as is N. F. Drake to Branner, 31 Dec. 1899, Branner Papers.

25 O. D. Rasmussen's *Tientsin* (Tientsin, 1935) quotes a William McLeish on the danger to Chang. John Agnew confirms the T'ang story in a memo dated 27 April 1938, Post-Presidential, Individual, Box 2, HHPL. There is an interview with T'ang in the *New York Herald-Tribune* of 15 Sept. 1929.

26 Lou Henry Hoover to Mary Austin, n.d., Austin Papers, Huntington Library; Lou Henry Hoover statement is in CRB files, ca 10/15. *Mining Journal* said Hoover and de Wouters are owed "a great deal of gratitude for making the business successful." N. F. Drake to Branner, 13 June 1900, Branner Papers; Hoover to Detring, 21 Aug. 1900, Bodleian Library; Ellsworth C. Carlson, *The Kaiping Mines, 1877–1912* (Cambridge, Mass., 1971), 2nd ed. I am obliged to Professor Carlson of Oberlin College for advice in a series of letters (1975–6) and for guidance in the use of Chinese sources.

27 Important Chinese sources which I have had translated are Yang Lu, *K'ai-lan-K'uang* . . . (Tientsin, 1932); Wang Hsi, *Chung-ying K'ai-P'ing* . . . (Taipei, 1963); Wang Liang, *Historical Materials* . . . (Peiping, 1933).

28 Hoover to Detring, 20 Jan. 1901 and 9 Feb. 1901, in Yang Lu, pp. 155–9; Carlson, *The Kaiping Mines, passim; London and China Telegraph,* 2 Dec. 1902; *Pallmall Gazette,* 2 Feb. 1903; the *Peking and Tientsin Times,* 4 Nov. 1902, 30 March 1904.

29 Hunt, "Hoover of the CRB," *World's Work,* June 1917, p. 165; *The Survey,* 2 Sept. 1916, p. 561.

30 De Wouters and Chang on 6 June 1901 did sign some documents that

provided for the two to work together. During that summer, however, the company hired about a dozen people, most of them Belgian, without Chinese permission.

[31] See *Australian Mail*, 4 Sept. 1902, p. 199, on the Francqui-Hoover conflict, and the Hoover-checked Arthur Train, *The Strange Attacks on Herbert Hoover* (New York, 1932). The letters of Hoover, de Wouters, and Detring cannot be found in British archives, but they do exist in Chinese. See Yang Lu, pp. 155–9 (Hoover to Detring, 20 Jan. and 9 Feb. 1901). Pro-Hoover articles include Edward Hunter, "The Kailan Mines and Hoover," *China Weekly Review*, 18 July 1931, pp. 262, 264–5, 280; G.B.R., "The Tragic Ending to a Daly Opera," *Far Eastern Review* (April 1932), pp. 153–5; Hoover's letter is in *North China Daily News*, 27 July 1902 (reprinted in *North China Herald*, 6 Aug. 1902).

[32] Shanghai *Daily Press*, 24 Nov. 1902.

[33] Foreign Office materials relating to the Chinese Engineering and Mining Company are in PRO 17/1759 and 17/1760. Townley's letter to F. Bertie is dated 3 Dec. 1902, pp. 127–9.

[34] Partial coverage of the trial is given in *The Times* (London), Jan.–March 1905, *passim;* see also *London and China Telegraph*, Dec. 1905, and "Memorandum on the K'AI P'ING MINING CASE" (Peking, 1908), 91 pp. Lou Henry Hoover's account is in a letter dated 1920 to Theodore Hoover, Reprint File, Jan.–Feb. 1920, HHPL; de Wouters to Francqui, 14 July 1901; Hoover to Moreing, 12 Feb. 1901; Hoover to Detring, 24 Jan. 1901, BM Papers, HHPL; *Memoirs*, I, 158.

[35] Carlson, *The Kaiping Mines*, passim.

[36] Delivery of 54,875 shares of stock by Moreing to Detring brought the German to the British Embassy in China to swear that he had "forgotten" that Moreing had promised him a share in the Syndicate's profits. There is no record of Detring contributing to the Chinese defense. One-fifth of the new company's 1 million shares were set aside for the promoters, including 50,000 each for Chang and Detring. Another 375,000 went to shareholders of the old company, who complained that the stock had been watered when the remaining shares were parceled out as enticements to purchasers of a fresh 500,000 bond issue. *Fortune* argued that the arrangement had operated to the advantage of the promoters rather than to that of the company, but the bonds might not have been sold without the stock dividend. Profits realized by the promoters were not more than were often made then on the Stock Exchange or on Wall Street. *Fortune*, Aug. 1932, pp. 33–5.

[37] In November 1905 the London *Chronicle* reported that the board thought Chinese laborers "a very poor lot indeed and certainly not worth the trouble and expense of bringing them out." But the shipments continued into 1906 with some 50,000 at work. The *Chronicle* also reprints Hoover's Chamber of Commerce speech opposing the use of Chinese labor. One oral history account claims that Hoover was sent to Africa to quiet racial tensions there. Frederick Terman, HHPL. *Mining Journal*, 17 Sept. 1904, p. 281; 25 Feb. 1905, p. 195; 28 Oct. 1905, p. 424; *Mining World*, 23 July 1904, p. 106.

[38] Again Hoover found time to compose technical articles: "Present Situation of the Mining Industry in China," *Engineering and Mining Journal*, 26 May

1900, pp. 619–20; "Metal Mining in the Provinces of Chi-Li and Shantung, China," *Transactions of the Institution of Mining and Metallurgy,* VIII (1900–1), 324–31; "The Kaiping Coal Mines and Coal Field, Chihle Province, North China," *Transactions of the Institution of Mining and Metallurgy,* X (1901–2).

CHAPTER III

1 Ephraim D. Adams recollected many early trips with Hoover in a speech he delivered at Stanford in 1928, Adams Papers.
2 Lou Henry Hoover to Mary Austin, 23 Mar. 1916, Austin Papers, Huntington Library; Austin, *Earth Horizon* (New York, 1932), pp. 311, 312, 314, 323–4.
3 W. J. Loring Interview, Liggett Papers; Hoover Calendars, HHPL.
4 J. W. McCarty, "British Investment in Western Australian Goldmining, 1894–1914," *University Studies in History* (Perth, 1961–2), p. 97; see also McCarty's Cambridge University doctoral dissertation of the same title (1960); New South Wales *Parliamentary Papers,* 1908, II, 834ff.; 1909, II, 738ff. *The Economist,* 3 Aug. 1907, pp. 1322–3; *Mining Magazine,* May 1912, p. 323; Robert Annan, Personal interview, 25 July 1968; Loring Interview, Liggett Papers.
5 *West Australian Mining, Building, and Engineering Journal,* 12 Sept. 1908, p. 51; *Australian Mining Standard* (Melbourne), 20 Sept. 1905; *Mining Journal,* 6 Jan. 1906, p. 19; 9 June 1906, pp. 773–4; 3 Aug. 1907, pp. 163–4; 18 July 1908, pp. 96–7; *Mining Magazine,* Oct. 1910, p. 234; *Engineering and Mining Journal,* 16 Jan. 1909, p. 219; interview with Amor Keene, Liggett Papers; Arthur A. Curtice, Oral history, HHPL; T. A. Rickard, ed., *Concentration by Flotation* (New York, 1921), pp. 12ff.
6 D. P. Mitchell to Bewick, Moreing, 17 July 1908, Bewick, Moreing Papers, HHPL, *passim;* Robert Annan, Personal interview, 22 Aug. 1968.
7 Geoffrey Blainey, ed., *If I Remember Rightly: Memoirs of W. S. Robinson* (Melbourne, 1968), pp. 39, 42, 108; *Mining Journal,* 9 June 1906, pp. 773–4; Mitchell to Bewick, Moreing, 17 July 1908, Bewick, Moreing Papers, HHPL.
8 *West Australian Mining, Building, and Engineering Journal,* 14 May 1902, p. 11; 30 April 1904, p. 6, 2 Dec. 1905, p. 25; *Mining Journal,* 6 Jan. 1905, p. 15.
9 *West Australian Mining, Building, and Engineering Journal,* 14 May 1902, p. 11; 6 June 1903, p. 11; 30 April 1904, p. 6; 2 Dec. 1905, p. 3; *Mining Journal,* 6 Jan. 1906, p. 15. For one motion to investigate the firm's monopolistic practices, see Western Australian *Parliamentary Papers* (Hansards), 26 (1904), 1557–9.
10 Storey was an old enemy of Hoover; see *West Australian Mining, Building, and Engineering Journal,* 6 June 1903; Bewick, Moreing Papers, HHPL.
11 *Report of the Royal Commission . . . to Inquire into . . . Great Boulder Perseverance . . . ,* Western Australian *Parliamentary Papers,* 6 (1905).
12 Blainey, "Herbert Hoover's Forgotten Years," *Business Archives and History,* III (Feb. 1963), 62.
13 On April 18, 1903, the *West Australian Mining, Building, and Engineering*

Journal criticized the company's policies on fire insurance and indemnity to miners against accidents. But more characteristic was perhaps the *Mining Journal*'s report that the firm moved its men to prevent unemployment, 12 Dec. 1905, p. 9; 6 Jan. 1906, pp. 15, 19; *Colonial Mining News* (London), 4 April 1907, p. 168; wage policies are discussed in *West Australian Mining, Building, and Engineering Journal,* 2 Dec. 1905.

14 Kalgoorlie *Miner,* 30 May 1904, p. 6; 2 May 1904, p. 2; 13 May 1904; 30 April 1904, p. 4; 20, 22, 26, and 28 April 1904; *Report of the Royal West Australian Parliament, Commission on the Immigration of Non-British Labor . . . 1904* (Perth, 1904), *Votes and Proceedings,* 2 (1904), 13, 14, 24, 26, 27, 44–6, 48, 49, 51, 52, 61–4, 67–84, 90, 91, 93–5; 26 (1904), 1558; 31 (1907), 1061, 1166–8. *Report of . . . Select Committee . . . into the Boiler Explosion on the Sons of Gwalia Mine* (Perth, 1906).

15 *Morning Herald* (Perth), 11 Sept. 1906; Coolgardie *Miner,* 10 Nov. 1905; 11 Nov. 1905; *Western Australian* (Perth), 10 Nov. 1905; H. C. Hoover, "Western Australia," *Engineering and Mining Journal,* 5 Jan. 1905, pp. 41–2.

16 A. C. Martin of Rangoon visited the slag heaps as early as 1891 and organized in 1904 the Great Eastern Mining Company in Mandalay, which sold its rights to Burma Mines. Blainey, ed., *If I Remember Rightly,* p. 132; John L. Christian, "Herbert Hoover and His Connection with Burma," *Journal of Burma Research Society,* XXVI (1930), 116–18; *Mining World,* 6 Nov. 1909, p. 599; *Engineering and Mining Journal,* 12 June 1909, p. 1292; 24 June 1922, pp. 1084–91; 28 April 1923, pp. 747, 757ff.

17 Lou Henry Hoover proudly recalled that the well-built Mandalay smelter had been erected entirely by woman labor; even the contracts were let to women. Lou Hoover to Mary Austin, n.d., Austin Papers, Huntington Library. *Report on the Great Eastern Mines, Burma,* 10 March 1905, Bewick, Moreing Papers, HHPL; *Mining Magazine,* Sept. 1912, p. 230; May 1914, pp. 327–8; Sept. 1914, p. 167.

18 Loring took over on about March 10, 1908; *West Australian Mining, Building, and Engineering Journal,* 7 March 1908, p. 4; *Mining Journal,* 12 Sept. 1903, p. 289; *Mining Magazine,* Dec. 1910, p. 395; Hoover to Agnew, Aug. 1908, Bewick, Moreing Papers, HHPL.

19 1910 M No. 9B, 1916 No. 1071B, King's Bench, PRO; Atwater and Loring interviews in Liggett Papers. Papers relating to both suits are in the microfilm of Bewick, Moreing Papers that I filmed in London in 1968 and that is now deposited in the HHPL.

20 As early as 1904, J. H. Curle, author of *Gold Mines of the World,* noted, "You will find [among investors] H. C. Hoover, Esq., the Capitalist." Curle called Hoover "one of the most brilliant men in the mining world today." Hoover let Curle use his Kensington flat while it was vacant. *Mining World,* 14 May 1904, p. 659; "Investment Speculation," *Mining Magazine,* Sept. 1909, pp. 39–41, 255, 285–7; Oct. 1909, p. 115, makes the authorship clear. Hoover in 1903 advised a Bewick, Moreing engineer in Kalgoorlie: "Share purchase by engineers has given me the greatest possible anxiety." After watching the West Australian market for seven years, Hoover wrote: "I do not know at the present time of anyone who has speculated in shares and is not worse off financially for having done so. . . . The way money is made

in mining is to secure interests in mines at their initiation and not when they come before the public." Hoover to D. E. Bigelow, 3 July 1903, Bigelow Papers.

21 Hoover complained to his secretary that an article in *Fortune* about his personal finances contained not "an accurate sentence." Judging from many sources, I suspect that the piece underestimates Hoover's personal worth. Certainly, having converted his assets into sound bonds in mid-1929, he was in superb financial condition after he left the Presidency. Theodore Joslin, *Hoover Off the Record* (Garden City, N.Y., 1934), p. 291. "The President's Fortune," *Fortune*, Aug. 1932, pp. 33–6, 82–3. Hoover to Colonel Wright, 2 Sept. 1914, HHPL. In a letter to Judge Curtis H. Lindley, Hoover remarked that he had been earning $100,000 annually for some years. 22 Nov. 1914, CRB Papers.

22 *Mining Magazine*, May 1914, pp. 327–8; Sept. 1914, p. 167; Amor Keene interview, Liggett Papers; *Engineering and Mining Journal*, 12 June 1909, p. 1292.

23 Others who worked with Hoover include James Cordner-James, R. Gilman Brown, Dean Mitchell, T. J. Jones, Louis Chevrillon, George P. Doolette, A. Chester Beatty (an American who did adopt British citizenship), A. N. Treadgold, John Hays Hammond, Edmund Davis, W. F. Turner, and R. Tilden-Smith. Hoover wasted months investigating Korean mines in 1910 for a group of Japanese bankers; *Engineering and Mining Journal*, 12 June 1909, p. 1292; Lancefield was Hoover's greatest failure; *Geological Survey of Victoria*, V, Pt. 3 (1906), 334; *Mining and Scientific Press*, 23 Nov. 1912, p. 672; *Mining Journal*, 6 Dec. 1909, p. 750; *Mining Magazine*, Nov. 1912, pp. 326–8; Nov. 1915, pp. 22–3; Oct. 1913; p. 241; *Mining World*, 11 Dec. 1909, p. 733.

24 Companies' House, London, holds skeletal records of all these companies.

25 There is considerable correspondence about Canadian mining ventures in the Bewick, Moreing microfilm, HHPL. The technical detail is from various issues of the mining press such as *Mining Journal*, 12 June 1909, p. 400.

26 Central State Historical Archives of the Soviet Union, M. U. Lachayeva, "On the History of Foreign Capital Penetration in the Non-ferrous Metallurgy of the Urals and Siberia at the Beginning of the XX Century," Moscow. Universitet, *Vestnik* Ser. 9: Istoria, XXX, 3 (May/June 1975), 81–96; Hoover explained in an unsent letter to Mrs. Urquhart that her husband had come to Washington, said that he had a chance to recover some of his property, and in view of Hoover's strong anti-communism, wanted to minimize his earlier connections with Russian enterprises. Urquhart, "Attacks on President Hoover," *Truth*, 25 May 1932, p. 811; Scott Turner, Mrs. Jameson Parker, and Hugh Moran, Oral history, HHPL; *Mining Magazine*, Feb. 1914, p. 97; *Engineering and Mining Journal*, 22 June 1912, pp. 1238–9; *Mining and Scientific Press*, 23 Nov. 1912, p. 672; Blainey, *Herbert Hoover's Forgotten Years;* Blainey, *Mines in the Spinifex* (Sydney, 1966), pp. 231–2; Mrs. Leslie Urquhart to Hoover, 5 June 1951 and 20 June 1951, HHPL; *Skinner's Mining Manual* (1913), pp. 730–1; Hoover *Memoirs*, I, 102–9.

27 *Mining Magazine*, June 1911, pp. 409–10; Aug. 1911, p. 155; Sept. 1911, p. 208; June 1912, p. 397; Sept. 1913, pp. 279–81; Oct. 1913, p. 309; Feb. 1914,

pp. 26, 150–1; Dec. 1914, pp. 348–50; Aug. 1915, p. 65; June 1913, p. 426; see also Hoover to Mrs. Urquhart, ca. 1954, not sent; *Skinner*, pp. 730–1; *Mining and Scientific Press*, 23 Nov. 1912, p. 672.

28 *World's Work*, April 1920, p. 579; *Mining Magazine*, Sept. 1911, p. 208; Feb. 1914, pp. 150–1; Dec. 1914, pp. 348–50; Aug. 1915, p. 65; Dec. 1917, p. 515. For additional information on Hoover and Russia, see the (London) *Financial Times*, 26 July 1912, and the Oral history reminiscences of Scott Turner and Hugh Moran, HHPL.

29 Scott Turner, Oral history, HHPL; Hoover, *Memoirs*, I, *passim*.

30 *Mining Magazine*, Nov. 1911, pp. 330–1; May 1912, p. 373; Dec. 1913, pp. 412–13, 463–4; June 1914, p. 30; Nov. 1914, pp. 287–8. Hoover to Wilbur, 16 June 1914, Wilbur Papers; T. A. Rickard, *The Romance of Mining* (Toronto, 1945), p. 314. In June 1913 *Mining Magazine* greeted Santa Gertrudis with enthusiasm reserved for those companies where "the technical advisors are holders of large blocks of shares." The magazine, remarking about the men who "engineered this deal," called this "an American phrase that expressed the useful work done by engineers who also act as promoters." Two years later, however, the world's leading mining journal objected to Hammond's "preposterous commission of £ 120,000" and complained of the secrecy under which the mine operated. Both Herbert and Theodore Hoover defended Hammond, but T. A. Rickard of *Mining Magazine* believed that mining engineers acting as promoters exerted a bad influence on the profession. See also *Mining Magazine*, Sept. 1909, p. 2; Jan. 1910, pp. 40–1; Dec. 1913, pp. 412–13, 463–4; Nov. 1914, pp. 287–8; Hoover to Ray Wilbur, 16 June 1914, Wilbur Papers.

31 Hoover helplessly wrote to a subordinate about some matter in 1914: "I do not know what to do about it as the case is a matter of detail." Hoover to John Lucey, 18 Dec. 1914, CRB Papers. Loring interview, T. A. Rickard, *Interviews with Mining Engineers* (San Francisco, 1922), p. 278.

32 *Mining Magazine*, Oct. 1909, p. 115.

33 On Hoover's ill health, see *Mining and Scientific Press*, 15 Feb. 1908, or *Mining Magazine* of 14 March 1908, which speaks of "continuous overwork," p. 314. Hoover to Theodore Hoover, 15 July 1903, 30 Aug. 1904, McLean Collection, HI.

34 The *New York Sun* interview of 18 Sept. 1912 is reprinted in *Mining Magazine*, Dec. 1910, pp. 304–5; Jordan, *The Days of a Man* (New York, 1922), II, 223.

35 Hoover to Charles C. Moore, 5, 18, and 27 July 1912, "Panama Pacific," Pre-Commerce, HHPL.

36 Hoover to *The Times* (London), 20 Aug. 1913; Hoover to Charles Moore, 21 Feb., 13 Oct., and 11 Nov. 1913, "Panama-Pacific Exposition," Pre-Commerce, HHPL.

37 Hoover to Meller-Zakometsky, 27 July 1912. Later he wrote, "the great success of the colonization of the Jews in Russia is an outstanding accomplishment." Hoover to Felix Warburg, 5 July 1927, Warburg Papers; Hoover to Barneson, 5 Dec. 1913; Hoover to Charles Moore, 27 July 1912, 2 April 1914; "Panama-Pacific Exposition," Pre-Commerce, HHPL; *The Times* (London), 31 Dec. 1913.

38 Craig Lloyd, *Aggressive Introvert* (Columbus, 1972), pp. 32–3; Goode to Charles C. Moore, 19 Dec. 1913; Hoover to Goode, 1 April 1914; Goode to Hoover, 28 Feb. 1914; Hoover to Moore, 2 April 1914; "Panama-Pacific Exposition," Pre-Commerce, HHPL.

CHAPTER IV

1 Hoover to Mary Austin [1913?], Austin Papers, Huntington Library.
2 At a New York dinner, for instance, Hoover complained that mining engineers had to take a position below the "parasitic" professions of theology, law, and war. *Engineering and Mining Journal*, 14 March 1914, p. 12.
3 "Permanence in Depth in Kalgoorlie," *Engineering and Mining Journal*, 31 Oct. 1903, p. 655; and "Ore Treatment at Kalgoorlie," *Engineering and Mining Journal*, 15 Aug. 1903, p. 228.
4 "The Valuation of Gold Mines," 19 May 1904, p. 801; "Mine Valuation," 7 July 1904; "Ore Treatment Capacities," 18 Aug. 1904, p. 253; "Gold Mine Accounts," 11 July 1903, 24 May 1904, 4 Aug. 1904; all in *Engineering and Mining Journal*; "The Economics of a Boom," *Mining Magazine*, May 1912, pp. 370–3.
5 "Mine Valuation and Mine Finance," *Mining Magazine*, VII (Oct. 1912), 275–7; "The Economics of a Boom," pp. 37–73; "Mine Valuation and Mine Finance," pp. 275–7; "Ore Treatment Capacities," p. 253.
6 *West Australia Mining, Building, and Engineering Journal*, 31 Mar. 1906; "Arbitration at Broken Hill," *Engineering and Mining Journal*, 17 April 1909; *Mining Magazine*, Sept. 1909.
7 *Principles of Mining* was published in New York in 1909. See pp. 125, 163, 165, 167–8. Harvard and the University of Wisconsin also invited Hoover to speak.
8 Loring interview, Liggett Papers; Hoover to Bigelow, 1905, Bigelow Papers. The Agnew letter and a selection of reviews are in Pre-Commerce, HHPL. *Mining Magazine*, Sept. 1909, pp. 37–8; Oct. 1909, pp. 113–14; *The Times* (London), 22 April 1909.
9 "The Training of the Mining Engineer," *Science*, XX (25 Nov. 1904), 716–19; *Mining Journal* (Sept. 1909), pp. 37–8; Hoover to Branner, 22 Sept. 1904, Branner Papers; Brooks Adams, *The New Empire* (Cleveland, 1902), p. vi.
10 Bauer himself was an eminent translator. As early as 1636, an English translation was unsuccessfully attempted. Some mining technicians in Butte, Montana—then a major center of copper extraction and mining research—were trying to undertake a translation around 1903. "De Re Metallica," Pre-Commerce, HHPL; Hazel Nickel, "A Chained Book—Now Free to All," *Canadian Mining and Metallurgical Bulletin*, 42 (June 1949), 303–6.
11 William B. Castle, Jr., "The Hoover Translation of *De Re Metallica*," *The Colophon*, Pt. 13 (1933); "De Re Metallica," Pre-Commerce, HHPL; Mrs. William Schockley, Oral history, HHPL.
12 David Kuhner, "The Herbert Hoover Collection: A Gift and a Story," *Honnold Library Record*, XII (Spring 1971), 2–6; Hoover to A. B. Parson, 7 Oct. 1942, "A.I.M.E.," HHPL; Mrs. William Schockley, Oral history;

Hoover, *List of Books Relating to Metals* (London, 1911); *Bulletin of the Seismological Society of America,* II (March 1912).
[13] Hoover to John Richardson, 9 May 1933, HHPL.

CHAPTER V

[1] Hoover, *Memoirs,* I, 135, 137; Hoover to Lindon Bates, 2 Oct. 1914, CRB Papers.
[2] Charlotte Kellogg, *Women of Belgium* (New York, 1916), p. 50.
[3] Hoover to Lindon Bates, 24 Jan. 1915, CRB Papers.
[4] Assistant Treasurer Bainbridge, Hoover observed, was "a more complete idiot than whom I have yet to discover in a public office." Hoover to Bates, 2 Oct. 1914; Hoover to Frederick van Duzer, 8 Aug. 1914; Hoover to Walter Hines Page, 23 Sept. 1914; Hoover to Judge Curtis H. Lindley, 22 Nov. 1914; Lou Henry Hoover, *Report of the Chairman of the American Women's Relief Committee,* CRB Papers; Hoover to Page, 23 Sept. 1914, American Legation, London, NA.
[5] Hoover had sent Page a copy of *De Re Metallica.* Hoover to Page, 22 Nov. 1913, Page Papers; Hoover, *An American Epic,* I, 3ff.; American Embassy, London, C8 15/189, V. CV (1915), *passim,* NA.
[6] Hoover to Bates, 17 Jan. 1915; 24 Jan. 1915, CRB Papers.
[7] Burton J. Hendrick, *The Life and Letters of Walter H. Page* (New York, 1922), II, 311–12; George I. Gay, *Statistical Review of Relief Operations* (Stanford, 1925); see also Gay, *Public Relations of the Commission for Relief in Belgium* (Stanford, 1929).
[8] Good secondary sources on Whitlock in Belgium are Robert M. Crunden's *A Hero in Spite of Himself: Brand Whitlock in Art, Politics and War* (New York, 1969), and John Wells Davidson, "The Diplomacy of Belgium Relief," *Prologue,* IV (Winter 1970), 145–60. Whitlock journal, 9 Jan. 1915, 3 Nov. 1932, Whitlock Papers, Library of Congress; Whitlock to Hoover, 18 Dec. 1914, CRB Papers.
[9] Hoover to Whitlock, 13 Jan. 1915, CRB Papers; Hoover to Whitlock, 28 Jan. 1916, file 848, and Hoover to Whitlock, Nov. 1916, file 519, Diplomatic Posts, Belgium; Whitlock to Page, 20 Nov. 1916, file C8 15/301, American Embassy, London, NA.
[10] Hoover to Whitlock, 13 Jan. 1915; Hoover to Wilson, 8 Feb. 1914, CRB Papers; Hoover to Gibson, 19 Feb. 1937, Gibson Papers; Whitlock journal, 2 Jan. 1915, 14 April 1932, Whitlock Papers, Library of Congress; Viscomtesse de Breughem, Oral history, HHPL; Ronald Swerczek, "The Diplomatic Career of Hugh Gibson, 1908–1938," unpublished doctoral dissertation, University of Iowa, 1973, pp. 67–8; Gibson to his mother, 2 May 1915, Gibson Papers, HI; Whitlock, *Belgium,* I (New York, 1919), 346–9.
[11] Whitlock journal, 29 Nov. 1914, Whitlock Papers, Library of Congress; Whitlock journal, 1 Aug. 1916, Nevins Papers; Whitlock, *Belgium,* I, 399.
[12] The successive directors of the CRB in Brussels were Albert Connett, Oscar Crosby, Vernon Kellogg, William Poland, Warren Gregory, and Prentiss Gray. William Honnold headed the London office, John White directed

shipping, and Ben Allen arranged publicity. Almost all were engineers. Lucey to Francqui, 13 Nov. 1914; Hoover to Doheny, 28 Nov. 1914; Hoover to Whitlock, 16 Dec. 1914; Lucey to Hoover, 29 Oct. 1914, CRB Papers; Whitlock, *Belgium*, I, 530; Gay, *Public Relations,* pp. 29–31; *Engineering and Mining Journal,* 30 Sept. 1916, p. 609; Hoover to Whitlock, 7 Dec. 1914, American Legation, Brussels, CB 12/12, NA.

13 Francqui to Hoover, 18 Nov. 1914, CRB Papers.

14 Hoover to Will Irwin, 18 Jan. 1915, Whitlock to Hoover, 12 Dec. 1914, CRB Papers; Whitlock journal, 7 Nov. 1914, Whitlock Papers, Library of Congress.

15 Gay, *Public Relations,* pp. 39–42, 44, 214–303; Hoover Memorandum, Dec. 1914; Whitlock to Hoover, 13 Jan. 1915, American Legation, Brussels, NA.

16 Whitlock to Hoover, 13 Jan. 1915, American Legation, Brussels, NA.

17 Gay, *Statistical Review, passim.*

18 John B. White to Tracy P. Kittredge, n.d.; Hoover to Will Irwin, 18 Jan. 1915; Hoover to Edward Curtis, 11 Nov. 1915, CRB Papers; Whitlock, *Belgium,* I, 234; Hoover, *An American Epic,* I, 149–53; Gibson to Shaler, 19 Dec. 1914, and Whitlock to Hoover, 17 Dec. 1914, American Legation, Brussels, NA.

19 Colonel House diary, 2 May 1915, House Papers; Hoover, *An American Epic,* I, *passim.*

20 Hoover to Adams, 16 June 1915; Hoover Memorandum, 19 Aug. 1915, CRB Papers; *The Nation,* 17 Oct. 1920, p. 388; Whitlock, *Belgium,* II, 234; Whitlock journal, 8 Jan. 1915, Whitlock Papers, Library of Congress; Hoover to Wilson, 13 May 1915, Francis O'Brien, ed., *The Hoover-Wilson Wartime Correspondence* (Ames, 1974), pp. 8–10.

21 Hoover to Crosby, 1 June 1915, CRB Papers; Hoover to Gerard, 5 Dec. 1914, American Embassy, London, C8 15/179, NA.

22 Hoover to Whitlock, 13 March 1915; Hoover memorandum, ca. 7 Dec. 1914, CRB Papers; Nevins, *The Letters and Journal of Brand Whitlock* (New York, 1936), pp. 18, 159; CAB 37/123/9, PRO; H. G. Chilton to Ronald [?], 15 Aug. 1928, FO 371/12839, PRO; Hoover to Whitlock, 13 March 1915, American Legation, Brussels, NA.

23 Edward Eyre Hunt, *War Bread* (New York, 1916), p. 195; *The Outlook,* 8 Sept. 1915, p. 6; Lloyd George, *Memoirs of the Peace Conference* (New Haven, 1939), I, 199; various attitudes of Britain toward the CRB are in FO 371, e.g., 1912/67903, 2283/117, 117/10179, 57767/15.

24 Hoover to Whitlock, 15 Aug. 1915, CRB Papers.

25 Hoover to Colonel House, 16 Aug. 1915; Gay, *Public Relations,* pp. 65, 508–606; Hoover, *An American Epic,* I, 241–2.

26 Francqui to Hoover, 4 Feb. 1916; Hoover to Poland, 24 Jan. 1916; Hoover to Percy, 4 July, 5 July, 24 Aug. 1915, 17 Feb. 1916; Percy to Hoover, 21 Jan. 1916; Hoover to Percy, 5 April 1916, CRB Papers; Gay, *Public Relations,* pp. 6–9, 58–60, 79; Hoover to Gerard, 27 March 1915, American Legation, Brussels, 848/658, NA; Hoover to Whitlock, 6 April 1915, American Legation, Brussels, 848/634, NA.

27 Hoover to Van Dyke, 4 Jan. 1915; Hoover to Percy, 18 Feb. 1916; Hoover

to Gerard, telegram, 19 March 1915, CRB Papers; Gay, *Public Relations,* pp. 53–4, 391–476; Whitlock journal, 6 March 1915, Whitlock Papers, Library of Congress; Gibson diary, 1 April 1915, Gibson Papers.

28 The Germans, by 1916, were engaged in the large-scale deportation of Belgians to forced-labor camps, chiefly in the Fatherland. Undoubtedly the Germans preferred Belgian control of relief, in the expectation that this would somehow ease the solution of their labor problems. Hoover wrote to Whitlock in November about "seizures of men . . . I fear it is the beginning of the end. Is it worth your considering . . . a full and strong protest? . . . This is a greater issue to the Belgian people than anything since the invasion and they look to you as to America for some strong action." He offered to inspect the camps in Belgium, but the CRB was under rigid instructions not to provide any such workers with food. Then, thanks to worldwide protests, and particularly those of Cardinal Mercier of Belgium, as well as the refusal of many Belgians to work at all, the deportations declined abruptly in December. Hoover to Whitlock, 14 Nov. 1914, American Legation, Brussels, C8 12/11, NA; Hoover to Jerome D. Green, 19 April 1915; Hoover to Lucey, 12 Nov. 1914, CRB Papers; "War Relief Work of the Rockefeller Foundation," Vols. 1, 2, 4, 11, 17, 22; Jerome D. Green to F. T. Gates, 29 Nov. 1915, Rockefeller Foundation Archives; Whitlock journal, 21 June 1915, Whitlock Papers, Library of Congress.

29 Hoover to Lansing, 6 June 1918, 860c.48/69, 860c.48/56, NA; Hoover to Whitlock, 14 Nov. 1914; Hoover memorandum of 26 May 1915 on Rockefeller Foundation and Poland; Hoover to CRB New York office, 15 and 29 Dec. 1915; Hoover to H. Beatty, 12 Jan. 1916, CRB Papers; Hoover to Colonel House, 23 Feb. 1916, House Papers; F. C. Walcott to Rockefeller Foundation, 20 and 23 Dec. 1915; Walcott to G. A. Bowden, 23 Feb. 1916, Walcott Papers; Page to State Department, 6 March 1916; Hoover to Page, 12 May 1916; Gerard to Page, 1 June 1916; Lord Grey to Page, 15 June 1916; Wilson to George V, 20 July 1916, American Legation, London, NA.

30 Page blamed the non-feeding of Poles on the Germans, Page Diary, 13 May 1916, Page Papers; Gay, *Public Relations,* pp. 83–126. That December Germany asked the CRB whether some work could be done for Serbia as well. For that job, which could be accomplished with fewer political difficulties than Polish relief, Hoover thought of Captain Lucey, who had business connections in Rumania. Hoover to Walcott, ca. Dec. 1915, Walcott Papers; Hoover to Beatty, 23 Dec. 1915; Beatty to Walcott, 28 Dec. 1915, Walcott Papers, Yale University Library. Hoover to Sir Edward Grey, 22 Dec. 1915, and Grey to Hoover, 6 Feb. 1916, are reprinted in George J. Lerski, *Herbert Hoover and Poland* (Stanford, 1977).

31 See FO 371/2586/58504 for important opinions, PRO; Hoover to Page, 15 April 1915; Kellogg to Whitlock, 3 Oct. 1916, American Legation, Brussels, C8 12/64 NA; Hoover to W. Honnold, 26 Oct. 1916; Hoover to Whitlock, 29 Dec. 1916, CRB Papers; Walter Hines Page diary, 25 Feb. 1916, Page Papers.

32 Hoover to Page, 10 and 12 May 1915, 24 Feb. 1916, Page Papers; Gay, *Public Relations,* pp. 90–2; Grey to Villalobar, 28 Feb. 1916, CRB Papers; Whitlock journal, 20 July 1915, Whitlock Papers, Library of Congress.

[33] Kellogg to Francqui, 9 Oct. 1916; Kellogg to Hoover, 24 Nov. 1916, CRB Papers.

[34] Hoover to Percy, 5 July 1915; Hoover to Whitlock, 13 Sept. 1915; Hoover to Page, 5 July 1915, American Embassy, London, C8 15/179, NA; Hoover to Jerome Greene, 19 April 1915, American Legation, Brussels, NA; Gay, *Public Relations,* pp. 31–82; CAB 37, 159/27, PRO.

[35] Francqui's point of view is expressed in a newspaper he controlled, *Libre Belgique,* particularly in the immediate postwar years. Kellogg to Francqui, 9 Oct. 1916; Kellogg to Hoover, 24 Nov. 1916; Percy to Hoover, 25 Nov. 1916; Hoover to Whitlock, 29 Dec. 1916; Memorandum of Agreement, CRB and CN, 12/16, CRB Papers.

[36] Hoover to Henry van Dyke, 28 Feb. 1915; Hoover to Bates, 9 Feb. 1915; Lucey to Hoover, 11 March 1915; Shaler to Edgar, 5 Oct. 1915, CRB Papers.

[37] Fund-raising letter to Mr. Honnold; Hoover to Carton de Wiart, 17 Feb. 1915; Hoover memorandum of 7 Nov. 1915 on Bates's charges, CRB Papers; House to Page, 29 Oct. 1915, Page Papers.

[38] Julius Barnes to Hoover, 4 Jan. 1918, CRB Papers; Goode to Page, 1 Nov. 1915; Page to Secretary of State, 2 Nov. 1915, American Embassy, London, C8 15/179, NA.

[39] Allen experienced much difficulty in obtaining his first photograph of Hoover: "Oh, how I wish the Chief would endure the limelight with more grace but how I do admire him for disliking it." Hoover to Bates, 19 Feb. 1915, CRB Papers. White's comment is quoted in Kittredge: see note 46.

[40] Hoover to Bates, 18 Feb. 1915, CRB Papers; Hoover to Van Tyne, 16 Sept. 1914, American Legation, London.

[41] Hoover to Francqui, 24 June 1915; Nevins, *Letters and Journal,* p. 262; Hoover to Jerome Greene, 9 April 1915, American Legation, Brussels, NA.

[42] Hoover to Whitlock, 23 Feb. 1915; Hoover to Francqui, 15 June 1915, and 28 June 1916; Page to Wilson, 12 Jan. 1915; see also an unsent letter to Wilson of 22 Feb. 1916 on Whitlock's nervous condition, Page Papers.

[43] Nevins, *Letters and Journal,* p. 358.

[44] Hoover to Whitlock, Jan. 1917; Gibson Memorandum, 9 Jan. 1917, CRB Papers; Whitlock to Baker, 17 Jan. 1917, Box 35, Whitlock Papers, Library of Congress; Hoover to House, 17 Feb. 1917, House Papers.

[45] Hoover to Penrose, 2 Feb. 1917, in Helen R. Fairbanks and Charles R. Berkey, eds., *Life and Letters of R. A. F. Penrose, Jr.* (New York, 1952), p. 524; Hoover to London office of the CRB, 6 Feb. and 11 March 1917; Hoover to House, 13 Feb. 1917; Hoover to W. H. Phillips, 25 Feb. 1917; Hoover to Whitlock, 21 April 1917; Hoover to Poland, 29 Aug. 1917, CRB Papers; Walter Hines Page diary, 25 Feb. 1917, Page Papers; Whitlock, *Belgium,* II, 731; Hoover to Page, 6, 13, and 27 Feb. 1917, American Legation, London, C8 15/402, NA.

[46] Three copies of the Kittredge book are at the Hoover Institution; the book was never circulated because it is critical of Francqui. *The History of the Commission for Relief in Belgium, 1914–1917,* p. 524. (There is a tedious statistical history of the CRB by Gay, *Statistical Review* . . . , cited earlier.) Hoover to William C. Edgar, n.d., Edgar Papers.

CHAPTER VI

1 House diary, 2 Nov. 1917; Hoover to House, 3 April 1917; House to Hoover, 7 April 1917, House Papers; Gibson diary, 5 April 1917, Gibson Papers. The standard published histories are William C. Mullendore, *History of the United States Food Administration, 1917–1919* (New York, 1941), and Frank M. Surface and Raymond L. Bland, *American Food in the World War and Reconstruction Period* . . . (Stanford, 1931). See also Tom G. Hall, "Wilson and the Food Crisis: Agricultural Price Control During World War I," *Agricultural History,* XLVII (Jan. 1973), 25–46. Hoover-Wilson letters may be found in Francis O'Brien, ed., *The Hoover-Wilson Wartime Correspondence* (Ames, 1974). Hoover summarizes the lessons on price controls that he learned in World War I in *Hearings,* Senate Committee on Banking and Currency, 16 Dec. 1941, pp. 409ff.

2 David Lloyd George, *War Memoirs,* III (London, 1934), 1341–3; House to Wilson, 2 April 1917, House Papers.

3 E. David Cronon, ed., *The Cabinet Diaries of Josephus Daniels, 1913–1921* (Lincoln, 1963), p. 148.

4 Robert D. Cuff, "Herbert Hoover, The Ideology of Voluntarism and War Organization During the Great War," *Journal of American History,* LXIV (Sept. 1977), 358–72; *Public Papers,* 1929, p. 6; House diary, 27 Dec. 1918, House Papers; *New Republic,* 30 June 1917, pp. 10–11; *The Outlook,* 27 June 1917, pp. 323–5.

5 "Production and Conservation of Food Supplies," Senate Committee on Agriculture and Forestry, V. 102, No. 6, pp. 373–425, 8–9 May 1917; 65th Congress, 1st Session; see also 19 June 1917, pp. 8ff. Other wartime congressional testimony by Hoover includes Senate, *Hearings,* V. 124, pp. 549–629 (scarcity of sugar); House, *Hearings,* V. 177, p. 3 (conservation of food); V. 179, p. 1148; V. 187, p. 2074; V. 205, p. 100 (minerals and metals); *Hearings,* 65th Congress, 1st Session, 19 June 1917, V. 102, No. 59.

6 Hoover to Hunt, 27 Dec. 1933, "Edward Eyre Hunt," HHPL; *Hearings,* 65th Cong., 19 June 1917.

7 Hoover, "Food Conservation and the War," *American Journal of Public Health,* Nov. 1917, p. 927.

8 Everett S. Brown, "The Food Administration," *The Historical Outlook* (May 1914), pp. 242–6; Hoover, "The Women's Call," *Independent,* 23 June 1917, p. 568; "School Leaflet for a Potato Campaign," United States Food Administration Pamphlets, March 1918, Library of Congress; Hoover to Alvin Johnson, 25 June 1947, "Alvin Johnson," HHPL.

9 Frederic Walcott to William Welch, 1 June 1917; Walcott to Mrs. F. S. Kellogg, 17 July 1917, Walcott Papers. The debate over the food bill is summarized in *Literary Digest,* 30 June 1917; it permanently soured Hoover's relations with many congressmen.

10 Tom G. Hall to the author, 11 Oct. 1977; Felix Frankfurter to M. B. Hammond, 17 June 1918, Box 64, Food Administration, HI.

11 The records of the U.S. Food Administration at Sutphin, Maryland, contrary to Hall's view, suggest the importance of state and local administration by the sheer volume of such materials.

[12] Leonard P. Dileanis, "Herbert Hoover's Use of Public Relations in the United States Food Administration, 1917–1919," master's essay, University of Wisconsin, 1969. A book financed by CRB funds is Edith Guerrier, *We Pledged Allegiance* (Stanford, 1941). Carol Reuss, "*The Ladies Home Journal* and Hoover's Food Program," *Journalism Quarterly* (Winter 1972), pp. 740–2; *Collier's*, 11 Aug. 1917, pp. 7–9; *World's Work*, June 1928, p. 140; Chief of Food Administration Speaking Division to Anna G. Murray of Waterproof, La., 26 Feb. 1918, Box 330, Food Administration Papers, Sutphin, Md.; John Dos Passos, *The Big Money* (Boston, 1937), p. 89.

[13] Tom G. Hall to author, 11 Oct. 1977.

[14] Hoover to Wilson, 1 Dec. 1917, O'Brien, *The Hoover-Wilson Wartime Correspondence*, pp. 117–18; Cronon, ed., *The Cabinet Diaries of Josephus Daniels*, p. 149; Hoover to James F. Bell, 4 April, 22 May, and 8 June 1918, Bell Papers.

[15] Alonzo Taylor to Frank Surface, 6 Nov. 1924, Taylor Papers, Box 1; Hoover to Alben Barkley, 25 Sept. 1918, Barkley Papers. An excellent work is Hall, "Cheap Bread from Dear Wheat: Herbert Hoover, the Wilson Administration, and the Management of Wheat Prices, 1916–1920," unpublished doctoral dissertation, University of California at Davis, 1971.

[16] Frank M. Surface, *The Grain Trade During the World War* (New York, 1928). Hoover wrote to Representative Lerer on 17 May 1917: "A fixed price is the only positive, absolute method of eliminating speculation," U.S. Food Administration Records, Box 5, Washington, D.C.; Hoover to Jouett Shouse, 25 Sept. 1918, Shouse Papers; Surface, "The Stabilization of the Price of Wheat During the War and Its Effect Upon the Returns to the Producer" (Washington, 1925).

[17] An excellent series of articles on the Food Administration in *The New Republic* discusses these and other issues, Jan.–March 1918. *Annual Report of the United States Food Administration for the Year 1918* (Washington, 1919), pp. 5–43; *Reports of the United States Food Administration and the United States Fuel Administration* (Washington, 1918), pp. 8–43; Lawrence Richey to Charles Brand, 2 Dec. 1925, Hoover Papers, HI; Hall, "Cheap Bread," *passim;* Samuel Jones of Omaha to "Gentlemen," [1928?], File 431, Chester Davis Papers.

[18] *Hearings*, Senate Subcommittee of the Committee on Manufactures, 2 and 3 Jan. 1918, pp. 549–707; Pinchot to Wallace, 17 Feb. 1918, Wallace Papers; *Congressional Record*, 20 April 1928, pp. 7121–30; *Literary Digest*, 12 Nov. 1927, pp. 11–12; Hoover to Wallace, 16 Feb. 1918, U.S. Food Administration Records, 1-H-C/GG, Sutphin, Md.; Pinchot to Wallace, telegrams, 25, 26 and 30 Sept. 1917; Wallace to Pinchot, 18 Oct. 1917, Wallace Papers; Senator George Norris to Luther Drake, 10 Feb. 1920, Tray 5, Box 1, Norris Papers; Kent to Hoover, 12 Sept. 1919, William Kent Papers.

[19] Allen to Baldwin, 12 July 1918, FA 12 HA-A6; Cronon, ed., *The Cabinet Diaries of Josephus Daniels*, p. 148; Hoover to Sheppard, 4 July 1918, Clippings, Pierre S. duPont Papers; *New York Times*, 27 May 1917.

[20] Hoover to McAdoo, 23 Feb. 1918, Food Administration Papers, Box 50, HI; Franklin G. Lane, Notes on cabinet meeting, 25 Feb. 1918, Anne W. Lane and Louise Walls, eds., *The Letters of Franklin K. Lane* (Boston, 1922); Josephus

Daniels, *The Wilson Era: Years of War and After, 1917–1923* (Chapel Hill, 1946), p. 318; McAdoo, *Crowded Years* (Boston, 1931).

[21] Frank M. Surface, *American Pork Production in the World War* (Chicago, 1926); Wallace to Hoover, 24 Oct. 1917, Wallace to Pinchot, 18 Oct. 1917, Wallace Papers; cf. Pinchot to Wallace, "Harding Papers," HHPL; Pinchot to House, 20 Oct. 1907, Pinchot Papers; Donald L. Winters, "The Hoover-Wallace Controversy During World War I," *Annals of Iowa,* XXXVI (Winter 1969), 586–97.

[22] Hoover to E. C. Lasater, 4 Dec. 1917; Hoover to Wallace, 3 Feb. 1918, 1-H-S, Food Administration Records, Sutphin, Md.; Lasater to Hoover, 12 Nov. 1917, Peek Papers; Pinchot to Henry C. Wallace, 20 Oct. 1917, 27 Feb. 1918, Wallace Papers; Pinchot's statement of resignation is in Herbert Lefkowitz to Peek, 20 Oct. 1928; Pinchot to Meyer Lissner, 1920, in Lefkowitz to Peek, 20 Oct. 1928, Peek Papers; Wallace to Hoover, 11 Feb. 1918, Hoover to Pinchot, 27 Oct. 1917, Pinchot Papers; Pinchot to Col. House, 20 Oct. and 29 Nov. 1917, "Harding Papers," HHPL. Pinchot thought it would only be a matter of time before Hoover "cracked up" under the strain, and Hoover agreed. Hoover to David R. Francis, 6 March 1918, Food Administration Records, Box 3, Sutphin, Md.

[23] *Hearings,* House Committee on Agriculture, 11 Feb. 1918, pp. 3–45; Urgent Deficiencies, House, V. 179, p. 1148, 31 Jan. 1918; Hoover to Carl Riddick, 22 May 1920.

[24] Walter T. Borg, "Food Administration Experience with Hogs, 1917–19," pp. 444–57, Box 292, Hoover Papers, HI; *New Republic,* 22 Feb. 1919, pp. 110–12; Lewis C. Gray, "Price-Fixing Policies of the Food Administration," *American Economic Review* (March 1919), pp. 252–77.

[25] Best, "Food Relief as Price Support: Hoover and American Pork, January–March 1919," *Agricultural History,* XLV (April 1971), 79–84. Or as Norman Davis put it, it was "difficult some times to draw the line between the requirements for relief and the requirements for an outlet for the surplus." Davis to Albert Rathbone, 3 Jan. 1919, Box 11, Norman Davis Papers; Hoover to Richey, 23 Dec. 1918, FA; FR, PPC, II, 789.

[26] *Hearings,* Senate Subcommittee of the Committee on Manufactures, 2 Jan. 1918, 3 Jan. 1918, pp. 549–707; Hoover to Federal Food Administrators, 11 June 1918, Box 459, Food Administration Records, Sutphin, Md.; *Literary Digest,* 12 June 1920, pp. 25–6.

[27] Nelson, "The Image of Herbert Hoover as Reflected in the American Press," unpublished doctoral dissertation, Stanford University, 1956; Austin to Hoover, 18 July 1917, FA; *The Nation,* 14 June 1920, p. 643.

[28] The concept of single administrators has been rejected by most experts on government administration. Hall to author, 11 Oct. 1977. *Hearings,* 68th Cong., 4 Dec. 1925.

CHAPTER VII

[1] An excellent doctoral dissertation, recently completed at the University of Michigan, provides intelligent argument, heavy documentation, and conclusions similar to those reached here: "Herbert Hoover and Food Relief," by

Leo Chavez (1976). The overhead cost of the postwar relief work, according to George I. Gay, was 43/100 of 1 percent. *Statistical Review of Relief Operations* (Stanford, 1925), preface. A major book of documents on postwar relief is Suda Bane and Ralph Lutz, eds., *Organization of American Relief in Europe, 1918–1919* (Stanford, 1943). Herman Bernstein, "Herbert Hoover," *McClure's,* Sept. 1925, pp. 666–79, Oct. 1925, pp. 869–84.

[2] Hoover to Page, telegram, 20 May 1918, State Department file 103, 97/200, NA; Hoover to Wilson, 27 Aug. 1918; Wilson to Hoover, 4 Nov. 1918; Francis O'Brien, *The Hoover-Wilson Wartime Correspondence* (Ames, 1974), pp. 237, 276–7, 283; *An American Epic,* 4 vols. (New York, 1959–64); *The Ordeal of Woodrow Wilson* (New York, 1955).

[3] Important congressional testimony by Hoover during the postwar period includes Senate, *Hearings,* V. 170, 23 Sept. 1920, p. 609; House, V. 250, 2 Sept. 1919, p. 527; V. 250–4, 12 Jan. 1920, p. 57; V. 277, 29 Oct. 1919, p. 1223; V. 234, 14 May 1920, p. 287; V. 262, 17 Jan. 1921 and 20 Jan. 1921, p. 893; V. 285, 20 Jan. 1921, p. 895. Hogan, "The United States and the Problem of International Economic Control: American Attitudes Toward European Reconstruction, 1918–1920," *Pacific Historical Review,* XLIV (1975), 85.

[4] Lord Reading to William Wiseman, 26 Nov. 1918, Reading Papers, FO 800/225, PRO; Hoover to Wilson, 11 Nov. 1918, Food Administration Records, Box 7 (RG4), Sutphin, Md.; Hoover statement, 10 Dec. 1918, FA; Hoover to House, 10 and 18 Dec. 1918; Hoover to Lord Reading, 16 Dec. 1919; Bliss to Hoover 30 Dec. 1918, Bliss Papers; Silvio Crespi, *Alla difensa d'Italia in guerra e a Versailles* (Milan, 1938), pp. 217–19; Étienne Clémentel, *La France et la politique économique interalliée* (New Haven, 1931), pp. 307–8.

[5] Allied Marine Transport Executive, HI, II, 1–15; ARA Documents, I, 31–3, 70–4, 80, 118–20, 134–8, 155, 255; Arthur Walworth, *America's Moment: 1918* (New York, 1977), p. 230; Cecil diary, 7 Jan. 1919, fol. 6^r, British Museum; Oscar Penn Fitzgerald IV, "The Supreme Economic Council and Germany," unpublished doctoral dissertation, Georgetown University, 1971.

[6] Wilson to Polk, 22 March 1919, State Department file 860, 48/1956, NA; House diary, 29 March 1919, House Papers; Jeffrey J. Safford, "Edward Hurley and American Shipping Policy: An Elaboration on Wilsonian Diplomacy, 1918–1919," *Historian,* XXXV (April 1974), 269–79; Bane and Lutz, eds., *Organization of American Relief . . . ,* pp. 2, 3; E. David Cronon, ed., *The Cabinet Diaries of Josephus Daniels, 1913–21* (Lincoln, 1963), p. 342; Hurley, *The Bridge to France* (Philadelphia, 1927), p. 267; FR, PPC, XI, 311.

[7] Atwood to Causey, 6 May 1919, "Atwood," ARA-Paris; Hoover to T. C. C. Gregory, 2 Feb. 1919, Gregory Papers; Shotwell, Oral history, Columbia University, p. 171. Hoover's chief lieutenants at the Hotel Crillon in Paris included Robert Taft, legal counsel and son of the former president; Colonel James Logan, chief of staff; Colonel A. A. Barber, distributor of supplies; Julius Barnes, grain executive; and Lewis Strauss, Hoover's secretary. Vernon Kellogg and Alonzo Taylor inspected various countries and helped to allocate food. Colonels W. G. Atwood and William B. Causey ran central Europe's railways; coal supplies came under the direction of Colonel Anson C.

Goodyear. Some of the more notable American food commissioners, who worked with Allied representatives in various places, included Howard Heinz (Constantinople), Magnus Swenson (Copenhagen), Captain T. C. C. Gregory (Trieste and Vienna), Arthur Ringland (Czechoslovakia), Colonel William Haskell (chiefly Armenia), and Captain Joseph Green (Rumania and Poland). See, for an example of instructions given subordinates, Hoover to Heinz, 26 Jan. 1919, ARA-Paris; Henry White to Hoover, 18 April 1919, Bliss Papers.

8 The Yale University House Collection is important for postwar Europe. Comments on Hoover are in the House diary, the Auchincloss diary, the Polk diary, the Miller diary, and the Norman Davis Papers. See also FO/800/207; CAB/23/17, PRO, and RG59, 103, 97/837, NA.

9 Edward Hurley's diary contains numerous hostile references to Hoover in 1918 and 1919. Gary Dean Best, "Food Relief as Price Support: Hoover and American Pork, January–March 1919," *Agricultural History*, XLV (April 1971), 79–84; Allan Nevins, *Henry White* (New York, 1930); *Epic*, II, 311; McCormick diary, 11 Jan. 1919; John Maynard Keynes, *Two Memoirs* (London, 1949); Jeffrey J. Safford, *Wilsonian Maritime Diplomacy, 1913–1921* (New Brunswick, 1977), pp. 184–8.

10 The administration's tack with Congress is well caught in Henry White's telegram to Henry Cabot Lodge: "Food relief only effective barrier . . . [against] . . . westward advance of Bolshevism." 18 Jan. 1919, State Department files, 861, 00/3608, NA. Cf. 840, 48/1912, and 840, 48/1919a. For congressional reviews, see *New Republic*, 8 Feb. 1918, pp. 43–5; Hoover, press statement, 25 April 1919, HHPL; Hoover to Wilson, 28 March 1919, HHPL; Arno J. Mayer, *Politics and Diplomacy of Peacemaking* (New York, 1967); Hoover to Norman Davis, 28 Feb. 1920, Davis Papers. Veblen's remarks are in Leon Ardzrooni, ed., *Thorstein Veblen: Essays* (New York, 1934), p. 37. Hoover press statement, 25 April 1919.

11 House diary, 27 March 1919, House Papers; Hoover to Wilson, 28 March 1919; Cronon, ed., *The Cabinet Diaries of Josephus Daniels*, 21 Dec. 1917, p. 254; Hoover to Wilson, 28 March 1919, and Address at Methodist Episcopal Church, Kingston, N.Y., 9 April 1920, "Public Statements," HHPL.

12 Hoover, Address to American Institute of Mining Engineers, 16 Sept. 1919, "Public Statements," HHPL; Hoover to Wilson, 28 March 1919, HHPL; William Webster to David R. Francis, 31 Jan. 1919, Francis Papers; Bane and Lutz, *Organization of American Relief*, pp. 50–3; Inga Floto, *Colonel House in Paris* (Aarhus, Denmark, 1973), p. 185; House diary, 27 March 1919; Beatrice Farnsworth, *William C. Bullitt and the Soviet Union* (Bloomington, 1967).

13 At the same time Hoover discouraged Quakers from going into Russia, and recommended Germany as a better place for their labors. Lucy Biddle Lewis to Lydia Lewis, 26 April 1919; Lucy Lewis to Wilbur Thomas, 30 April 1919, Swarthmore Quaker Collection. Lord Cecil to Lloyd George on interview with Hoover, 29 March 1919, F 6/6/20, Lloyd George Papers; Cecil diary, 29 March 1919, British Museum; Robert Lansing Desk Diary, 13 June 1918, Lansing Papers; FR, PPC, 1919, VII, 230–1.

14 Hoover said that Bolshevik atrocities in Odessa were frightful, but that Russian refugees there, living profligately, deserved their fate. Auchincloss diary, p. 542. Hoover to Wilson, 16 May 1919, HHPL; Harold H. Fisher, *The Famine in Soviet Russia* (New York, 1927), p. 27. Accounts of Hoover's role in the Nansen project that overemphasize anti-Bolshevism are contained in John M. Thompson, *Russia, Bolshevism and the Versailles Peace* (Princeton, 1966), and Mayer, *Politics and Diplomacy of Peacemaking*. Hoover, *The Ordeal of Woodrow Wilson*, pp. 116–23; Robert Lansing Desk Diary, 4 Feb. 1920, Lansing Papers; 840.48/2082, NA; Chicherin's response is recorded inaccurately in FR, 1919, Russia, pp. 111–15.

15 Hoover, 3 June 1920, "Public Statements," HHPL; Hoover, Address to American Institute of Mining and Metallurgical Engineers, 16 Sept. 1919, Reprint file, HHPL; Hoover to Wilson, 4 Feb. 1919, HHPL; Hoover to Baker, telegram, 28 Feb. 1919, Box 12, Baker Papers.

16 This interpretation is opposed to that of George W. Hopkins, "The Politics of Food: United States and Soviet Hungary, March–August, 1919," *Mid-America*, LV (Oct. 1973), 245–70. Hopkins cynically remarks that "the American relief policy was no altruistic 'Food for Peace' program but a convenient blend of anti-communism and profit, tinged with humanitarianism." Hoover to Wilson, 28 March 1919, HHPL; Rudolf Tökés, *Béla-Kun and the Hungarian Soviet Republic* (Stanford, 1967).

17 Gregory to Hoover, 22 April 1919, Box 68A, ARA-Paris.

18 Hoover to Wilson, 28 and 31 March, and 15 April 1919; Wilson to Hoover, 2 April 1919, HHPL; Nicholas Roosevelt, Oral history, HHPL; USFR, PPC, VII, 22; Bliss to Wilson, 28 March 1919, Bliss Papers. David Hunter Miller diary, VII, 260–1; XVI, 495. Gregory to Hoover, 29 March 1919, ARA-Paris.

19 The implication of a meeting of the economic group—Messrs. Hoover, House, Bliss, Benson, and Robinson—in Paris on April 2 is that the French were holding up Hoover's food shipments into Hungary against his will: "Colonel House thought that, in principle, our policy of feeding Hungary should be continued and that Mr. Hoover ought to be in a position to fight for this principle." Hoover to Gregory, 3 April 1919, ARA, VI, 43–4; Hoover to Wilson, 15 April 1919, HHPL; Hoover to Lansing, 1 July 1919, Lansing Papers; 840.48/2042, 840.48/2082, NA.

20 Hoover at Council of Five meeting, 7 July 1919, F/89/3/3, Lloyd George Papers, House of Lords; Minutes, Supreme Economic Council, 5 July 1919, HI; Minutes of the Daily Meetings of the Commissioners Plenipotentiary, 1 July 1919, USFR, PPC, 1919, VII, 20 ff.; XI, 259–60, 315–17. Gregory to Hoover, 14 June 1919; Hoover to Gregory, 9 June 1919; Hoover to Wilson, 9 June 1919, Box 2, Gregory Papers.

21 T. T. C. Gregory, "Stemming the Red Tide in Central Europe," *World's Work*, Sept. 1921, p. 229; Hoover to Oswald Garrison Villard, 17 Aug. 1921, ARA-Paris; Minutes of the Supreme Economic Council, 25 July 1919, 26 July 1919, 4 Aug. 1919, HHPL; Chavez, "Herbert Hoover and Food Relief," p. 229.

22 Gregory to Hoover, 5 Aug. 1919, 17 Aug. 1919; account by Hoover of situa-

tion in Hungary, 21 Aug. 1919, F/89/4/16, Lloyd George Papers; Causey to Hoover, 8 Aug. 1919; Minutes of the Supreme Economic Council, 21 Aug. 1919, HI.

23 The Manchester *Guardian* claimed that Hoover was responsible for stopping arms shipments to Rumania. 26 Aug. 1919. Powerful labor and social democratic groups opposed Archduke Joseph, but Hoover could not get the Czech patriot Masaryk to protest to him publicly about Joseph. Hoover to ARA, Vienna, 18 Aug. 1919, ARA-Paris; *The Nation*, 30 Aug. 1919, table of contents page; Hoover to Polk, 18 Aug. 1919; Hoover to Logan, 15 Aug. 1919, ARA-Paris; Polk diary, 21 Aug. 1919.

24 Hoover, *Memoirs*, I, 403–4; Hoover at Council of Five meeting, 21 Aug. 1919, F/89/4/16, Lloyd George Papers; *Literary Digest*, 13 Sept. 1919, pp. 16–17.

25 Hoover on economic situation in Vienna, 20 Jan. 1920; files 863.48/108; 863, 48/111, 840.48/2595a, State Department, NA; Causey to Atwood, 9 June 1919, "Atwood," ARA-Paris; Hoover, *An American Epic*, II, 121; Surface and Bland, *American Food*, pp. 153 ff; Gregory to Hoover, 22 April 1919, "Supreme Economic Council," ARA-Paris; FR, PPC, 1919, VII, 174.

26 Ammission (Hoover) to Polk, 28 Feb. 1919, State Department file 840, 48/1934, NA. Cf. 840, 48/6934. Hoover probably leaked to the press news of the holdup in Italy. Polk to Ammission, 10 March 1919, file 840, 48/1952B, NA; Hoover to Wilson, 12 Feb. 1919; Hoover to House, 19 Feb. 1919, ARA-Paris; Cecil diary, 4 March 1919, British Museum; Memorandum in Lloyd George Papers, 29 March 1919; FR, PPC, 1919, XI, 77–8.

27 Edward F. Willis, *Herbert Hoover and the Russian Prisoners of World War I* (Stanford, 1951).

28 John A. Gade, *Citoyen du Hainant, The Life of Cardinal Mercier* (New York, 1934), p. 197; Sharp to Polk, 13 March 1919, State Department file 840, 48/1946; Hoover to Wilson, 3 April 1919, HHPL; Suda Bane and Ralph Lutz, eds., *The Blockade of Germany after the Armistice* (Stanford, 1942); Edward F. Willis, "Herbert Hoover and the Blockade of Germany," in Frederick J. Cox et al., eds., *Studies in Modern European History* (New York, 1956), pp. 265–310; Minutes of the Supreme Economic Council, 22 Aug. 1919, HI.

29 Hurley epitomized those wishing to remodel the world in the capitalist image. See Hurley to Wilson, 3 March 1919, quoted in Safford, "Edward Hurley," pp. 568–86. Hoover to Brown, 28 Nov. 1918, American Legation, London; Charles E. Strickland, "American Aid to Germany, 1919 to 1921," *Wisconsin Magazine of History*, XLV (Summer 1962), 256–70; *Hearings*, House Committee on Expenditures in the War Department, 29 Oct. 1919, pp. 1233 ff; Hoover to Norman Davis, 24 Nov. 1919, "Davis," ARA-Paris; Oswald Garrison Villard, *Fighting Years* (New York, 1936), p. 446; Hoover to Groome, 24 June, 1919, telegram, Box 7, ARA-Paris; Sebastian Haffner, *Failure of a Revolution: Germany, 1918–19*, tr. Georg Rapp (London, 1973).

30 Strickland, "American Aid to Germany," pp. 266–9.

31 Louis Lochner, *Herbert Hoover and Germany* (New York, 1960); Hoover testimony, *Hearings*, House Committee on Foreign Affairs, 1924, V. 341, No. 4. Jane Addams is quoted in James Linn, *Jane Addams* (New York, 1935),

p. 345. Mary G. Cary, "Jane Addams Knew No 'Enemy,'" *American-German Review*, XXVI (Aug.–Sept. 1960), 4; Hoover to Rufus M. Jones, 1 Nov. 1919, 17 Nov. 1919, Swarthmore Peace Collection; John Forbes, "Quaker Relief and Government," unpublished doctoral dissertation, University of Pennsylvania. The Swarthmore Quaker Collection has numerous holdings on Hoover and Germany. See, for example, Lucy Biddle Lewis to her family, 9 May 1919, Biddle Papers.

32 The Frederic Walcott Papers at Yale are an excellent source for Polish relief. Other sources are collected in George J. Lerski, *Herbert Hoover and Poland* (Stanford, 1977); Adaline W. Fuller, Oral history, HHPL; Hoover, 27 Sept. 1920, File 861, 48/1930, State Department, NA; Surface and Bland, *American Food*, pp. 189 ff.; William R. Grove, *War's Aftermath* (New York, 1940).

33 There is one grand-scale study: Donald R. Van Patten, "The European Technical Advisers and Post-War Austria, 1919–1925," 2 vols., unpublished doctoral dissertation, Stanford University, 1943. A. B. Barber, *Report of ETA to Poland, 1919–1922* (New York, 1923); J. W. Krueger, "The Origin and Development of European Technical Advisers," Box 8, ETA Archives, HI.

34 Best, "Herbert Hoover's Technical Mission to Yugoslavia, 1919–20," *Annals of Iowa*, XLII (Fall 1975), 443–59; Hoover to Baruch, 5 April 1919, Baruch Papers.

35 A single dinner in New York City raised $3 million, a third of that sum coming from John D. Rockefeller, Jr. Hoover, *An American Epic*, II, 255–8; *New York Times*, 11 Nov. 1920.

36 Hoover had another viewpoint. He told the Manchester *Guardian* shortly before he left Europe that there would be no additional American financing "to enable people to live without work or work a part of the time, as they are doing all over Europe today." 26 Aug. 1919; *Memoirs*, I, 278–80; Surface and Bland, *American Food*, pp. 275, 281.

37 Hoover, Address before the American Bankers' Association, Chicago, 10 Dec. 1920, "Public Statements"; Hoover to Wilson, 27 June 1919; HHPL.

38 The two most important books on Hoover's relief activities in Russia are Benjamin Weissman, *Herbert Hoover and Famine Relief to Soviet Russia: 1921–1923* (Stanford, 1974), and Harold H. Fisher, *The Famine in Soviet Russia* (New York, 1927). Two dissertations of interest are Floyd J. Fithian, "Soviet-American Economic Relations, 1918–1933; American Business in Russia during the Period of Non-Recognition," Nebraska, 1964, and Ladislas F. Reitzer, "U.S.-Russian Economic Relations, 1917–1920," Chicago, 1950. See also Henry C. Wolfe, Oral history, HHPL; Weissman, "Herbert Hoover's, 'Treaty' with Soviet Russia: August 20, 1921," *Slavic Review*, 28 (Sept. 1969), 276–88; Hoover, Public statement to Newspaper Enterprise Association, 3 June 1920, HHPL.

39 *New York Times*, 23 July 1921. A detailed description of the working out of the Riga Agreement is given in Weissman's article in *Slavic Review*, pp. 276–88. See Nansen's comments on Hoover's plans for Russian relief, 2 Sept. 1921, F/34/2/5, Lloyd George Papers.

40 Weissman, *Herbert Hoover and Famine Relief*, pp. 34, 26–7, 43; Fisher, *The Famine*, pp. 35–6, 49. See the text of a telegram from Hoover to

Samuel Gompers dated 23 June 1922, "Public Statements," No. 244, and two other public statements on trade with Russia dated 21 March and 25 March 1921, "Public Statements," Nos. 138 and 138A. An early press statement denounces Bolshevism, issued 19 April 1919, "Public Statements," No. 18A, HHPL.

[41] See the series of letters from Haskell to Brown variously dated 7 Oct., 14 Oct., 14 Dec. 1921, 14 April 1922, 20 Feb. 1923, and the report to Hoover from Haskell sent in cipher, dated 18–20 Oct. 1921, HI; Fisher, *The Famine,* pp. 112–13; Frank Golder and Lincoln Hutchinson, *On the Trail of the Russian Famine* (Stanford, 1927), *passim.*

[42] Fisher, *The Famine,* pp. 82, 85, 173–87, *passim;* Surface and Bland, *American Food,* p. 245; Golder and Hutchinson, *On the Trail,* pp. 110, 137, and *passim.*

[43] Golder and Hutchinson, *On the Trail,* pp. 44, 214, 37, 137; Fisher, *The Famine,* pp. 106, 96–7; Weissman, *Herbert Hoover and Famine Relief,* p. 7; Boxes 9 and 11, George Barr Baker Papers.

[44] Hoover made these suggestions to Harding in a letter dated 20 Dec. 1921, "Harding Papers, Reparations Commission, Russia, Correspondence," HHPL; see also Hoover's reports to President Harding, dated 9 Feb. and 16 July 1922, "Harding Papers . . . ," HHPL. The statements are reprinted in Fisher, *The Famine,* pp. 150–1, and in Weissman, *Herbert Hoover and Famine Relief,* pp. 100, 102.

[45] Weissman, *Herbert Hoover and Famine Relief,* pp. 40–1, 49; John Forbes, "American Friends and Russian Relief," Friends' Historical Association *Bulletin,* XLI, 39–51, 121–32.

[46] Hoover to Mrs. Morgan Vining, 31 May 1957 with covering memoranda, "Post-Presidential Papers—Individual," HHPL; *New Republic,* 10 Aug. and 31 Aug. 1921, 14 Sept. 1921; Fisher, *The Famine,* pp. 46, 161, 328–9; *Freeman,* 28 June 1922; *The Nation,* 5 Sept. 1921.

[47] *New York World,* 14 May 1922; *Literary Digest,* 3 Sept. 1921, pp. 14–16.

[48] "Harding Papers, Russian Relief-Purchasing Commission," HHPL.

[49] Fisher, *The Famine,* pp. 318–25, 328–9; Weissman, *Herbert Hoover and Famine Relief,* pp. 132–4, 141–3, 148–50; Hoover's comments and draft of the manuscript of Mrs. Morgan Vining, 31 May 1957, "Post-Presidential Papers—Individual," HHPL.

[50] Weissman, *Herbert Hoover and Famine Relief,* pp. 180, 135–7, 152–4, 181; Hoover to C. V. Hibbard, 23 March 1923, reprinted in Fisher, *The Famine,* pp. 542–3; Hoover to Samuel Gompers, 23 June 1922, "Public Statements," No. 244, HHPL.

[51] Hoover to President Harding, 9 Feb. 1922 and 16 July 1922, "Harding Papers, Reparations Commission, Russia, Correspondence," HHPL, reprinted in Fisher, *The Famine,* pp. 544, 548; see also Fisher, p. 172, and Weissman, *Herbert Hoover and Famine Relief,* pp. 95, 130.

[52] Golder and Hutchinson, *On the Trail, passim.* For the Goodrich anecdote, see the article on Hoover and the American Relief Administration, in "ARA, History and Records Division," Reprint File, No. 879, HHPL; Hoover to Harding, 2 June 1922, "Harding Papers," HHPL.

[53] An article in Russian challenges Hoover's figures on food sent and notes that

the Soviets were in bad straits particularly because capitalists refused to trade with them. D. N. Stashevski, "The Bourgeois Literature of the U.S.A. Concerning American Aid to Soviet Russia," *Voprosy Istorii* (1966), 173–80. The whole text of the scroll is given by Hoover in his *Memoirs*, III, 514; see also Weissman, *Herbert Hoover and Famine Relief*, pp. 177–8; Kennan, *Russia and the West Under Stalin* (Boston, 1960), p. 180.

CHAPTER VIII

[1] Keynes, according to Joseph S. Davis, who was in Paris at the time, went astray in his analysis because Hoover, as a member of the Supreme Economic Council, "tended to credit more extreme statements and to underrate the possibility of improvement without major intervention"—Davis, Oral history, HHPL. Keynes, *The Economic Consequences of the Peace* (New York, 1920), p. 247.

[2] Burner, "1919—Prelude to Normalcy," John Braeman *et al.*, eds., *The 1920's Revisited: Change and Continuity in Twentieth-Century America* (Columbus, 1968), pp. 3–35. The Brandeis remark to Norman Hapgood is quoted in Lewis Strauss, Oral history, HHPL.

[3] Gary Dean Best, *The Politics of American Individualism: Herbert Hoover in Transition, 1918–1921* (Westport, 1975), *passim*.

[4] Quoted in Best, *The Politics of American Individualism*, p. 19.

[5] See *American Individualism* (New York, 1922).

[6] Layton, *The Revolt of the Engineers* (Cleveland, 1971), and Samuel Haber, *Efficiency and Uplift* (Chicago, 1964); Hoover to Richard Humphrey, 1 Feb. 1923; Hoover to Owen D. Young, 13 March 1923; "F.A.E.S., 1922–1924," HHPL; Hoover, Address to American Institute of Mining Engineers, Minneapolis, 27 Aug. 1920; "The Only Way Out," Inaugural Address to the American Institute of Mining Engineers, *Mining and Metallurgy* (March 1920), pp. 3–7; Address Before the Federated American Engineering Societies, 19 Nov. 1920, "Public Statements," HHPL; *Engineering and Mining Journal*, 4 Sept. 1920, p. 453.

[7] Hoover, Foreword to Elisha Friedman, *America and the New Era* (New York, 1920); Hoover, draft of public statement, 30 March 1920, "Public Statements," HHPL.

[8] Robert H. Zieger, "Herbert Hoover, the Wage Earner, and the 'New Economic System,' 1919–1929," *Business History Review*, LI (Summer 1977); Memorandum, Professor Taussig, 20 Oct. 1926, Owen D. Young Papers; Martin Glynn to Tumulty, 23 Dec. 1919, Wilson Papers, 4–5085.

[9] Report of the Industrial Conference Called by the President, 6 March 1920, in U.S. Department of Labor, *Annual Report, 1920* (Washington, 1921), pp. 236–71; Minutes, Second Industrial Conference, H1 and William B. Wilson Papers; Department of Labor, RG 174, NA; "2nd Industrial Conference," Pre-Commerce, HHPL. Manuscript sources—too numerous to list here—are in Gary Dean Best's "President Wilson's Second Industrial Conference, 1919–20," *Labor History*, XVI (Fall 1975), 505–20.

[10] An important source on the conference is Haggai Hurvitz, "The Meaning of Industrial Conflict in Some Ideologies of the Early 1920's: The AFL, Or-

ganized Employers and Herbert Hoover," unpublished doctoral dissertation, Columbia University, 1971; *Industrial Management,* LX (Feb. 1920), 94.

11 See Hoover's testimony on the Industrial Conference before the Senate Committee on Education and Labor, 14 May 1920, 66th Congress, 2nd Session, pp. 25–41; *Engineering News Record,* 25 Nov. 1920, p. 1052; Boston speech, 24 March 1920, "Public Statements," HHPL; *System,* July 1920, p. 10; *Trust Companies,* April 1920, pp. 349–52; Carroll E. French, *The Shop Committee in the United States* (Baltimore, 1923).

12 Gompers to Hoover, 13 Aug. 1920; Christian Herter (then Hoover's secretary) to Gompers, 17 Aug. 1920; Hoover to Gompers, 23 Oct. 1920, "F.A.E.S.-AFL, 1920," HHPL; Conference, 27 March 1921, President's Files, Box 57, AFL Papers; Cyrus S. Ching, *Review and Reflection* (New York, 1953).

13 "F.A.E.S.," Pre-Commerce, HHPL; *Industrial Management,* LX (Feb. 1920), 94.

14 *World's Work,* April 1920, p. 583; "F.A.E.S.," Pre-Commerce; Lawrence H. Wallace, Oral history, HHPL.

15 Hoover is quoted on "trusteeship" in Edward Eyre Hunt, "Hoover of the 'C.R.B.,' " *World's Work,* June 1917, p. 167; see also "America's Obligation in Belgian Relief," 1 Feb. 1917, CRB Papers.

16 Ruhl Bartlett underestimates Hoover's aggressive role: *The League to Enforce Peace* (Chapel Hill, 1949), pp. 151, 157; cf. Best, *The Politics of American Individualism,* pp. 31, 36.

17 "Public Statements," 15 Sept. 1920, HHPL.

18 Washington *Star,* 18 March 1920.

19 *New York Times,* 28 July 1919; George J. Lerski, *Herbert Hoover and Poland* (Stanford, 1977).

20 Address Before the Students of Stanford University, "Public Statements," HHPL; Taft is quoted in Best, *The Politics of American Individualism,* p. 29.

21 Breckinridge Long had a similar conversation with Hoover, 7 Feb. 1920, Long diary; Cummings diary, Box 3, Ray Stannard Baker Papers; Hoover to Frederic R. Coudert, 2 Nov. 1918, Pre-Commerce, HHPL; Box 1, Carol Green Papers; Lewis L. Strauss, *Men and Decisions* (Garden City, 1962), pp. 19–20, or Strauss, Oral history, HHPL; Robert Lansing Desk Diary, 27 June 1918, Lansing Papers.

22 Many manuscript sources cited in this account are in Gary Dean Best, "The Hoover-for-President Boom of 1920," *Mid-America,* LIII (Oct. 1971), 227–43; House diary, 25 Feb. 1920, House Papers; Baruch to McAdoo, 24 Oct. 1928, Baruch Papers.

23 Hoover to Wilson, 11 April 1919, "Public Statements," HHPL; Chicago *Daily Tribune,* 2 and 6 April 1920. On Wilson's alleged insanity, see Charles Hamlin diary, 8 Aug. 1932 (p. 75). "The failure of Mr. Wilson was pathological," said Hoover in a letter to William Allen White, 13 June 1924, White Papers; Hoover to Gibson, 2 Jan. 1920, Box 8A, Gibson Papers; David Houston to Lee S. Overman, 19 Sept. 1928, Overman Papers.

24 House diary, 25 Feb. 1920, House Papers; *Literary Digest,* 10 April 1920, pp. 22–3; *New York Times,* 2, 4, 7, 8, and 9 April 1920; Robinson, Oral history, HHPL.

[25] Hoover to Chester Murphy and O. C. Leiter, 13 May 1920, "Public Statements," HHPL; *Literary Digest,* 6 March 1920, p. 15.

[26] William Howard Taft observed that after California it was impossible for Hoover to be nominated. Memorandum, 16 May 1920, Taft Papers (at UCLA). Hoover to Warren Gregory, 30 March 1920, "Public Statements," HHPL; Ralph Arnold, "Laying Foundation Stones," The Historical Society of Southern California *Quarterly* (June 1955), pp. 99–124; see also Arnold's "Account of Hoover's Rise to the Presidency," Huntington Library; Richard D. Batman, "The Road to the Presidency: Hoover, Johnson, and the California Republican Party, 1920–1924," unpublished doctoral dissertation, University of Southern California, 1965, pp. 80–122; *New York Times,* 23 April 1920.

[27] Austin, "Hoover and Johnson," *The Nation,* 15 May 1920, p. 643.

[28] Louis Post commented to William Dodd on the vast improvement in the *Herald* under Hoover. 16 Feb. 1920, Box 16, Dodd Papers; the *Herald* remark is quoted in the *New York World,* 7 Dec. 1919; Gibson to Fred R. Dolbeare, 11 May 1920, Gibson Papers.

[29] Wilbur to Gibson ("flivver" story), 6 March 1920, Box 8, Gibson Papers; *Literary Digest,* 20 April 1920, p. 10; Walter Lippmann, *Early Writings* (New York, 1970), p. 191; Strauss, *Men and Decisions,* pp. 56–7; *New Republic,* 24 March 1920, p. 120.

[30] Hoover, Address at Rochester, New York, 22 Oct. 1920; Hoover, "Reorganization of the Federal Government," *Mining and Metallurgy* (May 1921), p. 9, Reprint file, HHPL.

[31] Hoover to A. Lawrence Lowell, 30 Sept. 1920; Hoover to Harding, 8 Aug. 1920, "General Campaign Correspondence, California, D-N," Pre-Presidential, HHPL.

[32] In 1923 Hoover apologized to Lord Cecil for his silence on the League: "You cannot do more than you can do." Cecil Diary, British Museum, pp. 24–5, fol. 151, 2; Hoover to Warren Harding, 8 and 27 Sept. 1920, "President Harding," HHPL; Hoover, Address Before the Columbia Club of Indianapolis, 9 Oct. 1920; "Treaty Statement," 9 Sept. 1920, "Public Statements," HHPL; Harding to Hoover, 21 Sept. 1920, Harding Papers; Hoover to Mrs. Robert A. Burdette, 29 Sept. 1920; Hoover to Will Hays, 20 Sept. 1920, Hays Papers.

[33] Hoover's telegram of acceptance is in the "Harding" file, Pre-Commerce, HHPL; Robert K. Murray, "President Harding and His Cabinet," *Ohio History,* LXXV (Spring–Summer 1966), 108–25; Anne W. Lane and Louise Wall, eds., *The Letters of Franklin K. Lane* (Boston, 1922); Lane to John W Hallowell, 21 Feb. 1921, Mark Sullivan to E. E. Smith, 17 Feb. 1921, Box 19, Sullivan Papers; J. R. Williams, "Hoover, Harding, and the Harding Image," *Northwest Ohio Quarterly* (Winter 1972/73), pp. 4–20.

[34] Austin, *Earth Horizon* (New York, 1932), p. 323.

CHAPTER IX

[1] One of the richest sources for an understanding of Hoover during the Commerce years is his testimony before numerous House and Senate committees.

Owing to space limitations, cumbersome citations to these hearings do not generally appear in the footnotes, even though the materials are used in the chapter. The scholar may consult the government index to congressional hearings to locate Hoover's testimony on the following diverse topics: the Webb-Pomerene Act, aircraft, crude rubber, coffee, potash, the foreign commerce service, pollution of navigable waters, the Colorado River Basin, railroad rate structures, reorganization of executive departments, future trading, coal distribution, trade with China, naval affairs, radio, inland waterways, the standardization of screw threads, flood control, rural credits, and so forth.

A thematic approach to the Commerce period is suggested in Carolyn Grin, "Herbert Hoover and the Social Responsibilities of the Expert: The Quantitatively-Trained Idealist," seminar paper, University of Iowa, 1971. For general views, see Hoover, Commencement Address, Penn College *Bulletin* (July 1925); Peri E. Arnold, "Herbert Hoover and the Department of Commerce: A Study of Ideology and Policy," unpublished doctoral dissertation, Chicago, 1972. For convenience see Arnold, "Herbert Hoover and the Continuity of American Public Policy," *Public Policy,* XX (Fall 1972), 525–44; J. Walter Drake, "How the Department of Commerce Works," *Journal of the National Education Association* (Jan. 1924), pp. 15–21; and Hoover, *Larger Purposes of the Department of Commerce* (New York, 1928). Hoover particularly lauded F. M. Feiker, "The Profession of Commerce in the Making," *Annals,* CI (May 1922), 203–7; Hoover to Feiker, 3 July 1922, Box 231, HHPL.

[2] Hunt, "The Cooperative Committee and the Conference System," a paper read before the Taylor Society of New York on 14 Dec. 1926, Box 161, Commerce Papers, HHPL; Joslin, *Hoover Off the Record* (Garden City, 1934), p. 50; *Kiplinger Washington Letter,* 9 June 1930.

[3] Total appropriations for the District of Columbia increased from $20 million in 1921–2 to $39 million in 1928–9.

[4] "Division of Simplified Practices, 1921–28," "Accomplishments," Commerce, HHPL.

[5] Hoover to Coolidge, 18 Dec. 1922, 14 Dec. 1923, Coolidge Papers; Memorandum, Hoover for Mr. O'Malley, 3 Oct. 1928; Hoover to Senator W. C. Jones, 25 June 1926; Secretary Hoover statement of 27 April 1924 in answer to [William Randolph] Hearst accusations; Hoover to Scott C. Bone, 14 Feb. 1923; Hoover to E. D. Clark, 20 Aug. 1923; Hoover to W. S. Greene, 7 Feb. 1924, "Alaska," HHPL; James J. Wadsworth to Hoover, 5 Jan. 1922, old numbering, 1–I/73, Commerce, HHPL; Harding to Hoover, 20 Oct. 1921, Harding Papers; Hoover to Harding, 6 April 1923, "Harding," HHPL.

[6] C. M. Jansky, Jr., "The Contribution of Herbert Hoover to Broadcasting," *Journal of Broadcasting,* I (Summer 1957), 241–9; Owen D. Young to Hoover, 2 Dec. 1925, Young Papers; Glenn A. Johnson, "Secretary of Commerce Herbert Clark Hoover: The First Regulator of American Broadcasting, 1921–1928," unpublished doctoral dissertation, University of Iowa, 1970.

[7] Roger E. Bilstein, "Technology and Commerce: Aviation in the Conduct of American Business, 1918–29," *Journal of Aviation* (July 1969), pp. 392–411; "The Vision of Hoover," *The Independent,* 28 Aug. 1926, pp. 229–31; "P.O. 1930 D," HHPL.

[8] For background, see Hoover, "Some Notes on Industrial Readjustment," *Saturday Evening Post,* 27 Dec. 1919, p. 39; Speech to Unemployment Conference, 26 Sept. 1921; Report of Economic Advisory Committee, 26 Sept. 1921, "Unemployment," HHPL.

[9] Meeting until mid-October 1922, the larger conference of eighty gave slight attention to permanent reform. Hoover himself later reflected that the long-run program for preventing unemployment had been overshadowed by the unemployment emergency. Report of Economic Advisory Committee, 26 Sept. 1921, "Unemployment—Advisory Committee," HHPL.

[10] The former socialist Hunt pronounced government-sponsored unemployment insurance "neither desirable nor practicable in America." Hunt, "The Washington Conference," 3 Jan. 1922; Hunt to Hoover, 1 Sept. 1922; Hoover to Henry S. Pritchett, 18 Nov. 1921; Woods's Staff Conferences, 2 Dec. 1921, 3 Jan. 1922; Woods to Mayors, 11 Oct. 1921, "Unemployment," HHPL.

[11] *Report of the President's Conference on Unemployment* (Washington, 1921); Mallery to Hoover, 9 Jan. 1926, 10 Feb. 1926, 10 May 1926, "Otto Mallery," HHPL; Mallery to Hoover, 7 Feb. 1928, "Owen D. Young," HHPL; Ellis Hawley, "Herbert Hoover and the Expansion of the Commerce Department: The Anti-Bureaucrat as Bureaucratic Empire-Builder," unpublished essay in possession of author, 1970; J. Joseph Huthmacher, *Senator Robert F. Wagner* (New York, 1968).

[12] Wesley C. Mitchell, *et al., Business Cycles and Unemployment: Report and Recommendations* (Washington, 1923); Committee on Recent Changes, *Recent Economic Changes in the United States,* 2 vols. (New York, 1929); Hoover, "Industrial Waste," *Bulletin* of the Taylor Society, VI (April 1921), 77; Carolyn Grin, "The Unemployment Conference of 1921: An Experiment in National Cooperative Planning," *Mid-America,* LV (April 1973), 83–107.

[13] In his own words, Hoover saw the Commerce Department as an "educational agency" to clear "a vast morass of economic illiteracy." Evan B. Metcalf, "Secretary Hoover and the Emergence of Macroeconomic Management," *Business History Review,* XLIX (Spring 1975), 60–80; cf. Donald Winch, *Economics and Policy* (New York, 1969).

[14] Lance E. Davis and Daniel J. Kevles, "The National Research Fund," *Minerva,* XII (April 1974), 207–20; Hoover to Coolidge, 10 Dec. 1925, old numbering, 1–I/241; Hoover to Young, 5 Dec. 1925, "Owen D. Young," Commerce, HHPL.

[15] James H. Shideler, *Farm Crisis, 1919–1923* (Berkeley, 1957), p. 293; "What of the Farmer's Future? An Interview with Secretary Hoover," *Commerce and Finance,* 18 Nov. 1925, pp. 2243–4; *The Washington Farmer,* 26 Sept. 1926, p. 3; Hoover, "Address on Agriculture," 7 Jan. 1925, "Public Statements"; Hoover to W. M. Jardine, 1 April 1926; Hoover to E. D. Funk, 31 May 1924, "Agriculture," HHPL; Gary Koerselman, "Herbert Hoover and the Farm Crisis of the Twenties," unpublished doctoral dissertation, Northern Illinois University, 1971.

[16] Joan Hoff Wilson, "Hoover's Agricultural Policies, 1921–1928," *Agricultural History,* LI (April 1977), 335–61. Hoover to Harding, 12 Jan. 1921, "Harding," HHPL.

[17] Edward L. Schapsmeier and Frederick H. Schapsmeier, "Disharmony in the

Harding Cabinet: Hoover-Wallace Controversy," *Ohio History,* LXXV (Spring/Summer 1966), 126–36.

[18] Hoover, *Memoirs,* II, 174; Taylor to Black, 16 Jan. 1928, Black Papers; Wallace to Coolidge, 8 April 1922; Hoover to Coolidge, 17 and 18 April 1924, Coolidge Papers; Donald L. Winters, *Henry C. Wallace as Secretary of Agriculture, 1921–1924* (Urbana, 1970).

[19] Edgar Rickard diary, 23 Jan. 1925.

[20] Koerselman, "Secretary Hoover and National Farm Policy," *Agricultural History,* LI (April 1977), 362–77. Hoover to Julian Friant, 12 June 1926; Hoover, Address, 14 Feb. 1927, "Agriculture," HHPL; Wilson, "Hoover's Agricultural Policies," pp. 335 ff.

[21] James Shideler, "Herbert Hoover and the Federal Farm Board Project," *Mississippi Valley Historical Review,* XLII (March 1956), 710–29; Jardine to Coolidge, 7 April 1924, and on the Federal Wheat Cooperative, Inc., old numbering 1–I/9Ag, HHPL; Stephen J. Adam to Frank Lowden, 3 Aug. 1927, Box 64, Series 3, Lowden Papers; Henry A. Wallace to Chester Davis, 2 Oct. 1928, Davis Papers; Wilson, "Hoover's Agricultural Policies," p. 347.

[22] Hoover to Everett Sanders, 7 March 1925, old numbering, 1–I/241, HHPL.

[23] William Allen White got at the notion of "individualistic cooperation" in a letter to Hoover of 18 Oct. 1920: "I believe it will solve a good many problems. Curiously enough you will find in it a strong drift and tendency away from what is known as Parliamentary or Congressional government. It sets up, in fact, an extra governmental life, quite apart from the government, somewhat regulated by it . . . but . . . a distinct institutional life"— White Papers; *The Washington Farmer,* 26 Aug. 1926, p. 3; Ivy L. Lee *Newsletter,* 7 Oct. 1926.

[24] Feiker, "The Profession of Commerce in the Making," pp. 203–7; *Hardware Age,* CX (5 Oct. 1922), 51–4; Feiker, "What the Government Is Doing for Industry," *Electrical World,* 14 Jan. 1922, p. 71; Louis Galambos, *Competition and Cooperation: The Emergence of a National Trade Association* (Baltimore, 1966).

[25] Robert Himmelberg, *The Origins of the National Recovery Administration* (New York, 1976); Hoover to W. W. McCullough, 20 Sept. 1922, and McCullough memorandum of 28 Sept. 1922 meeting with David L. Wing, Commerce, HHPL; *Electrical World,* 18 Feb. 1922, p. 349; Maple Flooring Assoc. *v.* U.S. 268 US 563; Cement Manufacturers Protective Assoc. *v.* U.S. 268 US 588; Hoover to Stone, 3 June 1925; Alpheus Mason, *Harlan Fiske Stone* (New York, 1950), p. 210; Stone to Hoover, 20 April 1925, Stone Papers.

[26] Hoover to Harry Garfield, 2 May 1922, "Coal," HHPL; Himmelberg, *Origins of the NRA,* p. 19; Louis P. Galambos, "The Cotton-Textile Institute and Government," *Business History Review* (Summer 1964), pp. 186–205; J. L. Dwyer, "Modify Anti-Trust Law Says Hoover," *Oil and Gas Journal,* 28 Oct. 1926, p. 29.

[27] The most recent and best treatment of Hoover's handling of labor matters is Robert H. Zieger, "Labor, Progressivism, and Herbert Hoover in the 1920's," *Wisconsin Magazine of History,* XLVII (Spring 1975), 196–208,

and "Herbert Hoover, the Wage-earner, and the 'New Economic System,' 1919–1923," *Business History Review,* LI (Summer 1977), 161–89. Zieger's *Republicans and Labor, 1919–1929* (Lexington, 1969) is standard. Barnes to Rickard, 1 Feb. 1929, Barnes Papers; Hoover, Address at Stanford, 22 June 1925, "Public Statements," HHPL.

28 The steel issue is well handled in Charles Hill, "Fighting the Twelve-hour Day in the American Steel Industry," *Labor History,* XV (Winter 1974), 19–35, in Zieger, *Republicans and Labor,* and in Haggar Hurvitz, "The Meaning of Industrial Conflict in Some Ideologies of the Early 1920's: The AFL, Organized Employers, and Herbert Hoover," unpublished doctoral dissertation, Columbia University, 1971. Hoover to Harding, 7 April and 4 May 1922, 13 June 1923, "Harding," HHPL. The importance of Hoover's role over that of Lindsay is emphasized in Henry A. Wallace, Oral history, Columbia University; Julius Barnes, Autobiography, Barnes Papers.

29 Ellis Hawley, "Secretary Hoover and the Bituminous Coal Problem, 1921–28," *Business History Review,* XLII (Autumn 1968), 253–70; Zieger, *Republicans and Labor,* pp. 15, 244, 275.

30 *Hearings,* House Committee on Interstate and Foreign Commerce, 14 May 1926; Hoover to Harding, 23 Aug. 1922, Harding Papers; San Francisco *Business,* 8 Dec. 1922, p. 20.

31 F. R. Wadleigh, "Herbert Hoover and the Coal Industry," *Coal Age,* XXXIII (April 1928), 213–14.

32 Hoover to J. P. Jackson, 12 Feb. 1926, "Anthracite," HHPL; Robert H. Zieger, "Pinchot and Coolidge: The Politics of the 1923 Anthracite Crisis," *Journal of American History,* LII (December 1965), 566–81; Robert H. Zieger, "Pennsylvania Coal and Politics: The Anthracite Strike of 1925–1926," *Pennsylvania Magazine of History and Biography* (April 1969), pp. 244–62.

33 Hawley, "Secretary Hoover," *passim;* Zieger, *Republicans and Labor,* pp. 230–6, 238–42, 245–7.

34 Hoover, "The Railways," 7 Nov. 1922, Box 5; Hoover to Harding, 11 July 1921, Harding Papers; *The Nation,* CXV (27 Sept. 1922), 297.

35 Hoover, "Railroad Reorganization," April 1923, "Railroad Consolidation," HHPL; Stephen J. Scheinberg, "The Development of Corporation Labor Policy, 1900–1940," unpublished doctoral dissertation, University of Wisconsin, 1966; Ross Runfola, "Herbert C. Hoover as Secretary of Commerce, 1921–1923: Domestic Economic Planning in the Harding Years," unpublished doctoral dissertation, S.U.N.Y. at Buffalo, 1973.

36 Two monographs disagree on Hoover's importance in the development of the Colorado River. Beverly Moeller finds many errors in the President's *Memoirs* and emphasizes the role of Congressman Phil Swing in *Phil Swing and Boulder Dam* (Berkeley, 1971); Norris Hundley gives more credit to Hoover in *Water and the West: The Colorado River Compact* (Berkeley, 1975).

37 Hundley, *Water and the West,* pp. xvi, xvii, 173, 188, 208–9, 212, 229, and *passim;* Hoover to William Allen White, 9 Dec. 1922, Commerce, HHPL; Hoover to Chester Rowell, 11 April 1925, Rowell Papers.

[38] Hundley, *Water and the West, passim.*

[39] The Utah state engineer wrote to Hoover on 5 Feb. 1923 of "how very, very much the fact of your approval helped in the matter of ratification. Somehow or other you are able to place on what you say and do the stamp of 'genuine' and the people are satisfied," "Colorado River," HHPL; Smoot to Coolidge, 21 Dec. 1928, Box 57; Smoot diary, 23 Feb. 1927, 23 April 1928, 5 May 1928, Smoot Papers.

[40] Senator Norris wrote Walter Lippmann on 9 Jan. 1925 that Boulder Canyon was in some respects more far-reaching than Muscle Shoals. Edgar Rickard diary, 3 Jan. 1925.

[41] Hoover to Coolidge, 2 June 1928, old numbering, 1–I/434, Commerce, HHPL; Hoover to Capper, 16 July 1926, Capper Papers.

[42] Hoover to Coolidge, 27 Dec. 1926, "Great Lakes–St. Lawrence"; Hoover to Warren F. Strong of Chicago *Daily News*, 29 Dec. 1926, "St. Lawrence," HHPL; *New York Herald*, 17 Jan. 1927; William R. Willoughby, *The St. Lawrence Waterway* (Madison, 1961).

[43] Richard N. Kottman, "Herbert Hoover and the St. Lawrence Seaway," *New York History*, LVI (July 1975), 314–46.

[44] *Hearings*, "Pollution of Navigable Waters," House Committee on Foreign Affairs, 67th Congress, 2nd Session, Oct. 1925, 7–8 Dec. 1921, and 15–22 Feb. 1922; Hoover to Harding, 25 June 1922, Harding Papers.

[45] Douglas C. Drake, "Herbert Hoover, Ecologist: The Politics of Oil Pollution Control, 1921–1926," *Mid-America*, LX (July 1973), 207–28.

[46] A monograph emphasizing the role of the bureau is Joseph Brandes, *Herbert Hoover and Economic Diplomacy* (Pittsburgh, 1962); Hoover to William Hard, 9 June 1921, old numbering, 1–I/242, HHPL; *Hearings* on State, Justice, Commerce, and Labor Appropriation Bill, "American Foreign Trade," House, 7 Jan. 1925, p. 213.

[47] Hoover to Hughes, 28 Feb. 1925; Hughes to Dearing, 3 May 1921; Hughes, Memorandum, 18 Dec. 1925—all in old numbering, 1–I/76, HHPL; Polk to Hughes, 9 April 1921; Hughes to Assistant Secretary Dearing, 3 May 1921, State Department Archives, 1110–78/79, NA; *New Republic*, 1 June 1927, pp. 43–4; Edgar Rickard diary, 21 Jan. 1925.

[48] On Hoover's earlier efforts to arrange a system of private overseeing of loans, see Michael Hogan, *Informal Entente* (Columbia, 1977), pp. 82–3; *Hearings*, House Committee on Interstate and Foreign Commerce, 18 Jan. 1926, pp. 292, 301.

[49] Hoover, *Memoirs*, II, 14, 56, 86. There is a good summary of U.S. foreign investment policy in Brandes, *Herbert Hoover*, pp. 151–91; Thomas Lamont to Hughes, 31 March 1932, Lamont Papers.

[50] Hoover, "What Government Can Do," *Nation's Business*, IX (June 1921), 11–13; *New York Times*, 3, 10, and 19 March 1926; *Nation's Business*, XIV (June 1926), 144; "Latin-America Strikes Back at Hoover," *Literary Digest*, 6 March 1926; Turner, Oral history, HHPL; Department of Commerce, 151:621/2; 82271/2, Box 533, NA. Texas deposits discovered at the instigation of Hoover were valuable during World War II.

[51] *New York Times*, 10 Jan. 1926; Young to Hoover, 5 Jan. 1926, Young Papers.

[52] The British were certain Hoover was courting public favor for the presidency by attacking them. FO 371/11167 and 12039, PRO. "D.W.," *The Passing Show* (London, ca. 1927); *Literary Digest,* 9 Jan. 1926, pp. 5–7.

[53] Hoover to Harding, 25 Nov. and 15 Dec. 1921, Harding Papers; *New Republic,* 21 Oct. 1925, p. 227; Hoover, Memoranda, 4 Feb. 1923, 23 Sept. 1925, "French Debts"; Hoover to Mellon, 6 Jan. 1923, "Treasury"; Hoover to Hughes, 23 Feb. 1923, HHPL; USFR, 1923, II, 67; Frank C. Costigliola, "The Politics of Financial Stabilization," unpublished doctoral dissertation, Cornell University, 1973; Benjamin Rhodes, "Reassessing 'Uncle Shylock': The United States and French War Debts," *Journal of American History,* LV (March 1969), 787–803; Rhodes, "Herbert Hoover and the War Debts, 1919–33," *Prologue,* VI (Summer 1974), 150–80.

[54] Hoover to Mellon, 6 Jan. 1923, "Treasury"; Hoover, Memoranda, 23, 28, 29, 30 Sept., and 1 Oct. 1925, "Debts, French (1)," HHPL; Rhodes, "The United States and the French War Debts"; Melvyn Leffler, "The Origins of Republican War Debt Policy, 1921–1923," *Journal of American History,* CIX (1972), 585–601.

[55] Young and Hoover disagreed about debts and national monopolies, Young believing the United States's inflexibility on debts drove foreign powers to create closed markets. Young to Hoover, 5 Jan. 1926, Young Papers; Mark Sullivan diary, 30 April 1922, Sullivan Papers. On British perception of Hoover's anti-European stand, see Sir Auckland Geddes to Lord Curzon, 17 Oct. 1922, FO 371/7283/A6613, PRO.

CHAPTER X

[1] *Fishing for Fun—And to Wash Your Soul* (New York, 1963). Donald R. McCoy has an excellent essay, "To the White House: Herbert Hoover, August 1927–March 1929," in Martin Fausold and George Mazuzan, eds., *The Hoover Presidency: A Reappraisal* (Albany, 1974), pp. 29–49.

[2] *New York Times,* 29 May 1924; Donald McCoy, *Calvin Coolidge* (New York, 1967), p. 247.

[3] Hoover to Cyrenus Cole, 6 Feb. 1934, "Post-Presidential, Individual," Calendars, HHPL; Lou Hoover to Denby, 18 Feb. 1924; Hoover to Denby, 14 March 1924, Denby Papers; Theodore Roosevelt, Jr., diary, 5 Feb. 1923.

[4] September 19, 1925.

[5] Hoover to Lindsay, 4 April 1924, HHPL; *Memoirs,* II, 56.

[6] Claude M. Fuess, *Calvin Coolidge* (Boston, 1940), p. 400; Bruce Lohof, "Herbert Hoover's Mississippi Valley Land Reform Memorandum: A Document," *Arkansas Historical Quarterly,* XXIX (Summer 1970), 112–19. Lohof's unpublished doctoral dissertation is "Hoover and the Mississippi Flood of 1927," Syracuse University, 1968; see also his "Herbert Hoover, Spokesman of Humane Efficiency: The Mississippi Flood of 1927," *American Quarterly,* XXII (Fall 1970), 690–700.

[7] James L. Fieser to Hoover, 27 Aug. 1927, gives the Red Cross's negative position on using its funds for the program. Hoover to W. D. Boies, 12 March 1928; Joseph Ransdell to Coolidge, 2 June 1928, "Mississippi Flood, 1928," HHPL; FO 371/12056, PRO.

[8] For an opposed interpretation, see Pete Daniel, *The Shadow of Slavery: Peonage in the South, 1901–1969* (Urbana, 1972) and *Deep 'N As It Comes: The 1927 Mississippi River Flood* (Knoxville, 1976); William H. Hughes and Frederick D. Patterson, *Robert Russa Moton* (Chapel Hill, 1956), pp. 200–3. Hoover to Arthur Kellogg, 6 July 1927; Hoover to Moton, 17 June, 29 Sept., 16 Dec. 1927; Hoover to H. C. Couch, 18 July 1927, "Mississippi Relief," HHPL; *The Afro-American,* 18 June 1927, p. 3; Kelly Miller to Hoover, 4 Oct. 1928, "Miller, Kelly," Pre-Presidential, HHPL; Moton to Joseph E. Bowman, 14 April 1928, Moton Papers.

[9] Hoover to H. C. Couch, 8 July 1927, "Mississippi Relief—Negroes," HHPL; Henry C. Taylor to Moton, 17 April 1928, copy in Black Papers; Hoover to Eugene Booze, n.d., "Mississippi Flood," HHPL; Lohof, "Herbert Hoover's Mississippi Valley Land Reform," pp. 112–19; Rickard diary, 11 July 1927.

[10] Washington *Post,* 31 March 1928; *Congressional Record,* Senate, 1928, p. 6397. A pair of articles reaches differing conclusions on the importance of race in the 1928 election: West Tennessee Historical Society *Papers,* XXVII (1973), 81–107.

[11] While Hoover was a student at Stanford, the college newspaper, reflecting a popular sentiment, complained that "the ubiquitous Jap found his way even into the library. One is now employed there in cutting the pages of new books"—*Daily Palo Alto,* 11 Oct. 1892. "Free institutions," President Jordan remarked, cannot "reclaim those whom heredity has debased or destroyed." Jordan thought there should be property and intellectual qualifications for immigration. *Daily Palo Alto,* 13 Feb. 1893. Hoover to Coolidge, draft of material conveyed verbally on 18 April 1924, old numbering, P/240; Paul L. Murphy, *The Meaning of Freedom of Speech* (Westport, 1972); Sacramento *Union,* 19 Aug. 1920.

[12] Hoover, "Address Before Polish Conference," Buffalo, 12 Nov. 1919, "Public Statements," HHPL.

[13] Lippmann, "The Peculiar Weakness of Mr. Hoover," *Harper's* (June 1930), p. 1.

[14] *Hearings,* Presidential Campaign Expenditures, Special Senate Committee, 70th Congress, 1st Session, 7 to 16 May 1928; George Akerson to Harry Hunt, 7 April 1928, "Political, H. B. Hunt"; Akerson to T. C. C. Gregory, 16 Feb. 1928, "Political, T. C. C. Gregory," Akerson Papers.

[15] Roy V. Peel and Thomas G. Donnelly, *The 1928 Campaign: An Analysis* (New York, 1931); Capper to Borah, 10 Nov. 1928, Borah Papers.

[16] William Howard Taft wrote of "Wall Street's" opposition to Hoover. Taft to Mrs. Frederick Manning, April 1928, Taft Papers; *Official Report of the Proceedings* [of the Republican National Convention] . . . *1928* (Washington, 1928); Work to Fred Root, 9 Nov. 1927, Work Papers; CAB 73/12811, PRO; Wald to Mary MacDowell, 27 Sept. 1928, Wald Papers; Morton Keller, *In Defense of Yesterday: James M. Beck* (New York, 1956), pp. 200–11.

[17] *Kiplinger Washington Letter,* 3 Sept. 1928; Adam McMullen to George Peek, 21 July 1928, and Peter Norbeck to Peek, 14 July 1928, Peek Papers.

[18] Smoot diary, 15 June 1928, Smoot Papers; Bess Furman, *Washington Byline* (New York, 1949), pp. 10–11.

[19] Kirk H. Porter, *National Party Platforms, 1840–1964* (Urbana, 1966); Richberg to Martin F. Ryan, 4 June 1928; D. B. Robertson to Richberg, 5 Aug. 1928, Richberg Papers.

[20] *Public Papers, 1929,* p. 498.

[21] Hoover's 1928 campaign speeches are published as *The New Day* (Stanford, 1928). The title is in harmony with a tradition encompassing Theodore Roosevelt's *New Nationalism* or Wilson's published volume of speeches, *The New Freedom.* Harlan Fiske Stone wrote at least some part of the acceptance speech: William Howard Taft to Samuel H. Fisher, 2 May 1929, Taft Papers.

[22] The campaign speeches are also collected in a modern edition: *Public Papers, 1929,* pp. 521–612. Silas Bent, *Strange Bedfellows* (New York, 1928), p. 22.

[23] Washington *News,* 8 Oct. 1928; Judson King to Hoover, 8 Oct. 1928, HHPL; Joseph G. Knapp, *The Advance of American Cooperative Enterprise: 1900–1945* (Danville, Ill., 1973); Hoover to Slemp, 11 Sept. 1928, Slemp Papers.

[24] A good analysis of the candidates is found in reports of the British Embassy to the Foreign Office, FO 371/12811, PRO; Glass to Robert Ailsworth, 14 July 1928; Glass to George Fort Milton, 3 Aug. 1928, Glass Papers; Paul A. Carter, *Another Part of the Twenties* (New York, 1977). Hoover, *Memoirs,* II, 199; Norris to Gifford Pinchot, 14 July 1928, and Norris to Lewis Gannett, 8 Sept. 1928, Norris Papers. New York City Democrats were notoriously anti-farmer in their congressional voting: Gilbert C. Fite, "The Agricultural Issue in the Presidential Campaign of 1928," *Mississippi Valley Historical Review,* XXVII (March 1951), 653–72; Borah to Walter McClenon, 6 Oct. 1928, Borah Papers; Seligman, "The Economics of Farm Relief," file 2063, Raskob Papers; Glass to G. F. Milton, 3 Aug. 1928, McAdoo Papers; *Literary Digest,* 25 Aug. 1926, p. 15.

[25] Burner, *The Politics of Provincialism: The Democratic Party in Transition, 1918–1932* (New York, 1968), Ch. VII.

[26] Carter, *Another Part of the Twenties, passim.*

[27] *Time,* 22 Aug. 1960, p. 10. Henry Allen told Bruce Barton that Hoover directed his staff not to attack Tammany and only to wage a positive campaign, 4 Sept. 1928, Barton Papers. Alfred Kirchofer, Oral history, HHPL; Hoover, *Memoirs,* II, 207–19; *New York Times,* 5 June, 6 June, 10 Sept., 2 Oct. 1928; *New York Evening Post,* 5 June 1929; *Time,* 8 Oct. 1928, p. 10; Raskob to Work, 31 Oct. 1928, Work Papers; Walter S. Ring to Moses, 13 Nov. 1928; Franklin Fort to Moses, 1 Aug. 1928, Moses Papers.

[28] Taft to Robert Taft, 4 Nov. 1928, Box 653, Taft Papers; Rickard to Gibson and enclosure, 6 Oct. 1928, Box 10, Gibson Papers; Hoover to Baruch, 19 Oct. 1928, "Selected Letters," Baruch Papers. Darrow is quoted in *Time,* 5 March 1928, p. 8.

[29] Kent Schofield, "The Figure of Herbert Hoover in the 1928 Campaign," unpublished doctoral dissertation, University of California at Riverside, 1966; *New York Times,* 7 March 1929.

[30] John L. McNab, "What Hoover Means to the West," *Sunset,* LXI (Oct. 1928), 12; *New York Times,* 1 Aug. 1928.

[31] Roosevelt to Melville, 21 Sept. 1928, Governor's file, Franklin D. Roosevelt Papers; James W. Linn, *Jane Addams* (New York, 1935); Clarke A. Chambers, *Seedtime of Reform* (Ann Arbor, 1967), pp. 140–1.

[32] O. Douglas Weeks, "The Election of 1928," *Political and Social Science Quarterly,* IX, 337–48; Overman to Colonel S. A. Ashe, Nov. 1928, Overman Papers. Views of Irish and German voting in 1928 appear in R. A. Burchell, "Did the Irish and German Voters Desert the Democrats in 1928?" *Journal of American Studies,* VI (August 1972), 153–64; and Burner, *Politics of Provincialism,* Ch. VIII.

[33] Robert H. Zieger, "The Career of James J. Davis," *Pennsylvania Magazine of History and Biography,* XCVIII (Jan. 1974), 74–84; John Bruce Dudler, "James J. Davis," unpublished doctoral dissertation, Ball State University, 1972; Daniel C. Roper, *Fifty Years of Public Life* (Durham, 1941), p. 239; Hoover to E. M. Poston, 2 Feb. 1928, "Cabinet Appointments," HHPL; Melvyn Dubofsky and Warren van Tine, *John L. Lewis* (New York, 1977).

[34] Hoover late in his life denied having offered the post of Secretary of State to Borah. Edgar Eugene Robinson, Oral history, HHPL; Hoover to Hughes, 18 Nov. 1928, Hughes Papers.

[35] Borah was strongly opposed to Donovan and recommended Mitchell. Mark Sullivan to Hoover, n.d., and Donovan to Hoover, n.d., "Attorney General," Pre-Presidential, HHPL. Dean Roscoe Pound of Harvard Law School called Mitchell the best-fitted candidate to be appointed Attorney General in thirty years. William E. Chadbourne to Hoover, 2 April 1928, "Justice, Misc.," HHPL; Taft to George Wickersham, 27 Dec. 1928, Box 657, Taft Papers.

[36] Jardine to F. D. Farrell, 24 May 1929, Jardine Papers; Robert T. Johnson, "Charles L. McNary . . . ," unpublished doctoral dissertation, University of Wisconsin, 1967; Hunt interview with Hoover, 8 Aug. 1933, Box 2, Hunt Papers; Neil MacNeil, Oral history, HHPL.

[37] Hand to Taft, 5 April 1928, Box 661, Taft Papers.

[38] Frederic Walcott, an old friend from relief days and now a Connecticut Republican senator, wrote: "Mr. Hoover goes into the presidency with the acclaim of the entire country. I am sorry for him because they probably expect too much of him. He is known as the Miracle Man and he is when he has his own organization." Walcott to T. B. Mott, 7 April 1929, Walcott Papers. Similarly, Mabel Walker Willebrandt wrote: "the public expects too much from you and expects it too soon," 8 Feb. 1929, "Attorney General," Pre-Presidential Papers, HHPL. Or Xenophon Caverno to George Peek, 11 Dec. 1928, Box 6, Peek Papers: "The whole country's expecting the impossible of Mr. Hoover . . . [if he cannot deliver,] he will be the most unhappy man in America." Willis J. Abbot, *Watching the World Go By* (Boston, 1933); cf. the *Monitor,* 27 Nov. 1932.

CHAPTER XI

[1] In his *Memoirs* Hoover wrote: "As adviser to Congress the President must demonstrate constant leadership by proposing social and economic reforms made necessary by the increasing complexity of American life"—II, 216. Hoover observed to a friend near Inauguration Day: the worst thing about the presidency was "that there are so many important jobs which ought to be done, and so few years in which to do them"—*Kiplinger Washington Letter,* 11 March 1929; Ray Henle in Bradley Nash's Oral history reminis-

cence, HHPL; Borah to Charles J. Carlson, Box 303, Borah Papers. "The truth is," Taft worried, "that Hoover is a progressive"—Taft to Horace Taft, 1 Jan. 1929, Box 74; Taft to Mrs. F. J. Manning, 13 Jan. 1929; Taft to Robert Taft, 4 Nov. 1928, 20 Jan. 1929, 7 April 1929, Box 653, Taft Papers; H. C. Taylor to Black, 27 March 1929, John D. Black Papers; Rickard diary, 21 Jan. 1927.

2 In late March Hoover invoked Section 10 of the Railway Labor Act and set up a board of inquiry under James G. Garfield to investigate a dispute by Texas and Pacific railroad workers. As a result, the company was forced to share losses by employees forced to move. "Mediation," Box 439, HHPL; *Congressional Record*, LXX, 1666, 2061–5, 2092–117, 2972, 5010; *Internal Revenue News* (April 1929), pp. 1–2; *New York World*, 15 March 1919; *Public Papers, 1929*, pp. 21, 25–30. See Hoover to Harding, 28 Nov. 1921, for an early formulation of this plan, "Harding," HHPL.

3 Hoover, said George Akerson speaking for the President, did not intend to engage in any "Red Hunt" when so many vital issues were before the country—*New York World*, 27 June 1929; *The Nation*, 24 July 1929, p. 10; Jane Addams to Lawrence Richey, 29 May 1929; Hoover to Addams, 9 Sept. 1929; Addams to Hoover, 28 Sept. 1929, "Amnesty, 1929," HHPL; Hoover to W. D. Mitchell, 23 April 1929; Mitchell to Hoover, 23 August 1929, "Justice, 1929—A and B"; Hoover to Mitchell, 18 Oct. 1930, HHPL; *New York World*, 27 June 1929; *Time*, XI (8 July 1929), 14; *New Republic*, LIX (10 July 1929), 19; "Communism—1929, Aug.–Dec.," HHPL.

4 *New York Times*, 24 April 1929; Clement H. Congdon to Hoover, 23 April 1929, Box 16; Hoover to Willebrandt, 28 May 1929, "Justice-Misc.-Willebrandt," HHPL; Burner, *The Politics of Provincialism* (New York, 1968), p. 205; *Public Papers, 1929*, pp. 156–9; Moses to M. S. Sherman, 29 Sept. 1928, Moses Papers.

5 Doak said: "There are a great many of these foreign born who have been admitted to our country who not only seem unwilling to live up to the requirements of citizenship but who seem bent upon doing their utmost to destroy our American civilization"—Washington *Sunday Star*, 24 Jan. 1932; Arthur Mann, *LaGuardia, A Fighter Against His Times* (Philadelphia, 1959); Pearson, "Immigration—1932," HHPL; Hoover to Mitchell, 30 Sept. 1943; Mitchell to Hoover, 4 Oct 1943, Mitchell Papers.

6 The White House belittled its role in the de Priest incident by announcing that "the incident was official, not social." Congressman de Priest agreed. Walter Newton to Henry W. Anderson, 20 June 1929; Carrie Butler Massenburg, Oral history, HHPL. Senator Coleman Blease called the White House a Caucasian symbol of dominance. Donald Lisio of Coe College is working on Hoover's Southern politics. On patronage, see Arthur Krock, "Hoover Brings Changes to Southern Politics," *New York Times*, 14 April 1929, 21 June 1929, 5 July 1929; Boxes 100–2, Presidential Papers, HHPL. The Nixons, by contrast, accepted a restrictive covenant in their deed. Mrs. Jameson Parker, Oral history, HHPL.

7 Hoover to Ferry Heath, 12 Sept. 1932, HHPL; *New York World*, 9 May 1929, 14 May 1930; "Colored Question, 1930B," HHPL; U.S. Department of the Interior, Annual Report (Washington, 1930), pp. 1024–30; Hoover to

Mitchell, 31 Dec. 1931, "Lynching," HHPL. A 12-to-1 student-teacher ratio was achieved at Howard. *New York Herald-Tribune,* 8 Aug. 1929; *Public Papers, 1930,* 23 Sept. 1930, p. 376.

8 Hoover to Moton, 31 Dec. 1931; Moton to Hoover, 6 Jan. 1932, Moton Papers; Walter Newton to Walter White, 20 Aug. 1930, HHPL.

9 Richard B. Sherman, *The Republican Party and Black America: From McKinley to Hoover, 1896–1933* (Charlottesville, 1973), pp. 246–7, 250.

10 Bates, *Prisons and Beyond* (New York, 1936), pp. 17–18, 100, 131, 134ff.; Mitchell to Wilbur, 24 June 1929, File 1-249, Pt. I, Interior Department, NA; Taylor/Gates Collection, file 200, HHPL; Willebrandt to Richey, 6 May 1929, "Justice-1929-A," HHPL.

11 Sanford Bates to Hoover, 27 April 1931, "Prisons," HHPL; Bureau of Prisons, Reports of the Director (1930–3); *American Political Science Review,* XXIV (1930), 913–46; Hoover to Bates, 28 Feb. 1928, HHPL.

12 Sons of Gwalia Letterbook, 14 Nov. 1898; Adalin W. Fuller, Roy St. Lewis, and Walter Trohan, Oral histories, HHPL; *Harper's* (Oct. 1930), p. 5.

13 Many of Hoover's associates were hard drinkers: George Akerson, Henry J. Allen, Bradley Nash, and most of his 1928 campaign staff and officers. Nash, Oral history, HHPL; Mrs. Henry W. Peabody to Borah, 5 Nov. 1928, Borah Papers.

14 In April 1929 Hoover wrote Taft that he regretted his pledge to appoint such a commission, for he lacked confidence in its members. Hoover to Taft, 7 April 1929 and 8 April 1929, quoted in Alpheus T. Mason, *William Howard Taft* (London, 1965). Mitchell wrote Wilbur on 3 Jan. 1936, Mitchell Papers: "We were so overwhelmed with the miserable task of dealing with prohibition, that everything else was submerged and whatever steps we tried to take . . . were lost or defeated in Congress because of the surge of other problems arising from the Depression. Much of the legislation recently put through Congress . . . with much favored publicity, was drafted and introduced during Mr. Hoover's administration"—File of the National Commission on Law Observance, Box 203, HHPL; *Harper's* (Oct. 1930), p. 5; *Outlook,* 29 Sept. 1930, p. 125; *Public Papers, 1930,* p. 266; *New York Times,* 1 April 1929; Stimson diary, 4 Nov. 1928, 28 Dec. 1930.

15 *The Nation,* CXXXIII (29 July 1931), 104; Rickard diary, 22 Jan. 1931; Lewis Strauss, Oral history, HHPL; National Committee on Law Observance and Enforcement, *Report* . . . (Washington, 1931).

16 Hoover claimed that the conferences were "sound processes for the search, production, and distribution of truth . . . they spread cooperation . . . not only in finding truth but . . . to get action upon it"—*Public Papers, 1930,* p. 17; *Literary Digest,* 15 Feb. 1930, pp. 10–11.

17 Hoover to Couzens, 6 March 1929, Box 97, HHPL; *Literary Digest,* 15 Feb. 1930, p. 10; *Public Papers, 1929,* pp. 208–12.

18 The purpose of the conference, according to Wilbur, was "to find facts, to define standards, to recommend changes." The Memphis *Commercial Appeal* termed the conference more important than the tariff or farm relief measures. *White House Conference on Child Health . . . 1930* (New York, 1931), Introduction, p. 5; Hoover to F. D. Roosevelt, 19 Aug. 1930, Roosevelt Papers.

[19] Perhaps the best account of the differences between Hoover and Grace Abbot is in Robert A. Karlsrud, "The Hoover Labor Department," unpublished doctoral dissertation, UCLA, 1972. Edgar Eugene Robinson, ed., *The Memoirs of Ray Lyman Wilbur* (Stanford, 1960), pp. 522 ff.; Clarke Chambers, *Seedtime of Reform* (Ann Arbor, 1967), p. 55; J. Stanley Lemons, *The Woman Citizen: Social Feminism in the 1920's* (Urbana, 1973); Joseph B. Chepaitis, "The First Federal Social Welfare Measure: The Sheppard-Turner Maternity and Infancy Act," unpublished doctoral dissertation, Georgetown University, 1963; Grace Abbot, Memorandum for the Secretary of Labor, 25 Nov. 1929, "Maternity Legislation"; Hoover to J. Dawson Roop, 16 Oct. 1929, Box 84; Hoover to Caroline Slade, 27 Feb. 1931; Hoover to Mrs. Ellis Yost, 15 Dec. 1930, HHPL; Grace Abbot to Julius Rosenwald, 25 April 1930, Rosenwald Papers; *Literary Digest*, 6 Dec. 1930, p. 10; *White House Conference on Child Health . . . 1930.*

[20] Lemons, *The Woman Citizen*, pp. 198, 231, 236–7, 243; Hoover to Caroline Slade, 27 Feb. 1931, and Hoover to Mrs. Ellis Yost, 15 Dec. 1930, HHPL.

[21] The Commerce Department in the 1920's did much to encourage better housing, particularly for lower income groups. Hoover wanted local communities to take on the responsibility of regulating the quality of housing and of requiring standard and simplified construction materials and tools that would make for lower prices. With a $40,000 appropriation from Congress he organized one hundred local conferences on housing, and with $50,000 more, a Division of Building and Housing had sprung to life in his department under John M. Gries of Harvard. Hoover also advanced an ambitious plan to provide cheap housing for government workers, but Washington's realtors prevented its enactment. He also became president of the important voluntary group, Better Homes in America; its 18,000 local committees supported the department's research and publications, and generally its efforts for the building of more and better houses more cheaply and the passage of zoning laws. Hoover persuaded the philanthropist Julius Rosenwald to undertake a pilot program of home financing, which showed banks the safety in higher mortgages. The department distributed 300,000 copies of a pamphlet called "How to Own Your Own Home." "Better Homes," HHPL; Washington *Star*, 10, 12, 13 Aug. 1926; Minutes of meeting of Better Homes, 9 Jan. 1929, Rosenwald Papers; *Public Papers, 1929*, p. 498.

[22] By 1932, for instance, thirty-seven states had made use of the "Standard State Zoning Enabling Act," prepared by the Advisory Committee on City Planning and Zoning of the Department of Commerce. Press release, 25 April 1929, Interior Department, NA; Hoover to Harding, 9 Feb. 1922, "President," HHPL; John M. Gries and James Ford, eds., *President's Conference on Home Building and Home Ownership*, 11 vols. (Washington, 1931); Lawrence Veiller, Oral history, Columbia University.

[23] Introduction, U.S. National Advisory Committee on Education, *Report* (Washington, 1930), I, 5; "Proposed Department of Health Education and Welfare," "Interior-1930-C," HHPL.

[24] *The Nation*, April 1, 1930, p. 111; Randolph C. Downes, "A Crusade for Indian Reform, 1929–1934," *Mississippi Valley Historical Review*, XXXII (Dec. 1945), 331–45.

[25] Report of C. J. Rhoads to Senator William King, 18 Jan. 1933, Taylor/Gates Collection, HHPL; Margaret Bacon, *The Quiet Rebels* (New York, 1969), p. 131; Wilcomb Washburn, *The Indian in America* (New York, 1970), p. 253.

[26] Lewis Meriam, *The Problem of Indian Administration* (Washington, 1928).

[27] Work's statement is in the *Saturday Evening Post*, 31 May 1924, p. 92; Rhoads to Hoover, 6 Aug. 1930; *Forum*, 6 Feb. 1924, p. 9; Wilbur to Work, 15 Dec. 1924, Wilbur Papers, HHPL; *Public Papers, 1930*, p. 6; Hoover speech file, 3 Jan. 1930, No. 1205, HHPL.

[28] Hoover to Scott Leavitt, 29 March 1930, File 5–3, pt. I, Interior Department, NA. In an article that I believe does not take seriously the Hoover Indian policies, Kenneth Philp argues that Rhoads gave Collier's program little support—"Herbert Hoover's New Era: A False Dawn for the American Indian, 1929–1932," *Rocky Mountain Social Science Journal*, IX (April 1972), 53–60; see also Philp, *John Collier's Crusade for Indian Reform* (Tucson, 1977); Wilbur, *Conservation in the Department of the Interior* (Washington, 1932); Neil McNeil, Oral history, HHPL.

[29] Year-by-year budget figures can be found in the U.S. Department of the Interior, *Annual Report;* Rhoads to Wilbur, 26 Oct. 1929; J. Clawson Roop to Hoover, 31 Oct. 1929, Wilbur Papers; Wilbur to Hoover, 7 Sept. 1929, HHPL; *Congressional Record, Senate,* 9 March 1932, p. 1656.

[30] Collier, "The Indian Bureau Record," *The Nation,* 5 Oct. 1932, pp. 303–5; Collier, *The Indians of the Americas* (New York, 1947), pp. 259–60; Haven Emerson to Hoover, 30 April 1930; Judson King to Wilbur, 27 March 1930; F. M. Kerr to Wilbur, 14 March 1930; Wilbur to Senator B. K. Wheeler, 12 March 1930; Patrick Hurley to Wilbur, 27 Feb. 1930; Scattergood to Wilbur, 3 March 1930; I. Parker Veasey, Jr., to Wilbur, 10 Feb. 1930; Northcutt Ely to Wilbur, 9 Jan. 1930, Wilbur Papers, HHPL; William Starr Myers and Walter H. Newton, *The Hoover Administration* (Stanford, 1935), pp. 391–2.

[31] Donald G. Swain, *Federal Conservation Policy, 1921–1933* (Berkeley, 1963), pp. 161, 165, and *passim;* Swain, *Wilderness Defender: Horace M. Albright and Conservation* (Chicago, 1970), pp. 189, 202.

[32] Secretary of Agriculture Hyde reduced the number of ducks and geese allowed to hunters—"Game Protection, 1929–1930"; Wilbur to A. J. Eager, 29 March 1929, file 2–37, Box 604; file 2–165, Box 813, RG 48, NA; Roy Chapin to Hoover, 6 Oct. 1932, "Lumber"; Frederick Weyerhauser to Hoover, 2 July 1931, "Agricultural Forest Service," HHPL.

[33] Beard's remark appears in *The Nation,* 22 July 1931, p. 83; Hoover to Secretary Good, 15 Aug. 1929, "States' Rights," HHPL; file 2–37, Box 684, RG 48, NA. Hoover termed himself a "lifelong friend of conservation"; Hoover to Coolidge, 31 Jan. 1925, Coolidge Papers; Hoover, *Public Papers, 1929,* pp. 423–4; *Public Papers, 1930,* pp. 220–1; Joseph Barnes, *Willkie* (New York, 1952), p. 81; *Annual Report of the Division of the National Park Service* (Washington, 1930); *Kiplinger Washington Letter,* 10 Jan. 1931; George Wharton Pepper, *Philadelphia Lawyer* (Philadelphia, 1944), p. 363; *U.S. v. Smith,* 286 U.S. 6 (1932).

[34] Phillip O. Foss, *Politics and Grass* (Seattle, 1960), pp. 47–8; John Carver Edwards, "Herbert Hoover's Public Lands Policy: A Struggle for Control of

the Western Domain," *Pacific Historian*, XX (Spring 1976), 34–35; Robinson, ed., *Memoirs of Ray Lyman Wilbur*, pp. 423–4; *New York Times*, 28 Aug. 1929; Hoover to Joseph M. Dixon, 21 Aug. 1929, contains his recommendations. Press releases, HHPL; *The Nation*, 12 Aug. 1931, pp. 151–3.

35 *New Republic*, 6 Nov. 1929, p. 509; Wilbur to Hoover, 2 Nov. 1931; Hoover to Governor James Rolph, Jr., 12 Feb. 1932, HHPL; Robinson, ed., *Memoirs of . . . Wilbur*, p. 416; Elwood Mead to Wilbur, 11 Oct. 1929, "Hoover Dam," Wilbur Papers; Hoover to Governor James Rolph, Jr., 12 Dec. 1932, "Irrigation," HHPL; Swain, *Federal Conservation Policy*, p. 92.

36 An early mention by Hoover of the St. Lawrence proposal is contained in "Address Before the Western Society of Engineers at Chicago," 28 Feb. 1920, "Public Statements," HHPL. Roosevelt recommended a federal-state agreement prior to an international agreement, quoted in Chicago *Tribune*, 10 July 1932. Hoover replaced Clarence Clark with John H. Bartlett on the Joint Commission—Hoover speech file, 23 Oct. 1929; Roosevelt to Hoover, 9 July 1932; Hoover to Roosevelt, 10 July 1932, "St. Lawrence River," HHPL; Great Lakes–St. Lawrence Tidewater Association correspondence, Barnes Papers; Carleton Mabee, *The Seaway Story* (New York, 1961); *Public Papers, 1929*, pp. 346–54; William R. Willoughby, *The Saint Lawrence Waterway* (Madison, 1961); Richard N. Kottman, "Herbert Hoover and the Saint Lawrence Seaway," *New York History*, LVI (July 1975), 314–46; Hoover to Stimson, 18 March 1931, NA 711.42157, Sa2a/742; Stimson diary, 28 Oct. 1931.

37 Secretary Hyde told Hoover there was no great demand for nitrogen, 24 Feb. 1931; Hoover to Secretary Hurley, 24 Feb. 1931, "Muscle Shoals", Attorney General Mitchell recommended a veto, 28 Feb. 1931, HHPL; Richard Lowitt, *George W. Norris: The Persistence of a Progressive, 1913–1933* (Urbana, 1971); Norman Zucker, *George W. Norris* (Urbana, 1966), pp. 22–3; *Public Papers, 1931*, p. 126.

38 Walter Newton to John Q. Tilson, 4 April 1931; Tilson to B. Carroll Reece, 8 July 1930; Governor B. M. Miller of Alabama to Hoover, telegram, 24 Feb. 1931, "Muscle Shoals," HHPL.

39 Wilbur to Hoover, 21 May 1929, 2 Nov. 1931; Governor Dan Moody of Texas to Hoover, telegram, 22 May 1929, "Oil," HHPL; Gerald D. Nash, *United States Oil Policy, 1890–1964* (Pittsburgh, 1968), pp. 91ff.; Mark Requa, "Colorado Springs Petroleum Conference," 13 June 1929, OF 56D, HHPL; Norman Nordhauser, "Origins of Federal Oil Regulation in the 1920's," *Business History Review* 47 (Spring 1973), pp. 53–71.

40 Robert Himmelberg, *The Origins of the National Recovery Administration* (New York, 1976); Hoover to James C. Stone, 18 Sept. 1929. Will Hays became apoplectic when O'Brian looked into the movie industry. Hays to Lawrence Richey by telephone, 17 March 1930, "Secretary's file," HHPL.

41 Raymond Clapper, interview with Hoover, Feb. 1931, HHPL; Ray Chapin to Hoover, 8 Oct. 1932, "National Timber Conservation Board," HHPL; *Public Papers, 1931*, p. 592; Hoover to Robert P. Lamont, 2 June 1931, "Oil Matters"; Wilbur to Mitchell, 20 March 1929, "Anti-Trust Laws 1929," HHPL; Stimson diary, 18 Nov. 1930.

42 Himmelberg, *The Origins of the National Recovery Administration;* Ellis

Hawley, "Herbert Hoover and American Corporatism, 1929–1933," in Martin Fausold and George Mazuzan, eds., *The Hoover Presidency: A Reappraisal* (Albany, 1974), pp. 101–19; Young to Mitchell, 1 Oct. 1931, Young Papers; John Lord O'Brian, Oral history, Columbia University; Young to Charles Neave, 23 Oct. 1931; Thomas Walsh to Hoover, 29 May 1931, "Endorsements, FRC," HHPL.

[43] Mitchell to Mark Sullivan, 26 July 1935, "Post-Presidential, Individual," HHPL; Ben R. Miller, "Politics and the Courts," ABA *Journal*, XLII (Oct. 1956), 942; Joel B. Grossman, *Lawyers and Judges* (New York, 1965).

[44] Hugh Edward Jones, "The Confirmation of Charles Evans Hughes as Chief Justice of the Supreme Court of the United States," unpublished master's essay, Duke University, 1962.

[45] William D. Mitchell to Mark Sullivan, 26 July 1935, Mitchell Papers; Glass to Baruch, 28 April 1930, Baruch Papers. On the Senate press gallery relishing its role in the defeat of Parker, see Fred F. Shedd to Verne Marshall, 20 May 1930, Box 202, HHPL; Richard L. Watson, Jr., "The Defeat of Judge Parker," *Mississippi Valley Historical Review*, L (Sept. 1963), 213–34; "Confirmation of John J. Parker," *Hearings,* United States Congress, Senate, 71st Congress, 2nd Sess., Judiciary Comm.

[46] Another judicial nominee, James H. Wilkerson, won Hoover's favor for his prosecution of Chicago gangsters, including Al Capone. Hoover nominated him for Circuit Court of Appeals, but liberal critics, complaining of his injunctions, forced the withdrawal of his name. Perhaps the nomination had been made to balance that of Cardozo. Speaking of Cardozo, according to Leonard Baker, Justices Butler and McReynolds pleaded with Hoover not to "afflict the Court with another Jew"—*Back to Back: The Duel Between FDR and the Supreme Court* (New York, 1967), p. 121; Ira H. Carmen, "The President, Politics, and the Power of Appointment: Hoover's Nomination of Mr. Justice Cardozo," *Virginia Law Review,* XL (1968), 616–59; this article, however, is undependable in some details. Franklin Fort to Hoover, 20 Jan. 1932; White to Norris, 19 Feb. 1932, Norris Papers; Hoover to Stone, 13 June 1941, HHPL.

[47] *Public Papers, 1932–1933,* 12 Jan. 1932, p. 75; Sumner H. Slichter to Norris, 21 April 1932, Norris Papers.

[48] Hoover said the export debenture plan would be a subsidy to grain dealers and speculators—*The Nation,* 1 May 1929, p. 6; Hoover to J. W. Duvel, 27 March 1929, HHPL; *Wallace's Farmer,* 8 Feb. 1929, p. 202. Hoover, according to James Shideler, has responsibility for "conception of the idea, nurturing of the policy, influencing the drafting of bills, and the promotion of legislation based upon that policy"—"Hoover and the Farm Board Project," *Mississippi Valley Historical Review,* LXII (March 1956), 710, 714; *Prairie Farmer,* 27 April 1929; Norbeck to G. J. Moen, 20 April 1929, Norbeck Papers.

[49] *Saturday Evening Post,* 21 June 1930, pp. 6–7, 110, 115. While Hoover favored the preservation of small farms, Legge believed any under 300 acres should be consolidated for the sake of efficiency—press clipping, 18 Oct. 1930, Box 309, Borah Papers.

[50] McKelvie to F. P. Heffelfinger, 25 Nov. 1929; McKelvie to J. C. Scott, 15

April 1931, "Presidential Papers—Grain," HHPL; *Public Papers, 1929,* pp. 75–8; Memorandum, McKelvie to F. P. Heffelfinger, 25 Nov. 1929; Hoover, *Memoirs,* II, 225.

51 Stone to Hoover, 29 July 1931, HHPL; David B. Miller, "Origins and Functions of the Federal Farm Board," unpublished doctoral dissertation, University of Kansas, 1973.

52 E. W. Dierecks to T. G. Winter, 21 Nov. 1929, "Presidential Papers," Box 160, HHPL; Baruch to Frank Kent, 23 May 1930, Baruch Papers; Hoover to Coolidge, 6 April 1928, Coolidge Papers.

53 Borah to Legge, 17 April 1930, Borah Papers; J. W. Duvel to Hoover, 27 March 1929, 16 July 1931, HHPL. To Barnes Hoover scrawled: "No President admits mistakes made," 18 Aug. 1931, Barnes Papers. Still later, in response to W. F. Schilling of the board, who remarked: "When dairy products get down to 22¢ it is time to step in," Hoover replied, "I admire your courage"—*Dairy Record,* 9 Dec. 1931, p. 1; Baruch to Frank Kent, 23 May 1930, Baruch Papers; Hoover to Barnes, 12 April 1932; Barnes to Hoover, 13 April 1932; Davis to Peek, 17 Nov. 1931, Davis Papers.

54 George T. Hill to Hoover, 5 Aug. 1931, HHPL; Forrest Crissen, *Alexander Legge* (Chicago, 1930), p. 190; *Congressional Record, Senate,* 16 April 1929, p. 42. For Barnes's viewpoint, see his "Notes Regarding Panic of 1929–1930," 12 July 1944, Barnes Papers.

55 John Coulter to Walter Newton, 26 June 1931; Hoover to Vice-President Curtis, 1 March 1932, "Grain," HHPL. McNary is quoted in a radiogram of 25 March 1931 from Walter Newton to Lawrence Richey, Richey Papers; "McK" to J. C. Scott, 15 April 1931, "Grain," HHPL; Ezekiel is quoted on p. 47 of William D. Rowley, *M. L. Wilson and the Campaign for Domestic Allotment* (Lincoln, 1970). An excellent critique of the Farm Board is in M. H. Greene to M. Evans, 1 Feb. 1932, John D. Black Papers; H. C. Taylor to Borah, 31 March 1931, Borah Papers.

56 *Memoirs,* III, 157; Peek to Clarence Ousley, 2 Jan. 1930, Peek Papers.

57 James C. Stone to F. J. Wilmer, 13 May 1931; Senator Arthur Capper to Hoover, 17 July 1931, Box 307a, HHPL; Peek to Clarence Ousley, 2 Jan. 1930, Peek Papers; Allen to Charles F. Scott, 5 May 1930, Allen Papers.

58 J. W. Duvel to Lawrence Richey, 27 March 1929, "Financial: Grain and Cotton Futures"; C. A. Ward to Hoover, 11 July 1931; C. B. Rogers to Stone, 3 July 1931; Stone to F. J. Wilmer, 13 May 1931, "Grain"; Hoover to Owen D. Young, 3 June 1932, Young Papers; Mitchell to Richey, 24 Oct. 1932, Richey White House files, HHPL; Legge to Hyde, 26 May 1932, quoted on p. 167 of William R. Johnson, "Herbert Hoover and the Regulation of Grain Futures," *Mid-America,* LI (July 1965), 155–74.

59 Walter Newton to John W. Summers, telegram, 1 Oct. 1932; Hoover, telegram to the Reverend Walter Mitchell, 6 Nov. 1931, "Grain," HHPL. The John D. Black Papers are excellent on administration policy in 1932. A congressional committee in 1930 had opposed sending surplus food to China. Hoover to Charles F. Scott, 18 April 1930, Scott Papers.

60 Stanley Reed, Oral history, HHPL; George S. Milner to Hoover, 10 April 1931, HHPL. On Black's important role, see Bernard M. Klass, "John D. Black, 1920–1942," unpublished doctoral dissertation, UCLA, 1969.

⁶¹ Hoover, who hoped the Farm Board would handle the farm surplus the way the Federal Reserve Board managed currency, would have liked the long view taken in Hendrik S. Houthakker, *Economic Policy for the Farm Sector* (Washington, 1967). Howard R. Tolley, Oral history, Columbia University; Ezekiel is quoted in William D. Rowley, "M. L. Wilson . . . ," unpublished doctoral dissertation, University of Nebraska, 1970.

CHAPTER XII

¹ As early as 1919 Hoover had asked for "a more vivid limelight on all . . . dealings in stocks"—*Saturday Evening Post,* 27 Dec. 1919, p. 15; Lenroot to Crissinger, 23 Nov. 1925, 23 Dec. 1925; Lenroot to Richey, 3 May 1933, HHPL; Herbert F. Margulies, "The Collaboration of Herbert Hoover and Irvine Lenroot, 1921–1928," *North Dakota Quarterly,* 45 (Summer 1977), 30–46; *Commercial and Financial Chronicle,* 1 Jan. 1926; Donald McCoy, *Calvin Coolidge* (New York, 1967), p. 319; Mrs. Jameson Parker, Oral history, HHPL.

² Elmus R. Wicker, *Federal Reserve Monetary Policy, 1917–33* (New York, 1966).

³ Hoover called Strong a "mental annex of Europe." Copies of the Norman-Strong correspondence are at the HHPL; Wicker, *Federal Reserve Monetary Policy,* emphasizes the role of Norman.

⁴ Donald McCoy, *Calvin Coolidge,* p. 290; Hoover to White, 24 June 1935, William Allen White Papers.

⁵ Merlo J. Pusey, *Eugene Meyer* (New York, 1974), pp. 201–3; Rickard diary, 14 April and 22 May 1928; Lamont to Hoover; Martin Egan to Lamont, Box 98, Lamont Papers; Mark Sullivan, Jr., Oral history, HHPL; Charles S. Hamlin diary, 12 Aug. 1929, Hamlin Papers.

⁶ The day after the banking pool was formed, on Nov. 13, the thirty standard industrials rose from $198 to $210 in a single session—Julius Barnes, "The Great Panic of 1929," Autobiography, Barnes Papers.

⁷ Herbert Stein, "Pre-Revolutionary Fiscal Policy: The Regime of Herbert Hoover," *Journal of Law and Economics,* IX (1966), 189–223; Stein, *The Fiscal Revolution in America* (Chicago, 1969). Stein argues that the Hoover administration suffered from a lack of cooperation from the Federal Reserve Board, the public's desire for a balanced budget, and inadequate information about employment.

⁸ Robert Sobel, *The Great Bull Market* (New York, 1968), p. 146; Peter Temin, *Did Monetary Forces Cause the Great Depression?* (New York, 1976), p. 178.

⁹ *Literary Digest,* 2 April 1932.

¹⁰ *Memoirs,* III.

¹¹ A severely technical up-to-date analysis of the Depression is Charles P. Kindleberger, *The World in Depression, 1929–1939* (London, 1973). Sobel, *The Great Bull Market.*

¹² The best general analyses of Hoover's presidency are Albert U. Romasco, *The Poverty of Abundance: Hoover, the Nation, the Depression* (New York,

1965), and Harris G. Warren, *Herbert Hoover and the Great Depression* (New York, 1959). See also the recent Edgar Eugene Robinson and Vaughn D. Bornet, *Herbert Hoover, President of the United States* (Stanford, 1975). *Chicago Journal of Commerce,* 19 June 1935; *Public Papers, 1930,* 2 Oct. and 2 Dec. 1930.

[13] Cf. Franklin Roosevelt's campaign remark of 25 Oct. 1932: "The crash came in October 1929. The President had at his disposal all the instrumentalities of government. . . . He did absolutely nothing"—quoted in Rexford Tugwell, "The Protagonists: Roosevelt and Hoover," *Antioch Review,* XIII (Dec. 1953), 419–42. For criticism of Hoover's actions, see *Financial Chronicle,* 28 Nov. 1931, p. 3502; Stein, *The Fiscal Revolution,* pp. 23–4; Hoover to Barnes, 7 Dec. 1929, "Unemployment"; Joslin to Edgar J. Rich, 11 June 1931, "Unemployment," HHPL; AFL Executive Council, Minutes, 6 May 1930.

[14] Henry J. Cadbury, "Interview with Hoover," *Friends' Journal,* 15 Nov. 1964.

[15] Fauneil J. Rinn, "President Hoover's Bad Press," *San Jose Studies,* I (1975), 32–34; Mark Sullivan, memorandum, March 1929, Sullivan Papers; *Outlook,* 24 Sept. 1930, pp. 123–5, 155; *Public Papers, 1929,* pp. 12–13, 20–1.

[16] *New Republic,* LXI (22 Jan. 1930), 249; *Public Papers, 1930,* pp. 349–50; Richard Oulahan to George Akerson, 8 April 1929, "Press," HHPL.

[17] Edward Clark wrote to Coolidge: "I do not think that there is any realization of the terrorism which the White House tried to exercise through Richey . . . I know personally that agencies of the Government were used for intimidation whenever possible." I have not been able to verify any such instances. 11 Nov. 1933, Clark Papers. Edgar Eugene Robinson, ed., *The Memoirs of Ray Lyman Wilbur* (Stanford, 1960), pp. 415–19.

[18] Oswald Garrison Villard to George Barr Baker, 5 Feb. 1929, Box 16, Baker Papers; *New York Herald-Tribune,* 6 March 1929; *Editor and Publisher,* 12 Jan. 1929, 9 March 1929; *New York World,* 7 March 1929; James Pollard, *The Presidents and the Press* (New York, 1947), pp. 737–55; Hoover to Roy Howard, telegram, 21 June 1931; Howard to Hoover, 23 June 1931, "United Press," HHPL.

[19] Edward Clark wrote to Coolidge of the "bitter personal hatred" which Hoover had inspired "in so many of the newspaper men"—Clark to Coolidge, 16 Sept. 1932, Clark Papers; *The Nation,* 14 Oct. 1931, p. 383; *Outlook,* 24 Sept. 1930, pp. 123–4; Kent Cooper, *Kent Cooper and the Associated Press* (New York, 1959); Elmer E. Carwell, Jr., *Presidential Leadership of Public Opinion* (Bloomington, 1965).

[20] Standard on Hoover and Congress is Jordan A. Schwarz, *The Interregnum of Despair: Hoover, Congress and the Depression* (Urbana, 1970); *Memoirs,* III, 127.

[21] C. David Tompkins, *Senator Arthur H. Vandenberg* (East Lansing, 1970), pp. 52 ff.

[22] Tompkins, *Senator Arthur H. Vandenberg,* pp. 76 ff.; Hoover to Representative Clarence F. Lea, 22 June 1931, "Congress . . . 1931," HHPL.

[23] Laird Archer to Allen, 15 Aug. 1931, Allen Papers.

[24] The first major test of Hoover's attitude came in a cabinet meeting discussion

of whether to give the Red Cross Farm Board surplus wheat, as Secretary Hyde suggested. Interestingly, Hoover first objected to the plan as an uneconomic distribution of wheat, and only later argued from principle. Stimson diary, 9 Jan. 1931. *The Nation,* 26 Aug. 1931, p. 199; William Starr Myers and Walter Newton, *The Hoover Administration* (New York, 1936), p. 53; *Public Papers, 1931,* pp. 405, 419; Hoover to Lamont, n.d., "Unemployment, October–November, 1930," HHPL.

25 The virtues Hoover urged for the restoration of the economy happened also to be prime Quaker virtues: thrift, simplicity of wants, and charity among neighbors. McAdoo to Borah, 18 Nov. 1930, Borah Papers.

26 Myers, *The Hoover Administration,* pp. 405–6, 475; Gerard Swope to Hoover, 20 June 1930, "Unemployment," HHPL; Marquis James, *The Metropolitan Life* (New York, 1947), p. 228.

27 William Green to Hoover, 12 and 20 March 1930; Hoover to Green, 13 March 1930; AFL Papers; *State Papers,* I, 579; Hoover to Wagner, telegram, 7 March 1931; Sumner H. Slichter to Doak, 6 April 1931; Doak to Slichter, 10 April 1931, HHPL; *The Nation,* 1 July 1931, p. 3, and 26 Aug. 1931, p. 199; *Public Papers, 1931,* pp. 132–8.

28 "Don't change barrels while going over Niagara," was another facetious argument for the administration. Josephine C. Brown, *Public Relief, 1929–1939* (New York, 1940); Joanna C. Colcord, *Emergency Work Relief* (New York, 1932); Edward A. Williams, *Federal Aid for Relief* (New York, 1939); Raskob is quoted in the *New York Times,* 28 Oct. 1930; *Forum* (Oct. 1930), pp. 146, 148.

29 Hoover described charity as "the obligation of the strong to the weak" and complained that "we attach too much importance to material and economic success"—5 Feb. 1930, *Public Papers, 1930,* p. 44.

30 Paul U. Kellogg, "Drought and the Red Cross," *The Survey,* 15 Feb. 1931, pp. 535–8, 572; Roger Lambert, "Hoover and the Red Cross in the Arkansas Drought of 1930," *Arkansas Historical Quarterly,* XL (April 1973), 18–35.

31 Edward Clark to Coolidge, 17 Jan. 1931, Clark Papers; Robert Cowley, "The Drought and the Dole," *American Heritage,* XXIII (Feb. 1973), 16 ff.; Payne Statement, 29 Jan. 1931, old numbering, file 1-E/113; Mark Sullivan, memorandum of talk with Borah, 17 Jan. 1931, Sullivan Papers; Stimson diary, 16 Jan. 1931.

32 *American Heritage,* XXIII (Feb. 1973), 99; *Public Papers, 1931,* pp. 272–7; Edward Clark to Coolidge, 9 Jan. 1931, Clark Papers; Mark Sullivan, notes on conversation with Senator Borah, 17 Jan. 1931, Borah Papers.

33 Stimson said Woods was appointed because Hoover feared congressional action. Diary, 21 Oct. 1930. Edward L. Bernays, who worked for Woods, said that he resigned because Hoover rejected his recommendations—*Biography of an Idea: Memoirs of Public Relations Counsel Edward L. Bernays* (New York, 1965), p. 467; Woods diary, 26 Jan., 11, 14 Feb., 4 April 1931; Woods to Payne, 14 Feb. 1931, "PECE"; Woods to Hoover, 21 and 26 Nov. 1930, "Unemployment—Emergency Comm.," HHPL; Erving P. Hayes, *Activities of the President's Emergency Committee for Employment* (Concord, 1936); Woods memorandum, 11 Feb. 1931, PECE, Reg. 73, Ser. 12, NA.

34 Gifford's remark to the subcommittee of the Senate Committee on Manufactures, 8 Jan. 1932, is quoted in Brown, *Public Relief, 1929–1939,* p. 88; see also 72nd Congress, 1st Session, 29 Dec. 1931, p. 124. Hoover to Gifford, 17 Aug. 1931, and 6 Jan. 1932; Lucey to Gifford, 7 Jan. 1932; Norman Thomas to Hoover, 23 April 1932; Gifford to Hoover, 29 July 1932; Frank Murphy to Hoover, 23 May 1932, "Unemployment," HHPL; Byron Price, Oral history, HHPL.

35 Constance Green, *Washington, Capital City, 1879–1950,* II (Princeton, 1963), 284–91; Simeon Fess to Sumner Fess, 27 Feb. 1932, Fess Papers; *Public Papers, 1929,* pp. 121–3, 417; *Public Papers, 1931,* pp. 67–9; Bernays, *Biography of an Idea,* p. 467; *Fortune,* July 1934.

36 Alfred Kazin wrote a spirited piece denying that "No One Has Starved," *Fortune,* VI (Sept. 1932), 19–88. *Literary Digest,* 2 April 1932; *Public Papers, 1931,* pp. 392–8; *Public Papers, 1932–1933,* pp. 64–5; *Journal of the American Medical Association,* 2 May 1977; "Joe Brown Starvation Story," Brown Papers.

37 Frank Connor to Fred Croxton, 7 April 1932, Box 1147; Frank Murphy to Hoover, 23 May 1932, "Unemployment," HHPL.

38 H. Thomas Johnson, "Postwar Optimism and the Rural Financial Crisis of the 1920's," *Explorations in Economic History* (Winter 1973), pp. 173–92.

39 A conference on the hoarding of currency met in February 1932; Hoover estimated that over $1 billion had gone into hiding during the previous year. *Public Papers, 1932–1933,* pp. 92–4.

40 Interview with Hoover, 20 April 1932, Krock Papers; Sumner Fess to Simeon Fess, 27 Nov. 1931, Fess Papers; Hoover to Mitchell, 26 Aug. 1931; Hoover to Young, 3 June 1932, "Federal Reserve Board," HHPL; John D. Lyle, "The United States Senate Career of Carter Glass," unpublished doctoral dissertation, University of South Carolina, 1974, pp. 200 ff.

41 Hoover to George Harrison, 5 Oct. 1931, "National Credit Corp.," HHPL; cf. Harrison to Hoover, 7 Oct. 1931, Mills Papers. Stimson diary, 22 Sept. 1931.

42 Senator Fess wrote to his son that when the NCC was proposed, "it took almost bludgeoning to bring the men who ought to be the first to cooperate to a position where they would be willing to put it in operation"—3 Nov. 1931, Fess Papers.

43 Hoover to Harrison, 5 Oct. 1931, Harrison Papers; Harrison to Hoover, 7 Oct. 1931, Mills Papers; Hoover to George H. Reynolds, 6 Nov. 1931, "National Credit Corporation"; Hoover to Thomas Watts, 31 Aug. 1931, "Real Estate," HHPL; James Olson, *Herbert Hoover and the Reconstruction Finance Corporation, 1931–1933* (Ames, 1977), pp. 24–32. Olson correctly portrays Hoover as ready to create the RFC once the NCC had failed. This displaces an older interpretation by Gerald D. Nash that shows Eugene Meyer persuading a grumbling, foot-dragging President to accept it. Nash, "Herbert Hoover and the Origins of the Reconstruction Finance Corporation," *Mississippi Valley Historical Review,* 46 (Dec. 1959), 455–65.

44 *Public Papers, 1931,* p. 590.

45 As late as 14 April 1932, Lawrence Richey was assuring correspondents on behalf of Hoover that virtually all loans were going to smaller banks. Richey

to Philip F. Apfel, "Financial-Banking," HHPL; Borah to Bryan Brown, 23 May 1932, Box 36, Borah Papers; Alfred Steinberg, *Sam Johnson's Boy* (New York, 1968), p. 73; Stanley Reed, Oral history, HHPL.

[46] Bascom Timmons, *Jesse H. Jones* (New York, 1956), p. 174; *The Nation,* 21 Oct. 1931, p. 421; *Kiplinger Washington Letter,* 28 Nov. 1931; Byron Price, Oral history, HHPL.

[47] Walter R. Livingston, Oral history, HHPL; James Olson, "The Philosophy of Herbert Hoover: A Contemporary Perspective," *Annals of Iowa,* 43 (Winter 1976), 181–91.

[48] *New York Times,* 20 May 1932; Hoover to Meyer, 8 Sept. 1931, and 23 July 1932, "Federal Reserve Board," HHPL; Wagner to Charles V. Bossert, 22 Dec. 1932, Wagner Papers.

[49] For criticism of the RFC as too generous, see Simeon to Sumner Fess, 31 Jan. 1933, Fess Papers; Olson, *Herbert Hoover, passim.*

[50] Simeon Fess to John T. Gribble, 5 Jan. 1932, Fess Papers; Olson, *Herbert Hoover,* pp. 61 ff.; Hamlin diary, *passim.*

[51] *New York Herald-Tribune,* 8 July 1932; *Public Papers, 1932–1933,* 6 July 1932, pp. 265–8, 272–6; Olson, *Herbert Hoover,* pp. 80 ff.

[52] Hastings to Hoover, 20 Aug. 1931, "Unemployment—Emergency Comm."; Pinchot to Hoover, 20 Sept. 1932, "Wagner Bills," HHPL; James Olson, "Gifford Pinchot and the Politics of Hunger, 1932–1933," *Pennsylvania Magazine of History & Biography* (Oct. 1972), pp. 508–20; "Pinchot's Years of Frustration," *Pennsylvania Magazine of History & Biography* (Winter 1974), 44–70.

[53] Glass to Colonel Robert W. Bingham, 20 Sept. 1932, Glass Papers.

[54] Hoover to Edward F. Hutton, 15 Oct. 1932, "Edward F. Hutton," HHPL; *Public Papers, 1932–1933,* 22 July 1932, pp. 291–2.

[55] *Financial Chronicle,* 3 Jan. 1931, p. 245; B. H. Meyer to Hoover, 25 Dec. 1932; William Z. Ripley to Hoover, 15 Nov. 1930; B. H. Meyer to Joslin, 25 Feb. 1932; Paul Shoup to Hoover, 20 Dec. 1931, and 31 Jan. 1932, "Railroads"; Mark Sullivan, Memorandum to Hoover, 2 Oct. 1931, and 14 Nov. 1931, "Mark Sullivan," HHPL.

[56] Olson, *Herbert Hoover, passim.*

[57] Edward Clark to Hoover, 9 Jan. 1932, Clark Papers; *Public Papers, 1930,* 29 July 1930, p. 304; Arthur Mann, *LaGuardia, A Fighter Against His Times* (Philadelphia, 1959), pp. 293–312, *passim.*

[58] For a mild statement of this view, see *Public Papers, 1930,* 3 Dec. 1930, p. 540; Washington *Evening Star,* 24 March 1932; Olson, *Herbert Hoover, passim.* Walter Lippmann argued against borrowing as a bad example to the world. *New York Herald-Tribune,* 10 Dec. 1931.

[59] The 1933 budget deficit, despite Hoover's attempts to cut spending and, with Speaker Garner's aid, to resurrect the sales tax, came to more than $2.5 billion. Walter Lippmann, like so many others, held the opinion in December that Hoover should have raised taxes "months ago"—*The Nation,* 23 Feb. 1931, p. 684. Borah to William A. Shuldberg, 6 Feb. 1932, Borah Papers; Norris to Frank D. Troop, 5 May 1932, Box 2, Norris Papers; Carl Shoup, *The Sales Tax in the American States* (New York, 1934), pp. 39 ff.; Hoover to

Baruch, 10 May 1932; Norris to Frank D. Throop, 8 May 1932, Tray 39, Box 4, Norris Papers; Clark to Coolidge, 19 Jan. 1932, Clark Papers; Long to Desha Breckinridge, 6 Jan. 1932, Long Papers.

60 Four years later LaGuardia as mayor of New York City enacted a sales tax on clothing and some foods. When Hoover chided him, LaGuardia replied: "You're no politician." Hoover, *Memoirs*, III, 138; Doughton to G. G. Allen, 19 March 1932; Doughton to F. J. Sizemore, Doughton Papers.

61 *Congressional Record*, 75 (1 April 1932), 7324.

62 Hoover had earlier worried that overtaxing in the upper brackets would impede recovery. Stimson diary, 26 May 1931. Irenée duPont to Hoover, 21 Oct. 1936, and 12 Dec. 1936; Hoover to duPont, 12 Nov. 1936, "duPont, Irenée," HHPL; see also Hoover to Samuel McCune Lindsey, 4 April 1924, Lindsey Papers; Hoover to Harding, 28 Nov. 1921, Harding Papers.

63 Albert U. Romasco, "Hoover, Roosevelt and the Great Depression," in J. Betal *et al.,* eds., *The New Deal: The National Level* (New York, 1975), p. 24.

CHAPTER XIII

1 Castle to Alanson Houghton, 7 Dec. 1925, Castle Papers; Joan Wilson's *Herbert Hoover* (Boston, 1975) is particularly strong on economic diplomacy; see also her "A Reevaluation of Herbert Hoover's Foreign Policy," in Martin Fausold and George Mazuzan, eds., *The Hoover Presidency: A Reappraisal* (Albany, 1974), pp. 164–86; and Thomas H. Dressler, "The Foreign Policies of American Individualism," unpublished doctoral dissertation, Brown University, 1973.

2 The standard study is Alexander DeConde, *Herbert Hoover's Latin American Policy* (Stanford, 1951); on Kellogg's rule, L. Ethan Ellis, *Frank B. Kellogg and American Foreign Relations, 1925–1929* (New Brunswick, 1961). The standard study of foreign affairs under Hoover is Robert H. Ferrell, *American Diplomacy in the Great Depression: Hoover-Stimson Foreign Policy, 1929–1933* (New Haven, 1957).

3 James M. Erdmann, "Some Aspects of the Latin American Policies of Herbert Hoover," unpublished master's essay, University of Chicago, 1947; Forbes diary, II, 12; Hoover, *Addresses Delivered During the Visit of Herbert Hoover to Central and South America* (Washington, 1929); Robert H. Denton, Oral history, HHPL; USFR, 1928, II, 527–30; 1929, I, 720–57, 811; FO 3334/14/12; 3390/3/15, PRO; A. N. Page, "United States Diplomacy in the Tacna-Arica Dispute, 1884–1929," unpublished doctoral dissertation, University of Oklahoma, 1958.

4 Edgar Rickard Diary, 5 March 1929; *New Republic*, 20 March 1929, p. 107; John J. Tierney, "The United States and Nicaragua, 1917–1932," unpublished doctoral dissertation, University of Pennsylvania, 1969; Sister Mary A. Schnitejam, "Henry L. Stimson's Latin American Policy, 1929–1933," unpublished master's essay, Georgetown University, 1967; Bryce Wood, *The Making of the Good Neighbor* (New York, 1961); Stimson, *American Policy in Nicaragua* (New York, 1927).

5 Robert M. Spector, "W. Cameron Forbes in Haiti," *Caribbean Studies*, VI

(1966), 28–45; Robert M. Spector, "W. Cameron Forbes and the Hoover Commissions to Haiti," unpublished doctoral dissertation, Boston University, 1961; *The Nation,* 12 March 1930, p. 400; *New Republic,* 26 March 1930, p. 137; Hans Schmidt, *The United States Occupation of Haiti, 1915–1934* (New Brunswick, 1971); United States President's Commission for Study and Review of Conditions in the Republic of Haiti, HHPL; Stimson diary, 21 Feb. 1931; Forbes diary, III, 63, 78–9.

[6] Hoover's Latin American policy also included, with one exception, the appointment of diplomats who spoke the native language. Only six of fifty worldwide appointments were not careerists; the six included the most important European posts, where the appointee had to spend $50,000 to $100,000 a year of his own money for living expenses. Stimson diary, 9 Feb. 1931; Ferrell, "Repudiation of a Repudiation," *Journal of American History,* LI (March 1965), 669–73; 710-11/1448A-1451, NA.

[7] *New York Times,* 30 Aug. 1928; Hoover's governor in the Virgin Islands, Leon Pearson, a Haverford teacher of public speaking, chose an all-white staff for the largely black island, Charles Jenkins Papers, Swarthmore College; Stimson diary, 2 Jan. 1931.

[8] Theodore Friend, *Between Two Empires: The Ordeal of the Philippines, 1924–1946* (New Haven, 1965); Friend, "Veto and Repassage of the Hare-Hawes-Cutting Act: A Catalogue of Motives," *Philippine Studies,* XII (1964), 666–80; Forbes diary, III, 492; Stimson diary, 28 Aug. 1930; Stimson to Root, 4 Jan. 1933, Stimson Papers.

[9] Richard N. Kottman, "Hoover and Canada: Diplomatic Appointments," *Canadian Historical Review,* LI (Sept. 1970), 292–309; Kottman, "The Hoover-Bennett Meeting of 1931: Mismanaged Summitry," *Annals of Iowa,* 42 (Winter 1974), 205–21; Stimson diary, 22 June 1929, 11 April 1931.

[10] "Nothing could be a finer or more vivid conversion of swords to plowshares" than saving money on armaments, Hoover had declared—*New York World,* 7 Sept. 1929. Undersecretary of State William R. Castle wrote in his diary on 10 Feb. 1931 that the Court was a matter of "extraordinary unimportance"; Hoover to Harding, 4 Jan. 1922, "Civil Service Commission," HHPL; Hoover to Charles F. Scott, 6 Dec. 1924, Scott Papers.

[11] During the car ride to the camp Hoover, still the businessman, had casually suggested trading Bermuda, British Honduras, and Trinidad for debt concessions; MacDonald showed little interest in any such idea. Hoover made a similar suggestion about taking some Caribbean islands as early as 1922: 16 March 1922, F/26/1/16, Lloyd George Papers; on the conflicting needs that separated Britain and the United States, and on Hoover's efforts to bridge them, see FO 3334/13/8, 3252/2/20, FO 321/13552, 3345/2/34, PRO; Walter Lippmann, *New York Herald-Tribune,* 22 Dec. 1932; Ferrell, *American Diplomacy in the Great Depression* pp. 68–86.

[12] J. H. Kitchens, Jr., "The Shearer Scandal and Its Origins: Big Navy Politics and Diplomacy in the 1920's," Ph.D. dissertation, University of Georgia, 1968, pp. 164, 255; Hoover to Stimson, 30 Aug. 1929, File SOUA15A1, Shearer, Department of State, NA; *Literary Digest,* 21 Sept. 1929, p. 7; *Public Papers, 1929,* pp. 274–8; *The Nation,* 18 Sept. 1929, p. 287.

13 *New York Times,* 7 Dec. 1930. On Gibson's role in 1930 and 1932, see Ronald Swerczek, "The Diplomatic Career of Hugh Gibson, 1908–38," Ph.D. dissertation, University of Iowa, 1972; Raymond G. O'Connor, *Perilous Equilibrium: The United States and the London Conference of 1930* (Lawrence, 1962).

14 Hoover experienced a brief flare-up with congressmen who demanded correspondence about the treaty, but the President resolutely refused on grounds of executive privilege. Borah to Arthur Capper, 18 Feb. 1930, Butler Papers; Robert A. Divine, "FDR and Collective Security, 1933," *Journal of American History,* 48 (June 1961), 45–6. Stimson, Lloyd George agreed, "will reflect Mr. Hoover's aim with literal accuracy," LG/26/1/9, Lloyd George Papers; FO 115/3395/2134/1; Stimson diary, 25 March 1930.

15 Christopher Thorne, *The Limits of Foreign Policy: The West, the League and the Far Eastern Crisis of 1931–1933* (London, 1972), p. 210. Brand Whitlock remarked that Hoover's message was "one of his typically impulsive and brutal acts . . . made no doubt for its political effect at home"—Journal, Whitlock Papers, Library of Congress. There are transcripts of numerous phone calls among Hoover, Stimson, Gibson, and Norman Davis, 21 and 22 June, 7 July 1932, "Foreign Affairs—Disarmament," HHPL; *Public Papers, 1932–1933,* 22 June 1932, pp. 247–52; Stimson diary, 5 Jan. 1932.

16 Herbert Spielman, "Henry L. Stimson and American Policy Toward the Chinese Eastern Railway Dispute of 1929," unpublished doctoral dissertation, University of Chicago, 1949; John W. Wheeler-Bennett, ed., *Documents on International Affairs* (London, 1930), p. 244. The best book on Hoover's Manchurian policy is now Thorne, *The Limits of Foreign Policy;* see also Armin Rappaport, *Henry L. Stimson and Japan, 1931–1933* (Chicago, 1963). Jerome Green sent the administration a good first-hand account of the incident, 21 Dec. 1931, "Foreign Affairs—Far East Incident," HHPL; in his *Memoirs* (II, 362) Hoover observed that the distinction between Japan's "morals and those of the older empires was one of timing." Stimson diary, 27 Feb. 1932; C. B. Hodges diary, 30 Oct. 1931.

17 As ambassador to England, "Hell 'N Maria" Dawes went in for practical jokes like hiring the comedian Leon Errol to act as a waiter for a 1931 embassy party. Pretending to be drunk, Errol corrected the guests' table manners, yanked their half-finished plates out of their hands, flung a cold lobster into the lap of a duchess, and crawled under the table with a lighted candle looking for no one knew what. Gary B. Ostrower, "The United States, the League of Nations, and Collective Security," unpublished doctoral dissertation, University of Rochester, 1970; Stimson diary, 9 Nov. 1931, 12 March 1932. Stimson termed Hoover's participation in the formulation of the Stimson Doctrine "very active and influential," and the President would take credit for it during the 1932 campaign. Lippmann is quoted in Stimson, *Turmoil and Tradition* (Boston, 1960), p. 384; Stimson's instructions to Gilbert are in a typescript of a phone conversation, 19 Oct. 1931, Box 1022, Presidential Papers, HHPL; Stimson's letter of 23 Feb. 1932 to Senator Borah was intended to warn Japan, Borah Papers; Richard N. Current, "The Stimson Doctrine and the Hoover Doctrine," *American His-*

torical Review, 59 (April 1954), 513–42; Current calls it the Hoover-Stimson doctrine because it was suggested by Hoover and formulated by Stimson. Stimson to Lippmann, 12 Jan. 1933.

18 At Hoover's "suggestion," Castle delivered a speech in the spring of 1932 announcing that the United States would not invoke sanctions. Hoover to Castle, 19 Feb. 1942, Castle Papers; Castle had replaced the deceased Joseph P. Cotton as Undersecretary, an appointment that would displease Stimson. Henry Misselwitz, interview with Hoover, 29 Feb. 1932, HHPL; Payson Treat, interview with Hoover, 8 April 1933, Treat Papers; "Memorandum of . . . telephone conversation between . . . Stimson and . . . MacDonald," 30 Jan. 1932, "Foreign Affairs—Disarmament"; Hurley to Hoover, 19 Jan. 1933; Wilbur to Hoover, 26 Jan. 1933, "Manchuria," HHPL; USFR, 1931–41, Japan, I, 83–7; George Homans, "Sailing with Uncle Charlie," *Proceedings of Massachusetts Historical Society,* LXXVI (1964), 55–67.

19 Manfred Jonas deemphasizes Stimson's bellicosity in "The United States and the Failure of Collective Security in the 1930's," in John Braeman *et al.,* eds., *Twentieth-Century American Foreign Policy* (Columbus, 1971), pp. 241–93. Jonas argues that Stimson merely wanted to keep the Japanese guessing, but Hoover preempted that strategy. See p. 244, lns. 11–16, of Stimson and McGeorge Bundy, *On Active Service in Peace and War* (New York, 1947); the last chapter of Stimson's *The Far Eastern Crisis* (New York, 1943); and Hoover to Charles Beard, 17 Dec. 1945, Castle Papers ("we agreed to disagree and my views prevailed over economic sanction"). See also Stimson diary, 27 Nov. 1931. Years later Hoover attacked the dropping of atomic bombs on Japan, while Stimson defended the actions. Hoover, *Memoirs,* II, 362; Simeon Fess to Sumner Fess, 27 Oct. 1931, Fess Papers; Williams, *New York Review of Books,* 13 Aug. 1970; Elting Morison, *Turmoil and Tradition* (Boston, 1960), p. 382; Harvey Bundy and Henry Stimson, Oral history, Columbia University; 24 Sept. 1930, Stimson diary.

20 Hoover to Bruce Barton, 12 June 1930, Barton Papers—"a most difficult problem," the President termed the tariff. *Outlook,* 24 Sept. 1930, p. 125; Stimson diary, 27 Feb., 30 March, 1 April 1931; Themistocles C. Rodis, "Russo-American Contacts During the Hoover Administration," *South Atlantic Quarterly,* LI (April 1952), 235–45.

21 Fletcher, memorandum on the tariff, 15 Aug. 1930; Fletcher to Hoover, 17 Nov. 1931, Fletcher Papers; *Public Papers, 1930,* 16 June 1930, p. 235; Myers, *Foreign Policies,* p. 406; White House press release, 24 Sept. 1929; Clark to Coolidge, 11 Sept. 1930, Clark Papers; Hoover to Lenroot, 10 June 1922, Lenroot Papers.

22 Julius Klein to Walter Newton, 13 May 1931, "Commerce—1931-A," HHPL; *Public Papers, 1930,* p. 235; Henry A. Wallace, Oral history, Columbia University.

23 On the tariff and agriculture, see Duane Guy, "The Influence of Agriculture on the Tariff Act of 1930," unpublished doctoral dissertation, University of Kansas, 1964, p. 28; Julius Barnes, unpublished autobiography, Barnes Papers; "Public Statements," Box 5, HHPL; *Public Papers, 1932–1933,* 11 May 1932, p. 203; O'Brian, Oral history, HHPL.

24 Benjamin Rhodes, "Herbert Hoover and the War Debts, 1919–33," VI, *Prologue* (Summer 1974), 150–80; Harry M. Creech to John S. Davis, 22 Dec. 1965, Davis Papers; Frank Costigliola, "The Other Side of Isolationism: The Establishment of the First World Bank, 1929–1930," *Journal of American History*, 59 (Dec. 1972), 610ff. Stimson to Owen D. Young, 15 April 1929, file 462–00, RG296/2773, Department of State, NA.

25 An excellent monograph on the 1931 financial crisis is Edward W. Bennett, *Germany and the Diplomacy of the Financial Crisis* (Cambridge, Mass., 1962); on the role of New York banks—America's unofficial diplomats—see, for instance, Preston Wolfe, Oral history, HHPL; Ambassador Sackett to Department of State, 11 July 1931, cable 121, "Federal Reserve Board," HHPL; Hunt, Hoover interview, 6 Nov. 1935, Hunt Papers; Hoover Memorandum, 1 Feb. 1933, Box 5495, Sullivan Papers; Stimson diary, *passim*.

26 Bennett, *Germany and the Diplomacy of the Financial Crisis, passim;* Clark to Coolidge, 25 June 1931, Coolidge Papers; see also Bernard V. Burke, "American Economic Diplomacy and the Weimar Republic," *Mid-America*, 54 (Oct. 1972), 211–33; Richard Lowitt, "Progressive Farm Leaders and Hoover's Moratorium," *Mid-America*, 50 (1968), 236–6; Walter Lippmann, "Stop, Look, and Listen," *New York Herald-Tribune*, 17 Nov. 1932; Glass to Josephus Daniels, 8 July 1931: "Hoover has no initiative," Glass observed, Glass Papers; Bascom Timmons, *Garner of Texas* (New York, 1948), pp. 132ff; Washington *Star*, 10 July 1931; Sackett to Hoover, 27 Dec. 1930; Hoover to Sackett, 12 Jan. 1931, "Foreign Affairs, Diplomats," HHPL.

27 *Public Papers, 1931*, pp. 657–79.

28 Walter E. Edge, *A Jerseyman's Journal* (Princeton, 1948). Connoisseurs looked forward to the sharp interchanges between Paul Claudel, the famous poet-ambassador, and Hoover. Hoover, Claudel remarked, was like an ass with two rear ends. Emmanuel Moonick, *Pour Mémoire* (Paris, 1970), pp. 40–2. Edgar Rickard diary, 23 July 1931; Thomas Lamont and Hoover, phone conversation, 29 June 1931, Lamont Papers; on Lord Reading's role, see Keynes, *Two Memoirs* (London, 1949), p. 7.

29 Charles L. Venable, "The Hoover-Laval Conference," Master's essay, University of Chicago, 1951; Rhodes, "Herbert Hoover and the War Debts," p. 138. Rhodes points out that Hoover shrewdly shifted the burden for future arrangements on the debts to France; Julius Barnes, unpublished autobiography, Barnes Papers; Mills to Senator David Reed, 5 Jan. 1933, "Treasury, 1973," HHPL; Arthur Krock interview with Hoover, 22 Jan. 1933, Krock Papers; Stimson diary, 20 Oct. 1931 and *passim;* Stimson to David Reed, 5 Jan. 1933, Stimson Papers. Hoover and Laval's discussion of ways to loosen trade restrictions and free frozen capital brought no results.

30 The feeling of many congressmen was caught in Senator George Norris' remark to Henry A. Wallace: "There is only one excuse for not paying it in full and that is if the country owing the debt is bankrupt," 21 Jan. 1932, Norris Papers. Stimson diary, 26 Nov. 1931 and 23 Nov. 1932; Michael Soper, "The Lausanne Conference of 1932," unpublished doctoral dissertation, University of Wisconsin, 1971.

31 James A. Moore, "History of the World Economic Conference, London, 1933," unpublished doctoral dissertation, SUNY at Stony Brook, New York, 1972.

CHAPTER XIV

[1] Moseley, "One Soldier's Journey," IV, 137, and Moseley to Corey, which advocated five years of martial law to rid the country of depression and crime; copy in Box 248, Charles Dawes Papers. Cf. Jules Archer, *The Plot to Seize the White House* (New York, 1973); John R. M. Wilson, "Herbert Hoover's Relations with the Military," *Military Affairs* (April 1974), 41–7.

[2] Walter Lippmann, "The Keynote Speech," *New York Herald-Tribune,* 15 June 1932.

[3] Richard Oulahan, *The Man Who . . . The Story of the 1932 Democratic National Convention* (New York, 1971); Republican Convention Committee, *The Book of the Republican Convention, 1932* (1932); *Official Report of the Proceedings of the Twentieth Republican National Convention* (New York, 1932).

[4] *The Nation,* CXXX (26 March 1930), 450; Daniel C. Roper, *Fifty Years of Public Life* (Durham, 1945), pp. 237–8; Philadelphia *Record,* 13 Dec. 1931; William R. Johnson, *Farm Policy in Transition: 1932* (Norman, 1963); Craig Lloyd, *Aggressive Introvert* (Columbus, 1972), pp. 172–3; Charles Hilles to LeRoy T. Vernon, 28 March 1930, Hilles Papers.

[5] Donald Lisio, *The President and Protest: Hoover, Conspiracy, and the Bonus Riot* (Columbia, 1974); Roger Daniels, *The Bonus March* (Westport, 1971); Hoover to Bruce Barton, 7 June 1932, Barton Papers.

[6] Unlike the growing "Hooverville" communities in the rest of the country, the shacks the veterans lived in were within sight of the Capitol, and thus of all Americans.

[7] Frank Hines to Hoover, 24 June 1932, Veterans Administration, NA; Hines to Hoover, 14 Jan., 21 and 25 June 1930, 15 April 1931; Hines to O. L. Bodenhamer, 29 Aug. 1930, "Veterans Bureau," HHPL.

[8] The BEF *News,* 9 July 1932, HHPL.

[9] Hoover to Luther Reichelderfer, 29 July 1932, "World War Veterans—Bonus," HHPL.

[10] Oral history recollections of Eisenhower, Flo Harriman, and F. Trubee Davison, HHPL. The Pulitzer Prize–winning reporter Lee McCardell described the scene as something different from a rout: "The veterans took their time about the retreat. And the regulars didn't press them any more than was necessary"—Baltimore *Evening Sun,* 29 July 1932; Hurley to MacArthur, 28 July 1932; Hurley to Governor James Rolph of California (unsent), 30 Nov. 1933, "World War Veterans—Bonus," HHPL.

[11] Lisio, *The President and Protest,* p. 56.

[12] D. Clayton James, *The Years of MacArthur,* I (Boston, 1970); Hoover to J. Edgar Hoover, 26 Aug. 1932, Box 6, Richey Papers; MacArthur, *Reminiscences* (New York, 1964), pp. 92–5.

[13] *The Nation,* CXXXV (10 Aug. 1932), 50.

[14] The kindly Bruce Barton called Roosevelt just "a name and a crutch"— Barton to Hoover, 21 Jan. 1932, Barton Papers; Rexford G. Tugwell, "Roosevelt and the Bonus Marchers of 1932," *Political Science Quarterly,* LXXXVII (Sept. 1972), 363–76; Simeon Fess to Sumner Fess, 22 Aug. 1932, Fess Papers; Frankfurter is quoted in G. Jackson, Oral history,

Columbia University, p. 369; on the Smith speech, see Sanders to Coolidge, 26 Oct. 1932, Coolidge Papers.

15 Johnson to Peter Norbeck, 3 Oct. 1932, Johnson Papers.

16 The convention platforms were remarkably similar; see Kirk H. Porter, *National Party Platforms, 1840–1964* (Urbana, 1966). On Hoover's character Stimson adds: "He presents a very curious combination of gruffness and aloofness based upon really his shyness, and yet . . . he doesn't ever do a mean thing." Stimson diary, 27 Feb., 5 Oct. 1932.

17 McKitrick to author, 5 Jan. 1972.

18 The St. Paul comment appears in several newspapers; see the *New York Times*, 6 Nov. 1932, p. 30. But this slightly different version comes from a stenographic report. *Public Papers, 1932–1933*, 5 Nov. 1932, p. 751; Charles Michaelson, *The Ghost Talks* (New York, 1944).

19 Howard W. Runkel, "Hoover's Speeches During His Presidency," unpublished doctoral dissertation, Stanford University, 1950.

20 Herbert Hoover and Calvin Coolidge, *Campaign Speeches of 1932* (Garden City, 1933). A better source, since it transcribes many speeches from sound recordings, is the *Public Papers, 1932–1933*. Turner Catledge, *My Life and The Times* (New York, 1971); Wayne S. Cole, *Charles A. Lindbergh and the Battle Against American Intervention in World War II* (New York, 1974); FO 115/232/17/32, PRO.

21 Michaelson, *The Ghost Talks*, p. 41; Hoover claimed that the grass did not grow because Roosevelt did not reduce tariffs as promised in the campaign. Hoover to William Starr Myers, 8 Jan. 1938, "Post-Presidential—Individual," HHPL; Stimson diary, 25 Sept. 1932.

22 James S. Olson, *Herbert Hoover and the Reconstruction Finance Corporation, 1931–1933* (Ames, 1977), *passim*.

23 *Public Papers, 1932–33*, 21 Nov. 1932; Hoover to Teagle, 21 Nov. 1932, "National Conference of Business and Industrial Commissions," HHPL.

24 Prohibition by no means assured the loyalty of dry progressive Republican Senators: see Ronald L. Feinman, "The Progressive Republican Bloc and the Presidential Election of 1932," *Mid-America*, 59 (April–July 1977), 73–91. Walter Lippmann, New York *Herald-Tribune*, 14 June 1932; Ray S. Peel and Thomas C. Donnelly, *The 1932 Campaign* (New York, 1935).

25 Charles H. Martin, "Negro Leaders, The Republican Party, and the Election of 1932," *Phylon*, XXXII (Spring 1971), 85–93.

26 Carol Green Wilson Papers, Box 5; Edmund W. Starling, *Starling at the White House* (New York, 1946); Motor Freight, Inc., to Hoover, 24 Sept. 1932; Edgar Eugene Robinson, Oral history, HHPL; Stevenson, *Babbitts and Bohemians* (New York, 1967). Whitlock thought Hoover the "most egregious, inept, ignorant, ill bred, boorish, tactless and incompetent President we have ever had," Journal, 10 Nov. 1932, 4 March 1933, Whitlock Papers.

27 For Hoover's reaction to the scandal books, see George Barr Baker Papers, Box 2, HI; Liggett Papers; Herbert Corey responded to the charges in *The Truth About Herbert Hoover* (New York, 1932); see also *New Republic*, 26 Aug. 1931, p. 45; "Report on the 'Smear Books,' " "Books by and about Herbert Hoover, Lists and Correspondence, 1942–64," HHPL, and Liggett *v.*

Corey and Houghton Mifflin, County Clerk's Archives, City of New York, Index 1040/33; John P. Robertson to A. D. Crowe, 27 Oct. 1932; Robertson to C. J. Rankin, 28 Oct. 1932, Norris Papers.

28 Hoover to Hurley, 11 Sept. 1934, "Post-Presidential—Individual," HHPL; John Robertson, *J. H. Scullin* (Nedlands, Australia, 1974).

29 James S. Olson, "Rehearsal for Disaster: Hoover, the R.F.C., and the Banking Crisis in Nevada, 1932–1933," *Western Historical Quarterly,* VI (April 1975), 149–61. See memorandum, 7 Nov. 1932, George Harrison Papers.

30 On these months, see Frank Freidel, "The Interregnum Struggle between Hoover and Roosevelt," Martin Fausold and George T. Mazuzan, eds., *The Hoover Presidency* (Albany, 1974), pp. 134–52; Freidel, "Hoover and Roosevelt and Historical Continuity," Hoover Centennial Paper, 1974, HHPL; and Freidel, *Franklin D. Roosevelt: Launching the New Deal* (Boston, 1973). The John R. Black Papers are particularly good on agricultural policy during the interregnum. See also the anti-Hoover Elliot A. Rosen, *Hoover, Roosevelt, and the Brains Trust* (New York, 1977).

31 Walter Lippmann, "The White House Conference," *New York Herald-Tribune,* 25 Nov. 1932; see also Lippmann, 13 Dec. 1932; memorandum, meeting with Roosevelt, 22 Nov. 1932, "Franklin D. Roosevelt," HHPL; Stimson diary, 20 Jan. 1933; Moley diary, 21 Jan. 1933, Moley Papers; Elliot A. Rosen, "Intranationalism vs. Internationalism: The Interregnum Struggle for the Sanctity of the New Deal," *Political Science Quarterly,* LXXXI (June 1966), 274–97; *Public Papers, 1932–1933,* 13 Nov. 1932, pp. 275–7.

32 Nor did anything come of correspondence between the two men in December 1932, *Public Papers, 1932–1933,* pp. 344–9; Bascom Timmons, Oral history, HHPL; Herbert Feis, *1933: Characters in Crisis* (Boston, 1966); Stimson diary, 22 Nov. 1932; Laurin Henry, *Presidential Transitions* (Washington, 1960), pp. 273–454.

33 For Hoover's memorandum on the Stimson/FDR talks, see 23 Dec. 1932, "Foreign Affairs, Financial—Monetary and Economic Conference," HHPL; Bernard Sternsher, "The Stimson Doctrine: FDR versus Moley and Tugwell," *Pacific Historical Review,* XXXI (1962), 282–9.

34 Lippmann, "The Hoover-Roosevelt Co-operation," *New York Herald-Tribune,* 28 Dec. 1932; Hoover's notes on the conference are in the "Franklin D. Roosevelt" file, HHPL; Stimson diary, 20 Jan. 1933; Moley diary, 21 Jan. 1933, Moley Papers; Freidel, "The Interregnum Struggle," *passim;* Hoover to Stimson, 15 Jan. 1933, Stimson Papers.

35 Susan Estabrook Kennedy has written the standard account, though she missed certain sources at the Hoover Library such as his diary of the banking crisis: *Public Papers, 1932–1933* (Washington, 1977). See her *Banking Crisis of 1933* (Lexington, 1973); see also Arthur Kemp, "Hoover and the Banking Crisis," Hoover Centennial Paper, 1974, HHPL; Bascom Timmons, *Jesse Jones* (New York, 1956), p. 181. Hoover's only success with the Lame Duck Congress (5 Dec. 1932 to 31 March 1933) was the passage in February of a modern bankruptcy act.

36 Francis G. Awalt, "Recollections of the Banking Crisis in 1933," *Business History Review,* XLIII (Autumn 1969), 349–71; C. David Tompkins, *Sena-*

tor Arthur H. Vandenberg (East Lansing, 1970), pp. 76–81; Susan Esta-
brook Kennedy, "The Michigan Banking Crisis of 1933," *Michigan History*,
LVII (Fall 1973), 237–64; Allan Nevins and Frank Hill, *Ford, Decline and
Rebirth, 1933–1962* (New York, 1962), pp. 11–15; "Statement of Interview
with Mr. Henry Ford in Detroit, February 13, 1933, by Secretary Roy D.
Chapin and Under Secretary A. A. Ballantine," Ballantine Papers, HHPL;
Howard R. Neville, "An Historical Study of the Collapse of Banking in
Detroit, 1929–1933," unpublished doctoral dissertation, Michigan State Uni-
versity, 1956.

37 Hoover's *Memoirs* claim that he tried unsuccessfully to reach FDR as early
as February 6. IV, 202. Hoover also pressured Senator Glass to obtain a
commitment from Roosevelt to stay on the gold standard. Hoover to Roosevelt, 18 Feb. 1933, Secretary's file, Roosevelt Library; Harry Barnard, *Independent Man: The Life of Senator James Couzens* (New York, 1958); memorandum on 1930's economic crisis, n.d., Box 94, Eugene Meyer Papers; *Public
Papers, 1932–1933*.

38 Hoover to Mills, 22 Feb. 1923, "Ogden L. Mills, Post-Presidential—Individual," HHPL; Hoover to the Governor and Members of the Federal
Reserve Board, 22 Feb. 1933, "Federal Reserve Board."

39 James S. Olson has the best account of this period: *Herbert Hoover and the
Reconstruction Finance Corporation, 1931–1933* (Ames, 1977), pp. 106–15.
Charles Hamlin diary, 2 March, 6 March 1933, Hamlin Papers; Mills's notes
on a March 2, 1933, meeting with Senators Glass and Robinson are in
"Ogden Mills, Post-Presidential—Individual"; Hoover to Miller, 14 May
1952, "Adolph Miller," HHPL; Hoover's note to Mills of 1 March 1933,
obviously intended for the historical record, is in the same file. Hoover was
some weeks quicker to adopt a bank deposits guarantee than was Roosevelt
—"James H. Douglas, Jr.," 1932, HHPL; Moley, Oral history, HHPL;
Arthur Krock, personal interview with Hoover, 28 Sept. 1937, Krock
Papers. In 1931 Hoover said: "Our people have a right to a banking system
in which their deposits shall be safeguarded"—"Public Statements," 8 Dec.
1931, HHPL. Stimson diary, 4 March 1932.

40 Transcript of phone conversations between Hoover and Mills, 10 March
1933, and Mills and Lawrence Richey, 9 March 1933, "Post-Presidential—
Individual," HHPL; Hoover to O'Laughlin, 25 March 1933, John Callan
O'Laughlin Papers.

EPILOGUE

1 Karl, "Presidential Planning and Social Science Research: Mr Hoover's
Experts," *Perspectives in American History*, III (1969), 347–409; cf. Karl,
Charles E. Merriam and the Study of Politics (Chicago, 1974).

2 See, for example, Mitchell to Merriam, 11 Aug. 1931, Merriam Papers.

3 Stuart A. Rice to W. F. Ogburn, 23 Feb. 1932, Merriam Papers.

4 Many of the "Hoover books" of the post-presidential era were supported
from the New York "Edgar Rickard" account of the Hoover War Library:
the Myers, Wilbur and Hyde, Mullendore, Guerrier, and other books, as well
as many of Hoover's own publications. Hoover to Rickard, 14 May 1919,

Box 274, Hoover Papers, HI; Claire Torrey, Oral history, HHPL; Ephraim D. Adams, *The Hoover War Collection* (Stanford, 1921); Hoover to Adams, 20 Oct. 1908, 22 Feb. 1912, Adams Papers; Gary N. Paul, "The Development of the Hoover Institution . . . 1919–1944," unpublished doctoral dissertation, University of California at Berkeley, 1974.

[5] Hoover to Walter E. Hope, 9 Aug. 1933, "Walter E. Hope"; Hoover to Joslin, 3 July and 2 Aug. 1933, "Theodore Joslin"; Hoover to Richard Lloyd Jones, 15 Dec. 1933, "Richard Lloyd Jones"; Hoover to Sullivan, 10 April 1933, "Mark Sullivan"; Edgar E. Robinson, Oral history, HHPL; Barnes, Autobiography, 21 April 1944, p. 51.

[6] Hoover later wrote to Arthur Vandenberg that "all the really free enterprise countries restored full employment by the end of 1934. The United States only did so by going to war in 1941," 20 Aug. 1949, "Vandenberg, Arthur"; Hoover to Jeremiah Milbank, 11 Sept. 1933, "Milbank, Jeremiah," HHPL; James T. Patterson, *Congressional Conservatism and the New Deal* (Lexington, 1967), p. 107; Leo E. Chavez, "Herbert Hoover and Food Relief," unpublished doctoral dissertation, University of Michigan, 1976, p. 269.

[7] Hoover remarked on Jan. 19, 1935, that the bank deposits guarantee was rotten theory but good in an emergency, that the Securities Act was good (he knew it was needed but did not wish to impede recovery, which he said was its effect), and that Roosevelt was not helping the little fellow. Instead of forcing stockholders to save banks, the New Deal was buying preferred stock. Fisher to John S. Davis, 24 June 1968, Davis Papers; Hoover to Sullivan, 18 Sept. 1938, Box 16A, Sullivan Papers; Hoover to L. W. Ainsworth, 3 Feb. 1936; Hoover to Chapin, 13 June 1933, Chapin Papers; Dewey, Oral history, HHPL.

[8] Hoover to Dawes, 1 Sept. 1934, "Dawes, Charles"; Hoover to Mrs. Lewis, 22 Oct. 1937, "Mrs. Sinclair Lewis," HHPL.

[9] Hoover is said to have remarked about Dewey: "A man can't wear a mustache like that without having an effective mind"—Joan Wilson, *Herbert Hoover* (Boston, 1974), p. 221; Lowden to Landon, 9 Oct. 1937, Series 1, Box 26, Lowden Papers; Theodore Rosenof, *Dogma, Depression and the New Deal* (Port Washington, N.Y., 1975), p. 236.

[10] Hoover to Samuel Crowther, 9 July 1939, "Crowther, Samuel," HHPL.

[11] There is an article in Russian arguing that Hoover, acting for Roosevelt, informed Germany, Austria, and Czechoslovakia of America's position about Hitler's plans: Iu. V. Arutiunian, *Voprosy Istorii*, VI (1954), 43–56. Lochner, *Herbert Hoover and Germany* (New York, 1960), pp. 133–5; Hoover to Hard, 6 Dec. 1938, "Hard, William"; Lydia Murray Huneke, Oral history; Frederick Terman, Oral history, HHPL; Fred Dearing to Franklin Roosevelt, 20 March 1938, Roosevelt Papers.

[12] Hoover to Sulzberger, 19 Dec. 1941, "Sulzberger, Arthur Hays"; Hoover to General Moseley, 2 Feb. 1938, "Moseley, George Van Horn," HHPL; William L. Langer and S. Everett Gleason, *The Challenge to Isolation, 1937–1940* (New York, 1952), p. 479; Hoover to Castle, 1 March 1941, Castle Papers.

[13] Noel Coward spent two hours with Hoover in August 1940 trying to per-

suade him to quit his campaign for feeding on the continent. Hoover was disgusted to learn that the British agent had never heard of the CRB. Lydia Huneke, Payson Treat, Oral history; Rickard to Galpin *et al.,* 25 Oct. 1940, Rickard Papers; Hoover to Hull, 27 March 1941, old numbering, 1–I/324; Hoover to Rickard, night letter, 13 Aug. 1940, old numbering, 1–K/396, HHPL; Hoover, *An American Epic,* IV; Hoover to Nicholas Roosevelt, 6 Dec. 1940, Nicholas Roosevelt Papers; Wayne S. Cole, *Senator Gerald P. Nye and American Foreign Relations* (Minneapolis, 1962).

14 For a rather detailed account of Hoover's views on Pearl Harbor, see the interviews with Hoover included in the Oral history reminiscence of Payson J. Treat, HHPL; Hoover to Landon, 5 June 1942, Landon Papers; Hull, *Memoirs* (New York, 1948), I, 183.

15 On May 13, 1945, Hoover told Stimson that it would be necessary to use food to fight communism after the war. What he meant by this, and whether or not he implemented his thinking, is an interesting question that historians must answer in future studies. Stimson Papers. Donald J. Mrozek, "Progressive Dissenter: Herbert Hoover's Opposition to Truman's Overseas Military Policy," *Annals of Iowa,* 43 (Spring 1976), 275–91; Benjamin Rogers, " 'Dear Mr. President': The Hoover-Truman Correspondence," *The Palimpsest,* LV (Sept./Oct. 1974), 152–8. Maurice Pate kept a comprehensive diary of the 1946 trip, Pate Papers; on Germany, see Hoover, recommendations on Germany, Gen. Acces. 298/1, Harry S. Truman Library; on Korea see, for example, Edward A. Keller, Oral history, HHPL; *Nation's Business* (Sept. 1974), pp. 305, 77–80.

16 *The Hoover Commission Report on Organization of the Executive Branch of the Government* (New York, 1949); *Hearings,* Joint Committee on the Reorganization of the Administrative Branch of the Government, 22 Jan. 1924; Bradley Nash and Cornelius Lynde, *A Hook in Leviathan* (New York, 1949).

17 Arnold, "The First Hoover Commission and the Managerial Presidency," *The Journal of Politics,* XXXVIII (1976), 46ff.

18 Neil McNeil, Oral history, HHPL; Eisenhower diary, 24 July 1953, Dwight D. Eisenhower Presidential Library; Robert J. Muckshorn, "Congressional Reaction to the Second Hoover Commission," unpublished doctoral dissertation, University of Iowa, 1957.

19 G. Keith Funston, Oral history; Admiral Ben Moreel, Oral history; Walter Trohan, Oral history, HHPL.

20 A sample passage from "Freedom Betrayed" (first entitled "The Crucifixion of Liberty") may be found in William C. Mullendore, Oral history, HHPL; reprinting not permitted by the Herbert Hoover Presidential Library Association. Robert Storey, a friend of Hoover from the Second Hoover Commission, said Hoover "made no reservations about the fact that he preferred President Johnson over Barry Goldwater," Oral history; Dr. Russel V. Lee, Oral history; Lewis Strauss, Oral history, HHPL; Lydia Huneke noted that Hoover in the spring of 1964 suggested another commission to reorganize the executive branch of government.

21 Wilson asked Creel what he thought of Hoover: "He always gave me the

feeling of a cockroach sliding around in a porcelain bathtub," was the reply—
Rebel at Large (New York, 1947), p. 265; Mrs. Jameson Parker, Oral history; Walter Livington, Oral history, HHPL.

22 Bernard Baruch speculated that Hoover's "lack of courage" stemmed from a desire not to hurt; Baruch also thought he was "inclined to have a persecution complex"—Baruch to Frank Kent, 15 May 1929, Selected correspondence, Baruch Papers; Alpheus Mason, *Harlan Fiske Stone* (New York, 1956), p. 270; Lippmann, "The Peculiar Weakness of Mr. Hoover," *Harper's* (June 1930), p. 3.

ACKNOWLEDGMENTS

I AM GRATEFUL for kind encouragement, after the passing of my doctoral sponsor, Richard Hofstadter, from Frank Freidel, Arthur S. Link, William Leuchtenburg, and Eric McKitrick. The research and writing of this book were furthered by the Guggenheim Foundation, the American Philosophical Society, and federal and New York State grants. Substantial help was contributed by Dwight M. Miller and Robert Wood of the Herbert Hoover Presidential Library, and Charles Palm of the Hoover Institution. I also wish to thank Ellis Hawley, Fred Weinstein, James Moore, Marian Wilson, Catherine West, James Patterson, Jordan Schwarz, John Williams, Julian Silva, Victoria Lebovics, Robert Crunden, James Olson, Jack Barnard, Neil Basen, Gary Dean Best, Craig Lloyd, William Haugaard, Laurence Lafore, David Chamberlain, Don Lisio, Todd Natkin, Richard Arsenault, Rupert Mitsch, Martin Fausold, Donald McCoy, Tom G. Hall, Don and Donna Reid, Richard Kuisel, Donn Neal, Emily and Norm Rosenberg, Bernard Semmel, David Trask, Charles Woody, Irwin Unger, Robert London, Meta Zimmeck, Dick Rapp, and many other colleagues, friendly and obliging librarians, and several students and typists. I owe an enormous debt to Thomas West of The Catholic University of America; he is virtual coauthor of this book. Robert Marcus gave me very useful advice and kept me going across seemingly hard times. Bob Burner gave invaluable assistance. My editor at Knopf, Ashbel Green, offered sound advice and useful criticisms. The book's copy-editor, Ann Adelman, production editor, Melvin Rosenthal, and proofreader, Tim Cleary, also made valuable contributions. My wife, Sandy, contributed very helpful editing and typing—and far more; Diane and Eric, tolerant, much-loved children, let me sleep late after nocturnal writing, for which I gratefully thank them.

DAVID BURNER
St. James, N.Y.

INDEX

A NOTE ABOUT THE AUTHOR

Dᴀᴠɪᴅ Bᴜʀɴᴇʀ was born in Cornwall, New York, in 1937. He received his B.A. from Hamilton College and his Ph.D. in history from Columbia University. He has taught at Colby College, Hunter College, City College of New York, and Oakland University, and is currently Professor of History at the State University of New York, Stony Brook. Mr. Burner is the author of *The Politics of Provincialism* (1968) and the co-author of several other works on American history. He has been the recipient of fellowships from the Guggenheim Foundation and the National Endowment for the Humanities. He and his family live in St. James, New York.

A NOTE ON THE TYPE

Tʜɪs ʙᴏᴏᴋ was set by computer in a face called Times Roman, designed by Stanley Morison for *The Times* (London) and first introduced by that newspaper in 1932.

Among typographers and designers of the twentieth century, Stanley Morison has been a strong forming influence, as typographical adviser to the English Monotype Corporation, as a director of two distinguished English publishing houses, and as a writer of sensibility, erudition, and keen practical sense.

Composed, printed, and bound
by American Book–Stratford Press, Saddle Brook, New Jersey

Typography and binding design by Camilla Filancia